FRENCH XX BIBLIOGRAPHY

A BIBLIOGRAPHY FOR THE STUDY OF FRENCH LITERATURE AND CULTURE SINCE 1885

VOLUME XIII, NO. 1, ISSUE NO.

61

COMPILED AND EDITED BY

WILLIAM J. THOMPSON
UNIVERSITY OF MEMPHIS

AFFILIATED WITH
THE AMERICAN ASSOCIATION
OF TEACHERS OF FRENCH

Selinsgrove
SUSQUEHANNA UNIVERSITY PRESS

Associated University Presses
2010 Eastpark Boulevard
Cranbury, NJ 08512

The paper used in this publication meets the requirements
of the American National Standard for Permanence of Paper
for Printed Library Materials Z39.48-1984.

ISBN 978-1-57591-137-3 (issue no. 61)
International Standard Serial Number 0085-0888
Library of Congress Catalog Card Number 77-648803

Printed in the United States of America

EDITORIAL OFFICE

William J. Thompson
Department of Foreign Languages and Literatures
Dunn Building, Room 375
University of Memphis
Memphis, Tennessee 38152

Editorial Assistant, Brock Terwilleger

CONTENTS

TABLE OF ABBREVIATIONS

BLF	*Bibliographie de la Littérature Française*
Cor	Cornell University
ILL	Inter-Library Loan
INIST	*Institute de l'Information Scientifique et Technique* (on-line database)
IR	Indirect Reference
LH	*Livres Hebdo*
McM	McMaster University
MLA	*MLA International Bibliography* (on-line version)
PC	Private Copy
UM	University of Memphis
VU	Vanderbilt University
WC	World Cat (on-line database)
Web	Information collected from Web site

COORDINATION TABLE

(for referring back to previous numbers of *French XX*)

Although the cross-reference system of *French XX* is simple and comprehensible at a moment's glance, time will be saved if this table is consulted before turning back to previous issues of *French XX*. When the cross-reference is expressed in terms of the sequential numbers of the entries or in terms of the pagination, it sometimes takes time to discover which annual issue is involved. This table will expedite such identification.

	Entries covered	*Pages*
Volume I (1949–1953)		
Publication No. 1	1 to 2007	1 to 106
Publication No. 2	2008 to 4058	107 to 210
Publication No. 3	4059 to 5131	211 to 273
Publication No. 4	5132 to 7082	275 to 372
Publication No. 5	7083 to 8654	379 to 466
Volume II (1954–1958)		
Sixth Publication (II, no. 1)	8655 to 10596	473 to 565
Seventh Publication (II, no. 2)	10597 to 12584	573 to 668
Eighth Publication (II, no. 3)	12585 to 14772	669 to 776
Ninth Publication (II, no. 4)	14773 to 16525	777 to 864
Tenth Publication (II, no. 5)	16526 to 18797	865 to 975
(with index to Vols. I & II)		977 to 1071
Volume III (1959–1963)		
Eleventh Publication (III, no. 1)	18798 to 20638	1073 to 1173
Twelfth Publication (III, no. 2)	20639 to 22779	1175 to 1282
Thirteenth Publication (III, no. 3)	22780 to 25212	1283 to 1406
Fourteenth Publication (III, no. 4)	25213 to 28188	1407 to 1551
Fifteenth Publication (III, no. 5)	28189 to 31409	1555 to 1711
Volume IV (1964–1968)		
Sixteenth Publication (IV, no. 1)	13410 to 37398	1713 to 1991
Vol. IV, no. 2, issue no. 17	37399 to 45169	1993 to 2406
Vol. IV, no. 3, issue no. 18	45170 to 52273	2407 to 2777
Vol. IV, no. 4, issue no. 19	52274 to 59024	2779 to 3123
Vol. IV, no. 5, issue no. 20	59025 to 65342	3125 to 3440
Index to Volumes III and IV		236 p.
Volume V (1969–1973)		
Vol. V, no. 1, issue no. 21	65343 to 73139	3441 to 3838
Vol. V, no. 2, issue no. 22	73140 to 78913	3841 to 4159
Vol. V, no. 3, issue no. 23	78914 to 87943	4167 to 4623
Vol. V, no. 4, issue no. 24	87944 to 94678	4625 to 4988
Vol. V, no. 5, issue no. 25	94679 to 102455	4989 to 5444
Index to Volume V		211 p.
Volume VI (1974–1978)		
Vol. VI, no. 1, issue no. 26	A1 to A6167	5445 to 5772
Vol. VI, no. 2, issue no. 27	A6168 to A12427	5773 to 6099
Vol. VI, no. 3, issue no. 28	A12428 to A18572	6101 to 6453

PART ONE

General Subjects

ANTHOLOGIES AND COLLECTIONS

GG1. ● *Amérique, Amériques!: écrit(s) du Québec, 1608-2008.* Ed., Michel Kneubühler, Thierry Renard. Genouilleux, France: Passe du vent; Québec: Instant même, 2008. *Haute mémoire.* 265 p. [Francophone]

GG2. ● *Anthology [An] of nineteenth-century women's poetry from France.* Ed. Gretchen Schultz; trans. by Anne Atik [et al.]. New York: MLA, 2008. *Texts and translations.* xl, 367 p.

GG3. ● Butor, Michel: *Anthologie de la littérature française.* Paris: Carnets nord, 2008. 145 p.

GG4. ● *Littérature africaine: une anthologie du monde noir.* Prés. Jacques Chevrier. Paris: Librio, 2008. 127 p. [Francophone]

GG5. ● Malinowski, Wieslaw Mateusz; Jerzy Styczynski: *La Pologne et les Polonais dans la littérature française, XIVe-XIXe siècles.* Paris: L'Harmattan, 2008. 516 p.

GG6. ● *Pluriel: une anthologie, des voix.* Sous la dir. de Marc Charron, Seymour Mayne et Christiane Melançon. Ottawa: Univ. of Ottawa Press, 2008. 284 p. [Francophone]

GG7. ● *Poésies de langue française: 144 poètes d'aujourd'hui autour du monde: anthologie.* Etablie par Stézphane Bataillon, Sylvestre Clancier et Bruno Doucey; préface de Bruno Doucey. Paris: Seghers, 2008. 479 p. [Francophone, Poetry]

GG8. ● *Québec 2008: 40 poètes du Québec et de France.* Compilé par Josyane De Jésus-Bergey, Bernard Pozier. Trois-Rivières, Québec: Ecrits des Forges, 2008. 210 p. [Francophone, Poetry]

GG9. ● Thélôt, Claude: *Anthologie de la littérature française sur la famille.* Paris: Le Cherche Midi, 2008. 490 p.

GG10. ● *XXe siècle: les grands auteurs français: anthologie et histoire littéraire.* André Lagarde, Laurent Michard, avec la collab. de Raoul Audibert, Henri Lemaitre, Thérèse Van Der Elst. Paris: Bordas, 2008. 896 p.

BIBLIOGRAPHY

GG11. ● *Bibliographie der französischen Literaturwissenschaft.* Hrsg. Astrid Klapp-Lehrmann. Frankfurt am Main: V. Klostermann, 2008. 1263 p.

GG12. ● Férey, Eric: *Bibliographie de la littérature française (XVIe-XXe siècle).* Paris: PUF, 2008. *Revue d'Histoire Littéraire de la France,* 108e année, no. hors série.

GG13. ● *Francesistica: bibliografia delle opere e degli studi di letteratura francese e francofona in Italia. IV, 2000-2004.* A cura di Novella Novelli. Torino; Paris: L'Harmattan, 2006. 876 p.

GG14. "Bibliographie sur la littérature guyanaise," *Nouvelles Etudes Francophones,* vol. 23, no. 2 (automne 2008), 163-177. [Francophone]

GG15. "Dix-neuvième siècle bibliographique," *Dix-Neuvième Siècle,* no. 47 (juin 2008), 146-186.

GG16. "Dix-neuvième siècle bibliographique," *Dix-Neuvième Siècle,* no. 48 (déc. 2008), 140-186.

GG17. "Recent Canadian theses," *Dalhousie French Studies,* vol. 84 (Fall 2008), 125-139.

BIBLIOPHILISM AND PUBLICATION

GG18. ● Dagan, Yaël: *La Nouvelle Revue Française entre guerre et paix: 1914-1925.* Paris: Tallandier, 2008. 425 p.

GG19. ● *Editions [Les] du Seuil, 70 ans d'histoires.* Exposition présentée au Centre Pompidou du 7 novembre 2007 au 4 février 2008. Dir. Hervé Serry. Paris: Seuil; IMEC, 2008. 207 p.

GG20. • *Histoire de la librairie française.* Sous la dir. de Patricia Sorel et Frédérique Leblanc. Paris: Editions du Cercle de la librairie, 2008. 719 p.

GG21. • Mollier, Jean-Yves: *Edition, presse et pouvoir en France au XXe siècle.* Paris: Fayard, 2008. 493 p.

GG22. • *Pensées critiques: dix itinéraires de la revue Mouvements, 1998-2008.* Paris: Découverte, 2008. 187 p. [Rancière]

GG23. • Perrin, Raymond: *Littérature de jeunesse et presse des jeunes au début du XXIe siècle.* Paris: L'Harmattan, 2008. 555 p.

GG24. • Samuelson, François Marie: *Il était une fois Libé . . . : reportage historique agrémenté de cinq entretiens.* Nouvelle préface de Bernard-Henri Lévy. Paris: J'ai lu, 2008. 413 p. [Foucault, Sartre]

GG25. • Silverman, Willa Z.: *The new bibliopolis: French book collectors and the culture of print, 1880-1914.* Toronto; Buffalo: Univ. of Toronto Press, 2008. *Studies in book and print culture.* xvii, 312 p.

GG26. • Simonin, Anne: *Les Editions de Minuit, 1942-1955: le devoir d'insoumission.* Paris: IMEC, 2008. Nouvelle édition. 523 p.

GG27. • *Situations de l'édition francophone d'enfance et de jeunesse.* Sous la dir. de Luc Pinhas. Paris: L'Harmattan, 2008. 343 p.

GG28. • Tudoret, Patrick: *L'écrivain sacrifié: vie et mort de l'émission littéraire.* Latresne: Bord de l'eau; Paris: Institut national de l'audiovisuel, 2008. *Penser les médias.* 252 p.

GG29. • Vigne, Eric: *Le livre et l'éditeur.* Paris: Klincksieck, 2008. *50 questions.* 178 p.

GG30. Buch Leander, Niels: "The colonial metropolis and its artistic adventure: Conrad, Congo, and the *Nouvelle Revue Française,*" *Romanic Review,* vol. 99, no. 1-2 (Jan.-March), 87-102.

GG31. Carbonnel, Marie: "Juges contre jurés. Les critiques et les prix littéraires (1903-1932)," *Mil Neuf Cent,* no. 26 (2008), 31-50.

GG32. Compagnon, Antoine: "L'antimodernisme de la *NRF,*" *Romanic Review,* vol. 99, no. 1-2 (Jan.-March), 27-44.

GG33. Dagan, Yaël: "La critique littéraire porteuse de discours politique. *La Nouvelle Revue Française,* 1919-1925," *Mil Neuf Cent,* no. 26 (2008), 125-142.

GG34. Drouin, Michel: "La fête et l'engagement: l'esprit de la *Revue Blanche,*" *Bulletin des Amis d'André Gide,* 41e année, vol. 36, no. 157 (janv. 2008), 115-120.

GG35. Fabre, Michel: "Oubliés par la *NRF*?: marginalité du modernisme noir," *Romanic Review,* vol. 99, no. 1-2 (Jan.-March), 133-141.

GG36. Hermetet, Anne-Rachel: "La question de la modernité se pose-t-elle dans la *Nouvelle Revue Française* (1919-1925)?," *Textuel,* no. 53 (2008), 59-71.

GG37. Marx, William: "Les deux modernismes: T. S. Eliot et la *NRF,*" *Romanic Review,* vol. 99, no. 1-2 (Jan.-March), 57-68.

GG38. Milne, Anna-Louise: "*La Nouvelle Revue Françaisse* in the age of modernism," *Romanic Review,* vol. 99, no. 1-2 (Jan.-March), 3-8.

GG39. Paulhan, Claire: "Henry Church et la revue *Mesures*: 'La ressource américaine'," *Romanic Review,* vol. 99, no. 1-2 (Jan.-March), 119-132.

GG40. Tadié, Benoît: " 'Au cœur de la lumière': T. S. Eliot, la *NRF* et Paris," *Romanic Review,* vol. 99, no. 1-2 (Jan.-March), 45-55.

FRANCOPHONE LITERATURE

See also 1, 4, 6, 7, 8,14, 1015, 1117.

GG41. • *A la carte: le roman québécois (2000-2005).* Gilles Dupuis, Klaus-Dieter Ertler, éds. Frankfurt: Peter Lang, 2007. 493 p.

GG42. • *Africa and trans-Atlantic memories: literary and aesthetic manifestations of diaspora and history.* Ed. Naana Opoku-Agyemang, Paul E. Lovejoy, David V. Trotman. Trenton, NJ: Africa World, 2008. vii, 477 p.

GG43.   • *African diasporas: ancestors, migrations and borders.* Ed. Robert Cancel, Winifred Woodhull. Trenton, NJ: Africa World, 2008. *African Literature Association annual series*, 14. iv, 455 p.

GG44.   • *Archives littéraires et manuscrits d'écrivains: politiques et usages du patrimoine.* Sous la dir. de Jacinthe Martel. Québec: Nota bene, 2008. 297 p. [Boschère, Desrochers, Ferron, Miron, G. Roy]

GG45.   • *Aux frontières de l'intime: le sujet lyrique dans la poésie québécoise actuelle.* Sous la dir. de Denise Brassard et Evelyne Gagnon. Montréal: Univ. du Québec à Montréal, Figura, 2007. 182 p. [Poetry]

GG46.   • Beaudry, Jacques: *La fatigue d'être: Saint-Denys Garneau, Claude Gauvreau, Hubert Aquin.* Montréal: Hurtubise, 2008. 140 p. [Aquin, Gauvreau, Saint-Denys Garneau]

GG47.   • *Belgique [La] entre deux siècles: laboratoire de la modernité, 1880-1914.* Ed. Nathalie Aubert [et al.]. Oxford: P. Lang, 2007. 272 p.

GG48.   • Biloa, Edmond: *Le français des romanciers négro-africains.* Paris: L'Harmattan, 2007. 461 p.

GG49.   • Bongie, Chris: *Friends and enemies: the scribal politics of post/colonial literature.* Liverpool: Liverpool Univ. Press, 2008. *Postcolonialism across the disciplines*, 3. xv, 412 p. [Condé, Debray, Glissant]

GG50.   • Braziel, Jana Evans: *Artists, performers, and black masculinity in the Haitian diaspora.* Bloomington: Indiana Univ. Press, 2008. *Blacks in the diaspora.* 300 p. [Laferrière, Peck]

GG51.   • Britton, Celia: *The sense of community in French Caribbean fiction.* Liverpool: Liverpool Univ. Press, 2008. vii, 190 p. [Chamoiseau, Condé, Glissant, Maximin, Placoly, Roumain, S. Schwarz-Bart]

GG52.   • *Cameroun [Le] au prisme de la littérature africaine, à l'ère du pluralisme sociopolitique, 1990-2006.* Ladislas Nzessé, M. Dassi, éds. Paris: L'Harmattan, 2008. 289 p.

GG53.   • *Caribbean(s) on the move; Archipélagos literarios del Caribe: a TransArea symposium.* Ed. Ottmar Ette. Frankfurt: Peter Lang, 2008. 167 p. [Chamoiseau, Confiant, Maalouf]

GG54.   • Chancé, Dominique: *Ecritures du chaos.* Saint-Denis: Presses univ. de Vincennes, 2008. 248 p. [Joël Des Rosiers, Frankétienne]

GG55.   • Cibalabala, Mutshipayi K.: *Les romanciers congolais et la satire.* Préface de Pius Ngandu Nkashama. Paris: L'Harmattan, 2008. 279 p.

GG56.   • Clerc, Jeanne-Marie; Liliane Nzé: *Le roman gabonais et la symbolique du silence et du bruit.* Paris: L'Harmattan, 2008. *Critiques littéraires.* 336 p. [Bessora, J. Divassa Nyama, Owondo]

GG57.   • Cloutier, Guy: *Le goût de l'autre: propos sur les poètes de l'Amérique française.* Montréal: Editions du Notoît, 2006. 236 p.

GG58.   • Collins, Walter P.: *Tracing personal expansion: reading selected novels as modern African Bildungsromane.* Lanham, MD: Univ. Press of America, 2006. 137 p. [Beyala]

GG59.   • Constant, Isabelle: *Les rêves dans le roman africain et antillais.* Paris: Karthala, 2008. *Lettres du Sud.* 246 p. [Bhêly-Qhenum, Depestre, Hampâté Bâ]

GG60.   • *Constructing vernacular culture in the trans-Caribbean.* Ed. Holger Henke, Karl-Heinz Magister. Lanham, MD: Lexington, 2008. *Caribbean studies.* xxiii, 407 p. [Chamoiseau]

GG61.   • *D'encre et d'exil 6: le Liban, entre rêve et cauchemar.* Paris: Bibliothèque publique d'information, Centre Pompidou, 2007. 184 p. [Khoury-Ghata, Stétié]

GG62.   • Diagana, M'Bouh Séta: *Eléments de la littérature mauritanienne de langue française: mon pays est une perle discrète.* Paris: L'Harmattan, 2008. 232 p.

GG63.   • Dion, Robert: *L'Allemagne de liberté: sur la germanophilie des intellectuels québécois.* Ottawa: Presses de l'Univ. d'Ottawa, 2007. xiv, 335 p.

GG64.   • Diop, Cheikh Mouhamadou: *Fondements et représentations identitaires chez Ahmadou Kourouma, Tahar Ben Jelloun et Abdourahman Waberi*. Paris: L'Harmattan, 2008. *Critiques littéraires*. [Ben Jelloun, Kourouma, Waberi]

GG65. ● Djungu-Simba Kamatenda, Charles: *Les écrivains du Congo-Zaïre: approches d'un champ littéraire africain*. Metz: Univ. Paul Verlaine-Metz, 2008. 329 p.

GG66. ● Dumont, Pierre: *La francophonie autrement, héritage senghorien?: et si le faire l'emportait sur le dire*. Paris: L'Harmattan, 2008. 246 p.

GG67. ● *Echoes of the Haitian revolution: 1804-2004*. Ed. Martin Munro, Elizabeth Walcott-Hackshaw. Kingston, Jamaica: Univ. of the West Indies Press, 2008. 189 p.

GG68. ● *Ecole [L'] des Belges: dix romanciers d'aujourd'hui: guide littéraire*. Sous la dir. de Francis Dannemark. Bordeaux: Castor astral, 2007. 143 p.

GG69. ● *Ecriture [L'] du corps dans la littérature québécoise depuis 1980*. Sous la dir. de Daniel Marcheix et Nathalie Watteyne. Limoges: PULIM, 2007. *Espaces humains*. 277 p.

GG70. ● Edwards, Carole: *Les dramaturges antillaises: cruauté, créolité, conscience féminine*. Paris: L'Harmattan, 2008. *Etudes transnationales, francophones et comparées*. 201 p. [I. Césaire, Condé, Dracius, S. Schwarz-Bart]

GG71. ● Egar, Emmanuel Edame: *The crisis of Negritude: a study of the Black movement against intellectual oppression in the early 20th century*. Boca Raton: Brown Walker, 2008.

GG72. ● *Enseigner le monde noir: mélanges offerts à Jacques Chevrier*. Prés. Beïda Chikhi. Paris: Maisonneuve & Larose, 2007. 620 p. [Beyala, Bhêly-Quenum, Bugul, Césaire, Chevrillon, Couao-Zotti, Diarra, Gauvin, Glissant, Hampâté Bâ, Kane, Monénembo, Moussirou-Mouyama, Senghor, Sissolo, Souza, Tchicaya, Waberi]

GG73. ● Fetscher, Doris: *Fez oder feutre?: koloniale Assimilationsdiskurse: zur Rekontextualisierung kolonialer Literatur am Beispiel "assimilierter" algerischer Autoren französischer Sprache, 1928-1961*. Frankfurt: IKO-Verlag, 2006. 360 p.

GG74. ● Föttinger, Gudrun: *Das Bild Frankreichs und der Französen in der neueren québecer Literatur (1941-1982) und seine identitätsbildende Funktion*. Frankfurt: Peter Lang, 2006. *Canadiana*, 4. 400 p.

GG75. ● *Francophonie [La] aujourd'hui*. Textes réunis par Karin Holter et Inge Skattum. Paris: L'Harmattan, 2008. 196 p. [Ducharme]

GG76. ● *Francophonie [La]: esthétique et dynamique de libération*. Sous la dir. de Ibrahim H. Badr. New York: Peter Lang, 2007. 211 p.

GG77. ● *Francophonie et interculturalité*. Dir. Jerzy Lis, Teresa Tomaszkiewicz. Lask: Oficyna Wydawnicza Leksem, 2008. 313 p. [Literary Themes, Alexakis, Djebar, Ernaux, Ferron, Laferrière, Lalonde, R. Robin]

GG78. ● Frindéthié, Martial K.: *The Black renaissance in Francophone African and Caribbean literature*. Jefferson, NC: McFarland & Company, 2008. v, 209 p. [Fanon]

GG79. ● *From Art nouveau to Surrealism: Belgian modernity in the making*. Ed. Nathalie Aubert, Pierre-Philippe Fraiture, Patrick McGuinness. London: Legenda, 2007. viii, 207 p. [Surrealism, Hergé, Maeterlinck, Jean Ray, Scutenaire, Simenon]

GG80. ● *Gender and displacement: 'home' in contemporary Francophone women's autobiography*. Ed. Natalie Edwards, Christopher Hogarth. Newcastle upon Tyne: Cambridge Scholars, 2008. ix, 141 p.

GG81. ● Giovannucci, Perri: *Literature and development in North Africa: the modernizing mission*. New York: Routledge, 2008. *Literary criticism and cultural theory*. vii, 245 p. [Camus, Djebar, Fanon, Memmi, Sartre]

GG82. ● Gorceix, Paul: *Le symbolisme en Belgique ou l'éveil à une identité culturelle: une si rare différence . . . : mélanges, tome I*. Paris: Eurédit, 2008. 321 p. [Literary History, Literary Theory, Literary Themes, Eekhoud, Lemonnier]

GG83. ● Gorceix, Paul: *Le symbolisme en Belgique ou l'éveil à une identité culturelle: une si rare différence . . . : mélanges, tome II*. Paris: Eurédit, 2008. 327 p. [Elskamp, Hellens, Rodenbach, Van Lerberghe, Verhaeren]

GG84. ● Gounongbé, Ari; Lilyan Kesteloot: *Les grandes figures de la négritude: paroles privées*. Paris: L'Harmattan, 2007. 162 p.

GG85. ● Hayward, Annette: *La querelle du régionalisme au Québec, 1904-1931: vers l'autonomisation de la littérature québécoise*. Ottawa: Le Nordir, 2006. 622 p.

GG86.   • Heady, Margaret: *Marvelous journeys: routes of identity in the Caribbean novel*. New York: Peter Lang, 2008. *Caribbean Studies*. 127 p. [Alexis, S. Schwarz-Bart]

GG87.   • *Identités: incursion tunisienne dans les lettres luxembourgeoises*. Sous la dir. de Marion Colas-blaise et Jalel el Gharbi. Esch-sur-Alzette (Luxembourg): PHI, 2006. 125 p.

GG88.   • *Image [L'] de l'Afrique dans les littératures coloniales et post-coloniales: actes du colloque international de Yaoundé, 15-17 décembre 2004*. Edition de Richard Laurent Omgba. Paris: L'Harmattan, 2008. 346 p.

GG89.   • Irele, Abiola: *Négritude et condition africaine*. Paris: Karthala, 2008. 189 p.

GG90.   • Jurney, Florence Ramond: *Voix/es libres: maternité et identité féminine dans la littérature antillaise*. Birmingham, AL: Summa, 2006. 251 p.

GG91.   • Kaussen, Valerie: *Migrant revolutions: Haitian literature, globalization, and U.S. imperialism*. Lanham, MD: Lexington Books, 2008. *After the empire*. xvi, 245 p. [Alexis, Chauvet, Roumain]

GG92.   • *Land and landscape in Francophone literature: remapping uncertain territories*. Ed. Magali Compan and Katarzyna Pieprzak. Newcastle-upon-Tyne: Cambridge Scholars, 2007. vi, 151 p. [Condé, Devi, Elalamy, Fanon, L. Gauvin, Lefèvre, Sembène]

GG93.   • *Langues dominantes, langues dominées: à la mémoire de Gérard Dallez*. Textes réunis par Laurence Villard, avec la collab. de Nicolas Ballier. Mont-Saint-Aignan: Publications des Univ. de Rouen et du Havre, 2008. 445 p.

GG94.   • Lapointe, Martine-Emmanuelle: *Emblèmes d'une littérature: Le Libraire, Prochain épisode et L'avalée des avalés*. Montréal: Fides, 2008. *Nouvelles études québécoises*. 357 p. [Aquin, Bessette, Ducharme]

GG95.   • Laronde, Michel: *Postcolonialiser la haute culture: à l'école de la République*. Paris: L'Harmattan, 2008. *Logiques sociales*. 299 p.

GG96.   • *Libres horizons: pour une approche comparatiste, lettres francophones imaginaires. Hommage à Arlette et Roger Chemain*. Ed. Micéala Symington, Béatrice Bonhomme; introd. Eva Kushner. Paris: L'Harmattan, 2008. 488 p.

GG97.   • *Littérature et cinéma au Québec: 1995-2005*. Dir. Carla Fratta. Bologna: Pendragon, 2008. 151 p.

GG98.   • *Littérature francophone, université et société au Congo-Zaïre: hommage à Victor Bol*. Sous la dir. de Nyunda ya Rubango et Bogumil Jewsiewicki. Paris: L'Harmattan, 2005. 308 p.

GG99.   • *Littératures et déchirures*. Sous la dir. de Clément Dili Palaï et Daouda Pare; préface de Romuald Fonkoua. Paris: L'Harmattan, 2008. *Etudes africaines*. 189 p. [Ben Jelloun, Glissant, Hampâté Bâ, Karone, Perec, Tournier, Yaya]

GG100.   • Lonergan, David: *Tintamarre: chroniques de littérature dans l'Acadie aujourd'hui*. Sudbury, Ont.: Prise de parole, 2008. 365 p.

GG101.   • Luthi, Jean-Jacques: *Entretiens avec des auteurs francophones d'Egypte: et fragments de correspondances*. Paris: L'Harmattan, 2008. 222 p.

GG102.   • Malela, Buata B.: *Les écrivains afro-antillais à Paris (1920-1960): stratégies et postures identitaires*. Paris: Karthala, 2008. *Lettres du Sud*. 465 p. [Beti, Césaire, Damas, Maran, Senghor]

GG103.   • *Mémoires et identités dans les littératures francophones*. Dir. Kanaté Dahouda, Sélom Komlan Gbanou. Paris: L'Harmattan, 2008. 264 p. [Chamoiseau, B. B. Diop, Djebar, Duras, Efoui, Glissant, Kane, Kokis, Kourouma, Labou, Lopes, Modiano, Ollivier, Tchicaya]

GG104.   • *Migrance comparée: les littératures du Canada et du Québec*. Ed. Marie Carrière, Catherine Khordoc. Bern; New York: Peter Lang, 2008. *Littératures de langue française*, 5. ix, 358 p.

GG105.   • Miller, Christopher L.: *The French Atlantic trangle: literature and culture of the slave trade*. Durham, NC: Duke Univ. Press, 2008. xvi, 571 p. [Césaire, Condé, Glissant]

GG106.   • Mokaddem, Hamid: *Littérature calédoniennes: la littérature océanienne francophone est-elle une littérature française?*. Marseille: La Courte Echelle; Transit, 2008. 62 p.

GG107. • *Mots [Les] du patrimoine: le Sénégal*. Sous la dir. de Geneviève N'Diaye Corréard. Paris: Archives Contemporaines, 2006. 600 p.

GG108. • Ngal, M. a M.: *Littératures congolaises de la RDC: 1482-2007: histoire et anthologie*. Paris: L'Harmattan, 2008. 2e édition corr. et augmentée. 339 p.

GG109. • Njoya, Wandia: *In search of El Dorado? Immigration, French ideals, and the African experience in contemporary African novels*. Saarbrücken: VDM Verlag, 2008. vi, 290 p. [Bessora, Fatou Diome, Nathalie Etoke, Mabanckou]

GG110. • Ogunyemi, Chikwenye Okonjo: *Juju fission: women's alternative fictions from the Sahara, the Kalahari, and the oases in-between*. New York: Peter Lang, 2008. *Society and politics in Africa*, 18. [Beyala, Djebar]

GG111. • *Orient [L'] dans le roman de la Caraïbe*. Sous la dir. de Mounia Benalil. Montréal: CIDIHCA, 2006. 220 p.

GG112. • Ostman, Margareta; Hans Ostman: *Au champ d'Apollon: écrits d'expression française produits en Suède, 1550-2006*. Stockholm: Académie royale suédoise des Belles-Lettres, de l'Histoire et des Antiquités, 2008. 432 p.

GG113. • Palmer, Eustace: *Of war and women, oppression and optimism: new essays on the African novel*. Trenton, NJ: Africa World Press, 2008. 367 p. [Bâ]

GG114. • Paravisini-Gebert, Lizabeth: *Literature of the Caribbean*. Westport, CT: Greenwood, 2008. viii, 244 p. [Condé, Confiant, S. Schwarz-Bart]

GG115. • *Parcours québécois. Introduction à la littérature du Québec*. Pierre Morel, éd. Bucaresti: Editura Cartier, 2007. 248 p.

GG116. • *Perspectives sur la littérature franco-ontarienne*. Sous la dir. de Ali Reguigui et Hédi Bouraoui. Sudbury, Ont.: Prise de parole, 2007. 2e éd. rev. et augm. 463 p.

GG117. • Pierre, Emeline: *Le caractère subversif de la femme antillaise dans un contexte (post)colonial*. Paris: L'Harmattan, 2008. *Approches littéraires*. 190 p. [Lucie Julia, G. Pineau]

GG118. • *Présences haïtiennes*. Textes réunis et présentés par Sylvie Bouffartigue [et al.]. Cergy-Pontoise: Univ. de Cergy-Pontoise, Centre de recherche textes et francophonies et civilisations et identités culturelles comparées, 2006. 456 p. [Depestre, Fignolé, Pasquet, Pulvar, Roumain, Trouillot, Victor]

GG119. • *Problématiques identitaires et discours de l'exil dans les littératures francophones*. Sous la dir. de Anissa Talahite-Moodley. Ottawa: Presses de l'Univ. d'Ottawa, 2007. *Transferts culturels*. v, 365 p.

GG120. • *Québec [Le] à l'aube du nouveau millénaire: entre tradition et modernité*. Sous la dir. de Marie-Christine Weidmann Koop. Québec: Presses de l'Univ. du Québec, 2008. xv, 418 p. [Beaulieu, Chen, Desautels, Farhoud, Hémon, Nepveu, Proulx, Ringuet, Sénécal, Vigneault, Cinema: Aubert, Poirier]

GG121. • *Reading(s) from a distance: European perspectives on Canadian women's writing*. Ed. Charlotte Sturgess, Martin Kuester. Augsburg: Wissner, 2008. *Studies in anglophone literatures and cultures*. 263 p. [Chen, S. Jacob]

GG122. • *Recharting the Black Atlantic: modern cultures, local communities, global connections*. Ed. Annalisa Oboe, Anna Scacchi. New York: Routledge, 2008. *Routledge research in Atlantic studies*, 1. ix, 423 p.

GG123. • *Réel et imaginaire de la femme dans la littérature du Maghreb au XXe siècle*. Coordination scientifique Hédia Khadhar. Carthage: Académie tunisienne des sciences, des lettres et des arts, Beït al-Hikma, 2004. 235 p.

GG124. • *Regards croisés sur l'histoire et la littérature acadiennes*. Dir. Madeleine Frédéric et Serge Jaumain. Bruxelles: P. Lang, 2006. 195 p.

GG125. • *Representing minorities: studies in literature and criticism*. Ed. Larbi Touaf, Soumia Boutkhil. Newcastle upon Tyne: Cambridge Scholars, 2008. xviii, 236 p.

GG126. • *Retours du colonial?: disculpation et réhabilitation de l'histoire coloniale française*. Sous la dir. de Catherine Coquio. Nantes: Atalante, 2008. *Comme un accordéon*. 380 p.

GG127. • Riesz, János: *De la littérature coloniale à la littérature africaine: prétextes, contextes, intertextes*. Paris: Karthala, 2007. *Lettres du Sud*. 421 p. [Beti, Delavignette, B. Diop, Grainville, Hazoumé, Randau, Sassine, Sembène]

GG128. ● *Roman [Le] policier belge.* Dir. Daniel Compère, Arnaud Huftier. Amiens: Association des amis du roman populaire, 2008.

GG129. ● *Romanciers français d'Algérie 1900-1950.* Textes réunis par Lucienne Martini et Jean-François Durand. Paris: Kailash, 2008. *Cahiers de la SIELEC,* 5. 394 p.

GG130. ● Schüller, Thorsten: *"Wo ist Afrika?": paratopische Ästhetik in der zeitgenössischen Romanliteratur des frankophonen Schwarzafrika.* Frankfurt: IKO, 2008. vi, 288 p.

GG131. ● *Scritture delle migrazioni: passagi e ospitalità. Ecritures des migrations: passages et hospitalité.* A cura di Laura Restuccia e Giovanni Saverio Santangelo. Palermo: Palumbo, 2008. 329 p. [Butor, Chraibi, Condé, Dib, Djebar, Houssi, Khatibi, Malinconi, Ouologuem, Semprun]

GG132. ● Sommer, Marcel: *Les villes et les livres: l'image de la ville dans la littérature africaine francophone.* Paris: L'Harmattan, 2007. 119 p.

GG133. ● *Tolérance [La] religieuse, reflet de l'aspiration d'une nation à la démocratie: dans la vie et l'œuvre de quatre auteurs sénégalais.* Dakar?: Fondation Konrad Adenauer; Société Goethe du Sénégal, 2007. 65 p. [Birago Diop, Cheikh Anta Diop, Abdoulaye Sadje, Senghor]

GG134. ● Toman, Cheryl: *Contemporary matriarchies in Cameroonian francophone literature: "on est ensemble".* Birmingham, AL: Summa, 2008. x, 187 p.

GG135. ● *Ton [Un], une voix, un texte: prix littéraires Radio-Canada (2001-2006).* Société Radio-Canada. Montréal: XYZ, 2008. 223 p.

GG136. ● *Traduire depuis les marges/Translating from the margins.* Ed. Denise Merkle [et al.]. Québec: Nota Bene, 2008. *Terre américaine.* 414 p. [Brossard, Daigle]

GG137. ● *Tree of liberty: cultural legacies of the Haitian Revolution in the Atlantic world.* Ed. Doris L. Garraway. Charlottesville: Univ. of Virginia Press, 2008. *New world studies.* vi, 280 p. [Césaire, Chauvet]

GG138. ● *Trois poètes québécois: poésie. Emile Nelligan, Hector de Saint-Denys Garneau, Anne Hébert.* Dossier d'accompagnement présenté par Marie-Thérèse Bataïni. Montréal: XYZ, 2008. 327 p. [Poetry, Hébert, Nelligan, Saint-Denys Garneau]

GG139. ● Tsitungu Kongolo, Antoine: *La présence belge dans les lettres congolaises: modèles culturels et littéraires.* Paris: L'Harmattan, 2008. 447 p.

GG140. ● *Utopia [La] mestiza: reflexion sobre sincretismo y multiculturalismo.* Coord. Maryse Renaud. Poitiers: Centre de recherches latino-américaines-Archivos, 2007. 469 p.

GG141. ● Vurgun, Sibel: *Voyages sans retour: Migration, Interkulturalität und Rückkehr in der frankophonen Literatur.* Bielefeld: Transcript, 2007. 318 p.

GG142. ● Wehrs, Donald R.: *Islam, ethics, revolt: politics and piety in Francophone West African and Maghreb narrative.* Lanham, MD: Lexington, 2008. x, 279 p. [Bâ, Boudjedra, Djebar, Kane, Kourouma, Laye, Ouologuem]

GG143. Abassi, Ali: "Une problématique identitaire de la littérature francophone en Tunisie: la femme et le féminin," *Revue de Littérature Comparée,* no. 327 [no. 3] (juillet-sept. 2008), 319-341.

GG144. Accad, Evelyne: "S'(écrire): des femmes francophones libanaises." In 119, 215-232.

GG145. Addino, Roberto: "De quelques inquiétants loups-garous: pour une définition du fantastique québécois," *Etudes Francophones,* vol. 23, no. 1-2 (printemps-automne 2008), 141-159.

GG146. Aksov, Ekrem: "La littérature d'expression française en Turquie," *Revue d'Histoire Littéraire de la France,* tome 108, no. 3 (juillet-sept. 2008), 633-644.

GG147. Akakuru, Iheanacho A.: "Le rejet du christianisme dans le roman africain d'expression française," *Neohelicon,* vol. 35, no. 1 (2008), 135-144.

GG147a. Alassane, Anne: "Le conflit père/fils à travers le roman francophone négro-africain et maghrébin." In 572, 217-226.

GG148. Alemdjrodo, Kangni Alem: "Images, mythes et figures dans les littératures du Maghreb et de l'Afrique noire: essai de littérature comparée," *Cultures Sud,* no. 169 (avril-juin 2008), 79-86.

GG148a. Amodeo, Immacolata: " 'Il n'est plus question de patrie': histoires de migration et leurs configurations esthétiques: de la littérature des auteurs francophones d'origine italienne au Canada." In 483, 153-161.

GG149.   Anyadike, Chima I.: "Modern African diaspora: the nervous conditions of ambiguous adventures." In 42, 331-342. [Hamidou Kane]

GG150.   Arino, Marc: "Images de Montréal dans la nouvelle québécoise du 20e siècle," *Etudes Canadiennes*, no. 64 (2008), 139-152.

GG151.   Azarian, Viviane: "L' 'irréel du passé' comme relief fictionnel dans les écritures de soi africaines," *Etudes Littéraires Africaines*, no. 26 (2008), 52-60. [Fily Dabo Sissoko, Birago Diop, Hampâté Bâ]

GG152.   Baker, Charlotte: "African and Maghreb literature," *Year's Work in Modern Language Studies*, vol. 69 (2007), 275-283.

GG153.   Banga Amvéné, Jean Désiré: "Polémique et accommodation de l'oralité francophone." In 99, 59-76.

GG153a.   Barbalosi, Laurence: "De la commémoration historique à la commémoration mémorielle à travers le théâtre grec et les nouvelles dramaturgies d'Afrique noire francophone." In 414, 511-520. [Efoui, Kwahulé]

GG154.   Baylee Toumi, Alek: "Actualités littéraires du Maghreb," *Nouvelles Etudes Francophones*, vol. 22, no. 2 (automne 2007), 220-223.

GG155.   Baylee Toumi, Alek: "Actualités littéraires du Maghreb," *Nouvelles Etudes Francophones*, vol. 23, no. 1 (printemps 2008), 227-231.

GG156.   Baylee Toumi, Alek: "Actualités littéraires du Maghreb," *Nouvelles Etudes Francophones*, vol. 23, no. 2 (automne 2008), 305-308.

GG157.   Baylee Toumi, Alek: "Actualités littéraires et cinématographiques du Maghreb," *Nouvelles Etudes Francophones*, vol. 22, no. 1 (printemps 2007), 217-220.

GG158.   Beaulé, Sophie: "Enfants du souvenir, enfants du devenir: facettes de l'expérience migrante dans la science-fiction québécoise." In 104, 123-138.

GG159.   Ben Saad, Nizar: "Ecrire dans la langue de l'Autre: risqué et enjeux," *Revue de Littérature Comparée*, no. 327 [no. 3] (juillet-sept. 2008), 289-298.

GG160.   Beniamino, Michel: "Ecritures féminines à l'île Maurice: une rupture postcoloniale?," *Nouvelles Etudes Francophones*, vol. 23, no. 1 (printemps 2008), 144-154.

GG161.   Bhêly-Quenum, Olympe: "Etre écrivain francophone et un étranger dans la littérature de langue française," *Présence Africaine*, no. 175-176-177 (2007-1er sem. 2008), 134-142. [Bhêly-Quenum]

GG162.   Bisanswa, Justin Kalulu: "Poétique du roman africain francophone contemporain." In 72, 135-155.

GG163.   Bitegue Dit Manga, Blaise: "La littérature guyanaise de demain, d'où vient-elle?," *Nouvelles Etudes Francophones*, vol. 23, no. 2 (automne 2008), 155-162.

GG164.   Bizek-Tatara, Renata: "Les avatars des rapports des écrivains belges francophones à la France." In 76, 187-195

GG165.   Blanco, Delia: "Haïti et République Dominicaine: convergences et divergences d'un espace littéraire," *Cultures Sud*, no. 168 (mars 2008), 96-107.

GG166.   Bokiba, André: "Le statut textuel du nom d'auteur: cas des écrivains congolais." In 96, 59-68.

GG167.   Bonn, Charles: "Le tragique de l'émergence littéraire maghrébine entre deux langues, ou le roman familial," *Nouvelles Etudes Francophones*, vol. 22, no. 1 (printemps 2007), 11-22.

GG168.   Bouguarche, Ahmed: "Critique de la religion et de la tradition dans la littérature maghrébine de langue française." In 43, 347-357.

GG169.   Boutkhil, Soumia: " 'The evil eye': re/presenting woman in Moroccan literature in French." In 125, 56-63. [Ben Jelloun, Serhane]

GG170.   Brancato, Sabrina: "Afro-European literature(s): a new discursive category?," *Research in African Literatures*, vol. 39, no. 3 (Fall 2008), 1-13.

GG171.   Brezault, Eloïse: "Qu'est-ce qu'un auteur 'francophone'? Aperçu sur un paysage éditorial." In 126, 347-357.

GG172.   Brogniez, Laurence; Charlyne Audin: "On the art of crossing borders: the double artist in Belgium." In 79, 30-40.

GG173.   Cajee, Zareen: "Le théâtre à la Réunion des années 1970 à nos jours," *Nouvelles Etudes Francophones*, vol. 23, no. 1 (printemps 2008), 94-108. [Theater]

GG173a.   Camoin, Cécilia: "Le cri derrière le masque. Le carnavalesque dans la littérature louisianaise francophone." In 441, 109-128.

GG173b.   Camoin-Nicolas, Cécilia: "Liens familiaux et quête des origines dans la littérature des Acadiens de Louisiane." In 571, 323-331.

GG174.   Caron, Pascal: "L'obsession du corps et la poésie québécoise," *Etudes Littéraires*, vol. 37, no. 2 (automne 2006), 93-106. [Michel Beaulieu, Claude Beausoleil, Brossard]

GG175.   Carrière, Marie: "Des méprises identitaires: migrance et écriture au Québec et au Canada anglais." In 104, 57-71.

GG176.   Cazenave, Odile: "Le roman africain et antillais: nouvelles formes d'engagement au féminin." In 72, 499-513.

GG177.   Chalaye, Sylvie: "Afrique noire francophone: dramaturgies contemporaines, dramaturgies *alien*." In 72, 421-431.

GG178.   Chalaye, Sylvie: "Pour une poétique des corps en écritures," *Esprit Créateur*, vol. 48, no. 3 (Fall 2008), 517.

GG179.   Charnley, Joy: "Ni ennemi, ni rivale: female friendship in works by Alice Rivaz, Anne-Lise Grobéty and Noëlle Revaz," *Forum for Modern Language Studies*, vol. 44, no. 1 (2008), 53-66. [Grobéty, Revaz, Rivaz]

GG180.   Charron, Marc; Christiane Melançon: "Altérité, migrance et traduction: les poésies contemporaines au Canada." In 104, 107-121.

GG181.   Chatti, Mounira: "Mythe, histoire et mémoire." In 96, 383-386. [Déwé Gorodé, Jean-Marie Tjibaou]

GG181a.   Chaulet-Achour, Christiane: "Des langues romanesques au cœur du plurilinguisme algérien." In 434, 77-88.

GG182.   Chaulet-Achour, Christiane: "En ligne de mire: le foulard et la scène. Humeur et humour 'maghrébins'," *Expressions Maghrébines*, vol. 7, no. 2 (hiver 2008), 129-141.

GG183.   Chaulet-Achour, Christiane: "Exils productifs. Quatre parcours méridiens." In 119, 37-55. [Bencheikh, Chahdortt Djavann, Huston, Sebbar]

GG184.   Chaulet-Achour, Christiane: "Machrek en feu: femmes/guerre/écriture," *Interculturel Francophonies*, no. 14 (2008), 163-182.

GG185.   Chemla, Yves: "Le roman haïtien: intertextualité, parentés, affinités," *Interculturel Francophones*, no. 12 (nov.-déc. 2007), 7-15.

GG186.   Chiwengo, Ngwarsungu: "When wounds and corpses fail to speak: narratives of violence and rape in Congo (DRC)," *Comparative Studies of South Asia, Africa and the Middle East*, vol. 28, no. 1 (2008), 78-92. [Tadjo]

GG187.   Clary, Françoise: "Paroles entravées et contre-discours: la résistance de la langue africaine dans l'espace caraïbe." In 93, 333-349.

GG188.   Clavaron, Yves: "Etudes francophones, postcolonial studies: entre mésentente cordiale et strategies partagées," *Neohelicon*, vol. 35, no. 2 (2008), 39-53.

GG189.   Constantini, Alessandro: "Des chiens et des hommes: de la métonymie individuelle à la métaphore collective," *Interculturel Francophones*, no. 12 (nov.-déc. 2007), 77-121.

GG190.   Coret, Laure: "Ecriture postcoloniale, écritures de soi: l'écriture au féminin dans la littérature antillaise." In 126, 331-345. [Chamoiseau, Maximin]

GG191.   Courcy, Nathalie: "Langue et plurilinguisme dans les œuvres camerounaises entre 1997 et 2001." In 52, 21-45.

GG192.   Croisy, Sophie: "Algerian history, Algerian literature, and critical theories," *Interdisciplinary Literary Studies*, vol. 10, no. 1 (Fall 2008), 84-106.

GG193.   Dalembert, Louis-Philippe: "Et la Caraïbe s'unit à la Méditerranée," *Cultures Sud*, no. 169 (avril-juin 2008), 111-113.

GG194.   Dash, J. Michael: "Fictions of displacement: locating modern Haitian narratives," *Small Axe*, no. 27 (Oct. 2008), 32-41. [Laferrière, Roumain]

GG195.   Davaille, Florence: "Quand une langue dominée tente de devenir dominante: la question du joual au Québec dans les années 1960-19770." In 93, 397-409.

GG196.   Davies Cordova, Sarah: "Raisonner ou résonner? Expressions de l'Histoire et je(ux) de la mémoire dans les récits féminins haïtiens contemporains," *Interculturel Francophones*, no. 12 (nov.-déc. 2007), 123-140.

GG197.   Décarie, David: "L'édition des textes fondamentaux de la littérature acadienne." In 44, 145-1554.

GG198.   De Luca, Ylenia: "Langage et malaise culturel de l'écrivain interculturel au Canada francophone," *Rivista di Studi Canadesi*, n. 20 (2007), 173-180.

GG199.   Détrez, Christine: Les écrivaines algériennes et l'écriture de la décennie noire," *Etudes Littéraires Africaines*, no. 26 (2008), 19-26.

GG199a.   Détrez, Christiane: "Le problématique nomadisme des romancières algériennes." In 539, 29-39.

GG199b.   Détrez, Christiane; Anne Simon: "La mémoire est-aussi-un mot féminin: construction d'une contre-mémoire chez les romancières algériennes." In 414, 419-428.

GG200.   Diagana, M'bouh Séta: "La rhétorique du nom de l'esclave dans le roman mauritanien francophone," *Itinéraires et Contacts de Cultures*, no. 39 (2007), 99-103.

GG201.   Dieng, Amady Ali: "Le 1er Congrès des écrivains et artistes noirs et les étudiants africains," *Présence Africaine*, no. 175-176-177 (2007-1er sem. 2008), 118-124.

GG202.   Douglas, Rachel: "Caribbean literature," *Year's Work in Modern Language Studies*, vol. 69 (2007), 269-274.

GG203.   Douider, Samira: "Les figures du fou et le malaise (romans maghrébins et sub-sahariens de langue française)." In 96, 159-164.

GG204.   Duclot-Clément, Nathalie: "Encres et ancrages: marquage du corps et dérives." In 96, 407-421.

GG205.   Dutton, Jacqueline: "*Littérature-monde* or Francophonie? From the manifesto to the great debate," *Essays in French Literature and Culture*, no. 45 (Nov. 2008), 43-68.

GG206.   Edwin, Shirin: "Subverting social customs: the representation of food in three West African Francophone novels," *Research in African Literatures*, vol. 39, no. 3 (Fall 2008), 39-50. [Bâ, Aminata Sow Fall, Kourouma]

GG206a.   El Hadrati, Latifa: "Les relations familiales dans les livres d'enfance et de jeunesse au Maroc." In 571, 367-380.

GG207.   Ertler, Klaus-Dieter: "Das literarische System der Provinz Québec: der Roman von 2000 bis 2006," *Zeitschrift für Kanada-Studien*, 28. Jahrgang, Heft 2 (2008), 67-89.

GG208.   Essohi Ewané, Christiane-Félicité: "Subjectivité et créativité lexicale dans *Temps de chien* de P. Nganang et *Bouillons de vies* de A. S. Bonono." In 52, 97-107. [Angéline Solange Bonono, P. Nganang]

GG209.   Fandio, Pierre: "Ambiguïtés et polyphonies: le mouvement des idées au Cameroun à l'ère de la transition démocratique." In 43, 426-442.

GG210.   Fonkoua, Romuald-Blaise: "Les écrivains antillais à *Présence Africaine*. Remarques sur le fonctionnement d'un champ littéraire," *Présence Africaine*, no. 175-176-177 (2007-1er sem. 2008), 528-545.

GG211.   Fontaine, Jean: "Romans tunisiens 2006," *IBLA*, no. 198 [no. 2] (2006), 265-285.

GG212.   Foulon, Jean-François: "La littérature en Belgique francophone est-elle belge, française ou wallonne?," *Presse Littéraire*, no. 11 (2007), 59-70.

GG213.   Fraiture, Pierre-Philippe: "Belgian 'Negro' fiction: modernist itinerary of a didactic genre." In 79, 41-56.

GG213a.   François, Cyrille: "Ecrire la mémoire sur un défaut d'histoire: le cas de la littérature francophone des Antilles." In 414, 439-447.

GG214.   Gaboury-Diallo, Lise: "Actualités littéraires de la francophonie nord-américaine (à l'exception du Québec)," *Nouvelles Etudes Francophones*, vol. 22, no. 1 (printemps 2007), 191-194.

GG215.   Gagnon, Daniel: "Poésie," *University of Toronto Quarterly*, vol. 77, no. 1 (Winter 2008), 510-530. [Poetry]

GG216.   Gauvin, Lise: "Filiations et filatures: modalités et usages de la parole chez deux écrivains migrants, Micone et Pasquali." In 119, 15-36. [Micone, Adrien Pasquali]

GG217.   Gauvin, Lise: "Situation des littératures francophones: à propos de quelques dénominations." In 75, 27-39.

GG218.   Gbanou, Sélom Komlan: "Réinventer Dionysos ou la théâtralité et le tragique dans le pouvoir politique en Afrique." In 72, 75-102.

GG219.   Gérin, Pierre M.: "Nationalisme et littérature au cours de la renaissance acadienne (1964-1930). Voix discordantes," *Studia Romanica Posnaniensia*, no. 35 (2008), 3-13.

GG220.   Ghamdi, Abdoulah Al: "La littérature francophone au Maghreb entre le figé et le mouvant." In 96, 171-174.

GG221.   Girard, Céline: "L'écriture de l'obsession du corps-vécu dans l'espace pulsionnel et impur de la ville." In 69, 247-259. [Pauline Harvey, Francine Noël, Lise Tremblay]

GG222.   Girard, Céline: "Entre tradition et modernité: la place de la femme dans la cité dans le roman féminin québécois." In 120, 277-281.

GG223.   Gorceix, Paul: "La Belgique, un balcon sur l'Europe." In 83, 291-302.

GG224.   Guedj, Colette: "A la croisée des chem(a)ins: autour de l'altérité." In 96, 389-396.

GG225.   Habrand, Tanguy; Denis Saint-Amand: "Actualités littéraires en Belgique francophone," *Nouvelles Etudes Francophones*, vol. 23, no. 1 (printemps 2008), 216-210.

GG226.   Halwani, Asma Chamly: "Eddé, Klat et Yazigi Najem ou trois voix féminines de la transgression," *Interculturel Francophonies*, no. 14 (2008), 183-202. [Dominique Eddé, Yasmine Klat, Tania Yazigi Najem]

GG227.   Hammouti, Abdellah: "Affirmation de soi, désir de l'autre et dissidence par l'écriture: cas de la littérature négro-africaine d'expression française." In 96, 97-104. [Adiaffi, Dadié, Hamidou Kane, Senghor]

GG228.   Hammouti, Abdellah: "De quelques manifestations de l'humour dans la littérature maghrébine d'expression française," *Expressions Maghrébines*, vol. 7, no. 2 (hiver 2008), 13-35.

GG229.   Hogarth, Christopher: "Representations of migrant 'homes' in France through Senegalese literature." In 80, 67-83.

GG230.   Hollosi, Szonja: "Réinterprétation de l'androgyne: du stéréotype aux métamorphoses dans l'imaginaire maghrébin francophone." In 96, 165-169. [Ben Jelloun, Boudjedra, N. Bouraoui, Khadra]

GG231.   Jeanneret, Sylvie: "Actualités littéraires de la Suisse romande," *Nouvelles Etudes Francophones*, vol. 22, no. 1 (printemps 2007), 231-234.

GG232.   Jolicœur, Louis: "Traduction littéraire et diffusion d'une culture littéraire nationale: le cas du Canada," *Rivista di Studi Canadesi*, n. 21 (2008), 95-103.

GG233.   Jonassaint, Jean: "Actualités littéraires d'Afrique et de la Caraïbe," *Nouvelles Etudes Francophones*, vol. 23, no. 1 (printemps 2008), 212-215.

GG234.   Jonassaint, Jean: "Actualités littéraires de l'Afrique subsaharienne," *Nouvelles Etudes Francophones*, vol. 22, no. 1 (printemps 2007), 189-190.

GG235.   Jonassaint, Jean: "Actualités littéraires des Caraïbes," *Nouvelles Etudes Francophones*, vol. 22, no. 1 (printemps 2007), 195-198.

GG236.   Jonassaint, Jean: "Toward new paradigms in Caribbean studies: the impact of the Haitian Revolution on our literatures." In 137, [n.p.]

GG237.   Jouve, Edmond: "Les écrivains et le rêve d'une Afrique unie." In 72, 53-66.

GG238.   Kabwe Wa Segatti, Désiré: "Enjeux du silence dans les littératures de la post-colonie," *French Studies in Southern Africa*, no. 38 (2008), 79-94.

GG239.   Karch, Pierre: "Roman," *University of Toronto Quarterly*, vol. 77, no. 1 (Winter 2008), 456-478. [Novel]

GG240.   Karmaoui, Ghazi: "Genèse(s) de la littérature judéo-tunisienne d'expression française," *Revue de Littérature Comparée*, no. 327 [no. 3] (juillet-sept. 2008), 299-317.

GG241.   Keown, Michelle: " 'Our seas of islands': migration and *métissage* in contemporary Polynesian writing," *International Journal of Francophone Studies*, vol. 11, no. 4 (2008), 503-522.

GG242.   Knutson, April A.: "The others' others: the perception of women in Caribbean literature," *CLA Journal*, vol. 51, no. 4 (June 2008), 378-393. [Beauvoir, Condé, S. Schwarz-Bart]

GG243. Kober, Marc: "La barque et la citadelle: les romans de la traversée clandestine," *Cultures Sud*, no. 169 (avril-juin 2008), 87-94.

GG244. Koné, Amadou: "Bilinguisme et émancipation du roman africain." In 72, 123-134.

GG245. Konkobo, Christophe: "Entre-deux, entre jeux: l'intermédialité dans les théâtres contemporains," *Esprit Créateur*, vol. 48, no. 3 (Fall 2008), 55-65.

GG246. Kouvouama, Abel: " 'Verre cassé' ou les figures de la transgression: de l'inspiration musicale à la production littéraire," *Études de Lettres*, no. 279 [no. 1] (2008), 119-132.

GG247. Kwaterko, Józef: "Ex-centricité et reterritorialisation: Montréal chez les écrivains haïtiens du Québec," *Etudes Canadiennes*, no. 64 (2008), 99-108.

GG248. Laforest, Daniel: "Fictions des temps en lutte: présences d'un passé indépassable." In 120, 318-324. [Quebec literature]

GG249. Lamar, Celite: "Entre sœurs: relations familiales au féminin dans l'œuvre dramatique de trois auteures québécoises," *Rivista di Studi Canadesi*, n. 21 (2008), 37-50. [Michelle Allen, Abla Farhoud, Marie Laberge]

GG250. Lapacherie, Jean-Gérard: "De l'oubli dans lequel s'abîme la littérature égyptienne de langue française," *Interculturel Francophonies*, no. 14 (2008), 121-130.

GG251. Lebdai, Benaouda: "Les littératures africaines: approche comparative," *Cultures Sud*, no. 169 (avril-juin 2008), 101-106.

GG252. Lepage, Élise: "Intertextualité dans la réception critique de la littérature québécoise au Canada anglais," *Québec Studies*, vol. 45 (Spring/Summer 2008), 133-151.

GG253. Levasseur, Jean: "Actualités littéraires de la francophonie," *Nouvelles Etudes Francophones*, vol. 22, no. 1 (printemps 2007), 185-188.

GG254. Levasseur, Jean: "Actualités littéraires du Québec," *Nouvelles Etudes Francophones*, vol. 22, no. 1 (printemps 2007), 221-230.

GG255. Levasseur, Jean: "Actualités littéraires du Québec," *Nouvelles Etudes Francophones*, vol. 22, no. 2 (automne 2007), 224-232.

GG256. Levasseur, Jean: "Actualités littéraires du Québec," *Nouvelles Etudes Francophones*, vol. 23, no. 1 (printemps 2008), 241-256.

GG257. Levasseur, Jean: "Actualités littéraires du Québec," *Nouvelles Etudes Francophones*, vol. 23, no. 2 (automne 2008), 309-320.

GG258. Lloret, Danielle Pastor: "Vers de nouveaux horizons." In 96, 225-238.

GG259. Lord, Michel: "Nouvelle," *University of Toronto Quarterly*, vol. 77, no. 1 (Winter 2008), 479-509.

GG260. Loum, Daouda: "Métis et métissages: l'éclairage littéraire en miroir," *French Colonial History*, vol. 9 (2008), 79-102. [Bâ, Ousmane Socé Diop, Abdoulaye Sadji, Senghor]

GG261. Lucas, Rafaël: "La mise en question de l'héroïsme dans la littérature haïtienne (1960-2000)." In 118, 391-420.

GG262. Maffesoli, Michel: "L'esthétique tribale." In 96, 375-382.

GG263. Magdelaine-Andrianjafitrimo, Valérie: "Actualités littéraires de l'Océan Indien," *Nouvelles Etudes Francophones*, vol. 23, no. 1 (printemps 2008), 232-240.

GG264. Magdelaine-Andrianjafitrimo, Valérie: "Les littératures réunionnaises: entre francophonie et Outre-Mer," *Nouvelles Etudes Francophones*, vol. 23, no. 1 (printemps 2008), 52-66.

GG265. Maggetti, Daniel: "Écrire en Suisse romande: pouvoir en faire à sa tête?," *Études de Lettres*, no. 279 [no. 1] (2008), 163-174.

GG266. Mahfoudh, Ahmed: "Etat et perspectives de la littérature maghrébine en Tunisie," *Cahiers de Tunisie*, tome 60, no. 196 (1er trim. 2006), 71-90.

GG267. Mambenga-Ylangou, Frédéric: "Français et imaginaire populaires ou la poétique du social urbain dans la littérature africaine francophone," *Itinéraires et Contacts de Cultures*, no. 39 (2007), 135-151.

GG268. Mangeon, Anthony: "Ecrire l'Afrique, penser l'histoire." In 126, 303-329. [Kourouma, Ouologuem]

GG269.　Marimoutou, Carpanin: "Parler des opprimés. Le roman réunionnais francophone des années 1970," *Nouvelles Etudes Francophones*, vol. 23, no. 1 (printemps 2008), 67-81.

GG270.　Marimoutou, Félix: "Chanson et poésie: Ile de la Réunion," *Nouvelles Etudes Francophones*, vol. 23, no. 1 (printemps 2008), 109-126. [Poetry]

GG271.　Marshall, Bill: "Cayenne et l'Atlantique français," *Nouvelles Etudes Francophones*, vol. 23, no. 2 (automne 2008), 55-69.

GG272.　Mboudjeke, Jean-Guy: "La poésie acadienne: entre esthéthique et l'hybridité et intraduisibilité." In 136, 75-92.

GG273.　McGuinness, Patrick: "Belgian literature and the symbolism of the double." In 79, 8-22.

GG273a.　Mertz-Baumgartner, Birgit: "Les écrivains algériens contemporains face à la guerre d'Algérie (1954-1962)." In 483, 41-51. [Latifa Ben Mansour, Maïssa Bey]

GG274.　Miller, Christopher: "Césaire, Glissant, Condé: reimagining the Atlantic African 'silence'." In 105. [Césaire, Condé, Glissant]

GG275.　Mokam, David: "Le pluralisme politique au Cameroun de 1951 à 1992: le regard de la littérature depuis 1990." In 52, 231-255.

GG276.　Morel, Pierre: "Coup d'œil sur l'histoire de la littérature du Québec." In 115, 14-19.

GG277.　Moura, Jean-Marc: "Sur la situation des études postcoloniales francophones," *Neohelicon*, vol. 35, no. 2 (2008), 55-61.

GG278.　Mouralis, Bernard: "La colonisation chez quelques écrivains africains depuis 1990." In 126, 187-210. [Beti, Hampâté Bâ, Kourouma, Monénembo, Mudimbe]

GG279.　Mouralis, Bernard: "Négritude et mondialisation," *Présence Africaine*, no. 175-176-177 (2007-1er sem. 2008), 258-265.

GG280.　Munro, Martin: "L'exil et l'innocence dans le discours politique et littéraire d'Haïti." In 119, 131-150.

GG281.　Munro, Martin: "Hatred Chérie: history, silence and animosity in three Haitian novels." In 67, 163-175. [Chauvet, Yanick Lahens, Lyonel Trouillot]

GG282.　Murphy, David: "Birth of a nation? The origins of Senegalese literature in French," *Research in African Literatures*, vol. 39, no. 1 (Spring 2008), 48-69.

GG283.　Nardout-Lafarge, Élisabeth: "Texte, livre et œuvre dans l'histoire littéraire du Québec," *Études de Lettres*, no. 279 [no. 1] (2008), 55-70.

GG284.　Ngalasso, Mwatha Musangi: "La question linguistique au 1er Congrès des écrivains et artistes noirs," *Présence Africaine*, no. 175-176-177 (2007-1er sem. 2008), 143-162.

GG285.　Nguyen, Nathalie: "Actualités littéraires de la francophonie vietnamienne," *Nouvelles Etudes Francophones*, vol. 22, no. 1 (printemps 2007), 235-236.

285a.　Nonnenmacher, Hartmut: "La (re-)construction de l'histoire de 'l'Algérie française' dans la série de B.D. *Les carnets d'Orient* de Jacques Ferrandez." In 483, 101-126.

GG286.　Nouschi, André: "Culture et éducation au Maghreb de 1914 à 1974," *Awal*, no. 37 (2008), 3-21.

GG287.　Novivor, Ayelevi: "Les relations à l'autre dans le roman antillais contemporain," *Nouvelles Etudes Francophones*, vol. 23, no. 2 (automne 2008), 234-245.

GG288.　Okai, Atukwei: "The writer as the compass finger of the people's consciousness. The mid-century imperatives of African literature in a globalised world," *Présence Africaine*, no. 175-176-177 (2007-1er sem. 2008), 574-584.

GG289.　O'Neill-Karch, Mariel: "Théâtre," *University of Toronto Quarterly*, vol. 77, no. 1 (Winter 2008), 531-542. [Theater]

GG290.　Oprea, Denisa-Adriana: "Une poétique du personnage dans cinq romans québécois contemporains au féminin (1980-2000): métaféminisme et postmoderne." Diss., Univ. Laval, 2008. 375 p. [Brossard, Monique Larue, Proulx, Lise Tremblay]

GG291.　Orlando, Valérie K.: "Writing in/on the front lines of exile: political dissidence, memory and cultural (dis)location in Francophone literature of the Maghreb." In 125, 170-182.

GG292. Pangop Kameni, Alain Cyr: "L'écriture du trauma postcolonial en Afrique subsaharienne." In 99, 105-121.

GG293. Parisot, Yolaine: "L'écrivaine haïtienne en son miroir." In 118, 313-324. [Chauvet, Y. Lahens]

GG294. Pavel, Maria: "Les écrivains québécois et la langue. Option et illustration." In 115, 56-71.

GG295. Penrod, Lynn: "Quebec children's literature: a cultural trump card." In 120, 231-237.

GG296. Pessini, Alba: "Dialogue d'enfances dans la littérature haïtienne de l'exil," *Interculturel Francophones*, no. 12 (nov.-déc. 2007), 229-247.

GG297. Pinçonnat, Crystel: "Passé oublié, passé regagné: de l'émergence d'une génération d'héritiers," *Expressions Maghrébines*, vol. 7, no. 1 (été 2008), 13-31.

GG298. Piret, Pierre: "Representation and subjectivity: Belgian playwrights and modernity." In 79, 68-77.

GG299. Pliya, José: "Haïti, Guadeloupe, Dominique: nouvelles écritures théâtrales," *Cultures Sud*, no. 168 (mars 2008), 306-315.

GG300. Pouliot, Suzanne; Noëlle Sorin: "Les mutations du discours éditorial sur la lecture des jeunes Québécois de 1920 à aujourd'hui." In 120, 222-230.

GG301. Quaghebeur, Marc: "Voici venu le temps des migrations au sein de notre langue." In 131, 149-163.

GG302. Raïssi, Rachid: "Littérature maghrébine entre déterminisme et désir d'authenticité," *Algérie Littérature/Action*, no. 121-122 (mai-juin 2008), 42-46.

GG303. Ramsay, Raylene: "In the belly of the canoe with Ihimaera, Hulme and Gorodé. The waka as a locus of hybridity," *International Journal of Francophone Studies*, vol. 11, no. 4 (2008), 559-579.

GG304. Ranaivoson, Dominique: "L'écriture malgache contemporaine: insulaire avant tout?," *Nouvelles Etudes Francophones*, vol. 23, no. 1 (printemps 2008), 35-51.

GG305. Ranaivoson, Dominique: "Madagascar 1947: le roman ouvre-t-il les pages scellées de l'Histoire?," *Etudes Littéraires Africaines*, no. 26 (2008), 61-69.

GG306. Ransom, Amy J.: "Sexuality, horror, and postmodernism in Québec's *Littératures du genre*," *Contemporary French Civilization*, vol. 32, no. 1 (Winter/Spring 2008), 157-182.

GG306a. Reichardt, Dagmar: "Drames sur drames: de la relation entre la fiction historique et l'histoire coloniale dans le théâtre francophone de l'Algérie et des Antilles des années 1950 et 1960." In 483, 137-152. [Césaire, Yacine]

GG307. Reswch, Y.: "L'étrangeté de l'écrivain migrant, cet Autre québécois." In 75, 167-176.

GG308. Riesz, János: "Les écrivains africains dans leurs portraits." In 127, 381-396.

GG309. Riesz, János: "Les littératures d'Afrique noire vues du côté de la réception." In 1127, 365-380.

GG310. Rochmann, Marie-Christine: "Le roman historique guyanais contemporain, ou les miroitements d'une temporalité hétérogène," *Nouvelles Etudes Francophones*, vol. 23, no. 2 (automne 2008), 70-84. [Novel]

GG311. Rosenstreich, Susan L.: "God the father or Mother Earth?: *Nouvelle France* in two Québec novels of the 1980s," *Esprit Créateur*, vol. 48, no. 1 (Spring 2008), 120-130. [Hébert, Poulin]

GG312. Rousselot, Elodie: "French Canadian literature," *Year's Work in Modern Language Studies*, vol. 69 (2007), 263-268.

GG313. Rudacogora, Augustin: "La littérature rwandaise après 1994," *Itinéraires et Contacts de Cultures*, no. 39 (2007), 77-83.

GG314. Saint-Martin, Lori: "The body politic and the erotic body: the (male) novel of the Quiet Revolution in Quebec," *British Journal of Canadian Studies*, vol. 21, no. 2 (2008), 195-217.

GG314a. Saint-Martin, Lori: "Des pères absents aux filles meurtrières et au-delà: le rapport père-fille en littérature québécoise." In 572, 13-26.

GG315. Saint-Martin, Lori: "Inceste père-fille, corps vivant, corps du texte." In 69, 71-84.

GG316. Sasu, Voichita-Maria: "Les retouches de l'intime." In 69, 215-225.

GG317. Scepi, Henri: "Métissage et autoexotisme dans le roman antillais contemporain." In 140, 359-366.

GG317a. Serrano, Richard: "Not your uncle: text, sex, and the globalized Moroccan author." In 629.

GG318. Sinanga, Judith Ohlman: "Pensée de la négritude et identitaire 'post-colonial'." In 96, 83-91. [Senghor]

GG319. Sissao, Alain: "Figures charismatiques et démocratie chez quelques romanciers de l'Afrique de l'Ouest." In 72, 181-203.

GG320. Sol, Antoinette Marie: "Histoire(s) et traumatisme(s): l'infanticide dans le roman féminin antillais," *French Review*, vol. 81, no. 5 (April 2008), 967-984.

GG321. Souza, Pascale de; H. Adlai Murdoch: "Oceanic routes: migrations and *métissages* in South Pacific literatures and travelogues," *International Journal of Francophone Studies*, vol. 11, no. 4 (2008), 481-502.

GG322. Stétié, Salah: "Le Liban au cœur du français," *Interculturel Francophonies*, no. 14 (2008), 13-33.

GG322a. Suhonen, Katri: "Mères marchandes et fils 'a-mères' dans la littérature québécoise, ou les vestiges d'un ordre social patriacal?" In 571, 137-145.

GG323. Sy, Kalidou: "L'écrivain francophone ou 'le paradoxe du comédien'," *Études de Lettres*, no. 279 [no. 1] (2008), 85-102.

GG323a. ten Kortenaar, Neil: "Œdipe et les fils des indépendances africaines." In 572, 153-161.

GG324. Tennier, Julie: "Ressemblance et étrangeté: l'altérité dans quelques œuvres franco-ontariennes," *LittéRéalité*, vol. 20, no. 1 (printemps/été 2008), 59-73. [Catherine Caron, Patrice Desbiens, Pierre Paul Karch]

GG325. Tessonneau, Alex Louise: "La littérature haïtienne de 1873 à 1906." In 118, 55-74.

GG326. Thérond, Emmanuel: "Littérature et intégration," *Algérie Littérature/Action*, no. 121-122 (mai-juin 2008), 36-38.

GG327. Thibault, Bruno: "Actualités littéraires de l'Europe de l'Ouest," *Nouvelles Etudes Francophones*, vol. 23, no. 2 (automne 2008), 286-304.

GG328. Thibault, Bruno; Jean Levasseur: "Actualités littéraires de la francophonie," *Nouvelles Etudes Francophones*, vol. 22, no. 2 (automne 2007), 198-201.

GG329. Thomas, Jean-Pierre: "Vers la modernité: l'impact de la figure de l'étranger dans la littérature québécoise." In 120, 245-253.

GG330. Tonyé, Alphonse J.: "Littérature camerounaise d'expression française." In 52, 81-95.

GG331. Topor, Hélène d'Almeida: "Les lettres et les arts dans les timbres-poste du Congo et du Togo." In 96, 397-406.

GG332. Toro, Alfonso de: "Au-delà de la francophonie: représentation de la pensée hybride au Maghreb," *Neohelicon*, vol. 35, no. 2 (2008), 63-86. [Djebar, Khatibi]

GG333. Traoré, Dominique: "Corps, voix et voies du dialogue," *Esprit Créateur*, vol. 48, no. 3 (Fall 2008), 41-54.

GG334. "Trois écrivains guyanais parlent librement de la littérature guyanaise," *Nouvelles Etudes Francophones*, vol. 23, no. 2 (automne 2008), 31-43. [André Paradis, Serge Patient, Elie Stephenson]

GG335. Tshitungu Kongolo, Antoine: "Littérature congolaise: des pionniers à l'essor actuel," *Carnet et les Instants*, no. 150 (2008), 37-42.

GG336. Turin, Gaspard: "Guerres et républiques d'enfants. L'enfance autonome dans la littérature francophone contemporaine." In 99, 151-164.

GG337. Vigier, Stéphanie: "La fiction au passé: histoire, mémoire et espace-temps dans la fiction littéraire océanienne contemporaine." Diss., Univ. of Auckland, 2008. 412 p.

GG338. Virolle, Marie: "Ecrivains algériens: le troisième pays." In 119, 57-103.

GG339. Vitali, Ilaria: "La bibliothèque de Shéhérazade en voyage: reprises et réécritures d'un livre-édifice dans la littérature algérienne contemporaine," *Voix Plurielles*, vol. 5, no. 1 (mai 2008), [n.p.]. [Djebar, Sebbar]

GG339a.   Vitali-Volant, Maria G.: "Une bibliothèque 'cabinet de curiosités' à Bamako (Mali)." In 414, 165-172.

GG340.   Voldrichová Beránková, Eva: "Identité et altérité dans le roman québécois," *Studia Romanica Posnaniensia*, no. 35 (2008), 103-111.

GG341.   Voldrichová Beránková, Eva: "Le roman québécois entre la francophonie et l'américanité." In 76, 305-313.

GG342.   West, Heather A.: "Le succès des Haïtiens dans le domaine de la production culturelle au Québec depuis la Révolution tranquille." In 120, 348-357.

GG343.   Woodsworth, Judith: "Translating identity in Northern Ontario." In 136, 95-120.

GG344.   Xanthos, Nicolas: "Fiction du contemporain: d'une structure énigmatique et de sa pensée du temps." In 120, 325-337.

GG345.   Yilancioglu, Seza: "Personnages en quête d'identité: voix féminines." In 96, 183-193. [N. Bouraoui]

GG346.   Yotova, Rennie: "Le langage comme impouvoir? 'Le monstre de carrefour'," *Études de Lettres*, no. 279 [no. 1] (2008), 133-147.

GG347.   Zrizi, Hassan: "Narrating domestic frontiers: unbecoming daughters of patriarchy: Moroccan women writers of French expression." In 125, 64-73. [Siham Benchekroun, Touria Oulehri]

LITERARY HISTORY: FRANCE

GG348.   • *Action [L'] française: culture, société, politique.* Dir. Michel Leymarie et Jacques Prévotat. Villeneuve d'Ascq: Presses univ. du Septentrion, 2008. 434 p. [Blondel, Maritain, Maurras]

GG349.   • Baecque, Antoine de: *Crises dans la culture française.* Paris: Bayard, 2008. 244 p. [Malraux]

GG350.   • Barilier, Etienne: *Ils liront dans mon âme: les écrivains face à Dreyfus.* Genève: Zoé, 2008. 230 p.

GG351.   • Breuil, Eddie: *Les littératures "fin de siècle".* Paris: Gallimard, 2008. 124 p.

GG352.   • Burke, David: *Writers in Paris.* Berkeley, CA: Counterpoint, 2008. 248 p.

GG353.   • Butor, Michel: *Petite histoire de la littérature française.* Paris: Carnets nord, 2008. 145 p.

GG354.   • Combes, Patrick: *Mai 68, les écrivains, la littérature.* Paris: L'Harmattan, 2008. 325 p.

GG355.   • Danesi, Fabien: *Le mythe brisé de l'Internationale situationniste.* Dijon: Presses du reel, 2008. 333 p.

GG356.   • *Décadence [La] dans la culture et la pensée politiques: Espagne, France et Italie, XVIIIe-Xxe siècle.* Etudes réunies par Jean-Yves Frétigné et François Jankowiak. Rome: Ecole française de Rome, 2008. viii, 360 p.

GG357.   • *Histoire de la littérature française du XXe siècle. Tome II, après 1940.* Dir. Michèle Touret. Rennes: Presses univ. de Rennes, 2008. 539 p.

GG358.   • Julaud, Jean-Joseph: *La littérature française pour les nuls. Du XIXe siècle à nos jours.* Paris: First, 2008. xvi, 464 p.

GG359.   • Malinovich, Nadia: *French and Jewish: culture and the politics of identity in early twentieth-century France.* Oxford; Portland, OR: Littman Library of Jewish Civilization, 2007.

GG360.   • *Qu'est-ce qu'un événement littéraire au XIXe siècle?.* Dir. Carinne Saminadayar-Perrin. Saint-Etienne: Publications de l'Univ. de Saint-Etienne, 2008. 320 p. [Goncourt, Verne]

GG361.   • Spotts, Frederic: *The shameful peace: how French artists and intellectuals survived the Nazi occupation.* New Haven; London: Yale Univ. Press, 2008. 283 p.

GG362.   • Viart, Dominique; Bruno Vercier: *La littérature française au présent:*

héritage, modernité, mutations. Avec la collaboration de Franck Evrard. Paris: Bordas, 2008. 2e éd. augm. 543 p.

GG362a.   Arend, Elisabeth: "Histoire, littérature et l'écriture de l'histoire." In 483, 15-32.

GG363.   Chartier, Anne-Marie: "When French schoolchildren were introduced to literature (1920-1940)," *Yale French Studies*, no. 113 (2008), 60-76.

GG364.   Demaeseneer, Rony: "Les Archives et Musée de la littérature: éclairage sur dix lustres d'existence," *Carnet et les Instants*, no. 154 (2008-2009), 41-43.

GG365.   Di Meo, Nicolas: "Mal politique ou fatalité historique? Le mythe de la decadence pendant l'entre-deux-guerres," *Modernités*, no. 29 (2008), 333-344.

GG366.   Durand, Jean-François: "Littératures coloniales, littératures d'Empire?," *Romantisme*, no. 139 (1er trim. 2008), 47-58.

GG367.   Evans, David; Meredith Lynch: "The nineteenth century (post-Romantic)," *Year's Work in Modern Language Studies*, vol. 69 (2007), 176-193.

GG368.   Gauvin, Lise: "Les littératures de langue française à l'heure de la mondialisation," *Ecrits*, no. 124 (déc. 2008), 7-14.

GG369.   Houdart-Mérot, Violaine: "Literary education in the lycée: crisis, continuity, and upheaval since 1880," *Yale French Studies*, no. 113 (2008), 29-45.

GG370.   Ippolito, Christophe: "Literature, 1900-1945," *Year's Work in Modern Language Studies*, vol. 69 (2007), 194-218.

GG371.   Jeannerod, Dominique: "Literature, 1945 to the present day," *Year's Work in Modern Language Studies*, vol. 69 (2007), 219-262.

GG372.   Klein, Jean-François; Marie-Albane de Suremain: "Clio et les colonies. Retour sur des historiographies en situation," *Romantisme*, no. 139 (1er trim. 2008), 59-80.

GG373.   Seillan, Jean-Marie: "La (para)littérature (pré)coloniale à la fin du XIXe siècle," *Romantisme*, no. 139 (1er trim. 2008), 33-45.

GG374.   Serry, Hervé: "Le double jugement de l'art est-il possible? Les impasses d'une critique catholique dans trois polémiques littéraires et religieuses de l'entre-deux-guerres," *Mil Neuf Cent*, no. 26 (2008), 91-104.

GG375.   Thibault, Bruno: "Actualités littéraires de l'Europe de l'Ouest," *Nouvelles Etudes Francophones*, vol. 22, no. 1 (printemps 2007), 202-216.

GG376.   Thibault, Bruno: "Actualités littéraires de l'Europe de l'Ouest," *Nouvelles Etudes Francophones*, vol. 22, no. 2 (automne 2007), 202-219.

GG377.   Verdaguer, Pierre: "Les genres du déclin," *Contemporary French Civilization*, vol. 32, no. 1 (Winter/Spring 2008), 129-155.

GG378.   Weltman-Aron, Brigitte: "The pedagogy of colonial Algeria: Djebar, Cixous, Derrida," *Yale French Studies*, no. 113 (2008), 132-146. [Cixous, Derrida, Djebar]

LITERARY THEMES AND TOPICS

GG379.   ● *Admirable tremblement du temps: le vieillir et le créer.* Etudes rassemblées et prés. par Marie-Christine Paillard. Clermont-Ferrand: Presses univ. Blaise Pascal, 2008. 337 p. [Barrès, Caillois, Guibert, Harpman, Hellens, Ionesco, Leiris, Mac Orlan, Malraux, Oberle, Valéry]

GG380.   ● *An den Rändern der Moral: Studien zur literarischen Ethik.* Hrsg. Ulrich Kinzel. Würzburg: Königshausen & Neumann, 2008. 202 p. [Levinas, Marker]

GG381.   ● *Art and life in aestheticism: de-humanizing and re-humanizing art, the artist, and the artistic receptor.* Ed. Kelly Comfort. Basingstoke: Palgrace Macmillan, 2008. xii, 240 p. [Barthes, Huysmans]

GG382.   ● *Art [L'] du peu.* Textes réunis par Christine Dupouy. Paris: L'Harmattan, 2008. 485 p. [Poetry, Barthes, Beckett, Bonnefoy, P. Denis, Des Forêts, Dupin, Emaz, Guillevic, Jaccottet, Klébaner, Lemaire, Michaux, Munier, Perrier, Quignard, Seynes, Vernet]

GG383.   ● *Automne [L'].* Etudes réunies par Alain Montandon. Clermont-Ferrand: Presses univ. Blaise Pascal, 2007. [Apollinaire, Brault, Gracq, Laforgue, Lorrain, Louis-Combet, Mauclair, Maupassant, Ponge, Proust]

GG384. • *Autour des écrivains franco-russes.* Dir. Murielle Lucie Clément. Paris: L'Harmattan, 2008. 272 p. [Arban, Gary, Gracq, Makine, Némirovsky, Rawicz, Sarraute, Triolet]

GG385. • *Autre [L'] tel qu'on le traduit.* Textes réunis par Maryla Laurent. Paris: Numilog, 2008. 297 p. [Queneau]

GG386. • *Aux confins de l'ailleurs: voyage, altérité, utopie: hommages offerts au professeur Jean-Michel Racault.* Dir. Marie-Françoise Bosquet, Serge Meitinger, Bernard Terramorsi. Paris: Klincksieck, 2008. 395 p. [France, Valéry, Vinaver]

GG387. • Badiou, Alain: *Conditions.* Trans. Steven Corcoran. London; New York: Continuum, 2008. xlv, 314 p. [Beckett, Lacan, Mallarmé, Rimbaud]

GG388. • Barilier, Etienne: *Ils liront dans mon âme: les écrivains face à Dreyfus.* Genève: Zoé, 2008. 230 p. [Barrès, Bernanos, J.-R. Bloch, Daudet, France, Gyp, Martin du Gard, Mirbeau, Péguy, Proust, Rolland, Zola]

GG389. • Baumann, Henrik: *Die autobiographische Rückkehr.* München: Meidenbauer, 2008. 333 p. [Doubrovsky, Guibert, Rouaud]

GG390. • Binder, Anne-Berenike: *"Mon ombre est restée là-bas": literarische und mediale Formen des Erinnerns in Raum und Zeit.* Tübingen: Niemeyer, 2008. *Romania Judaica.* xi, 348 p. [Aaron, Delbo, Gary, Resnais]

GG391. • *Biographie et intimité des Lumières à nos jours.* Etudes réunies par Daniel Madelenat. Clermont-Ferrand: Presses univ. Blaise Pascal, 2008. 282 p. [Barrès, Chaillou, Cixous, Macé, Proust, Rimbaud]

GG392. • *Black womanhood: images, icons, and ideologies of the African body.* Ed. Barbara Thompson. Hanover, NH: Hood Museum of Art, Dartmouth College in association with University of Washington Press, 2008. [Beyala]

GG393. • *Blanc [Le] en littérature.* Textes réunis par Daniel Leuwers. Paris: EST, 2006. 126 p. [Apollinaire, Di Manno, Jouve, Senghor]

GG394. • Blanckeman, Bruno: *Les récits indécidables.* Villeneuve-d'Ascq: Presses univ. du Septentrion, 2008. *Perspectives.* 222 p. [Echenoz, Guibert, Quignard]

GG395. • *Bodies and voices: the force-field of representation and discourse in colonial and postcolonial studies.* Ed. Merete Falck Borch, Eva Knudsen Rask, Bruce Clunies Ross. Amsterdam: Rodopi, 2008. *Cross/cultures,* 94. xl, 459 p. [Bataille, N. Bouraoui]

GG396. • Bonhomme, Béatrice: *Mémoire et chemins vers le monde.* Colomars: Melis Editions, 2008. 212 p. [Bonnefoy, du Bouchet, Emaz, Jaccottet, B. Noël, Réda, Jean-Claude Renard, Sacré, Stéfan, Stétié]

GG397. • Boodakian, Florence Dee: *Resisting nudities: a study in the aesthetics of eroticism.* New York: Peter Lang, 2008. 102 p. [Bataille, Derrida, Foucault, Nancy]

GG398. • Bouveresse, Jacques: *La connaissance de l'écrivain: sur la littérature, la vérité et la vie.* Marseille: Agone, 2008. 237 p. [Maupassant, Proust, Zola]

GG399. • Bové, Paul A.: *Poetry against torture: criticism, history, and the human.* Hong Kong: Hong Kong Univ. Press, 2008. xvi, 159 p. [Foucault]

GG400. • Boyle, Claire: *Consuming autobiographies: reading and writing the self in post-war France.* Leeds: Legenda, 2007. x, 176 p. [Memoirs, Cixous, Genet, Perec, Sarraute]

GG401. • Brin, David: *Through stranger eyes: reviews, introductions, tributes and iconoclastic essays.* Ann Arbor, MI: Nimble Books, 2008. 215 p. [Verne]

GG402. • Brook, Timothy; Jérôme Bourgon; Gregory Blue: *Death by a thousand cuts.* Cambridge, MA: Harvard Univ. Press, 2008. xi, 320 p. [Bataille]

GG403. • Buat, Christian: *Le connétable, le régent et son ombre: Jules Barbey d'Aurevilly vu par Remy de Gourmont, Jean de Gourmont et le Mercure de France.* Agneaux: Frisson esthétique, 2008. 188 p. [Gourmont]

GG404. • Cany, Bruno: *Fossiles de mémoire: poésie et philosophie, de Homère à Jacques Roubaud.* Paris: Hermann, 2008. 166 p. [Roubaud]

GG405. • Chaitin, Gilbert D.: *The enemy within: culture wars and political identity in novels of the French Third Republic.* Columbus: The Ohio State Univ. Press, 2008. 314 p. [Barrès, Bourget, France, Zola]

GG406. • Charlesworth, Michael: *Landscape and vision in nineteenth-century Britain and France.* Aldershot; Burlington, VT: Ashgate, 2008. xvi, 186 p. [Mallarmé]

GG407. ● *Citer la langue de l'autre: mots étrangers dans le roman, de Proust à W. G. Sebald.* Textes réunis par Danielle Perrot-Corpet, Christine Queffélec. Lyon: Presses univ. de Lyon, 2007. [Chamoiseau, Escholier, Federman, Proust]

GG408. ● Clavaron, Yves: *Le génie de l'Italie: géographie littéraire de l'Italie à partir des littératures américaine, brittanique et française, 1890-1940.* Paris: Connaissances et Savoirs, 2006. 557 p.

GG409. ● Cohen, Maxime: *Promenades sous la lune.* Paris: Grasset, 2008. 382 p. [Proust]

GG410. ● *Cohérence et discours.* Sous la dir. de Frédéric Calas. Paris: PUPS, 2006. 436 p. [Camus, Gracq, Novarina, Proust, Sarraute, Simon, Zola]

GG411. ● Constantin, Danielle: *Masques et mirages: genèse du roman chez Cortázar, Perec et Villemaire.* New York: Peter Lang, 2008. *Comparative Romance languages and literatures,* 162. x, 192 p. [Perec, Villemaire]

GG412. ● *Contemporary Jewish writing in Europe: a guide.* Ed. Vivian Liska and Thomas Nolden. Bloomington: Indiana Univ. Press, 2008. *Jewish literature and culture.* xxxiii, 224 p.

GG413. ● Cornille, Jean-Louis: *Plagiat et créativité (treize enquêtes sur l'auteur et son autre).* Amsterdam; New York: Rodopi, 2008. *Faux titre,* 319. 217 p. [Breton, Céline, Echenoz, Leiris, Lindon, Maupassant, Perec, Proust, Rimbaud, Roussel, Zola]

GG414. ● *Culture et mémoire: représentations contemporaines de la mémoire dans les espaces mémoriels, les arts du visuel, la littérature et le théâtre.* Dir. Carola Hähnel-Mesnard, Marie-Liénard-Yeterian, Cristina Marinas. Paris: Ecole Polytechnique, 2008. 534 p. [Francophone, Theater, Modiano, Cinema]

GG415. ● *Culture wars and literature in the French Third Republic.* Ed. Gilbert D. Chaitin. Newcastle upon Tyne: Cambridge Scholars, 2008. vi, 224 p. [Novel, Rachilde]

GG416. ● David-de Palacio, Marie-France: *Ecce Tiberius ou la réhabilitation historique et littéraire d'un empereur décadent: Allemagne-France 1850-1930.* Paris: H. Champion, 2006. 286 p.

GG417. ● *De l'amer.* Textes réunis par Véronique Duche-Gavet et Jean-Gérard Lapacherie. Biarritz: Atlantica, 2008. 242 p. [Claudel, Loti, Saint-John Perse, Weil]

GG418. ● *De la plume au pinceau: écrivains dessinateurs et peintres depuis le romantisme.* Etudes réunies par Serge Linarès. Valenciennes: CAMELIA; Presses univ. de Valenciennes, 2007. 415 p. [Arp, Bauchau, Breton, Cheng, Clerc, Des Forêts, Dorgelès, Jarry, Pinget, Richez, Valéry, Zola]

GG419. ● *De l'éventail à la plume: mélanges offerts à Roger Marchal.* Textes réunis par France Marchal-Ninosque, Lise Sabourin et Eric Francalanza. Nancy: Presses univ. de Nancy, 2007. 459 p. [Chedid, Gadenne, Gyp, Louis-Combet, F. Mauriac, Proust]

GG420. ● Déchanet-Platz, Fanny: *L'écrivain, le sommeil et les rêves: 1800-1945.* Paris: Gallimard, 2008. *Bibliothèque des idées.* 384 p. [H. Bosco, Breton, Cocteau, Desnos, Eluard, Giraudoux, Huysmans, Jouve, Leiris, Michaux, Proust, Semprun, Supervielle, Valéry, Yourcenar]

GG421. ● Delville, Michel: *Food, poetry, and the aesthetics of consumption: eating the avant-garde.* New York: Routledge, 2008. *Routledge studies in twentieth-century literature.* x, 150 p.

GG422. ● Demanze, Laurent: *Encres orphelines.* Paris: Corti, 2008. 403 p. [Bergounioux, Macé, Michon]

GG423. ● *Des îles en archipel: flottements autour du thème insulaire en hommage à Carminella Biondi.* Dir. Carmelina Imbroscio, Nadia Minerva et Patrizia Oppici. Bern: P. Lang, 2008. 559 p. [Audisio, Benabou, Blais, Colette, Delembert, Giraudoux, Glissant, Henry-Valmore, Labou, Maximin, Poulin, Tournier, Trouillot, Verne, Yourcenar]

GG424. ● Destais, Alexandra: *L'émergence de littérature érographique féminine en France: 1954-1975.* Paris: ANRT, 2008. 2 vols.

GG425. ● *Détectives [Les] de l'étrange. Tome II, Quête en enquête.* Dir. Lauric Guillaud et Jean-Pierre Picot. Paris: Le Manuscrit, 2007. 306 p. [Leblanc, J. Ray]

GG426. ● Detienne, Marcel: *Comparing the incomparable.* Stanford: Stanford Univ. Press, 2008. *Cultural memory in the present.* ix, 108 p. [M. Bloch, Dumézil]

GG427. • *Dialogue [Le] d'idées et ses formes littéraires.* Textes réunis par Marie-Françoise Bosquet et Jean-Michel Racault. Paris: L'Harmattan, 2008. 256 p. [Beti]

GG428. • *Diasporic literature and theory: where now?.* Ed. Mark Shackleton. Newcastle upon Tyne: Cambridge Scholars, 2008. xiv, 199 p. [Cinema: Pontecorvo]

GG429. • *Dinge [Die] und die Zeichen: Dimensionen des Realistischen in der Erzählliteratur des 19. Jahrhunderts.* Hrsg. Sabine Schneider, Barbara Hunfeld. Würzburg: Königshausen & Neumann, 2008. 412 p. [Améry]

GG430. • Dirda, Michael: *Classics for pleasure.* Orlando: Harcourt, 2008. vii, 341 p. [Céline, Huysmans, Malraux, Verne, Zola]

GG431. • *Don [Le] de Shahrazad: la mémoire des Mille et une nuits dans la littérature contemporaine.* Textes réunis par Cyrille François. Amiens: Encrage; Certy-Pontoise: Univ. de Cergy-Pontoise, 2008. 216 p. [Chedid, Hassani, Magani]

GG432. • *Don Juans insolites.* Dir. Pierre Brunel. Paris: PUPS, 2008. 222 p. [M. Noël, Schmitt, Topor]

GG433. • Dotoli, Giovanni: *Parole et liberté: la langue et écriture de mai 68.* Paris: Hermann, 2008. 150 p.

GG434. • *Du littéraire: analyses sociolinguistiques et pratiques didactiques.* Tayeb Bouguerra, coord. Montpellier: Presses univ. de la Méditerranée, 2007. 228 p. [Francophone, Apollinaire]

GG435. • Durmelat, Sylvie: *Fictions de l'intégration: du mot beur.* Paris: L'Harmattan, 2008. 328 p.

GG436. • *Ecrire l'énigme.* Christelle Reggiani, Bernard Magné, dir. Paris: Presses de l'Univ. Paris-Sorbonne, 2007. *Travaux de stylistique et de linguistique françaises.* 347 p.

GG437. • *Ecrire, mai 68.* Emmanuel Adely [et al.]. Paris: Argol, 2008. 299 p.

GG438. • *Ecriture [L'] et le souci de la langue: écrivains, linguistes.* Dir. Irène Fenoglio. Louvain-le-Neuve: Academia Bruylant, 2007. 198 p. [Balpé, Pingaud]

GG439. • *Ecritures insolites.* Dir. Arlette Bouloumié. Angers: Presses de l'univ. d'Angers, 2008. 239 p. [Char, Desnos, Dhôtel, Laforgue, Schwob, Verhaeren, Villiers, Volodine, Zola]

GG440. • *Ecritures transculturelles: kulturelle Differenz und Geschlechterdifferenz im französischsprachigen Gegenwartsroman.* Hrsg. Gisela Febel, Karen Struve, Natascha Lueckmann. Tübingen: G. Narr, 2007. 237 p. [Francophone, Agnant, Ben Jelloun, Beyala, N. Bouraoui, Cixous, Djebar, Duras, Genet, Glissant, Pineau, N. Simon]

GG441. • *Ecrivain [L'] masqué.* Beïda Chikhi, dir. Paris: Presses de l'Univ. Paris-Sorbonne, 2008. *Lettres francophones.* 260 p.

GG442. • *Ecrivains franco-russes.* Sous la dir. de Murielle Lucie Clément. Amsterdam: Rodopi, 2008. *Faux titre,* 318. 236 p.

GG443. • *Education, culture, littérature.* Sous la dir. d'Anne Baudry Scubbi. Paris: Orizons, 2008. [Antelme, Barjavel, Gide, Réda, Scheinert]

GG444. • Edwards, Paul: *Soleil noir: photographie et littérature des origines au surréalisme.* Rennes: Presses univ. de Rennes, 2008. 565 p. [Surrealism]

GG445. • Elpers, Susanne: *Autobiographische Spiele: Texte von Frauen der Avantgarde.* Bielefeld: Aisthesis, 2008. 282 p. [Cahun]

GG446. • *Emotions et discours: l'usage des passions dans la langue.* Sous la dir. de Michael Rinn. Rennes: Presses univ. de Rennes, 2008. 371 p. [Césaire, Delbo]

GG447. • *Empreinte [L'] des choses.* Marie-Christine Lemardeley et André Topia, éds. Paris: Presses Sorbonne Nouvelle, 2007. 184 p. [Beckett]

GG448. • *Enfance [L'] des héros: l'enfance dans les épopées et les traditions orales en Afrique et en Europe.* Etudes réunies par Jean-Pierre Martin [et al.]. Arras: Artois presses université, 2008. 331 p. [Beti, Chamoiseau]

GG449. • *Entre hommes: French and Francophone masculinities in culture and theory.* Ed. Todd W. Reeser, Lewis C. Seifert. Newark: Univ. of Delaware Press, 2008. 289 p. [Alleg, Antelme, Colette, Hocquenghem, Laye, Sartre]

GG450. • Erler, Katja: *Deutschlandbilder in der französischen Literatur nach dem Fall der Berliner Mauer.* Berlin: Erich Schmidt, 2004. 232 p.

GG451. • *Eros: zur Asthetisierung eines (neu)platonischen Philosophems in Neu-*

zeit und Moderne. Hrsg. Maria Moog-Grünewald. Heidelberg: Winter, 2006. viii, 226 p. [Breton]

GG452. ● *Esculape et Dionysos: mélanges en l'honneur de Jean Céard.* Etudes réunies par Jean Dupèbe [et al.]. Genève: Droz, 2008. 1214 p. [Bernanos]

GG453. ● *Ethnographes et voyageuers: les défis de l'écriture.* Dir. Tiphaine Barthélémy et Maria Courocli. Paris: CTHS, 2008. 286 p. [Bouvier, Le Clézio, Lévi-Strauss, Maillart]

GG454. ● Farasse, Gérard: *Lettres de château.* Villeneuve d'Ascq: Presses univ. du Septentrion, 2008. *Objet.* 192 p. [Barthes, Delvaux, Follain, Ghil, Hyvernaud, Jaccottet, Ponge, Quignard, Reverdy, Tardieu, Villiers de l'Isle-Adam]

GG455. ● Farbman, Herschel: *The other night: dreaming, writing, and restlessness in twentieth-century literature.* New York: Fordham Univ. Press, 2008. ix, 152 p. [Beckett, Blanchot]

GG456. ● *Fiction et engagement littéraire: la représentation du parti et du militant dans le roman et le théâtre du XXe siècle.* Sous la dir. de Jeanyves Guérin. Paris: Sorbonne nouvelle, 2008. 277 p.

GG457. ● *Figures du pouvoir: l'arbitraire et le droit de Machiavel au XXe siècle.* Sous la dir. de Jean-Marie Paul. Angers: Presses de l'Univ. d'Angers, 2008. 183 p. [Proust]

GG458. ● *Flesh [The] in the text.* Ed. Thomas Baldwin, James Fowler, Shane Weller. Oxford: Peter Lang, 2007. 289 p. [Beckett, Djebar, Nothomb, Proust]

GG459. ● *Formes [Les] du temps: rythme, histoire, temporalité.* Réunis par Paule Petitier et Gisèle Séginger. Strasbourg: Presses univ. de Strasbourg, 2007. 416 p. [Aragon, Camus, Goux, Gracq, Huysmans, Ionesco, Proust, Simon]

GG460. ● Forsdick, Charles; Feroza Basu; Siobhán Shilton: *New approaches to twentieth-century travel literature in French: genre, history, theory.* New York: Peter Lang, 2006. vi, 235 p. [Boudjedra, N. Bouvier, Gilles Lapouge, Lévi-Strauss, Loti, Segalen, Ousmane Socé]

GG461. ● Foucart, Claude: *Visions françaises de l'Allemagne: de Léon Bloy à Pascal Quignard.* Paris: Klincksieck, 2008. 439 p. [Bedel, Benoit, Bernanos, Bloy, Cabanis, Gide, Mallarmé, Tournier, Vercors]

GG462. ● *Framed!: essays in French studies.* Ed. Lucy Bolton, Gerri Kimber, Ann Lewis, Michael Seabrook. Oxford: P. Lang, 2007. 235 p. [Surrealism, Ernaux, Frankétienne, Genet, Mallarmé]

GG463. ● *France: a traveler's literary companion.* Ed. William Rodarmor and Anna Livia. Berkeley, CA: Whereabouts Press, 2008. xii, 244 p.

GG464. ● *Frankreich und der deutsche Expressionismus = France and German expressionism.* Frank Krause, Hrsg. Göttingen: V&R Unipress, 2008. 201 p. [Demasy]

GG465. ● *Frontières [Les] littéraires de l'économie (XVIIe-XIXe siècles).* Dir. Martial Poirson, Yves Citton et Christian Biet. Paris: Desjonquères, 2008. 217 p. [Proust, Zola]

GG466. ● *Ganymède, ou, L'échanson: rapt, ravissement et ivresse poétique.* Sous la dir. de Véronique Gély. Nanterre: Presses de l'Univ. de Paris 10, Nanterre, 2008. 295 p. [Genet]

GG467. ● Garelli, Jacques: *Fragments d'un corps en archipel; suivi de, Perception et imaginaire: réflexions sur un poème oublié de Rimbaud.* Paris: Corti, 2008. 167 p. [Rimbaud]

GG468. ● Gay, Peter: *Modernism: the lure of heresy: from Baudelaire to Beckett and beyond.* New York: W. W. Norton, 2008. xxii, 610 p. [Beckett, Jarry, Proust]

GG469. ● Gendron, Sarah: *Repetition, difference, and knowledge in the work of Samuel Beckett, Jacques Derrida, and Gilles Deleuze.* New York: Peter Lang, 2008. *Studies in literary criticism and theory,* 19. xxiii, 182 p. [Beckett, Deleuze, Derrida]

GG470. ● Glutz-Ruedin, Brigitte: *Sept écrivains célèbres en Valais.* Sierre: Monographic, 2008. 232 p. [Giono, Simenon, Yourcenar]

GG471. ● Gontard, Marc: *La langue muette: littérature bretonne de langue française.* Rennes: Presses univ. de Rennes, 2008. 158 p.

GG472. ● *Gouvernement des hommes, gouvernement des âmes: mélanges de langue et littérature françaises offerts au professeur Charles Brucker.* Etudes réunies par Venceslas Bubenicek et Roger Marchal. Nancy: Presses univ. de Nancy, 2007. 522 p. [Deville]

GG473. ● *Grande [La] guerre: un siècle de fictions romanesques: actes du colloque 13-15 mars 2008, Université de Gand, In Flanders Fields Museum, Ypres.* Pierre Schoentjes, éd., avec la collab. de Griet Theeten. Genève: Droz, 2008. *Romanica Gandensia,* 36. 438 p. [Novel, Apollinaire, Barbusse, Cendrars, Dorgelès, Giono, Proust, Simon, Werth]

GG474. ● Granier, Caroline: *Les briseurs de formules: les écrivains anarchistes en France à la fin du XIXe siècle.* Cœuvres: Ressouvenances, 2008. 469 p.

GG475. ● Granier, Caroline: *Quitter son point de vue: quelques utopies anarcho-littéraires d'il y a un siècle.* Paris: Monde libertaire, 2007. 117 p.

GG476. ● Greaney, Patrick: *Untimely beggar: poverty and power from Baudelaire to Benjamin.* Minneapolis: Univ. of Minnesota Press, 2008. xxiii, 227 p. [Mallarmé]

GG477. ● Grossman, Evelyne: *L'angoisse de penser.* Paris: Minuit, 2008. *Paradoxe.* 156 p. [Beckett, Blanchot]

GG478. ● Guthmüller, Marie: *Der Kampf um den Autor: Abgranzungen und Interaktionen zwischen französischen Literaturkritik und Psychophysiologie 1858-1910.* Tübingen: A. Francke, 2007. 425 p.

GG479. ● Harst, Joachim: *Textspalten: Fetischismus als literarische Strategie.* Heidelberg: Winter, 2007. 141 p. [Maupassant]

GG480. ● Hatem, Jad: *La genèse du monde fantastique en littérature.* Bucharest: Zeta, 2008. 167 p.

GG481. ● Hawley, Richard A.: *Beyond the Icarus factor: releasing the free spirit of boys.* Rochester, VT: Park Street, 2008. ix, 166 p. [Saint-Exupéry]

GG482. ● *Hélène de Troie dans les lettres françaises.* A cura di Liana Nissim e Alessandra Preda. Milano: Cisalpino, 2008. 405 p. [Poetry, Camus, Giraudoux, Sartre, Verhaeren]

GG483. ● *Histoires inventées: la représentation du passé et de l'histoire dans les littératures françaises et francophones.* Sous la dir. de Elisabeth Arend, Dagmar Reichardt, Elke Richter. Frankfurt: Peter Lang, 2008. 269 p.

GG484. ● Hoffmann, Dieter: *Prosa des Absurden: Themen, Strukturen, geistige Grundlagen: von Beckett bis Bernhard.* Tübingen: Francke, 2006. xviii, 513 p. [Beckett, Camus, Sartre]

GG485. ● Indiana, Gary: *Utopia's debris: selected essays.* New York: Basic, 2008. xi, 315 p. [Carrère, Simenon, Cinema: Bresson]

GG486. ● Janis, Michael: *Africa and modernism: transitions in literature, media, and philosophy.* New York: Routledge, 2008. *Routledge studies in cultural history.* x, 280 p. [Leiris, Ouologuem]

GG487. ● *Jardins et intimité dans la littérature européenne (1750-1920).* Clermont-Ferrand: Presses univ. Blaise Pascal, 2008. 552 p. [Barrès, Gide, Gourmont, Maupassant, Péguy, Zola]

GG488. ● *"Je suis l'écho", l'écriture et la voix: hommage offert à Giuditta Isotti.* Sous la dir. de Camillo Faverzani. Saint-Denis: Univ. Paris 8-Vincennes-Saint-Denis, 2008. 329 p. [Duras]

GG489. ● Jenny, Laurent: *Je suis la révolution: histoire d'une métaphore (1830-1975).* Paris: Belin, 2008. 220 p. [Barthes, Blanchot, Breton, Maurras, Paulhan, Sollers]

GG490. ● Jourde, Pierre: *Littérature monstre: études sur la modernité littéraire.* Paris: Esprit des péninsules, 2008. 715 p.

GG491. ● Julliard, Jacques: *L'argent, Dieu et le diable: face au monde moderne avec Péguy, Bernanos, Claudel.* Paris: Flammarion, 2008. 229 p. [Bernanos, Claudel, Péguy]

GG492. ● Kalinarczyk, Pierre-Henri: *Le pays natal dans les œuvres poétiques de René Char, Aimé Césaire et Tchicaya U Tam'si.* Rennes: Presses univ. de Rennes, 2008. *Interférences.* 254 p. [Césaire, Char, Tchicaya]

GG493. ● Keskinen, Mikko: *Audio book: essays on sound technologies in narrative fiction.* Lanham, MD: Lexington, 2008. 157 p. [Tournier]

GG494. ● Koberich, Nicolas: *Merlin, l'enchanteur romantique.* Paris: L'Harmattan, 2008. 473 p. [Lorrain]

GG495. ● König, Alexandra: *Littérature féminine?: französische Romanautorinnen der dreissiger Jahre.* München: M Press, 2005. 276 p.

GG496. ● *Langage, temps, temporalité.* Dir. Pierre Marillaud, Robert Gauthier.

Toulouse: CALS-CPST, 2008. [Novel, Beauvoir, Butor, Camus, Ernaux, Follain, Hébert, Weil]

GG497. • Laügt, Elodie: *L'Orient du signe: rêves et dérives chez Victor Segalen, Henri Michaux et Emile Cioran*. Oxford: Peter Lang, 2008. *Modern French identities*, 75. 242 p. [Cioran, Michaux, Segalen]

GG498. • LeBlanc, Julie Diane: *Genèse de soi: l'écriture du sujet féminin dans quelques journaux d'écrivaines*. Montréal: Editions du Remue-ménage, 2008. 238 p.

GG499. • Le Bot, Marie-Claude; Martine Schuwer; Elisabeth Richard: *La reformulation: marqueurs linguistiques, stratégies énonciatives*. Rennes: Presses univ. de Rennes, 2008. 264 p. [Beti, Gaspar]

GG500. • Lebow, Alisa: *First person Jewish*. Minneapolis: Univ. of Minnesota Press, 2008. *Visible evidence*. xxxiii, 203 p. [Akerman]

GG501. • *Lectures psychanalytiques croisées: prosse et poésie contemporaines d'Europe et d'Amériques*. Coord. Sadi Lakhdari. Paris: Indigo et Côté-femmes, 2008. 262 p. [Gide, Michaux]

GG502. • *Lieux magiques, magie des lieux: mélanges offerts à Claude Foucart*. Etudes réunies et prés. par Simone Bernard-Griffiths et Angels Santa. Clermont-Ferrand: Presses univ. Blaise Pascal, 2008. *Révolutions et romantismes*, 11. 226 p. [Cixous, Crevel, Dabit, Jabès, Verne]

GG503. • *Linguista sum: mélanges offerts à Marc Dominicy à l'occasion de son soixantième anniversaire*. Paris: L'Harmattan, 2008. 421 p. [Goscinny, Saint-John Perse, Verhaeren, Verlaine]

GG504. • *Literarische Medienreflexionen: Künste und Medien im Fokus moderner und postmoderner Literatur*. Hrsg. Sandra Poppe, Sascha Seiler. Berlin: Schmidt, 2008. *Philologische Studien und Quellen*. 239 p. [Mallarmé]

GG505. • *Literatur der Jahrtausendwende: Themen, Schreibverfahren und Buchmarkt um 2000*. Hrs. Evi Zemanek, Susanna Krones. Bielefeld: Transcript, 2008. 453 p. [Nothomb]

GG506. • *Littérature [La] dépliée: reprise, répétition, réécriture*. Sous la dir. de Jean-Paul Engelibert, Yen-Mai Tran-Gervat. Rennes: Presses univ. de Rennes, 2008. [Bauchau, Giono, Lefebvre, R. Millet, Perec, Proust, Simon, Stéfan, Streeman]

GG507. • *Littérature et identités sexuelles*. Sous la dir. d'Anne Tomiche et Pierre Zoberman. Paris: SFLGC, 2007. 191 p. [Cixous]

GG508. • *Littérature et photographie*. Sous la dir. de Jean-Pierre Montier, Liliane Louvel, Danièle Meaux et Philippe Ortel. Rennes: Presses univ. de Rennes, 2008. 572 p. [Barthes, Bouvier, Calle, Ernaux, Houellebecq, Lambrichs, Levé, Maspero, C. Mauriac, Roussel, Zola]

GG509. • *Littérature [La], le XVIIe siècle et nous: dialogue transatlantique*. Sous la dir. d'Hélène Merlin-Kajman. Paris: Sorbonne nouvelle, 2008. [Deleuze, Guattari, Lacan]

GG510. • *Livre [Le] de sagesse: supports, médiations, usages:*. Dir. Nicolas Brucker. Bern: P. Lang, 2008. 368 p. [Francophone, Cossery, Hampâté Bâ, Maeterlinck, Michaux]

GG511. • Lowrie, Joyce O.: *Sightings: mirrors in texts-texts in mirrors*. Amsterdam; New York: Rodopi, 2008. *At the interface/probing the boundaries*. xi, 228 p. [Lorrain, Maupassant, Pieyre de Mandiargues, Rodenbach]

GG512. • Maldonado Torres, Nelson: *Against war: views from the underside of modernity*. Durham: Duke Univ. Press, 2008. *Latin American otherwise*. xvi, 342 p. [Fanon]

GG513. • Mansfield, Charlie: *Traversing Paris: French travel writing practices in the late twentieth century*. Saarbrücken: VDM, 2008. 79 p. [Ernaux, François Maspero, Jean Rolin]

GG514. • Marzel, Shoshana-Rose: *L'esprit du chiffon: le vêtement dans le roman français du XIXe siècle*. Bern: Peter Lang, 2005. x, 384 p.

GG515. • *Méditerranée de Audisio à Roy*. Dir. Guy Dugas. Alger: Mémoire de la Méditerranée; Houilles: Manucius, 2008. 299 p. [J. Amrouche, Audisio, H. Bosco, Camus, Fréminville, A. Guibert, Pélégri, J. Roy, Sénac]

GG516. • *Mémoire et oubli dans le lyrisme européen: hommage à John E. Jackson*. Réunis par Dagmar Wieser et Patrick Labarthe. Paris: H. Champion, 2008. 652 p. [Bonnefoy, Caillois, Mallarmé, Michaux, Proust, Saint-John Perse]

GG517. • *Mémoires, traces, récits. Volume 1, Le passé revisité.* Sous la dir. de Anne Prouteau. Paris: L'Harmattan, 2008. 163 p. [Camus]

GG518. • *Merveilleux [Le] et son bestiaire.* Sous la dir. de Anne Besson [et al.]. Paris: L'Harmattan, 2008. 265 p. [Apollinaire]

GG519. • Mesnard, Philippe: *Témoignage en résistance.* Paris: Stock, 2007. *Un ordre d'idées.* 419 p. [Antelme, Cayrol, Delbo, Perec, Rawicz, Wiesel]

GG520. • *Métamorphoses du mythe: réécritures anciennes et modernes des mythes antiques.* Dir. Peter Schnyder. Paris: Orizons, 2008. 920 p. [Theater, Apollinaire, Bonnefoy, H. Bosco, Cheng, Cocteau, Desnos, Dupuis, Gide, Giono, Grosjean, Hébert, Klossowski, Le Clézio, Liking, Montherlant, Ost, Rachilde]

GG521. • *Métissage [Le] en littérature.* Textes réunis par Daniel Leuwers. Paris: EST, 2007. [Baron Supervielle, Lopes, Luca, Mallarmé, Senghor]

GG522. • Meynier-Heydenrich, Frederic: *Die Literatur der Anderen: fünf Jahr deutsch-französische Literaturkritik (1995-1999).* Frankfurt: Peter Lang, 2004. 384 p.

GG523. • Michel, Alain; Arlette Michel: *La littérature française et la connaissance de Dieu (1800-2000). Volume III, La modernité: différences, compréhensions, dialogues.* Paris: Editions du Cerf, 2008. 1414 p.

GG524. • *Migrations of gesture.* Ed. Carrie Noland, Sally Ann Ness. Minneapolis: Univ. of Minnesota Press, 2008. 296 p. [Mallarmé, Michaux]

GG525. • Miletic, Tijana: *European literary immigration into the French language: readings of Gary, Kristof, Kundera and Semprun.* Amsterdam: Rodopi, 2008. *Faux titre,* 313. 372 p. [Gary, Kristof, Kundera, Semprun]

GG526. • *Modernism on file: writers, artists, and the FBI, 1920-1950.* Ed. Claire A. Culleton, Karen Leick. New York: Palgrave Macmillan, 2008. vi, 269 p. [Renoir]

GG527. • *Monstres et monstrueux littéraires.* Sous la dir. de Marie-Hélène Larochelle. Québec: Presses de l'Univ. Laval, 2008. xviii, 243 p. [Novel, Bessette, Giono, Hergé, Sartre, Zola]

GG528. • *Monuments [Les] du passé: traces et représentations d'une histoire dans la littérature.* Sous la dir. de Fiona McIntosh-Varjabédian, Joëlle Prungnaud. Villeneuve d'Ascq: Univ. Charles de Gaulle-Lille 3, 2008. 195 p. [Bourget, O. Rolin]

GG529. • *Morale [La] élémentaire_: aventures d'une forme poétique: Queneau, Oulipo, etc..* Textes réunis et prés. par Jacques Jouet, Pierre Martin et Dominique Moncond'huy. Rennes: Presses universitaires de Rennes, 2008. 338 p. *Licorne.* [Oulipo, Queneau]

GG530. • *Mourir pour des idées.* Textes réunis par Caroline Cazanave et France Marchal-Ninosque. Besançon: Presses univ. de Franche-Comté, 2008. 493 p. [Rostand]

GG531. • Munier, Brigitte: *Quand Paris était un roman: du mythe de Babylone au culte de la vitesse.* Paris: Différence, 2007. 478 p.

GG532. • *Mythe [Le] des Bohémiens dans la littérature et les arts en Europe.* Dir. Sarga Moussa. Paris: L'Harmattan, 2008. 384 p. [Vallès]

GG533. • *Narration et identité: de la philosophie à la bioéthique.* Ed. Marie-Geneviève Pinsart. Paris: Vrin, 2008. 173 p. [Kourouma]

GG534. • *Neo-colonial mentalities in contemporary Europe? Language and discourse in the construction of identities.* Ed. Guido Rings, Anne Ife. Newcastle upon Tyne: Cambridge Scholars, 2008. vii, 253 p. [Sebbar]

GG535. • *New interpretations in the history of French literature: from Marie de France to Beckett and Cioran.* Ed. Aleksandra Gruzinska; Allan H. Pasco, foreword. Lewiston, NY: Mellen, 2008. xv, 280 p. [Beauvoir, Beckett, Cioran, Cocteau, David-Néel]

GG536. • Niderst, Alain: *De Rabelais à Sartre: mélanges.* Paris: Eurédit, 2008. [Giraudoux, Ponge, Sartre, Valéry]

GG537. • *1968: episodes of culture in context.* Ed. Cathy Crane, Nicholas Muellner. Newcastle: Cambridge Scholars, 2008. xviii, 208 p. [Akerman]

GG538. • Nissim, Liana; Claude Benoit: *Etudes sur le vieillir dans la littérature française.* Clermont-Ferrand: Presses univ. Blaise Pascal, CRLMC, 2008. 194 p. [Colette]

GG539. • *Nomadismes des romancières contemporaines de langue française.* Dir. Audrey Lasserre, Anne Simon. Paris: Sorbonne nouvelle, 2008. 220 p.

GG540. • *Novel stages: drama and the novel in nineteenth-century France.* Ed. Pratima Prasad, Susan McCready. Newark: Univ. of Delaware Press, 2007. 242 p. [Goncourt, Zola]

GG541. ● *Nowhere is perfect: French and Francophone utopias/dystopias*. Ed. John West-Sooby. Newark: Univ. of Delaware Press, 2008. *Monash Romance Studies*. vi, 252 p.

GG542. ● Nuti, Marco: *Et in pictura fabulator: Paul Cézanne et le dialogue créateur entre peinture, littérature et philosophie de Balzac à Maldiney*. Fasano: Schena; Paris: Alain Baudry, 2008. [Surrealism, Bonnefoy, Merleau-Ponty, Simon, Zola]

GG543. ● *Obscène, obscénités*. Sous la dir. de Steven Bernas et Jamil Dakhlia. Paris: L'Harmattan, 2008. 254 p. [Bataille, Houellebecq]

GG544. ● Orjinta, Ikechukwu: *Women in world religions and literatures*. Münster: ImPrint, 2008. 184 p. [Aminata Sow Fall]

GG545. ● *Oscar Wilde and the making of modern culture: the making of a legend*. Ed. Joseph Bristow. Athens: Ohio Univ. Press, 2008. xlii, 355 p. [Cahun, Mirbeau, Proust]

GG546. ● Ouellette-Michalska, Madeleine: *Autofiction et dévoilement de soi*. Montréal: XYZ, 2007. *Documents*. 152 p. [Arcan, Bianciotti, Chen, Duras, Ernaux, C. Millet, Marie José Thériault]

GG547. ● *Paris Review [The] interviews. III*. Introd. Margaret Atwood. New York: Picador, 2008. xii, 446 p. [Simenon]

GG548. ● Parisse, Lydie: *La "parole trouée": Beckett, Tardieu, Novarina*. Caen: Lettres Modernes Minard, 2008. *Archives des lettres modernes*, 292. 158 p. [Beckett, Novarina, Tardieu]

GG549. ● Patterson, Anita: *Race, American literature and transnational modernisms*. Cambridge: Cambridge Univ. Press, 2008. *Cambridge studies in American literature and culture*. vi, 241 p. [Laforgue, Roumain, Saint-John Perse]

GG550. ● *Penser les métaphores*. Ed. Ursula Bähler [et al.]. Limoges: Lambert-Lucas, 2008. 116 p. [Jaccottet, Weil]

GG551. ● Pernot, Denis: *La jeunesse en discours (1880-1925): discours social et création littéraire*. Paris: Champion, 2007. 288 p.

GG552. ● Perruche, Mariane: *J.-B. Pontalis: une œuvre, trois rencontres: Sartre, Lacan, Perec*. Paris: L'Harmattan, 2008. *L'œuvre et la psyché*. 297 p. [Lacan, Perec, Sartre]

GG553. ● *Personnages [Les] autour du Graal*. Textes réunis par Claude Lachet. Lyon: CEDIC, 2008. 320 p. [Benoit, Dumont, Gracq, Rio]

GG554. ● *Perturbations et réajustements: langue et langage*. Ed. Béatrice Vaxelaire [et al.]. Strasbourg: Univ. Marc Bloch-Strasbourg 2, 2007. 341 p. [Guérin, Roubaud]

GG555. ● *Peser les mots*. Textes réunis par Gérard Danou. Limoges: Lambert-Lucas, 2008. 226 p. [Ferron, Michaux, M. Roche]

GG556. ● *Phrase [La] littéraire*. Dir. Ridha Bourkhis, Mohammed Benjelloun. Louvain-la-Neuve: Academia-Bruylant, 2008. 254 p. [Genet, Giono, Le Clézio, Rimbaud, Saint-John Perse, Schehadé]

GG557. ● Picconi, Lucia: *Il romanzo beur fra emigrazione e mito del ritorno*. Nouvelle éd. mise à jour. Roma: Aracne, 2008. 287 p.

GG558. ● Pinson, Guillaume: *Fiction du monde: de la presse mondaine à Marcel Proust*. Montréal: Presses de l'Univ. de Montréal, 2008. *Socius*. 365 p. [Bourget, Lorrain, Maupassant, Proust]

GG559. ● *Pleasure and pain in nineteenth-century French literature and culture*. Ed. David Evans, Kate Griffiths. Amsterdam: Rodopi, 2008. *Faux titre*, 324. 286 p.

GG560. ● Poliak, Claude F.: *Aux frontières du champ littéraire: sociologie des écrivains amateurs*. Paris: Economica, 2006. 305 p.

GG561. ● *Présences du passé dans le roman français contemporain*. Dir. Gianfranco Rubino. Roma: Bulzoni, 2007. 244 p. [Cathala, Michon, Rambaud, Robbe-Grillet, O. Rolin, Rouaud, Salvayre]

GG562. ● Prungnaud, Joëlle: *Figures littéraires de la cathédrale: 1880-1918*. Villeneuve d'Ascq: Presses universitaires du Septentrion, 2008. 269 p.

GG563. ● *Quand les écrivains se font critiques des autres arts*. Dir. Erik Pesenti Rossi. Strasbourg: Centre interdisciplinaire de recherches sur l'Italie de l'Univ. de Strasbourg, 2008. 130 p. [Barrès, Breton, Djebar, Du Bouchet, Frénaud, Proust, Valéry, Yourcenar]

GG564. ● *Querelles et invectives*. Textes réunis par Jean-Jacques Lefrère et Michel

Pierssens. Tusson: Du Lérot, 2007. 265 p. [Aragon, Brisset, Céline, L. Daudet, Debord, Fargue, Michaux, Prigent, A. Robin, Sartre, Soupault]

GG565. • Rabatel, Alain: *Homo narrans*. Limoges: Lambert-Lucas, 2008. 2 vols. [R. Camus, Ernaux, Maupassant, Semprun]

GG566. • Rashkin, Esther: *Unspeakable secrets and the psychoanalysis of culture*. Albany: SUNY Press, 2008. *SUNY series in psychoanalysis and culture*. xii, 260 p. [Villiers de l'Isle-Adam]

GG567. • *Reconstructing pain and joy: linguistic, literary and cultural perspectives*. Ed. Chryssoula Lascaratou, Anna Despotopoulou, Elly Ifantidou. Newcastle upon Tyne: Cambridge Scholars, 2008. 464 p. [Beckett]

GG568. • Redfern, W. D.: *French laughter: literary humour from Diderot to Tournier*. Oxford: Oxford Univ. Press, 2008. ix, 245 p. [Beckett, Céline, Huysmans, Sartre, Tournier, Vallès]

GG569. • *Re-embroidering the robe: faith, myth and literary creation since 1850*. Ed. Suzanne Bray, Adrienne E. Gavin, Peter Merchant. Newcastle upon Tyne: Cambridge Scholars, 2008. ix, 278 p. [Giono, Mallarmé, Yourcenar]

GG570. • *Reflections: new directions in modern languages and cultures*. Ed. Sarah Buxton [et al]. Newcastle upon Tyne: Cambridge Scholars, 2008. [Goncourt, Sallenave]

GG571. • *Relations familiales dans les littératures française et francophone des XXe et XXIe siècles. Volume I: La figure de la mère*. Sous la dir. de Murielle Lucie Clément et Sabine van Wesemael. Paris: L'Harmattan, 2008. 393 p.

GG572. • *Relations familiales dans les littératures française et francophone des XXe et XXIe siècles. Volume II: La figure du père*. Sous la dir. de Murielle Lucie Clément et Sabine van Wesemael. Paris: L'Harmattan, 2008. 365 p.

GG573. • *Resilient [The] female body: health and malaise in twentieth-century France*. Maggie Allison, Yvette Rocheron, eds. Oxford; New York: Peter Lang, 2007. 230 p. [Aragon, Duras, Hyvrard]

GG574. • *Review of national literatures: selected essays (1970-2001): the European spectrum*. Selected by Anne Paolucci. Middle Village, NY: Griffon House Publications, 2008. vi, 315 p. [Claudel]

GG575. • *Rhythms: essays in French literature, thought and culture*. Ed. Elizabeth Lindley, Laura McMahon. Oxford: Peter Lang, 2008. *Modern French identities*, 68. 238 p.

GG576. • *Richesses du français et géographie linguistique. Volume I*. Etudes rassemblées par Pierre Rézeau. Bruxelles: De boeck-Duculot, 2007. 501 p. [Picard, Quint]

GG577. • *Riots in literature*. Ed. David Bell, Gerald Porter. Newcastle upon Tyne: Cambridge Scholars, 2008. vi, 178 p. [Artaud]

GG578. • Rothenberg, Jerome: *Poetics and polemics, 1980-2005*. Selected and ed. by Jerome Rothenberg and Steven Clar; introd. Hank Lazer. Tuscaloosa: Univ. of Alabama Press, 2008. *Modern and comparative poetics*. xvii, 310 p. [Surrealism, Jabès]

GG579. • Roshwald, Mordecai: *Dreams and nightmares: science and technology in myth and fiction*. Jefferson, NC: McFarland & Co., 2008. *Critical explorations in science fiction and fantasy*. v, 221 p. [Verne]

GG580. • Rossow, Francis C.: *Gospel patterns in literature: familiar truths in unexpected places*. Minneapolis: Lutheran Univ. Press, 2008. 196 p. [Camus]

GG581. • Rothenberg, Jerome: *Poetics and polemics, 1980-2005*. Selected and edited by Jerome Rothenberg and Steven Clay. Tuscaloosa: Univ. of Alabama Press, 2008. xvii, 310 p. [Surrealism, Jabès]

GG582. • Rouart, Marie-France: *Les structures de l'aliénation*. Paris: Publibook, 2008. *Lettres & langues*. 313 p. [Camus, Gide, Malraux, Proust]

GG583. • Russo, Adelaide M.: *Le peintre comme modèle: du surréalisme à l'extrême contemporain*. Villeneuve d'Ascq: Presses univ. du Septentrion, 20087. *Perspectives*. 302 p.

GG584. • Salvadon, Marjorie: *Fictions of childhood: the roots of identity in contemporary French narratives*. Lanham, MD: Rowman & Littlefield, 2008. *After the empire*. xxvii, 97 p. [N. Bouraoui, Lê, Pineau]

GG585. • Schulte Nordholt, Annelies: *Perec, Modiano, Raczymow: la génération d'après et la mémoire de la Shoah*. Amsterdam; New York: Rodopi, 2008. *Faux titre*, 315. 335 p.

GG586. ● *Scritture delle migrazioni: passaggi e ospitalità*. A cura di Laura Restuccia, Giovanni Saverio Santangelo. Palermo: Palumbo, 2008. 329 p. [Butor, Chraïbi, Condé, Djebar, El Houssi, Malinconi, Ouologuem, Semprun]

GG587. ● *Se figurer l'origine ou la spécificité humaine*. Collectif sous la dir. de Isabelle Dalcourt, Olivier Dionne, Jean-Sébastien Trudel. Québec: GIFRIC, 2008. *Nœud*. 199 p. [Goncourt, Michaux]

GG588. ● *Seeking the self—encountering the other: diasporic narrative and the ethics of representation*. Ed. Tuomas Huttunen [et al.]. Newcastle upon Tyne: Cambridge Scholars, 2008. xxii, 364 p. [Levinas]

GG589. ● *Seelengespräche*. Hrsg. Béatrice Jakobs, Volker Kapp. Berlin: Duncker & Humblot, 2008. 289 p. [Bernanos]

GG590. ● *Sens [Le] de l'événement dans la littérature française des XIXe et XXe siècles*. Etudes réunies par Pierre Glaudes et Helmut Meter. Bern: P. Lang, 2008. 308 p. [Duras, Echenoz, Michaux, Pujade-Renaud, Queneau, Simon]

GG591. ● Serra, Maurizio: *Les frères séparés: Drieu La Rochelle, Aragon, Malraux face à l'histoire*. Traduit de l'italien par Carole Cavallera; préface de Pierre Assouline. Paris: Table ronde, 2008. viii, 319 p. [Aragon, Drieu, Malraux]

GG592. ● *Silences fin-de-siècle: hommage à Jean de Palacio*. Dir. André Guyaux. Paris: PUPS, 2008. 264 p. [Bernhardt, Bloy, Cassou, Goncourt, Gourmont, Lorrain, Maeterlinck, Villiers]

GG593. ● Singer, Régis: *L'ordre des Arts et des Lettres*. Versailles: Mémoire et documents, 2006. 101 p.

GG594. ● *Sinographies: writing China*. Ed. Eric Hayot, Haun Saussy, Steven Yao. Minneapolis: Univ. of Minnesota Press, 2008. xxi, 381 p. [Claudel, Segalen, Teilhard de Chardin]

GG595. ● Sobanet, Andrew: *Jail sentences: representing prison in twentieth-century French fiction*. Lincoln: Univ. of Nebraska Press, 2008. *Stages*. xii, 254 p. [F. Bon, Genet, Sarrazin, V. Serge]

GG596. ● Spies, Werner: *Mit Skalpell und Farbmaschine: Porträts von Max Ernst bis Gerhard Richter*. München: Hanser, 2008. *Edition Akzente*. 194 p. [Beckett, Calle, Lévi-Strauss, Michaux, Sarraute]

GG597. ● *Spiritualité [La] des écrivains*. Dir. Olivier Millet. Boulogne: ADIREL, 2008. 542 p. [Barrès, H. Bosco, Cheng, Claudel, Dadelsen, Jaccottet, La Tour du Pin, Massignon, Péguy, Saint-Pol-Roux, Suarès]

GG598. ● Steinmetz, Jean-Luc: *Reconnaissances*. Nantes: Défaut, 2008. 389 p. [Mallarmé, Rimbaud]

GG599. ● *Styles, genres, auteurs. 8*. Dir. Christelle Reggiani, Claire Stolz, Laurent Susini. Paris: PUPS, 2008. 256 p. [Bernanos]

GG600. ● Suleiman, Susan Rubin: *Crises of memory and the second World War*. Cambridge: Harvard Univ. Press, 2008. x, 286 p. [Aubrac, Malraux, Perec, Sartre, Semprun, Wiesel, Cinema: Ophuls]

GG601. ● *Teaching life writing texts*. Ed. Miriam Fuchs, Craig Howes. New York: MLA, 2008. *Options for teaching*. xi, 400 p. [Genet, Loti, Michon]

GG602. ● *Témoignages de l'après-Auschwitz dans la littérature juive-française d'aujourd'hui: enfants de survivants et survivants-enfants*. Dir. Annelise Schulte Nordholt. Amsterdam: Rodopi, 2008. *Faux titre*, 327. 269 p.

GG603. ● *Territories of evil*. Ed. Nancy Billias. Amsterdam: Rodopi, 2008. *At the interface/Probing the boundaries*, 45. 252 p. [Beigbeder]

GG604. ● *Testifying to the Holocaust*. Ed. Pam Maclean, Michele Langfield, Dvir Abramovich. Sydney: Australian Assn. of Jewish Studies, 2008. 226 p . [Levinas]

GG605. ● *Texte [Le] didascalique à l'épreuve de la lecture et de la représentation*. Textes réunis par Frédéric Calas, Romdhane Elouri, Saïda Hamzaoul. Pessac: Presses univ. de Bordeaux; Tunis: Sud Editions, 2007. 543 p. [Artaud, Camus, Césaire, Claudel, Feydeau, Gabily, Gary, Ghelderode, Giono, Ionesco, Koltès, Maeterlinck, Rosenthal, Rostand, Sartre, Visdei]

GG606. ● Thévenin, Paule: *Textes (1962-1993)*. Textes réunis par Hélène Milliex; préface de Bernard Noël. Paris: Lignes & Manifestes, 2005. 237 p. [Adamov, Artaud, Blin, Breton, Derrida, Des Forêts, Genet, Ponge]

GG607. ● Thomas, Jean-Paul: *La plume et le scalpel: la médecine au prisme de la littérature*. Paris: PUF, 2008. viii, 254 p.

GG608. ● *Translating selves: experience and identity between languages and literatures*. Ed. Paschalis Nikolaou, Maria-Venetia Kyritsi. London: Continuum, 2008. xiv, 202 p. [Apollinaire, Ricœur]

GG609. ● *Translation and censorship in different times and landscapes*. Ed. Teresa Seruya, Maria Moniz Lin. Newcastle upon Tyne: Cambridge Scholars, 2008. xix, 344 p. [Beauvoir, Semprun]

GG610. ● *Transmissions: essays in French literature, thought and cinema*. Ed. Isabelle McNeill and Bradley Stephens. Bern: Peter Lang, 2007. 221 p. [Surrealism, Barthes, Derrida, Huston, Ndiaye, Proust, Cinema: Denis, Resnais]

GG611. ● *Trauma et texte*. Peter Kuon, éd. Frankfurt: Peter Lang, 2008. *KZ-memoria scripta*, 4. 330 p. [Bauchau, Cahun, Simon]

GG612. ● *Traversée [Une] du XXe siècle: arts, littérature, philosophie: hommages à Jean Burgos*. Dir. Barbara Meazzi, Jean-Pol Madou et Jean-Paul Gavard-Perret. Chambéry: Univ. de Savoie, 2008. 433 p. [Poetry, Apollinaire, Beauvoir, Dermée, Duhamel, Giono, M. Henry, Martin du Gard, Maulpoix, Michaux, Prévert, Roubaud, Salmon, Verhaeren]

GG613. ● *Unwege: Ästhetik und Poetik exzentrischer Reisen*. Hrsg. Bernd Blaschke [et al.]. Bielefeld: Aisthesis, 2008. *Reisen Texte Metropolen*, 7. 311 p. [Camus, Segalen]

GG614. ● Vadé, Yves: *Pour un tombeau de Merlin: du barde celte à la poésie moderne*. Paris: Corti, 2008. 304 p. [Breton, Michaux]

GG615. ● Vallury, Rajeshwari S.: *Surfacing the politics of desire: literature, feminism, and myth*. Toronto: Univ. of Toronto Press, 2008. ix, 234 p. [Deleuze, Maupassant]

GG616. ● *Villes [Les] du symbolisme*. Organisé par Marc Quaghebeur et Marie-France Renard. Bruxelles: P. Lang, 2007. 302 p. [Literary History, Barrès, Claudel, Elskamp, Fargue, Hellens, Rachilde, Rodenbach, Rosny]

GG617. ● *Violence in French and Francophone literature and film*. Ed. James T. Day. Amsterdam: Rodopi, 2008. *French literature series*, 35. 177 p.

GG618. ● *Visages du temps: parcours critiques dans la littérature française du XXe siècle*. Textes réunis par Daniela Fabiani. Macerata: EUM, 2006. 167 p. [H. Bosco, Claudel, Juliet, Sulivan]

GG619. ● *Voix [La] du peuple et leurs fictions*. Dir. André Petitjean et Jean-Marie Privat. Metz: Univ. Paul Verlaine, 2007. 506 p. [Francophone, Theater, F. Bon, Cohen, Ernaux, Pinget, Simon, Vallès, Vinaver]

GG620. ● *Voyage [Le] au féminin: perspectives historiques et littéraires, XVIIIe-XXe siècles*. Sous la dir. de Nicolas Bourguinat. Strasbourg: Presses univ. de Strasbourg, 2008. *Sciences de l'histoire*. 152 p. [Noailles]

GG621. ● Walls, Alison M. K.: *The sentiment of spending: intimate relationships and the consumerist environment in the works of Zola, Rachilde, Maupassant and Huysmans*. New York: Peter Lang, 2008. *Currents in Comparative Romance Languages and Literatures*. xi, 150 p. [Huysmans, Maupassant, Rachilde, Zola]

GG622. ● *War, virtual war and society: the challenge to communities*. Ed. Andrew R. Wilson, Mark L. Perry. Amsterdam: Rodopi, 2008. *At the interface/Probing the boundaries*. xii, 170 p. [Duras, Resnais]

GG623. ● Warnod, Jeanine: *Chez la baronne d'Oettingen: Paris russe et avant-gardes, 1913-1935*. Paris: Conti, 2008. 143 p. [Apollinaire, Cendrars, Jacob]

GG624. ● Watt, Daniel: *Fragmentary futures: Blanchot, Beckett, Coetzee*. Ashby-de-la-Zouch: InkerMen Press, 2007. 180 p. [Beckett, Blanchot]

GG625. ● Westley, Hannah: *The body as medium and metaphor*. Amsterdam; New York: Rodopi, 2008. *Faux titre*. 212 p. [Leiris, B. Noël, Prassinos]

GG626. ● *Wie die Welt lacht: Lachkulturen im Vergleich*. Hrsg. Waltraud Wende. Würzburg: Königshausen & Neumann, 2008. 349 p. [Gary]

GG627. ● Winkiel, Laura: *Modernism, race, and manifestos*. Cambridge: Cambridge Univ. Press, 2008. x, 242 p. [Césaire]

GG628.   • *Women's studies, diasporas and cultural diversity: essays in literary criticism and culture*. Ed. Mamadou Kandji. Dakar: Presses univ. de Dakar, 2008. *Bridges*, 12. 431 p. [A. Sow Fall, S. Schwarz-Bart, Sembène, Senghor]

GG629.   • *World writing: poetics, ethics, globalization*. Ed. Mary Gallagher. Toronto; Buffalo: Univ. of Toronto Press, 2008. *Cultural spaces*. x, 262 p. [Francophone, Literary Theory, Blanchot, Glissant, Levinas, Malraux]

GG630.   • *Writers' houses and the making of memory*. Ed. Harald Hendrix. New York: Routledge, 2008. vii, 284 p. [Goncourt, Loti, Proust]

GG631.   • Yeazell, Ruth Bernard: *Art of the everyday: Dutch painting and the realist novel*. Princeton, NJ: Princeton Univ. Press, 2008. xx, 252 p. [Proust]

GG632.   • Yilmaz, Selim: *Les figures de style en français et leur traduction en turc*. München: LINCOM, 2008. 112 p. [Michaux]

GG633.   • Zuccarino, Giuseppe: *Il dialogo e il silenzio*. Parian di Prato: Campanotto, 2008. *Le carte francesi*. 175 p. [Blanchot, Jabès, Mallarmé]

GG634.   Abramov, Tamar: "To catch a spy: explorations in subjectivity." Diss., Harvard Univ., 2008. viii, 208 p. [Echenoz, Robbe-Grillet]

GG635.   Allamand, Carole: "Amies mortelles: autobiographie et résistance à la psychanalyse," *Modern Language Notes*, vol. 123, no. 4 (Sept. 2008), 777-796.

GG636.   Armbrecht, Thomas J. D.: "The whole picture: using nonliterary forms of artistic production to teach life writing." In 601, 151-160. [Loti]

GG637.   Bacholle-Boskovic, Michèle: "Et les enfants, alors? Une littérature beure de jeunesse?," *Expressions Maghrébines*, vol. 7, no. 1 (été 2008), 159-176.

GG637a.   Baker, Charlotte: "Writing over the illness: the symbolic representation of albinism." In 867, 115-127. [Didier Destremau, Grainville, Sassine]

GG638.   Barclay, Fiona J.: "Postcolonial France?: the problematisation of Frenchness through North African immigration: a literary study of metropolitan novels 1980-2000." Diss., Univ. of Glasgow, 2006. 276 p. [Cardinal, Cixous]

GG639.   Barnett, R.-L. Etienne: "Les enjeux de la parole," *Neohelicon*, vol. 35, no. 2 (2008), 181-189. [Leiris, Quignard]

GG640.   Baudet, Marion: "Le jardin décadent: de l'intimité dévoilée à l'intimité dévoyée." In 487, 357-369.

GG641.   Beaupré, Nicolas: "Nécrologies d'écrivains: la survie littéraire des écrivains français morts à la guerre." In 473, 113-132.

GG642.   Bélisle, Mathieu: "Le drôle de roman: rire et imaginaire dans les œuvres de Marcel Aymé, Albert Cohen et Raymond Queneau." Diss., 2008. vii, 351 p. [Aymé, Cohen, Queneau]

GG643.   Berheri, Afifa: "Quand l'histoire glisse dans le littéraire: procédés d'écriture et représentations idéologiques." In 483, 127-134. [Amrouche, Rimbaud, Yacine]

GG644.   Bonord, Aude: "Usages et métamorphoses du livre de sagesse à la fin du XXe siècle." In 510, 165-181. [Christian Bobin, Louis-Combet]

GG645.   Boucharenc, Myriam: "A quoi rêvent les jeunes filles?," *Revue des Sciences Humaines*, no. 289 [no. 1] (2008), 199-211.

GG646.   Bouju, Emmanuel: "Forme et responsabilité. Rhétorique et éthique de l'engagement littéraire contemporain," *Etudes Françaises*, vol. 44, no. 1 (2008), 9-23.

GG647.   Boumelha, Penny: "Regeneration: time, place and gender in fin-de-siècle utopian narrative." In 541, 123-138.

GG648.   Bourdieu, Séverine: "Un air de famille: l'histoire familiale à l'épreuve de la mémoire et des photographies." In 572, 295-304.

GG649.   Bozzetto, Roger: "Rêves et doubles dans les textes 'fantastiques' chinois et français," *Etudes Francophones*, vol. 23, no. 1-2 (printemps-automne 2008), 120-126.

GG650.   Bralove, Alicia: "The road not taken: portrayal of women in ten French novels on the Spanish Civil War (1936-1939)." Diss., City Univ. of New York, 2008. xi, 201 p.

GG651.   Buignet, Christine: "Tropismes photographiques." In 508, 497-514.

GG652.   Caine, Philippa: "Marvellous bodies? Srange sex(es)?: fantastic genre in recent French fiction," *Forum for Modern Language Studies*, vol. 44, no. 4 (2008), 427-444.

GG653.   Cairns, Lucille: "Dissidences charnelles: the female body in revolt." In 458, 205-225.

GG654.   Caron, David: "The queerness of male group friendship." In 449, 251-266. [Antelme, Hocquenghem]

GG655.   Casta, Isabelle: "Les chasses fantastiques, motif récurrent du romanesque corse?," *Etudes Francophones*, vol. 23, no. 1-2 (printemps-automne 2008), 73-81.

GG656.   Chahinian, Talar: "The Paris attempt: rearticulation of (national) belonging and the inscription of aftermath experience in French Armenian literature between the wars." Diss., UCLA, 2008. x, 239 p.

GG657.   Chitrit, Annelle: "Poétique du temps: le temps poétique et la parole singulière." In 496, 253-262. [Desnos, Jabès, Jaccottet, Proust]

GG658.   Cryle, Peter: "Building a sexological concept through fictional narrative: the case of 'frigidity' in late nineteenth-century France," *French Cultural Studies*, vol. 19, no. 2 (June 2008), 115-140.

GG659.   DalMolin, Eliane: "Vouloir montrer: le spectacle de la réalité chez Annie Ernaux, Lydie Salvayre et Amélie Nothomb." In 539, 103-113. [Ernaux, Nothomb, Salvayre]

GG660.   David-de Palacio, Marie-France: " 'Je parle et je suis mort': l'épitaphe latine dans les textes fin-de-siècle." In 592, 113-129.

GG661.   Delville, Michel: "Minimalists and anorexics." In 421. [Beckett, Robbe-Grillet]

GG662.   Delville, Michel: "Pop serialism: soup cans, pie counters, and things that look like meat." In 421. [Ponge]

GG663.   Delville, Michel: "Tasting is believing: a few thoughts on still life poetics." In 421. [Claudel, Ponge]

GG664.   Demanze, Laurent: "Mélancolie des origines." In 572, 315-323.

GG665.   Détrez, Christine: "Conjugalisme et familialisme de l'immoral chez les romancières contemporaines." In 571, 333-341.

GG666.   Diop, Cheikh M. S.: "L'écrivain, 'fils de sa mère': de la représentation sociale à la symbolisation." In 571, 167-177.

GG667.   Ducas, Sylvie: "Père ou fils de ses œuvres?" In 572, 173-184.

GG668.   Enderlein, Isabelle: "En attendant le déluge: la dissimulation de l'écriture de guerre." In 483, 181-195. [Gracq, Queneau, Sartre]

GG669.   Fabbiano, Giulia: "Les voies de la mémoire dans la production littéraire des descendants de harkis." In 414, 429-437.

GG670.   Forestier, louis: "Trois artistes aux pieds d'Hélène." In 482, 231-245. [Huysmans, Laforgue]

GG671.   François, Cyrille: "Shahrâzâd désœuvrée: du mythe à son actualité." In 421, 165-178.

GG672.   Fratta, Carla: "Spazi sognati." In 423. [Césaire, Glissant, Laferrière]

GG673.   Frédéric, Madeleine: "L'écriture de l'événement chez Le Clézio, Rouaud et Hanotte." In 473, 291-302. [Hanotte, Le Clézio, Rouaud]

GG674.   Gale, Beth W.: "Education, literature and the battle over female identity in Third Republic France." In 415, 103-127.

GG675.   Geay, Ian: "A la tombée des nues: une esthétique fin de siècle," *Revue des Sciences Humaines*, no. 289 [no. 1] (2008), 139-152.

GG676.   Gefen, Alexandre: " 'Parlant de lui, c'est de moi que je parle'. Privatisation identitaire et empathie mémorielle dans la fiction biographique contemporaine." In 391, 231-240.

GG677.   Geiser, Myriam: "La 'littérature beur' comme écriture de la post-migration et forme de 'littérature-monde'," *Expressions Maghrébines*, vol. 7, no. 1 (été 2008), 121-139.

GG678.   Giovannucci, Perri: "Camus, Djebar, and the 'non-color' of nonviolence." In 81, 71-100. [Camus, Djebar]

GG679.   Giovannucci, Perri: "North Africa and the anti-colonial critics." In 81, 41-70. [Camus, Fanon, Memmi, Sartre]

GG680.   Gorceix, Paul: "La constitution du 'mythe nordique' chez les symbolistes belges." In 82, 161-172.

GG681. Granjean, Valérie: "Les *ymagiers* fin-de-siècle," *Etudes Littéraires*, vol. 38, no. 2 (automne 2007), 167-185. [Elskamp, Gourmont, Maeterlinck]

GG682. Green, Eldred Ibibiem: "Morality and the beggar's question in Ousmane Sembène's *Xala* and Aminata Sow Fall's *The Beggars' Strike*." In 628, 273-282. [Fall, Sembène]

GG683. Guiney, M. Martin: "Literary Pedagogy and the limits of assimilation in France since the Third Republic." In 415, 44-63.

GG684. Guiyoba, François: "Autour de *Cœur des ténèbres*: l'intertextualité revisitée." In 506, 363-372. [Céline, Gide]

GG685. Hargreaves, Alec G.: "La littérature issue de l'immigration maghrébine en France: recensement et évolution du corpus narratif," *Expressions Maghrébines*, vol. 7, no. 1 (été 2008), 193-213.

GG686. Hartford, Jason J.: "Queer martyr-figures in fiction in French, 1876-1985." Diss., Univ. of Oxford, 2008. viii, 303 p.

GG687. Hartje, Hans: "Relations orageuses. L'adolescent et ses parents dans la fiction de langue française du XXe siècle." In 571, 381-389.

GG688. Hébert, Louis: 'Petite sémiotique du monstre." In 527, 121-139. [Hergé, Matthieu Ricard]

GG689. Irvine, Margot: "Spousal collaborations in naturalist fiction and in practice," *Nineteenth-Century French Studies*, vol. 37, no. 1-2 (Fall-Winter 2008-2009), 67-80. [Daudet, Goncourt, Maupassant, Zola]

GG690. Jaccomard, Hélène: "Guerre d'Algérie dans la littérature *beur*: traces et trous de mémoire," *Australian Journal of French Studies*, vol. 45, no. 2 (May-Aug. 2008), 150-163.

GG691. Jaccomard, Hélène: " 'Tu rêves?': utopies, dystopies et hétérotopies dans quelques écrits beurs." In 541, 240-252.

GG691a. Kapp, Volker: "Die Rhetorik des Fragmentarischen als Auseinandersetzung mit Grenzerfahrungen." In 589, 245-278. [Bonnefoy, Claudel, Annie Le Brun, M. Noël]

GG692. Kaye, Richard A.: "Oscar Wilde and the politics of posthumous sainthood." In 545. [Mirbeau, Proust]

GG693. Lahanque, Reynald: "Le goût de l'obscène en littérature." In 543, 175-186.

GG694. Lambrecht, Anne: "Le mythe de Cassandre." In 520, 183-195. [Giraudoux, Sartre]

GG695. Laroussi, Farid: "La littérature 'beur' et le paradoxe de l'authenticité," *Expressions Maghrébines*, vol. 7, no. 1 (été 2008), 109-120.

GG696. Ledoux-Beaugrand, Evelyne: "Filles du père? Le spectre paternel chez quelques auteurs contemporaines." In 572, 49-57.

GG697. Leroy, Claude: "Eros géographe." In 612, 165-181.

GG698. Lestringant, Frank: "Insulaires en mouvement." In 423. [Glissant, Michaux, Saint-Exupéry]

GG699. Liao, Jun-Pei: "L'intertexte des contes fantastiques chinois chez Segalen, Claudel et Morand," *Etudes Francophones*, vol. 23, no. 1-2 (printemps-automne 2008), 96-119. [Claudel, Morand, Segalen]

GG700. Lindaman, Dana Kristofor: "Mapping the geographies of French identity: 1871-1914." Diss., Harvard Univ., 2008. vi, 190 p. [Verne]

GG701. Louwagie, Fransiska: " 'Métastases' d'Auschwitz: modalités et limites d'une tradition testimoniale." In 602, 171-185.

GG702. Lyle, Louise: "*Le struggleforlife*: contesting Balzac through Darwin in Zola, Bourget, and Barrès," *Nineteenth-Century French Studies*, vol. 36, no. 3-4 (Spring-Summer 2008), 305-319. [Barrès, Bourget, Zola]

GG703. Mairesse, Anne N.: "La traversée du genre: le héros-narrateur chez les romancières contemporaines." In 539, 93-102. [Garréta, Salvayre]

GG704. Malinowski, Wieslaw Mateusz: "La spiritualité des symbolistes: paradigme romanesque," *Travaux de Littérature*, tome 21 (2008), 307-321.

GG704a. Marks, Elaine: "Women and literature in France." In 4744.

GG705. Martin, Jean-Pierre: "Le militant et l'apostat." In 456, 191-199. [Duras, Nizan, Sartre, Vailland]

GG706. Martinez, Frédéric: "Faux comme l'Antique ou les ambiguïtés du néoclassicisme," *Revue d'Histoire Littéraire de la France*, tome 108, no. 1 (janv.-mars 2008), 101-132. [Barrès, Louÿs]

GG707. Mathieu, Jean-Claude: "La main passe." In 516, 375-408.

GG708. Meaux, Danièle: "L'écriture à l'épreuve de l'image enregistrée." In 508, 311-324. [F. Bon, Echenoz, Michon]

GG709. Mersch, Dieter: "Differenz und Augenblick: Überlegungen zum französischen Ereignisdenken." In 380, 25-36.

GG710. Mesch, Rachel: "Sexual healing: power and pleasure in fin-de-siècle women's writing." In 559, 159-171. [Colette, Delarue-Mardrus, Noailles]

GG711. Miguet-Ollagnier, Marie: "Les mythes revisités." In 520, 465-475. [Céline, Cixous, Louis-Combet, Proust, Schmitt, Simon, Tournier]

GG712. Minucci, Marina: "Un héros du passé: le militant communiste." In 561, 85-101.

GG713. Miraglia, Anne Marie: "Les figures du père immigré dans le texte dit 'beur'," *Francofonia*, n. 55 (autunno 2008), 21-32.

GG714. Modenesi, Marco: " 'Je fermerai partout portières et volets.' Le silence dans le texte narratif décadent." In 592, 241-249.

GG715. Montémont, Véronique: "Dites voir (sur l'*ekphrasis*)." In 508, 457-472.

GG716. Moore, Alison: "Pathologizing female sexual frigidity in fin-de-siècle France." In 559, 187-200.

GG717. Mouchenik, Yoram: "Passeurs de mémoire: élaboration et transmission, soixante ans plus tard, chez les enfants juifs, traqués et cachés en France." In 602, 47-62.

GG718. Naudier, Delphine: "Assignation à 'résidence sexuée' et nomadisme chez les écrivaines." In 539, 51-62.

GG719. Nøjgaard, Morten: *Splendor corporis-splendor veritatis*?: le corps féminin comme démonstration ou subversion de la vérité," *Excavatio*, no. 1-2 (2008), 74-90. [A. Daudet, Goncourt, Huysmans, Rachilde, Zola]

GG720. Nolden, Thomas: "A la recherche du judaïsme perdu: contemporary Jewish writing in France." In 412.

GG721. Nordholt, Annelies Schulte: "Perec, Modiano, Raczymow et les lieux comme ancrages de la postmémoire." In 602, 243-256. [Modiano, Perec, Raczymow]

GG722. Ojalvo, Catherine: "Une mémoire lacunaire mais fondatrice." In 602, 187-203. [Raczymow, Gérard Wajcman]

GG723. Olsson, Kenneth: "L'effet beur. La littérature beure face à la réception journalistique," *Expressions Maghrébines*, vol. 7, no. 1 (été 2008), 93-107.

GG724. Ortel, Philippe: "Trois dispositifs photo-littéraires: l'exemple symboliste." In 508, 17-35. [Huysmans, Rodenbach]

GG725. Pflüger, Christine: "L'opinion officielle distinguait deux camps . . . : la représentation de l'Occupation allemande 1940-1944 dans le roman et dans la recherche historique." In 414, 393-400.

GG726. Popa-Liseanu, Doina: "Où les langues se lient et se délient." In 521, 37-44.

GG727. Poulton, Leslee: "Les mères russes vues par leurs fils francophones." In 384, 169-182. [Bosquet, Gary, Troyat]

GG728. Prigent, Gaël: "Spiritualité décadente," *Travaux de Littérature*, tome 21 (2008), 323-335.

GG729. Riesz, Janós: "L'ethnologie coloniale ou le refus de l'assimiliation. Les 'races' dans le roman colonial." In 127, 147-159.

GG730. Riesz, Janós: "Identité 'à la carte'. Représentations littéraires de papiers d'identité en Afrique." In 127, 189-208.

GG731. Riesz, Janós: "Les métamorphoses d'un livre. Textes et images dans la littérature coloniale française." In 127, 133-146.

GG732. Robaey, Jean: "De la Ville morte à la Ville éternelle: petit voyage symboliste en France, en Belgique et en Italie." In 616, 89-109.

GG733. Rochmann, Marie-Christine: "L'éruption de la Montagne Pelée: une mise en fiction problématique," *Cartes Blanches*, no. 3 (2008), 203-218. [Audiberti, J. Bioret, R. Tardon, M. Tauriac]

GG734. Rubino, Gianfranco: "Visions de l'entre-deux-guerres." In 473, 237-250. [Martin du Gard, Romains]

GG735. Russo, Adelaide M.: "De l'amour: Fenosa quatre fois." In 583, 179-196. [Jean-Marie Gleize, B. Noël, Ponge, Vargaftig]

GG736. Russo, Adelaide M.: "L'hospitalité du texte du surréalisme à l'extrême contemporain: le poète ami du peintre." In 583, 265-278. [Surrealism, Deguy, B. Noël]

GG737. Russo, Adelaide M.: "Salutations et étrennes: circulation des valeurs." In 583, 221-263. [Derrida, Leiris, Georges Limbour, B. Noël]

GG738. Sallager, Edgar: "Ecritures de la Commune." In 590, 57-70. [Goncourt, Vallès, Zola]

GG739. Schaepdrijver, Sophie de: "Rancœurs et grands cœurs: les fictions d'occupation en Belgique." In 473, 183-201.

GG740. Schoentjes, Pierre: "Les véritables écrivains de guerre ont-ils 'rarement dépeint ce qu'ils avaient vu'? In 473, 17-43.

GG741. Schultz, Gretchen: "Gender, sexuality and the poetics of identification," *Nottingham French Studies*, vol. 47, no. 3 (Autumn 2008), 91-102. [Verlaine]

GG742. Schultz, Gretchen: "La rage du plaisir et la rage de la douleur: lesbian pleasure and suffering in fin-de-siècle French literature and sexology." In 559, 175-186. [Mendès]

GG743. Silverman, Max: "Interconnected histories: Holocaust and empire in the culture imaginary," *French Studies*, vol. 62, no. 4 (Oct. 2008), 417-428. [Modiano, Perec]

GG744. Simon, Anne: "Embryon, femme, médecin: accouchement et avortement chez les romancières contemporaines." In 573, 115-132.

GG745. Sirvent, Michel: "Entre Oulipo et nouveau roman textuel: pour une approche transformelle du texte contraint," *Esprit Créateur*, vol. 48, no. 2 (Summer 2008), 18-31. [Novel, Oulipo]

GG746. Smith, Leonard V.: " 'Ce que finir veut dire': l'*explicit* dans le roman de la Grande Guerre des années 30." In 473, 251-262.

GG747. Soncini Fratta, Anna: "L'Hercule stéréotypé en Belgique à la fin du XIXe siècle." In 520, 421-432.

GG748. Spandonis, Sophie: "Du politique dans le poétique: le discours idéologique de quelques écrivains de la décadence en France à la fin du XIXe siècle." In 356, 205-219.

GG749. Stephens, Elizabeth: "Redefining sexual excess as a medical disorder: fin-de-siècle representations of hysteria and spermatorrhoea." In 559, 201-212.

GG750. Stobierska, Agnieszka: "Le père chassé par la mère: des exclusions du père de la relation mère/fille dans la littérature féminine." In 571, 95-105.

GG751. Susini-Anastopoulos, Françoise: "Le fragment, histoire d'une exigence." In 382, 41-58.

GG752. Sussner, Daniel Maxwell: "Projections: the visual structure of French history." Diss., Harvard Univ., 2008. viii, 300 p. [Cinema: Resnais]

GG753. Tamburini, Grazia: "Le passé au présent: quelques remarques sur l'emploi des temps dans le récit contemporain." In 561, 179-191. [Michon, Quignard]

GG754. Tlemsani-Cantin, Jawad: "Lumières sur le sujet contemporain," *Information Littéraire*, 60e année, no. 4 (oct.-déc. 2008), 44-47. [Delay, Macé, Michon, Quignard]

GG755. Van Den Hoven, Adrian: "*Nekrassov* de Sartre, satire de sa propre philosophie, d'une certaine presse, de Beckett et de Camus." In 96, 239-250. [Beckett, Camus, Sartre]

GG756. Véray, Stéphane: "La Grande Guerre à l'écran: entre reconstruction du passé et lecture du présent." In 473, 355-379. [Cinema]

GG757. Viart, Dominique: "En quête du passé: la Grande Guerre dans la littérature contemporaine." In 473, 325-344.

GG758. Viart, Dominique: "Témoignage et restitution. Le traitement de l'Histoire dans la littérature contemporaine." In 561, 43-64.

GG759. Viers, Carole Anne: "The OULIPO and art as retrieval: copyists and translators in the novels of Raymond Queneau, Italo Calvino, Harry Mathews, and Georges Perec." Diss., UCLA, 2008. xii, 270 p. [Perec, Queneau]

GG760. Villeneuve, Lisa A.: "Dwelling space in post-war French fiction." Diss., Univ. of Oxford, 2008. xiii, 293 p. [Camus, Perec, Sollers]

GG761. Vray, Jean-Bernard: "Photographie et 'revenances de l'histoire' dans la littérature narrative contemporaine." In 561, 193-215. [Bon, Modiano, O. Rolin, Vautrin]

GG762. Wrigley-Brown, Lynette: "S'anéantir ou s'épanouir: avatars d'ascétisme
anorexique dans la littérature française du XIXe au XXIe siècle." Diss., Univ. of Auckland,
2008. ix, 227 p.

GG763. Young, Sylvie: "Les scandaleuses rêveries du célibataire fin de siècle: la
représentation textuelle des mécanismes auto-érotiques." Diss., UCLA, 2008. x, 290 p.
[Gourmont, Huysmans, Villiers de l'Isle-Adam]

LITERARY THEORY AND ESTHETICS

GG764. ● *Argumentation et narration.* Ed. Emmanuelle Danblon [et al.]. Bruxelles:
Editions de l'Univ. de Bruxelles, 2008. 210 p. [Cendrars]

GG765. ● *Authority matters: rethinking the theory and practice of authorship.* Ed.
Stephen Donovan, Danuta Fjellestad, Rold Lundén. Amsterdam: Rodopi, 2008. *DQR: Studies
in literature*, 43. 302 p. [Barthes, Foucault, Mallarmé]

GG766. ● *D'un genre littéraire à l'autre.* Sous la dir. de Michèle Guéret-Laferte,
Daniel Mortier. Mont-Saint-Aignan: Publications des Université de Rouen et du Havre, 2008.
359 p. [Giraudoux, Graeve, Grumberg, Mallarmé, Sardou, Zola]

GG767. ● Huglo, Marie-Pascale: *Le sens du récit: pour une approche esthétique de
la narrativité contemporaine.* Villeneuve d'Ascq: Presses univ. du Septentrion, 2007. 184 p.

GG768. ● *Idée [L'] et ses fables: le rôle du genre.* Etudes réunies par Geneviève
Artigas-Ménant et Alain Couprie. Paris: H. Champion, 2008. 339 p. [Malaquais, Malraux]

GG769. ● Juvan, Marko; Timothy Pogacar: *History and poetics of intertextuality.*
West Lafayette, IN: Purdue Univ. Press, 2008. *Comparative cultural studies.* viii, 218 p.
[Kristeva]

GG770. ● *Metaphor and cognition.* Ed. Zdzislaw Wasik, Tomasz Komendzinski.
Frankfurt: Peter Lang, 2008. 178 p. [Saussure]

GG771. ● *Metaphor and gesture.* Ed. Alan Cienki, Cornelia Müller. Amsterdam:
Benjamins, 2008. *Gesture studies*, 3. ix, 306 p. [Derrida]

GG772. ● *Narrative beginnings: theories and practices.* Ed. Brian Richardson. Lincoln: Univ. of Nebraska Press, 2008. xi, 281 p. [Beckett]

GG773. ● Toudoire-Surlapierre, Frédérique: *Que fait la critique?.* Paris: Klincksieck, 2008. 180 p.

GG774. Gorceix, Paul: "De nouveaux concepts esthétiques: symbolisation, sugges-
tion et ambiguïté." In 82, 105-123.

GG775. Juvan, Marko; Tomothy Pogacar: "Trajectories of intertextuality from Kristeva to Holthuis." In 769. [Kristeva]

GG776. Kristeva, Julia: "French theory." In 629.

GG777. Orsini, Elisabetta: "La poesia prima della poesia. Teoria dell'influenza poetica in Roland Barthes, Harold Bloom e Gilles Deleuze," *Francofonia*, n. 55 (autunno 2008),
3-20. [Barthes, Deleuze]

GG778. Pennanech, Florian: "Le formalisme dans la nouvelle critique française,"
Esprit Créateur, vol. 48, no. 2 (Summer 2008), 101-114.

MEMOIRS AND AUTOBIOGRAPHY

GG779. ● Jeannelle, Jean-Louis: *Ecrire ses mémoires au XXe siècle: déclin et renouveau.* Paris: Gallimard, 2008. 427 p. [Barthes, Beauvoir, Malraux, Martin du Gard, Mauriac, Ricœur, Sartre, Valéry, Yourcenar]

GG780. ● *"Moi public" et "moi privé" dans les mémoires et les écrits autobiographiques du XVIIe siècle à nos jours.* Etudes réunies et prés. par Rolf Wintermeyer. Mont-
Saint-Aignan: Publications des Universités de Rouen et du Havre, 2008. 443 p. [Semprun]

GG781.   Boyle, Claire: "Autobiography: orthodoxies and paradoxes." In 400, 11-29.
GG782.   Brunel, Pierre: "Introduction aux autobiographies," *Revue de Littérature Comparée*, no. 325 [no. 1] (janv.-mars 2008), 7-22.
GG783.   Grève, Marcel de: "L'autobiographie, genre littéraire?," *Revue de Littérature Comparée*, no. 325 [no. 1] (janv.-mars 2008), 23-31.
GG784.   Lejeune, Philippe: "L'autobiographie et l'aveu sexuel," *Revue de Littérature Comparée*, no. 325 [no. 1] (janv.-mars 2008), 37-51.
GG785.   Madelénat, Daniel: "Moi, biographe: m'as-tu vu?," *Revue de Littérature Comparée*, no. 325 [no. 1] (janv.-mars 2008), 95-108.

MISCELLANEOUS

GG786.   • Acocella, Joan Ross: *Twenty-eight artists and two saints*. New York: Vintage, 2008. xix, 540 p. [Beauvoir, Yourcenar]
GG787.   • *American and Canadian literature and culture: across a latitudinal line*. Ed. Klaus Martens, Paul Morris. Saarbrücken: Nordamerikanische Literatur und Kultur, 2008. 231 p. [Gervais, Gide]
GG788.   • *Approaches to teaching Pynchon's The Crying of Lot 49 and other works*. Ed. Thomas H. Schaub. New York: MLA, 2008. xiii, 195 p. [Lyotard]
GG789.   • *Approaches to teaching Poe's prose and poetry*. Jeffrey Andrew Weinstock, ed. New York: MLA, 2008. ix, 241 p. [Lacan]
GG790.   • *Architects [The] of Vatican II: they think they've won*. Foreword by John Vennari. Kansas City, MO: Angelus Press, 2008. [Blondel, Lubac]
GG791.   • *Asian Canadian writing beyond autoethnography*. Eleanor Ty, Christl Verduyn, eds. Waterloo, Ont.: Wilfrid Laurier Univ. Press, 2008. viii, 330 p. [Chen]
GG792.   • *Augustine and history*. Ed. Christopher T. Daly [et al.]. Lanham, MD: Lexington Books, 2008. xiii, 326 p. [Ricœur]
GG793.   • Ausseur, Christine: *Répertoire de l'exil*. Paris: Scali, 2008. 351 p. [Zola]
GG794.   • *Autour des langues et du langage: perspective pluridisciplinaire*. Ouvrage coord. par Mathieu Loiseau [et al.]. Grenoble: PUG, 2008. [Viollier]
GG795.   • Bacherich, Martine: *La passion d'être soi: cinq portraits*. Paris: Gallimard, 2008. 169 p. [Pozzi]
GG796.   • Barnes, Julian: *Nothing to be afraid of*. New York: Alfred A. Knopf, 2008. 243 p. [Renard]
GG797.   • Bates, Robin E.: *Shakespeare and the cultural colonization of Ireland*. New York: Routledge, 2008. vii, 170 p. [Beckett]
GG798.   • Belliotti, Raymond A.: *Watching baseball, seeing philosophy: the great thinkers at play on the diamond*. Jefferson, NC: McFarland & Co., 2008. ix, 187 p. [Camus]
GG799.   • Birnbaum, Pierre: *Geography of hope: exile, the Enlightenment, disassimilation*. Stanford: Stanford Univ. Press, 2008. 479 p. [Durkheim]
GG800.   • *Blick.Spiel.Feld*. Hrsg. Malda Denana [et al.]. Würzburg: Königshausen & Neumann, 2008. 376 p. [Barthes]
GG801.   • *Brian Ferneyhough*. Hrsg. Ulrich Tadday. München: Text + Kritik, 2008. *Musik-Konzepte*. 109 p. [Lévi-Strauss]
GG802.   • *Cambridge [The] companion to Kate Chopin*. Janet Beer, ed. Cambridge: Cambridge Univ. Press, 2008. xii, 184 p. [Maupassant]
GG803.   • *Cambridge [The] companion to W. E. B. Du Bois*. Shamoon Zamir, ed. Cambridge: Cambridge Univ. Press, 2008. xx, 172 p. [Fanon]
GG804.   • *Camille Claudel: de la vie à l'œuvre: regards croisés: actes du colloque*. Réunis par Silke Schauder. Paris: L'Harmattan, 2008. 369 p. [Claudel, Mirbeau]
GG805.   • *Changing the nation: Günter Grass in international perspective*. Ed. Rebecca Braun, Frank Brunssen. Würzburg: Königshausen & Neumann, 2008. 224 p. [Lacan]
GG806.   • Chiles, James R.: *The god machine: from boomerangs to black hawks, the story of the helicopter*. New York: Bantam Dell, 2008. 354 p. [Verne]

GG807. • *Conceptos y objetos de la retórica ayer y hoy.* Ed. Gerardo Ramírez Vidal, Silvia Aquino. México: Univ. Nacional Autónoma de México, 2008. 345 p. [Ricœur]

GG808. • *Consuming symbolic goods: identity and commitment, values and economics.* Ed. Wilfred Dolfsma. Milton Park, Abingdon; New York: Routledge, 2008. 155 p. [Bourdieu]

GG809. • *Contraddizione [La] virtuosa: il problema educativo, don Milani e Il forteto.* A cura di Giuseppe Fornari, Nicola Casanova; con un'intervista a René Girard. Bologna: Il Mulino, 2008. 181 p. [Girard]

GG810. • Curle, Clinton T.: *New directions in human rights.* Camrose, Alberta: Chester Ronning Centre for the Study of Religion and Public Life, 2008. *Augustana distinguished lectures.* 45 p. [Bergson]

GG811. • *Cutting-edge issues in business ethics.* Ed. Mollie Painter-Morland, Patricia Werhane. Dordrecht: Springer, 2008. xiv, 228 p. [Sartre]

GG812. • Delaunay, Sonia: *Sonia Delaunays Welt der Kunst.* Hrsg. Jutta Hülsewig-Johnen. Bielefeld: Kerber Verlag Bielefeld, 2008. 303 p. [Tzara]

GG813. • De Lissovoy, Noah: *Power, crisis, and education for liberation.* New York: Palgrave Macmillan, 2008. 209 p. [Fanon]

GG814. • *Distorsión [La] del espejo: estrategias de la representación en textos de literature argentina y comparada.* María Minellono, compiladora. La Plata: Ediciones al Margen, 2008. 350 p. [Bianciotti]

GG815. • Dufournet, Jean: *Dernières recherches sur Villon.* Paris: Champion, 2008. 205 p. [Schwob, P. Toussaint]

GG816. • *Ecstasy and understanding: religious awareness in English poetry from the late Victorian to the modern period.* Ed. Adrian Grafe. London: Continuum, 2008. xi, 183 p. [S. Weil]

GG817. • *Edgar G. Ulmer: detour on poverty row.* Ed. Gary D. Rhodes. Lexington: Lanham, 2008. xiii, 335 p. [Benoît]

GG818. • *Eduquer, instruire et former à Bordeaux et en Bordelais de l'Ancien Régime à nos jours.* Bordeaux: Univ. Michel de Montaigne, 2008. *Revue historique de Bordeaux et du département de la Gironde,* 3e série, no. 13-14, 2008. 242 p. [Durkheim]

GG819. • *E-Formes: écritures visuelles sur supports numériques.* Dir. Alexandra Saemmer und Monique Maza. Saint-Etienne: Publications de l'Univ. de Saint-Etienne, 2008. 220 p. [F. Bon, Sadin]

GG820. • *Elfriede Jelinek: Sprache, Geschlecht und Herrschaft.* Hrsg. Françoise Rétif und Johann Sonnleitner. Würzburg: Königshausen & Neumann, 2008. 168 p. [Angot, Bataille]

GG821. • *Embodied practices in historical geography.* High Point, NC: Historical Geography Specialty Group, Association of American Geographers, 2008. 283 p. [Beckett]

GG822. • *Emmett Till in literary memory and imagination.* Ed. Harriet Pollack, Christopher Metress. Baton Rouge: Louisiana State Univ. Press, 2008. viii, 262 p. [Césaire]

GG823. • *Empire and its discontents.* Foreword and short essays by Amy Ingrid Schlegel; essay by Rhonda Saad. Medford, MA: Tufts Univ. Art Gallery, 2008. 72 p. [Satrapi]

GG824. • *Erinnerung als Herkunft der Zukunft.* Hrsg. Verena Lenzen. Bern: Peter Lang, 2008. 168 p. [Derrida]

GG825. • Falk, Avner: *Anti-Semitism: a history and psychoanalysis of contemporary hatred.* Westport, CT: Praeger, 2008. vii, 303 p. [Améry]

GG826. • *Festschrift zum 75. Geburtstag von Norbert Linke.* Hrsg. Eva-Maria Houben und Joachim Dorfmüller. Dortmund: NonEM-Verlag, 2008. 268 p. [Baudrillard]

GG827. • Fitzgerald, Michael: *Attention deficit hyperactivity disorder: creativity, novelty seeking and risk.* New York: Nova Science, 2008. 189 p. [Verne]

GG828. • *Food and morality.* Susan R. Friedland, ed. Totnes, England: Prospect, 2008. 320 p. [Sartre]

GG829. • *French music: culture and national identity, 1870-1939.* Ed. Barbara L. Kelly. Rochester: Univ. of Rochester Press, 2008. 260 p. [Zola]

GG830. • Gauntlett, David: *Media, gender and identity.* London; New York: Routledge, 2008. 2nd ed. xii, 317 p. [Foucault]

GG831. • *Gedächtnis und Identität*. Hrsg. Fabrizio Cambi. Würzburg: Königshausen & Neumann, 2008. 354 p. [Goldschmidt]

GG832. • *Genealogies of Orientalism*. Ed. Edmund Burke, III, David Prochaska. xi, 446 p. [Eberhardt]

GG833. • *Germanistik im Konflikt der Kulturen, Band 11*. Hrs. Jean-Marie Valentin [et al.]. Bern: Peter Lang, 2008. 399 p. [Surrealism]

GG834. • *Gothic and modernism: essaying dark literary modernity*. Ed. John Paul Riquelme. Baltimore: Johns Hopkins Univ. Press, 2008. viii, 236 p. [Beckett]

GG835. • Gross, Benjamin: *The holy tongue and how it changed the course of history*. New York: Devora, 2008. ix, 315 p. [Levinas]

GG836. • *Henry Irving: a re-evaluation of the pre-eminent Victorian actor-manager*. Ed. Richard Foulkes. Aldershot: Ashgate, 2008. xiv, 212 p. [Sardou]

GG837. • *History and politics in French language comics and graphic novels*. Ed. Mark McKinney. Jackson: Univ. Press of Mississippi, 2008. xv, 300 p. [Hergé]

GG838. • Kunin, Madeleine: *Pearls, politics, and power: how women can win and lead*. White River Junction, VT: Chelsea Green, 2008. xiv, 233 p. [Beauvoir]

GG839. • *Letzte [Die] Schlacht gewinnen wir!: 40 Jahre 1968*. Hrsg. Elmar Altvater. Hamburg: VSA, 2008. 237 p. [Fanon]

GG840. • *"Lichtersprache aus den Rissen": Nelly Sachs: Werk und Wirkung*. Hrsg. Ariane Huml. Göttingen: Wallstein, 2008. 335 p. [S. Weil]

GG841. • *Life and learning XVII: proceedings of the seventeenth University Faculty for Life conference at Villanova University, 2007*. Ed. Joseph W. Koterski. Washington: Univ. Faculty for Life, 2008. xiv, 698 p. [Zola]

GG842. • *Liminal borderlands in Irish literature and culture*. Ed. Irene Gilsenan Nordin and Elin Holmsten. New York: Peter Lang, 2008. 207 p. [Beckett]

GG843. • *Literatur im Krebsgang*. Hrsg. Arne Winde, Anke Gilleir. Amsterdam: Rodopi, 2008. 363 p. [Breton]

GG844. • *Macht [Die] der Erinnerung*. Hrsg. Ottmar Fuchs, Bernd Janowski. Neukirchen-Vluyn: Neukirchener Verlag, 2008. xii, 482 p. [Ricœur]

GG845. • *Mechademia 3: limits of the human*. Ed. Frenchy Lunning. Minneapolis: Univ. of Minnesota Press, 2008. xvi, 287 p. [Villiers de l'Isle-Adam]

GG846. • *Memoria histórica, género e interdisciplinariedad*. Dir. Santiago Juan-Navarro, Joan Torres-Pou. Madrid: biblioteca Nueva, 2008. [n.p.]. [Deleuze]

GG847. • Morrison, Toni: *What moves at the margin: selected nonfiction*. Jackson: Univ. Press of Mississippi, 2008. xxvi, 215 p. [Laye]

GG848. • *Native Shakespeares*. Ed. Craig Dionne, Parmita Kapadia. Aldershot: Ashgate, 2008. ix, 247 p. [Césaire]

GG849. • *Networked disease*. Ed. S. Harris Ali and Roger Keil. Malden, MA; Oxford: Wiley-Blackwell, 2008. xxii, 356 p. [Foucault]

GG850. • *New direction in American reception study*. Ed. Philip Goldstein and James L. Machor. Oxford; New York: Oxford Univ. Press, 2008. xxviii, 379 p. [Bourdieu]

GG851. • *Olivier Messiaen: music, art and literature*. Ed. Christopher Philip Dingle. Aldershot: Ashgate, 2008. xxv, 351 p. [Cocteau]

GG852. • Peppiatt, Michael: *Francis Bacon: studies for a portrait*. New Haven: Yale Univ. Press, 2008. vii, 272 p. [Leiris]

GG853. • *Philosophy [The] of TV noir*. Ed. Steven Sanders, Aeon J. Skoble. Lexington: Univ. Press of Kentucky, 2008. viii, 272 p. [Camus]

GG854. • Pound, Ezra: *Instigations of Ezra Pound*. Whitefish, MT: Kessinger, 2008. *Kessinger Publishing's rare reprints*. viii, 388 p. [Gourmont]

GG855. • *Primo Levi à l'œuvre: la réception de l'œuvre de Primo Levi dans le monde*. Sous la dir. de Philippe Mesnard et Yannis Thanassekos. Paris: Kimé, 2008. *Détours littéraires*. 525 p. [Francophone, Cinema]

GG856. • *Puppet [The] show*. Curated by Ingrid Schaffner and Carin Kuoni. Philadelphia: Institute of Contemporary Art, Univ. of Pennsylvania, 2008. 127 p. [Jarry]

GG857. • Ratcliffe, Sophie: *On sympathy*. Oxford: Clarendon Press; New York: Oxford Univ. Press, 2008. *Oxford English monographs*. xi, 266 p. [Beckett]

GG858. • *Reading Jude with new eyes.* Ed. Robert L. Webb, Peter H. Davids. London; New York: T & T Clark, 2008. *Library of New Testament Studies.* viii, 154 p. [Bourdieu]

GG859. • *Reception [The] of Charles Darwin in Europe.* Ed. Eve-Marie Engels, Thomas F. Glick. London: Continuum, 2008. lxxii, 659 p. [Teilhard de Chardin]

GG860. • *Routledge companion to directors' Shakespeare.* Ed. John Russell Brown. London: Routledge, 2008. xiii, 588 p. [Lepage]

GG861. • *Royaume [Le] intermédiaire: psychanalyse, littérature, autour de J.-B. Pontalis.* Avant-propos de François Gantheret et Jean-Michel Delacomptée. Paris: Gallimard, 2007. 501 p. [Garcin, Germain, Grenier]

GG862. • *Salvation goods and religious markers.* Ed. Jörg Stolz. Bern; New York: Peter Lang, 2008. 287 p. [Bourdieu]

GG863. • Savage, Jon: *Teenage: the prehistory of youth culture, 1875-1945.* London: Penguin, 2008. 551 p. [Bashkirtseff]

GG864. • Scott, David: *Critical essays on major curriculum theorists.* London; New York: Routledge, 2008. viii, 162 p. [Foucault]

GG865. • Sewell, Elizabeth: *Lewis Carroll: voices from France.* New York: Lewis Carroll Society of North America, 2008. xl, 212 p. [Mallarmé]

GG866. • *Sites of female terror.* Ed. Ana Antón-Pacheco Bravo [et al.]. Cizur Menor: Aranzadi, 2008. vi, 405 p. [Feydeau]

GG867. • *Social studies of health, illness and disease.* Ed. Peter L. Twohig, Vera Kalitzkus. Amsterdam: Rodopi, 2008. 243 p. [Literary themes]

GG868. • Sontag, Susan: *At the same time.* Ed. Paolo Dilonardo and Anne Jump. New York: Picador, 2008. xvii, 235 p. [V. Serge]

GG869. • Spieker, Sven: *The big archive: art from bureaucracy.* Cambridge, MA: MIT Press, 2008. xiii, 219 p. [Breton]

GG870. • *Steven Spielberg and philosophy: We're gonna need a bigger book.* Ed. Dean Kowalski. Lexington: Univ. Press of Kentucky, 2008. vii, 274 p. [Levinas]

GG871. • *Sub/versions: cultural status, genre and critique.* Ed. Pauline MacPherson [et al.]. Newcastle upon Tyne: Cambridge Scholars, 2008. xi, 182 p. [Wittig]

GG872. • Surette, Leon: *The modern dilemma: Wallace Stevens, T. S. Eliot and humanism.* Montréal: McGill-Queen's Univ. Press, 2008. xi, 416 p. [Maurras]

GG873. • *Swift's travels.* Ed. Nicholas Hudson, Aaron Santesso. Cambridge: Cambridge Univ. Press, 2008. xiii, 304 p. [Beckett]

GG874. • Taylor, Andrew: *Books that changed the world: the 50 most influential books.* London: Quercus, 2008. 207 p. [Beauvoir]

GG875. • *Tränen.* Hrsg. Beate Söntgen, Beraldine Spiekermann. München: Fink, 2008. 308 p. [Zola]

GG876. • *Turgenev and Russian culture.* Ed. Joe Andrew, Derek Offord, Robert Reid. Amsterdam: Rodopi, 2008. 372 p. [Beckett]

GG877. • Twain, Mark: *In defense of Harriet Shelley and other essays.* Whitefish, MT: Kessinger, 2008. 404 p. [Bourget]

GG878. • *Victorial freaks.* Ed. Marlene Tromp. Columbus: Ohio State Univ. Press, 2008. xiii, 328 p. [Levinas]

GG879. • *Visualizing medieval performance: perspectives, histories, contexts.* Ed. Elina Gertsman. Aldershot; Burlington, VT: Ashgate, 2008. xiv, 348 p. [Certeau]

GG880. • *What rough beasts?: Irish and Scottish studies in the new millennium.* Ed. Shane Alcobia-Murphy. Newcastle upon Tyne: Cambridge Scholars, 2008. xv, 219 p. [Beckett]

GG881. • White, Harry: *Music and the Irish literary imagination.* Oxford; New York: Oxford Univ. Press, 2008. xiv, 260 p. [Beckett]

GG882. • *Why work?: the perceptions of a real job and the rhetoric of work through the ages.* Robin Patric Clair [et al.]. West Lafayette, IN: Purdue Univ. Press, 2008. xv, 196 p. [Durkheim]

GG883. • *Y todo el resto es literatura: ensayos sobre Osvaldo Lamborghini.* Dir. Juan Pablo Dabove, Natalia Brizuela. Buenos Aires: Interzona, 2008. 282 p. [Beckett]

GG884. • Zaleznik, Abraham: *Hedgehogs and foxes.* New York: Palgrave Macmillan, 2008. xiii, 250 p. [Fanon]

GG885.   Amsallem, Daniela: "Primo Levi et la France." In 855.

GG886.   Arnaud, Celka: "Primo Levi en Belgique francophone." In 855.

GG887.   Baetens, Jan: "Of graphic novels and minor cultures: the Fréon Collective," *Yale French Studies*, no. 114 (2008), 95-115.

GG888.   Brownlie, Siobhan: "Resistance and non-resistance to boundary crossing in translation research," *Target*, vol. 20, no. 2 (2008), 333-347. [Cixous, Huston, Zola]

GG889.   Dalle, Matthieu: "Contre la 'BD': la bande dessinée indépendante depuis 1990," *Contemporary French Civilization*, vol. 32, no. 1 (Winter/Spring 2008), 1-29.

GG890.   Keating, Kelle Lyn: " 'Je me souviens de rien': political discourse in Québec's modern *chanson engagée*." In 120, 358-389.

NOVEL AND SHORT STORY

See also 239, 310, 745.

GG891.   ● Ablamowicz, Aleksander: *Ecrits sur le roman et le romanesque*. Ostrava: Ostravská univerzita v Ostrave, Filozofická fakulta, 2008. 262 p. [Robbe-Grillet]

GG892.   ● *Assises internationales du roman: le roman, quelle invention!*. Préface de Guy Walter. Paris: C. bourgois, 2008. 460 p. [Sagan]

GG893.   ● Daunais, Isabelle: *Les grandes disparitions: essai sur la mémoire du roman*. Saint-Denis: Presses univ. de Vincennes, 2008. 129 p.

GG894.   ● *D'un conte à l'autre, d'une génération à l'autre*. Etudes réunies par Catherine d'Humières. Clermont-Ferrand: Presses univ. Blaise Pascal, 2008. 329 p. [Literary Themes, Blais, Bruckner, Fleutiaux, Nothomb, Sadji, Silhol]

GG895.   ● Godenne, René: *Etudes sur la nouvelle de langue française. III*. Genève: Slatkine, 2005. 462 p.

GG896.   ● Godenne, René: *La nouvelle de A à Z, ou un troisième tour du monde de la nouvelle de langue française*. Auxerre: Rhubarbe, 2008. 150 p.

GG897.   ● Hamon, Philippe; Alexandrine Viboud: *Dictionnaire thématique du roman de mœurs en France, 1814-1914*. Paris: Presses Sorbonne nouvelle, 2008. 2 vols.

GG898.   ● Lantelme, Michel: *Le roman contemporain: Janus postmoderne*. Paris: L'Harmattan, 2008. *Critiques littéraires*. 207 p.

GG899.   ● Michelet Jacquod, Valérie: *Le roman symboliste: un art de l'extrême conscience*. Genève: Droz, 2008. *Histoire des idées et critique littéraire*. 506 p. [E. Dujardin, Gide, Gourmont, Schwob]

GG900.   ● Motte, Warren F.: *Fiction now: the French novel in the twenty-first century*. Champaign, IL: Dalkey Archive Press, 2008. 237 p. [Echenoz, Gailly, Gavarry, Lapeyre, Lenoir, Montalbetti, Redonnet, Salvayre]

GG901.   ● Müller, Elfriede: *Histoire noire: Geschichtsschreibung im französischen Kriminal roman nach 1968*. Bielefeld: Transcript, 2007. 396 p.

GG902.   ● *Nouveau [Le] roman en questions 6: vers un écriture des normes?*. Textes réunis par Johan Faerber. Caen: Lettres modernes Minard, 2008. *Revue des Lettres Modernes*. [Beckett, Duras, Jauffret, C. Mauriac, Ollier, Pinget, Robbe-Grillet, Sarraute, Simon]

GG903.   ● *Présences du passé dans le roman français contemporain*. Sous la dir. de Gianfranco Rubino. Roma: Bulzoni, 2007. 244 p.

GG904.   ● *Problèmes du roman historique*. Textes réunis par Aude Deruelle et Alain Tassel. Paris: L'Harmattan, 2008. 418 p. [Francophone, Barrès, Gary, Martin du Gard, Quignard, Simon, Yourcenar]

GG905.   ● Reggiani, Christelle: *Eloquence du roman: rhétorique, littérature et politique aux XIXe et XXe siècles*. Genève: Droz, 2008. *Histoire des idées et critique littéraire*, 439. 230 p.

GG906.   ● Reiser, Frank: *Andere Räume, entschwindende Subjekte: das Gefängnis und seine Literarisierung im französischen Roman des ausgehenden 20. Jahrhunderts*. Heidelberg: Synchron, 2007. 188 p.

GG907.   ● *Roman [Le] populaire: des premiers feuilletons aux adaptations télévisuelles, 1836-1960*. Sous la dir. de Loïc Artiaga. Paris: Autrement, 2008. 186 p.

GG908. ● *Romanesque et histoire.* Sous la dir. de Christophe Reffait. Amiens: Centre d'études du roman et du romanesque de l'Univ. de Picardie-Jules Verne, 2008. 259 p. [Literary Themes, Bourget, Gracq, Littell, Zola]

GG909. Belhadin, Anissa: "Le roman noir, un espace privilégié pour le romanesque de l'histoire." In 908, 205-219.

GG910. Chaitin, Gilbert D.: "The thesis novel as weapon in the education wars of the Third Republic." In 415, 20-43.

GG911. Dugast-Portes, Francine: "Le 'nouveau roman': éléments d'une esthétique des ruines." In 902, 37-50.

GG912. Faerber, Johan: "Ce que les enfants disent ou le 'nouveau roman' au regard de la littérature contemporaine." In 902, 218-224.

GG913. Faerber, Johan: "La modification ou vers un bilan critique du 'nouveau roman'." In 902, 258-267.

GG914. Ferreira-Meyers, Karen: "Autofiction, problème de définition, ou problème de légitimité d'un genre?," *French Studies in Southern Africa*, no. 38 (2008), 63-78.

GG915. Godenne, René: "De la lecture de la nouvelle française," *Estudios de Lengua y Literatura Francesas*, no. 16 (2005), 33-40.

GG916. Goulet, Andrea: "Malet's maps and Butor's Bleston: city-space and formal play in the *roman policier*," *Esprit Créateur*, vol. 48, no. 2 (Summer 2008), 46-59. [Butor, Malet]

GG917. James, Alison: "Grids and transparencies," *Esprit Créateur*, vol. 48, no. 2 (Summer 2008), 74-85.

GG918. Panaïté, Oana: "La discipline du refus: sur le formalism des écrivains," *Esprit Créateur*, vol. 48, no. 2 (Summer 2008), 60-73.

GG919. Panaïté, Oana: "Poétiques de récupération, poétiques de créolisation," *Littérature*, no. 151 (sept. 2008), 52-74.

GG920. Piat, Julien: "L'expérimentation syntaxique dans l'écriture du Nouveau Roman (1950-1960)," *Information Grammaticale*, no. 116 (2008), 53-54. [Beckett, Pinget, Simon]

GG921. Theeten, Griet: " 'Une remontée dans les traces.' La représentation de la Première Guerre mondiale dans le roman policier français contemporain." In 473, 303-324.

GG922. Verdaguer, Pierre: "Proximité temporelle et évocation de l'horreur. Tendances actuelles dans le roman policier français." In 527, 101-116.

PHILOSOPHY, PSYCHOLOGY, AND RELIGION

See also 4787.

GG923. ● Allen, Amy: *The politics of our selves: power, autonomy, and gender in contemporary critical theory*. New York: Columbia Univ. Press, 2008. *New directions in critical theory*. xi, 230 p. [Foucault]

GG924. ● *Antisemitism and philosemitism in the twentieth and twenty-first centuries*. Ed. Phyllis Lassner and Lara Trubowitz. Newark: Univ. of Delaware Press, 2008. 248 p. [Sartre]

GG925. ● Aron, Raymond: *Main currents in sociological thought. Vol. 2, Durkheim, Pareto, Weber*. Trans. Richard Howard and Helen Weaver; with a new introduction by Daniel J. Mahoney and Brian C. Anderson. Reprint. New Brunswick, NJ; London: Transaction Publishers, 2008. xxi, 346 p. [Aron, Durkheim]

GG926. ● Arrivé, Michel: *Le linguiste et l'inconscient*. Paris: PUF, 2008. *Formes sémiotiques*. 187 p. [Lacan, Saussure]

GG927. ● Badiou, Alain: *Petit Panthéon portatif*. Paris: La Fabrique, 2008. 177 p. [Althusser, Badiou, Canguilhem, Cavaillès, Deleuze, Derrida, Foucault, Lacan, Lacoue-Labarthe, Lyotard, Sartre]

GG928. ● Bahlmann, Katharina: *Können Kunstwerke ein Antlitz haben?*. Wien: Passagen, 2008. 157 p. [Levinas, Lyotard]

GG929.　● *Bausteine zu einer Ethik des Strafens*. Hrsg. Hans-Helmuth Gender [et al.]. Würzburg: Ergon, 2008. viii, 328 p. [Foucault]

GG930.　● Bellinger, Charles K.: *The trinitarian self: the key to the puzzle of violence*. Eugene, OR: Pickwick, 2008. xx, 167 p. [Girard]

GG931.　● Bennett, Tony: *Critical trajectories: culture, society, intellectuals*. Oxford: Blackwell, 2008. ix, 207 p. [Bourdieu]

GG932.　● Braunstein, Néstor A.: *Depuis Freud, après Lacan: déconstruction dans la psychanalyse*. Trad. Daniel Koren. Fenouillet: Erès, 2008. 213 p. [Lacan]

GG933.　● Burke, Sean: *The death and return of the author: criticism and subjectivity in Barthes, Foucault and Derrida*. Third edition. Edinburgh: Edinburgh Univ. Press, 2008. xxiv, 283 p. [Barthes, Derrida, Foucault]

GG934.　● Burke, Sean: *The ethics of writing: authorship and legacy in Plato and Nietzsche*. Edinburgh: Edinburgh Univ. Press, 2008. xii, 243 p. [Derrida, Levinas]

GG935.　● Calarco, Matthew: *Zoographies: the question of the animal from Heidegger to Derrida*. New York: Columbia Univ. Press, 2008. 169 p. [Derrida]

GG936.　● Carter, J. Kameron: *Race: a theological account*. Oxford: Oxford Univ. Press, 2008. xiv, 489 p. [Foucault]

GG937.　● Chimisso, Cristina: *Writing the history of the mind: philosophy and science in France, 1900 to 1960s*. Aldershot; Burlington, VT: Ashgate, 2008. vi, 209 p. [Bachelard, Canguilhem]

GG938.　● *China-West interculture: toward the philosophy of world integration: essays on Wu Kuang-Ming's thinking*. Ed. Jay Goulding. New York: Global Scholarly Publications, 2008. [Merleau-Ponty]

GG939.　● Cusset, François: *French theory: how Foucault, Derrida, Deleuze, & Co. transformed the intellectual life of the United States*. Trans. Jeff Fort with Josephine Berganza and Marlon Jones. Minneapolis: Univ. of Minnesota Press, 2008. xxi, 388 p. [Barthes, Baudrillard, Bourdieu, Deleuze, Derrida, Foucault, Guattari, Lacan, Lyotard, de Man]

GG940.　● *Deconstruction reading politics*. Martin McQuillan, ed. Basingstoke: Palgrave Macmillan, 2008. x, 225 p. [Badiou, Beckett, Derrida]

GG941.　● Deflem, Mathieu: *Sociology of law: visions of a scholarly tradition*. Cambridge; New York: Cambridge Univ. Press, 2008. x, 348 p. [Durkheim]

GG942.　● Depoortere, Frederiek: *The death of God: an investigation into the history of the Western concept of God*. London: T & T Clark, 2008. xi, 207 p. [Girard]

GG943.　● *Desire of the analysts: psychoanalysis and cultural criticism*. Ed. Greg Forter, Paul Allen Miller. Albany: SUNY Press, 2008. vii, 258 p. [Lacan, Sartre]

GG944.　● *Encounter between eastern orthodoxy and radical orthodoxy: transfiguring the world through the Word*. Ed. Adrian Pabst and Christoph Schneider. Aldershot; Burlington, VT: Ashgate, 2008. [Lacan]

GG945.　● *Evolution [The] of evil*. Gaymon Bennett [et al.], eds. Göttingen: Vandenhoeck & Ruprecht, 2008. 368 p. [Girard, Ricœur]

GG946.　● Farley, Margaret A.: *Just love: a framework for Christian sexual ethics*. London: Continuum, 2008. xiii, 322 p. [Foucault]

GG947.　● Fazio, Mariano: *Cristianos en la encrucijada: los intelectuales cristianos en el periodo de entreguerras*. Madrid: Rialp, 2008. *Vértice*. 304 p. [Maritain, Mounier]

GG948.　● Feinmann, José Pablo: *El filosofía y el barro de la historia*. Buenos Aires: Planeta, 2008. 814 p. [Foucault, Sartre]

GG949.　● Ferrero Carracedo, Luis: *Razón dramática y pensamiento*. Madrid: Fundación Universitaria Española, 2008. 328 p. [Blanchot, Deleuze, Foucault, Levinas]

GG950.　● Gillissen, Matthias: *Philosophie des Engagements: Bergson, Husserl, Sartre, Merleau-Ponty*. Freiburg im Breisgau: Alber, 2008. 341 p. [Bergson, Merleau-Ponty, Sartre]

GG951.　● Goddard, Jean-Christophe: *Violence et subjectivité: Derrida, Deleuze, Maldiney*. Paris: Vrin, 2008. *Moments philosophiques*. 180 p. [Artaud, Bataille, Deleuze, Derrida, Lacan]

GG952.　● Green, Anna: *Cultural history*. Houndsmills; New York: Palgrave Macmillan, 2008. *Theory and history*. viii, 163 p. [Foucault]

GG953. • Habib, Rafey: *A history of literary criticism and theory: from Plato to the present*. Malden, MA: Blackwell, 2008. ix, 838 p.

GG954. • *Horizontes existenciários da filosofía: Søren Kierkegaard and philosophy today*. Ed. João Vila-Chã. Braga: Revista Portuguesa de Filosofía, 2008. *Revista portuguesa de filosofía*, t. 64, fasc. 2-4 (2008). viii, 701 p. [Derrida, Levinas, Sartre]

GG955. • Ingram, Penelope: *The signifying body: toward an ethics of sexual and racial difference*. Albany: SUNY Press, 2008. *SUNY Series in Gender Theory*. xxxv, 154 p. [Fanon, Irigaray, Lacan]

GG956. • *Jesus and philosophy*. Ed. Paul K. Moser. Cambridge; New York: Cambridge Univ. Press, 2008. ix, 236 p. [Ricœur]

GG957. • Joas, Hans: *Do we need religion?*. Trans. Alex Skinner. Boulder, CO: Paradigm, 2008. *Yale cultural sociology series*. x, 153 p. [Ricœur]

GG958. • Judt, Tony: *Reappraisals: reflections on the forgotten twentieth century*. New York: Penguin, 2008. xiv, 448 p. [Althusser, Camus]

GG959. • Lievens, Thierry: *L'éthique comme vocation: se laisser choisir pour choisir*. Bruxelles: Lessius, 2008. *Donner raison*. 282 p. [Ladrière, Levinas, Ricœur]

GG960. • Juisetti, Federico: *Estetica dell'immanenza: saggi sulle immagini, le parole e le macchine*. Roma: Aracne, 2008. 241 p. [Bergson]

GG961. • *Marxist feminist criticism of the Bible*. Ed. Roland Boer and Jorunn Okland. Sheffield: Sheffield Phoenix Press, 2008. 252 p. [Beauvoir, Kristeva]

GG962. • Mohia, Nadia: *L'expérience de terrain: pour une approche relationnelle dans les sciences sociales*. Paris: Découverte, 2008. 304 p. [Leiris, Lévi-Strauss]

GG963. • Monville, Aymeric: *Misère du nietzschéisme de gauche*. Bruxelles: Aden, 2007. 104 p. [Bataille, Camus, Deleuze, Derrida]

GG964. • *Moraliste [Le], la politique et l'histoire: de La Rochefoucauld à Derrida*. Sous la dir. de Jean-Charles Darmon. Paris: Desjonquères, 2007. 238 p. [Cioran, Derrida]

GG965. • *Mulheres, filosofía ou coisas do gênero*. Org. Marcia Tiburi, Bárbara Valle. Santa Cruz do Sul: EDUNISC, 2008. 224 p. [Levinas]

GG966. • Murchland, Bernard: *The arrow that flies by day: existential images of the human condition from Socrates to Hannah Arendt*. Lanham, MD: Univ. Press of America, 2008. xiii, 143 p. [Camus, Marcel, Sartre]

GG967. • Noudelmann, François: *Le toucher des philosophes: Sartre, Nietzsche et Barthes au piano*. Paris: Gallimard, 2008. 177 p. [Barthes, Sartre]

GG968. • *The Office and philosophy: scenes from the unexamined life*. Ed. Jeremy Wisnewski. Malden, MA: Blackwell, 2008. xiii, 310 p. [Baudrillard, Sartre]

GG969. • Oldmeadow, Harry: *Mediations: essays on religious pluralism and the perennial philosophy*. San Rafael, CA: Sophia Perennis, 2008. [Eliade, Guénon]

GG970. • Osborne, Thomas: *The structure of modern cultural theory*. Manchester; New York: Manchester Univ. Press, 2008. 168 p. [Bourdieu, Foucault]

GG971. • Oventile, Robert Savino: *Deconstruction: an introduction for college students*. Los Angeles: Learn Perfect, 2008. iii, 155 p. [Derrida]

GG972. • *Participatory [The] turn: spirituality, mysticism, religious studies*. Ed. Jorge N. Ferrer, Jacob H. Sherman. Albany: SUNY Press, 2008. vii, 388 p. [Bergson]

GG973. • Powell, Jim: *Deconstruction for beginners*. New York: For Beginners; London: Turnaround, 2008. [Derrida]

GG974. • *Religion: beyond a concept*. Ed. Hent de Vries. New York: Fordham Univ. Press, 2008. *The future of the religious past*. xiv, 1006 p. [Levinas]

GG975. • Ritter, Henning: *Die Eroberer: Denker des 20. Jahrhunderts*. München: Beck, 221 p. [Kojève, Lévi-Strauss, Malraux]

GG976. • Roudinesco, Elisabeth: *Philosophy in turbulent times*. Trans. William McCuaig. New York: Columbia Univ. Press, 2008. xvi, 184 p. [Althusser, Canguilhem, Deleuze, Derrida, Foucault, Sartre]

GG977. • *Routledge [The] companion to twentieth-century philosophy*. Dermot Moran, ed. London: Routledge, 2008. xvi, 1024 p.

GG978. • Rubenstein, Mary-Jane: *Strange wonder: the closure of metaphysics and the opening of awe*. New York: Columbia Univ. Press, 2008. *Insurrections*. xii, 256 p. [Derrida, Levinas, Nancy]

GG979.   ● Schweizer, Harold: *On waiting*. London; New York: Routledge, 2008. *Thinking in action*. x, 152 p. [Bergson]

GG980.   ● Searle, Alison: *"The eyes of your heart": literary and theological trajectories of imagining biblically*. Colorado Springs: Paternoster, 2008. xiv, 231 p. [Ricœur]

GG981.   ● Seidman, Steven: *Contested knowledge: social theory today*. Malden, MA: Blackwell, 2008. Fourth edition. xv, 310 p. [Baudrillard, Bourdieu, Derrida, Lyotard]

GG982.   ● Shaw, Spencer: *Film consciousness: from phenomenology to Deleuze*. Jefferson, NC: McFarland & Co., 2008. x, 217 p. [Surrealism, Bergson, Deleuze, Merleau-Ponty, Cinema: Bazin]

GG983.   ● Shults, F. LeRon: *Christology and science*. Grand Rapids, MI: William B. Eerdmans, 2008. *Ashgate science and religion series*. x, 171 p. [Girard]

GG984.   ● *Spiritual leaders who changed the world*. Ed. Ira Rifkin. Woodstock, VT: SkyLight Paths, 2008. xviii, 277 p. [Eliade, S. Weil]

GG985.   ● Susam-Sarajeva, Sebnem: *Theories on the move: translation's role in the travels of literary theories*. Amsterdam; New York: Rodopi, 2006. *Approaches to translation studies*. ix, 241 p. [Barthes, Cixous]

GG986.   ● Thomassen, Lasse: *Deconstructing Habermas*. New York: Routledge, 2008. *Routledge studies in social and political thought*. xi, 186 p. [Lyotard, Mouffe]

GG987.   ● *Transforming philosophy and religion: love's wisdom*. Ed. Norman Wirzba and Bruce Ellis Benson. Bloomington: Indiana Univ. Press, 2008. vi, 263 p. [Marion, Ricœur]

GG988.   ● Vaughan, William: *Detours in philosophy: controversies in the continental tradition*. New York: Peter Lang, 2008. *Phenomenology and literature*. vi, 366 p. [Bataille, Derrida, Levinas, Sartre, S. Weil]

GG989.   ● Weller, Shane: *Literature, philosophy, nihilism: the uncanniest of guests*. New York: Palgrave Macmillan, 2008. x, 234 p. [Badiou, Blanchot, Derrida]

GG990.   ● Wills, David: *Dorsality: thinking back through technology and politics*. Minneapolis: Univ. of Minnesota Press, 2008. *Posthumanities*. ix, 269 p. [Derrida, Levinas, Rimbaud]

GG991.   ● Wilson, Scott: *The order of joy: beyond the cultural politics of enjoyment*. Albany: SUNY Press, 2008. *SUNY series in psychoanalysis and culture*. xviii, 188 p. [Bataille, Deleuze, Guattari, Lacan]

GG992.   ● Wolf, Kurt: *Philosophie der Gabe: Meditationen über die Liebe in der französischen Gegenwartsphilosophie*. Stuttgart: Kohlhammer, 2006. 198 p.

GG993.   Berman, Michael: "Still looking for the image in French philosophy," *European Legacy*, vol. 13, no. 5 (Aug. 2008), 645-649.

GG994.   Botha, Catherine F.: "From Destruktion to deconstruction: a response to Moran," *South African Journal of Philosophy*, vol. 27, no. 1 (2008), 52-68. [Derrida]

GG995.   Choplin, Hugues: "De la force à la confiance," *Revue de Métaphysique et de Morale*, no. 4 (oct. 2008), 461-472.

GG996.   Constantinou, Marios; Maria Margaroni: "Continental philosophy," *Year's Work in Critical and Cultural Theory*, vol. 16 (2008), 22-49. [Badiou, Deleuze, Lacan, Rancière]

GG996a.   Gallop, Jane; Carolyn Burke: "Psychoanalysis and feminism in France." In 4744.

GG996b.   Goldberg Moses, Claire: "Made in America: 'French feminism' in academia." In 4787.

GG997.   Goldfelder, Matthew S.: "The art of failure: Hannah Arendt, Michel Foucault, E. M. Cioran and the role of aesthetics in politics." Diss., Univ. of Virginia, 2008. iv, 278 p. [Cioran, Foucault]

GG997a.   Greenstein Burke, Carolyn: "Report from Paris: women's writing and the women's movement." In 4744.

GG998.   Gutting, Gary: "French philosophy in the twentieth century." In 977.

GG999.   Habib, Rafey: "Feminist criticism." In 953. [Beauvoir, Cixous, Kristeva]

GG1000.   Habib, Rafey: "Heterological thinkers." In 953. [Bergson]

GG1001.   Habib, Rafey: "New historicism." In 953. [Foucault]

GG1002.   Habib, Rafey: "Postcolonial criticism." In 953. [Fanon]

GG1003.   Habib, Rafey: "Structuralism." In 953. [Barthes, Saussure]

GG1004.   Hammerschlag, Sarah: "Reading May 68 through a Levinasian lens: Alain Finkielkraut, Maurice Blanchot, and the politics of identity," *Jewish Quarterly Review*, vol. 98, no. 4 (Fall 2008), 522-551. [Blanchot, Finkielkraut, Levinas]

GG1005.   Kamuf, Peggy: "Deconstruction," *Year's Work in Critical and Cultural Theory*, vol. 16 (2008), 1-21. [Derrida]

GG1006.   Mansker, Andrea: " 'Vive 'Mademoiselle'!' The politics of singleness in early twentieth-century French feminism," *Feminist Studies*, vol. 33, no. 3 (Fall 2007), 632-658.

GG1007.   Schrift, Alan D.: "The effects of the *aggregation de philosophie* on twentieth-century French philosophy," *Journal of the History of Philosophy*, vol. 46, no. 3 (July 2008), 449-473.

GG1008.   Seidman, Steven: "The postmodern world of Jacques Derrida, Jean-François Lyotatrd and Jean Baudrillard." In 981. [Baudrillard, Derrida, Lyotard]

GG1008a.   Shukla, B. A.: "The history of French feminism." In 1500.

GG1008b.   Shukla, B. A.: "Major influences on French feminists." In 1500.

GG1008c.   Susam-Sarajeva, Sebnem: "Structuralism and semiotics in Turkey and French feminism in Anglo-America." In 985, 17-52.

POETRY

See also 7, 8, 45, 215, 270, 7536.

GG1009.   ● Annese, Venanzia: *L'œil et la poésie: Desnos, Jouve, Schehadé, Stétié*. Fasano: Schena, 2008. 124 p. [Desnos, Jouve, Schehadé, Stétié]

GG1010.   ● Bennett, Guy; Béatrice Mousli: *Poésies des deux mondes: un dialogue franco-américain à travers les revues, 1850-2004*. Trad. par Marina Dick et Jean-Michel Epistallier. Paris: Ent'revues, 2004. Ed. revue et mise à jour. 238 p.

GG1011.   ● Coenen-Mennemeier, Brigitta: *Dichter und Gedicht im lyrischen Selbstverweis: zur Poetologie des französischen Symbolismus*. Baden-Baden: Deutscher Wissenschafts-Verlag, 2007. 110 p.

GG1012.   ● Dazzan, Eric: *Poétiques de la finitude*. Lille: ANRT, 2008. *Thèse à la carte*. 525 p. [Bonnefoy, Jaccottet, Jean Malrieu, Gaston Puel]

GG1013.   ● Elfakir, Véronique: *Le ravissement de la langue: la question du poète*. Paris: L'Harmattan, 2008. 128 p. [Michaux, Segalen]

GG1014.   ● *Eloge [L'] lyrique*. Sous la dir. d'Alain Genetiot. Nancy: Presses univ. de Nancy, 2008. 503 p. [Bonnefoy, Claudel, Mallarmé, Saint-John Perse]

GG1015.   ● Hébert, François: *Dans le noir du poème: les aléas de la transcendance*. Montréal: Fides, 2007. 214 p. [Francophone]

GG1016.   ● Hénault, Gilles: *Interventions critiques: essais, notes et entretiens*. Edition préparée par Karim Larose et Manon Plante. Montréal: Editions Sémaphore, 2008. *La vie courante*. 503 p.

GG1017.   ● Jouve, Pierre-Jean: *Apologie du poète: suivi de Six lectures*. Saint-Clément-de-Rivière: Fata Morgana, 2006. 93 p. [Nouvelle édition]

GG1018.   ● Kelly, Michael G.: *Strands of utopia: spaces of poetic work in twentieth-century France*. London: Legenda, 2008. x, 269 p. [Bonnefoy, Daumal, Segalen]

GG1019.   ● Lacoste, Frédéric: *L'oiseau dans la poésie de Saint-John Perse, Kenneth White et Philippe Jaccottet*. Lille: ANRT, 2008. *Thèse à la carte*. 470 p. [Jaccottet, Saint-John Perse, White]

GG1020.   ● Murat, Michel: *Le vers libre*. Paris: H. Champion, 2008. 329 p. [Breton, Claudel, Larbaud, Péguy]

GG1021.   ● Petterson, James: *Poetry proscribed: twentieth-century (re)visions of the trials of poetry in France*. Lewisburg, PA: Bucknell Univ. Press, 2008. 195 p. [Breton]

GG1022.   ● *Poésie contemporaine et tensions de l'identification: de 1985 à nos jours*. Ed. Antonio Rodriguez. Lausanne: Archipel, 2008. 196 p.

GG1023. ● *Poètes [Les] symbolistes: recueil de poèmes choisis*. Prés., Michel Frankland. Saint-Laurent, Québec: Editions du Renouveau pédagogique, 2008. xxi, 74 p.

GG1024. ● *Poetry criticism*. Michelle Lee, ed. Detroit: Thomson/Gale, 2008. xiii, 460 p. [Brossard]

GG1025. ● *Poetry for students. Vol. 28*. Ira Mark Milne, project editor. Detroit: Gale/ Cengage Learning, 2008. xxi, 345 p. [Rimbaud]

GG1026. ● *Rêve [Le] et la ruse dans la traduction de poésie*. Textes réunis et prés. par Béatrice Bonhomme et Micéala Symington. Paris: H. Champion, 2008. 340 p. [Artaud, Meschonnic, H. Thomas]

GG1027. ● Scepi, Henri: *Poésie vacante: Nerval, Mallarmé, Laforgue*. Lyon: ENS éditions, 2008. *Signes*. 243 p. [Laforgue, Mallarmé]

GG1028. ● *Sprachen der Lyrik: von der Antike bis zur digitalen Poesie*. Hrsg. Klaus W. Hempfer. Stuttgart: Steiner, 2008. *Text und Kontext*, 27. 464 p. [Bonnefoy, Céline, Levinas, Maulpoix, Ponge]

GG1029. ● Vaillant, Alain: *La poésie: introduction à l'analyse des textes poétiques*. 2e éd. entièrement refondue. Paris: A. Colin, 2008. 127 p.

GG1030. ● Warren, Rosanna: *Fables of the self: studies in lyric poetry*. New York: Norton, 2008. xxiii, 343 p. [Apollinaire, Jacob, Mallarmé, Rimbaud]

GG1031. Bobillot, Jean-Pierre: "La poésie écrite a-t-elle encore lieu d'être?," *Mélusine*, no. 28 (2008), 197-210.

GG1032. Collini, Maria Benedetta: " 'Elle apparaît divine aux lueurs du couchant': Hélène dans la poésie fin-de-siècle." In 482, 261-277.

GG1033. Collot, Michel: "Blancs et silences dans la poésie moderne." In 382, 137-148. [Du Bouchet, Mallarmé, Reverdy]

GG1034. Debreuille, Jean-Yves: "Un âge d'or de la poésie? Les dix premières années de la collection 'Poètes d'aujourd'hui' de Pierre Seghers, 1944-1954." In 612, 231-244.

GG1035. Delorenzo, Christian: "Le sonnet régulier, le sonnet libre et le sonnet potentiel," *Formules*, no. 12 (2008), 95-104.

GG1036. Disson, Agnès: "Turbulences et mutations: la poésie française contemporaine des années 50 aux années 2000," *Gallia*, no. 47 (2007), 109-118.

GG1037. Dotoli, Giovanni: "Pour une nouvelle poésie européenne." In 612, 245-257.

GG1038. Espitallier, Jean-Michel: "Politique du poétique," *Etudes Françaises*, vol. 44, no. 1 (2008), 111-117.

GG1039. Kruse, Margot: " 'Ut musica poesis': zur Bedeutung der Analogie zur Musik in der Dichtungstheorie des französischen Symbolismus." In 1028, 169-180.

GG1040. Maulpoix, Jean-Michel: "Un impossible éloge?" In 1014, 941-949.

GG1041. Modenesi, Marco: "1900-1950: intermittences de la figure d'Hélène dans la poésie française." In 482, 295-309.

GG1042. Moncond'huy, Dominique: "D'Aragon à Roubaud et Hocquard: le sonnet comme espace," *Formules*, no. 12 (2008), 11-21. [Aragon, Hocquard, Roubaud]

GG1043. Moog-Grünewald, Maria: "Zur Poiëtik der modernen Lyrik." In 1028, 381-397. [Bonnefoy, Ponge]

GG1044. Murphy, Steve: "Versifications 'parnassiennes' (?)," *Romantisme*, no. 140 (2e trim. 2008), 67-84.

GG1045. Parish, Nina: "From book to page to screen: poetry and new media," *Yale French Studies*, no. 114 (2008), 51-66.

GG1046. Rodriguez, Antonio: "Verset et déstabilisation narrative dans la poésie contemporaine," *Etudes Littéraires*, vol. 38, no. 2 (automne 2007), 109-124.

GG1047. Sabourin, Lise: "L'éloge du poète face à la modernité." In 1014, 437-448.

GG1048. Scott, Clive: "Re-conceiving voice in modern verse," *Comparative Critical Studies*, vol. 5, no. 1 (2008), 5-20. [Calaferte, Du Bouchet, Reverdy]

SURREALISM

See also 444, 736, 1331, 4204, 6905.

GG1049. ● Baker, Simon: *Surrealism, history and revolution*. Bern: Peter Lang, 2007.

GG1050. • Colombet, Marie J. A.: *L'humour objectif: Roussel, Duchamp, "sous le capot": l'objectivation du surréalisme.* Paris: Publibook.com, 2008. 547 p. [Breton, Roussel]

GG1051. • Duwa, Jérôme: *Surréalistes et situationnistes, vies parallèles.* Paris: Dilecta, 2008. 237 p.

GG1052. • Eburne, Jonathan P.: *Surrealism and the art of crime.* Ithaca, NY: Cornell Univ. Press, 2008. xi, 324 p.

GG1053. • Flahutez, Fabrice: *Nouveau monde et nouveau mythe: mutations du surréalisme.* Dijon: Presses du réel, 2007. 525 p.

GG1054. • Forest, Philippe: *Introduction au surréalisme.* Paris: Vuibert, 2008. 120 p.

GG1055. • Gonçalves, Marco Antonio: *O real imaginado: etnografía, cinema e surrealismo.* Rio de Janeiro: Topbooks, 2008. 239 p. [Cinema: Rouch]

GG1056. • *Intellectuel surréaliste (après 1945).* Dir. Nathalie Limat-Letellier, Maryse Vassevière. Paris: Association pour l'étude du surréalisme et les auteurs, 2008. 239 p.

GG1057. • *Main [La] à plume: anthologie du surréalisme sous l'Occupation.* Etablie par Anne Vernay et Richard Walter; préface de Gérard Durozoi. Paris: Syllepse, 2008. *Les Archipels du surréalisme.* 350 p.

GG1058. • Parkinson, Gavin: *Surrealism, art, and modern science: relativity, quantum mechanics, epistemology.* New Haven: Yale Univ. Press, 2008. viii, 294 p. [Bachelard, Bataille, Breton, Caillois]

GG1059. • *Razonado desorden: textos y declaraciones surrealistas, 1924/1939.* Edición, prólogo, traducción y notas Angel Pariente. Logroño: Pepitas de calabaza, 2008. 298 p.

GG1060. Aubert, Nathalie: "Twenty years on—distances: Belgian and French surrealists and 'the' revolution." In 79, 174-189.

GG1061. Béhar, Henri: "Une correspondance d'Outre-Manche. Lettres d'André Breton, Paul Éluard et Georges Hugnet à Herbert Read," *Mélusine*, no. 28 (2008), 267-294. [Breton, Éluard, Hugnet]

GG1062. Clavez, Bertrand: "Fluxus et le surréalisme, entre meurtre du père et redite historiciste," *Mélusine*, no. 28 (2008), 183-196.

GG1062a. Coombs, Neil: "Surrealism and fantasy cinema." In 7973.

GG1062b. Coombs, Neil: "What is surrealism?" In 7973.

GG1063. Forcer, Stephen: " 'Ceci n'est pas une transmission': Dada and surrealism in work by Jean-Luc Godard and Anne-Marie Miéville." In 610, 179-198. [Cinema: Godard, Miéville]

GG1064. Fréché, Bibiane: "Surrealism in Belgium between the Wars." In 79-, 161-173.

GG1065. Gorrillot, Bénédicte: "Les TXT et l'héritage surréaliste," *Mélusine*, no. 28 (2008), 249-264.

GG1066. Leclercq, Sophie: "Le colonialisme mis à nu. Quand les surréalistes démythifiaient la France coloniale (1919-1962)," *Revue Historique*, no. 646 (avril 2008), 315-336.

GG1067. Nuti, Marco: "Le cerveau du fruitier: l'impossible surréalisme cézannien." In 542, 109-127.

GG1068. Ottinger, Didier: "Dada est-il soluble dans le surréalisme? Breton/Tzara: comment l'amitié écrit l'histoire," *Cahiers du Musée National d'Art Moderne*, no. 102 (hiver 2007-2008), 64-77. [Breton, Tzara]

GG1069. Parkinson, Gavin: "Coda: nuclear physics and the cold war: surrealism and Salvador Dali." In 1058.

GG1070. Pennone, Florence: "Abschied vom Wunderbaren: Paul Celan und der französische Surrealismus." In 833, 189-198. [Breton]

GG1071. Polizzotti, Mark: "Profound occultation (surrealism)," *Parnassus*, vol. 30, no. 1-2 (2008), 1-37.

GG1072. Rothenberg, Jerome: "Three modernist movements: Dadaism, futurism, surrealism." In 581.

GG1073. Rubio, Emmanuel: "Du surréalisme à l'IS, l'*Esthétique* en héritage," *Mélusine*, no. 28 (2008), 95-108.

GG1073a. Shaw, Spencer: "Benjamin and surrealism." In 982.

GG1074. Vrydaghs, David: " 'Cela ne s'imposait pas. Cela, je l'impose': l'immixtion de l'invective dans les pratiques du groupe surréaliste français," *Etudes Littéraires*, vol. 39, no. 1 (hiver 2008), 113-124.

GG1075. Westbrook, John: "Reorienting surrealism," *French Review*, vol. 81, no. 4 (March 2008), 707-719.

THEATER

See also 173, 289.

GG1076. • Angel-Perez, Elisabeth: *Voyages au bout du possible: les théâtres du traumatisme de Samuel Beckett à Sarah Kane*. Paris: Klincksieck, 2006. 248 p. [Beckett]

GG1077. • Bonnevie, Serge: *Le sujet dans le théâtre contemporain*. Paris: L'Harmattan, 2007. 239 p.

GG1078. • Bradby, David; Annabel Poincheval: *Le théâtre en France de 1968 à 2000*. Paris: H. Champion, 2007. 752 p.

GG1079. • Charle, Christophe: *Théâtres en capitales: naissance de la société du spectacle à Paris, Berlin, Londres et Vienne: 1860-1914*. Paris: A. Michel, 2008. 572 p.

GG1080. • Corey, Paul: *Messiahs and Machiavellians: depicting evil in the modern theatre*. Notre Dame, IN: Univ. of Notre Dame Press, 2008. xvi, 357 p. [Beckett, Camus]

GG1081. • Curran, Beverley: *Theatre translation theory and performance in contemporary Japan: native voices, foreign bodies*. Manchester; Kinderhook, NY: St. Jerome, 2008. vi, 159 p. [Michel Marc Bouchard]

GG1082. • DiGaetani, John Louis: *Stages of struggle: modern playwrights and their psychological inspirations*. Jefferson, NC: McFarland & Co., 2008. ix, 197 p. [Beckett]

GG1083. • *Drama for students. Volume 25*. Project editor, Ira Mark Milne. Detroit: Gale/Cengage Learning, 2008. xix, 350 p. [Ionesco]

GG1084. • Felbeck, Christine: *Erinnerungsspiele: memoriale Vermittlung des Zweiten Weltkrieges im französischsprachigen Gegenwartsdrama*. Tübingen: Francke, 2008. 377 p.

GG1085. • *France-Italie, un dialogue théâtral depuis 1950*. Ed. Marie-José Tramuta et Yannick Butel. Bern: P. Lang, 2008. x, 195 p.

GG1086. • Gidel, Henry: *Gens de théâtre: biographies*. Paris: Omnibus, 2008. ii, 1079 p. [Bernhardt, Feydeau, Guitry]

GG1087. • Haney, William S.: *Integral drama: culture, consciousness and identity*. Amsterdam; New York: Rodopi, 2008. *Consciousness, literature and the arts*. 184 p. [Genet, Ionesco]

GG1088. • Heinrici, Sandra: *Maskenwahnsinn: Darstellungsformen des Wahnsinns im europäischen Theater des 20. Jahrhunderts*. Bonn: Bouvier Verlag, 2008. *Junges Forum Literatur*. 176 p. [Beckett]

GG1089. • *Histoire [Une] du spectacle militant: théâtre et cinéma militants 1966-1981*. Sous la dir. de Christian Biet et Olivier Neveux. Vic la Gardiole: L'Entretemps, 2007. 463 p.

GG1090. • Horde, Jean-Marie: *Un directeur de théâtre: pour un théâtre singulier*. Besançon: Les Solitaires intempestifs, 2008. 187 p.

GG1091. • Hubert, Marie-Claude: *Le nouveau théâtre: 1950-1968*. Paris: Champion, 2008. *Dictionnaires et références*. 413 p.

GG1092. • Laplace-Claverie, Hélène: *Modernes féeries: le théâtre français du XXe siècle, entre réenchangement et désenchantement*. Paris: H. Champion, 2007. 316 p.

GG1093. • Malachy, Thérèse: *Le théâtre dans la cité: un recueil d'articles*. Saint-Genouph: Nizet, 2008. 230 p. [Anouilh, Beckett, Claudel, Ghelderode, Giraudoux, Vitez, Yourcenar]

GG1094. • Martin-Fugier, Anne: *Comédiennes: les actrices en France au XIXe siècle*. Paris: Complexe, 2008. 408 p. [Bernhardt] [Orig. ed., 2001]

GG1095. • Moss, Leonard: *The evolutionary sequence in tragedy and the Bible*. Aurora, CO: Davies Group, 2008. [Beckett]

GG1096. ● Philips, Henry; Aude Pichon; Louis-Georges Tin: *Le théâtre catholique en France au XXe siècle*. Paris: H. Champion, 2007. 903 p.

GG1097. ● Rauch, Marie-Ange: *Le théâtre en France en 1968: crise d'une histoire, histoire d'une crise*. Paris: Editions de l'Amandier, 2008. 562 p.

GG1098. ● Saurel, Renée: *Le théâtre face au pouvoir: chroniques d'une relation orageuse, les temps modernes, 1965-1984*. Préface et notes par Robert Abirached. Paris: L'Harmattan, 2008. 295 p.

GG1099. ● *State on stage: the impact of public policies on the performing arts in Europe*. Hans Onno van den Berg [et al.]. Amsterdam: Boekmanstudies, 2008. 240 p.

GG1100. ● *Théâtre des minorités: mises en scène de la marge à l'époque contemporaine*. Textes réunis par Patrice Brasseur et Madelena Gonzalez. Paris: L'Harmattan, 2008. [Francophone, Astalos, Barbeau, Chaurette, Prescott, Yacine]

GG1101. ● *Théâtre [Le] monte au front*. Dir. Chantal Meyer-Plantureux. Paris: Complexe, 2008. 417 p. [Rolland]

GG1102. ● *TNM [Le], d'hier à aujourd'hui*. Sous la dir. de Lorraine Pintal. Montréal: Lanctôt, 2006. 197 p.

GG1103. ● *Traditions et transformations dans le théâtre en France et au Japon du XVe au XXe siècle*. Aurillac: Publications orientalistes de France, 2008. 171 p.

GG1104. Asso, Annick: "Le témoignage comme mode de représentation de la Shoah au théâtre." In 414, 491-499. [Michel Dubois, Cécile Guillemot]

GG1105. Borie, Monique: "La scène du XXe siècle et le défi du dialogue avec les morts," *Alternatives Théâtrales*, no. 99 (2008), 13-17. [Genet, Vitez]

GG1106. Bost, Bernadette: "Histoire, idéologie, musique: dialogues de morts dans le théâtre français contemporain," *Otrante*, no. 22 (2007), 129-138.

GG1107. Bouchard, Michel-Marc: "Le théâtre au cinéma ou le dramaturge devient scénariste!" In 97, 43-52. [Bouchard]

GG1108. Chalaye, Sylvie: "La cérémonie théâtrale comme levée de corps dans les dramaturgies contemporaines des diasporas," *Alternatives Théâtrales*, no. 99 (2008), 41-44. [Efoui, Kwahulé, Mouawad]

GG1109. Daniels, Barry: "Paris theatre, Fall 2007," *Western European Stages*, vol. 20, no. 1 (Winter 2008), 55-64.

GG1110. Daniels, Barry: "Paris theatre, January-April 2008," *Western European Stages*, vol. 20, no. 2 (Spring 2008), 25-30.

GG1111. Daniels, Barry: "Paris theatre, summer 2008," *Western European Stages*, vol. 20, no. 3 (Fall 2008), 67-70.

GG1112. Decock, Jean: "Avignon OFF 2008: the noise of people around," *Western European Stages*, vol. 20, no. 3 (Fall 2008), 43-52.

GG1113. Faivre-Zellner, Catherine: "De la troupe du Théâtre-Libre," *Revue d'Histoire du Théâtre*, no. 239 [no. 3] (2008), 263-272.

GG1114. Glytzouris, Antonis: "On the emergence of European avant-garde theatre," *Theatre History Studies*, vol. 28 (2008), 131-146.

GG1115. Guidicelli, Carole: "Le théâtre documentaire: pour la constitution d'une mémoire commune?" In 414, 501-509. [Py]

GG1116. Leal-Duart, Juli: "Le nu dans le théâtre," *Revue des Sciences Humaines*, no. 289 [no. 1] (2008), 189-198.

GG1117. Léger, Danielle: "Le théâtre français au Québec. Une histoire singulière," *Revue de la Bibliothèque Nationale de France*, no. 30 (2008), 63-72. [Francophone]

GG1118. Négrier, Emmanuel: "Urban and regional cooperation for cultural democratisation: public policies for the performing arts in France." In 1099.

GG1119. Parisse, Lydie: "Défaut des langues et parole trouée au théâtre," *Etudes de Linguistique Appliquée*, no. 147 (2007), 297-305. [Beckett, Novarina, Tardieu]

GG1120. Petitjean, André: "Effets d'oralité et de parlure populaire dans les textes dramatiques contemporains." In 619, 355-395. [X. Durringer, D. Lemahieu]

GG1121. Phillips, Henry: "Le théâtre catholique en Europe et au Canada: un milieu réuni dans la dispersion," *Revue de Littérature Comparée*, no. 326 [no. 2] (avril-juin 2008), 175-194.

GG1122. Razgonnikoff, Jacqueline: "Itinéraires de découverte dans les archives de la Comédie-Française," *Revue d'Histoire du Théâtre*, no. 240 [no. 4] (2008), 379-386.

GG1123. Scherer, Colette: "Notes sur les archives de théâtre en France en 2007," *Revue d'Histoire du Théâtre*, no. 237 [no. 1] (2008), 37-42.

GG1124. Schwartz-Gastine, Isabelle: "Shakespeare for all seasons? *Richard II* en Avignon: de Jean Vilar (1957) à Ariane Mnouchkine (1982)," *Revue LISA*, vol. 6, no. 3 (2008), 291-304. [Mnouchkine, Vilar]

GG1125. Sowerwine, Charles; Gabrielle Wolf: "Echoes of Paris in the Antipodes: French theatre and opera in Melbourne (1850-1914)," *Australian Journal of French Studies*, vol. 45, no. 1 (Jan.-April 2008), 81-98.

GG1126. Van Staeyen, Jef: "La virgule est un trait d'union. Le théâtre transfrontalier à Tourcoing et Meuscron," *Franse Nederlanden*, 32ste jaarboek (2007), 169-177.

GG1127. Wehle, Philippa: "Avignon 2008: children, babies, and even some dogs," *Western European Stages*, vol. 20, no. 3 (Fall 2008), 33-42.

GG1128. Weigel, Philippe: "Le nouveau visage d'Orphée dans le théâtre contemporain." In 520, 560-570.

GG1129. Zatlin, Phyllis: "April in Paris: in search of the past," *Western European Stages*, vol. 20, no. 2 (Spring 2008), 31-36.

PART TWO

Author-Subjects

ABA, Noureddine.

GG1130.   Ouardi, Brahim: "Noureddine Aba: un parcours, une œuvre," *Algérie Littérature/Action*, no. 119-120 (mars-avril 2008), 27-34.

AARON, Soazig.

GG1131.   Binder, Anne-Berenike: "Soazig Aaron, *Le non de Klara.*" In 390, 117-169.

GG1132.   Obergöker, Timo: "Shoah et récit fictionnel, un champ de force délicat: *Le non de Klara* de Soazig Aaron." In 602, 205-218.

ABÉGA, Séverin-Cécile.

GG1133.   Abomo-Maurin, Marie-rose: "Séverin-Cécile Abéga, humaniste engagé, patriote révolté," *Cultures Sud*, no. 170 (sept. 2008), 21-26.

GG1134.   Atangana-Abola, Marthe-Isabelle: "*Le Sein t'est pris* de Séverin-Cécile Abéga: une lecture du personnage féminin." In 52, 257-273.

ACCAD, Évelyne.

GG1135.   ● *On Evelyne Accad: essays in literature, feminism, and cultural studies.* Cheryl Toman, ed. Birmingham, AL: Summa, 2007. xix, 420 p.

GG1136.   Ben Aba, Amel: "On Evelyne Accad, the friend." In 1135.

GG1137.   Capshew, Thomas F.: "Trauma and transformation in the fiction of Evelyne Accad." In 1135.

GG1138.   Cooke, Miriam: "Dying to be free: wilderness writing from Lebanon, Arabia, and Libya." In 1135.

GG1139.   diLiberti, Julia: "Excising sleep and subverting the patriarchy: creativity in the novels of Accad and Chedid." In 1135. [Chedid]

GG1140.   El Atia, Samira: "A window on polygamy in Morocco: Accad's creative writing style as a tool of female empowerment." In 1135.

GG1141.   Figueira, Dorothy: "Excised from a profession." In 1135.

GG1142.   Hahn, Cynthia: "On translating Evelyne Accad." In 1135.

GG1143.   Handal, Nathalie: "Reflections on sex, silence, and feminism." In 1135.

GG1144.   Harb, Sirène: "Love, transgression, and femihumanism in *Sitt Marie Rose.*" In 1135.

GG1145.   Heistad, Dennis: "Unraveling the self to discover the other." In 1135.

GG1146.   Hottell, Ruth A.: "Evelyne Accad: traveling through mutation and mutilation of the other." In 1135.

GG1147.   MacGillivray, Catherine A. F.: "Translating Evelyne Accad." In 1135.

GG1148.   Rice, Alison: "Women writers from the 'Arab world' in tune with the times." In 1135. [Chedid, Djebar]

GG1149.   Saba Yared, Nazik: "Evelyne Accad on women excised." In 1135.

GG1150.   Solheim, Jennifer: " 'Tenter de les évoquer': testimony and écriture féminine in Evelyne Accad's *Coquelicot du massacre.*" In 1135.

GG1151.   Sullivan, Zohreh T.: "The body and the city: Evelyne Accad's and Etel Adnan's Beirut." In 1135.

GG1152.   Toman, Cheryl: "Evelyne Accad and Dubravka Ugresic: feminism, war, and Mediterranean sisterhood." In 1135.

GG1153.   Verthuy, Maïr: "Evelyne Accad, or the hijacking of sexuality." In 1135.

GG1154.   Vieille, Paul: "An account of a round table on the war." In 1135.

GG1155.   Zahnd, Elizabeth A.: "The oil-pot or the 'Elvis torch'?: Evelyne Accad between tradition and modernity." In 1135.

GG1156.   Zupancic, Metka: "Healing the goddess: the way out of *The wounded breast.*" In 1135.

ADAM, Paul.

GG1157. Fornasiero, Jean: "Mécènes de l'utopie fin-de-siècle: le cas de Paul Adam et d'Emile Zola." In 541, 108-122.

ADAMOV, Arthur. See also 606.

GG1158. Hubert, Marie-Claude: "La grande et la petite manœuvre ou la 'révolution trahie'." In 456, 159-168.

GG1159. Kostanyan, Ani: "Le théâtre d'Arthur Adamov." In 442, 121-129.

ADIAFFI, Jean-Marie. See 227.

AGÉNOR, Monique.

GG1160. Hourau, Stéphane: "Ecrire entre l'Océan Indien et l'Europe: la négociation de la distance chez Monique Agénor et Jean Lods," *Nouvelles Etudes Francophones*, vol. 23, no. 1 (printemps 2008), 82-93. [Lods]

AGNANT, Marie-Célie

GG1161. Branach-Kallas, Anna: "Maroon mothers, motherless daughters." In 104, 153-169.

GG1162. Schuchardt, Beatrice: "Deux couleurs bleu: opacité et différence dans *Le Livre d'Emma* de Marie-Célie Agnant." In 440, 189-204.

ALAGBÉ, Yvan.

GG1163. Frey, Hugo: " 'For all to see': Yvan Alagbé's *Nègres jaunes* and the representation of the contemporary social crisis in the *banlieue*," *Yale French Studies*, no. 114 (2008), 116-129.

ALAIN [Emile Auguste Charier]. See 4162.

ALAIN-FOURNIER.

GG1164. • Alain-Fournier: *Le grand Meaulnes*. Edition établie, prés. et annotée par Sophie Basch. Paris: Fayard; Librairie Générale Française, 2008. Nouvelle edition. 348 p.

GG1165. • Cordier, Marcel: *Un grand amour: Alain-Fournier et Le Grand Meaulnes*. Paris: Pierron, 2008. 271 p.

GG1166. Autrand, Michel: "*Le Grand Meaulnes* au cinéma (suite). Les lettres d'Isabelle Rivière," *Bulletin des Amis de Jacques Rivière et d'Alain-Fournier*, no. 120 (2e sem. 2008), 81-110.

GG1167. Blanchard, Pascal: "*Le Grand Meaulnes*: un roman à indices," *Bulletin des Amis de Jacques Rivière et d'Alain-Fournier*, no. 120 (2e sem. 2008), 51-71.

GG1168. Cetin, Gulser: "L'espace réel et l'espace onirique dans *Le Grand Meaulnes* d'Alain-Fournier," *Studi Francesi*, anno 52, fasc. 2 (maggio-agosto 2008), 405-412.

GG1169. Grenet, Guy: "Bonheur, malheur, couleurs dans *Le Grand Meaulnes*," *Bulletin des Amis de Jacques Rivière et d'Alain-Fournier*, no. 120 (2e sem. 2008), 37-50.

GG1170. Zahra, May Abou: "Un livre vivant: perspective linguistique," *Bulletin des Amis de Jacques Rivière et d'Alain-Fournier*, no. 120 (2e sem. 2008), 73-80.

ALBERT-BIROT, Pierre.

GG1171. Langley, Joanne: "Pierre Albert-Birot: a new mimesis, another modernism," *Nottingham French Studies*, vol. 47, no. 1 (Spring 2008), 89-102.

ALBIACH, Anne-Marie. See also 6875.

GG1172. Noël, Bernard: "Anne-Marie Albiach ou la nudité obscure," *Critique*, tome 64, no. 735-736 (août-sept. 2008), 583-586.

ALECHINSKY, Pierre.

GG1173. • Peyré, Yves: *Pierre Alechinsky ou la pluralité du geste*. Paris: Virgile, 2008. *Carnet d'ailleurs*. 145 p.

GG1174. Sicard, Michel: "Alechinsky, surréaliste à la marge," *Mélusine*, no. 28 (2008), 33-46.

ALEXAKIS, Vassilis.

GG1175. Chatzidimitrious, Ioanna: " 'I have no history': negotiating language in Vassilis Alexakis's *The Mother Tongue*," *Comparatist*, vol. 40 (May 2006), 101-112.

GG1176. Halloran-Bessy, Marianne: "Vassilis Alexakis: bilinguisme littéraire et autotraduction. Parcours linguistique et itinéraire identitaire," *Essays in French Literature and Culture*, no. 45 (Nov. 2008), 69-87.

GG1177. Sadkokwski, Piotr: "La surconscience linguistique du romancier bilingue." In 76, 281-288.

GG1178.   Sawas, Stéphane: "La quête de la langue maternelle chez Vassilis Alexakis et Denis Lachaud." In 571, 87-93. [Lachaud]

ALEXIS, Jacques-Stéphen.

GG1179.   Anglade, Georges: "Le dernier codicille d'Alexis. Sur le parcours de Jacques-Stéphen Alexis dans la théorie littéraire," *Présence Africaine*, no. 175-176-177 (2007-1er sem. 2008), 546-573.

GG1180.   Heady, Margaret: *Les arbres musiciens*: a marvelous-realist initiation into Marxist consciousness." In 86, 51-65.

GG1181.   Heady, Margaret: "Jacques-Stéphen Alexis and the foundations of *le réalisme merveilleux des Haïtiens.*" In 86, 42-50.

GG1182.   Kaussen, Valerie: "Slaves, viejos, and the Internationale: the Marxist novels of Jacques Roumain and Jacques-Stéphen Alexis." In 91. [Roumain]

ALFERI, Pierre.

GG1183.   Leblond-Schrader, Ellen: "Le lyrisme purement visuel: le dessin dans la poésie de Pierre Alféri," *Formules*, no. 12 (2008), 191-199.

GG1184.   Pesty, Eric: "Pierre Alferi. 'Pas un geste inutile/pas un qui ne soit libre'," *Critique*, tome 64, no. 735-736 (août-sept. 2008), 612-624.

ALLAIN, Marcel. See also 8189.

GG1185.   ● Allain, Marcel; Pierre Souvestre: *Fantomas: the corpse who kills*. Introduction and translation by Candice Black. ?: Solar Books, 2008. New edition. 254 p. [Souvestre]

GG1186.   Duflo, Colas: "*Fantômas*, un feuilleton théorique (épisode 3)," *Rocambole*, no. 42 (2008), 132-138.

GG1187.   Duflo, Colas: "*Fantômas*, un feuilleton théorique (épisode 4)," *Rocambole*, no. 45 (2008), 136-142.

ALLAIS, Alphonse.

GG1188.   ● *Alphonse Allais lu par les livreurs*. Sous la dir. de Pierre Jourde. Apt: Archange Minotaure, 2008. 29 p.

ALLEG, Henri.

GG1189.   Chambers, Ross: "Ordeals of pain (concerning Henri Alleg's *La question*)." In 449, 207-223.

ALLEN, Michelle. See 249.

ALLIX, Guy.

GG1190.   ● *Guy Allix: portrait, bibliographie, anthologie*. Prés. Jean-Luc Maxence. Paris: Le Nouvel Athanor, 2008. 107 p.

ALTHUSSER, Louis.

GG1191.   ● *Althusser: une lecture de Marx*. Coordonné par Jean-Claude Bourdin. Paris: PUF, 2008. *Débats philosophiques*. 227 p.

GG1192.   ● Pardi, Aldo: *Campo di battaglia: teoria, produzione e conflitto in Louis Althusser*. Verona: Ombre corte, 2008. *Culture*. 243 p.

GG1193.   ● *Penser Louis Althusser*. Pantin: Temps des cerises, 2006. 197 p.

GG1194.   ● *Rileggere il Capitale: la lezione di Louis Althusser: Venezia, 9-10-11 novembre 2006, atti del convegno*. A cura di Maria Turchetto. Milano: Mimesis, 2007. 210 p.

GG1195.   Bidet, Jacques: "Fécondité et ambiguïté du concept d'aliénation. *Le Capital* après Althusser." In 1191, 57-86.

GG1196.   Bourdin, Jean-Claude: "Matérialisme aléatoire et pensée de la conjoncture." In 1191, 193-226.

GG1197.   Fischbach, Franck: " 'Les sujets marchent tout seuls . . .'. Althusser et l'interpellation." In 1191, 113-145.

GG1198.   Garo, Issabelle: "La coupure impossible. L'idéologie en mouvement, entre philosophie et politique dans la pensée de Louis Althusser." In 1191, 31-56.

GG1199.   Henninger, Max: "Facticity and contigency in Louis Althusser's aleatory materialism," *Pli: The Warwick Journal of Philosophy*, vol. 18 (2007), 34-59.

GG1200.   Judt, Tony: "Elucubrations: the 'Marxism' of Louis Althusser." In 958.

GG1201.   Lewis, William S.: "Concrete analysis and pragmatic social theory: notes towards an Althusserian critical theory," *International Studies in Philosophy*, vol. 39, no. 2 (2007), 97-116.

GG1202. Nigro, Roberto: "La question de l'anthropologie dans l'interprétation althussérienne de Marx." In 1191, 87-111.

GG1203. Roudinesco, Elisabeth: "Louis Althusser: the murder scene." In 976, 97-131.

GG1204. Vargas, Yves: "L'horreur dialectique." In 1191, 147-192.

AMÉRY, Jean.

GG1205. ● Améry, Jean: *Intellettuale a Auschwitz*. Pres. di Claudio Magris. Trad. di Enrico Ganni. Torino: Ballati Boringhieri, 2008. 150 p.

GG1206. ● Améry, Jean: *Materialen*. Hrsg. von Irene Heidelberger-Leonard; mit einem Bibliographie und einem Register von Gudrun Bernhardt. Stuttgart: Klett-Cotta, 2008. *Werke*, Band 9. 897 p.

GG1207. ● Brudholm, Thomas: *Resentment's virtue: Jean Améry and the refusal to forgive*. Foreword by Jeffrie G. Murphy. Philadelphia: Temple Univ. Press, 2008. *Politics, history, and social change*. xv, 235 p.

GG1208. ● Heidelberger-Leonard, Irene: *Jean Améry*. Trad. de l'allemand par Sacha Zilberfarb. Arles: Actes Sud, 2008. 364 p.

GG1209. Falk, Avner: "Holocaust survivors: 'Jean Améry,' Simon Wiesenthal, Leon Wieslicer." In 825.

GG1210. Hutchinson, Ben: " 'Ich bin Ich im Altern durch meinen Körper und gegen ihn': Jean Amérys Grammatik des Alterns als Dialog mit der französischen Philosophie," *Jahrbuch für Internationale Germanistik*, 40. Jahrgang, Heft 1 (2008), 119-132.

GG1211. Lütkehaus, Ludger: "Jean Améry nach dreißig Jahren," *Neue Gesellschaft Frankfurter Hefte*, Nr. 6 (2008), 61-64.

GG1212. Siguan, Marisa: "Jean Amérys Realismuskritik." In 429, 391-401.

AMROUCHE, Jean. See also 643, 3954, 4118.

GG1213. Masson, Pierre: "Jean Amrouche, un homme entre deux rives." In 515, 163-173.

AMROUCHE, Taos.

GG1214. Ribstein, Ada: "L'énonciation autobiographique: *Jacinthe noire*, de Taos Amrouche," *Awal*, no. 37 (2008), 63-81.

ANDRIS, Colette.

GG1215. Loetscher, Michel: "A la recherche de Colette Andris," *Presse Littéraire*, no. 16 (2008), 115-118.

ANGOT, Christine.

GG1216. Kandioler, Nicole: "Radikales und mimetisches Ich des Kollektivs. Elfriede Jelinek und Christine Angot." In 820.

ANOUILH, Jean.

GG1217. ● Anouilh, Jean: *Antigone. Texte et documents*. Stuttgard: Klett Sprachen, 2008. 81 p.

GG1218. ● Anouilh, Jean: *La grotte*. Présentation, notes et dossier par Benjamin Girault. Paris: Flammarion, 2008. *Etonnants classiques*. 195 p.

GG1219. ● Anouilh, Jean: *La sauvage*. Edition présentée, établie et annotée par Bernard Beugnot. Paris: Gallimard, 2008. *Folio/Théâtre*. 235 p.

GG1220. Barut, Benoît: " 'Prendre la futilité au sérieux': *La Répétition* ou l'acte manqué de Jean Anouilh," *Revue d'Histoire Littéraire de la France*, tome 108, no. 1 (janv.-mars 2008), 159-182.

GG1221. "Jean Anouilh," *Twentieth-Century Literary Criticism*, vol. 195 (2008), 1-77.

GG1222. Malachy, Thérèse: "*Antigone* d'Anouilh: une déviation du tragique." In 1093.

GG1223. Malachy, Thérèse: "L'idée de bonheur dans le théâtre d'Anouilh." In 1093.

GG1224. Malachy, Thérèse: "Ornifle d'Anouilh dans la tradition du mythe de Don Juan." In 1093.

GG1225. Malachy, Thérèse: "*Pauvre Bitos* d'Anouilh: l'éclatement théâtral d'un mythe." In 1093.

ANTELME, Robert. See also 2023.

GG1226. Bertrand, Lucie: " 'Récit concentrationnaire' et 'prose d'idées': ce qu'apporte la désignation des œuvres inclassables de la 'littérature des camps' par l'appellatif de 'prose d'idées': l'exemple de *L'Espèce humaine* de Robert Antelme," *Cahiers de Narratologie*, no. 14 (févr. 2008), [n.p.].

GG1227. Guyer, Sara: "Before *The Human Race*: Robert Antelme's anthropomorphic poetry," *Critical Survey*, vol. 20, no. 2 (2008), 31-42.

GG1228. Heissler, Deborah: "L'usage du blanc, et de cela que rien ne mesure." In 443, 155-163.

GG1229. Lachapelle, Louise: "L'intérieur est l'asile où l'art se réfugie," *Voix Plurielles*, vol. 5, no. 1 (mai 2008), [n.p.].

APOLLINAIRE, Guillaume. See also 623, 3560.

GG1230. ● Apollinaire, Guillaume: *Du coton dans les Oreilles: carnet de tir*. Prés. Jean-Jacques Lebel. Paris: IMEC, 2008. 55 p.

GG1231. ● Apollinaire, Guillaume: *Poésies libres*. Préface et annoté par Michel Décaudin. Paris: Points, 2008. 106 p.

GG1232. ● Debon, Claude: *Calligrammes dans tous ses états: edition critique du receuil de Guillaume Apollinaire*. Vanves: Calliopées, 2008. 384 p.

GG1233. ● *Dessins [Les] de Guillaume Apollinaire*. Réunis et presents par Claude Debon et Peter Read. Paris: Buchet/Chastel, 2008. *Cahiers dessinés*. 157 p.

GG1234. ● Dubus Vaillant, Nicole: *Guillaume Apollinaire, l'Italo-Polonais*. Nice: Vaillant, 2008. 206 p.

GG1235. ● Fongaro, Antoine: *Culture et sexualité dans la poésie d'Apollinaire*. Paris: Champion, 2008. 460 p.

GG1236. ● Read, Peter: *Picasso and Apollinaire: the persistence of memory*. Berkeley: Univ. of California Press, 2008. xvi, 317 p.

GG1237. ● Roessler, Kurt: *Der Dichter Guillaume Apollinaire und Honnef: Weltliteratur und rheinische Poesie, 1901-1902*. Hrsg. von Werner Osterbrink und Paul-Georg Gutermuth. Bornheim: Verein zur Förderung der Kunst und Kultur in Bad Honnef, 2008. 214 p.

GG1238. Absalon, Patrick: "Fantaisies animalières dans *L'Enchanteur pourrissant* et *Le Bestiaire ou Cortège d'Orphée* de Guillaume Apollinaire." In 518, 137-150.

GG1239. Barbéris, Jeanne-Marie: "Avec Apollinaire, dans 'la petite auto': figures du temps, figures du sujet." In 434, 51-75.

GG1240. Becker, Annette: "*Le poète assassiné*: Apollinaire entre blessure, fiction et commémoration." In 473, 77-99.

GG1241. Caizergues, Pierre: "*Le Poète assassiné* au théâtre ou un suicide d'Apollinaire évité." In 612, 37-42.

GG1242. Debon, Claude: "Les blancs ou la mise en scène poétique dans *Calligrammes*." In 612, 55-67.

GG1243. Debon, Claude: "Le massacre des blancs dans *Calligrammes* d'Apollinaire." In 393, 61-68.

GG1244. Delbreil, Daniel: "Lecture d' 'Un soir' de Guillaume Apollinaire." In 612, 69-84.

GG1245. Dubois, Jacques: "Apollinaire et l'automne triomphal des vendanges." In 383, 453-463.

GG1246. Fraisse, Luc: "Les 'mythes personnels' d'Apollinaire." In 520, 765-772.

GG1247. Metlica, Alessanddro: "Il primo orfismo. Il poeta second Apollinaire all'altezza del 'Bestiaire'," *Studi Francesi*, anno 52, fasc. 1 (genn.-aprile 2008), 136-147.

GG1248. Orlandini, Franco: "Figure di bambini nella poesia di Apollinaire," *Silarus*, anno 48, no. 259 (sett.-ott. 2008), 59-61.

GG1249. Read, Peter: " 'Vous pensez à une belle perle': Apollinaire, Picasso et Cléopâtre en 1918." In 612, 85-93.

GG1250. Richter, Mario: "Apollinaire et Soffici, deux amis, deux vies parallèles." In 612, 95-108.

GG1251. Richter, M.: "Da Clément Marot a Apollinaire. Un'esperienza di critica letteraria," *Rivista di Letterature Moderne e Comparate*, vol. 61, fasc. 2 (aprile-guigno 2008), 211-226.

GG1252. Scott, Clive: "Translating the art of seeing in Apollinaire's 'Les fenêtres'." In 608, 37-51.

GG1253. ter Horst, Eleanor E.: "Urban pastoral: tradition and innovation in Apollinaire's 'Zone' and Rilke's 'Zehnte Duineser Elegie'," *Studies in Twentieth and Twenty-First Century Literature*, vol. 32, no. 1 (Winter 2008), 142-178.

GG1254. Warren, Rosanna: "Orpheus the painter: Apollinaire and Robert Delaunay." In 1030.

APPANAH, Nathacha.

GG1255. Rice, Alison: " 'Le français, langue exotique.' Entretien avec Nathacha Appanah," *Nouvelles Etudes Francophones*, vol. 23, no. 1 (printemps 2008), 184-197.

APRIL, J. P.

GG1256. Tremblay, Nicolas: "J. P. April, *Mon père a tué la terre*," *XYZ: La Revue de la Nouvelle*, no. 96 (hiver 2008), 83-86.

AQUIN, Hubert. See also 46, 94.

GG1257. Harvey, François: "Coupures enchaînées. La dynamique générique dans *Neige noire* d'Hubert Aquin," *Etudes Littéraires*, vol. 39, no. 1 (hiver 2008), 141-152.

ARAGON, Louis. See also 591, 1042, 4663, 7451, 7486.

GG1258. ● Aragon, Louis: *Œuvres romanesques completes, IV.* Edition publiée sous la direction de Daniel Bougnoux; avec, pour ce volume, la collaboration de Bernard Leuilliot et de Nathalie Piégay-Gros. Paris: Gallimard, 2008. *Bibliothèque de la Pléiade*, 545. lxviii, 1691 p.

GG1259. ● Kimyongür, Angela: *Memory and politics: representations of war in the work of Louis Aragon.* Cardiff: Univ. of Wales Press, 2008. *French and Francophone Studies.* xiv, 207 p.

GG1260. ● Tossou, Okri Pascal: *Le mentir-vrai de l'engagement chez Louis Aragon romancier: des Cloches de Bâle à Servitude et grandeur des Français.* Lille: Atelier national de reproduction des theses, 2008. 431 p.

GG1261. Grenouillet, Corinne: "Les militants ouvriers et communistes dans *Le monde réel* d'Aragon." In 456, 61-73.

GG1262. Kasbi, François: "Aragon manifeste," *Nouvelle Revue Française*, no. 584 (janv. 2008), 199-206.

GG1263. Kimyongür, Angela: "Towards a healthy social status for women? Capitalism and the figure of the prostitute in the novels of Louis Aragon." In 573, 101-114.

GG1264. Morel, Jean-Paul: "Aragonade: la querelle du réalisme." In 564, 77-81.

GG1265. Russo, Adelaide M.: "L'ekphrasis dans *Les Collages* de Louis Aragon." In 583, 45-59.

GG1266. Schaffner, Alain: "Flux, rythme et répétition dans *Aurélien*." In 459, 211-221.

GG1267. Stauder, Thomas: " 'Ceci n'est pas un roman historique': considérations sur le genre de *La Semaine Sainte* d'Aragon (1958)." In 483, 211-227.

GG1268. Vaugeois, Dominique: "Aragon et la grandeur (1945-1982)," *Histoires Littéraires*, no. 33 (janv.-févr.-mars 2008), 79-101.

ARBAN, Dominique.

GG1269. Di Mattia, Francesca: "Le germe de l'écriture. Créations et interactions dans l'œuvre de Dominique Arban." In 384, 233-244.

ARCAN, Nelly. See also 546, 925.

GG1270. Abdelmoumen, Mélikah: "*Folle* de Nelly Arcan." In 41, 19-38.

GG1271. Boisclair, Isabelle: "Accession à la subjectivité et autoréification: statut paradoxal de la prostituée dans *Putain* de Nelly Arcan." In 69, 111-123.

GG1272. Prus, Elena: " 'Scandaleusement intime': *Putain* de Nelly Arcan." In 115, 208-216.

GG1273. Resch, Yannick: "Violence du corps, violence culturelle: *Putain* de Nelly Arcan." In 69, 179-183.

ARCHAMBAULT, Gilles.

GG1274. Cuerrier, Alain: "Gilles Archaubault à l'écoute de la fragilité du monde," *Lettres Québécoises*, no. 131 (automne 2008), 6-8.

ARCOS, René.

GG1275. Gondre, Odile: "La bibliothèque de René Arcos," *Cahiers de l'Abbaye de Créteil*, no. 26 (2007), 5-102.

ARNOTHY, Christine.

GG1276. ● Parent, Anne Martine: *Etude sur J'ai quinze ans et je ne veux pas mourir de Christine Arnothy*. Carouge-Genève: Zoé, 2008. 112 p.

ARON, Raymond.

GG1277. ● Oppermann, Matthias: *Raymond Aron und Deutschland: die Verteidigung der Freiheit und das Problem des Totalitarismus*. Ostfildern: Thorbecke, 2008. *Beihefte der Francia*, 68. 622 p.

GG1278. ● *Raymond Aron et la démocratie au XXIe siècle: centenaire de la naissance de Raymond Aron*. Réunis par Elisabeth Dutartre. Paris: Fallois, 2007. 265 p.

GG1279. ● *Raymond Aron, philosophe dans l'histoire, "armer la sagesse"*. Sous la dir. de Serge Audier [et al.]. Paris: Fallois, 2008. 234.

GG1280. ● Verstraeten, Pierre: *L'anti-Aron*. Paris: La Différence, 2008. 121 p.

GG1281. ● Völkel, Evelyn: *Der totalitäre Staat: das Produkt einer säkularen Religion?*. Baden-Baden: Nomos, 2008. 455 p.

GG1282. Likin, Max: " 'Nothing fails like success': the Marxism of Raymond Aron," *French Politics, Culture and Society*, vol. 26, no. 3 (Winter 2008), 43-60.

ARP, Jean.

GG1283. ● *Art is Arp: dessins, collages, reliefs, sculptures, poésie*. Exhibition catalog. Strasbourg: Editions des Musées de Strasbourg, 2008. 343 p.

GG1284. ● *Hans Arp: die Natur der Dinge*. Hrsg. Klaus Gallwitz. Düsseldorf: Richter; Remagen: Arp Museum Bahnhof Rolandseck, 2007. 235 p.

GG1285. ● Hausmann, Raoul: *Hans, Jean Arp*. München: Belleville, 2008. 148 p.

GG1286. Sachs-Galey, Pénélope: "Cummings et Arp dans la plasticité de l'écrit." In 418, 279-291.

ARRABAL, Fernando.

GG1287. Zigrino, Damiano Augusto: *Il teatro di Fernando Arrabal*. Città di Castello: Edimond, 2008. 212 p.

GG1288. Penot-Lacassagne, Olivier: "Arrabal ou l'adieu au surréalisme," *Mélusine*, no. 28 (2008), 175-182.

ARTAUD, Antonin. See also 606, 951, 2970, 3290, 8007.

GG1289. ● Artaud, Antonin: *50 drawings to murder magic*. Edited with a preface by Evelyne Grossman; trans. by Donald Nicholson-Smith. London; New York: Seagull Books, 2008. *The French List*. xv, 82 p.

GG1290. ● *Attention Artaud*. Hrsg. Anton Rey. Zürich: Zürcher Hochschule der Künste. 52 p.

GG1291. ● Barber, Stephen: *Artaud: terminal curses: the notebooks, 1945-1948*. Los Angeles: Solar, 2008. 149 p.

GG1292. ● Barber, Stephen: *The last words of Antonin Artaud*. London: Reaktion Books, 2008. 160 p.

GG1293. ● Galibert, Thierry: *La bestialité*. Cabrid: Sulliver, 2008. 571 p.

GG1294. ● Margel, Serge: *Aliénation: Antonin Artaud, les généalogies hybrides*. Paris: Galilée, 2008. *La philosophie en effet*. 126 p.

GG1295. ● Mèredieu, Florence de: *Antonin Artaud: portraits et gris-gris; suivi de Artaud/Balthus; Artaud/graffiti*. Paris: Blusson, 2008. Nouvelle edition. 119 p.

GG1296. ● Saba, Wilson: *Il punto fosforoso: Antonin Artaud e la cultura eternale*. Con un testo introduttivo di Paolo Terni. Macerata: Quodlibet, 2008. 132 p.

GG1297. ● *Tentativa Artaud*. Catalog of an exhibition held April-May, 2008 at the Museo Nacional de Bellas Artes, Santiago Chile. Textos y fotografias, Ronald Kay. Santiago de Chile: Museo Nacional de Bellas Artes, 2008.

GG1298. Alix, Christophe: "Les didascalies dans *Le jet de sang* d'Antonin Artaud, expression de la mise en scène moderne au théâtre." In 605, 295-306.

GG1299. Andréo, Benjamin: "Le retour de la momie: entre Corps sans Organes et corps sacré," *Dalhousie French Studies*, vol. 83 (Summer 2008), 99-108.

GG1300. Arrien, Sophie-Jan: "Ipséité et passivité: le montage narratif du soi," *Laval Théologique et Philosophique*, vol. 63, no. 3 (oct. 2007), 445-458. [Ricœur]

GG1301. Forest, Philippe: "Artaud Bataille encore," *Mélusine*, no. 28 (2008), 223-234. [Bataille]

GG1302. Goux, Jean-Joseph: "Antonin Artaud and the promise of a great therapeutic," *Angelaki*, vol. 13, no. 3 (Dec. 2008), 17-24.

GG1303. Moore, Charlotte X.: "The aesthetics of Antonin Artaud," *Kinesis*, vol. 35, no. 1 (Spring 2008), 43-60.

GG1304. Russo, Adelaide M.: "Art et oscillation: 'l'œil d'un certain philosophe'." In 583, 123-140.

GG1305. Singleton, Brian: "The performance of Artaud in Ireland," *Etudes Irlandaises*, vol. 33, no. 2 (automne 2008), 43-52.

GG1306. Tomiche, Anne: "Artaud traducteur d'Edgar Poe." In 1026, 197-222.

GG1307. Walker, Ruth: "Antonin Artaud's avant-garde aesthetics of disturbance and audio-visual anarchy." In 577, 151-172.

ASSOULINE, Pierre. See 7256.

ASTALOS, Georges.

GG1308. Vuillemin, Alain: "La ruse contre la dictature dans le théâtre de Georges Astalos." In 1100, 111-115.

AUBRAC, Lucie.

GG1309. ● Reid, Donald: *Germaine Tillion, Lucie Aubrac, and the politics of memories of the French Resistance.* Newcastle: Cambridge Scholars, 2008. xi, 192 p. [Tillion]

GG1310. Suleiman, Susan Rubin: "Narrative desire: the 'Aubrac affair' and national memory of the French Resistance." In 600.

AUDE. See 4543.

AUDET, Noël.

GG1311. Forget, Danielle: "En pieces détachés et déplacées. *Frontières, ou Tableaux d'Amérique* de Noël Audet," *Etudes Françaises*, vol. 44, no. 1 (2008), 73-87.

AUDIBERTI, Jacques. See also 733.

GG1312. Bienaimé, Dora: "Jacques Audiberti traduce Torquato Tasso," *Studi Francesi*, anno 52, fasc. 2 (maggio-agosto 2008), 361-370.

AUDISIO, Gabriel. See also 3954, 7199.

GG1313. Arend, Elisabeth: "Epistémologie méditerranéenne de Gabriel Audisio." In 515, 147-162.

GG1314. Gnocchi, Maria Chiara: "L'archipel méditerranéen de Gabriel Audisio." In 423.

GG1315. Guedj, Colette: "La Méditerranée solaire de Gabriel Audisio." In 515, 211-221.

AUDOUX, Marguerite.

GG1316. Garreau, Bernard-Marie: "La veuve: personnage emblématique de l'univers de Marguerite Audoux." In 571, 245-251.

GG1317. Roe, David: "Un conte retrouvé: *Madame Jean*," *Amis de Charles-Louis Philippe*, no. 64 (2008), 55-61.

AYMÉ, Marcel. See also 642.

GG1318. ● Aymé, Marcel: *Clérambard.* Mise en scène de Nicolas Briançon. Paris: L'Avant-Scène Théâtre, 2008. *L'Avant-Scène Théâtre*, no. 1249. 124 p.

AZAMA, Michel.

GG1319. Taylor, Scott D.: "French tragic farce in an age of interpellation: Michel Azama's *Croisades* and Hervé Blutsch's *Anatole Felde*," *Modern Drama*, vol. 51, no. 2 (Summer 2008), 2742-88. [Blutsch]

BÂ, Mariama. See also 206, 260.

GG1320. ● Bâ, Mariama: *So long a letter.* Trans. Modupé Bodé-Thomas. Harlow: Heinemann, 2008. *African writers series.* x, 96 p.

GG1321. Asaah, Augustine H.: "L'éthique de la différence en traduction: le cas de deux romans africains francophones et de leur restitution en anglais," *Présence Francophone*, no. 70 (2008), 113-135. [Kourouma]

GG1322. Engelking, Tama Lea: "Senegalese women, education, and polygamy in *Une si longue lettre* and *Faat Kiné*," *French Review*, vol. 82, no. 2 (Dec. 2008), 326-341. [Sembène]

GG1323. Njoya, Wandia: "On Mariama Bâ's novels, stereotypes, and silence," *Comparative Studies of South Asia, Africa and the Middle East*, vol. 27, no. 2 (2007), 450-462.

GG1324. Palmer, Eustace: "Mariama Bâ: *So long a letter.*" In 113.

GG1325. Wehrs, Donald R.: "Incorporating the female subject: revolt, despair, and madness in Bâ's *Un chant écarlate.*" In 142.

BACHELARD, Gaston. See also 937.

GG1326. ● *Bachelard et Bergson, continuité et discontinuité?*. Sous la dir. de Frédéric Worms et Jean-Jacques Wunenburger. Paris: PUF, 2008. 293 p. [Bergson]

GG1327. Alexander, Nelson: "Gaston Bachelard and the dialectics of scientific inquiry," *Kinesis*, vol. 34, no. 2 (Fall 2007), 34-44.

GG1328. Casey, Edward S.: "Taking Bachelard from the instant to the edge," *Philosophy Today*, vol. 52, supplement (2008), 31-37.

GG1329. Chimisso, Cristina: "Gaston Bachelard and the history of the scientific mind." In 937, 139-152.

GG1330. Kearney, Richard: "Bachelard and the epiphanic instant," *Philosophy Today*, vol. 52, supplement (2008), 38-45.

GG1331. Parkinson, Gavin: "Epistemology of physics and politics: Gaston Bachelard and surrealism." In 1058. [Surrealism]

GG1332. Parkinson, Gavin: "Relativity and epistemology: André Breton and Gaston Bachelard." In 1058. [Breton]

GG1333. Pouliquen, Jean-Luc: "Bachelard, Berdiaeff et l'imagination," *Sapienza*, vol. 61, no. 2 (2008), 235-241.

GG1334. Rizo-Patron, Eileen: "*Regressus ad uterum*: Bachelard's alchemical hermeneutic," *Philosophy Today*, vol. 52, supplement (2008), 21-30.

BACHI, Salim.

GG1335. Vitali, Ilaria: " 'Shéhérazade ne s'arrête jamais': entretien avec Salim Bachi," *Francofonia*, n. 55 (autunno 2008), 97-102.

BADIOU, Alain. See also 996, 3143.

GG1336. ● *Alain Badiou: penser le multiple: actes du Colloque de Bordeaux, 12-23 octobre 1999.* Réunis et édités par Charles Ramond. Paris: L'Harmattan, 2002. *La philosophie en commun.* 575 p.

GG1337. ● Bac, Rémy: *La soustraction de l'être: la question ontologique de la vérité, de Heidegger à Badiou.* Paris: Le Grand Souffle, 2008. *La contrée.* 362 p.

GG1338. ● *Ecrits aurout de la pensée d'Alain Badiou.* Sous la dir. de Bruno Besana et Oliver Feltham. Paris: L'Harmattan, 2007. 246 p.

GG1339. ● Feltham, Oliver: *Alain Badiou: live theory.* London; New York: Continuum, 2008. 159 p.

GG1340. ● Gillespie, Sam: *The mathematics of novelty: Badiou's minimalist metaphysics.* Melbourne: Re.Press, 2008. *Anamnesis.* 159 p.

GG1341. ● Miller, Adam: *Badiou, Marion and St. Paul: immanent grace.* London; New York: Continuum, 2008. *Continuum Studies in Continental Philosophy.* 162 p. [Marion]

GG1342. Calcagno, Antonio: "Alain Badiou: the event of becoming a political subject," *Philosophy and Social Criticism*, vol. 34, no. 9 (Nov. 2008), 1051-1070.

GG1343. Gibson, Andrew: "Badiou and deconstruction: the politics of reading Beckett." In 940, 146-160. [Beckett]

GG1344. Johnston, Adrian: "What matter(s) in ontology: Alain Badiou, the Hebb-event, and materialism split from within," *Angelaki*, vol. 13, no. 1 (April 2008), 27-49.

GG1345. Kaufman, Eleanor: "The Saturday of Messianic time (Agamben and Badiou on the apostle Paul)," *South Atlantic Quarterly*, vol. 107, no. 1 (Jan. 2008), 37-54.

GG1346. Weller, Shane: "The denial of (Greek) thought: Alain Badiou." In 989.

GG1347. Wright, Colin: "Event or exception?: disentangling Badiou from Schmitt, or, Towards a politics of the void," *Theory and Event*, vol. 11, no. 2 (2008), [n.p.].

GG1348. Wright, Colin: "Resurrection and reaction in Alain Badiou: towards an eventual historiography," *Culture, Theory and Critique*, vol. 19, no. 1 (April 2008), 73-92.

BALIBAR, Étienne.

GG1349. Reid, Don: "Etienne Balibar: Algeria, Althusser and *altereuropéenisation*," *South Central Review*, vol. 25, no. 3 (Fall 2008), 68-85.

BALPE, Jean-Pierre.

GG1350. Balpe, Jean-Pierre: "Ecriture sans manuscrit, brouillon absent." In 438, 149-165.

BANCQUART, Marie-Claire.

GG1351. • Broome, Peter: *In the flesh of the text: the poetry of Marie-Claire Bancquart.* Amsterdam; New York: Rodopi, 2008. *Collection monographique Rodopi en littérature française contemporaine*, 47. 270 p.

BARBEAU, Jean.

GG1352. Jakubczuk, Renata: "Minorité féministe dans *Citrouille* de Jean Barbeau." In 1100, 77-83.

BARBUSSE, Henri. See also 2510.

GG1353. Becker, Karin: "*Le Feu* de Barbusse et *Les croix de bois* de Dorgelès: deux romans de guerre à la lumière de nouvelles approches historiques." In 483, 165-179. [Dorgelès]

GG1354. Kaempfer, Jean: "Le témoin, le crieur, le peintre: Henri Barbusse, romancier de la Grande Guerre." In 473, 133-149.

BARCELO, François.

GG1355. Barcelo, François: "Garder mes distances." In 97, 31-41.

BARJAVEL, René.

GG1356. Lysøe, Eric: "Dernier clin d'œil à Eurydice." In 443, 51-68.

BARON SUPERVIELLE, Silvia.

GG1357. Michel, Jacqueline: "Silvia Baron Supervielle: 'Suis-je un écrivain argentin?'." In 521, 33-35.

BARRÈS, Maurice. See also 702, 706.

GG1358. Barilier, Etienne: "La vérité et la justice françaises." In 388, 99-110.

GG1359. Basch, Sophie: "*Le Voyage de Sparte* ou la quatrième 'station de psychothérapie' de Maurice Barrès," *Ritm*, no. 38 (2007), 147-159.

GG1360. Bompaire-Evesque, Claire: "Barrès et la psychologie religieuse, dans *La Colline inspirée*," *Ritm*, no. 38 (2007), 129-145.

GG1361. Bompaire-Evesque, Claire: "Les récits de voyage de Barrès ou 'l'art de découvrir le divin dans le monde'," *Travaux de Littérature*, tome 21 (2008), 337-352.

GG1362. Chaitin, Gilbert D.: "The novel of national energy, by Maurice Barrès." In 405.

GG1363. Giraud, Nadine: "Barrès et les *ultima verba*." In 379, 187-193.

GG1364. Giraud, Nadine: " 'Une impératrice de la solitude' dans *Amori et dolori sacrum* de Maurice Barrès." In 391, 187-193.

GG1365. Hilaire, Maud: "L'Histoire, instrument de propagande dans *Les Déracinés*." In 904, 369-385.

GG1366. Pernot, Denis: "Chez M. Barrès," *Revue des Sciences Humaines*, no. 292 [no. 4] (2008), 107-122.

GG1367. Rambaud, Vital: "Barrès: père et fils," *Nouveau Cahiers François Mauriac*, no. 16 (2008), 133-144.

GG1368. Rambaud, Vital: "Culte du moi et culte des jardins dans l'œuvre de Maurice Barrès." In 487, 401-410.

GG1369. Tucci, Patrizio: "Bayreuth, Venise(s)." In 616, 59-74.

GG1370. Wittmann, Jean-Michel: "La critique d'art au service de l'égotisme littéraire: la peinture italienne dans les premières œuvres de Barrès." In 563, 63-69.

BARTHES, Roland. See also 489, 777, 779, 933, 967, 1003, 2027, 3607, 6463, 7602.

GG1371. • Pommier, René: *Le Sur Racine de Roland Barthes: nouvelle edition, revue, corrigée et augmentée.* Paris: Eurédit, 2008. *Théâtre du monde entier.* 495 p.

GG1372. • *Roland Barthes.* Préface de Catherine Clément et Bernard Pingaud. Paris: Inculte, 2007. 244 p.

GG1373. Allen, Graham: "Transparency, incalculability, *Mythologies* today," *Nottingham French Studies*, vol. 47, no. 2 (Summer 2008), 71-82.

GG1374. Andersen, Wayne: "Moving constants, in the West," *Common Knowledge*, vol. 14, no. 3 (Fall 2008), 384-395.

GG1375. Bellon, Guillaume: "Le vivre et mourir en ligne du *Vivre ensemble* de Roland Barthes," *Recherches et Travaux, Université Stendhal, UFR de Lettres*, no. 72 (2008), 217-226.

GG1376. Buse, Peter: "Photography degree zero: cultural history of the polaroid image," *New Formations*, no. 62 (Autumn 2007), 29-44.

GG1377. Cassar, Ignaz: "Envisioning inversion," *Parallax*, vol. 14, no. 2 [no. 47] (April-June 2008), 1-6.

GG1378. Coste, Claude: "Ceci est mon corps," *Europe*, no. 952-953 (août-sept. 2008), 267-280.

GG1379. Coste, Claude: "Comment vivre ensemble de Roland Barthes: vie et mort d'un site littéraire," *Recherches et Travaux, Université Stendhal, UFR de Lettres*, no. 72 (2008), 201-215.

1379a. Demanze, Laurent: "Roland Barthes: une écriture orpheline." In 2652, 127-135.

GG1380. Farasse, Gérard: "Or, un soir de novembre." In 454, 177-192.

GG1381. Fisher, Andrew: "Beyond Barthes: rethinking the phenomenology of photography," *Radical Philosophy*, no. 148 (March/April 2008), 19-29.

GG1382. Foster, Nicola: "Photography and the gaze: the ethics of vision inverted," *Parallax*, vol. 14, no. 2 [no. 47] (April-June 2008), [n.p.]. [Levinas]

GG1383. Garland, Sarah: " 'This temptation to be undone . . .': Sontag, Barthes, and the uses of style." In 381, 189-207.

GG1384. Garson, Charlotte: "Barthes ver luisant: le cinéma comme écran," *Europe*, no. 952-953 (août-sept. 2008), 227-233.

GG1385. Grove, Laurence: "*Bande dessinée*: the missing *Mythologie*," *Nottingham French Studies*, vol. 47, no. 2 (Summer 2008), 29-40.

GG1386. Guilbard, Anne-Cécile: "Le roman du regardeur en 1980." In 508, 259-275. [Guibert]

GG1387. Guittard, Jacqueline: "Roland Barthes: une aventure avec la photographie," *Revue des Sciences Humaines*, no. 292 [no. 4] (2008), 203-224.

GG1388. Hawthorn, Jeremy: "Authority and the death of the author." In 765, 65-88. [Foucault]

GG1389. Hegarty, Paul: "The time of myth, here, now: reviewing the time of *Mythologies*," *Nottingham French Studies*, vol. 47, no. 2 (Summer 2008), 52-59.

GG1390. Joly, Martine: "Du symbole au ninisme: vie ou mort du mythe, aujourd'hui?," *Nottingham French Studies*, vol. 47, no. 2 (Summer 2008), 60-760.

GG1391. Jouan, Yves: "Le chef-d'œuvre invisible," *Europe*, no. 952-953 (août-sept. 2008), 179-184.

GG1392. Kheshti, Roshanak: "Inversion, significance and the loss of the self in sound," *Parallax*, vol. 14, no. 2 [no. 47] (April-June 2008), 68-77.

GG1393. Lavers, Annette: "Barthes et Sartre: distance et proximité," *Europe*, no. 952-953 (août-sept. 2008), 198-206. [Sartre]

GG1394. Lindenberg, Judith: " 'La langue travaillée par le pouvoir': Franco Fortini et Roland Barthes face à Brecht," *Revue de Littérature Comparée*, no. 382 [82e année, no. 4] (oct.-déc. 2008), 429-442.

GG1395. MacLeod, Sheila: "Le tragique dans *La chambre claire*," *Europe*, no. 952-953 (août-sept. 2008), 249-254.

GG1396. Marty, Eric: "Science de la littérature et plaisir du texte," *Europe*, no. 952-953 (août-sept. 2008), 185-197.

GG1397. Mégevand, Martin: "Barthes et le théâtre: les variations du sujet," *Europe*, no. 952-953 (août-sept. 2008), 214-226.

GG1398. Nachtergael, Magali: "Roland Barthes et les artistes des mythologies individuelles: la création de soi par la photographie entre 1970 et 1975." In 508, 349-360.

GG1399. Nitsche, Jessica: "Dem Tod ins Auge (ge)sehen: Protagonistinnen der Fotografietheoriebei Döblin, Kracauer, Barthes und Benjamin." In 800, 93-109.

GG1400. Noguez, Dominique: "Mythologie de la mythologie," *Europe*, no. 952-953 (août-sept. 2008), 288-291.

GG1401. Noguez, Dominique: "R. B. de S à Z.," *Europe*, no. 952-953 (août-sept. 2008), 176-178.

GG1402. O'Meara, Lucy: " 'L'affaire Barthes' and ownership of the voice." In 610, 141-160.

GG1403. Parvulescu, Anca: "The professor's desire," *Diacritics*, vol. 37, no. 1 (Spring 2007), 32-39.

GG1404. Piégay-Gros, Nathalie: "L'art de lire," *Europe*, no. 952-953 (août-sept. 2008), 207-213.

GG1405. Quillier, Patrick: "Roland Barthes à l'oreille," *Europe*, no. 952-953 (août-sept. 2008), 255-266.

GG1406. Renouard, Madeleine: "Barthes pour tous?," *Europe*, no. 952-953 (août-sept. 2008), 172-175.

GG1407. Ribière, Mireille: "Barthes réaliste," *Europe*, no. 952-953 (août-sept. 2008), 241-248.

GG1408. Rouffiat, Françoise: "Entre plein et délié: l'écriture de *L'Empire des signes*." In 382, 77-93.

GG1409. Smirnova, Larysa: "Roland Barthes in search of an epic modernity: Barthes's evaluation of intellectual legacy of Bertolt Brecht and the question of modernity." Diss., Yale Univ., 2007. i, 230 p.

GG1410. Smith, Douglas: "Introduction: Barthes's (im)pertinence," *Nottingham French Studies*, vol. 47, no. 2 (Summer 2008), 1-5.

GG1411. Smith, Douglas: "*Sens de la cuisine ou cuisine du sens?*: food and meaning in *Mythologies*," *Nottingham French Studies*, vol. 47, no. 2 (Summer 2008), 41-51.

GG1412. Sollers, Philippe: "Vérité de Barthes," *Infini*, no. 105 (hiver 2008), 22-25.

GG1413. Stafford, Andy: "Barthes, Londres, Mai 68," *Europe*, no. 952-953 (août-sept. 2008), 281-287.

GG1414. Stafford, Andy: "Dialectics of form(s) in Roland Barthes's *Mythologies*," *Nottingham French Studies*, vol. 47, no. 2 (Summer 2008), 6-18.

GG1415. Susam-Sarajeva, Sebnem: "Image formation: 'Turkish Barthes' and 'Anglo-American Cixous'." In 985, 85-134. [Cixous]

GG1416. Susam-Sarajeva, Sebnem: "Multiple-entry visa to travelling theory." In 985, 135-172.

GG1417. Susam-Sarajeva, Sebnem: "Translating theory into politics." In 985, 173-204.

GG1418. Tholen, Toni: "Asthetik der Existenz. Zur literarischen Ethik des späten Roland Barthes," *Romantische Zeitschrift für Literaturgeschichte*, 32. Jahrgang, Heft 3-4 (2008), 393-412.

GG1419. Welbourn, Sally: "Barthes/Robbe-Grillet, nouveau roman/nouvelle critique," *Europe*, no. 952-953 (août-sept. 2008), 234-240. [Robbe-Grillet]

GG1420. Welch, Edward: " 'Une reconciliation du reel et des hommes': *Mythologies* and the politics of things," *Nottingham French Studies*, vol. 47, no. 2 (Summer 2008), 19-28.

BASTIDE, François-Régis.

GG1421. ● Garcin, Jérôme: *Son excellence, monsieur mon ami*. Paris: Gallimard, 2008. 202 p.

BATAILLE, Georges. See also 397, 951, 963, 991, 1301, 2026, 2326, 7296, 7448.

GG1422. ● Bataille, Georges: *L'archangélique et autres poèmes*. Préface de Bernard Noël; notes de Bernard Noël et Thadée Klossowski. Paris: Gallimard, 2008. *Poésie*. 209 p.

GG1423. ● Bataille, Georges; Michel Leiris: *Correspondence*. Edited with notes by Louis Yvert; afterword by Bernard Noël; trans. Liz Heron. Calcutta; New York: Seagull Books, 2008. *The French list*. 298 p. [Leiris]

GG1424. ● Lippi, Silvia: *Transgressions: Bataille, Lacan*. Ramonville Saint-Ange: Erès, 2008. *Point hors ligne*. 258 p.

GG1425. ● Louvrier, Pascal: *Georges Bataille: la fascination du mal*. Monaco: Editions du Rocher, 2008. 198 p.

GG1426. ● Tauchert, Ashley: *Against transgression*. Malden, MA: Wiley-Blackwell, 2008. *Critical quarterly*. 149 p.

GG1427. Brook, Timothy: "Georges Bataille's interpretation." In 402.

GG1428. Brunot, Chantal: "Le corps sacrifié ou le nu athéologique dans les œuvres de Sade et de Bataille," *Revue des Sciences Humaines*, no. 289 [no. 1] (2008), 43-53.

GG1429. de la Torre, José María: "The smeared metaphor: viscosity and fluidity in Bataille's *Story of the Eye*." In 395, 381-387.

GG1430. Finas, Lucette: "B. de l'égarement au délire face à la Loi aux cheveux raides," *Littérature*, no. 152 (déc. 2008), 7-16.

GG1431. Forest, Philippe: "Le *Dianus* de Frazer: de Faulkner à Bataille," *Littérature*, no. 152 (déc. 2008), 35-45.

GG1432. Louette, Jean-François: "*Informitas* de l'univers et figures humaines. Bataille entre Queneau et Leiris," *Littérature*, no. 152 (déc. 2008), 119-133. [Leiris, Queneau]

GG1433. Lyotard, Dolorès: "Judas," *Revue des Sciences Humaines*, no. 292 [no. 4] (2008), 73-103. [Leiris]

GG1434. Marmande, Francis: "Le Pur bonheur," *Littérature*, no. 152 (déc. 2008), 17-33.

GG1435. Parkinson, Gavin: "Astrophysics and mysticism: Georges Bataille and Arthur Eddington." In 1058.

GG1436. Rétif, Françoise: "Die Lust des Obszönen bei Georges Bataille und Elfriede Jelinek." In 820.

GG1437. Santi, Sylvain: "L'œil d'Edwarda," *Littérature*, no. 152 (déc. 2008), 65-77.

GG1438. Sweedler, Milo: "The politics of sacrifice: Mel Gibson and Georges Bataille," *Intertexts*, vol. 11, no. 2 (Fall 2007), 157-171.

GG1439. Swoboda, Tomasz: "Entre absence et jouissance: la famille dans les récits de Georges Bataille." In 572, 351-359.

GG1440. Swoboda, Tomasz: "Le silence de l'obscène: Bataille et Manet." In 543, 161-173.

GG1441. Trécherel, Sylvie: "Lire après Bataille: 'un intérêt d'ordre littéraire," *Littérature*, no. 152 (déc. 2008), 95-103.

GG1442. Vaughan, William: "Mysticism, gift, and Bataille." In 988.

GG1443. Vivès, Vincent: "Anarchipel: poésie et désordre philosophique," *Littérature*, no. 152 (déc. 2008), 47-63.

GG1444. Wald Lasowski, Aliocha: "A la faveur de la pénombre," *Littérature*, no. 152 (déc. 2008), 79-94.

GG1445. Zimmermann, Laurent: "Bataille fantôme," *Littérature*, no. 152 (déc. 2008), 105-117.

BAUCHAU, Henry. See also 3454.

GG1446. ● Bauchau, Henry: *Un arbre de mots: entretien avec Indira De Bie.* Clichy: Editions de Corlevour, 2008. 61 p.

GG1447. ● Duchenne, Geneviève; Vincent Dujardin; Myriam Watthée-Delmotte: *Henry Bauchau dans la tourmente du XXe siècle: configurations historiques et imaginaires.* Bruxelles: Le Cri, 2008. *Biographie.* 208 p.

GG1448. Demangeat, Michel: "Le traumatisme chez Freud et selon Freud: la déchirure d'Henry Bauchau." In 611.

GG1449. Ferry, Ariane: "En finir avec le théâtre: transmodalisation et renouvellement de la réécriture mythique." In 506, 141-150.

GG1450. Mastroianni, Michele: "Simmetrie e intertestualità teoretiche. Henry Bauchau fra dinamiche di elaborazione poetica e stilemi teologici," *Studi Francesi*, anno 52, fasc. 2 (maggio-agosto 2008), 336-359.

GG1451. Watthee-Delmotte, Myriam: "Henry Bauchau: le passage de l'image." In 418, 357-371.

BAUDRILLARD, Jean. See also 981, 1008, 1822.

GG1452. ● Baudrillard, Jean: *Fatal strategies.* Introduction by Dominic Pettman; trans. Philippe Beitchman and W. G. J. Niesluchowski. Los Angeles: Semiotext(e), 2008. 230 p.

GG1453. ● Córdoba Elías, Juan Pablo: *Baudrillard.* Prólogo de Francisco Carballo. México: UNAM, Facultad de Ciencias Políticas y Sociales, 2008.

GG1454. ● Gauthier, Alain: *Jean Baudrillard, une pensée singulière.* Paris: Nouvelles editions Lignes, 2008. 185 p.

GG1455. ● *Jean Baudrillard: fatal theories.* Ed. David B. Clarke [et al.]. London: Routledge, 2008.

GG1456. ● Redhead, Steve: *The Jean Baudrillard reader*. Edinburgh: Edinburgh Univ. Press; New York: Columbia Univ. Press, 2008. *European perspectives*. vii, 226 p.

GG1457. ● Schuster, Marc: *Don DeLillo, Jean Baudrillard, and the consumer conundrum*. Youngstown, NY: Cambria Press, 2008. xii, 214 p.

GG1458. Abbinnett, Ross: "The spectre and the simulacrum: history after Baudrillard," *Theory, Culture and Society*, vol. 25, no. 6 (Nov. 2008), 69-87.

GG1459. Almeida, Ivan: "Borges à la carte (tres citas de Baudrillard)," *Variaciones Borges*, n. 25 (2008), 25-51.

GG1460. Baldwin, Jon: "Lessons from Witchetty Grubs and Eskimos: the French anthropological context of Jean Baudrillard," *French Cultural Studies*, vol. 19, no. 3 (Oct. 2008), 333-346.

GG1461. Gane, Mike: "*Cool memories*: Baudrillard and the crisis of reading," *French Cultural Studies*, vol. 19, no. 3 (Oct. 2008), 305-316.

GG1462. Gonzalez, Madelena: "Pourquoi y a-t-il Baudrillard plutôt que rien?: the reception and perception of Jean Baudrillard in France," *French Cultural Studies*, vol. 19, no. 3 (Oct. 2008), 287-304.

GG1463. Grace, Victoria: "Baudrillard's illusions: the seduction of feminism," *French Cultural Studies*, vol. 19, no. 3 (Oct. 2008), 347-362.

GG1464. Hegarty, Paul: "Constructing (in) the 'real' world: simulation and architecture in Baudrillard," *French Cultural Studies*, vol. 19, no. 3 (Oct. 2008), 317-332.

GG1465. Hessler, Hans-Joachim: "Das Verschwinden der Musik, oder: Papst Gregor I. und Madonna, die Göttin der Liebe, suchen Jean Baudrillard, irhen Verführer." In 826.

GG1466. Manning, Russell: "A boy who swims faster than a shark: Jean Baudrillard visits *The Office*." In 968.

GG1467. Martins Rosa, Jorge: "A misreading gone too far? Baudrillard meets Philip K. Dick," *Science Fiction Studies*, vol. 35, no. 1 [no. 104] (March 2008), 60-71.

GG1468. Merrin, William: "Baudrillard's future," *French Cultural Studies*, vol. 19, no. 3 (Oct. 2008), 255-272.

GG1469. Taylor, Paul: "Baudrillard's Gallic shrug: reality fundamentalism and the Heineken effect," *French Cultural Studies*, vol. 19, no. 3 (Oct. 2008), 273-286.

BAZIÉ, Jacques Prosper.

GG1470. Sanou, Salaka: "L'écriture-vérité de Jacques Prosper Bazié," *Cultures Sud*, no. 170 (sept. 2008), 27-32.

BEAUCHEMIN, Jean-François.

GG1471. Lohse, Rolf: "*Le jour des corneilles* de Jean-François Beauchemin." In 41, 39-56.

BEAUCHEMIN, Yves.

GG1472. ● Beauchemin, Yves: *The alley cat*. Trans. Sheila Fischman; afterword by Kenneth Radu. Toronto: M & S, 2008. *New Canadian Library*. 602 p.

BEAULIEU, Michel. See 174.

BEAUPRÉ, Normand.

GG1473. Pacini, Peggy: "Hériter, transmettre et écrire: une affaire de famille(s) chez Normand Beaupré et Robert B. Perreault." In 572, 325-333. [Perreault]

BEAUSOLEIL, Claude. See 174.

BEAUVOIR, Simone de. See also 242, 779, 999, 7196.

GG1474. ● Beauvoir, Simone de: *Cahiers de jeunesse: 1926-1930*. Texte établi, édité et présenté par Sylvie Le Bon de Beauvoir. Paris: Gallimard, 2008. 849 p.

GG1475. ● Beauvoir, Simone de: *L'existentialisme et la sagesse des nations*. Prés. Michel Kail. Paris: Gallimard, 2008. ix, 110 p.

GG1476. ● Beauvoir, Simone de: *La femme indépendante: extraits du Deuxième sexe*. Edition établie et présentée par Martine Reid. Paris: Gallimard, 2008. *Folio*. 137 p.

GG1477. ● Beauvoir, Simone de: *Lettres à Nelson Algren: un amour transatlantique, 1947-1964*. Texte établi, trad. de l'anglais et annoté par Sylvie Le Bon de Beauvoir. Paris: Gallimard, 2008. *Folio*. 910 p.

GG1478. ● Beauvoir, Simone de: *Tout connaître du monde*. Textes choisis et presents par Eric Levéel. Paris: Quinzaine littéraire-Louis Vuitton, 2008. 267 p.

GG1479. ● Deguy, Jacques; Sylvie Le Bon de Beauvoir: *Simone de Beauvoir: écrire la liberté*. Paris: Gallimard, 2008. *Découvertes*. 127 p.

GG1480. ● Deutscher, Penelope: *The philosophy of Simone de Beauvoir: ambiguity, conversion, resistance*. Cambridge: Cambridge Univ. Press, 2008. *Ideas in context*, 91.

GG1481. ● Eaubonne, Françoise d': *Une femme nommée Castor: mon amie Simone de Beauvoir*. Paris: L'Harmattan, 2008. 389 p. [Orig. ed., 1986]

GG1482. ● *Eigensinnige Frauen*. Rapperswil: Du Kulturmedian AG, 2008. 122 p.

GG1483. ● Fraisse, Geneviève: *Le privilege de Simone de Beauvoir: suivi de Une mort douce*. Arles: Actes Sud, 2008. 122 p.

GG1484. ● *French feminists: critical evaluations in cultural theory. Vol. 1: Simone de Beauvoir*. Ed. Jennifer Hansen, Ann Cahill. London; New York: Routledge, 2008. xxvii, 386 p.

GG1485. ● Fullbrook, Edward; Kate Fullbrook: *Sex and philosophy: rethinking de Beauvoir and Sartre*. London: Continuum, 2008. xvii, 269 p. [Sartre]

GG1486. ● Gleichauf, Ingeborg: *Sein wie keine andere Simone de Beauvoir: Schriftstellerin und Philosophin*. 2. Aufl. München: Dt. Taschenbuch-Verlag, 2008. 298 p.

GG1487. ● Lacoin, Elisabeth: *Zaza: 1907-1929; amie de Simone de Beauvoir*. Paris: L'Harmattan, 2008. 355 p.

GG1488. ● Lecarme-Tabone, Eliane: *Eliane Lecarme-Tabone commente Le deuxième sexe de Simone de Beauvoir*. Paris: Gallimard, 2008. *Foliothèque*. 303 p.

GG1489. ● Moreau, Jean-Luc: *Simone de Beauvoir: le goût d'une vie*. Paris: Ecriture, 2008. 368 p.

GG1490. ● Moricourt, Guillaume: *Simone de Beauvoir: l'envers du mythe*. Paaris: Picollec, 2008. 330 p.

GG1491. ● Moricourt, Guillaume: *Simone de Beauvoir: une femme méconnue*. Jargeau: Dorval, 2008. 319 p.

GG1492. ● Moser, Susanne: *Freedom and recognition in the work of Simone de Beauvoir*. Frankfurt: Peter Lang, 2008. *Philosophy, phenomenology and hermeneutics of values*, 3. 220 p.

GG1493. ● *(Re)découvrir l'œuvre de Simone de Beauvoir: du "Deuxième sexe" à "La cérémonie des adieux"*. Sous la dir. de Julia Kristeva. Latresne: Bord de l'eau, 2008. 474 p.

GG1494. ● Sallenave, Danièle: *Castor de guerre*. Paris: Gallimard, 2008. *Nrf*. 610 p.

GG1495. ● Schwarzer, Alice: *Entretiens avec Simone de Beauvoir*. Paris: Mercure de France, 2008. 124 p.

GG1496. ● Schwarzer, Alice: *Simone de Beauvoir: ein Lesebuch mit Bildern*. Reinbek bei Hamburg: Rowohlt-Taschenbuch-Verlag, 2008. 334 p.

GG1497. ● Schwarzer, Alice: *Simone de Beauvoir: Weggefährtinnen im Gespräch*. Köln: Kiepenheuer & Witsch, 2008. 2. Aufl. 121 p.

GG1498. ● *Segunda [La] mirada: memoria del Coloquio "Simone de Beauvoir y loes Estudios de Género"*. Doris Moromisato, ed. Lima: Flora Tristán, 2008. 182 p.

GG1499. ● Seymouru-Jones, Carole: *A dangerous liaison*. London: Century, 2008. [Sartre]

GG1500. ● Shukla, B. A.: *The French feminists and The Second Sex*. Jaipur, India: Book Enclave, 2008. iv, 274 p.

GG1501. ● *Simone de Beauvoir: alles welbeschouwd*. Joke J. Hermsen, red. Kampen: Klement; Kapellen: Pelckmans, 2008. 168 p.

GG1502. ● *Simone de Beauvoir cent ans après sa naissance: contributions interdisciplinaires de cinq continents*. Thomas Stauder, éd. Tübingen: G. Narr, 2008. 380 p.

GG1503. ● *Simone de Beauvoir, une femme actuelle*. Paris: Arte, 2008.

GG1504. Acocella, Joan Ross: "The frog and the crocodile: Simone de Beauvoir." In 786.

GG1505. Altman, Meryl: "Simone de Beauvoir and lesbian lived experience." In 1484, 33-53.

GG1506. Arnold, Anastassia: "Le piège de douleur." In 1493, 47-52.

GG1507. Arp, Kristana: "The joys of disclosure: Simone de Beauvoir and the phenomenological tradition." In 1484, 332-344.

GG1508. Arp, Kristana: "Simone de Beauvoir and the joys of existence," *Simone de Beauvoir Studies*, vol. 25 (2008-2009), 38-49.

GG1509. Bair, Deirdre: "Seeing it now: Simone de Beauvoir's 'truth of the story'." In 1493, 53-57.

GG1510. Barnes, Hazel: "Response to Margaret Simons." In 1484, 260-267.

GG1511. Bauer, Nancy: "Beauvoir on the allure of self-objectification." In 1493, 269-276.

GG1512. Bauer, Nancy: "Being-with as being-against: Heidegger meets Hegel in *The Second Sex*." In 1484, 312-331.

GG1513. Bauer, Nancy: "Must we read Simone de Beauvoir?" In 1484, 203-220

GG1514. Bergoffen, Debra: "Finitude et justice: *Tous les hommes sont mortels*, par Simone de Beauvoir," *Lendemains*, 33. Jahrgang, Heft 132 (2008), 49-57.

GG1515. Bergoffen, Debra B.: "Marriage, autonomy, and the feminine protest." In 1484, 347-363.

GG1516. Biagini Sabelli, Enza: "La mort donnée: *Les bouches inutiles* de Simone de Beauvoir." In 1493, 141-154.

GG1517. Bjørsnøs, Annlang: "Beauvoir et Ricœur—l'identité narrative: analyse d'une crise identitaire dans *L'Invitée* de Simone de Beauvoir," *Revue Romane*, vol. 43, no. 1 (2008), 107-123. [Ricœur]

GG1518. Bjørnøs, Annlang: "Femmes du nord et femmes du sud: dialogue ou guerre idéologique." In 1493, 277-284.

GG1519. Bonal, Gérard: "Simone de Beauvoir-Colette." In 1493, 351-355. [Colette]

GG1520. Borde, Constance; Sheila Malovany Chevallier: "Research and development in the translation of *Le Deuxième sexe*," *Simone de Beauvoir Studies*, vol. 25 (2008-2009), 5-12.

GG1521. Bras, Pierre: "La propriété privée est-elle *arrivée?*" In 1493, 155-164

GG1522. Brisac, Geneviève: "Simone de Beauvoir 'en temps réel'. Une écriture de l'instantané." In 1493, 58-61.

GG1523. Bruera, Franca: "Le jeu des 'je': présence et désignation de l'autre dans *Les bouches inutiles* de Simone de Beauvoir." In 612, 305-317.

GG1524. Brun, Danièle: "Une zone d'ombre dans l'amitié." In 1493, 62-66.

GG1525. Brydon, James: " 'Cette autre guerre qui s'appelle la paix': *Le sang des autres* de Beauvoir et *Les Epées* de Nimier," *Roman 20-50*, no. 46 (2008), 123-133. [Nimier]

GG1526. Butler, Judith: "Sex and gender in Simone de Beauvoir's *Second Sex*." In 1484, 128-140.

GG1527. Cabestan, Philippe: "Simone de Beauvoir et l'énigme de la différance sexuelle." In 1493, 165-169.

GG1528. Calado, Eliana: "La construction de l'identité dans *Mémoires d'une jeune fille rangée*." In 1493, 67-72.

GG1529. Castro Vazquez, Olga: "(Para)translated ideologies in Simone de Beauvoir's *Le deuxième sexe*." In 609, 130-146.

GG1530. Chafiq, Chahla: "Simone de Beauvoir à travers le miroir iranien," *Lendemains*, 33. Jahrgang, Heft 132 (2008), 40-48.

GG1531. Chaperon, Sylvie: "Les études beauvoiriennes aujourd'hui." In 1493, 467-470.

GG1532. Clayton, Cameron: "Beauvoir, Sartre, temporality and the question of influence," *Simone de Beauvoir Studies*, vol. 25 (2008-2009), 50-62. [Sartre]

GG1533. Cohen Shabot, Sara; Yaki Menschenfreund: "Is existentialist authenticity unethical? De Beauvoir on ethics, authenticity, and embodiment," *Philosophy Today*, vol. 52, no. 2 (Summer 2008), 150-156.

GG1534. Corbí Saéz, María Isabel: "*Les belles images*: annonciatrices de la rupture du discours maître," *Simone de Beauvoir Studies*, vol. 25 (2008-2009), 20-30.

GG1535. Daigle, Christine: "Beauvoir philosophe." In 1493, 170-178.

GG1536. Dallery, Arleen B.: "Sexual embodiment: Beauvoir and French feminism." In 1484, 117-127.

GG1537. Decousu, Cécile: "La philosophie du *Deuxième sexe*." In 1493, 179-186.

GG1538. Dijkstra, Sandra: "Simone de Beauvoir and Betty Friedan." In 1484, 7-19.

GG1539. Domínguez González, Francisco: "*Le Deuxième Sexe* dans *Les Mandarins*," *Lendemains*, 33. Jahrgang, Heft 132 (2008), 58-69.

GG1540. Fallaize, Elizabeth: "Le temps des femmes: Simone de Beauvoir et la femme indépendante." In 1493, 285-291.

GG1541. Fleury, Danièle: "A propos de la réception de *L'Invitée* et des *Bouches inutiles*." In 1493, 457-466.

GG1542. Fransch, Chet: "Simone de Beauvoir, *Le deuxième sexe*: (re)naissance en Afrique du Sud." In 1493, 339-350.

GG1543. Fullbrook, Edward; Kate Fullbrook: "Whose ethics: Sartre's or Beauvoir's?" In 1484, 221-231. [Sartre]

GG1544. Gagnon, Carolle: "Resistance and rescue in Beauvoir's *The Blood of Others* and *The Mandarins*," *Semiotica*, vol. 172, no. 1-4 (2008), 233-259.

GG1545. Gagnon, Carolle: "Survie et amour accompli dans *Les Mandarins*." In 1493, 356-364.

GG1546. Gervais-Linon, Laurence: "Un infranchissable océan, correspondance de Simone de Beauvoir et Nelson Algren de 1947 à 1964," *Résonances*, no. 9 (févr. 2008), 15-27.

GG1547. Golay, Annabelle: " 'Ça m'atteignait', ou quand l'affect est politique." In 1493, 292-300.

GG1548. Gothlin, Eva: "Simone de Beauvoir's existential phenomenology and philosophy of history in *Le deuxième sexe*." In 1484, 302-311.

GG1549. Gramatzki, Susanne: "Le *skandalon* d'être vieux: une relecture critique de *La vieillesse* de Simone de Beauvoir," *Lendemains*, 33. Jahrgang, Heft 132 (2008), 81-91.

GG1550. Gray, Margaret E.: "Narcissism, abjection and the reader(e) of Simone de Beauvoir's *Les Belles Images*," *Studies in Twentieth and Twenty-First Century Literature*, vol. 32, no. 1 (Winter 2008), 37-52.

GG1551. Grimwood, Tom: "Re-reading *The Second Sex*'s 'Simone de Beauvoir'," *British Journal for the History of Philosophy*, vol. 16, no. 1 (Feb. 2008), 197-213.

GG1552. Guyot-Bender, Martine: "*Les belles images*: 'Sottisier', roman prémonitoire ou récit universel?," *Lendemains*, 33. Jahrgang, Heft 132 (2008), 70-80.

GG1553. Hamel, Yan: "Entre tourisme et engagement." In 1493, 301-309.

GG1554. Heinamaa, Sara: "Simone de Beauvoir's phenomenology of sexual difference." In 1484, 283-301.

GG1555. Heinamaa, Sara: "What is a woman? Butler and Beauvoir on the foundations of the sexual difference." In 1484, 162-181.

GG1556. Hernández Alvarez, Vicenta: "Simone de Beauvoir: deux points pour une ouverture graphique à la vie." In 1493, 35-46.

GG1557. Holland, Alison T.: "La voix chancelante dans le monologue intérieur de Anne dans *Les Mandarins*." In 1493, 365-369.

GG1558. Holveck, Eleanore: "Can a woman be a philosopher? Reflections of a Beauvoirian housemaid." In 1484, 232-241.

GG1559. Hurezanu, Daniela: "New York: un mythe français." In 535, 157-165.

GG1560. Jeannelle, Jean-Louis: "Les mémoires comme 'institution de soi'." In 1493, 73-83.

GG1561. Jeannelle, Jean-Louis: "La prose de l'histoire dans les mémoires: Beauvoir et la Guerre d'Algérie," *Elseneur*, no. 22 (2008), [n.p.].

GG1562. Kadoglou, Triantafyllia: "*Les Mandarins*: un témoignage sociopolitique de signification universelle." In 1493, 370-379.

GG1563. Kail, Michel: "Beauvoir et Sartre, l'enjeu de l'altérité." In 1493, 187-196. [Sartre]

GG1564. Kiran, Ayse: "Les belles images françaises des années soixante." In 1493, 380-391.

GG1565. Klaw, Barbara: "Simone de Beauvoir, cousin Jacques du journal intime à l'autobiographie." In 1493, 84-91.

GG1566. Klein, Judith: "Présence de la philosophie dans quelques écrits posthumes de Simone de Beauvoir." In 1493, 92-97.

GG1567. Klein, Judith: "Simone de Beauvoirs Jugentagebücher," *Neue Gesellschaft Frankfurter Hefte*, Nr. 9 (2008), 72-74.

GG1568.   Kruks, Sonia: "Gender and subjectivity: Simone de Beauvoir and contemporary feminism." In 1484, 141-161.

GG1569.   Kruks, Sonia: "Pour une politique de l'ambiguïté." In 1493, 197-201.

GG1570.   Kunin, Madeleine: "Profile: Simone de Beauvoir." In 838.

GG1571.   La Londe, Suzanne: "Une perspective psychanalytique de 'La femme rompue' et du journal intime," *Simone de Beauvoir Studies*, vol. 25 (2008-2009), 31-37.

GG1572.   Lanzmann, Claude: "Le sherpa du 11bis." In 1493, 19-22.

GG1573.   Larsson, Bjørn: "Simone de Beauvoir vingt ans après." In 1493, 392-396.

GG1574.   Lazar, Liliane: "Le combat de Simone de Beauvoir contre l'antisémitisme." In 1493, 310-315.

GG1575.   Le Dœuff, Michèle: "Simone de Beauvoir and existentialism." In 1484, 271-282.

GG1576.   Le Dœuff, Michèle: "Towards a friendly, transatlantic critique of *The Second Sex*." In 1484, 20-32.

GG1577.   Levéel, Eric C. G.: "Le tout voir beauvoirien ou pour une philosophie des voyages." In 1493, 202-207.

GG1578.   Mann, Bonnie: "Beauvoir and the question of a woman's point of view," *Philosophy Today*, vol. 52, no. 2 (Summer 2008), 136-149.

GG1579.   Marillaud, Pierre: "Quand un passé composé en rappelle un autre." In 496, 269-280.

GG1580.   Martin, Tiphaine: "*Deuxième sexe* et *Femme rompue*: une écriture parallèle?" In 1493, 397-406

GG1581.   Ménégaki, Maria: "L'impact du *Deuxième sexe* en Grèce." In 1493, 316-323.

GG1582.   Miao, Xin: "Simone de Beauvoir et *Le deuxième sexe* en Chine." In 1493, 432-434.

GG1583.   Miyasaki, Donovan: "La violence politique comme mauvaise foi dans *Le sang des autres*." In 1493, 407-413.

GG1584.   Moberg, Asa: "Perdu dans la traduction." In 1493, 324-328.

GG1585.   Moberg, Asa: "Why did Simone de Beauvoir make no mention of Florence Nightingale in *The Second Sex*?," *Simone de Beauvoir Studies*, vol. 25 (2008-2009), 13-19.

GG1586.   Moi, Toril: "While we wait: the English translation of *The Second Sex*." In 1484, 78-106.

GG1587.   Mokry, Adélaïde: "Le double 'je' des *Mandarins*." In 1493, 414-422.

GG1588.   Monteil, Claudine: "Simone de Beauvoir et le mouvement féministe français et international," *Lendemains*, 33. Jahrgang, Heft 132 (2008), 28-39.

GG1589.   Morgan, Anne: "Simone de Beauvoir's ethics of freedom and absolute evil," *Hypatia*, vol. 23, no. 4 (Fall 2008), [n.p.].

GG1590.   Økland, Jorunn: "Textual reproduction as surplus value: Paul on pleasing Christ and spouses, in light of Simone de Beauvoir." In 961.

GG1591.   Patterson, Yolanda Astarita: "Simone de Beauvoir et la génération dite silencieuse d'Américaines diplômées dans les années 50." In 1493, 133-140.

GG1592.   Patterson, Yolanda Astarita: "Who was this H. M. Parshley? The saga of translating Simone de Beauvoir's *The Second Sex*." In 1484, 67-77.

GG1593.   Patterson, Yolanda Astarita: " 'You've come a long way, baby!'," *Simone de Beauvoir Studies*, vol. 25 (2008-2009), 86-99.

GG1594.   Persson, Ann-Sofie: "De la narration du spectacle au spectacle de la narration: *L'Invitée* de Simone de Beauvoir." In 1493, 435-447.

GG1595.   Pettersen, Tove: "La joie existentielle et l'angoisse dans la philosophie morale de Simone de Beauvoir." In 1493, 220-233.

GG1596.   Purtschert, Patricia: "Anerkennung als Kampf um Repräsentation. Hegel lessen mit Simone de Beauvoir und Frantz Fanon," *Deutsche Zeitschrift für Philosophie*, 56. Jahrgang, Heft 6 (2008), 923-933. [Fanon]

GG1597.   Reid, Martine: "Anatomie d'une réception: *Le Deuxième sexe*." In 1493, 208-215.

GG1598.   Reineke, Sandra: "Border crossings: Simone de Beauvoir, feminist intellectual exchanges, and the organization of women's studies programs in France, Germany, and the United States," *Simone de Beauvoir Studies*, vol. 25 (2008-2009), 63-80.

GG1599. Risse, David: "Philosophie beauvoirienne de la sexualité?" In 1493, 234-268

GG1600. Rowley, Hazel: "Modèles ou monstres? Le célèbre 'pacte'." In 1493, 98-104.

GG1601. Rowley, Hazel: "What Simone de Beauvoir has meant to me," *Simone de Beauvoir Studies*, vol. 25 (2008-2009), 81-85.

GG1602. Sallenave, Danièle: "Pourquoi 'castor de guerre'." In 1493, 29-34.

GG1603. Saugues, Sylviane: "L'incipit du manuscrit des *Mémoires d'une jeune fille rangée*." In 1493, 105-112.

GG1604. Seltzer, David: "An eye for an eye: Beauvoir and Levinas on retributive justice," *International Studies in Philosophy*, vol. 39, no. 1 (2007), 59-77. [Levinas]

GG1605. Shukla, B. A.: "Simone de Beauvoir: a feminist study." In 1500.

GG1606. Shukla, B. A.: "Simone de Beauvoir's *The second sex*: an introduction." In 1500.

GG1607. Simons, Margaret A.: "Beauvoir's philosophical independence in a dialogue with Sartre." In 1484, 242-259. [Sartre]

GG1608. Simons, Margaret A.: "Du solipsisme à la solidarité: la philosophie de guerre de Beauvoir." In 1493, 216-219.

GG1609. Simons, Margaret A.: "The silencing of Simone de Beauvoir." In 1484, 57-66.

GG1610. Sollers, Philippe: "Beauvoir de Sade," *Infini*, no. 105 (hiver 2008), 17-21. [Also in 1493, 23-28]

GG1611. Stauder, Thomas: "Les dernières publications autour de Simone de Beauvoir en France et en Allemagne," *Lendemains*, 33. Jahrgang, Heft 132 (2008), 6-17.

GG1612. Stauder, Thomas: "Simone de Beauvoir et ses héritières." In 1493, 448-456.

GG1613. Stemmer, Valérie: "Formes du romanesque dans *L'Invitée*." In 1493, 423-431.

GG1614. Story, Amy E.: "Simone de Beauvoir and *Antigone*: feminism and the conflict between ethics and politics," *Mosaic*, vol. 41, no. 3 (Sept. 2008), 169-184.

GG1615. Strasser, Anne: "Les figures du 'je' ou la question de l'identité dans les écrits autobiographiques de Simone de Beauvoir." In 1493, 113-123.

GG1616. Sugier, Annie; Kahina Benziane: "Nos chemins se sont croisés." In 1493, 329-334.

GG1617. Taylor, Andrew: "*The Second Sex* (1949, Simone de Beauvoir)." In 874.

GG1618. Tidd, Ursula: "*Etat present*: Simone de Beauvoir studies," *French Studies*, vol. 62, no. 2 (April 2008), 200-208.

GG1619. Vagnarelli, Gianluca: "Sartre féministe grâce à Simone de Beauvoir?," *Lendemains*, 33. Jahrgang, Heft 132 (2008), 18-27. [Sartre]

GG1620. Veltman, Andrea: "The Sisyphean torture of housework: Simone de Beauvoir and inequitable divisions of domestic work in marriage." In 1484, 364-386.

GG1621. Viollet, Catherine: " 'Mon amour pour vous, c'est l'ordre en moi.' Correspondance Violette Leduc/Simone de Beauvoir, 1945-1972." In 1493, 124-132. [Leduc]

GG1622. Ward, Julie K.: "Beauvoir's two senses of 'body' in *The Second Sex*." In 1484, 182-199.

GG1623. Wittig, Monique: "One is not born a woman." In 1484, 109-116.

GG1624. Zelensky, Anne: "Simone ou la cohérence d'une vie." In 1493, 335-336.

GG1625. Zhang, Sophie: "Beauvoir et la Chine." In 1493, 337-338.

BÉCHEUR, Ali.

GG1626. Bonnet, Véronique: "Ali Bécheur, lumière et nostalgie," *Cultures Sud*, no. 170 (sept. 2008), 33-38.

BECK, Béatrix.

GG1627. "In memoriam, Béatrix Beck," *Simone de Beauvoir Studies*, vol. 25 (2008-2009), 102-106.

BECKETT, Samuel. See also 477, 484, 548, 624, 661, 755, 1076, 1080, 1082, 1088, 1095, 1119, 1343, 2902, 3233, 7288.

GG1628. ● Adorno, Theodor: *Notes sur Beckett.* Trad. Christophe David et prés. par Rolf Tiedemann. Caen: Nous, 2008. 169 p.

GG1629. ● Beckett, Samuel: *Proust y otros ensayos.* Prólogo de S. E. Gontarski. Santiago: Univ. Diego Portales, Salesianos, 2008. 115 p.

GG1630. ● *Beckett and ethics.* Ed. Russell Smith. London: Continuum, 2008. ix, 186 p.

GG1631. ● *Beckett at 100: revolving it all.* Ed. Linda Ben-Yvi and Angela Moorjani. Oxford; New York: Oxford Univ. Press, 2008. xiv, 334 p.

GG1632. ● *Beckett: écrans de silence/Beckett: screens of silence.* Ed. Irene Gilsenan Nordin, Véronique Simon; preface Don Sparling. Santiago de Compostela: Compostela Group of Universities, 2008. *European issues.* 153 p.

GG1633. ● *Beckett & puppet: studi e scene tra Samuel Beckett e il teatro di figura.* A cura di Fernando Marchiori. Pisa: Titivillus, 2007. 211 p.

GG1634. ● *Beckett's literary legacies.* Ed. Matthew Feldman and Mark Nixon. New-castle: Cambridge Scholars, 2007. 244 p.

GG1635. ● Boulter, Jonathan: *Beckett: a guide for the perplexed.* London; New York: Continuum, 2008. 186 p.

GG1636. ● Branigan, Kevin: *Radio Beckett: musicality in the radio plays of Samuel Beckett.* Bern; Oxford: Peter Lang, 2008. 268 p.

GG1637. ● Brown, Llewelyn: *Beckett: les fictions brèves: voir et dire.* Caen: Lettres moderns Minard, 2008. 230 p.

GG1638. ● Carpentier, Aline: *Théâtres d'ondes: les pièces radiophoniques de Beckett, Tardieu et Pinter.* Bruxelles: De Boeck; Paris: INA, 2008. 144 p.

GG1639. ● *Companion [A] to Samuel Beckett.* S. E. Gontarski, ed. Oxford: Wiley-Blackwell, 2008. 512 p.

GG1640. ● *Drama of the mind: papers from Beckett in Kraków 2006 conference.* Ed. Krystyna Stamirowska, Katarzyna Bazarnik. Kraków: Wydawnictwo Uniwersytetu Jagiello-nskiego, 2008. 86 p.

GG1641. ● *En attendant Godot de Samuel Beckett: 1952-1961.* Textes réunis par André Derval. Paris: 10-18, 2007. 287 p.

GG1642. ● Federman, Raymond: *The Sam book.* Trans. Sharon Blackie. Ullapool, Ross-Shire: Two Ravens Press, 2008. 149 p.

GG1643. ● Gatti, Guido: *Aspettare Godot?: trace di speranza nei drammi di Samuel Beckett.* Con un'intervista a Franco Branciaroli. Milano: Ancora, 2008. 112 p.

GG1644. ● Grossman, Evelyne: *L'angoisse de penser.* Paris: Minuit, 2008. *Para-doxe.* 156 p.

GG1645. ● Hulle, Dirk van: *Manuscript genetics, Joyce's know-how, Beckett's nohow.* Gainesville: Univ. Press of Florida, 2008. *Florida James Joyce Series.* xvi, 230 p.

GG1646. ● Kunkel, Michael: *"Dire cela, sans savoir quoi": Samuel Beckett in der Musik von György Kurtág und Heinz Holliger.* Saarbrücken: Pfau, 2008. 290 p.

GG1647. ● Lawley, Paul: *Waiting for Godot: character studies.* London; New York: Continuum, 2008. xi, 126 p.

GG1648. ● Le Juez, Brigitte: *Beckett before Beckett: Samuel Beckett's lectures on French literature.* Trans. Ros Schwartz. London: Souvenir, 2008. 80 p.

GG1649. ● MacKenzie, Gina Masucci: *The theatre of the real: Yeats, Beckett, and Sondheim.* Columbus: Ohio State Univ. Press, 2008. x, 173 p.

GG1650. ● Mével, Yann: *L'imaginaire mélancolique de Samuel Beckett, de Murphy à Comment c'est.* Amsterdam; New York: Rodopi, 2008. 432 p.

GG1651. ● Oppo, Andrea: *Philosophical aesthetics and Samuel Beckett.* Bern; Ox-ford: Peter Lang, 2008. 268 p.

GG1652. ● Ost, Isabelle: *Samuel Beckett et Gilles Deleuze: cartographie de deux parcours d'écriture.* Bruxelles: Facultés Universitaires Saint-Louis, 2008. 444 p.

GG1653. ● Pothast, Ulrich: *The metaphysical vision: Arthur Schopenhauer's philo-sophy of art and life and Samuel Beckett's own way to make use of it.* New York: Peter Lang, 2008. xiv, 246 p.

GG1654. • *Samuel Beckett*. Dargestellt von Friedhelm Rathjen. Reinbek bei Hamburg: Rowohlt, 2006. 155 p.

GG1655. • *Samuel Beckett und die Medien*. Peter Seibert, Hrsg. Bielefeld: Transcript, 2008. 223 p.

GG1656. • *Samuel Beckett's Waiting for Godot*. Ed., introd. Harold Bloom. New edition. New York: Bloom's literary criticism, 2008. vii, 172 p.

GG1657. • Schoell, Konrad: *Uber Samuel Becketts Werk: Essays und Studien*. Kassel: Kassel Univ. Press, 2008. 101 p.

GG1658. • Taylor-Batty, Mark; Juliette Taylor-Batty: *Samuel Beckett's Waiting for Godot*. London; New York: Continuum, 2008. *Modern theatre guides*. viii, 115 p.

GG1659. • *Tra le lingue tra i linguaggi: cent'anni di Samuel Beckett: Milano, 30 novembre-1 dicembre 2006*. A cura di Mariacristina Cavecchi e Caroline Patey. Milano: Cisalpino, 2007. *Quaderni di acme*. 581 p.

GG1660. • *Tullio Pericoli's many Becketts*. Ed. Maria Anita Stefanelli. Firenze: Centro Di, 2008. 95 p.

GG1661. • Uhlmann, Anthony: *Beckett and poststructuralism*. Cambridge; Melbourne: Cambridge Univ. Press, 2008. x, 202 p. [Deleuze, Derrida, Foucault, Guattari, Levinas]

GG1662. • *Verder: Beckett en de 21e eeuw*. Red. Matthijs Engelberts, Onno Kosters. Amsterdam: Amsterdam Univ. Press, 2008. 94 p.

GG1663. • *Warten auf Godot: das Absurde und die Geschichte*. Hrsg. Denis Thouard, Tim Trzaskalik. Berlin: Matthes & Seitz, 2008. 187 p.

GG1664. Abbott, H. Porter: " 'I am not a philosopher'." In 1631, 81-92.

GG1665. Ackerley, Chris: " 'The last ditch': shades of Swift in Samuel Beckett's 'Fingal'," *Eighteenth-Century Life*, vol. 32, no. 2 (Spring 2008), 60-67.

GG1666. Badiou, Alain: "Writing of the generic: Samuel Beckett." In 387.

GG1667. Barry, Elizabeth: "Beckett, language and the mind," *Journal of Beckett Studies*, vol. 17, no. 1-2 (2008), 1-8.

GG1668. Barry, Elizabeth: "Beckett, Sarah Kane and the theatre of catastrophe." In 1634, 169-187.

GG1669. Barry, Elizabeth: "One's own company: agency, identity and the middle voice in the work of Samuel Beckett," *Journal of Modern Literature*, vol. 31, no. 2 (Winter 2008), 115-132.

GG1670. Ben-Zvi, Linda: "Beckett, McLuhan, and television: the medium, the message, and 'the mess'." In 1631, 271-284.

GG1671. Bertrand, Michel: "L'être de boue ne saurait être un être debout: l'eau et la terre dans *Molloy* de Samuel Beckett," *Samuel Beckett Today/Aujourd'hui*, vol. 20 (2008), 83-95.

GG1672. Blackman, Jackie: "Post-war Beckett: resistance, commitment or communist krap?" In 1630, 68-85.

GG1673. Blanckeman, Bruno: "Les filiations ruinées du théâtre de Samuel Beckett ou 'l'oncle incarné'." In 902, 225-240.

GG1674. Blau, Herbert: "Apnea and true illusion: Breath(less) in Beckett." In 1631, 35-53.

GG1675. Bonafous-Murat, Carle: "De l'espèce à la marque: l'art beckettien de mal penser les choses." In 447, 115-128.

GG1676. Bousquet, Mireille: "La boue dans *Comment c'est*: 'petits paquets grammaire d'oiseau'," *Samuel Beckett Today/Aujourd'hui*, vol. 20 (2008), 71-82.

GG1677. Boxall, Peter: "From Joyce to Beckett." In 1630, 147-162.

GG1678. Boxall, Peter: " 'There's no lack of void': waste and abundance in Beckett and DeLillo," *Substance*, vol. 37, no. 2 [no. 116] (2008), 56-70.

GG1679. Boyce, Brynhildur: "(Im)possible worlds: dissociated sound in Samuel Beckett's radio drama." In 1632, 129-143.

GG1680. Brater, Enoch: "Beckett's romanticism." In 1631, 139-151.

GG1681. Bryden, Mary: "The midcentury *Godot*: Beckett and Saroyan." In 1631, 259-270.

GG1682. Butler, Thomas: "The ethics of an expressionless gaze: Samuel Beckett's

Ohio Impromptu," *Journal of Dramatic Theory and Criticism,* vol. 23, no. 1 (Fall 2008), 5-20.

GG1683. Campbell, Julie: "Beckett and Paul Auster." In 1631, 299-310.

GG1684. Chan, Paul: "*Waiting for Godot:* in New Orleans: an artist's statement," *Beckett Circle,* vol. 31, no. 1 (2008), 1-3.

GG1685. Chaudier, Stéphane: "*L'Innommable* de Samuel Beckett ou les ruines sont une fête." In 902, 69-90.

GG1686. Chevaillier, Flore: " 'Something wrong there': punning in *Comment c'est,*" *Journal of Modern Literature,* vol. 31, no. 2 (Winter 2008), 133-142.

GG1687. Chestier, Alain: "Samuel Beckett: le théâtre du silence ou l'écriture à la recherche de l'être assassiné." In 1632, 23-34.

GG1688. Connor, Steven: "Beckett and Bion," *Journal of Beckett Studies,* vol. 17, no. 1-2 (2008), 9-34.

GG1689. Connor, Steven: "Beckett and the world." In 1630, 134-146.

GG1690. Cordingley, Anthony: "Samuel Beckett's *Comment c'est/How it is:* a philosophy of composition." Diss., Univ. of Sydney, 2008. 329 p.

GG1691. Corey, Paul: "Messianism and the age of senility: perpetual expectation in Beckett's *Waiting for Godot.*" In 1080.

GG1692. Corey, Paul: "The two 'nothings' of *Caligula* and *Waiting for Godot.*" In 1080. [Camus]

GG1693. Cornwell, Neil: "First loves and last rites." In 876, 157-174.

GG1694. Culik, Hugh: "Raining and midnight: the limits of representation," *Journal of Beckett Studies,* vol. 17, no. 1-2 (2008), 127-152.

GG1695. Cunningham, David: " 'We have our being in justice': formalism, abstraction and Beckett's 'ethics'." In 1630, 21-37.

GG1696. Czarnecki, Kristin: " 'Signs I don't understand': language and abjection in *Molloy,*" *Journal of Beckett Studies,* vol. 17, no. 1-2 (2008), 52-77.

GG1697. Degani-Raz, Irit: "The spear of Telephus in *Krapp's Last Tape.*" In 1631, 190-201.

GG1698. Diamond, Elin: "Beckett and Caryl Churchill along the Möbius strip." In 1631, 285-298.

GG1699. DiGaetani, John Louis: "Samuel Beckett: decadence and the suicidal impulse." In 1082.

GG1700. Doga, U.: "*Finali di partita,* Paul Celan e Samuel Beckett," *Rivista di Letterature Moderne e Comparate,* vol. 61, fasc. 2 (aprile-guigno 2008), 227-242.

GG1701. Dospinescu, Liviu: "Beckett, l'espace vide et le théâtre phénoménologique," *Samuel Beckett Today/Aujourd'hui,* vol. 20 (2008), 279-293.

GG1702. Dospinescu, Ovidiu Liviu: "Pour une théorie de l'espace vide: strategies énonciatives de la mise en scène dans les *Pièces pour la télévision* de Samuel Beckett." Diss., Univ. du Québec à Montréal, 2008.

GG1703. Dowd, Garin: "Prolegomena to a critique of excavatory reason: reply to Matthew Feldman," *Samuel Beckett Today/Aujourd'hui,* vol. 20 (2008), 375-388.

GG1704. Eigenmann, Eric: "Etre de poussière et de souffle: l'intertexte biblique de l'anthropologie beckettienne," *Samuel Beckett Today/Aujourd'hui,* vol. 20 (2008), 217-232.

GG1705. Einarsson, Charlotta Palmstierna: "Voice as self/not self in two of Beckett's short plays." In 1632, 145-153.

GG1706. Einarsson, Lotta P.: "Movement as text: text as movement: the choreographic writing of Samuel Beckett." In 842.

GG1707. Engelberts, Matthijs: "*Film* and *Film:* Beckett and early film theory." In 1631, 152-165.

GG1708. Eubanks, Peter: "Redemption, order, and the undoing of plot in Samuel Beckett's *Molloy,*" *Literature and Belief,* vol. 27, no. 1 (2007), 43-53.

GG1709. Farbman, Herschel: "Beckett's restlessness." In 455.

GG1710. Feldman, Matthew: "In defence of empirical knowledge: rejoinder to 'A critique of excavatory reason'," *Samuel Beckett Today/Aujourd'hui,* vol. 20 (2008), 389-399.

GG1711. Feldman, Matthew: " 'A suitable engine of destruction'? Samuel Beckett and Arnold Geulincx's *Ethics.*" In 1630, 38-56.

GG1712. Fifield, Peter: "Beckett, Cotard's syndrome and the narrative patient," *Journal of Beckett Studies*, vol. 17, no. 1-2 (2008), 169-186.

GG1713. García Hubard, Gabriela: "En traversant l'aphasie," *Samuel Beckett Today/Aujourd'hui*, vol. 20 (2008), 335-345.

GG1714. Germoni, Karine: "*Le Dépeupleur*: des éléments absents/présents ou l'ambiguïté de l'antiromantisme beckettien," *Samuel Beckett Today/Aujourd'hui*, vol. 20 (2008), 189-201.

GG1715. Giesler, Daina: "*Krapp's Last Tape*: an actor's perspective," *Beckett Circle*, vol. 31, no. 2 (Fall 2008), 5-8.

GG1716. Giles, Jana María: " 'The aesthetics of relinquishment': natural and social contracts in Beckett's 'The End'," *Samuel Beckett Today/Aujourd'hui*, vol. 20 (2008), 175-188.

GG1717. Godeau, Florence: "Figures d'exclus, figures exclues chez Franz Kafka et Samuel Beckett," *Samuel Beckett Today/Aujourd'hui*, vol. 20 (2008), 347-358.

GG1718. Gontarski, S. E.: "Recovering Beckett's Bergsonism." In 1631, 93-106. [Bergson]

GG1719. Grene, Nicholas: "Beckett and Irish drama: an offstage presence." In 1632, 93-106.

GG1720. Grene, Nicholas: "The Hibernicization of *En attendant Godot*," *Etudes Irlandaises*, vol. 33, no. 2 (automne 2008), 135-144.

GG1721. Gribben, Darren: "Beckett's other revelation: the capital of the ruins," *Irish University Review*, vol. 38, no. 2 (Autumn-Winter 2008), 263-273.

GG1722. Gruzinska, Aleksandra: "Une amitié: Samuel Beckett vu par E. M. Cioran." In 535, 205-217. [Cioran]

GG1723. Guilbard, Anne-Cécile: "Traces du regard: dioptrique de Beckett," *Samuel Beckett Today/Aujourd'hui*, vol. 20 (2008), 295-306.

GG1724. Gunn, Leslie Ann Hart: "*Arrested Development* and the theatre of the absurd," *Velox*, vol. 2, no. 1 (2008), 14-20

GG1725. Hansen, Jim: "Samuel Beckett's *Catastrophe* and the theater of pure means," *Comparative Literature Studies*, vol. 45, no. 4 (2008), [n.p.].

GG1726. Hendrickson, Suzanne Bader: "Samuel Beckett's *Fin de partie/Endgame/Endspiel*: a dynamic evolving reality." In 535, 135-156.

GG1727. Hendrickson, Suzanne; William Hendrickson: "A conversation with Samuel Beckett (Paris, April 16, 1983)." In 535, 273-280.

GG1728. Hoffert, Yannick: "Aspects de l'eau dans le théâtre de Beckett," *Samuel Beckett Today/Aujourd'hui*, vol. 20 (2008), 49-60.

GG1729. Houppermans, Sjef: "Père de pierre," *Samuel Beckett Today/Aujourd'hui*, vol. 20 (2008), 107-118.

GG1730. Houston Jones, David: "From contumacy to shame: reading Beckett's testimonies with Agamben." In 1631, 54-67.

GG1731. Houston Jones, David: " 'So fluctuant a death': entropy and survival in *The Lost Ones* and *Long Observation of the Ray*." In 1630, 118-133.

GG1732. Hubert, Marie-Claude: "La mise en scène des éléments," *Samuel Beckett Today/Aujourd'hui*, vol. 20 (2008), 155-164.

GG1733. Hunkeler, Thomas: " 'Quelque chose d'arborescent ou de céleste': poésie et poétique selon le jeune Beckett," *Samuel Beckett Today/Aujourd'hui*, vol. 20 (2008), 133-142.

GG1734. Inkel, Stéphane: "Figure de mère et image de pierre," *Samuel Beckett Today/Aujourd'hui*, vol. 20 (2008), 119-130.

GG1735. Jenkins, Cecil: "Waiting for Beckett," *Critical Engagements*, vol. 2, no. 1 (Summer 2008), 9-58.

GG1736. Kalb, Jonathan: "Beckett after Beckett," *Salmagundi*, no. 160-161 (Fall 2008-Winter 2009), 140-150.

GG1737. Katz, Daniel: "Writing in the disciplinary borderlands," *MFS*, vol. 54, no. 4 (Winter 2008), 853-861.

GG1738. Keatinge, Benjamin: "Beckett and language pathology," *Journal of Modern Literature*, vol. 31, no. 4 (Summer 2008), 86-101.

GG1739. Kimoliatis, Evdokia: "Samuel Beckett, des histoires sans vie en attendant la mort." In 1632, 35-48.

GG1740. Kirschen, Robert M.: "The influences of and on Samuel Beckett," *Journal of Modern Literature*, vol. 31, no. 2 (Winter 2008), 142-148.

GG1741. Knowlson, James: "*All that Fall* on stage," *Beckett Circle*, vol. 31, no. 2 (Fall 2008), 9-11.

GG1742. Knowlson, James: "Beckett the tourist: Bamberg and Würzburg." In 1631, 21-31.

GG1743. Knowlson, Jim: "Beckett's passion for art: a biographical note," *Beckett Circle*, vol. 31, no. 1 (2008), 7-9.

GG1744. Laddaga, Reinaldo: "La detención de la escritura: Samuel Beckett en Osvaldo Lamborghini." In 883.

GG1745. Lawlor, Seán: "Brook's *Fragments* at the Young Vic," *Beckett Circle*, vol. 31, no. 1 (2008), 3-4.

GG1746. Laws, Catherine: "Beckett—Feldman—Johns." In 1631, 230-245.

GG1747. Le Cam, Brigitte: "D'*Eleutheria* à *Godot* ou comment réussir l'échec." In 1632, 49-64.

GG1748. Lecossois, Hélène: "Les vestiges du corps dans le théâtre de Samuel Beckett," *Samuel Beckett Today/Aujourd'hui*, vol. 20 (2008), 259-269.

GG1749. Locatelli, Carla: "Projections: Beckett's *Krapp's Last Tape* and *Not I* as autobiographies." In 1631, 68-80.

GG1750. Malachy, Thérèse: "*En attendant Godot*: une lecture politique." In 1093.

GG1751. Malachy, Thérèse: "Samuel Beckett: la culpabilité sans Dieu." In 1093.

GG1752. Malachy, Thérèse: "Samuel Beckett: pourquoi le théâtre?" In 1093.

GG1753. Maude, Ulrika: "Centennial Beckett: the gray canon and the fusion of horizons," *Modernism/Modernity*, vol. 15, no. 1 (Jan. 2008), 179-187.

GG1754. Maude, Ulrika: " 'A stirring beyond coming and going': Beckett and Tourette's," *Journal of Beckett Studies*, vol. 17, no. 1-2 (2008), 153-168.

GG1755. McMullan, Anna: "Beckett's theater: embodying alterity." In 1631, 166-176.

GG1756. Mével, Yann: "Beckett et le devenir du paysage," *Samuel Beckett Today/Aujourd'hui*, vol. 20 (2008), 143-154.

GG1757. Montini, Chiara: "Sinking in the mud: *From an abandoned work* et le difficile retour à l'anglais," *Samuel Beckett Today/Aujourd'hui*, vol. 20 (2008), 63-69.

GG1758. Mooney, Sinead: "Ghost writer: Beckett's Irish Gothic." In 880, 167-182.

GG1759. Mooney, Sinéad: " 'I say I': Beckett, translation, ventriloquism." In 1632, 107-128.

GG1760. Moorjani, Angela: "Le complexe de Prométhée ou sous le signe du feu: tyrannie et volonté de savoir chez Beckett," *Samuel Beckett Today/Aujourd'hui*, vol. 20 (2008), 23-32.

GG1761. Moorjani, Angela: "Deictic projection of the *I* and eye in Beckett's fiction and *Film*," *Journal of Beckett Studies*, vol. 17, no. 1-2 (2008), 35-51.

GG1762. Moorjani, Angela: " 'Just looking': ne(i)ther-world icons, Elsheimer nocturnes, and other simultaneities in Beckett's *Play*." In 1631, 123-138.

GG1763. Morgan Wortham, Simon: "Anonymity writing pedagogy: Beckett, Descartes, Derrida," *Symploke*, vol. 16, no. 1-2 (2008), 93-105. [Derrida]

GG1764. Mori, Naoya: " 'No body is at rest': the legacy of Leibniz's *Force* in Beckett's œuvre." In 1631, 107-120.

GG1765. Moss, Leonard: "*Waiting for Godot*: the end of evolution?" In 1095.

GG1766. Mount, Nick: "*Waiting for Godot* without existentialism," *Raritan*, vol. 28, no. 2 (Fall 2008), 24-34.

GG1767. Naito, Jonathan Tadashi: "The postimperial imagination: the emergence of a transnational literary space, from Samuel Beckett to Hanif Kureishi." Diss., UCLA, 2008. x, 230 p.

GG1768. Nixon, Mark: " 'Infernal streams': Beckett's rivers," *Samuel Beckett Today/Aujourd'hui*, vol. 20 (2008), 33-47.

GG1769.   Novén, Bengt: "Samuel Beckett et 'les splendeurs polyglottes'." In 1632, 65-84.

GG1770.   Okamuro, Minako: *"Words and music, . . . but the clouds . . .*, and Yeat's 'The Tower'." In 1631, 217-229.

GG1771.   Oppenheim, Lois: "A twenty-first century perspective on a play by Samuel Beckett," *Journal of Beckett Studies*, vol. 17, no. 1-2 (2008), 187-198.

GG1772.   Ost, Isabelle: " 'Et rêve d'un espace sans ici ni ailleurs': parcours en terre beckettienne," *Samuel Beckett Today/Aujourd'hui*, vol. 20 (2008), 97-106.

GG1773.   Panagopoulos, Nic: "Beckett and Bakhtin: carnival abuse as universal uncrowning in *Waiting for Godot*." In 567, 371-393.

GG1774.   Parrott, Jeremy: " 'Change all the names': a Samuel Beckett onomasticon," *Nome Nel Testo (II)*, no. 8 (2006), 611-620.

GG1775.   Penet-Astbury, Herlen: "Limbo of (in)different language(s): Samuel Beckett/Nancy Huston," *Essays in French Literature and Culture*, no. 45 (Nov. 2008), 105-124. [Huston]

GG1776.   Penet-Astbury, Helen: *"Rough for Theatre I* and *II* and why they stayed that way, or when Beckett's French theatre became Irish again," *Etudes Irlandaises*, vol. 33, no. 2 (automne 2008), 125-133.

GG1777.   Perloff, Marjorie: "Beckett in the country of the Houyhnhnms." In 873, 280-299.

GG1778.   Phillips, Doug: "Classroom drama: Beckett for the high school set," *Text and Presentation*, supplement 5 (2008), 123-131.

GG1779.   Ratcliffe, Sophie: "Samuel Beckett: 'humanity in ruins'." In 857.

GG1780.   Redfern, Walter: "Bad jokes and Beckett." In 568.

GG1781.   Redfern, Walter: "A little bird tells us." In 568. [Queneau]

GG1782.   Reginio, Robert J.: "The problem of memory in modernism: gestures of memory in Virginia Woolf, Wallace Stevens, Marcel Duchamp, and Samuel Beckett." Diss., Univ. of Massachusetts Amherst, 2008. x, 277 p.

GG1783.   Richardson, Brian: "A theory of narrative beginnings and the beginnings of 'The Dead' and *Molloy*." In 772, 113-126.

GG1784.   Rimoldi, Lucas: "Un paradigma local de posdramatismo: variaciones sobre B . . . ," *telondefondo*, n. 8 (2008), 1-15.

GG1785.   Rinhaug, Aino: "Is the absurd a male-dominated terrain? Pessoa and Beckett as case studies," *Portuguese Studies*, vol. 24, no. 1 (2008), 41-55.

GG1786.   Riquelme, John Paul: "Dark modernity from Mary Shelley to Samuel Beckett: gothic history, the gothic tradition, and modernism." In 834.

GG1787.   Rodríguez-Gago, Antonia: "Re-figuring the stage body through the mechanical re-production of memory." In 1631, 202-213.

GG1788.   "Round table: 'Staging Beckett in France'," *Etudes Irlandaises*, vol. 33, no. 2 (automne 2008), 145-155.

GG1789.   Salisbury, Laura: " 'Throw up for good': gagging, compulsion and a comedy of ethics in the *Trilogy*." In 1630, 163-180.

GG1790.   Salisbury, Laura: " 'What is the word': Beckett's aphasic modernism," *Journal of Beckett Studies*, vol. 17, no. 1-2 (2008), 78-126.

GG1791.   Sardin, Pascale: "The spectral logic of *Eh Joe/dis Joe*: from reception to genesis and back," *Samuel Beckett Today/Aujourd'hui*, vol. 20 (2008), 307-319.

GG1792.   Sheehan, Paul: "A world without memory: Beckett and the ethics of cruelty." In 1630, 86-101.

GG1793.   Siboni, Julia: "Des cendres à la poussière, une ontologie résiduelle," *Samuel Beckett Today/Aujourd'hui*, vol. 20 (2008), 359-369.

GG1794.   Siess, Jürgen: "Beckett's *Posture* in the French literary field." In 1631, 177-189.

GG1795.   Sivetidou, Aphrodite: "L'expression terrestre de la 'réalité humaine' chez Beckett," *Samuel Beckett Today/Aujourd'hui*, vol. 20 (2008), 165-174.

GG1796.   Soenen, Dimitri: " 'No final script': sur les carnets de mise en scène de Samuel Beckett," *Samuel Beckett Today/Aujourd'hui*, vol. 20 (2008), 271-277.

GG1797.   Spector, Donald: "Distinguishing the multiverse from an echo: quantum mechanics and *Waiting for Godot*," *Samuel Beckett Today/Aujourd'hui*, vol. 20 (2008), 245-257.

GG1798. Spies, Werner: "Samuel Beckett." In 596.

GG1799. Tanaka, Mariko Hori: "Ontological fear and anxiety in the theater of Beckett, Betsuyaku, and Pinter." In 1631, 246-258.

GG1800. Tokarev, Dimitri: "Le rôle et les métamorphoses des quatre éléments dans *La Nausée* de Sartre et *La Fin* de Beckett," *Samuel Beckett Today/Aujourd'hui*, vol. 20 (2008), 233-241. [Sartre]

GG1801. Travis, Charles: "Beyond the Cartesian pale: travels with Samuel Beckett, 1928-1946." In 821.

GG1802. Uhlmann, Anthony: "Withholding assent: Beckett in the light of stoic ethics." In 1630, 57-67.

GG1803. Van Hulle, Dirk: "Les manuscrits bilingues de Beckett: la combinaison des approches 'documentaire' et 'textuelle' dans une édition numérique," *Recherches et Travaux, Université Stendhal, UFR de Lettres*, no. 72 (2008), 53-58.

GG1804. Van Hulle, Dirk: " 'World stuff': éléments présocratiques dans la genèse de l'œuvre beckettienne," *Samuel Beckett Today/Aujourd'hui*, vol. 20 (2008), 203-216.

GG1805. Warner, Marina: " 'Who can shave an egg?': Beckett, Mallarmé, and foreign tongues," *Raritan*, vol. 27, no. 4 (Spring 2008), 62-89. [Mallarmé]

GG1806. Weller, Shane: "The anetics of desire: Beckett, Racine, Sade." In 1630, 102-117.

GG1807. Weller, Shane: " 'Gnawing to be naught': Beckett and pre-Socratic nihilism," *Samuel Beckett Today/Aujourd'hui*, vol. 20 (2008), 321-333.

GG1808. Weller, Shane: "The politics of body language: the Beckett embrace." In 458, 141-159.

GG1809. Wessler, Ereic: "L' 'art du peu' comme héritage du romantisme." In 382, 311-326.

GG1810. White, Harry: "Words after music: Samuel Beckett after Joyce." In 881.

GG1811. Yeh, Tzu-ching: " 'Close your eyes and listen to it, what would you think it was?': the uncanny and the mechanical in *All That Fall* and *Embers*," *NTU Studies in Language and Literature*, no. 20 (Dec. 2008), 149-178.

GG1812. Zeifman, Hersh: "Staging Sam: Beckett as dramatic character." In 1631, 311-318.

BEDEL, Maurice.

GG1813. Foucart, Claude: "Maurice Bedel: *Monsieur Hitler*, 1937." In 461, 355-365.

BEGAG, Azouz.

GG1814. ● Rogers, Sheila: *Azouz Begag, Le gone du Chaâba*. Glasgow: Univ. of Glasgow French and German Publications, 2008. *Glasgow introductory guides to French literature*, 55. viii, 60 p.

GG1815. Lay-Chenchabi, Kathryn; Tess Do: "Guilt and betrayal in the works of Azouz Begag and Linda Lê," *French Cultural Studies*, vol. 19, no. 1 (Feb. 2008), 39-56. [Lê]

GG1816. Talahite-Moodley, Anissa: " 'Les deux pieds dans le ciment': deuil et surplus identitaire dans *Le Marteau pique-cœur* de Azouz Begag." In 119, 151-171.

GG1817. Talahite-Moodley, Anissa: "Deux romans de la rupture et du renouvellement: *Le Marteau pique-cœur* d'Azouz Begag et *Le Dromadaire de Bonaparte* de Tassadit Imache," *Expressions Maghrébines*, vol. 7, no. 1 (été 2008), 177-192. [Tassadit Imache]

BÉGIA, Christian.

GG1818. Belzil, Patricia: "Dernière (s)cène. Pi . . . ?!," *Jeu: Cahiers de Théâtre*, no. 129 [no. 4] (2008), 14-18.

BEIGBEDER, Frédéric.

GG1819. ● Beigbeder, Frédéric: *Au secours pardon*. Préface de Marin de Viry. Paris: Librairie générale française, 2008. *Le livre de poche*. 316 p.

GG1820. ● *Frédéric Beigbeder et ses doubles*. Alain-Philippe Durand, ed. Amsterdam: Rodopi, 2008. *CRIN*, 51. 208 p.

GG1821. ● Martin, Jenny: *"Haben Sie keine Angst vor dem Glück, es existiert nicht": der Traum vom Glück und sein Scheitern bei Houellebecq und Beigbeder*. Bonn: Bouvier, 2008. 224 p. [Houellebecq]

GG1822. Cloonan, William: "L'image comme image: le (possible) triomphe du simulacre dans l'univers de Beigbeder." In 1820, 127-138. [Baudrillard]

GG1823. Delvaux, Martine: "L'égoïsme romantique de Frédéric Beigbeder." In 1820, 93-105.

GG1824. Durand, Alain-Philippe: "Défense de Narcisse." In 1820, 61-71.

GG1825. Durand, Alain-Philippe: "Entretien avec Frédéric Beigbeder." In 1820, 17-36.

GG1826. Durand, Alain-Philippe: "Exhiber la violence de l'événement: l'exemple du onze septembre." In 617, 365-376.

GG1827. Duteurtre, Benoît: "Beigbeder et son contraire." In 1820, 51-57.

GG1828. Hernández, Ramiro Martín: "Frédéric Beigbeder, un nuevo topi de novelista para un nuevo tipo de lector?," *Cuadernos de Filologia Francesa*, vol. 19 (2008), 165-183.

GG1829. La Quérière, Yves de: "L'écume des nuits: vacances dans le coma de Frédéric Beigbeder." In 1820, 139-154.

GG1830. Le Naire, Olivier: "Le croisé et le ruse, entretien avec Frédéric Beigbeder et Richard Millet." In 1820, 39-42. [Millet]

GG1831. Mandel, Naomi: "Fiction et fidélité: *Windows on the World*." In 1820, 107-126.

GG1832. McIntyre, Richard: "Shopping with Octave." In 1820, 185-203.

GG1833. Powers, Scott M.: "Post-modern narratives of evil and 9-11: the case of Frédéric Beigbeder." In 603, 133-150.

GG1834. Schoolcraft, Ralph, III: "Pour prendre au sérieux Frédéric Beigbeder." In 1820, 73-91.

GG1835. van Wesemael, Sabine: "Le potentiel transgressif de l'art contemporain." In 1820, 155-183.

GG1836. Vilain, Philippe: "L'égo beigbederien." In 1820, 59-60.

BELAÏD, Lakhdar.

GG1837. Durmelat, Sylvie: "The Algerian war and its afterlives painted noir in *Sérail Killers* by Lakhdar Belaïd: Beur literature or *roman noir*?," *Expressions Maghrébines*, vol. 7, no. 1 (été 2008), 141-157.

BÉNABOU, Marcel.

GG1838. Brignoli, Laura: "La multiplicité des points de germination de l'écriture dans l'*Epopée familiale* de Marcel Bénabou." In 423.

BENCHEIKH, Jamal Eddine. See 183.

BENCHEKROUN, Siham. See 347.

BÉNÉZET, Mathieu.

GG1839. Garron, Isabelle: "Mathieu Bénézet," *Critique*, tome 64, no. 735-736 (août-sept. 2008), 689-696.

GG1840. Stout, John: "Entretien avec Mathieu Bénézet," *LittéRéalité*, vol. 20, no. 1 (printemps/été 2008), 39-47.

BEN JELLOUN, Tahar. See also 64, 169, 230.

GG1841. • Ader, Wolfgang: *Tahar Ben Jelloun, Les raisins de la galère*. Rev. Ausg. Stuttgart: Reclam, 2008. 79 p.

GG1842. • Ben Jelloun, Tahar: *Les raisins de la galère*. Hrsg. Johannes Röhrig. Stuttgart: Reclam, 2008. 175 p.

GG1843. • Farouk, May: *Tahar Ben Jelloun: étude des enjeux réflexifs dans l'œuvre*. Paris: L'Harmattan, 2008. *Approches littéraires*. 220 p.

GG1844. Bourget, Carine: "9/11 and the affair of the Muslim headscarf in essays by Tahar Ben Jelloun and Abdelwahab Meddeb," *French Cultural Studies*, vol. 19, no. 1 (Feb. 2008), 71-84. [Meddeb]

GG1845. El Hadji, Camara: "Le double identitaire ou la quête de soi dans *L'Enfant de sable* de Tahar Ben Jelloun et *La Goutte d'Or* de Michel Tournier." In 99, 91-104. [Tournier]

GG1846. Gilleir, Anke: "Habeas corpus: on the meaning of the 'ethnic' body in the writing of Tahar Ben Jelloun and Feridun Zaimoglu." In 588, 198-210.

GG1847. Lezra, Esther: "(Ab)errant bodies/(ab)erring stories/remembering bodies/disordering stories in *The Pagoda* and *The Sand Child*." In 43, 80-106.

GG1848. Lombardi-Diop, Cristina: "Ghosts of memories, spirits of ancestors: slavery, the Mediterranean, and the Atlantic." In 122, 162-180.

GG1849. Semsch, Klaus: "Androgynität im Erzählwerk Tahar Ben Jellouns als Spiel mit Differenzen." In 440, 91-100.

GG1850. Urbani, Bernard: "Entre humour et dérision: *Moha le fou Moha le sage* de Tahar Ben Jelloun," *Expressions Maghrébines*, vol. 7, no. 2 (hiver 2008), 37-49.

GG1851. West-Pavlov, Russell: "The fictions of clandestinity: dream and reality in Ben Jelloun and Skif," *Australian Journal of French Studies*, vol. 45, no. 2 (May-Aug. 2008), 164-178. [Hamid Skif]

BEN MANSOUR, Latifa. See 273a.

BENMILOUD, Yassir.

GG1852. Swamy, Vinay: "The telereal republic: nation, narration, and popular culture in Benmiloud's *Allah superstar*," *Yale French Studies*, no. 114 (2008), 130-143.

GG1853. Vitali, Ilaria: " 'Qui est qui et qui pense quoi?' Autofiction et masques chez Y. B." In 441, 129-137.

BENOIT, Pierre.

GG1854. ● Benoit, Pierre; Georges Lecomte: *La rencontre de Pierre Benoît et Georges Lecomte de l'Académie Française avec le Liban: correspondances inédites.* Ed. Hyam Mallat. Paris: Geuthner, 2008. 170 p.

GG1855. Figuerola, Carme: "Ecriture et signification de la Quête chez Pierre Benoit." In 553, 255-269.

GG1856. Foucart, Claude: "L'Allemand et le paysage germanique dans les romans de Pierre Benoit." In 461, 311-320.

GG1857. Hefferman, Kevin: " 'A sword and sandal gone screwy' or, Edgar G. Ulmer's journey to the lost city, *L'Atlantide*." In 817, 263-271.

BENS, Jacques.

GG1858. Tassou, Bertrand: "Les *Sonnets irrationnels* de Jacques Bens," *Formules*, no. 12 (2008), 67-80.

BÉRAUD, Henri.

GG1859. ● Béraud, Henri: *Le Merle blanc: écrits 1919-1922*. Textes réunis par Pierrette et Georges Dupont. Tusson: Du Lérot, 2008. 284 p.

GG1860. Dussert, Eric: "Le métier de flâner," *Matricule des Anges*, no. 84 (2007), 49.

BERGER, Yves.

GG1861. ● Berger, Yves: *Œuvre romanesque*. Préface de Dominique Fernandez. Paris: B. Grasset, 2008. 1204 p.

BERGOUNIOUX, Pierre. See also 422.

GG1862. Duffy, Jean H.: "Commemoration, initiation and art in Pierre Bergounioux: *La Mort de Brune* and *Kpélié*," *Word and Image*, vol. 24, no. 4 (Oct.-Dec. 2008), 439-460.

GG1863. Duffy, Jean H.: "Family comes first: I-identity and we-identity in Pierre Bergounioux," *Modern Language Review*, vol. 103, part 1 (Jan. 2008), 57-75.

BERGSON, Henri. See also 950, 960, 979, 1000, 1326, 3027, 3092, 4612, 5242, 5832, 7210.

GG1864. ● Bergson, Henri: *Cours de psychologie de 1892-1893 au lycée Henri-IV.* Edité par Sylvain Matton; prés. par Alain Panero. Paris: Séha; Milan: Arché, 2008. 276 p.

GG1865. ● Bergson, Henri: *La politesse et autres essais*. Préface de Frédéric Worms. Paris: Payot et Rivages, 2008. 76 p.

GG1866. ● *Bergson et la religion: nouvelles perspectives sur Les deux sources de la morale et de la religion.* Sous la dir. de Ghislain Waterlot. Paris: PUF, 2008. 496 p.

GG1867. ● *Dio, la vita, il nulla: L'Evoluzione creatrice di Henri Bergson a cento anni dalla pubblicazione: atti del Colloquio internazionale, Bari, 4 maggio 2007.* A cura di Giusi Strummiello. Bari: Edizioni di Pagina, 2008. 165 p.

GG1868. ● Dittmann, Lorenz: *Matisse begegnet Bergson: Reflexionen zu Kunst und Philosophie.* Köln: Böhlau, 2008. *Studien zur Kunst*, 10. 279 p.

GG1869. ● François, Arnaud: *Bergson*. Paris: Ellipses, 2008. *Philo-philosophes*. 128 p.

GG1870. ● François, Arnaud: *Bergson, Schopenhauer, Nietzsche: volonté et réalité.* Paris: PUF, 2008. *Philosophie d'aujourd'hui*. 284 p.

GG1871. • Giribone, Jean-Luc: *Le rire étrange: Bergson avec Freud*. Paris: Ed. du Sandre, 2008. 60 p.

GG1872. • Godani, Paolo: *Bergson e la filosofia*. Pisa: ETS, 2008. *Philosophica*. 172 p.

GG1873. • Jankélévitch, Vladimir: *Henri Bergson*. Paris: PUF, 2008. 3e édition. *Quadrige*. 299 p.

GG1874. • Lindsay, A. D.: *The philosophy of Bergson*. Whitefish, MT: Kessinger, 2008. 247 p. [Originally published, 1911]

GG1875. • Moulard-Leonard, Valentine: *Bergson-Deleuze encounters: transcendental experience and the thought of the virtual*. Albany: SUNY Press, 2008. *SUNY series in contemporary French thought*. x, 197 p. [Deleuze]

GG1876. • Ramanujam, A. Appan.: *Reflections on Bergson's philosophy*. Delhi: Sharada, 2008. x, 222 p.

GG1877. • Wilm, Emil Carl: *Henri Bergson: a study in radical evolution*. Whitefish, MT: Kessinger Publishing, 2008. *Kessinger Publishing's Rare Reprints*. xv, 193 p. [Original edition, 1914]

GG1878. Barnard, G. William: "Pulsating with life: the paradoxical intuitions of Henri Bergson." In 972.

GG1879. Barreau, Hervé: "Bergson face à Spencer. Vers un nouveau positivisme," *Archives de Philosophie*, tome 71, cahier 2 (avril-juin 2008), 219-243.

GG1880. Bergson, Henri: "Trois lettres 'inédites' de Henri Bergson à Gilles Deleuze, proposées par Elie During," *Critique*, tome 64, no. 732 (mai 2008), 398-409. [Deleuze]

GG1881. Bernet, Rudolf: "Bergson over het driftmatig karakter van bewustzijn en leven," *Tijdschrift voor Filosofie*, 70ste Jaargang, Nr. 1 (2008), 51-85.

GG1882. Bernet, Rudolf: "Bergson sul potere creatore della coscienza e della vita." In 1867, 57-96.

GG1883. Blencowe, Claire: "Destroying duration: the critical situation of Bergsonism in Benjamin's analysis of modern experience," *Theory, Culture and Society*, vol. 25, no. 4 (July 2008), 139-158.

GG1884. Boyer, Alain: "Popper, Bergson: l'intuition et l'ouvert," *Revue Philosophique de la France et de l'Etranger*, no. 2 (avril-juin 2008), 187-203.

GG1885. Breeur, Roland: "Het niets en de materie bij Bergson," *Tijdschrift voor Filosofie*, 70ste Jaargang, Nr. 1 (2008), 87-108.

GG1886. Breeur, Roland: "La vita e il nulla." In 1867, 97-122.

GG1887. Burton, James: "Machines making Gods: Philip K. Dick, Henri Bergson, Saint Paul," *Theory, Culture and Society*, vol. 25, no. 7-8 (Dec. 2008), 262-284.

GG1888. Caron, Maxence: "Sur la question du corps dans la pensée de Heidgger. De *Sein und Zeit* aux *Séminaires de Zollikon*," *Archives de Philosophie*, tome 71, cahier 2 (avril-juin 2008), 309-329.

GG1889. Cherniavsky, Axel: "La expresión de la *durée* en la filosofía de Bergson," *Revista Latinoamericana de Filosofía*, vol. 34, n. 1 (otoño 2008), 93-123.

GG1890. Curle, Clinton T.: " 'One of the most important books I have ever read': John Humphrey, Henri Bergson and international human rights." In 810.

GG1891. Degraeuwe, Jan: "Verscheidenheid en eenheid in de creatieve evolutie volgens Bergson," *Tijdschrift voor Filosofie*, 70ste Jaargang, Nr. 1 (2008), 27-49.

GG1892. Doucot, Julien: "Le vivant en activité. Besoin, problème et créativité chez Henri Bergson," *Archives de Philosophie*, tome 71, cahier 2 (avril-juin 2008), 269-288.

GG1893. Jones, Donna: "The eleatic Bergson," *Diacritics*, vol. 37, no. 1 (Spring 2007), 21-31.

1893a. Lefebvre, Alexandre: "The time of law." In 3027.

GG1894. Narbone, Jean-Marc: "I Greci nel pensiero religioso di Bergson." In 1867, 19-36.

GG1895. Panero, Alain: "Kant, précurseur manqué de Bergson," *Revue Philosophique de la France et de l'Etranger*, no. 2 (avril-juin 2008), 133-145.

GG1896. Ragghianti, Renzo: "Trois lettres d'Henri Bergson à René Helleu," *Giornale Storica della Filosofia Italiana*, fasc. 1, anno 87 (genn.-aprile 2008), 134-144.

GG1897.   Riquier, Camille: "Bergson (d')après Deleuze," *Critique*, tome 64, no. 732 (mai 2008), 356-371. [Deleuze]

GG1898.   Ronchi, Rocco: "L'oro e gli spiccioli." In 1867, 37-56.

GG1899.   Schweizer, Harold: "A brief theory of waiting: Henri Bergson's lump of sugar." In 979.

GG1900.   Sehgal, Melanie: "Das Kriterium der Intimität. William James als Leser Bergson," *Revue Philosophique de la France et de l'Etranger*, no. 2 (avril-juin 2008), 173-186.

GG1901.   Shaw, Spencer: "Bergson: movement and intermediate imagery." In 982.

GG1902.   Sitbon-Peillon, Brigitte: "A la suite de *L'évolution créatrice*: Les deux sources de la morale et de la religion. L'entropie, un principe social?," *Archives de Philosophie*, tome 71, cahier 2 (avril-juin 2008), 289-308.

GG1903.   Slegers, Rosa: "A phenomenological groundwork for involuntary memory: Henri Bergson's aesthetics and Marcel Proust's *A la recherche du temps perdu*," *International Studies in Philosophy*, vol. 39, no. 1 (2007), 79-91. [Proust]

GG1904.   Strummiello, Giusi: "*Deux sive vita*? Il divino e il vitale ne *L'Evoluzione creatrice*." In 1867, 123-148.

GG1905.   Tasdelen, Demet Kurtoglu: "The role of closed morality in achieving rational communication: the possibility of rational communication within Bergson's non-rationalist morality," *Kaygi*, no. 10 (2008), 71-82.

GG1906.   Trabichet, Luc: "La ponctuation de l'absolu: nature, saisie et expression de l'absolu chez Hegel et Bergson," *Revue des Sciences Religieuses et Théologiques*, tome 92, no. 4 (oct.-déc. 2008), 773-797.

GG1907.   Vieillard-Baron, Jean-Louis: "L'événement et le tout: Windelbrand lecteur de Bergson," *Revue Philosophique de la France et de l'Etranger*, no. 2 (avril-juin 2008), 157-171.

GG1908.   Vieillard-Baron, Jean-Louis: "Réflexion sur la réception théorique de *L'évolution créatrice*," *Archives de Philosophie*, tome 71, cahier 2 (avril-juin 2008), 207-217.

GG1909.   Vittorio Macri, Rocco: "Che cos'è il tempo?: Bergson, Maritain, Dingle a confronto con Einstein," *Sapienza*, vol. 61, no. 1 (2008), 3-51. [Maritain]

GG1910.   Waterlot, Ghislain: "Dieu est-il transcendant? Examen critique des objections de P. de Tonquedec adressées à 'l'auteur de *L'évolution créatrice*'," *Archives de Philosophie*, tome 71, cahier 2 (avril-juin 2008), 269-288.

GG1911.   Windelband, Wilhelm: "En guise d'introduction à *Matière et mémoire* de Bergson," *Revue Philosophique de la France et de l'Etranger*, no. 2 (avril-juin 2008), 147-156.

GG1912.   Worms, Frédéric: "Quale vitalismo al di là di quale nichilismo? Da *L'evoluzione creatrice* ad oggi." In 1867, 149-?.

BERNANOS, Georges. See also 491, 2840, 4188.

GG1913.   ● Baudelle, Yves; Françoise Rullier-Theuret: *Bernanos: le rayonnement de l'invisible. Sous le soleil de Satan*. Paris: CNED, 2008. 222 p.

GG1914.   ● Bernanos, Georges: *Les grands cimetières sous la lune*. Préface de Michel del Castillo. Bordeaux: Castor Astral, 2008. 307 p.

GG1915.   ● Bernanos, Georges: *Monsieur Ouine*. Préface de Pierre-Robert Leclercq. Bordeaux: Castor astral, 2008. 309 p.

GG1916.   ● Bernanos, Georges: *Sous le soleil de Satan*. Préface de Sébastien Lapaque. Bordeaux: Castor astral, 2008. 333 p.

GG1917.   ● *Georges Bernanos: Sous le soleil de Satan*. Etudes réunies par Yves Baudelle et Paul Renard. Vimy: Société 20-50, 2008. *Roman 20-50*, hors série, no. 4 140 p.

GG1918.   ● Gil, Marie: *Les deux écritures: étude sur Bernanos*. Paris: Cerf, 2008. 228 p.

GG1919.   ● Gosselin-Noat, Monique; Bérengère Moricheau-Airaud: *Bernanos, Sous le soleil de Satan*. Neuilly: Atlande, 2008. *Clefs concours*. 255 p.

GG1920.   Asensio, Juan: "La figure de Satan dans *Sous le soleil de Satan*: une ambiguïté et une complexité fondamentales," *Archives des Lettres Modernes*, no. 293 (2008), 5-61.

GG1921. Barilier, Etienne: "L'île du Diable, villégiature monotone mais conforta-ble." In 388, 178-189. [Céline]

GG1922. Bordas, Eric: "Prolepses dans *Sous le soleil de Satan* de Bernanos," *Information Grammaticale*, no. 119 (2008), 49-53.

GG1923. Foucart, Claude: "Bernanos face à Hitler." In 461, 367-376.

GG1924. Gosselin-Noat, Monique: "Bernanos et Luther." In 452, 865-881.

GG1925. Guyot-Jeannin, Arnaud: "Georges Bernanos contre les bien-pensants," *Spectacle du Monde*, no. 547 (juillet-août 2008), 68-73.

GG1926. Kidd, William: "*Sous le soleil de Satan*: une influence 'normande' (Bernanos et Flaubert)," *Archives des Lettres Modernes*, no. 293 (2008), 63-74.

GG1927. Morello, André-Alain: " 'Il n'y a rien ici pour les professeurs'. Note sur les défis de Bernanos dans *Sous le soleil de Satan*," *Littératures*, no. 58-59 (2008), 321-332.

GG1928. Ouellette, Julie: "Ecrire 'à partir de la fin': l'écriture de l'agonie," *Archives des Lettres Modernes*, no. 293 (2008), 75-99.

GG1929. Sarocchi, Jean: "Monsieur Ouine ou la puissance bétifiante du mal," *Modernités*, no. 29 (2008), 229-260.

GG1930. Smadja, Stéphanie: "L'adjectif dans *Sous le soleil de Satan*." In 599, 213-226.

GG1931. Subbotina, Galina: "L'image du diable dans *Sous le soleil de Satan* de Georges Bernanos et *Le Maître et Marguerite* de Mikhaïl Boulgakov," *Roman 20-50*, no. 46 (2008), 115-122.

GG1932. Teuber, Bernhard: "Selbstgespräch-Zwiegespräch-Seelengespräch: zur Ökonomie spiritueller Kommunikation." In 589, 57-79.

GG1933. Watine, Marie-Albane: "Ellipse et cohérence dans *Sous le soleil de Satan*." In 599, 227-246.

BERNANOS, Michel.

GG1934. • Bernanos, Michel: *La Montagne morte de la vie*. Préface Stéphane Aude-guy; postface Dominique de Roux. Paris: La Table ronde, 2008. 174 p.

BERNHARDT, Sarah. See also 1086, 1094.

GG1935. • *Sarah Bernhardt: the art of high drama*. Carol Ockman and Kenneth E. Silver. New Haven; London: Yale Univ. Press, 2006. xv, 216 p. [Published to accompany the exhibition held at The Jewish Museum, New York, 2 Dec. 2005 to 2 April 2006]

GG1936. Ducrey, Guy: "Quand Sarah Bernhardt se tait." In 592, 155-166.

GG1937. Kuch, Peter: "Sarah Bernhardt, the Irish, et le pays de Kangaroo," *Etudes Irlandaises*, vol. 33, no. 2 (automne 2008), 31-41.

BESNACI-LANCOU, Fatima.

GG1938. Enjelvin, Géraldine: "A Harki's daughter offline and online 'parole cicatri-sante'," *Australian Journal of French Studies*, vol. 45, no. 2 (May-Aug. 2008), 136-149.

BESSETTE, Gérard. See also 94.

GG1939. Rangarajan, Sudarsan: "A Foucauldian study of space and discourse in Gé-rard Bessette's *Le Libraire*," *Cincinnati Romance Review*, vol. 27 (2008), 125-134.

GG1940. Urquhart, Steven: "L'esthétique du monstreux dans *Le Libraire* (1960) de Gérard Bessette." In 527, 173-192.

BESSETTE, Hélène.

GG1941. • Doussinault, Julien: *Hélène Bessette*. Paris: L. Scheer, 2008. 302 p.

GG1942. Dussert, Eric: "Le phrase Bessette," *Matricule des Anges*, no. 77 (2006), 49.

BESSORA. See also 109, 1958.

GG1943. Bouchard, Jen Westmoreland: "Representing 'les multitudes': resisting nor-mative definitions of gender and sexuality in Bessora's *Deux bébés et l'addition*," *Journal of African Literature and Culture*, vol. 5 (2008), 305-322.

GG1944. Clerc, Jeanne-Marie; Liliane Nzé: "Bessora et son roman *Petroleum*." In 56.

BETI, Mongo. See also 278.

GG1945. • Beti, Mongo: *Le rebelle. III: Suivi de les obsèques de Mongo Beti par Odile Biyidi*. Textes réunis et prés. par André Djiffack; préface de Boniface Mongo Mboussa. Paris: Gallimard, 2008. *Continents noirs*. 388 p.

GG1946. ● Owono-Kouma, Auguste: *Mongo Beti et la confrontation: rôle et importance des personnages auxiliaires.* Paris: L'Harmattan, 2008. *Etudes africaines.* 272 p.

GG1947. Abomo-Maurin, Marie-Rose: "L'onomastique dans le roman de Mongo Beti," *Interculturel Francophonies,* no. 13 (juin-juillet), 61-75.

GG1948. Aït-Aarab, Mohamed: "Dialogues romanesques et débats idéologiques dans deux romans de Mongo Beti." In 427, 245-253.

GG1949. Aït-Aarab, Mohamed: "Mongo Beti ou le tragique de l'écriture engagée," *Interculturel Francophonies,* no. 13 (juin-juillet), 101-110.

GG1950. Basabose, Philippe: "Mongo Beti: l'art du polémotexte," *Interculturel Francophonies,* no. 13 (juin-juillet), 31-43.

GG1951. Briot, Frédéric: "Enfances travesties dans *La Ruine presque cocasse d'un polichinelle* de Mongo Beti." In 448, 253-261.

GG1952. Cali, Andrea: "Du drame individuel à la tragédie collective: une lecture de *Perpétue ou l'habitude du malheur,*" *Interculturel Francophonies,* no. 13 (juin-juillet), 89-99.

GG1953. Dassi, Etienne: "Le romancier africain et sa responsabilité énonciative: le cas de Mongo Beti." In 499, 237-250.

GG1954. Diouf, Mbaye: "Rire du pouvoir. L'ultime (r)appel de Beti," *Interculturel Francophonies,* no. 13 (juin-juillet), 143-157.

GG1955. Dolisane-Ebosse, Cécile: "Le personnage androgyne chez Mongo Beti: jeu littéraire ou mystique révolutionnaire?," *Interculturel Francophonies,* no. 13 (juin-juillet), 77-87.

GG1956. Kitenge-Ngoy, Tunda: "Mongo Beti et la mise en scène de l'énonciation dans *Mission terminée, Trop de soleil tue l'amour* et *Branle-bas en noir et blanc,*" *Interculturel Francophonies,* no. 13 (juin-juillet), 113-127.

GG1957. Magnier, Julien: "*L'Histoire du fou*: le roman politique postcolonial." In 52, 189-202.

GG1958. Magnier, Julien: "La tension babélienne dans le roman africain francophone de Mongo Beti à Bessora," *Interculturel Francophonies,* no. 13 (juin-juillet), 2211-226. [Bessora]

GG1959. Malela, Buata B.: "Mongo Beti et l'expérience de l'art social." In 102, 367-416.

GG1960. Mambenga, Frédéric: "Mongo Beti: la pertinence réaliste et militante," *Interculturel Francophonies,* no. 13 (juin-juillet), 9-28.

GG1961. Mbondé-Mouangué, Auguste Léopole: "*Branle-bas en noir et blanc* de Mongo Beti ou la représentation d'un monde ébranlé," *Interculturel Francophonies,* no. 13 (juin-juillet), 159-173.

GG1962. Nouago, Marcel: "L'écriture du refus dans *L'Histoire du fou* de Mongo Beti," *Interculturel Francophonies,* no. 13 (juin-juillet), 129-142.

GG1963. Raharimanana, Jean-Luc: "Mongo Beti, l'écriture sans concession. Entretien avec Odile Tobner Biyidi," *Interculturel Francophonies,* no. 13 (juin-juillet), 227-240.

GG1964. Riesz, János: "Les 'filles mères' et la sixa dans *Le Pauvre Christ de Bomba* de Mongo Beti." In 127, 297-317.

GG1965. Tegomo, Guy: "L'autre Mongo Beti: un passeur de savoirs." In 52, 203-213.

GG1966. Tomas, Ilda: "Fornication et évangélisation . . . ou l'art d'aimer chez Mongo Beti," *Interculturel Francophonies,* no. 13 (juin-juillet), 45-59.

GG1967. Vokeng, Guilioh: "Mongo Beti: du roman au polar, ou l'itinéraire d'une dynamique romanesque protéiforme," *Interculturel Francophonies,* no. 13 (juin-juillet), 193-210.

GG1968. Volet, Jean-Marie: "Mongo Beti et la revue *Peuples Noirs-Peuples Africains,*" *Interculturel Francophonies,* no. 13 (juin-juillet), 175-190.

BEY, Maïssa. See also 273a.

GG1969. Bey, Maïssa: "Les cicatrices de l'histoire." In 483, 33-37.

GG1970. Kelle, Michel: "Maïssa Bey, fiction et Histoire," *Algérie Littérature/Action,* no. 119-120 (mars-avril 2008), 55-62.

GG1971. Richter, Elke: " 'Construire mon histoire': Entwürfe des Weiblichen in *Cette fille-là* von Maïssas Bey." In 440, 137-150.

GG1972. Soler, Ana: "La parole au féminin: la narratrice de *Cette fille-là* de Maïssa Bey," *Présence Francophone*, no. 70 (2008), 169-183.

BEYALA, Calixthe.

GG1973. Abomo-Maurin, Marie-Rose: "Jacques Chevrier, lecteur de *C'est le soleil qui m'a brûlée* de Calixthe Beyala." In 72, 481-498.

GG1974. Amabiamina, Flora: "La crise des valeurs: l'éducation désacralisée dans *L'homme qui m'offrait le ciel* de Calixthe Beyala," *LittéRéalité*, vol. 20, no. 2 (automne/hiver 2008), 21-44.

GG1975. Brown, Caroline: "A divine madness: the secret language of trauma in the novels of Bessie Head and Calixthe Beyala," *Comparative Studies of South Asia, Africa and the Middle East*, vol. 28, no. 1 (2008), 93-108.

GG1976. Coly, Ayo Abiétou: "Housing and homing the black female body in France: Calixthe Beyala and the legacy of Sarah Baartman and Josephine Baker." In 392.

GG1977. De Meyer, Bernard: "Tu t'appelleras Beyala, ou la vision de Calixthe," *French Studies in Southern Africa*, no. 38 (2008), 44-62.

GG1978. Ogunyemi, Chikwenye Okonjo: " 'Lunatic writing': the speaking space between the present and the future." In 110.

GG1979. Sarr, Awa: "Mères exigeantes, filles rebelles: une lutte peut en cacher une autre," *Tropos*, no. 34 (printemps 2008), 90-103.

BHÊLY-QUENUM, Olympe. See also 59, 161.

GG1980. Lozes, Guillaume: "*As-tu vu Kokolie?* Une œuvre à part dans l'œuvre d'Olympe Bhêly-Quenum." In 72, 355-364.

BIANCIOTTI, Hector. See also 546.

GG1981. Moronell, El retrato de si mismo en la escritura autobiográfica de Héctor Bianciotti." In 814.

BIORET, J. See 733.

BIYAOULA, Daniel.

GG1982. Cévaër, Françoise: "Les stéréotypes, vecteurs de la *constriction* identitaire chez Biyaoula," *Présence Francophone*, no. 71 (2008), 101-120.

BLAIS, Marie-Claire. See also 4483.

GG1983. • Blais, Marie-Claire: *The collected stage dramas of Marie-Claire Blais.* Trans. and with an introd. by Nigel Spencer. Toronto: Cormorant, 2008.

GG1984. • Blais, Marie-Claire: *Mad shadows.* Trans. Merloyd Lawrence; afterword by Daphne Marlatt. Toronto: McClelland & Stewart, 2008. 135 p.

GG1985. • Blais, Marie-Claire: *A season in the life of Emmanuel.* Trans. Derek Coltman; introd. Priscila Uppal; essay by Kirsty Bell. Holstein, Ont.: Exile Editions, 2008. 161 p.

GG1986. • Blais, Marie-Claire: *The Wolf.* Trans. Sheila Fischman; introd. Shyam Selvadurai. Holstein, Ont.: Exile Editions, 2008. xii, 129 p.

GG1987. • *Visions poétiques de Marie-Claire Blais.* Ed. Janine Ricouart, Roseanna Dufault; préface de Nicole Brossard. Montréal: Remue-Ménage, 2008. 323 p.

GG1988. Bell, Kirsty: "Portraits d'Héloïse dans l'édition illustrée d'*Une saison dans la vie d'Emmanuel*." In 1987, 52-69.

GG1989. Bolanger, Ghislaine: "L'une passe-t-elle sans l'autre? Le problème des solidarités identitaires dans *L'Ange de la solitude*." In 1987, 211-229.

GG1990. Dufault, Roseanna: "Comment immortaliser les martyrs des années 1960?" In 1987, 181-192.

GG1991. Egloff, Karin: "Un jeu d'enfants: *L'Exécution* de Marie-Claire Blais." In 1987, 161-171.

GG1992. Lamar, Celita: "Amour et haine sous un soleil éclatant." In 1987, 172-180.

GG1993. Leblanc, Julie: "Des carnets d'écriture aux tapuscrits annotés: vers une étude de la genèse du Testament de Jean-Le-Maigre à ses frères." In 1987, 70-89.

GG1994. Maclennan, Oriel C. L.; John A. Barnstead: "Marie-Claire Blais et Dostoïevski." In 1987, 136-160.

GG1995. Oore, Irène: "Le désert dans l'œuvre romanesque de Marie-Claire Blais." In 1987, 123-135.

GG1996.   Pich Ponce, Eva: "La haine de Cendrillon ou la ré-écriture du conte dans *La Belle Bête* de Marie-Claire Blais." In 894, 221-234.

GG1997.   Ricouart, Janine: "Bibliographie sur Marie-Claire Blais." In 1987, 262-319.

GG1998.   Ricouart, Janine: "Poète et politique: entretien avec Marie-Claire Blais." In 1987, 26-34.

GG1999.   Ricouart, Janine: "Vision politique de Marie-Claire Blais." In 1987, 243-261.

GG2000.   Roy, Nathalie: "La caractérisation de l'espace dans *Soifs*." In 1987, 90-107.

GG2001.   Suhonen, Katri: "De l'humour noir au rire jaune: les mécanismes textuels de l'ironie chez Marie-Claire Blais et Rosa Liksom," *Tangence*, no. 84 (2007), [n.p.].

GG2002.   Suhonen, Katri: " 'L'obscène présence de l'hiver' dans la fiction de Marie-Claire Blais." In 1987, 108-122.

GG2003.   Tardif, Karine: "La bibliothèque imaginaire de l'humanité souffrante dans la trilogie *Soifs* de Marie-Claire Blais," *Etudes Françaies*, vol. 44, no. 3 (2008), 141-157.

GG2004.   Vaucher Gravili, Anne de: "L'île paradisiaque de Marie-Claire Blais." In 423.

GG2005.   Vaucher Gravili, Anne de: "La lumière des eaux dans l'imaginaire de Marie-Claire Blais." In 1987, 230-242.

GG2006.   Vergereau-Dewey, S. Pascale: "Vision blaisienne de l'enfance: le salut par l'écriture." In 1987, 37-51.

GG2007.   Woodhull, Winifred: "Figurations littéraires et cinématographiques de la toxicomanie." In 1987, 193-210.

BLANCHARD, Maurice. See 6785.

BLANCHOT, Maurice. See also 477, 624, 633, 949, 1004, 3154, 3632, 4574.

GG2008.   ● Bident, Christophe: *Maurice Blanchot: partenaire invisible: essai biographique*. Seyssel: Champ Vallon, 2008. 634 p. [Original edition, 1998]

GG2009.   ● Blanchot, Maurice: *Ecrits politiques: 1953-1993*. Textes choisis, établis et annotés par Ereic Hoppenot. Paris: Gallimard, 2008. *Les cahiers de la NRF*. 266 p.

GG2010.   ● Blanchot, Maurice: *Das Neutrale: Philosophische Schriften und Fragment*. Kommentiert und übers. von Marcus Coelen. Berlin: Diaphanes, 2008. *TransPositionen*. 272 p.

GG2011.   ● Gilonne, Yves: *La rhétorique du sublime dans l'œuvre de Maurice Blanchot*. Paris: L'Harmattan, 2008. *Ouverture philosophique*. 274 p.

GG2012.   ● Kai, Gohara: *Il y a de l'image: Maurice Blanchot et l'image minimale de la littérature*. Lille: ANRT, 2008. *Thèse à la carte*. 389 p.

GG2013.   ● Lannoy, Jean-Luc: *Langage, perception, mouvement: Blanchot et Merleau-Ponty*. Grenoble: J. Millon, 2008. *Krisis*. 347 p. [Merleau-Ponty]

GG2014.   ● *Maurice Blanchot, de proche en proche*. Dir. Eric Hoppenot, coord. par Daiana Manoury. Paris: Complicités, 2008. *Compagnie de Maurice Blanchot*. 284 p.

GG2015.   ● Yasuhara, Shinichiro: *Maurice Blanchot dans les années 1930: la dissidence politique et la perfection littéraire*. Lille ANRT, 2008. *Thèse à la carte*. 363 p.

GG2016.   Antonioli, Manola: "Entre Blanchot et Derrida," *Chimères: Revue des Schizoanalyses*, no. 66-67 (2007-2008), 133-144. [Derrida]

GG2017.   Antonioli, Manola: "Blanchot et Michel Foucault." In 2014, 131-151. [Foucault]

GG2018.   Benjamin, Andrew: "Another naming, a living animal: Blanchot's community," *Substance*, vol. 37, no. 3 [no. 117] (2008), 207-227.

GG2019.   Bietlot, Mathieu: "Blanchot et Hegel." In 2014, 11-30.

GG2020.   Bird, Gregory: "Community beyond hypostasis: Nancy responds to Blanchot," *Angelaki*, vol. 13, no. 1 (April 2008), 3-26.

GG2021.   Chan, Wai-chung: "The insistence of literature in Blanchot and Derrida." Diss., Univ. of Hong Kong, 2008. vi, 219 p. [Derrida]

GG2022.   Cools, Arthur: "Blanchot et Levinas." In 2014, 31-47. [Levinas]

GG2023.   Durand, Thierry: "Blanchot, Antelme, Levinas." In 2014, 49-70. [Antelme, Levinas]

GG2024.   Farbman, Herschel: "Dream and writing in Blanchot." In 455.

GG2025.   Gilonne, Yves: "Blanchot lecteur de Paulhan." In 2014, 153-174. [Paulhan]

GG2026. Halsberghe, Christophe: "Blanchot et Bataille ou les limites d'une entente." In 2014, 245-263. [Bataille]

GG2027. Hoppenot, Eric: "Ecriture et fatigue dans les œuvres de Barthes et Blanchot." In 2014, 175-192. [Barthes]

GG2028. Just, Daniel: "The politics of the novel and Maurice Blanchot's theory of the *récit*, 1954-1964," *French Forum*, vol. 33, no. 1-2 (2008), 121-139. .

GG2029. Just, Daniel: "Weakness as a form of engagement: Maurice Blanchot on the figure of the last man," *Forum for Modern Language Studies*, vol. 44, no. 1 (2008), 40-52.

GG2030. Lavauzelle, Stéphane: "Claude Louis-Combet et Blanchot." In 2014, 103-127. [Louis-Combet]

GG2031. Manoury, Daiana: "Blanchot, Michaux et Butor." In 2014, 193-208. [Butor, Michaux]

GG2032. Milon, Alain: "Blanchot, lecteur de René Char." In 2014, 209-220. [Char]

GG2033. Opelz, Hannes: "Blanchot, Valéry et 'l'œuvre'." In 2014, 71-86. [Valéry]

GG2034. Secchieri, Filippo: "Poetica e fenomenologia del frammento in Maurice Blanchot," *Strumenti Critici*, anno 23, n. 118 (sett. 2008), 389-416.

GG2035. Smith, Douglas: "Redrawing the hexagon: the space of culture in Malraux and Blanchot." In 629. [Malraux]

GG2036. Sollers, Philippe: "Blanchot l'extrême," *Infini*, no. 104 (automne 2008), 9-11.

GG2037. Sweedler, Milo: "Tabula rasa: Blanchot and the terror." In 617, 95-103.

GG2038. Teixeira, Vincent: "Blanchot et Paul Celan." In 2014, 221-242.

GG2039. Tremblay, Thierry: "La part divine: Blanchot et Klossowski." In 2014, 265-281. [Klossowski]

GG2040. Vande Veire, Frank: " 'La peur, le manque de peur': quotidienneté, angoisse et mort chez Heidegger et Blanchot." In 2014, 87-102.

GG2041. Venturino, Steven J.: "The notorious jumping reader of Calaveras County: Twain, Blanchot, and a dialectic of storytelling," *Midwest Quarterly*, vol. 49, no. 4 (Summer 2008), 374-387.

GG2042. Weller, Shane: " 'Ce mot sec et latin par surcroît': Maurice Blanchot, literature and nihilisme," *Forum for Modern Language Studies*, vol. 44, no. 3 (2008), 307-321.

GG2043. Weller, Shane: "The naïve calculation of the negative." In 989.

GG2044. Zanetta, Julien: "Lois de l'aveugle: notes sur *La Folie du jour*," *MLN*, vol. 123, no. 5 (Dec. 2008), 1127-1140.

BLANZAT, Jean.

GG2045. ● Lagarde-Escoffier, Christine: *Jean Blanzat: de l'héritage à l'hérésie.* Limoges: PULIM, 2008. 346 p.

BLIN, Roger. See 606.

BLOCH, Jean-Richard.

GG2046. ● Bloch, Jean-Richard: *Un théâtre engagé.* Prés. d'Antoinette Blum. Bruxelles: Complexe, 2008. 206 p.

GG2047. Autrand, Michel: "Le bureau de Jean-Richard Bloch," *Etudes Jean-Richard Bloch*, no. 14 (2008), 188-207.

GG2048. Barilier, Etienne: "Je suis un aryen, entendez-vous?" In 388, 145-152.

GG2049. Bouju, Marie-Cécile: "Jean-Richard Bloch dans le champ éditorial français de la Libération," *Etudes Jean-Richard Bloch*, no. 14 (2008), 137-151.

GG2050. Cœuré, Sophie: "Intellectuels 'en certitude'? Jean-Richard Bloch et les engagements communistes à la veille de la Guerre froide," *Etudes Jean-Richard Bloch*, no. 14 (2008), 165-173.

GG2051. Courban, Alexandre: "*Ce soir*, un quotidien communiste 'indépendant' entre guerre et Guerre froide," *Etudes Jean-Richard Bloch*, no. 14 (2008), 153-163.

GG2052. Fhima, Catherine: "Jean-Richard Bloch, ou comment concilier judaïsme et socialisme," *Etudes Jean-Richard Bloch*, no. 14 (2008), 61-83.

GG2053. Gorilovics, Tivadar: "Jean-Richard Bloch dans les dictionnaires de littérature," *Etudes Jean-Richard Bloch*, no. 14 (2008), 215-222.

GG2054. Gorilovics, Tivadar: "Un poème de jeunesse d'inspiration religieuse de Jean-Richard Bloch," *Etudes Jean-Richard Bloch*, no. 14 (2008), 59-62.

GG2055. Niogret, Philippe: "Jean-Richard Bloch et quelques intellectuels chrétiens," *Etudes Jean-Richard Bloch*, no. 14 (2008), 208-214.

GG2056. Poulaille, Henry: "Jean-Richard Bloch, l'homme et l'écrivain," *Etudes Jean-Richard Bloch*, no. 14 (2008), 70-76.

GG2057. Scaviner, Isabelle: "La pièce *Toulon*," *Etudes Jean-Richard Bloch*, no. 14 (2008), 84-101.

GG2058. Stern, Ludmila: " 'Prisonnier d'amitié': Jean-Richard Bloch et ses correspondants soviétiques," *Etudes Jean-Richard Bloch*, no. 14 (2008), 103-121.

GG2059. Trébitsch, Michel: "Jean-Richard Bloch et la défense de la culture," *Etudes Jean-Richard Bloch*, no. 14 (2008), 12-28.

GG2060. Vamos, Eva: " 'De Paris à Prague à tire-d'aile dans les nuées'. Jean-Richard Bloch et les écrivains d'Europe centrale," *Etudes Jean-Richard Bloch*, no. 14 (2008), 123-135.

GG2061. Vamos, Eva: "La mémoire d'une famille: une contribution au destin du roman . . . *Et Compagnie*," *Etudes Jean-Richard Bloch*, no. 14 (2008), 63-66.

BLOCH, Marc.

GG2062. Detienne, Marcel; Janet Lloyd: "Saint Marc Bloch." In 426.

BLONDEL, Maurice. See also 5406.

GG2063. ● Bernardi, Peter J.: *Maurice Blondel, social Catholicism, and Action française: the clash over the church's role in society during the modernist era.* Washington: Catholic Univ. of America, 2008.

GG2064. ● *Maurice Blondel, dignité du politique et philosophie de l'action.* Ed. Marie-Jeanne Coutagne et Pierre de Cointet. Paris: Parole et silence, 2006.

GG2065. ● Müller, Andreas Uwe: *Christlicher Glaube und historische Kritik: Maurice Blondel und Alfred Loisy im Ringen um das Verhältnis von Schrift und Tradition.* Freiburg: Herder, 2008. *Freiburger theologische Studien.* 357 p.

GG2066. ● Murgia, Daniela: *La filosofia dell'azione di Maurice Blondel.* Napoli: Luciano, 2008. 244 p.

GG2067. Mandolini, Clara: "Action, work, and education in Blondel," *Analecta Husserliana*, vol. 95 (2008), 163-194.

GG2068. "The new philosophy of Maurice Blondel." In 790.

GG2069. Sutton, Michael: "Des opposants à l'Action française: Maurice Blondel, son influence, et le repositionnement de Jacques Maritain." In 348. [Maritain]

BLONDIN, Antoine.

GG2070. Dambre, Marc: "Du militant au libertin: les premiers romans de Blondin et de Nimier." In 456, 147-157. [Nimier]

BLOY, Léon.

GG2071. ● *Léon Bloy en verve.* Prés. et choix Hubert Juin. Paris: Horay, 2008. 124 p.

GG2072. ● *Sur Le Désespéré. Dossier 1.* Textes réunis par Pierre Glaudes. Caen: Lettres modernes Minard, 2008. *Revue des Lettres Modernes*; *Léon Bloy*, 7. 261 p.

GG2073. ● *Sur Le Désespéré. Dossier 2.* Textes réunis par Pierre Glaudes. Caen: Lettres modernes Minard, 2008. *Revue des Lettres Modernes*; *Léon Bloy*, 8. 231 p.

GG2074. Berg, Christian: "Abjections de Bloy." In 592, 45-58.

GG2075. "Le cas Bloy: polémique en Belgique." In 2072, 238-259.

GG2076. Fontana, Michèle: "*Le Désespéré*, un monstre de roman." In 2072, 61-74.

GG2077. Foucart, Claude: "Léon Bloy et l'Allemagne." In 461, 33-42.

GG2078. Galpérine, Alexis: "Léon Bloy et la musique." In 2072, 165-208.

GG2079. Galpérine-Gilles de Pelichy, Natacha: "Liberté et solidarité chez Bloy et Dostoïevski." In 2073, 197-228.

GG2080. Georges-Métral, Alice de: "Pour une poétique bloyenne." In 2073, 83-101.

GG2081. Giné Janer, Marta: "Léon Bloy dans le journal de Ricardo Viñes." In 2072, 209-220.

GG2082. Glaudes, Pierre: "Le sublime et le grotesque dans *Le Désespéré*." In 2072, 127-144.

GG2083. Glenisson, Jean-Louis: "Les manuscrits bloyens dans les collections publiques françaises." In 2073, 165-196.

GG2084.	Griffiths, Richard: "Désespoir romantique et douleur chrétienne." In 2072, 93-105.

GG2085.	Guyot, Gaëlle: *"Le Désespéré*, roman épistolaire?" In 2073, 11-31.

GG2086.	Huet-Brichard, Marie-Catherine: *"Le Désespéré*, une écriture de la révolte." In 2072, 47-60.

GG2087.	Massoulier, Nicolas: "La question du père." In 2073, 49-68.

GG2088.	Melmoux-Montaubin, Marie-Françoise: *"Le Désespéré*, roman de Marchenoir?" In 2072, 75-92.

GG2089.	Millet-Gérard, Dominique: "Bloy et Huysmans." In 2073, 103-118. [Huysmans]

GG2090.	Negrello, Gilles: *"Le Désespéré*, roman générationnel." In 2073, 33-48.

GG2091.	Novakovic, Jelena: "Ivo Andric, lecteur du *Désespéré*." In 2073, 149-162.

GG2092.	Parisse, Lydie: *"Le Désespéré* de Léon Bloy: le *pur amour* comme modèle herméneutique." In 2072, 145-161.

GG2093.	Parisse, Lydie: "Une figure de convertisseur à l'aube du XXe siècle. Léon Bloy, de la conversionn religieuse à la 'métanoïa'," *Manchette*, no. 3 (2004), 229-239.

GG2094.	Royer, Joseph: "Un parricide laborieux. Etude génétique de l'incipit dans *Le Désespéré*." In 2072, 13-46.

GG2095.	Solal, Jérôme: "Bloy romancier: différence sexuelle et destruction volontaire." In 2073, 69-82.

GG2096.	Van Balberghe, Emile: "La conspiration du silence." In 2073, 119-135.

GG2097.	Van den Heede, Philippe: "Un 'hors norme' normatif: Léon Bloy dans la critique littéraire de Léopold Levaux." In 2072, 221-235.

GG2098.	Vibert, Bertrand: "Ceci n'est pas de la littérature, ou l'expérience tragique de *Désespéré*." In 2072, 107-126.

GG2099.	Walbecq, Eric: "Présence du *Désespéré* dans le *Journal*." In 2073, 137-148.

BLUTSCH, Hervé. See 1319.

BOBIN, Christian. See also 644.

GG2100.	Martineau, Anne; "Albain et la dame du lac gelé: essai sur *Geai* de Christian Bobin." In 96, 197-204.

BODART, Roger.

GG2101.	Fréché, Bibiane: "Pouvoir, littérature et réseaux en Belgique francophone: Roger Bodart (1910-1973)," *Études de Lettres*, no. 279 [no. 1] (2008), 55-70.

BON, François. See also 595, 708, 761.

GG2102.	• Viart, Dominique: *François Bon: étude de l'œuvre.* Paris: Bordas, 2008. *Ecrivains au présent.* 191 p.

GG2103.	Korthals Altes, Liesbeth: "Traces: writing the visual in *Daewoo* by François Bon," *Yale French Studies*, no. 114 (2008), 80-94.

GG2104.	Krebs, Constance: "Archaïsmes et nouveauté." In 819, 171-183.

GG2105.	Michel, Raymond: "François Bon, *Daewoo*: le bonheur des mots pour dire le malheur du corps." In 619, 107-141.

BONI, Tanella.

GG2106.	Boni, Tanella: "Ecrire en état d'urgence: texte et contexte." In 96, 47-57.

BONNEFOY, Yves. See also 691a, 1012, 1018, 1043, 2295, 6977.

GG2107.	• Buchs, Arnaud: *Une pensée en mouvement: trois essais sur Yves Bonnefoy.* Paris: Galilée, 2008. *Lignes fictives.* 107 p.

GG2108.	• Dotoli, Giovanni: *Yves Bonnefoy dans la fabrique de la traduction.* Paris: Hermann, 2008. *Savoir.* 165 p.

GG2109.	• *Poétique et ontologie: colloque international Yves Bonnefoy.* Yves Bonnefoy [et al.]. Bordeaux: ARDUA; William Blake, 2008. 255 p.

GG2110.	Aquien, Michèle: "Le langage 'en rêve' d'Yves Bonnefoy: une lecture de *Rue Traversière*." In 516, 253-278.

GG2111.	Avice, Jean-Paul: "Sur un poème déchiré d'Yves Bonnefoy." In 521, 279-298.

GG2112.	Canadas, Serge: "Arcadies, ou comment habiter la terre en poète." In 2109, 29-47.

GG2113.   Cavallini, Concetta: "Le nom et la nomination chez Yves Bonnefoy," *Studi Francesi*, anno 52, fasc. 2 (maggio-agosto 2008), 413-424.

GG2114.   Cavallini, Concetta: "Yves Bonnefoy poète de la 'mélancolie'," *Bérénice*, anno 15, n. 40-41 (nov. 2008), 168-183.

GG2115.   Caws, Mary-Ann: "Yves Bonnefoy en communication." In 2109, 133-140.

GG2116.   Demangeat, Michel: "Dans le leurre du seuil. Désir d'être au-delà." In 2109, 61-72.

GG2117.   Drouet, Pascale: " 'Elle prend vie, elle va parler': Shakespeare et Bonnefoy à l'écoute de voix féminines," *Littérature*, no. 150 (juin 2008), 40-55.

GG2118.   Edwards, Michael: "Yves Bonnefoy et les *Sonnets* de Shakespeare," *Littérature*, no. 150 (juin 2008), 25-39.

GG2119.   Grun, Jean-Paul: "La machinerie picturale dans *L'Arrière-pays*." In 2109, 197-216.

GG2120.   Himy, Olivier: "Temps du souvenir et temps du rêve chez Yves Bonnefoy." In 2109, 217-229.

GG2121.   Khodr, Fadi: "Yves Bonnefoy et la réécriture du mythe." In 520, 787-795.

GG2122.   Labarthe, Patrick: "La cérémonie de l'obscur: Yves Bonnefoy et Racine." In 2109, 95-110.

GG2123.   Labarthe, Patrick: " 'N'allons pas plus avant . . .': un vers de *Phèdre* dans l'œuvre de Bonnefoy," *Versants*, vol. 55, no. 1 (2008), 143-159.

GG2124.   Labarthe, Patrick: "Yves Bonnefoy et la question de l'éloge lyrique." In 1014, 449-467.

GG2125.   Lafond, Natacha: "A l'écoute du 'peu sonore' dans la poésie d'Yves Bonnefoy." In 382, 353-366.

GG2126.   Landi, Michela: "Yves Bonnefoy et la traduction: l'enseignement et l'exemple de l'Italie," *Littérature*, no. 150 (juin 2008), 56-69.

GG2127.   Legrand, Yolande: "Yves Bonnefoy et Alfred de Vigny." In 2109, 111-122.

GG2128.   Martínez, Patricia: "Critique et poésie." In 2109, 165-179.

GG2129.   Michaud, Stéphane: "Bonnefoy et Deguy," *Nouvelle Revue Française*, no. 585 (avril 2008), 267-271. [Deguy]

GG2130.   Michel, Jean-Paul: "Yves Bonnefoy, *Goya, Les peintures noires*." In 2109, 141-147.

GG2131.   Naughton, John: "L'autobiographie de l'autre." In 2109, 189-196.

GG2132.   Navarri, Roger: "Situation d'Yves Bonnefoy." In 2109, 21-28.

GG2133.   Née, Patrick: "De la *critique poétique* selon Yves Bonnefoy," *Littérature*, no. 150 (juin 2008), 85-124.

GG2134.   Née, Patrick: "Du rôle de l'art." In 2109, 73-94.

GG2135.   Nuti, Marco: "Poétique de la présence: Cézanne et l'épiphanie de la vision chez Bonnefoy." In 542, 141-162.

GG2136.   Rabaté, Dominique: "L'appel des voix." In 2109, 231-245.

GG2137.   Scotto, Fabio: "Yves Bonnefoy traducteur de Leopardi et de Pétrarque," *Littérature*, no. 150 (juin 2008), 70-83.

GG2138.   Seilhean, Alain: "Le miroir poétique et la quête originelle." In 2109, 49-60.

GG2139.   Tucoo-Chala, Jean: "Georges Séféris et Yves Bonnefoy à l'écoute des pierres du *Roi d'Asiné*." In 2109, 123-131.

GG2140.   Verret, Guy: "Yves Bonnefoy, poète de la traduction." In 2109, 181-187.

GG2141.   Verret, Monique: "Du dessin à la poésie." In 2109, 247-254.

GG2142.   Vouilloux, Bernard: "Une histoire d'art en quête de sens." In 2109, 149-164.

GG2143.   Zach, Matthias: "Rhythms in poetic translation: Bonnefoy and Shakespeare." In 575, 43-57.

BONONO, Angéline Solange. See 208.

BORY, Jean-François.

GG2144.   Lespiau, David: "Jean-François Bory. D'une nuit du signe à l'image," *Critique*, tome 64, no. 735-736 (août-sept. 2008), 677-688.

BOSCHÈRE, Jean de.

GG2145. Jago-Antoine, Véronique: "L'obscur entre mots et images: le fond Jean de Boschère aux Archives et Musée de la littérature de Bruxelles." In 44, 123-143.

BOSCO, Henri. See also 420, 7590.

GG2146. ● *Henri Bosco et le métier de romancier*. Textes réunis par Alain Tassel. Paris: L'Harmattan, 2008. 289 p.

GG2147. Arouimi, Michel: "La quête mythique d'Henri Bosco dans *L'Enfant et la Rivière*." In 520, 617-629.

GG2148. Mariani, Marinella: "De l'autre côté de l'écriture: Bosco rêveur de temps dans les récits d'enfance." In 618.

GG2149. Neiss, Benoît: "Un romancier inactuel, Bosco devant Dieu," *Travaux de Littérature*, tome 21 (2008), 441-457.

GG2150. Riegert, Guy: "De Naples à Lourmarin, une amitié méditerranéenne." In 515, 49-55. [Jean Grenier]

BOSQUET, Alain. See also 727.

GG2151. Poulton, Leslee: "L'influence des 'autres' dans l'œuvre d'Alain Bosquet." In 442, 151-161.

BOUCHARD, Hervé.

GG2152. Bouchard, Hervé: "Lecteurs et amis sont invités à y assister," *Liberté*, no. 277 (2007), 79-88. [Entretien]

GG2153. Canty, Daniel: "Le livre de boue et la robe de bois," *Liberté*, no. 277 (2007), 63-78.

BOUCHARD, Michel Marc. See also 1107.

GG2154. Curran, Beverley: "Speaking lily-white: Michel Marc Bouchard's *Les feluettes* as JQ translation." In 1081.

BOUDJEDRA, Rachid. See also 230, 2396, 4254, 6171.

GG2155. ● Lotodé, Valérie: *Le lecteur virtuel de Rachid Boudjedra*. Lille: ANRT, 2008. 450 p.

GG2156. Calargé, Carla A.: "Le carnaval," *Cincinnati Romance Review*, vol. 26 (2007), 10-23.

BOUNDZEKI, Emmanuel.

GG2157. Coulibaly, Moussa: "Paradoxes de l'identité: de la déconstruction à la construction identitaire dans *Les petits garçons naissent aussi des étoiles* d'Emmanuel Boundzeki," *LittéRéalité*, vol. 20, no. 2 (automne/hiver 2008), 45-57.

BOURAOUI, Hédi.

GG2158. ● Bouraoui, Hédi: *Puglia with open arms*. Trans., introd. Elizabeth Sabiston. Toronto: CMC, 2008. 77 p.

GG2159. ● Bouraoui, Hédi: *Thus speaks the CN tower*. Trans., preface Elizabeth Sabiston. Toronto: CMC, 2008. 319 p.

GG2160. ● *Perspectives critiques: l'œuvre d'Hédi Bouraoui*. Sous la dir. de Elizabeth Sabiston et Suzanne Crosta. Sudbury, Ont.: Université Laurentienne, 2007. viii, 415 p.

GG2161. Buono, Angela: "Hédi Bouraoui: l'écriture en mouvement," *Rivista di Studi Canadesi*, n. 20 (2007), 135-142.

GG2162. Buono, Angela: "Un modèle d'écriture migratoire: *La Transpoétique* d'Hédi Bouraoui." In 104, 237-248.

GG2163. D'Ambrosio, Nicola: "Entretien avec Hédi Bouraoui," *Rivista di Studi Canadesi*, n. 21 (2008), 123-130.

GG2164. D'Ambrosio, Nicola: "Il mosaico canadese in *Ainsi parle la tour CN* di Hédi Bouraouoi," *Rivista di Studi Canadesi*, n. 20 (2007), 113-127.

BOURAOUI, Nina. See also 230, 345, 584.

GG2165. Höfer, Bernadette: "Regard, violence et mutisme: la relation père-filles dans *La Voyeuse interdite* de Nina Bouraoui." In 572, 125-133.

GG2166. Lebadi, Benaouda: "Identity: bodies and voices in Coetzee's *Disgrace* and Bouraoui's *Garçon manqué*." In 395, 33-43.

GG2167. Struve, Karen: " 'Je passe de Yasmina à Nina. De Nina à Ahmed. D'Ahmed à Brio': Überlegungen zu einer *écriture transculturelle* am Beispiel von Nina bouraouis *Garçon manqué*." In 440, 119-136.

BOURDIEU, Pierre. See also 970, 981.

GG2168. ● Bongaerts, Gregor: *Verdrängungen des Ökonomischen: Bourdieus Theorie der Moderne*. Bielefeld: Transcript, 2008. *Sozialtheorie*. 382 p.

GG2169. ● Bourdieu, Pierre: *Language and symbolic power*. Ed. and introd. John B. Thompson. Cambridge: Polity Press, 2008. ix, 302 p.

GG2170. ● Bourdieu, Pierre: *Political interventions: social science and political action*. Texts selected and introduced by Franck Poupeau and Thierry Discepolo; trans. David Fernbach. London; New York: Verso, 2008. xviii, 398 p.

GG2171. ● *Bourdieu und die Linke: Politik, Ökonomie, Kultur*. Effi Böhlke, Rainer Rilling, Hrsg. Berlin: Dietz, 2007. 319 p.

GG2172. ● Champagne, Patrick: *Pierre Bourdieu*. Toulouse: Milan, 2008. 63 p.

GG2173. ● Hanks, William: *Língua como prática social: das relações entre língua, cultura e sociedade a partir de Bourdieu e Bakhtin*. Sã Paolo: Cortez Editora, 2008. 280 p.

GG2174. ● Jurt, Joseph: *Bourdieu*. Stuttgart: Reclam, 2008. 129 p.

GG2175. ● Kajetzke, Laura: *Wissen im Diskurs: ein Theorienvergleich von Bourdieu und Foucault*. Wiesbaden: Verlag für Sozialwissenschaft, 2008. 199 p. [Foucault]

GG2176. ● Lescourret, Marie-Anne: *Pierre Bourdieu: vers une économie du bonheur*. Paris: Flammarion, 2008. *Grandes biographies*. 538 p.

GG2177. ● Marqués Perales, Ildefonso: *Génesis de la teoría social de Pierre Bourdieu*. Madrid: Centro de Investigaciones Sociológicas, 2008. 368 p.

GG2178. ● Martin-Criado, Enrique: *Les deux Algéries de Pierre Bourdieu*. Trad. Hélène Bretin. Bellecombe-en-Bauges: Croquant, 2008. 125 p.

GG2179. ● *Nach Bourdieu: Visualität, Kunst, Politik*. HRsg. Beatrice von Bismarck, Therese Kaurmann, Ulf Wuggenig. Wien: Turia + Kant, 2008. 361 p.

GG2180. ● *Pierre Bourdieu and literary education*. Ed. James Albright and Allan Luke. New York: Routledge, 2008. xii, 380 p.

GG2181. ● *Pierre Bourdieu: key concepts*. Ed. Michael Grenfell. Stocksfield: Acumen, 2008. viii, 248 p.

GG2182. ● *Pierre Bourdieu: son œuvre, son héritage*. Auxerre: Sciences humaines, 2008. 127 p.

GG2183. ● *Politik-Programme-Projekte: menschenorientierte Entwicklungszusammenarbeit im Sinne von Bourdieu*. Hrsg. Elisabeth Gotschi, Andreas Hunger, Klaus Zapotoczky. Linz: Trauner, 2007. vi, 197 p.

GG2184. ● *Symbolische Gewalt: Herrschaftsanalyse nach Pierre Bourdieu*. Hrsg. Robert Schmidt, Volker Woltersdorff. Konstanz: UVK Verlagsgesellschaft, 2008. 316 p.

GG2185. ● Wolfreys, Jim: *Political Bourdieu: anti-capitalism and the public intellectual*. London: Pluto, 2008.

GG2186. Aisenberg, Andrew: "Bourdieu, ambiguity, and the significance of events," *Differences*, vol. 19, no. 2 (Summer 2008), 82-98.

GG2187. Bennett, Tony: "Habitus clivé: aesthetics and politics in the work of Pierre Bourdieu." In 850.

GG2188. Bennett, Tony: "The historical universal: the role of cultural value in the historical sociology of Pierre Bourdieu." In 931.

GG2189. Bosteels, Bruno: "Translator's introduction: staging Bourdieu," *Theatre Survey*, vol. 49, no. 2 (Nov. 2008), 183-186.

GG2190. Bruun, Hans Henrik: "Objectivity, value spheres, and 'inherent laws': on some suggestive isomorphisms between Weber, Bourdieu, and Luhmann," *Philosophy of the Social Sciences*, vol. 38, no. 1 (March 2008), 97-120.

GG2191. Dobbin, F.: "The poverty of organizational theory: Comment on: 'Bourdieu and organizational analysis'," *Theory and Society*, vol. 37, no. 1 (Feb. 2008), 53-63.

GG2192. Eagleton, Mary: "Mapping contemporary women's fiction after Bourdieu," *Women: A Cultural Review*, vol. 19, no. 1 (Spring 2008), 5-20.

GG2193. Emirbayer, M.; V. Johnson: "Bourdieu and organizational analysis," *Theory and Society*, vol. 37, no. 1 (Feb. 2008), 1-44.

GG2194. Grant, Rachel; Shelley Wong: "Critical race perspectives: Bourdieu and language education." In 2180.

GG2195. Heller, Monica: "Bourdieu and 'literary education'." In 2180.

GG2196. Hultin, Jeremy F.: "Bourdieu reads Jude." In 858.

GG2197. Kramsch, Claire: "Pierre Bourdieu: a biographical memoir." In 2180.

GG2198. Lamont Hill, Marc: "Towards a pedagogy of the popular: Bourdieu, hip-hop, and out-of-school literacies." In 2180.

GG2199. Luke, Allan: "Using Bourdieu to make policy." In 2180.

GG2200. Markham, Tim: "Bourdieusian political theory and social science: the field of war correspondence 1990-2003." Diss., Univ. of Oxford, 2008. 237 p.

GG2201. Osborne, Thomas: "Bourdieu, ethics and reflexivity." In 970.

GG2202. Schultheis, Franz: "Salvation goods and domination: Pierre Bourdieu's sociology of the religious field." In 862.

GG2203. Swartz, D. L.: "Bringing Bourdieu's master concepts into organizational analysis," *Theory and Society*, vol. 37, no. 1 (Feb. 2008), 45-52.

GG2204. Trigg, Andrew B.: "Deriving the Engel curve: Pierre Bourdieu and the social critique of Maslow's hierarchy of needs." In 808.

GG2205. Vaughan, D.: "Bourdieu and organizations: the empirical challenge," *Theory and Society*, vol. 37, no. 1 (Feb. 2008), 65-81.

BOURDOUXHE, Madeleine. See also 7302.

GG2206. Kovacshazy, Cécile: "Relire Madeleine Bourdouxhe," *Roman 20-50*, no. 45 (2008), 159-172.

BOURGEAT, François.

GG2207. Richter, Elke: "Réalité et construction imaginaire de l'Histoire dans *La Nuit Algérie* de François Bourgeat." In 483, 53-68.

BOURGET, Paul. See also 558, 702, 5713, 6395.

GG2208. Chaitin, Gilbert D.: "*The disciple*, by Paul Bourget: a dangerous experiment in education." In 405.

GG2209. Clavaron, Yves: "La colonne solitaire de Capo Colonna: herméneutique d'un martyre archéologique par Bourget, Gissing et Douglas." In 528, 103-112.

GG2210. Hibbitt, Richard: "Le roman d'analyse et le romanesque: la représentation de l'héritage psychologique chez Paul Bourget." In 908, 175-189.

GG2211. Twain, Mark: "A little note to M. Paul Bourget." In 877.

GG2212. Twain, Mark: "What Paul Bourget thinks of us." In 877.

GG2213. Wittman, Laura: "Mystical insight and psychology in the fin-de-siècle novel," *Forum Italicum*, vol. 42, no. 1 (Spring 2008), 30-51. [Huysmans]

BOUSQUET, Joë. See also 7709.

GG2214. ● Bousquet, Joë: *Lettres à une jeune fille*. Introduction et notes de Nicolas Brimo. Paris: B. Grasset, 2008. 312 p.

BOUVIER, Nicolas.

GG2215. ● Bouvier, Nicolas: *L'œil du voyageur*. Introd. Daniel Girardin. Paris: Hoëbeke; Lausanne: Musée de l'Elysée, 2008. 117 p.

GG2216. ● Laut, François: *Nicolas Bouvier: l'œil qui écrit*. Paris: Payot, 2008. 318 p.

GG2217. ● Lecloux, Frédéric: *L'usure du monde: hommage à Nicolas Bouvier*. Préface d'Eliane Bouvier; postface de Christian Caujolle. Manosque: Bec en l'air, 2008. 238 p.

GG2218. ● *Oreille [L'] du voyageur: Nicolas Bouvier de Genève à Tokyo*. Dir. Hervé Guyader. Carouge: Zoé, 2008. 143 p.

GG2219. Guyon, Laurence: " 'C'que c'est beau la photographie!'." In 508, 487-495.

GG2220. Taguchi, Aki: "Nicolas Bouvier et le Japon." In 453, 269-279.

BOVE, Emmanuel.

GG2221. Macho Vargas, Azucena: "*La dernière nuit* d'Emmanuel Bove: culpabilité sans regret," *Thélème*, no. 23 (2008), 75-85.

BRASSENS, Georges.

GG2222. ● Agid, Didier: *Brassens*. Reims: Fradet, 2008. 154 p.

GG2223. ● Brassens, Georges: *Les chemins qui ne mènent pas à Rome: réflexions et maximes d'un libertaire*. Edition établie et prés. par Jean-Paul Liégeois. Paris: Cherche midi, 2008. *Brassens d'abord*. 158 p.

BRAULT, Jacques.

GG2224. ● *Précarités de Brault*. Sous la dir. de François Hébert et Nathalie Watteyne. Québec: Nota Bene, 2008. 214 p.

GG2225. Urs, Luminita: "Variations automnales dans la poésie de Jacques Brault." In 383, 151-157.

GG2226. Watteyne, Nathalie: "Corps cachés et jeux d'ombres dans la poésie récente de Jacques Brault et d'Anne Hébert." In 69, 139-149. [Hébert]

BREL, Jacques. See also 7253.

GG2227. ● Crocq, Philippe: *Jacques Brel*. Paris: Albin Michel, 2008. *Nostalgie*. 143 p.

GG2228. ● Le Vaillant, Serge: *Jacques Brel: l'éternel adolescent*. Paris: Textuel, 2008. 191 p.

GG2229. ● Przybylski, Eddy: *Jacques Brel: la valse à mille rêves*. Paris: L'Archipel, 2008. 765 p.

GG2230. ● Quint, Michel: *Sur les pas de Jacques Brel*. Paris: Presses de la Renaissance, 2008. 93 p.

GG2231. ● Vincendet, Serge: *Jacques Brel: l'impossible rêve*. Monaco: Alphée, 2008. 359 p.

GG2232. ● Wodrascka, Alain: *Jacques Brel: voyage au bout du rêve*. Paris: Didier Carpentier, 2008. 141 p.

BRETON, André. See also 420, 489, 606, 1020, 1021, 1050, 1061, 1068, 1070, 1332, 6905.

GG2233. ● *Album André Breton*. Iconographie choisie et commentée par Robert Kopp. Paris: Gallimard, 2008. *Bibliothèque de la Pléiade*. 330 p.

GG2234. ● Arlotta, Ivan: *L'esotismo nella poesia di André Breton*. Roma: Aracne, 2008. 121 p.

GG2235. ● Berthet, Dominique: *André Breton, l'éloge de la rencontre: Antilles, Amérique, Océanie*. Paris: HC, 2008. 159 p.

GG2236. ● Breton, André: *Arcane 17*. Edition préparée et présentée par Henri Béhar. Paris: Biro, 2008. 251, xlviii p.

GG2237. ● Breton, André: *Martinique: snake charmer*. Trans. David Seaman; introd. Franklin Rosemont. Austin: Univ. of Texas Press, 2008. *Surrealist revolution*. x, 117 p.

GG2238. ● Breton, André: *Œuvres complètes. IV, Ecrits sur l'art et autres textes*. Edition de Marguerite Bonnet; publié, pour ce volume, sous la dir. d'Etienne-Alain Hubert, avec la collab. de Philippe Bernier et Marie-Claire Dumas. Paris: Gallimard, 2008. *Bibliothèque de la Pléiade*. lv, 1527 p.

GG2239. ● Török, Jean-Paul: *André Breton, ou, La hantise de l'absolu*. Grez-sur-Loing: Pardès, 2008. 352 p.

GG2240. Aleksic, Branko: "The unpublished correspondence of Henry Miller and André Breton, the 'Steady Rock', 1947-1950," *Nexus: The International Henry Miller Journal*, no. 5 (2008), 150-172.

GG2241. Devereux Herbeck, Mariah: "André Breton's *Nadja*: a *vagabonde* in a *femme fatale's* narrative," *Dalhousie French Studies*, vol. 82 (Spring 2008), 163-171.

GG2242. Dumas, Marie-Claire: "Le 'poème-objet' selon André Breton." In 418, 91-103.

GG2243. Duwa, Jérôme: "Arshile Gorky et son double: la rencontre avec Breton," *Cahiers du Musée National d'Art Moderne*, no. 102 (hiver 2007-2008), 102-117.

GG2244. Lemaître, Sylvie: "André Breton critique d'Alberto Giacometti." In 563, 54-61.

GG2245. Masschelein, Anneleen: "Negative Hände: die Darstellung der Negativität in Bretons *Nadja* und Sebalds *Austerlitz*." In 843, 319-350.

GG2246. Née, Patrick: "Le 'hasard objectif': une allégorèse problématique (André Breton, *L'amour fou*)," *Revue d'Histoire Littéraire de la France*, tome 108, no. 1 (janv.-mars 2008), 133-157.

GG2247. Petterson, James: "André Breton *contra* all." In 1021, 117-155.

GG2248. Russo, Adelaide M.: "André Breton et les dispositifs du jugement: spéculaire, spéculatif." In 583, 61-81.

GG2249. Schlesier, Renate: "D'Eros et de la lutte contre Eros: zur Poetisierung von Freuds Trieblehre in Bretons *L'Amour fou*." In 451, 193-207.

GG2250. Sequi, Caterina: "Le premier sexe: la figura femminile in Breton e Savinio," *Ponte*, anno 44, n. 5 (maggio 2008), 142-150.

GG2251. Spieker, Sven: "1924: the bureaucracy of the unconscious." In 869.

GG2252. Vadé, Yves: "André Breton et l'ombre de Merlin." In 614, 221-259.

BRIOT, Geneviève.

GG2253. Le Boucher, Dominique: "La douleur devenue oiseau," *Algérie Littérature/Action*, no. 117-118 (janv.-févr. 2008), 54-55.

BRISSET, Jean-Pierre.

GG2254. Decimo, Marc: "Bagarre d'Angers." In 564, 189-197.

GG2255. Decimo, Marc: "Comment s'y prendre avec les grenouilles qui sexpriment: actualités autour de Jean-Pierre Brisset (1837-1919)," *Cahiers de l'Institut*, no. 1 (2008), 22-39.

BRISVILLE, Jean-Claude.

GG2256. ● Brisville, Jean-Claude: *L'Antichambre*. Paris: Avant-Scène Théâtre, 2008. *Avant-Scène Théâtre*, no. 1238 (15 févr. 2008). 93 p.

BROCHU, André.

GG2257. ● *André Brochu, écrivain*. Sous la dir. de Micheline Cambron et Laurent Mailhot. Montréal: Hurtubise, 2006. 223 p.

BROSSARD, Jacques.

GG2258. Ransom, Amy J.: "Critical reception and postmodern violation of generic conventions in Jacques Brossard's 'Monument aux marges': *L'oiseau de feu*," *Studies in Canadian Literature*, vol. 33, no. 1 (2008), 229-256.

BROSSARD, Nicole. See also 174, 290.

GG2259. ● Brossard, Nicole: *D'aube et de civilisation: poèmes choisis, 1965-2007*. Choix et préface de Louise Dupré. Montréal: Typo, 2008. 451 p.

GG2260. Fourcaut, Laurent: "Désir et corps de l'écriture dans *A tout regard* de Nicole Brossard." In 69, 199-212.

GG2261. Hernandez, Julie Gerk: "Fertile theoretical ground: an ecocritical reading of Nicole Brossard's *Mauve desert*," *Critique*, vol. 49, no. 3 (Spring 2008), 255-272.

GG2262. Hubbell, Amy L.: "Genre trouble in Nicole Brossard's *Un livre*," *Women in French Studies*, no. 18 (2008), 116-123.

GG2263. "Nicole Brossard, 1943: Canadian poet, novelist, and essayist." In 1024.

GG2264. Snauwaert, Maïté: "*Hier* de Nicole Brossard." In 41, 57-78.

GG2265. Wheeler, Anne-Marie: "Accent in the translation of Nicole Brossard." In 136, 269-290.

BRUCKNER, Pascal.

GG2266. Constantinescu, Muguras: "Les contes de Pascal Bruckner, réécriture d'un genre, écriture de la problématique intergénératioinnelle." In 894, 467-479.

BUGUL, Ken. See also 3534.

GG2267. ● Bugul, Ken: *The abandoned baobab*. Trans. Marjolijn de Jager; afterword by Jeanne Garane. Charlottesville: Univ. of Virginia Press, 2008. *CARAF books*. 180 p.

GG2268. ● *Emerging perspectives on Ken Bugul: from alternative choices to oppositional practices*. Ed. Ada Uzoamaka Azodo and Jeanne-Sarah de Larquier. Trenton, NJ: Africa World, 2008. 371 p.

GG2269. Edwards, Natalie: "In search of lost home: Ken Bugul's *Le Baobab fou* and Buchi Emecheta's *Second Class Citizen*." In 80, 84-98.

GG2270. Sanvee, Mathieu: "Le mal de mère: étude de l'abjection dans *Le Baobab fou* de Ken Bugul." In 72, 467-479.

BUTOR, Michel. See also 916, 2031.

GG2271. ● Butor, Michel: *Œuvres complètes de Michel Butor. VII, Le génie du lieu, 3*. Sous la dir. de Mireille Calle-Gruber. Paris: Différence, 2008. 958 p.

GG2272. ● Butor, Michel: *Œuvres complètes de Michel Butor. VIII, Matière de rêves*. Sous la dir. de Mireille Calle-Gruber. Paris: Différence, 2008. 1050 p.

GG2273. ● *Michel Butor: déménagements de la littérature*. Ed. Mireille Calle-Gruber. Paris: Sorbonne nouvelle, 2008. 310 p.

GG2274. Assadollahi-Tejaragh, Allahchokr: "Temporalité arithmétique dans *La Modification* de Michel Butor." In 496, 189-195.

GG2275.   Bourjea, Serge: "Butor/Alechinsky." In 2273, 133-151.
GG2276.   Calle-Gruber, Mireille: "Cantique de Michel Butor mendiant et hospitalier." In 2273, 47-56.
GG2277.   Camarero, Jesús: "Ut pictura poesis chez Michel Butor." In 2273, 173-188.
GG2278.   Collot, Michel: "Le génie des lieux." In 2273, 73-84.
GG2279.   Coulibeuf, Pierre: "Dédoublements." In 2273, 207-210.
GG2280.   Deguy, Michel: "Plaque tournante." In 2273, 17-29.
GG2281.   Desoubeaux, Henri: "Littérature: ça déménage sur le net avec Michel Butor." In 2273, 223-229.
GG2282.   Faerber, Johan: "Le déni du lieu ou l'utopie baroque dans l'œuvre de Michel Butor." In 2273, 271-287.
GG2283.   Geerts, Walter: "Ecritures des migrations: Santocono, Butor, Consolo." In 586, 117-124.
GG2284.   Giraudo, Lucien: "Michel Butor et les œuvres d'art en collaboration." In 2273, 235-240.
GG2285.   Lancry, Yehuda: "Echographie idéologico-politique en terre butorienne." In 2273, 31-46.
GG2286.   Mennan, Zeynep; Eminge Bogenç Demirel: "Du mythe antique du labyrinthe au mythe moderne: *L'Emploi du temps* et *Les Gommes*," *Edebiyat Fakültesi Dergisi*, vol. 25, no. 1 (2008), 115-127. [Robbe-Grillet]
GG2287.   Minssieux-Chamonard, Marie: "Exposer Butor." In 2273, 231-233.
GG2288.   Noël, Bernard: "Michel Butor, 'l'homme qui fait seul de beaux livres'." In 2273, 89-91.
GG2289.   Ogawa, Midori: "Dialogue/dialogue, Butor/Beethoven." In 2273, 189-205.
GG2290.   Oppenheim, Lois: "D'après-coup en après coup: lecture de textes butoriens." In 2273, 259-269.
GG2291.   Roudaut, Jean: "Salut," *Théodore Balmoral*, no. 56-57 (2008), 184-199. [also in 2273, 57-72]
GG2292.   Russo, Adelaide: "Miroitements du livre." In 2273, 153-171.
GG2293.   Skimao, Christian: "L'heure des mots: illustration pratique d'une collaboration artistique entre Michel Butor et Patrice Pouperon." In 2273, 213-221.
GG2294.   Starobinski, Jean: "Lettre à Michel Butor sur un cinquantenaire." In 2273, 13-15.
GG2295.   Weiand, Christof: "Ravenne: Bonnefoy/Butor." In 2273, 289-297. [Bonnefoy]

CABANIS, José. See also 5750.
GG2296.   Alexandre, Didier: "José Cabanis et *La Nouvelle Revue Française*," *Cahiers José Cabanis*, no. 3 (2007), 177-195.
GG2297.   Bayle, Françoise: "L'ironie comme expression de l'herméneutique cabanisienne," *Cahiers José Cabanis*, no. 3 (2007), 77-99.
GG2298.   Braud, Michel: "Le journal à deux voix de José Cabanis," *Cahiers José Cabanis*, no. 3 (2007), 121-135.
GG2299.   Bressolette, Michel: "José Cabanis et les catholiques libéraux," *Cahiers José Cabanis*, no. 3 (2007), 265-280.
GG2300.   Degout, Bernard: "De l'histoire à la fable—et retour: José Cabanis lecteur de Chateaubriand," *Cahiers José Cabanis*, no. 3 (2007), 247-263.
GG2301.   Deschaux, Jocelyne: "Les manuscrits de José Cabanis," *Cahiers José Cabanis*, no. 3 (2007), 333-339.
GG2302.   Foucart, Claude: "José Cabanis et le monde germanique." In 461, 321-335.
GG2303.   Huet-Brichard, Marie-Catherine: " 'La vraie vie est absente': le désir et la mélancolie dans *Les Jeux de la nuit* et *La Bataille de Toulouse*," *Cahiers José Cabanis*, no. 3 (2007), 53-75.
GG2304.   Labadié, Robert: "Julien Green et José Cabanis," *Cahiers José Cabanis*, no. 3 (2007), 281-290. [Green]
GG2305.   Lanavère, Alain: "Les romans de *L'Age ingrat* (1952-1958)," *Cahiers José Cabanis*, no. 3 (2007), 15-52.

GG2306. Lassalle, Jean-Pierre: "José Cabanis et l'Académie des Jeux floraux," *Cahiers José Cabanis*, no. 3 (2007), 319-332.

GG2307. Mailhos, Georges: "José Cabanis et Saint-Simon," *Cahiers José Cabanis*, no. 3 (2007), 229-246.

GG2308. Mansau, Andrée: "Cabanis, amateur d'art," *Cahiers José Cabanis*, no. 3 (2007), 215-228.

GG2309. Meter, Helmut: "Lectures dialogiques. José Cabanis critique littéraire," *Cahiers José Cabanis*, no. 3 (2007), 197-214.

GG2310. Nouilhan, Pierre: "Du *Fils* au *Magnificat*: une révélation annoncée," *Cahiers José Cabanis*, no. 3 (2007), 165-175.

GG2311. Sarocchi, Jean: "Monsieur de la Trappe," *Cahiers José Cabanis*, no. 3 (2007), 137-164.

GG2312. Steinhart, Wolfgang: "José Cabanis, requis du STO: expériences et conséquences du séjour en Allemagne," *Cahiers José Cabanis*, no. 3 (2007), 303-317.

GG2313. Tinti Ladu, Mariella: "Cabanis et l'écriture du moi," *Cahiers José Cabanis*, no. 3 (2007), 101-120.

GG2314. Touzot, Jean: "De François à Claude Mauriac," *Cahiers José Cabanis*, no. 3 (2007), 291-302. [C. Mauriac, F. Mauriac]

CAGE-FLORENTINY, Nicole.

GG2315. Vété-Congolo, Hanétha: "Idéal romantique et projet social dans *C'est vole que je vole* de Nicole Cage-Florentiny," *Présence Francophone*, no. 71 (2008), 139-164.

GG2316. Vété-Congolo, Hanétha: "Sexual pleasure and eroticism in Nicole Cage-Florentiny's 'Amours marines ou Erótico mar': toward a postmodern writing of women's body and sexuality," *Dalhousie French Studies*, vol. 83 (Summer 2008), 127-139.

CAHUN, Claude.

GG2317. • Cahun, Claude: *Disavowals, or, Cancelled confessions*. Préf. Pierre Mac Orlan; introd. Jennifer Mundy; afterword François Leperlier; trans. Susan de Muth. Cambridge, MA: MIT Press, 2008. xxvi, 226 p.

GG2318. Lhermitte, Agnès: "Paroles d'une 'sur-vivante': les récits de rêve dans les écrits autobiographiques de Claude Cahun." In 611.

GG2319. Thynne, Lizzie: " 'Surely you are not claiming to be more homosexual than I?' Claude Cahun and Oscar Wilde." In 545.

CAILLOIS, Roger.

GG2320. • Bridet, Guillaume: *Littérature et sciences humaines: autour de Roger Caillois*. Paris: Honoré Champion, 2008. *Bibliothèque de littérature générale et comparée*, 75. 589 p.

GG2321. • Caillois, Roger: *Le champ des signes*. Préface de Jean-Clarence Lambert. Paris: Hermann, 2008. *Littérature*. vi, 93 p.

GG2322. • Caillois, Roger: *Œuvres*. Edition établie et prés. par Dominique Rabourdin. Paris: Gallimard, 2008. *Quarto*. 1189 p.

GG2323. Laserra, A.: "Aspetti di un universo unitario in Roger Caillois," *Rivista di Letterature Moderne e Comparate*, vol. 61, fasc. 2 (aprile-guigno 2008), 175-184.

GG2324. Parkinson, Gavin: "Relativity and the fourth dimension: Salvador Dali and Roger Caillois." In 1058.

GG2325. Rigoli, Juan: "Caillois, le lapidaire intime." In 516, 409-436.

GG2326. Swoboda, Tomasz: "Testaments d'hommes du sacré." In 379, 303-313. [Bataille]

CALAFERTE, Louis. See 1048.

CALET, Henri. See 6309.

CALLE, Sophie.

GG2327. • Kittner, Alma: *Visuelle Autobiographien: Sammeln als Selbstentwurf bei Hannah Höch, Sophie Calle und Annette Messager*. Bielefeld: Transcript, 2008. 300 p.

GG2328. Camart, Cécile: "Les stratégies éditoriales de Sophie Calle: livres de photographies, photo-roman, livres d'artiste." In 508, 373-389.

GG2329. Conant, Chloé: "Histoires d'images et de textes les œuvres photo-fictionnelles de Sophie Calle et d'Edouard Levé." In 508, 361-372. [Levé]

GG2330. Hersant, Yves: "L'autorité de Sophie Calle," *Critique*, tome 64, no. 731 (avril 2008), 341-349.

GG2331. Spies, Werner: "Sophie Calle." In 596.

CAMUS, Albert. See also 81, 484, 678, 679, 755, 760, 963, 966, 1080, 7199, 7200.

GG2332. ● *Albert Camus: dissidences et liberté: solidarité avec les opposants de l'Europe de l'Est, 1945-1960*. Rencontres méditerranéennes Albert Camus. Aix-en-Provence: Edisud, 2008. 129 p.

GG2333. ● *Albert Camus et la pensée de Midi*. Sous la dir. de Jean-François Mattéi. Nice: Ovadia, 2008. *Chemins de pensée*. 221 p.

GG2334. ● *Albert Camus in the 21st century: a reassessment of his thinking at the dawn of the new millennium*. Ed. Christine Margerrison, Mark Orme, Lissa Lincoln. Amsterdam: Rodopi, 2008. *Faux titre*, 308. 295 p.

GG2335. ● *Albert Camus's The Stranger*. Ed., and with an intro. by Harold Bloom. New York: Bloom's Literary Criticism, 2008. 93 p.

GG2336. ● Camus, Albert: *Albert Camus et les libertaires (1949-1960): écrits rassemblés*. Ed. Lou Marin. Marseille: Egrégores, 2008. 361 p.

GG2337. ● Camus, Albert: *La chute*. Dossier et notes réalisés par Sophie Doudet; lecture d'image par Alain Jaubert. Paris: Gallimard, 2008. *Folioplus*. 212 p.

GG2338. ● Camus, Albert: *Der Fall*. Mit Kommentaren von Brigitte Ständig und Sven Grotendiek. Berlin: BWV, 2008. 105 p.

GG2339. ● Camus, Albert: *Les justes*. Edition prés., établie et annotée par Pierre-Louis Rey. Paris: Gallimard, 2008. *Folio théâtre*. 220 p.

GG2340. ● Camus, Albert: *Notebooks: 1951-1959*. Trans., introd., and afterword by Ryan Bloom. Chicago: Dee, 2008. xix, 264 p.

GG2341. ● Camus, Albert: *Œuvres complètes. III, 1949-1956*. Edition publiée sous la dir. de Raymond Gay-Crosier; avec, pour ce volume, la collab. de Robert Dengler [et al.]. Paris: Gallimard, 2008. *Bibliothèque de la Pléiade*. xx, 1481 p.

GG2342. ● Camus, Albert: *Œuvres complètes. IV, 1957-1959*. Edition publiée sous la dir. de Raymond Gay-Crosier; avec, pour ce volume, la collab. de Robert Dengler [et al.]. Paris: Gallimard, 2008. *Bibliothèque de la Pléiade*. xiv, 1600 p.

GG2343. ● Camus, Albert: *La peste*. Dossier et notes réalisés par Mériam Korichi; lecture d'image par Bertrand Leclair. Paris: Gallimard, 2008. *Folioplus*. 391 p.

GG2344. ● Camus, Albert: *Réflexions sur la guillotine*. Dossier et notes réalisés par Marc-Henri Arfeux. Lecture d'image par Christian Hubert-Rodier. Paris: Gallimard, 2008. *Folioplus*. 168 p.

GG2345. ● Chandra, Sharad: *Albert Camus et l'Inde*. Trad. Sylvie Crossman. Montpellier: Indigène, 2008. 233 p.

GG2346. ● Figuero, Javier: *Albert Camus ou l'Espagne exaltée*. Trad. Marie-Hélène Carbonel. Gemenos: Autre temps, 2008. 277 p.

GG2347. ● Foley, John: *Albert Camus: from the absurd to revolt*. Montréal: McGill-Queen's Univ. Press, 2008. xiv, 239 p.

GG2348. ● Halfmann, Roman: *Kafka kann einen Schriftsteller lähmen: dargestellt an Albert Camus, Philip Roth, Peter Handke und Thomas Bernhard*. Berlin: Lit, 2008. *Germanistik*. 250 p.

GG2349. ● Isaac, Jeffrey C.: *Arendt, Camus, and modern rebellion*. New Haven: Yale Univ. Press, 2008. xi, 320 p. [Orig. ed., 1992]

GG2350. ● *Je me révolte donc nous sommes: Albert Camus, à hauteur d'homme*. Sylvie Arnaud-Gomez [et al.]. Paris: Cerf, 2008. *Cause Commune*, no. 4. 267 p.

GG2351. ● Maldonado Ortega, Rubén: *Absurdo y rebelión: una lectura de contemporaneidad en la obra de Albert Camus*. Barraquilla: Uninorte, 2008. 200 p.

GG2352. ● Margerrison, Christine: *Ces forces obscures de l'âme: women, race and origins in the writings of Albert Camus*. Amsterdam: Rodopi, 2008. *Faux titre*, 311. 356 p.

GG2353. ● *Œuvre [L'] d'Albert Camus en 100 reliures de création*. Préface de Catherine Camus; introd. Florent Rousseau. Dijon: Faton, 2008. 143 p.

GG2354. ● Parker, Emmet: *Albert Camus, the artist in the arena*. Madison: Univ. of Wisconsin Press, 2008. xv, 245 p. [Orig. ed., 1966]

GG2355. ● Poppe, Reiner: *Erläuterungen zu Albert Camus, Der Fremde.* 4. Aufl. Hollfed: Bange, 2008. 86 p.

GG2356. ● Porz, Rouven: *Zwischen Entscheidung und Entfremdung: Patienten-perspektiven in der Gendiagnostik und Albert Camus' Konzepte zum Absurden.* Paderborn: Mentis, 2008. 373 p.

GG2357. ● Prouteau, Anne: *Albert Camus, ou, Le présent impérissable.* Paris: Orizons, 2008. 282 p.

GG2358. ● Rey, Pierre-Louis: *Pierre-Louis Rey commente Le Premier homme d'Albert Camus.* Paris: Gallimard, 2008. *Foliothèque.* 216 p.

GG2359. ● Sauvage, Pierre; Nicole Maritzen: *Albert Camus, L'Etranger.* Stuttgart; Düsseldorf: Klett, 2008. 4. Aufl. 96 p.

GG2360. ● Sessler, Tal: *Levinas and Camus: humanism for the twenty-first century.* London: Continuum, 2008. *Studies in Continental Philosophy.* ix, 114 p. [Levinas]

GG2361. Alpozzo, Marc: "Etranger à soi-même, étranger au monde? Une lecture de *L'Etranger* de Camus," *Presse littéraire,* no. 11 (2007), 27-36.

GG2362. Basset, Guy: "Une proximité à l'œuvre: autour des refus communs de Koestler et Camus." In 2332.

GG2363. Belliott, Raymond A.: "First inning: Ted Williams and Albert Camus." In 798.

GG2364. Bondarenco, Anna: "Le temps et la temporalité du stéréotype et de l'événement." In 496, 215-227.

GG2365. Chae, Sookhee: "Albert Camus et le bouddhisme." In 96, 131-140.

GG2366. Chebchoub, Zahida: "Le silence dans la vie et l'œuvre de Camus." In 571, 127-135.

GG2367. Chijiwa, Yasuko: "Le corps déchu de Clamence: tentative de relecture de *La Chute,*" *Etudes Camusiennes,* no. 8 (2008), 93-109.

GG2368. Cielens, Isabelle: "Camus sous l'occupation soviétique en Lettonie." In 2332.

GG2369. Ciocärlie, Livius: "Liberté et indifférence." In 2332.

GG2370. Corey, Paul: "The Gnostic Caesar: radical eschatology in Albert Camus's *Caligula.*" In 1080.

GG2371. Crespo, Gérard: "Camus, Audisio et la Méditerranée." In 2333.

GG2372. Fosty, Andrée: "Les rencontres méditerranéennes." In 2332.

GG2373. Foulon, Jean-François: "Albert Camus ou l'ambiguïté d'une révolte," *Presse littéraire,* no. 11 (2007), 9-26.

GG2374. Géraud, Violaine: "Cohérence et discohérence chronologiques dans *L'Etranger* de Camus." In 410, 371-380.

GG2375. Hamel, Yan: "Camus pour la jeunesse. *Les justes,*" *Jeu: Cahiers de Théâtre,* no. 128 [no. 3] (2008), 44-46.

GG2376. Horváth, Andor: " 'Parier pour la renaissance': en marge de Camus penseur politique." In 2332.

GG2377. Inada, Harutoshi: "Meursault et la dimension transcendantale," *Etudes Camusiennes,* no. 8 (2008), 72-92.

GG2378. Ivaldi, Jean-Pierre: "L'exil et le royaume." In 2333.

GG2379. Joyaux, Evelyne: "*Le premier homme*: le révolte et l'innocence." In 2333.

GG2380. Judt, Tony: "Albert Camus: 'the best man in France'." In 958.

GG2381. Kouchkine, Evgueni: "Camus et la Russie: pour une renaissance." In 2332.

GG2382. Lapeyre, Christian: "Camus ou la fidélité." In 2333.

GG2383. Leparulo, William E.: "Il trionfo della 'misura' e della letteratura nelle opere di Albert Camus," *Silarus,* anno 48, no. 257-258 (maggio-agosto 2008), 145-152.

GG2384. Lubrich, Oliver: "Über die Grenze der Bedeutung: Albert Camus in Nazi-Deutschland." In 613, 227-248.

GG2385. Lund, Hans Peter: "Le *Prométhée enchaîné* de Camus," *Romanistische Zeitschrift für Literaturgeschichte,* 32. Jahrgang, Heft 1-2 (2008), 83-103.

GG2386. Lyotard, Dolorès: "*L'Etranger* en personne," *Elseneur,* no. 22 (2008), [n.p.].

GG2387. Martinez, Louis: "Camus dans Paris." In 2333.

GG2388. Mattéi, Jean-Françoise: "Albert Camus et la terre natale." In 2333.

GG2389. Mattéi, Jean-Françoise: "La tendre indifférence du monde." In 2333.

GG2390. McMahon, Jennifer L.: "*24* and the existential man of revolt." In 853, 115-129.

GG2391. Murchland, Bernard: "Between solitude and solidarity: the two worlds of Albert Camus." In 966.

GG2392. Musso, Frédéric: "Albert Camus, écrivain et poète." In 2333.

GG2393. O'Brien, Stephen M.: "God and the Devil are fighting: the scandal of evil in Dostoyevsky and Camus." Diss., CUNY, 2008. xiii, 423 p.

GG2394. Prouteau, Anne: "*Le Premier homme* d'Albert Camus: le mémorial des anonymes." In 517, 125-137.

GG2395. Puleio, Maria Teresa: " 'L'exil d'Hélène' d'Albert Camus ou le tragique solaire de la Méditerranée." In 482, 337-353.

GG2396. Raïssi, Rachid: "L'insolation comme motif du 'texte fou' dans *L'Etranger* d'Albert Camus et *L'insolation* de Rachid Boudjedra," *Algérie Littérature/Action*, no. 117-118 (janv.-févr. 2008), 40-43. [Boudjedra]

GG2397. Ramírez Medina, Angel: "Anti-Teodicea y ateísmo en Albert Camus," *Pensamiento*, vol. 64, núm. 241 (sept.-dic. 2008), 487-498.

GG2398. Repse, Gundega: "Camus en Lettonie occupée." In 2332.

GG2399. Rey, Pierre-Louis: "Aspects du temps dans *La Chute* d'Albert Camus." In 459, 379-384.

GG2400. Rey, Pierre-Louis: "Militants amoureux chez Camus." In 456, 169-177.

GG2401. Rodan, Martin: "*Le Mythe de Sisyphe* et Kierkegaard," *Etudes Camusiennes*, no. 8 (2008), 110-129.

GG2402. Rossow, Francis C.: "*The Fall* by Albert Camus." In 580.

GG2403. Rouart, Marie-France: "Camus, *L'Etranger*." In 582, 193-220.

GG2404. Rufat, Hélène: "A propos des dernières rencontres camusiennes: l'archipel méditerranéen d'Albert Camus." In 515, 35-45.

GG2405. Samama, Guy: "Albert Camus: un équilibre des contraires," *Esprit*, no. 341 (janv. 2008), 22-35.

GG2406. Sändig, Brigitte: "La réception de Camus et la chute du mur." In 2332.

GG2407. Santoni, Ronald E.: "Camus on Sartre's 'freedom': another 'misunderstanding'," *Review of Metaphysics*, vol. 61, no. 4 (June 2008), 785-813. [Sartre]

GG2408. Sarrochi, Jean: "Redevenir enfant?" In 2333.

GG2409. Smola, Julia: "La dimension politique du langage. L'exemple de l'Argentine," *Itinéraires et Contacts de Cultures*, no. 39 (2007), 209-219.

GG2410. Stora, Benjamin: "Albert Camus, prix Nobel au cœur de la tourmente algérienne," *Esprit*, no. 341 (janv. 2008), 11-21.

GG2411. Trabelsi, Mustapha: "Poétique de la didascalie dans *L'Etat de siège* d'Albert Camus." In 605, 321-333.

GG2412. Viallaneix, Paul: "*Le Mythe de Sisyphe*: une pensée problématique," *Etudes Camusiennes*, no. 8 (2008), 130-139.

CAMUS, Renaud. See also 6427.

GG2413. Baetens, Jan: "Les hommes, les œuvres, les lieux. Passages de l'art dans le *Journal* de Renaud Camus," *Cuadernos de Filologia Francesa*, vol. 19 (2008), 13-25.

GG2414. Rabatel, Alain: "Autobiographie et auto-citations dans *Du sens* et *La campagne de France* de Renaud Camus." In 565, 550-574.

CANGUILHEM, Georges. See also 937.

GG2415. ● Canguilhem, Georges: *Knowledge of life.* Ed. Paola Marrati and Todd Meyers; trans. Stefanos Geroulanos, Daniela Ginsburg. New York: Fordham Univ. Press, 2008. xx, 202 p.

GG2416. ● Lecourt, Dominique: *Georges Canguilhem.* Paris: PUF, 2008. *Que sais-je?.* 125 p.

GG2417. ● Muhle, Maria: *Eine Genealogie der Biopolitik zum Begriff des Lebens bei Foucault und Canghuilhem.* Bielefeld: Transcript, 2008. 301 p. [Foucault]

GG2418. ● Pénisson, Guillaume: *Le vivant et l'épistoméologie des concepts: essai sur le normal et le pathologique de Georges Canguilhem.* Paris: L'Harmattan, 2008. *Ouverture philosophique.* 122 p.

GG2419. ● *Philosophie et médecine: en hommage à Georges Canguilhem.* Sous la dir. d'Anne Fagot-Largeault, Claude Debru et Michel Morange. Paris: J. Vrin, 2008. 240 p.

GG2420. Andersen, Sven: "L'idéalisation de la 'schizophrénie' par un (anti)psychiatre, Roland Laing," *Annales de l'Institut de Philosophie de Bruxelles* (2008), 157-172.

GG2421. Carroy, Jacqueline: "Observation, expérimentation et clinique de soi: haschich, folie, rêve et hystérie au XIXe siècle," *Annales de l'Institut de Philosophie de Bruxelles* (2008), 53-71.

GG2422. Chimisso, Cristina: "George Canguilhem between concepts and the living being." In 937, 152-166.

GG2423. Coffin, Jean-Christophe: "La réhabilitation de la folie dans l'œuvre d'Henri Ey," *Annales de l'Institut de Philosophie de Bruxelles* (2008), 141-156.

GG2424. Daled, Pierre F.: "L'envers de la raison, du 'principe de Broussais' à Foucault via Canguilhem," *Annales de l'Institut de Philosophie de Bruxelles* (2008), 7-16. [Foucault]

GG2425. Daled, Pierre F.: "Santé, folie et vérité aux XIXe et XXe siècles: Nietzsche, Canguilhem et Foucault," *Annales de l'Institut de Philosophie de Bruxelles* (2008), 115-140. [Foucault]

GG2426. Ebke, Thomas: "Lebenswissenschaft bei Georges Canguilhem," *Philosophische Rundschau*, Band 55, Heft 3 (Sept. 2008), 252-261.

GG2427. Fauvel, Aude: " 'Par rapport à moi tous les autres hommes sont des singes'. L'internement du baron Seillière (1887-1889) et les témoignages d'aliénés," *Annales de l'Institut de Philosophie de Bruxelles* (2008), 97-114.

GG2428. Han, Hee-Jin: "La philosophie de la médecine chez Canguilhem," *Annales de l'Institut de Philosophie de Bruxelles* (2008), 173-190.

GG2429. Le Blanc, Guillaume: "L'homme sauvage, le primitif et l'idiot," *Annales de l'Institut de Philosophie de Bruxelles* (2008), 17-34.

GG2430. Lefève, Céline: "La lecture épistémologique de la psychanalyse de Maine de Biran par Georges Canguilhem," *Annales de l'Institut de Philosophie de Bruxelles* (2008), 35-52.

GG2431. Rigoli, Juan: "Aux sources de la folie: Moreau de Tours et l' 'observation intime'," *Annales de l'Institut de Philosophie de Bruxelles* (2008), 73-95.

GG2432. Roudinesco, Elisabeth: "George Canguilhem: a philosophy of heroism." In 976, 1-32.

CARCO, Francis. See also 4653.

GG2433. Carco, Francis: *Primavera de España.* Trad. y epílogo de Yoland Morató. Cordoba: Almuzara, 2008. 263 p.

CARDINAL, Marie. See also 638.

GG2434. Hubbell, Amy L.: "Slipping home in Marie Cardinal's *Ecoutez la mer.*" In 80.

GG2435. Ring, Annie Grace Helena: "Ecrire le patriarcat, le corps et la topographie du désordre: *Les Mots pour le dire* et *Détruire, dit-elle,*" *French Studies Bulletin,* no. 107 (Summer 2008), 31-39. [Duras]

CARON, Catherine. See 324.

CARRÈRE, Emmanuel.

GG2436. Carrère, Emmanuel: "Généalogie d'une délivrance," *Matricule des Anges,* no. 82 (2007), 18-23. [Entretien]

GG2437. Favre, Emmanuel: "Le temps retrouvé," *Matricule des Anges,* no. 82 (2007), 14-17.

GG2438. Indiana, Gary: "Emmanuel Carrère's counterfeiters." In 485.

GG2439. Marion, Esther N.: "The narrator-perpetrator and the infectious crime scene: Emmanuel Carrère's *L'Adversaire.*" In 617, 59-70.

CASSOU, Jean.

GG2440. ● Cassou, Jean: *The madness of Amadis; and other poems.* Intro. and trans. Timothy Adès; foreword by Harry Guest. Mayfield, East Sussex: Agenda, 2008. 87 p.

GG2441. Basch, Sophie: "Silences de Jean Cassou." In 592, 29-44.

GG2442. Lafond, Natacha: "Le sonnet dans l'œuvre de Jean Cassou," *Formules*, no. 12 (2008), 23-34.

CASTILLO DURANTE, Michel

GG2443. Tremblay, Emmanuelle: *"La passion des nomades* de Michel Castillo Durante." In 41, 79-86.

CATHALA, Frédéric.

GG2444. Cordiner, Valerio: "Le théorème de Marmouset, ou la langue (peu) tranchante du Léviathan." In 561, 119-139.

CAU, Jean.

GG2445. Benoist, Alain de: "Jean Cau contre la décadence," *Spectacle du Monde*, no. 541 (janv. 2008), 56-60.

CAVAILLÈS, Jean.

GG2446. ● Centrone, Marino: *La scalata al cielo: il pensiero filosofico di Jean Cavaillès.* Bari: Levante, 2008. 231 p.

CAYROL, Jean. See also 519.

GG2447. Coquio, Catherine: "Qu'est-ce qu'une littérature lazaréenne? Jean Cayrol au présent," *Licorne*, no. 78 (2006), 291-307.

GG2448. Leutrat, Jean-Louis: "Le coup de grâce," *Trafic*, no. 67 (automne 2008), 86-93.

GG2449. Liandrat-Guigues, Suzanne: "L'élégance selon Jean Cayrol," *Trafic*, no. 67 (automne 2008), 79-85.

CÉLINE, Louis-Ferdinand. See also 684, 711, 1921, 4397, 6510.

GG2450. ● Aebersold, Denise: *"Goétie de Céline.* Paris: Société d'Etudes Céliniennes, 2008. 413 p.

GG2451. ● Alliot, David; Daniel Renard: *Céline à Bezons: 1940-1944.* Monaco: Rocher, 2008. 235 p.

GG2452. ● Alliot, David; François Marchetti: *Céline au Danemark: 1945-1951.* Monaco: Rocher, 2008. 119 p.

GG2453. ● Alméras, Philippe: *Sur Céline.* Versailles: Editions de Paris, 2008. 253 p.

GG2454. ● Cadier, Marc Henri: *En lisant Louis-Ferdinand Céline.* Saint-Etienne: MHC, 2008. 305 p.

GG2455. ● Céline, Louis-Ferdinand: *Da un castello all'altro.* Introd. di Gianni Celati; trad. di Giuseppe Guglielmi. Torino: Einaudi, 2008. xvii, 360 p.

GG2456. ● Céline, Louis-Ferdinand: *Lettres à Marie Canavaggia: 1936-1960.* Ed. établie et annotée par Jean Paul Louis. Paris: Gallimard, 2008. Ed. rev. et corr. *Cahiers Céline*, 9. 758 p.

GG2457. ● Céline, Louis-Ferdinand: *Semmelweis.* Intro. Philippe Sollers; trans. John Harman. London: Atlas Press, 2008. 109 p.

GG2458. ● *Céline-Paulhan: questions sur la responsabilité de l'écrivain au sortir de la Seconde Guerre mondiale: première Journée d'étude Céline-Paulhan, Paris, 20 novembre 2007.* Paris: Société d'études céliniennes, 2008. 110 p. [Paulhan]

GG2459. ● Geyersbach, Ulf: *Louis-Ferdinand Céline.* Reinbek bei Hamburg: Rowohlt Taschenbuch Verlag, 2008. 160 p.

GG2460. ● Godard, Henri: *Un autre Céline.* Paris: Textuel, 2008. 2 vols.

GG2461. ● Hausmann, Frank-Rutger: *L.-F. Céline et Karl Epting.* Bruxelles: Le Bulletin célinien, 2008. 140 p.

GG2462. ● *Louis-Ferdinand Céline.* Dargest. von Uulf Geyersbach. Reinbek bei Hamburg: Rowohlt, 2008. 157 p.

GG2463. ● Richard, Gaël: *Dictionnaire des personnages: des noms de personnes, figures et référents culturels dans l'œuvre romanesque de Louis-Ferdinand Céline.* Tusson: Du Lérot, 2008. 528 p.

GG2464. ● Richard, Jean-Pierre: *Nausée de Céline.* Ed. rev. et corr. Lagrasse: Verdier, 2008. 87 p.

GG2465. ● Roych, Fabrizio: *L'angelo sinistro: la vita e l'opera di Louis-Ferdinand Céline.* Scandicci, Firenze: Firenze Atheneum, 2008. 87 p.

GG2466. ● Stasková, Alice: *Nächte der Aufklärung: Studien zur Ästhetik, Ethik und*

Erkenntnistheorie in "Voyage au bout de la nuit" von Louis-Ferdinand Céline und "Die Schlafwandler" von Hermann Broch. Tübingen: Max Niemeyer, 2008. ix, 342 p.

GG2467. ● Thomas, Merlin: *Louis-Ferdinand Céline.* New York: New Directions, 2008.

GG2468. ● Trovato, Loredana: *Armonia della forma, alchimie della lingua: Guignol's band di Louis-Ferdinand Céline.* Acireale: Bonanno, 2008. 335 p.

GG2469. ● Vitoux, Frédéric: *Bébert: le chat de Louis-Ferdinand Céline.* Paris: Grasset & Fasquelle, 2008. 133 p.

GG2470. ● Vitoux, Frédéric: *Céline, l'homme en colère.* Ed. rev. et mise à jour. Montréal: Ecriture, 2008. 310 p.

GG2471. Anton, Sonia: "Relevé des lettres mentionnées dans l'œuvre de Céline," *Année Céline* (2007), 163-171.

GG2472. Baillaud, Bernard: "Louis-Ferdinand Céline au miroir du fonds Paulhan." In 2458, 19-34. [Paulhan]

GG2473. Bénard, Johanne: "Céline transposé: l'adaptation des romans de Céline au théâtre," *Etudes Céliniennes*, no. 4 (2008), 5-24.

GG2474. Brami, Emile: "Céline et le cinéma," *Etudes Céliniennes*, no. 4 (2008), 41-53.

GG2475. Céline, Louis-Ferdinand: "Textes," *Année Céline* (2007), 9-102.

GG2476. Cornille, Jean-Louis: "Série noire." In 413.

GG2477. Cornille, Jean-Louis: "Les soirées de Meudon." In 413. [Zola]

GG2478. Décarie, David; Joël Boilard: "Figures et roman dans *Voyage au bout de la nuit*," *Etudes Céliniennes*, no. 4 (2008), 55-66.

GG2479. Dirda, Michel: "Louis-Ferdinand Céline." In 430.

GG2480. Gaillard, Françoise: "Quand le mot 'fiente' sent le caca." In 564, 205-210.

GG2481. Gibault, François: "Céline, Paulhan et Dubuffet." In 2458, 11-17. [Paulhan]

GG2482. Hartmann, Marie: "La responsabilité des écrivains." In 2458, 71-82.

GG2483. Latterner, Jean-Pierre: "Céline propriétaire à Saint-Leu-la-Forêt: lettres à André et Madeleine Pinson," *Année Céline* (2007), 19-55.

GG2484. Marchetti, François: "Lang og folk," *Année Céline* (2007), 155-159.

GG2485. Mazet, Eric: "Céline au pays des danseuses, des prêcheurs et des gangsters: le voyage de février 1937 à New York," *Etudes Céliniennes*, no. 4 (2008), 69-81.

GG2486. Mikkonen, Kai: " 'It is not the fully conscious mind which chooses West Africa in preference to Switzerland': the rhetoric of the mad African forest in Conrad, Céline and Greene," *Comparative Critical Studies*, vol. 5, no. 2-3 (2008), 301-315.

GG2487. Oesterreicher, Wulf: "Die Stimme im Text-die Schrift in der Rede." In 1028, 209-236.

GG2488. Rabier, Michaël: "Louis-Ferdinand Céline, l'éternel retour," *Spectacle du Monde*, no. 544 (avril 2008), 60-65.

GG2489. Redfern, Walter: "Upping the anti/e: exaggeration in Céline and Vallès." In 568. [Vallès]

GG2490. Rihard-Diamond, Fabienne: "Le rigodon du *Voyage*: la satire célinienne entre danse et silence," *Modernités*, no. 27 (2008), 407-418.

GG2491. Roussin, Philippe: "Céline et Paulhan: terreur ou rhétorique." In 2458, 53-69. [Paulhan]

GG2492. Sapiro, Gisèle: "L'intellectuel a-t-il le droit à l'erreur?" In 2458, 83-105.

GG2493. Sautermeister, Christine: " 'Avec les mots on ne se méfie jamais suffisamment' ou la dynamique de l'invective chez Louis-Ferdinand Céline," *Etudes Littéraires*, vol. 39, no. 1 (hiver 2008), 83-98.

GG2494. Seba-Collett, Anne Elizabeth: "The genesis of poetic prose in the works of Louis-Ferdinand Céline through the transgressive and maieutic agency of the figure of the double." Diss., Univ. of Cape Town, 2008. 343 p.

GG2495. Simon, Laurent: "Bibliophilie," *Année Céline* (2007), 173-181.

GG2496. Simon, Laurent; Gaël Richard: "Retour au Cameroun," *Année Céline* (2007), 107-153.

GG2497. Staskova, Alice: "*Professor Y* à la Berliner Volksbühne," *Etudes Céliniennes*, no. 4 (2008), 140-142.

GG2498. Staskova, Alice: "Une soirée Céline à l'Institut français de Prague," *Etudes Céliniennes*, no. 4 (2008), 143-144.

GG2499. Sugiura, Yoriko: "Stratégie de l'humour chez Céline," *Etudes Céliniennes*, no. 4 (2008), 25-39.

GG2500. Vargas Llosa, Mario: "Céline: le dernier maudit," *Nouvelle Revue Française*, no. 587 (oct. 2008), 75-80.

CENDRARS, Blaise. See also 623, 4308.

GG2501. ● Bienne, Gisèle: *La ferme de Navarin*. Paris: Gallimard, 2008. 129 p.

GG2502. ● *Blaise Cendrars, un imaginaire du crime*. Sous la dir. de David Martens. Paris: L'Harmattan, 2008. *Structures et pouvoirs des imaginaires*. 137 p.

GG2503. Bienne, Gisèle: "Cendrars: *La main coupée*, le grand livre." In 473, 101-109.

GG2504. Campa, Laurence: "Cendrars à Granville," *Continent Cendrars*, no. 13 (2008), 39-44.

GG2505. Cendrars, Blaise: "Deux cartes, trois lettres à Louis Brun et autres documents de la collection Anacréon," *Continent Cendrars*, no. 13 (2008), 45-69.

GG2506. Cendrars, Blaise: "Entretiens de Bruxelles (1949)," *Continent Cendrars*, no. 13 (2008), 17-38.

GG2507. Flückiger, Jean-Carlo: "A la lumière de deux photos," *Continent Cendrars*, no. 13 (2008), 98-101.

GG2508. Flückiger, Jean-Carlo: "La tête à couper." In 2502, 11-34.

GG2509. Frédéric, Madeleine: "Cendrars: de la légalisation à l'autojustification du meurtre." In 2502, 35-47.

GG2510. Frédéric, Madeleine: "Témoignages de guerre et méandres génériques: la guerre de 14 selon Barbusse et Cendrars." In 764, 129-138. [Barbusse]

GG2511. Guyon, Laurence: "Le lépreux de 'Gênes'." In 2502, 93-105.

GG2512. Le Quellec Cottier, Christine: "Nouvelles de la famille Sauser: Cendrars entre famille et fiction . . . ou 'de l'existence des Sauser'," *Continent Cendrars*, no. 13 (2008), 78-96.

GG2513. Martens, David: "Blaise Cendrars vous salue . . . ," *Continent Cendrars*, no. 13 (2008), 11-14.

GG2514. Martens, David: "Portrait du traducteur en hors la loi: Blaise Cendrars et Al Jennings." In 2502, 63-79.

GG2515. Montrosset, Luisa: "*Panorama de la pègre*: un stellionat dans l'œuvre cendrarsienne?" In 2502, 81-92.

GG2516. Ravet, David: "Arthur Honegger et Blaise Cendrars: une interprétation musicale des *Pâques à New York*," *Continent Cendrars*, no. 13 (2008), 106-122.

GG2517. Russo, Maria Teresa: "Entre crime et démesure, le Paris-palimpseste de Cendrars." In 2502, 123-137.

GG2518. Schoolcraft, Ralph: "Mort d'Icare—Deuil de Cendrars." In 2502, 107-121.

GG2519. Temple, Frédéric Jacques: "Voyage et divagabondage," *Continent Cendrars*, no. 13 (2008), 123-131.

GG2520. Touret, Michèle: "Et si nous parlions des victimes?" In 2502, 49-61.

GG2521. Touret, Michèle: "Questions de cadrage dans *La Guerre au Luxembourg*, poème de Blaise Cendrars avec cinq dessins de Moïse Kisling," *Degrés*, 36e année, no. 133 (printemps 2008), e1-e5.

CERTEAU, Michel de.

GG2522. ● *Lire Michel de Certeau: la formalité des pratiques*. Hrsg. Philippe Büttgen, Christian Jouhaud. Frankfurt: Vittorio Klostermann, 2008. *Zeitsprünge*, Band 12, Heft 1/2. 270 p.

GG2523. ● Mboukou, Serge: *Michel de Certeau, l'intelligence de la sensibilité*. Strasbourg: Le Portique, 2008. 151 p.

GG2524. ● *Michel de Certeau: Geschichte-Kultur-Religion*. Hrsg. Marian Füssel. Konstanz: UVK Verlagsgesellschaft, 2007. 371 p.

GG2525. ● *Sulla traccia di Michel de Certeau*. A cura di Barnaba Maj, Rossana Lista. Macerata: Quodlibet, 2008. 214 p.

GG2526. ● York, George B.: *Michel de Certeau or union in difference*. ?: Gracewing, 2008. *Inigo texts series*. 109 p.

GG2527. Frohlich, Mary: "The space of Christic performance: Teresa of Avila through the lens of Michel de Certeau." In 879.

GG2528. Orylski, Tomas: "L'itinéraire du croire dans la démarche de Michel de Certeau," *Revue des Sciences Religieuses*, 82e année, no. 2 (avril 2008), 245-251.

CÉSAIRE, Aimé. See also 105, 274, 306a, 492, 672, 2930, 7060.

GG2529. ● Alliot, David: *Aimé Césaire: le nègre universel*. Gollion: Infolio, 2008. 255 p.

GG2530. ● Césaire, Aimé: *Ferrements et autres poèmes*. Préface par Daniel Maximin. Paris: Seuil, 2008. *Points*. 200 p.

GG2531. ● Césaire, Aimé: *Nègre je suis, nègre je resterai: entretiens avec Françoise Vergès*. Paris: Michell, 2008. 148 p.

GG2532. ● Davis, Gregson: *Aimé Césaire*. Cambridge: Cambridge Univ. Press, 2008. *Cambridge studies in African and Caribbean literature*, 5. [Orig. ed., 1997]

GG2533. ● Hénane, René: *Les armes miraculeuses d'Aimé Césaire*. Paris: L'Harmattan, 2008. *Critiques littéraires*. 352 p.

GG2534. ● Kalamba Nsapo, Sylvain: *La négritude vue par un théologien africain: tradition bimwenyienne: hommage à Aimé Césaire*. Paris: Menaibuc, 2008. 121 p.

GG2535. ● Kalamba Nsapo, Sylvain: *Retour au pays natal de la prière: hommage à Aimé Césaire*. Paris: Menaibuc, 2008. 35 p.

GG2536. ● Kesteloot, Lilyan: *Comprendre le Cahier d'un retour au pays natal d'Aimé Césaire*. Paris: L'Harmattan, 2008. *Comprendre*. Nouv. éd. 127 p.

GG2537. ● Monthieux, Yves-Léopold: *ContreChroniques de la vie politique martiniquaise: Aimé Césaire: le verbe et l'action*. Fort-de-France: Désormeaux, 2008. 382 p.

GG2538. ● Pépin, Ernest; Ali Babar Kenjah: *Quelques mots sur Aimé Césaire*. Brissac: Petit pavé, 2008. 45 p.

GG2539. ● Pestre de Almeida, Lilian: *Aimé Césaire: Cahier d'un retour au pays natal*. Paris: L'Harmattan, 2008. *Classiques francophones*. 188 p.

GG2540. ● Ribbe, Claude: *Le nègre vous emmerde*. Paris: Buchet/Chastel, 2008. 135 p.

GG2541. ● Riemann, Marianne: *Hommage für Aimé Césaire*. Berlin: Forschungsinst. der IWVWW, 2008. 20 p.

GG2542. ● Shima, Eric: *Aimé Césaire, Cahier d'un retour au pays natal et Tchicaya U Tam'si, Epitomé: étude comparative*. Paris: L'Harmattan, 2008. *Approches littéraires*. 213 p.

GG2543. ● Vilar, Pierre: *Les armes miraculeuses d'Aimé Césaire*. Carouge: Zoé, 2008. *Le cippe*. 112 p.

GG2544. Arnold, A. James: "Beyond postcolonial Césaire: reading *Cahier d'un retour au pays natal* historically," *Forum for Modern Language Studies*

GG2545. Arnold, A. James: "Forty years with Césaire, 1968-2008," *Small Axe*, no. 27 (2008), 128-141.

GG2546. Bonhomme, Marc: "Les figures pathétiques dans le pamphlet." In 446, 165-175.

GG2547. Bouvier, Pierre: "Aimé Césaire, la négritude et l'ouverture poétique," *Esprit*, no. 346 (juillet 2008), 15-28.

GG2548. Cailler, Bernadette: "Histoires . . . à tout petits mots. Chassé-croisé entre Aimé Césaire et Lorand Gaspar," *Nouvelles Etudes Francophones*, vol. 22, no. 1 (printemps 2007), 37-46. [Gaspar]

GG2549. Chamoiseau, Patrick: "Césaire? Ma liberté: hommage à Aimé Césaire," *PEN International*, vol. 58, no. 2 (Autumn-Winter 2008), 6-9.

GG2550. Chaulet Achour, Christiane: "Pour Aimé Césaire," *Caribbean Studies*, vol. 36, no. 1 (Jan.-June 2008), 103-127.

GG2551. Eshleman, Clayton: "Aimé Césaire's lost, found, scattered body," *Callaloo*, vol. 31, no. 4 (Fall 2008), 983-986.

GG2552. Frassinelli, Pier Paolo: "Shakespeare and transculturation: Aimé Césaire's *A Tempest*." In 848, 173-186.

GG2553. Glissant, Edouard: "Aimé Césaire: the poet's passion," *Small Axe*, no. 27 (2008), 118-123.

GG2554.   Hamzaoui, Saïda: "Didascalies et engagement dans le théâtre de Césaire." In 605, 365-378.

GG2555.   Hurley, E. Anthony: " 'Is he, am I, a hero?': self-referentiality and the colonial legacy in Aimé Césaire's Toussaint Louverture." In 137.

GG2556.   Irele, F. Abiola: "Homage to Césaire," *Présence Africaine*, no. 174 (2008), 91-94.

GG2557.   Irele, F. Abiola: "Homage to Aimé Césaire," *Small Axe*, no. 27 (2008), 124-127.

GG2558.   Kandé, Sylvie: "This corpse so small left unavenged: Nicolás Guillén and Aimé Césaire on Emmett Till's lynching." In 822, 143-160.

GG2559.   Malela, Buata B.: "Césaire nomothète." In 102, 274-320.

GG2560.   Nnaemeka, Obioma: "Racialization and the colonial architecture," *PMLA*, vol. 123, no. 5 (Oct. 2008), 1748-1751.

GG2561.   Price, Richard: "Martinique, memory, Césaire," *Caribbean Studies*, vol. 36, no. 1 (Jan.-June 2008), 211-214.

GG2562.   Rowell, Charles H.: "It is through poetry that one copes with solitude: an interview with Aimé Césaire," *Callaloo*, vol. 31, no. 4 (Fall 2008), 989-997.

GG2563.   Scharfman, Ronnie: "Homage to Aimé Césaire, 1913-2008," *Callaloo*, vol. 31, no. 4 (Fall 2008), 976-980.

GG2564.   Smith, Phyllis A.: "A meeting with Aimé Césaire," *Callaloo*, vol. 31, no. 4 (Fall 2008), 987-988.

GG2565.   Stétié, Salah: "Moi qui Krakatoa." In 72, 561-573.

GG2566.   Winkiel, Laura: "Reading across the color line." In 627. [S. Césaire]

CÉSAIRE, Ina. See 70.

CÉSAIRE, Suzanne. See also 2566.

GG2567.   Rabbitt, Kara M.: "The geography of identity in Suzanne Césaire's 'Le grand camouflage'," *Research in African Literatures*, vol. 39, no. 3 (Fall 2008), 121-131.

CHADOURNE, Marc.

GG2568.   Renard, Paul: "Marc Chadourne (1895-1975), l'absent," *Roman 20-50*, no. 46 (2008), 105-113.

GG2569.   Madelénat, Daniel: "Biographie et intimité entre Lumières et romantisme dans *Le Matamore ébouriffé* de Michel Chaillou." In 391, 69-80.

CHAINAS, Antoine.

GG2570.   Leroy, Jérôme: "*Versus*, de A. Chainas," *Nouvelle Revue Française*, no. 587 (oct. 2008), 216-220.

CHAMOISEAU, Patrick. See also 190, 4250.

GG2571.   ● *Autour de Patrick Chamoiseau*. Ed. Tomasz Swoboda, Ewa Wierzbowska, Olga Wronska. Sopot: Uniwersytetu Gdanskiego, 2008. 190 p.

GG2572.   ● Lutas, Liviu: *Biblique des derniers gestes de Patrick Chamoiseau: fantastique et histoire*. Lund: Språk-och litteraturvetenskapligt centrum, Lunds universitet, 2008. *Etudes romanes de Lund*. 235 p.

GG2573.   Bérard, Stéphanie: "Le théâtre de Patrick Chamoiseau. Entretien avec le dramaturge martiniquais," *Nouvelles Etudes Francophones*, vol. 22, no. 2 (automne 2007), 165-178.

GG2574.   Bloch, Béatrice: "Un livre-monde, entre l'utopie libératoire et la fidélité enchantée." In 96, 317-324.

GG2575.   Britton, Celia: "Conquering the town: stories and myth in Patrick Chamoiseau's *Texaco*." In 51, 93-110.

GG2576.   Chamoiseau, Patrick: "Entretien public avec Anne Douaire." In 441, 231-247.

GG2577.   Cordobés, Fernando: "Vivir la aventura de la diversidad del mundo," *Cuadernos Hispanoamericanos*, n. 694 (2008), [n.p.].

GG2578.   Delmeule, Jean-Christophe: "Enfance réelle, enfance rêvée: *Une enfance créole* de Patrick Chamoiseau." In 448, 139-148.

GG2579.   Douaire, Anne: "Marqueur de paroles, en réalité sans profession?" In 441, 87-95.

GG2580. Exner, Isabel: "Lo limpio y lo sucio: movimientos textuales críticos en Patrick Chamoiseau y Pedro Juan Gutiérrez." In 53, 79-91.

GG2581. Gauvin, Lise: "Autor in fabula: pérégrinisme et paratexte." In 407, 113-129.

GG2582. Knepper, Wendy: "Patrick Chamoiseau's seascapes and the trans-Caribbean imagery." In 60.

GG2583. Knepper, Wendy: "Remapping the crime novel in the Francophone Caribbean: the case of Patrick Chamoiseau's *Solibo Magnifique*," *PMLA*, vol. 122, no. 5 (Oct. 2007), 1431-1446.

GG2584. Maisier, Véronique: "Texte et pré(-)textes dans *Texaco* de Patrick Chamoiseau." In 617, 83-94.

GG2585. Morgan, Janice: "Re-imagining diversity and connection in the chaos-world: an interview with Patrick Chamoiseau," *Callaloo*, vol. 31, no. 2 (Spring 2008), 443-453.

GG2586. Ndiaye, Cheikh M.: "Marronnage, oralité et écriture dans *Solibo magnifique* de Patrick Chamoiseau," *Nouvelles Etudes Francophones*, vol. 22, no. 2 (automne 2007), 112-121.

GG2587. Pilorget, Jean-Paul: "Densifier le lieu: enjeux de l'intertextualité dans *Biblique des derniers gestes* de Patrick Chamoiseau," *Nouvelles Etudes Francophones*, vol. 23, no. 2 (automne 2008), 246-261.

GG2588. Stafford, Andy: "Patrick Chamoiseau and Rodolphe Hammadi in the penal colony. Photo-text and memory-traces," *Postcolonial Studies*, vol. 11, no. 1 (March 2008), 27-38.

GG2589. Tremblay, Emmanuelle: "De la mémoire autobiographique au théâtre de la mémoire chez Patrick Chamoiseau." In 103, 173-191.

CHAMSON, André. See 5578.

CHAPELLE, Marie-Louis.

GG2590. Cohen-Halimi, Michèle: "Marie-Louise Chapelle. Volonté de chance," *Critique*, tome 64, no. 735-736 (août-sept. 2008), 605-611.

CHAR, René.

GG2591. ● *Dire René Char: actes du colloque du 10 mai 2007.* Buc: SCEREN-CRDP, 2008. 112 p.

GG2592. ● Hahn, Kurt: *Ethopoetik des Elementaren: Zum Schreiben als Lebensform in der Lyrik von René Char, Paul Celan und Octavio Paz.* Paderborn: Fink, 2008. 384 p.

GG2593. ● Marty, Eric: *L'engagement extatique sur René Char: suivi de commentaire du fragment 178 des Feuillets d'Hypnos.* Houilles: Manucius, 2008. 67 p.

GG2594. ● *René Char.* Dir. Dominique Fourcade. Paris: L'Harne, 2007. 175 p.

GG2595. ● *René Char dans le miroir des eaux.* Catalogue raisonné du fonds René Char conserve au Musée Pétrarque à Fontaine-de-Vaucluse établi par Sandra Chastel. Sous la dir. d'Eve Duperray; texts de Didier Alexandre [et al.]. Paris: Beauchesne, 2008. 184 p.

GG2596. Brackenbury, Rosalind: "On the trail of René Char," *Brick*, no. 81 (Summer 2008), 42-?.

GG2597. Charbagi, Haydée: "Dire René Char: la sonorité de la pensée." In 2591, 23-30.

GG2598. Charvet, Pascal: "Atelier: Char entre lyrisme et aphorisme." In 2591, 81-92.

GG2599. Dimanche, Thierry: "*Point d'orgue pour les poulpes*: extraits, précédés de trois petites gloses," *Liberté*, no. 277 (2007), 39-46.

GG2600. Dumont, François: "Char carnettiste," *Liberté*, no. 277 (2007), 35-38.

GG2601. Gomez, Françoise: "Atelier: le théâtre et René Char, panoramique autour de *Claire*." In 2591, 59-71.

GG2602. Hahn, Kurt: "Lyrische Historiographie und Trauerarbeit: René Chars *écriture contre le désastre*," *Romantische Zeitschrift für Literaturgeschichte*, 32. Jahrgang, Heft 3-4 (2008), 375-392.

GG2603. Lancrey-Javal, Romain; Marie-Françoise Delecroix: "Redonnez-leur . . . René Char: quelles préoccupations pédagogiques?" In 2591, 15-21.

GG2604. Laroche, Yves: "L'inespéré de René Char," *Liberté*, no. 277 (2007), 47-54.

GG2605. Loayza, Daniel: "Fulgurant lapidaire: René Char ou le trait de poème." In 2591, 93-112.

GG2606. Morier-Genoud, Philippe: "*Claire*, mémoires d'une création théâtrale." In 2591, 73-79.

GG2607. Plante, Manon: "Se délier la langue," *Liberté*, no. 277 (2007), 22-28.

GG2608. Riou, Nathalie: "La mise à nuit de la métaphore dans la poésie de René Char," *LittéRéalité*, vol. 20, no. 2 (automne/hiver 2008), 59-76.

GG2609. Rasoamanana, Linda: "Une recontre insolite de René Char." In 439, 113-123.

GG2610. Riva, Claude: "Aborder René Char en ateliers de création et d'écriture." In 2591, 41-57.

GG2611. Thibault, Louis-Jean: "Faire un homme," *Liberté*, no. 277 (2007), 29-34.

GG2612. Villemaine, Pierre Antoine: "Pour une lecture créative." In 2591, 33-38.

CHARCHOUNE, Serge.

GG2613. Morard, Annick: "Serge Charchoune dadaïste, ou le français sans complexe." In 442, 49-57.

CHARDONNE, Jacques.

GG2614. Authier, François-Jean: "Espaces *destinés*: la topographie *sentimentale* de Jacques Chardonne," *Roman 20-50*, no. 45 (2008), 73-84.

GG2615. Cornick, Martyn: "Jacques Chardonne et *La Nouvelle Revue Française*," *Roman 20-50*, no. 45 (2008), 9-23.

GG2616. Dambre, Marc: "Vivre à Buc-Chalo," *Roman 20-50*, no. 45 (2008), 85-95.

GG2617. Dantal, Didier: "Chardonne ou l'art de ne pas finir," *Roman 20-50*, no. 45 (2008), 97-106.

GG2618. Douzou, Catherine: "*Une jeunesse charentaise*: le 'roman par images' de Jacques Chardonne," *Roman 20-50*, no. 45 (2008), 118-121.

GG2619. Durafour, Jean-Michel: " 'Est-ce un film?': l'adaptation cinématographique des *Destinées sentimentales* par Olivier Assayas," *Roman 20-50*, no. 45 (2008), 63-72. [Assayas]

GG2620. Lecarme, Jacques: "L'éthique protestante et le roman du capitalisme," *Roman 20-50*, no. 45 (2008), 25-35.

GG2621. Mattiussi, Laurent: "Le lourd secret de vivre ensemble," *Roman 20-50*, no. 45 (2008), 107-117.

GG2622. Montfort, Frédéric; Stéphane Chaudier: "*Soli Deo gloria*: Chardonne à l'épreuve de la foi," *Roman 20-50*, no. 45 (2008), 49-62.

GG2623. Tonolo, Alain: "L'esprit ancien du capitalisme," *Roman 20-50*, no. 45 (2008), 37-48.

CHAREF, Mehdi.

GG2624. ● Brokopf, Ellen: *Schreiben als kultureller Widerstand die 2. Generation in der Migration am Beispiel von zwei Romanen aus Deutschland und Frankreich*. Berlin: Lit, 2008. *FOLIES*, 6. 147 p.

CHASSAY, Jean-François.

GG2625. Nareau, Michel: "*Les taches solaires* de Jean-François Chassay." In 41, 87-106.

CHAURETTE, Normand.

GG2626. Monah, Dana: "La réécriture de *Richard III* dans *Les Reines* de Normand Chaurette." In 1100, 69-76.

GG2627. Popovic, Pierre: "Tant crie-t-on au loup qu'il vient. *Ce qui meurt en dernier*," *Jeu: Cahiers de Théâtre*, no. 127 [no. 2] (2008), 7-11.

CHAUVET, Marie. See also 281, 293.

GG2628. Kaussen, Valerie: "Decolonization, revolution, and postmodernity in Marie Chauvet's *Amour*." In 91.

GG2629. Kaussen, Valerie: "Irrational revolutions: colonial intersubjectivity and dialects in Marie Chauvet's *Amour*." In 137.

CHAWAF, Chantal.

GG2630. Schwertdner, Karin: "Mémoire traumatisante, parole réparatrice: Chawaf," *Etudes Littéraires*, vol. 37, no. 2 (automne 2006), 37-47.

CHAZAL, Malcolm de.

GG2631. • Chazal, Malcolm: *Autobiographie spirituelle*. Ouvrage coordonné par Robert Furlong. Paris: L'Harmattan, 2008. *L'Afrique au cœur des lettres*. 105 p.

GG2632. • Chazal, Malcolm de: *Moïse*. Ouvrage coordonné par Christophe Cassiau-Haurie. Paris: L'Harmattan, 2008. *L'Afrique au cœur des lettres*. 93 p.

GG2633. • Chazal, Malcolm de: *Sens-plastique*. Trans. with an introduction by Irving Weiss; foreword by W. H. Auden. København; Los Angeles: Green Integer; Saint Paul, 2008. 779 p. [Orig. ed., 1948]

CHEDID, Andrée. See also 1139, 1148.

GG2634. Bednárová, Katarína: "Représentations du pre dans l'imaginaire du fils et structures narratives dans le récit de vie *Géricault* par Andrée Chedid." In 572, 245-256.

GG2635. Boustani, Carmen: "Fiction biographique: Andrée Chedid," *Interculturel Francophonies*, no. 14 (2008), 143-161.

GG2636. Calle-Gruber, Mireille: "L'écriture anachorète: *Les Marches de sable* d'Andrée Chedid." In 539, 199-207.

GG2637. Chaulet Achour, Christiane: "Archives du passé et travail d'écriture dans *Les marches de sable* d'Andrée Chedid," *Etudes Littéraires Africaines*, no. 26 (2008), 10-18.

GG2638. Darwiche, Jabbour Zahida: "Terre et poésie: lecture de *Cavernes et soleils* d'Andrée Chedid." In 96.

GG2639. Grépat-Michel, Nicole: "Andrée Chedid et le discret déni des *Nuits*." In 431, 115-131.

GG2640. Houriez, Jacques: "Andrée Chedid, un univers de la féminité." In 419, 233-244.

CHEN, Ying. See also 492, 546.

GG2641. Andrei, Carmen: "Ying Chen, *Les lettres chinoises*." In 115, 180-191.

GG2642. Diego, Rosa de: "Ying Chen: à la recherche d'une mémoire." In 119, 299-317.

GG2643. Lapointe, Martine-Emmanuelle: "Entre le propre et l'étranger: la réception québécoise des œuvres de Ying Chen et de David Homel." In 120, 204-213.

GG2644. Lorre, Christine: "The poetics of exile: a comparative study of the reception of Ying Chen's recent novels in Canada and in France." In 121.

GG2645. Lorre, Christine: "Ying Chen's 'poetic rebellion'." In 791, 267-295.

GG2646. Meadwell, Kenneth: "La migrance de l'Autre dans le récit canadien d'expression française: *La Mémoire de l'eau* de Ying Chen." In 104, 91-106.

GG2647. Parent, Anne Martine: "Origines manquantes, origines en trop: héritage et filiation dans l'œuvre de Ying Chen." In 572, 287-294.

CHENG, François.

GG2648. Bertaud, Madeleine: "*L'ardent face-à-face / des presences entre-croisées*, François Cheng," *Travaux de Littérature*, tome 21 (2008), 501-518.

GG2649. Bertaud, Madeleine: " 'Leurs yeux se rencontrèrent', mais . . . Un autre mythe de l'amour." In 520, 727-738.

GG2650. Mascarou, Alain: "François Cheng ou l'exil du trait." In 418, 313-323.

GG2651. Nabert, Nathalie: "*Laudatio* de François Cheng," *Transversalités*, no. 105 (2008), 163-166.

CHEVILLARD, Eric.

GG2652. • *Chevillard, Echenoz: filiations insolites*. Ed. Aline Mura-Brunel. Amsterdam: Rodopi, 2008. *CRIN*, 50. 140 p. [Echenoz]

GG2653. André, Marie-Odile: "Filiation insolite: un vaillant petit Chevillard." In 2652, 117-126.

GG2654. Audet, René: "Eric Chevillard et l'écriture du déplacement." In 2652, 105-116.

GG2655. Audet, René: " 'Et si la littérature . . . ?' Des auteurs en quête d'événements racontent des histoires littéraires," *Roman 20-50*, no. 46 (2008), 23-32.

GG2656. Bessard-Banquy, Olivier: "Moi, je, pas tellement: l'autobiographie selon Chevillard," *Roman 20-50*, no. 46 (2008), 33-42.

GG2657.	Blanckeman, Bruno: " 'L'écrivain marche sur le papier': une étude du *Hérisson*," *Roman 20-50*, no. 46 (2008), 67-76.

GG2658.	Chevillard, Eric: "Des leurres ou des hommes de paille: entretien," *Roman 20-50*, no. 46 (2008), 11-22.

GG2659.	Cotea, Lidia: "Eric Chevillard: le roman, une mythologie de notre temps," *Studies on Lucette Desvignes and the Twentieth Century*, no. 18 (2008), 201-214.

GG2660.	De Smet, Stijn: "Portrait de l'écrivain en orang-outang. Les origines dans l'œuvre d'Eric Chevillard," *Littératures*, no. 58-59 (2008), 333-353.

GG2661.	Havercroft, Barbara; Pascal Riendeau: "Les jeux intertextuels d'Eric Chevillard ou comment (faire) démolir Nisard par lui-même," *Roman 20-50*, no. 46 (2008), 77-89.

GG2662.	Lapacherie, Jean-Gérard: "Quand le roman représente les conventions qui le régissent." In 2652, 15-25. [Echenoz]

GG2663.	Michelucci, Pascal: "Démolir la métafiction?," *Roman 20-50*, no. 46 (2008), 55-66.

GG2664.	Papillon, Joëlle: "Marges et mutineries," *Roman 20-50*, no. 46 (2008), 43-53.

GG2665.	Schaffner, Alain: "*Démolir Nisard*: variations sur la mort de l'auteur," *Roman 20-50*, no. 46 (2008), 91-99.

GG2666.	Tobiassen, Elin Beate: "Promenades de lecteuers dans *Le Vaillant Petit Tailleur* d'Eric Chevillard," *French Studies*, vol. 62, no. 3 (July 2008), 313-327.

CHEVRILLON, André.

GG2667.	Durand, Jean-François: "Regards sur la culture arabo-musulmane dans le récit de l'ère coloniale." In 72, 29-52.

CHRAÏBI, Driss.

GG2668.	● Chraïbi, Driss; Abdeslam Kadiri: *Une vie sans concessions: entretiens avec Driss Chraïbi*. Casablanca: Tarik, 2008. 126 p.

GG2669.	● Fouet, Jeanne: *La mère du printemps de Driss Chraïbi*. Paris: L'Harmattan, 2008. *Approches littéraires*. 91 p.

GG2670.	Alexandre Madonia, Francesco Paolo: "Tradurre il plurilinguismo: francese mescidato e calchi dall'arabo in *Naissance à l'aube* di Driss Chraïbi." In 586, 181-191.

GG2671.	Cipriano, Manuela: "Una nuova 'auscultazione' della contemporaneità: I romanzi polizieschi di Andrea Camilleri e di Driss Chraïbi." In 586, 249-259.

GG2672.	Graiouid, Said: "We have not buried the simple past: the public sphere and post-colonial literature in Morocco," *Journal of African Cultural Studies*, vol. 20, no. 2 (Dec. 2008), 145-158.

GG2673.	Karzazi, Wafae: "Les mécanismes de l'ironie dans *Une enquête au pays* de Driss Chraïbi," *Expressions Maghrébines*, vol. 7, no. 2 (hiver 2008), 99-112.

GG2674.	Roblès, Emmanuel: "Hommage à Driss Chraïbi," *CELAAN*, vol. 6, no. 3 (Fall 2008), 7-17. [Suivi d'un interview de Driss Chraïbi accordée à Lionel Dubois]

CINGRIA, Charles-Albert.

GG2675.	● Chessex, Jacques: *Charles-Albert Cingria: l'instant et l'intemporel*. Lausanne: Age d'homme, 2008. *Poche suisse*. 89 p.

CIORAN, Émile-Michel. See also 497, 997, 1722.

GG2676.	● Sarca, Maria Ioana: *Aussenseitertum und metaphysisches Exil: eine vergleichende Auseinandersetzung mit den Werken Emil Ciorans und Josef Winklers*. Frankfurt: Peter Lang, 2008. 133 p.

GG2677.	● Zanaz, Hamid: *La mélancolie joyeuse: excursions dans la philosophie de Cioran*. Paris: Aparis, 2008. 81 p.

GG2678.	Bulger, Raymonde A.: "Le poids du peu ou l'aphorisme chez E. M. Cioran." In 535, 193-204.

GG2679.	David, Sylvain: "Cioran et le 'pamphlet *sans objet*'. Paradoxes d'une poétique de l'excès," *Etudes Littéraires*, vol. 39, no. 1 (hiver 2008), 47-58.

GG2680.	Frosin, Constantin: "Cioran et le rire," *Revue de Littérature Comparée*, no. 382 [82e année, no. 4] (oct.-déc. 2008), 475-487.

GG2681.	Jarrety, Michel: "Cioran et la chute dans l'Histoire." In 964, 215-225.

GG2682.	Nicorescu, Liliana: "Cioran lecteur de Cioran." In 535, 219-243.

GG2683. Roman, Aurélia: "E. M. Cioran: music in my soul." In 535, 245-270.

CIXOUS, Hélène. See also 378, 638, 711, 888, 999, 1415.

GG2684. ● Cixous, Hélène: *White ink: interviews on sex, text and politics.* Ed. Susan Sellers. New York: Columbia Univ. Press, 2008. *European perspectives.* xvi, 199 p. [Derrida, Duras, Foucault]

GG2685. ● *French feminists: critical evaluations in cultural theory. Vol. II: Hélène Cixous.* Ed. Jennifer Hansen, Ann Cahill. London; New York: Routledge, 2008. xi, 385 p.

GG2686. ● Ives, Kelly: *Hélène Cixous, I love you: the jouissance of writing.* 2nd edition. Maidstone: Crescent Moon, 2008. *European writers.* 165 p.

GG2687. ● Schäfer, Elisabeth: *Die offene Seite der Schrift: J. D. und H. C. côte à côte.* Wien: Passagen-Verlag, 2008. 144 p. [Derrida]

GG2688. ● Spanfelner, Deborah L. Calabro: *Hélène Cixous, a space for the other: in between forgetting, remembering and rewriting.* Saarbrücken: VDM, 2008. 147 p.

GG2689. Allen, Jeffner: "Poetic politics: how the Amazons took the Acropolis." In 2685.

GG2690. Aneja, Anu: "The Medusa's slip: Hélène Cixous and the underpinnings of *écriture féminine.*" In 2685.

GG2691. Boyle, Claire: "Hélène Cixous: autobiography, the ethics of knowledge and strategies of self-writing." In 400, 125-151.

GG2692. Calle, Mireille: "Hélène Cixous's writing-thinking." In 2685.

GG2693. Calle-Gruber, Mireille: "Les villes imaginaires d'Hélène Cixous." In 502.

GG2694. Cixous, Hélène: "From the word of life, with Jacques Derrida." In 2684. [Derrida]

GG2695. Cixous, Hélène: "On Marguerite Duras, with Michel Foucault." In 2684. [Duras, Foucault]

GG2696. Colebrook, Claire: "Friendship, seduction and text: Cixous and Derrida," *Angelaki,* vol. 13, no. 2 (2008), 109-124. [Derrida]

GG2697. Cooper, Sarah: "Bisexual textual economies: reading sexuality through Hélène Cixous's writing." In 2685.

GG2698. Crevier Goulet, Sarah-Anaïs: "De l'ectogenèse au corps post-humain: pour une redéfinition de la singularité chez Hélène Cixous." In 440, 69-78.

GG2699. Crolla, Adriana Cristina: "Derrida-Cixous-Lispector: velos y desvelos en el paradigma intraducible de la tra-dicción," *Cuadernos de Filologia Francesa,* no. 19 (2008), 65-82. [Derrida]

GG2700. Debrauwere-Miller, Nathalie: "Hélène Cixous, la passante de l'histoire," *Dalhousie French Studies,* vol. 84 (Fall 2008), 101-111.

GG2701. Dobson, Julia: "The scene of writing: the representation of poetic identity in Cixous's recent theatre." In 2685.

GG2702. Freeman, Barbara: "Plus corps donc plus écriture: Hélène Cixous and the mind-body problem." In 2685.

GG2703. Garnier, Marie-Dominique: "Writing, dreaming Freud, Fliess, Fluff and Cixous," *Journal of European Studies,* vol. 38, no. 4 (Dec. 2008), 361-372.

GG2704. Hanrahan, Mairead: "Of altobiography." In 2685.

GG2705. "Hélène Cixous," *Contemporary Literary Criticism,* vol. 253 (2008), 1-112.

GG2706. Jones, Ann Rosalind: "Writing the body: toward an understanding of *l'écriture féminine.*" In 2685.

GG2707. Kamuf, Peggy: "To give place: semi-approaches to Hélène Cixous." In 2685.

GG2708. Laillou Savona, Jeannelle: "Hélène Cixous and utopian thought." In 2685.

GG2709. Lydon, Mary: "Re-translating no re-reading no, rather: rejoycing (with) Hélène Cixous." In 2685.

GG2710. Manners, Marilyn: "Hélène Cixous names woman, mother, other." In 2685.

GG2711. McQuillan, Martin: "The girl who steps along, or, 10 steps on the ladder to reading Cixous." In 2685.

GG2712. Moi, Toril: "Hélène Cixous: an imaginary utopia." In 2685.

GG2713. Penrod, Lynn: "Algeriance, exile, and Hélène Cixous." In 2685.

GG2714. Regard, Frédéric: "L'intime en déconstruction: le portrait biographique selon Hélène Cixous." In 391, 241-251.

GG2715. Regard, Frédéric: "On Cixous's tongue." In 2685.

GG2716. Regard, Frédéric: "Pas de deux: les styles du féminin." In 507, 29-46. [Althusser, Derrida]

GG2717. Running-Johnson, Cynthia: "The Medusa's tale: feminine writing and 'La Genet'." In 2685.

GG2718. Setti, Nadia: "The outsider society: potentialité de l'impuissance," *Résonances*, no. 9 (févr. 2008), 117-125.

GG2719. Shiach, Morag: "Their 'symbolic' exists, it holds power—we, the sowers of disorder, know it only too well." In 2685.

GG2720. Shukla, B. A.: "Hélène Cixous and poststructuralist feminist theory." In 1500.

GG2721. Shukla, B. A.: "Hélène Cixous on the position of women." In 1500.

GG2722. Shukla, B. A.: "Hélène Cixous on 'Women: the longest revolution'." In 1500.

GG2723. Shukla, B. A.: "Introduction to Hélène Cixous." In 1500.

GG2724. Spivak, Gayatri Chakravorty: "Cixous without borders." In 2685.

GG2725. Stanton, Domna C.: "Difference on trial: a critique of the maternal metaphor in Cixous, Irigaray, and Kristeva." In 2685. [Irigaray, Kristeva]

GG2726. Stevens, Christa: "Hélène Cixous et le livre du frère: de *Tours promises* aux *Rêveries de la femme sauvage*." In 571, 353-365.

GG2727. Thomas, Sue: "Difference, intersubjectivity and agency in the colonial and decolonizing spaces of Hélène Cixous's 'sorties'." In 2685.

GG2728. Walsh, Lisa: "Writing (into) the symbolic: the maternal metaphor in Hélène Cixous." In 2685.

GG2729. Wilson, Emma: "Hélène Cixous: an erotics of the feminine." In 2685.

GG2730. Wilson, Emma: "Identification and melancholia: the inner cinema of Hélène Cixous." In 2685.

CLANCIER, Georges-Emmanuel.

GG2731. ● Clancier, Georges-Emmanuel: *Le Paysan céleste, suivi de Notre part d'ombre*. Préface d'André Dhôtel. Paris: Gallimard, 2008. 418 p.

CLAUDEL, Paul. See also 491, 663, 691a, 699, 1020, 5395, 5405, 7659.

GG2732. ● Bona, Dominique: *Camille et Paul: la passion Claudel*. Paris: Librairie générale française, 2008. *Livre de poche*. 442 p.

GG2733. ● Bona, Dominique: *Camille und Paul: Kunst und Leben der Geschwister Claudel*. Aus dem Franz. von Eva Moldenhauer. München: Knaus, 2008. 383 p.

GG2734. ● Claudel, Paul: *Psaumes: traductions, 1918-1953*. Texte établi et annoté par Renée Nantet et Jacques Petit; avant-propos de Pierre Claudel; préface de Guy Goffette. Paris: Gallimard, 2008. *NRF*. 320 p.

GG2735. ● Claudel, Paul: *Le sacrement du monde et l'intention de gloire: correspondance de Paul Claudel avec les ecclésiastiques de son temps*. Ed. Dominique Millet-Gérard. Paris: Champion, 2008. 2 vols.

GG2736. ● Lubac, Henri de: *Claudel et Péguy*. Paris: Cerf, 2008. *Œuvres complètes, Henri de Lubac*, 30. xi, 213 p. [Péguy]

GG2737. ● *Paul Claudel 2005: perspectives critiques*. Textes réunis par Sergio Villani. Ottawa: Legas, 2008. 232 p.

GG2738. ● Wasserman, Michel: *D'or et de neige: Paul Claudel et le Japon*. Paris: Gallimard, 2008. *Les cahiers de la NRF*. 232 p.

GG2739. Alexandre, Didier: "Le *Bulletin de la Société Paul Claudel* a 50 ans," *Bulletin de la Société Paul Claudel*, no. 192 (4e trim. 2008), 10-20.

GG2740. Alexandre, Didier: "Les villes de Paul Claudel." In 616, 225-236.

GG2741. Alexandre-Bergues, Pascale: "Entretien avec le metteur en scène Yves Beaunesne," *Bulletin de la Société Paul Claudel*, no. 190 (2e trim. 2008), 7-22.

GG2742. Aquien, Michèle: "Une forme paradoxale: le verset claudélien dans *Tête d'Or*," *Etudes Littéraires*, vol. 38, no. 2 (automne 2007), 83-92.

GG2743. Barrault, Jean-Louis: "Familiar memories of Paul Claudel." In 574, 205-215.

GG2744. Boly, Joseph: "*L'Échange* de Paul Claudel," *Bulletin Société Paul Claudel en Belgique*, no. 53 (2008), 4-6.

GG2745. Bompaire-Evesque, Claire: "Une lettre de Paul Claudel à Hélène Berthelot," *Bulletin de la Société Paul Claudel*, no. 192 (4e trim. 2008), 42-47.

GG2746. Brémeau, Catherine: "*Partage de Midi* par Vladimir Agueev, suivi d'un commentaire de Claude Frioux," *Bulletin de la Société Paul Claudel*, no. 190 (2e trim. 2008), 63-65.

GG2747. Brethenoux, Michel: "Camille et Paul Claudel: génies et enfers." In 804, 241-269.

GG2748. Bush, Christopher: "Reading and difference: image, allegory, and the invention of Chinese." In 594, 34-63.

GG2749. Edwards, Michael: "La littérature et l'espoir du lieu," *Études*, 152e année, no. 4081 (janv. 2008), 69-79.

GG2750. Fleury, Raphaèle: "Le projet du marionnettiste Georges Lafaye pour *L'Ours et la Lune*," *Bulletin de la Société Paul Claudel*, no. 191 (3e trim. 2008), 20-30.

GG2751. Garbagnati, Lucile: "Claudel et la crise de 1929," *Bulletin de la Société Paul Claudel*, no. 192 (4e trim. 2008), 29-41.

GG2752. Glon, Thierry: "Théophanique *Tête d'Or*," *Bulletin de la Société Paul Claudel*, no. 189 (1er trim. 2008), 29-43.

GG2753. Guérin, Jeanyves: "Ce soir on improvise ou les didascalies dans *Le Soulier de satin*." In 605, 279-294.

GG2754. Hassanein, Y. Taha: "Un art fabuleux de voir le feu." In 96, 325-335.

GG2755. Kaes, Emmanuelle: "Poéetique de la comparaison dans *Tête d'Or*," *Champs du Signe*, no. 21 (2006), 45-65.

GG2756. Langslet, Lars Roar: "Paul Claudel et la Norvège," *Bulletin de la Société Paul Claudel*, no. 190 (2e trim. 2008), 2-6.

GG2757. Lioure, Michel: "A propos du 'Théophanique *Tête d'Or*' de Thierry Glon," *Bulletin de la Société Paul Claudel*, no. 189 (1er trim. 2008), 43-46.

GG2758. Livry, Anatoly: "*Tête d'or* et *Hélios Roi*, la rupture du cercle de l'éternel retour," *Bulletin de l'Association Guillaume Budé*, no. 2 (2008), 167-193.

GG2759. Malachy, Thérèse: "Paul Claudel: le ravissement de Scapin." In 1093.

GG2760. Marcerou, Philippe: "La naissance du 'théâtre d'art'," *Bulletin de la Société Paul Claudel*, no. 191 (3e trim. 2008), 2-7.

GG2761. Martin-Schmets, Victor: "Le triangle Claudel-Maeterlinck-Mockel," *Bulletin de la Société Paul Claudel*, no. 191 (3e trim. 2008), 8-19.

GG2762. Millet-Gérard, Dominique: "Connaissance et écriture du temps chez Paul Claudel." In 618.

GG2763. Millet-Gérard, Dominique: "De saint Bernard à Claudel: le *Cantique des Cantiques* et les paradoxes de l'éloge lyrique." In 1014, 391-401.

GG2764. Millet-Gérard, Dominique: "Paul Claudel au croisement des familles spirituelles," *Travaux de Littérature*, tome 21 (2008), 391-410.

GG2765. Mourlevat, Thérèse: "Destins croisés: Camille, Paul, Rosalie." In 804, 271-292.

GG2766. Narjoux, Cécile: " 'Il faut que je m'élève comme la flamme enracinée': la comparaison dans *Tête d'Or*," *Champs du Signe*, no. 22 (2006), 29-50.

GG2767. Peyre, Henri: "Paul Claudel: bibliographical spectrum." In 574, 216-243.

GG2768. Poli, Gianni: "La (veritable) creation du *Livre de Christophe Colomb* de Paul Claudel," *Revue d'Histoire du Théâtre*, no. 239 [no. 3] (2008), 287-298.

GG2769. Rivière, Anne: "Les bustes de Paul Claudel par Camille Claudel," *Bulletin de la Société Paul Claudel*, no. 191 (3e trim. 2008), 31-40.

GG2770. Weber-Caflisch, Antoinette: "Cheminements de l'imagination claudélienne," *Bulletin de la Société Paul Claudel*, no. 189 (1er trim. 2008), 47-59.

CLAVEL, Maurice. See also 5750.

GG2771. Le Corre, Elisabeth: "*Les Paroissiens de Palente* de Maurice Clavel: le c(h)œur des militants." In 456, 101-111.

CLAVER AKENDENGUÉ, Pierre.

GG2772. ● Tindy-Poaty, Juste Joris: *Pierre Claver Akendengué ou l'épreuve du miroir.* Paris: L'Harmattan, 2008. *Points de vue.* 232 p.

CLIFF, William.

GG2773. Cliff, William: "Dans l'intimité d'une bibliothèque d'écrivain: chez William Cliff," *Carnet et les Instants*, no. 150 (2008), 33-36.

GG2774. Fourcaut, Laurent: "*Autobiographie* de William Cliff: le sonnet comme (in)-discipline," *Formules*, no. 12 (2008), 167-178.

GG2775. Guichard, Thierry: "Les chemins sauvages," *Matricule des Anges*, no. 83 (2007), 14-17.

GG2776. Guichard, Thierry: "Jouissifs carcans," *Matricule des Anges*, no. 83 (2007), 18-19.

CLOUTIER, Cécile.

GG2777. Paparo, Immacolata: "Avec Cécile Cloutier: souvenirs d'une rencontre," *Rivista di Studi Canadesi*, n. 20 (2007), 129-134.

COCTEAU, Jean. See also 420, 5751, 6033, 7252.

GG2778. ● *Adaptations [Les].* Textes réunis et prés. par Serge Linarès. Caen: Lettres modernes Minard, 2008. *Revue des Lettres Modernes; Jean Cocteau*, 5. 189 p.

GG2779. ● Castronovo, Enrico: *Jean Cocteau, le seuil et l'intervalle: hantise de la mort et assimilation du fantastique.* Avant-propos de Jean Touzot. Paris: L'Harmattan, 2008. *Critiques littéraires.* 322 p.

GG2780. ● *Cocteau avant le Potomak.* Sous la dir. scientifique de David Gullentops. Paris: M. de Maule, 2008. *Cahiers Jean Cocteau.* 160 p.

GG2781. ● *Cocteau et l'Italie; Démarche d'un poète.* Sous la dir. de David Gullentops. Paris: M. de Maule, 2007. *Cahiers Jean Cocteau*, nouvelle série, no. 5. 177 p.

GG2782. ● *Derek Jarman, Jean Cocteau: alchimie.* Sous la dir. de Dominique Bax, avec la collab. de Cyril Béghin. Bobigny: Magic cinéma, 2008. 255 p.

GG2783. ● Eynat-Confino, Irène: *On the uses of the fantastic in modern theatre: Cocteau, Oedipus, and the monster.* New York: Palgrave Macmillan, 2008. *Palgrave studies in theatre and performance history.* 198 p.

GG2784. ● *Jean Cocteau et le monde de l'enfance.* Bruxelles: Théâtre La montagne magique, 2007. 64 p.

GG2785. ● Jih, Jong-Hyun: *Jean Cocteau, le corps-écriture.* Lille: ANRT, 2008. *Thèse à la carte.* 529 p.

GG2786. ● Rodríguez, Luis Sancho: *Una tinta de luz: la poesía cinematográfica de Jean Cocteau.* Bilbao: Univ. del País Vasco, 2008. 210 p.

GG2787. ● Williams, James S.: *Jean Cocteau.* London: Reaktion, 2008. *Critical lives.* 253 p.

GG2788. Armbrecht, Thomas: " 'La dixième muse' meets 'un monstre sacré': theatricality and the cinema in Jean Cocteau's *L'Aigle à deux têtes*," *Quarterly Review of Film and Video*, vol. 25, no. 1 (2008), 37-51.

GG2789. Bertrand, Solène: "*L'Eternel retour*, ou le retour éternel de la légende tristanienne." In 2778, 39-52.

GG2790. Bourdin, Monique: "Jean Cocteau et le mariage princier de Monaco." In 2780.

GG2791. Broad, Stephen: "Messiaen and Cocteau." In 851.

GG2792. Bruera, Franca: "De la récréation à la recréation: le mythe antique dans le théâtre français de l'entre-deux-guerres." In 520, 549-560.

GG2793. Caizergues, Pierre: "De *Dear Liar* à *Cher menteur*: Jean Cocteau et 'le mur des langues'." In 2778, 33-38.

GG2794. Caizergues, Pierre; Pierre Chanel: "La correspondance Jean Cocteau-Jacques Renaud." In 2780.

GG2795. Campo, Isa: "Jean Cocteau: el arte de vencer un don," *Quimera*, n. 296-297 (julio-agosto 2008), 40-43.

GG2796. Canovas, Frédéric: "The 'frivolous prince' or Jean Cocteau's art of metamorphoses." In 535, 111-133.

GG2797. Castonovo, Enrico: "Jean Cocteau et les mythes de mort." In 520, 505-516.

GG2798.   Chaperon, Danielle: "*Les Parents terribles* et *L'Aigle à deux têtes* au cinéma." In 2778, 131-148.

GG2799.   Chapuis, Bérengère: "La figure de l'ange chez Cocteau." In 520, 533-548.

GG2799a.   Coombs, Neil: "Jean Cocteau and Orphée." In 7973.

GG2800.   Dixon, Wheeler Winston: "The power of resistance: *Les dames du Bois de Boulogne*," *Senses of Cinema*, no. 46 (2008), [n.p.]. [Bresson]

GG2801.   Fermi, Elena: "Jean Cocteau et l'Italie." In 2781.

GG2802.   Gullentops, David: "Autour de la séance du théâtre Fémina." In 2780.

GG2803.   Gullentops, David: "La Chapelle de Villefranche." In 2780.

GG2804.   Gullentops, David: "Cocteau dans les périodiques *Comœdia* et *Comœdia illustré*." In 2780.

GG2805.   Gullentops, David: "Démarche d'un poète: une édition critique." In 2780.

GG2806.   Gullentops, David; Gérard Langlet: "La correspondance Jean Cocteau-René Rocher." In 2780.

GG2807.   Köppen, Manuel: "Das Genie im Spiegel: Melancholie und Künstlerträume in Jean Cocteaus *Orphée* (1949)," *Zeitschrift für Germanistik*, 18. Jahrgang, Heft 1 (2008), 119-132.

GG2808.   Linares, Serge: " 'La Crucifixion' de J(ean) C(octeau)," *Studi Francesi*, anno 52, fasc. 2 (maggio-agosto 2008), 324-335.

GG2809.   Linares, Serge: "D'après l'antique?" In 2778, 13-31.

GG2810.   Martin, Christophe: "Une parole 'soufflée'." In 2778, 53-71. [Cinema: Bresson]

GG2811.   Mourier, Maurice: "*La Belle et la bête* ou l'enfance de l'art." In 2778, 73-89.

GG2812.   Nabli, Moncef: "*Judith et Holopherne* de Jean Cocteau, de la référence biblique au traitement poétique." In 2778, 167-178.

GG2813.   Naugrette, Florence: "Cocteau adaptateur de *Ruy Blas*." In 2778, 91-109.

GG2814.   Penot-Lacassagne, Olivier: " 'Une sorte de sorcellerie verbale': Artaud/Cocteau, 1931-1932." In 2778, 155-165.

GG2815.   Poiana, Peter: "Seduction and scandal: two kinds of relation with the thing," *Angelaki*, vol. 13, no. 3 (Dec. 2008), 53-65.

GG2816.   Rouget, François: "Jean Cocteau correcteur de ses vers." In 2778, 179-189.

GG2817.   Van Steerthem, Angie: "Jean Cocteau collaborateur de Jean Delannoy pour *La Princesse de Clèves*." In 2778, 111-129.

GG2818.   Zemignan, Roberto: "De *Romantici a Venezia* à *Venise et ses amants*." In 2780.

COHEN, Albert. See also 642.

GG2819.   ● Goergen, Bertrand: *Dialogues et dialogisme dans l'œuvre d'Albert Cohen*. Lille: ANRT, 2008. *Thèse à la carte*. 2 vols.

GG2820.   ● Maisier-Eynon, Véronique: *L'inspiration picaresque dans l'œuvre romanesque d'Albert Cohen*. Lille: ANRT, 2008. *Thèse à la carte*. 574 p.

GG2821.   Abecassis, Jack I.: "La gnose sans gnosis d'Albert Cohen," *Cahiers Albert Cohen*, no. 18 (2008), 131-140.

GG2822.   Auroy, Carole: "*Belle du Seigneur*: la blessure de l'altérité," *Cahiers Albert Cohen*, no. 8 (2008), 129-185.

GG2823.   Cabot, Jérôme: "Le Marseillais, le petit bourgeois et la bonne: paroles populaires dans les romans d'Albert Cohen." In 619, 397-427.

GG2824.   Conceatu, Marius: "Les humains-bêtes de Cohen et Proust entre la jungle et le jardin d'acclimatation," *Cahiers Albert Cohen*, no. 18 (2008), 67-81. [Proust]

GG2825.   Davies, J. Marina: "Le parasite et le cosmopolite chez Albert Cohen," *Cahiers Albert Cohen*, no. 18 (2008), 83-97.

GG2826.   Decout, Maxime: "L'animal dans le social," *Cahiers Albert Cohen*, no. 18 (2008), 99-116.

GG2827.   Duprey, Véronique: "*Belle du Seigneur*: un défi au bon sens," *Cahiers Albert Cohen*, no. 8 (2008), 287-301.

GG2828.   Fix-Combe, Nathalie: "Mariette, la reinette: un autre visage de la maternité," *Cahiers Albert Cohen*, no. 8 (2008), 43-67.

GG2829. Fix-Combe, Nathalie: "Sous le soleil de Solal: regard brûlant sur la féminité," *Cahiers Albert Cohen*, no. 8 (2008), 101-127.

GG2830. Georgen, Bertrand: "Normes et anti-normes: *Belle du Seigneur* ou le pari d'un écheveau normatif," *Cahiers Albert Cohen*, no. 8 (2008), 211-245.

GG2831. Lannegrand, Sylvie: "Ecrire la mère disparue: Albert Cohen et Charles Juliet." In 571, 29-35. [Juliet]

GG2832. Lewy-Bertaut, Evelyne: "Mais où sont passés les Valeureux dans *Belle du Seigneur?*," *Cahiers Albert Cohen*, no. 8 (2008), 19-41.

GG2833. Maisier, Véronique: "Albert Cohen, Annie Ernaux et le portrait problématique de la mère," *Women in French Studies*, no. 16 (2008), 51-63. [Ernaux]

GG2834. Mathis, Mail-Anne: "Le bestiaire dans *Belle du Seigneur*," *Cahiers Albert Cohen*, no. 8 (2008), 69-95.

GG2835. Michon-Bertout, Laure: "Les lettres dans *Belle du Seigneur*," *Cahiers Albert Cohen*, no. 8 (2008), 267-286.

GG2836. Milkovitch-Rioux, Catherine: "La guerre, c'est là qu'on voit l'homme," *Cahiers Albert Cohen*, no. 8 (2008), 191-210.

GG2837. Noudelmann, François: " 'Ariane est son nom': les jeux de la lettre dans *Belle du Seigneur*," *Cahiers Albert Cohen*, no. 8 (2008), 379-392.

GG2838. Ozwald, Thierry: "Ecriture romanesque et retournement satirique chez Albert Cohen," *Modernités*, no. 27 (2008), 431-444.

GG2839. Romestaing, Alain: "Fouet, fauves et peluches: figures de la lutte contre l'animal dans *solal* et *Belle du Seigneur*," *Cahiers Albert Cohen*, no. 18 (2008), 45-65.

GG2840. Sandler, Julie: "Bernanos et Cohen: deux écritures du commencement," *Cahiers Albert Cohen*, no. 18 (2008), 143-156. [Bernanos]

GG2841. Schaffner, Alain: "L'amour des animaux dans *Belle du Seigneur*," *Cahiers Albert Cohen*, no. 18 (2008), 117-130.

GG2842. Schaffner, Alain: "*Belle du Seigneur*, roman à thèse ou roman expérimental?," *Cahiers Albert Cohen*, no. 8 (2008), 247-263.

GG2843. Simon, Anne: "Bêtes, 'homme naturel' et 'homme humain' chez Albert Cohen," *Cahiers Albert Cohen*, no. 18 (2008), 13-25.

GG2844. Stolz, Claire: "*Churchill d'Angleterre* d'Albert Cohen," *Estudios de Lengua y Literatura Francesas*, no. 16 (2005), 105-116

GG2845. Stolz, Claire: "Esthétique de la phrase dans *Belle du Seigneur* (I): la phrase de récit," *Cahiers Albert Cohen*, no. 8 (2008), 303-335.

GG2846. Stolz, Claire: "Esthétique de la phrase dans *Belle du Seigneur* (I): la phrase de discours," *Cahiers Albert Cohen*, no. 8 (2008), 337-377.

GG2847. Zagury-Benhattar, Joëlle: "Le duo métaphorique de l'animal et de l'homme dans le chapitre 35 de *Belle du Seigneur*," *Cahiers Albert Cohen*, no. 18 (2008), 27-43.

COHEN, Marcel.

GG2848. "Dossier Marcel Cohen," *Préau des Collines*, no. 7 (2005).

GG2849. Jaron, Steven: "Le témoignage discret de Marcel Cohen." In 602, 63-79.

COLETTE, Sidonie Gabrielle. See also 710, 4999.

GG2850. ● Fiore de Feo, Ester: *Colette e il giornalismo letterario del Novecento*. Fasano: Schena, 2008. 307 p.

GG2851. ● Lazard, Madeleine: *Colette*. Paris: Gallimard, 2008. 398 p.

GG2852. ● Michineau, Stéphanie: *L'autofiction dans l'œuvre de Colette*. Paris: Publibook, 2008. 371 p.

GG2853. Benoit, Charles: "L'art de 'bien vieillir' chez deux grandes femmes de lettres: G. Sand et Colette." In 538, 141-161.

GG2854. Brechemier, Dominique: "Rencontres: Colette et Annie de Pène," *Cahiers Colette*, no. 30 (2008), 93-103.

GG2855. Delcroix, Maurice: " 'Où sont les enfants?'. La première nouvelle de *La Maison de Claudine*," *Cahiers Colette*, no. 30 (2008), 137-168.

GG2856. Delesalle, Simone: "La phrase de Colette. Incises et suspens," *Cahiers Colette*, no. 30 (2008), 169-180.

GG2857. Engelking, Tama Lea: "Ceci n'est pas Colette: writing, performance and identity in Colette's *Mes apprentissages*," *Women in French Studies* (2008), 124-134.

GG2858. Freadman, Anne: "Being there: Colette in the crowd," *French Cultural Studies*, vol. 19, no. 1 (Feb. 2008), 5-16.

GG2859. Licari, Carmen: "Les maisons de Colette à Paris." In 423.

GG2860. Marzel, Shoshana-Rose: "La mode substitut de la parole dans *Gigi* de Colette." In 571, 195-203.

GG2861. Michineau, Stéphanie: "L'autofiction dans l'œuvre de Colette," *Cahiers Colette*, no. 30 (2008), 123-136.

GG2862. Resch, Yannick: "Colette et ses masques." In 441, 141-148.

GG2863. Rico, Josette: "La maison et le livre dans *La Maison de Claudine* de Colette," *Voix Plurielles*, vol. 5, no. 1 (mai 2008), [n.p.].

GG2864. Schehr, Lawrence R.: "Colette and androcentrism." In 449, 158-178.

GG2865. Tsuda, Nanaé: "La fonction du 'chat' dans les premières œuvres de Colette," *Cahiers Colette*, no. 30 (2008), 105-122.

COLLOBERT, Danielle.

GG2866. Bénézet, Mathieu: "D. C.," *Critique*, tome 64, no. 735-736 (août-sept. 2008), 600-604.

COMTE-SPONVILLE, André.

GG2867. ● Tellez, Jean: *Etre moderne: introduction à la pensée d'Andre Comte-Sponville, et entretien avec André Comte-Sponville*. Meaux: Germina, 2008. 150 p.

CONDÉ, Maryse. See also 70, 105, 242, 274.

GG2868. ● Cisse, Mouhamadou: *Identité créole et écriture métissée dans les romans de Maryse Condé et Simone Schwarz-Bart*. Lille: ANRT, 2008. 536 p. [S. Schwarz-Bart]

GG2869. ● Fulton, Dawn: *Signs of dissent: Maryse Condé and postcolonial criticism*. Charlottesville: Univ. of Virginia Press, 2008. *New world studies*. 185 p.

GG2870. ● Simek, Nicole: *Eating well, reading well: Maryse Condé and the ethics of interpretation*. Amsterdam: Rodopi, 2008. *Francopolyphonies*, 7. 235 p.

GG2871. Bongie, Chris: "Withering heights: Maryse Condé and the postcolonial middlebrow." In 49.

GG2872. Britton, Celia: "On not belonging: surrogate families and marginalized communities in Maryse Condé's *Desirada*." In 51.

GG2873. Condé, Maryse: "Mode d'emploi. Comment devenir une écrivaine que l'on dit antillaise," *Nouvelles Etudes Francophones*, vol. 22, no. 1 (printemps 2007), 47-51.

GG2874. Costa Ragusa, Giuliana: "Le peregrinazioni di una schiava in *Moi, Tituba sorcière . . . Noire de Salem* di Maryse Condé." In 586, 97-113.

GG2875. Ionescu, Mariana C.: "*Histoire de la femme cannibale*: du collage à l'auto-fiction," *Nouvelles Etudes Francophones*, vol. 22, no. 1 (printemps 2007), 155-169.

GG2876. Johnson, Erica L.: "Departures and arrivals: home in Maryse Condé's *Le Cœur à rire et à pleurer*." In 80, 15-33.

GG2877. Leservot, Typhaine: "Murder or accident? Condé's postcolonial detective novels," *Women in French Studies*, no. 16 (2008), 85-99.

GG2878. Léticee, Marie: "My body, my land: redefining and rediscovering the Guadeloupean Creole woman," *CLA Journal*, vol. 51, no. 2 (Dec. 2007), 133-154.

GG2879. "Maryse Condé," *Contemporary Literary Criticism*, vol. 247 (2008), 57-138.

GG2880. McCormick, Jr., Robert H.: "Spero's 'Sittin' on the dock of the bay': Maryse Condé's *The Last of the African Kings*," *Research in African Literatures*, vol. 39, no. 3 (Fall 2008), 132-148.

GG2881. Paravisini-Gebert, Lizabeth: "Maryse Condé's *I, Tituba, black witch of Salem*." In 114.

GG2882. Phaëton, Jacqueline: "Mère-abîme, mère-miroir, les relations mère-fille dans *Desirada* de Maryse Condé." In 571, 77-85.

GG2883. Poteau-Tralie, Mary: "Landscape, identity, and sexuality: Tituba as Candide in Maryse Condé's *Moi, Tituba, sorcière . . . Noire de Salem*." In 92, 27-40.

GG2884. Reyes-Santos, Irmary: "Witch or feminist: Anowa and Tituba." In 43, 115-123.

GG2885. Schon, Nathalie: "Voyages d'île en île." In 43, 308-322.

GG2886. Veldwachter, Nadège: "Les nouvelles expositions coloniales: quand les couvertures se dévoilent," *Nouvelles Etudes Francophones*, vol. 23, no. 2 (automne 2008), 262-275. [Chamoiseau]

CONFIANT, Raphaël.

GG2887.   Arnold, Josephine Valenza: "From sea to shining sea: comment peut-on être Martiniquais?" In 53, 61-66.

GG2888.   Herbeck, Jason: "Raphaël Confiant's *Le Meurtre du Samedi-Gloria_*: crime and testimony," *French Review*, vol. 82, no. 2 (Dec. 2008), 342-352.

GG2889.   Paravisini-Gebert, Lizabeth: "Raphaël Confiant's *Mamzelle Dragonfly*." In 114.

GG2890.   Ramond Jurney, Florence: "Représentations de la violence et sexualité féminine dans l'œuvre de Raphaël Confiant," *Nouvelles Etudes Francophones*, vol. 22, no. 1 (printemps 2007), 170-184.

CONSTANT, Paule.

GG2891.   Edwards, Natalie: "The perversity of whiteness: Paule Constant's *White Spirit* as a gendered rewriting of Joseph Conrad's *Heart of Darkness*," *Women in French Studies*, no. 16 (2008), 73-84.

COPEAU, Jacques. See also 6772.

GG2892.   ● Donahue, Thomas John: *Jacques Copeau's friends and disciples: the Théâtre du Vieux-Colombier in New York City, 1917-1919*. New York: Peter Lang, 2008. *Francophone cultures and literatures*, 54. xii, 168 p.

GG2893.   Copeau, Jacques: "Un essai de rénovation dramatique: le Théâtre du Vieux Colombier," *Bulletin des Amis de Jacques Rivière et d'Alain-Fournier*, no. 119 (1er sem. 2008), 49-63. [Theater]

GG2894.   Malkin, Shira: "L'école et la troupe: aspects de la pédagogie théâtrale de George Sand et de Jacques Copeau," *George Sand Studies*, no. 27 (2008), 77-94.

GG2895.   Rivière, Jacques: "Le drame après l'époque symboliste. Jacques Copeau et le Théâtre du Vieux Colombier," *Bulletin des Amis de Jacques Rivière et d'Alain-Fournier*, no. 119 (1er sem. 2008), 7-44. [Prés. Michel Autrand] [Rivière]

CORMANN, Enzo.

GG2896.   Pilorget, Jean-Paul: "Un théâtre pavé d'horreur et de folie: *Toujours l'orage* de Enzo Cormann." In 602, 219-230.

COSSERY, Albert.

GG2897.   Fili-Tullon, Touriya: "L'Orient de Cossery: à la recherche de l'orient perdu," *Interculturel Francophonies*, no. 14 (2008), 131-141.

GG2898.   Parris, David L.: "Note on the death of Albert Cossery (1913-2008)," *International Journal of Francophone Studies*, vol. 11, no. 4 (2008), 653-655.

GG2899.   Tritsmans, Bruno: "Sagesses d'Orient? De Khalil Gibran à Albert Cossery." In 510, 321-333.

COUAO-ZOTTI, Florent.

GG2900.   Kakpo, Mahougnon: "Les *moi-vides*, les *moi-débris* ou l'esthétique des débris humains chez Florent Couao-Zotti." In 72, 327-354.

COURTOT, Claude.

GG2901.   Buono, Angela: "Claude Courtot, surrealista 'dans les ruines'," *Annali, Università degli Studi di Napoli "L'Orientale", Sezione Romanza*, anno 50, n. 2 (2008), 381-391.

COUSSE, Raymond.

GG2902.   Germoni, Karine: "Traces et empreintes beckettiennes: *Péripéties, Rencontres* et *Lever de rideau* de Raymond Cousse, *pantomimes* beckettiennes_?," *Revue d'Histoire Littéraire de la France*, tome 108, no. 3 (juillet-sept. 2008), 621-632. [Beckett]

CRASSAS, Théo.

GG2903.   Aranjo, Daniel: "Un poète grec francophone: Théo Crassas," *Babel*, no. 18 (2008), 59-63.

CRAVAN, Arthur. See also 4125.

GG2904.   Burke, Carolyn: "Au Mexique," *Nouvelle Revue Française*, no. 587 (oct. 2008), 289-316.

CREVEL, René.

GG2905. Guéraud, François: "Métamorphose du corps et de la ville chez René Crevel." In 502.

CRICKILLON, Jacques.

GG2906. Van Rossom, Christophe: "Jacques Crickillon ou les territoires de l'Indien," *Carnet et les Instants*, no. 151 (2008), 2-8.

DABEL, Verly.

GG2907. Parisot, Yolaine: "Verly Dabel ou la mémoire immédiate," *Cultures Sud*, no. 170 (sept. 2008), 39-44.

DABIT, Eugène.

GG2908. ● Dabit, Eugène: *Train de vies, suivi de Velazquez*. Préface de Pierre-Edmond Robert; avant-propos de Joseph Macé-Scaron. Paris: Buchet-Chastel, 2008. 334 p.

GG2909. Figuerola, Carme: "Lieux magiques ou maudits? Autour du Paris d'Eugène Dabit." In 502.

DADELSEN, Jean-Paul de.

GG2910. Guyot-Rouge, Gaëlle: "Le protestantisme dans l'œuvre de Jean-Paul de Dadelsen," *Travaux de Littérature*, tome 21 (2008), 473-487.

DADIÉ, Bernard. See also 227.

GG2911. ● Lemaire, Frédéric: *Bernard Dadié: itinéraire d'un écrivain africain dans la première moitié du XXe siècle*. Paris: L'Harmattan, 2008. *Grandes figures d'Afrique*. 207 p.

DAENINCKX, Didier.

GG2912. Blatt, Ari J.: "The revolution will be televised, or Didier Daeninckx's Cathode fictions," *Yale French Studies*, no. 114 (2008), 144-155.

DAI, Sijie.

GG2913. ● Plaquette, Haud: *Etude sur Dai Sijie, Balzac et la petite tailleuse chinoise*. Paris: Ellipses, 2008. *Résonances*. 128 p.

GG2914. Xavier, Subha: "China and its other: the economy of writing in Dai Sijie's *Le complexe de Di*," *Concentric*, vol. 34, no. 2 (Sept. 2008), 63-85.

DAIGLE, France.

GG2915. Doyon-Gosselin, Benoit: "Pour une herméneutique de l'espace: l'œuvre romanesque de J. R. Léveillé et France Daigle." Diss., Univ. de Moncton, 2008. [Léveillé]

GG2916. Leclerc, Catherine: "Le Chiac, le Yi King, et l'entrecroisement des marges." In 136, 163-192.

GG2917. Paré, François: "*Un fin passage* de France Daigle." In 41, 107-121.

DAIVE, Jean.

GG2918. Cohen, Francis: "Dans l'audition de l'éthique," *Critique*, tome 64, no. 735-736 (août-sept. 2008), 625-637.

GG2919. Cohen, Francis: "Transfert," *CCP: Cahier Critique de Poésie*, no. 14 (2007), 27-34.

GG2920. Czermak, Marcel: "A Jean, pour continuer à chercher la femme," *CCP: Cahier Critique de Poésie*, no. 14 (2007), 39-47.

GG2921. Garron, Isabelle: "Cet objet phsique à son négatif seul," *CCP: Cahier Critique de Poésie*, no. 14 (2007), 19-23.

GG2922. Hamacher, Werner: "Brouillon d'une fantaisie sur le feu et la parole pour saluer Jean Daive," *CCP: Cahier Critique de Poésie*, no. 14 (2007), 72-78.

GG2923. Houser, Eric: "Comptez quatre, roman," *CCP: Cahier Critique de Poésie*, no. 14 (2007), 48-51.

GG2924. Lespiau, David: "Partition jaune," *CCP: Cahier Critique de Poésie*, no. 14 (2007), 25-26.

GG2925. Roubaud, Jacques: "36 vues de *Décimale blanche*," *CCP: Cahier Critique de Poésie*, no. 14 (2007), 15-17.

DALEMBERT, Louis-Philippe.

GG2926. Gyssels, Kathleen; Gaëlle Cooreman: "Intertextualité et ironie dans l'écriture de Louis-Philippe Dalembert," *Essays in French Literature and Culture*, no. 45 (Nov. 2008), 129-148.

GG2927. Pessini, Elena: "Présences insulaires dans l'œuvre de Louis-Philippe Dalembert." In 423.

DAMAS, Léon-Gontran.

GG2928. Gyssels, Kathleen: " 'La persistance de la mémoire': l'exil chez Léon Damas." In 119, 173-191.

GG2929. "Léon-Gontran Damas," *Twentieth-Century Literary Criticism*, vol. 204 (2008), 184-210.

GG2930. Malela, Buata B.: "Du marronnage littéraire: Damas et Césaire contestataires." In 102, 169-210. [Césaire]

GG2931. Rano, Daniel Jonas: "Créolitude: prolégomènes à l'intégration socioculturelle et littéraire afro-créole: le cas de Léon-Gontran Damas." Diss., Univ. de Paris XII. 449 p.

DAMBURY, Gerty.

GG2932. Bérard, Stéphanie: "Percussion et repercussion des voix dans le théâtre de Gerty Dambury," *Esprit Créateur*, vol. 48, no. 3 (Fall 2008), 76-88.

DANIS, Daniel.

GG2933. Bertin, Raymond: "Le réveil du père. *Terre océane*," *Jeu: Cahiers de Théâtre*, no. 126 (mars 2008), 12-15.

DARD, Frédéric, *pseud.* San-Antonio.

GG2934. ● Rullier-Theuret, Françoise: *Faut pas pisser sur les vieilles recettes: San-Antonio, ou, La fascination pour le genre romanesque.* Louvain-la-Neuve: Academia-Bruylant, 2008. 230 p.

DARIEN, Georges.

GG2935. Melmoux-Montaubin, Marie-Françoise: "L'œuvre de Georges Darien ou la satire au péril de la fiction," *Modernités*, no. 27 (2008), 205-220.

DARRIEUSSECQ, Marie.

GG2936. Kemp, Simon: "Darrieussecq's mind," *French Studies*, vol. 62, no. 4 (Oct. 2008), 429-441.

GG2937. Kemp, Simon: "Homeland: voyageurs et patrie dans les romans de Marie Darrieussecq." In 539, 159-166.

GG2938. Marrone, Claire: "Rewriting the writing mother in Marie Darrieussecq's *Le Bébé*," *Studies in Twentieth and Twenty-First Century Literature*, vol. 32, no. 1 (Winter 2008), 77-99.

GG2939. Willocq, Philippe: "*White* de Marie Darrieussecq ou les géographies du vide," *Etudes Francophones*, vol. 23, no. 1-2 (printemps-automne 2008), 160-170.

GG2940. Wronska, Olga: "Ménage-à-trois: maman-bébé-psychanalyse." In 571, 227-234.

GG2941. Zimmermann, Margarete: "Histoire(s) de famille sous le signe de la mondialisation: Marie Darrieussecq, *Le Pays* (2005)," *Lendemains*, 33. Jahrgang, Heft 132 (2008), 109-118.

DAUDET, Alphonse. See also 689, 719.

GG2942. ● Daudet, Alphonse: *Lettres de mon moulin*. Préface, notes et annexes de Louis Forestier. Paris: Librairie Générale Française, 2008. *Livre de poche*. Nouv. éd. illustrée. 234 p.

GG2943. ● Daudet, Alphonse: *Little what's-his-name*. Trans. and introd. W. P. Trent. New York: Mondial, 2008. *French classics*. vi, 206 p.

GG2944. ● Droit, Isabelle: *La mise en mots de la mort: l'œuvre d'Alphonse Daudet*. Lille: ANRT, 2008. *Thèse à la carte*. 416, 72 p.

GG2945. Becker, Colette: "Daudet, Zola et le naturalisme," *Petit Chose*, no. 97 (2008), 139-150. [Zola]

GG2946. Bonnin-Ponnier, Joëlle: "La femme dans les romans d'Alphonse Daudet," *Petit Chose*, no. 97 (2008), 63-76.

GG2947. Branthomme, Michel: "Zola et le théâtre de Daudet," *Petit Chose*, no. 97 (2008), 129-138. [Zola]

GG2948. Chamand-Debenest, Christiane: "L'érotisme chez Alphonse Daudet," *Petit Chose*, no. 97 (2008), 51-61.

GG2949. Clap, Vincent: "Daudet entre réalisme et naturalisme: le cas de *Jack*," *Petit Chose*, no. 97 (2008), 7-19.

GG2950. Droit, Isabelle: "Le traitement de la mort est-il naturaliste dans *Fromont jeune et Risler aîné*," *Petit Chose*, no. 97 (2008), 21-36.

GG2951. Dufief, Anne-Simone: "L'abeille et le fumier," *Petit Chose*, no. 97 (2008), 37-49.

GG2952. Dufief, Anne-Simone: "Avec un microscope," *Petit Chose*, no. 97 (2008), 87-98.

GG2953. Hernández Alvarez, María Vicenta: "Alphonse Daudet: la tradición oral, fábrica de los cuentos," *Anales de Filología Francesa*, n. 15 (2006-2007), 159-174.

GG2954. Hirchwald-Mélison, Gabrielle: "Roman de mœurs et naturalisme chez Daudet," *Petit Chose*, no. 97 (2008), 109-118.

GG2955. Not, André: "Daudet et le reportage," *Petit Chose*, no. 97 (2008), 99-108.

GG2956. Ribes, Angels: "Alphonse Daudet et le naturalisme en Catalogne," *Petit Chose*, no. 97 (2008), 119-128.

GG2957. Ripoll, Roger: "A propos de *Rose et Ninette*: une interview d'Alphonse Daudet," *Petit Chose*, no. 97 (2008), 152-157.

GG2958. Ripoll, Roger: "Des livres poignants de réalité triste," *Petit Chose*, no. 97 (2008), 77-85.

GG2959. Ripoll, Roger; Anne-Simone Dufief: "Alphonse Daudet, de la Provence à Paris," *Petit Chose*, no. 97 (2008), 159-175.

DAUDET, Léon.

GG2960. Barilier, Etienne: "Couleur traître." In 388, 22-38. [Barrès]

GG2961. Carnevali, Barbara: " 'Aura' e 'ambiance': Léon Daudet tra Proust e Benjamin," *Rivista di Estetica*, anno. 46, no. 3 [no. 33] (2006), 117-141. [Proust]

GG2962. Trombert-Grivel, Adeline: "Léon Daudet, diffamateur outré." In 564, 131-135.

DAUMAL, René. See also 1018.

GG2963. ● Daumal, René: *Correspondance avec les Cahiers du Sud*. Clermont-Ferrand: Au signe de la licorne, 2008. *Le grand jeu*. 197 p.

GG2964. ● *René Daumal: l'ascension continue: catalogue de l'exposition présentée du 28 novembre 2008 au 10 janvier 2009*. Sous la dir. de Xavier Dandoy de Casabianca. Charleville-Mézières: Médiathèque Voyelles, 2008. 190 p.

GG2965. ● *René Daumal, ou, Le perpétuel incandescent*. Sous la dir. de Basarab Nicolescu et de Jean-Philippe de tonnac; édition, Christian Le Mellec. L'Isle-sur-la-Sorgue: Bois d'Orion, 2008. 283 p.

GG2966. Bianu, Zéno: "René Daumal dans l'œil analogue d'un poète contemporain." In 2965, 15-24.

GG2967. Bonnasse, Pierre: "L'éveil est un acte. Daumal et le Travail sur soi." In 2965, 137-152.

GG2968. Daumal, Myriam: "L'ami Daumal." In 2965, 169-176.

GG2969. Ferrick Rosenblatt, Kathleen: "René Daumal vu des Etats-Unis." In 2965, 163-167.

GG2970. Galluci, Marcello: "Théâtre et technologie du soi: Daumal et Artaud." In 2965, 119-136. [Artaud]

GG2971. Le Mellec, Christian: "René Daumal, poète indien." In 2965, 99-118.

GG2972. Lipsey, Roger: "Monsieur Daumal et Monsieur Gurdjieff." In 2965, 153-162.

GG2973. Masui, Jacques: "René Daumal et l'Inde." In 2965, 205-212.

GG2974. Nicolescu, Basarab: "Le grand jeu et la transdisciplinarité." In 2965, 25-38.

GG2975. Pascault, Olivier: "Daumal, philosophe de l'irrévérence." In 2965, 39-53.

GG2976. Penot-Lacassagne, Olivier: "Grand jeu et petits jeux surréalistes." In 2965, 55-63.

GG2977. Pouilloux, Jean-Yves: "Les pouvoirs de la fable. Lecture de *Mont Analogue*." In 2965, 65-74.

GG2978. Richaud, Frédéric: "Daumal-Dietrich: une amitié au travail." In 2965, 89-97.

GG2979. Rolland de Renéville, André: "Souvenir de René Daumal." In 2965, 195-198.

GG2980. Rubio, Emmanuel: "Ecrire et défaire *Le Mont Analogue*." In 2965, 75-87.

DAVID-NÉEL, Alexandra.

GG2981. James, Geneviève: "L'aventure selon Alexandra David-Néel." In 535, 167-192.

DEBORD, Guy. See also 3647.

GG2982. ● Danesi, Fabien: *Le mythe brisé de l'International situationniste*. Dijon: Presses du réel, 2008. 333 p.

GG2983. ● Debord, Guy: *Correspondance. Volume VII, janvier 1988-novembre 1994*. Paris: Fayard, 2008. 472 p.

GG2984. ● *Guy Debord: dal superamento dell'arte alla realizzazione della filosofia*. A cura di Antonio Gasbarrini. L'Aquila: Angelus novus, 2008. 95 p.

GG2985. ● Jacquemond, Olivier: *Les 3 secrets*. Paris: Sens & Tonka, 2008. 183 p.

GG2986. ● Zagdanski, Stéphane: *Debord, ou, La diffraction du temps*. Paris: Gallimard, 2008. 244 p.

GG2987. Donné, Boris: "Debord et Chtcheglov, bois et charbons," *Mélusine*, no. 28 (2008), 109-124.

GG2988. Kaufmann, Vincent: "Guy Debord: nécessité de l'insulte." In 564, 141-144.

DEBRAY, Régis.

GG2989. Bongie, Chris: "Chroniques de la francophonie triomphante: the dutiful memories of Régis Debray." In 49.

DEBURAUX, Édouard.

GG2990. Seillan, Jean-Marie: "Réflexions sur un genre mineur: le *Roman aérostatique* de Léo Dex." In 96, 423-432.

DEGUY, Michel. See also 736, 2129, 3281.

GG2991. ● Deguy, Michel: *Gegebend Gedichte*. Aus dem Franz. übers. und mit einem Vorwort vers. von Leopold Federmair. Mit einem Text von Andrea Zanzotto. Wien: Bozen Folio-Verlag, 2008. 160 p.

DELARUE-MARDRUS, Lucie. See also 710.

GG2992. ● Delarue-Mardrus, Lucie: *Nos secrètes amours*. Texte établi et annoté par Mirande Lucien, en collab. avec la revue *Inverses*. Cassaninouze: Erosonyx, 2008. 87 p.

DELAUME, Chloé.

GG2993. Décimo, Marc: "De quelques histoires de famille à la naissance de Chloé Delaume: traumas et usage singulier de la langue." In 571, 315-322.

DELAVIGNETTE, Robert. See also 6561.

GG2994. Riesz, János: "*Les Paysans noirs*, roman modèle ou modèle de roman(s)?" In 127, 269-285.

DELAY, Florence. See 754.

DELBO, Charlotte. See also 519.

GG2995. Binder, Anne-Berenike: "Charlotte Delbo, *Auschwitz et après*." In 390, 40-116.

GG2996. Brunetaux, Audrey: "Charlotte Delbo: une écriture du silence." Diss., Michigan State Univ., 2008. viii, 262 p.

GG2997. Dufiet, Jean-Paul: "Le pathos dans la langue de la représentation du camp nazi." In 446, 205-218.

DEL CASTILLO, Michel.

GG2998. Rasson, Luc: " 'Je suis un produit de cette guerre': Michel del Castillo et la guerre civile espagnole," *Roman 20-50*, no. 45 (2008), 135-144.

DELECROIX, Vincent.

GG2999. Glaux, Raphaële: "Vincent Delecroix, écrivain solitaire," *Spectacle du Monde*, no. 543 (mars 2008), 66-68.

DELERM, Philippe.

GG3000. Cavallero, Claude: "Les florilèges du quotidien de Philippe Delerm," *Etudes Littéraires*, vol. 37, no. 1 (automne 2005), 145-156.

DELEUZE, Gilles. See also 469, 777, 949, 951, 963, 991, 996, 1652, 1875, 1880, 1897, 3185, 3237, 3238, 3276, 3293, 3317, 3328, 3341, 3353, 3376, 3640, 5420, 5839, 5885, 6339, 6577, 8326.

GG3001. ● Abiusi, Luigi: *Tempo di Campana: divenire della poesia tra Nietzsche e Deleuze*. Bari: B. A. Graphis, 2008. xxiii, 103 p.

GG3002. ● Abou-Rihan, Fadi: *Deleuze and Guattari: a psychoanalytic itinerary*. London; New York: Continuum, 2008. *Studies in continental philosophy*. x, 166 p. [Guattari]

GG3003. ● *Ateliers sur l'Anti-Œdipe*. Ed. Nicolas Cornibert, Jean-Christophe Goddard. Milan: Mimesis; Genève: MetisPresses, 2008. 302 p.

GG3004. ● Barroso Ramos, Moisés: *La piedra de toque: filosofia de la inmanencia y de la naturaleza en Gilles Deleuze*. Madrid: Biblioteca Nueva, 2008. 240 p.

GG3005. ● Borghi, Simone: *La casa e il cosmo: il ritornello e la musica nel pensiero di Deleuze e Guattari*. Verona: Ombre corte, 2008. 126 p. [Guattari]

GG3006. ● Bryant, Levi R.: *Difference and giveness: Deleuze's transcendental empiricism and the ontology of immanence*. Evanston: Northwestern Univ. Press, 2008. *Topics in historical philosophy*. xiii, 278 p.

GG3007. ● Buchanan, Ian: *Deleuze and Guattari's Anti-Œdipus: a reader's guide*. London: Continuum, 2008. xii, 168 p. [Guattari]

GG3008. ● *Canone Deleuze: la storia della filosofia come divenire del pensiero*. A cura di Manlio Iofrida [et al.]. Firenze: Clinamen, 2008. 166 p.

GG3009. ● Cantone, Damiano: *Cinema, tempo e soggetto: il sublime kantiano secondo Deleuze*. Milano: Mimesis, 2008. *Filosofie*. 172 p.

GG3010. ● *Deleuze and gender*. Ed. Claire Colebrook and Jami Weinstein. Edinburgh: Edinburgh Univ. Press, 2008. iv, 153 p.

GG3011. ● *Deleuze and politics*. Ed. Ian Buchanan, Nicholas Thoburn. Edinburgh: Edinburgh Univ. Press, 2008. *Deleuze connections*. vi, 262 p.

GG3012. ● *Deleuze and the schizoanalysis of cinema*. Ed. Ian Buchanan and Patricia MacCormack. London; New York: Continuum, 2008. xi, 159 p.

GG3013. ● *Deleuze, Guattari and the production of the new*. Ed. Simon O'Sullivan, Stephen Zepke. London; New York: Continuum, 2008. ix, 245 p.

GG3014. ● *Deleuze und die Künste*. Hrsg. von Peter Gente und Peter Weibel. Frankfurt: Suhrkamp, 2007. 261 p.

GG3015. ● *Deleuzian encounters: studies in contemporary moral issues*. Ed. Anna Hickey-Moody, Peta Malins. New York: Palgrave Macmillan, 2008.

GG3016. ● Engelhardt, Miriam: *Deleuze als Methode: ein Seismograph für theorische Innovationen durchgeführt an Beispielen des feministischen Diskurses*. München: W. Fink, 2008. 231 p.

GG3017. ● *Falsi raccordi: cinema e filosofia in Deleuze*. A cura di Paolo Godani e Delfo Cecchi. Pisa: ETS, 2007. 154 p.

GG3018. ● Faulkner, Keith W.: *Force of time: an introduction to Deleuze through Proust*. Lanham, MD: Univ. Press of America, 2008. xiv, 169 p. [Proust]

GG3019. ● Friedrichs, Werner: *Passagen der Pädagogik: zur Fassung des pädagogischen Moments im Anschluss an Niklas Luhmann und Gilles Deleuze*. Bielefeld: Transcript, 2008. *Theorie bilden*, 13. 303 p.

GG3020. ● Gil, José: *O imperceptível devir da imanência: sobre a filosofia de Deleuze*. Lisboa: Relógio d'Agua, 2008. 263 p.

GG3021. ● *Gilles Deleuze et les images*. Sous la dir. de François Dosse et Jean-Michel Frodon. Paris: Cahiers du cinéma; Institut national de l'audiovisuel, 2008. 200 p.

GG3022. ● *Gilles Deleuze, Félix Guattari et le politique*. Sous la dir. de Manola Antonioli [et al.]. Paris: Sandre, 2007. 334 p. [Guattari]

GG3023. ● *Gilles Deleuze, immanence et vie*. Collège international de philosophie. Paris: PUF, 2006. 157 p. [Original ed., 1998]

GG3024. ● Goddard, Jean-Christophe: *Violence et subjectivité: Derrida, Deleuze, Maldiney*. Paris: Vrin, 2008. *Moments philosophiques*. 180 p. [Derrida]

GG3025. ● Grosz, Elizabeth: *Chaos, territory, art: Deleuze and the framing of the earth*. New York: Columbia Univ. Press, 2008. xi, 116 p.

GG3026. ● Hughes, Joe: *Deleuze and the genesis of representation*. London; New York: Continuum, 2008. *Studies in Continental philosophy*. 192 p.

GG3027. ● Lefebvre, Alexandre: *The image of law: Deleuze, Bergson, Spinoza*. Stanford: Stanford Univ. Press, 2008. *Cultural memory in the present*. xix, 305 p. [Bergson]

GG3028. ● Marrati, Paola: *Gilles Deleuze: cinema and philosophy*. Trans. Alisa Hartz. Baltimore: Johns Hopkins Univ. Press, 2008. *Parallax*. xix, 138 p.

GG3029. ● Martin-Jones, David: *Deleuze, cinema and national identity*. Edinburgh: Edinburgh Univ. Press, 2008. ix, 244 p.

GG3030. ● *Metamorfosi del trascendentale: percorsi filosofici tra Kant e Deleuze*. A cura di Gaetano Rametta. Padova: CLEUP, 2008. 376 p.

GG3031. ● Monaco, Beatrice: *Machinic modernism: the Deleuzian literary machines of Woolf, Lawrence and Joyce*. Basingstoke; New York: Palgrave Macmillan, 2008. viii, 213 p.

GG3032. ● Montebello, Pierre: *Deleuze: la passion de la pensée*. Paris: J. Vrin, 2008. 256 p.

GG3033. ● Nancy, Jean-Luc; René Schérer: *Ouvertüren: Texte zu Gilles Deleuze*. Zsgest. und übers. von Christoph Dittrich. Zürich; Berlin: Diaphanes, 2008. 64 p.

GG3034. ● *Nomadic education: variations on a theme by Deleuze and Guattari*. Ed. Inna Semetsky. Rotterdam: Sense publishers, 2008. *Educational futures*. xxi, 199 p. [Guattari]

GG3035. ● Olsson, Liselott: *Experiments in young children's learning: Deleuze and a virtual child*. London: Routledge, 2008. *Contesting early childhood*.

GG3036. ● Parr, Adrian: *Deleuze and memorial culture: desire, singular memory and the politics of trauma*. Edinburgh: Edinburgh Univ. Press, 2008. 199 p.

GG3037. ● Rawes, Peg: *Space, geometry and aesthetics: through Kant and towards Deleuze*. Houndmills; New York: Palgrave Macmillan, 2008. *Renewing philosophy*. xviii, 218 p.

GG3038. ● Río, Elena del: *Deleuze and the cinemas of performance: powers of affection*. Edinburgh: Edinburgh Univ. Press, 2008. viii, 240 p.

GG3039. ● Romein, Ed; Marc Schuilenburg; Sjoerd van Tuinen: *Deleuze compendium*. Meppel: Boom Distributie Centrum, 2008. 384 p.

GG3040. ● Salin, Sophie: *Kryptologie des Unbewussten: Nietzsche, Freud und Deleuze im Wunderland*. Würzburg: Königshausen & Neumann, 2008. *Epistemata*. 330 p.

GG3041. ● Stivale, Charles J.: *Gilles Deleuze's ABCs: the folds of friendship*. Baltimore: Johns Hopkins Univ. Press, 2008. *Parallax*. xix, 180 p. [Derrida, Foucault]

GG3042. ● Sutton, Damian; David Martin-Jones: *Deleuze reframed: a guide for the arts student*. London; New York: I. B. Tauris, 2008. 149 p.

GG3043. ● Teschke, Henning: *Sprünge der Differenz: Literatur und Philosophie bei Deleuze*. Berlin: Matthes & Seitz, 2008. *Traversen*. 550 p.

GG3044. ● Thiele, Kathrin: *The thought of becoming: Gilles Deleuze's poetics of life*. Zürich: Diaphanes, 2008. 208 p.

GG3045. ● Uhlig, Ingo: *Poetologien des Ereignisses bei Gilles Deleuze*. Würzburg: Königshausen & Neumann, 2008. 197 p.

GG3046. ● *(Un)likely [An] alliance: thinking environment(s) with Deleuze/Guattari*. Ed. Bernd Herzogenrath. Newcastle upon Tyne: Cambridge Scholars, 2008. 367 p. [Guattari]

GG3047. ● Williams, James: *Gilles Deleuze's Logic of sense: a critical introduction and guide*. Edinburgh: Edinburgh Univ. Press, 2008. xi, 219 p.

GG3048. Albrecht-Crane, Christa; Jennifer Daryl Slack: "Toward a pedagogy of affect." In 3015.

GG3049. Alliez, Eric; Jean-Claude Bonne: "Matisse with Dewey and Deleuze," *Pli: The Warwick Journal of Philosophy*, vol. 18 (2007), 1-19.

GG3050. Arsic, Branka: "The experimental ordinary: Deleuze on eating and anorexic elegance," *Deleuze Studies*, vol. 2 [supplement] (2008), 34-59.

GG3051. Aubron, Hervé: "Clichés vivants." In 3021, 85-95.

GG3052. Béghin, Cyril: "Le couteau de Gilles Deleuze." In 3021, 163-172.

GG3053. Bergala, Alain: "Stratégie critique, tactique pédagogique." In 3021, 37-42.

GG3054. Bignall, Simone: "Indigenous peoples and a Deleuzian theory of practice." In 3015.

GG3055. Bignall, Simone: "Postcolonial agency and poststructuralist thought: Deleuze and Foucault on desire and power," *Angelaki*, vol. 13, no. 1 (2008), 127-147. [Foucault]

GG3056. Binetti, María J.: "Mediación o repetición: de Hegel a Kierkegaard y Deleuze," *Daimon*, núm. 45 (sept.-dic. 2008), 125-139.

GG3057. Bogue, Ronald: "Search, swim and see: Deleuze's apprenticeship in signs and pedagogy of images." In 3034.

GG3058. Bonitzer, Pascal; André Téchiné: "Gilles Deleuze et nous." In 3021, 31-36. [Téchiné]

GG3059. Brassier, Ray: "The expression of meaning in Deleuze's ontological proposition," *Pli: The Warwick Journal of Philosophy*, vol. 19 (2008), 1-29.

GG3060. Brito, Vanessa: "L'île déserte et le peuple qui manque." In 3021, 65-74.

GG3061. Buchanan, Ian: "Power, theory and praxis." In 3011.

GG3062. Buchanan, Ian; Nicholas Thoburn: "Deleuze and politics." In 3011.

GG3063. Chesters, Graeme: "Complex and minor: Deleuze and the alter globalization movement(s)." In 3015.

GG3064. Clark, Tim: "Becoming everyone: the politics of sympathy in Deleuze and Rorty," *Radical Philosophy*, no. 147 (Jan./Feb. 2008), 33-44.

GG3065. Cole, David R.: "Deleuze and the narrative forms of educational otherness." In 3034.

GG3066. Colebrook, Claire: "Bourgeois thermodynamics." In 3011.

GG3067. Colebrook, Claire: "Leading out, leading on: the souul of education." In 3034.

GG3068. Collins, Lorna: "Sensations spill a deluge over the figure," *Deleuze Studies*, vol. 2, no. 1 (2008), 49-73.

GG3069. Colman, Felicity: "Affective terrorism." In 3015.

GG3070. Connolly, William E.: "Habermas, Deleuze and capitalism," *Theory and Event*, vol. 11, no. 4 (2008), [n.p.].

GG3071. Daignault, Jacques: "Pedagogy and Deleuze's concept of the virtual." In 3034.

GG3072. Dean, Kenneth; Thomas Lamarre: "Microsociology and the ritual event." In 3015.

GG3073. DeLanda, Manuel: "Deleuze, materialism and politics." In 3011.

GG3074. Evans, Fred: "Deleuze, Bakhtin, and the 'clamour of voices'," *Deleuze Studies*, vol. 2, no. 2 (2008), 178-200.

GG3075. Fargier, Jean-Paul: "Comment j'ai raté Deleuze." In 3021, 53-60.

GG3076. Ferreyra, Julián: "Los pliegues del inconsciente: la metafísica materialista de Deleuze y Guattari," *Revista de Filosofía* (México), n. 119 (mayo-agosto 2007), 131-161. [Guattari]

GG3077. Flaxman, Gregory: "A politics of non-being." In 3015.

GG3078. Flaxman, Gregory; Elena Oxman: "Losing face." In 3012.

GG3079. Frichot, Helene: "Holey space and the smooth and striated body of the refugee." In 3015.

GG3080. Frodon, Jean-Michel: "Aimer/mettre en résonance." In 3021, 11-20.

GG3081. Fujita, Jun: "Pourquoi les images refusent de travailler." In 3021, 75-84.

GG3082. Garo, Isabelle: "Molecular revolutions: the paradox of politics in the work of Gilles Deleuze." In 3011.

GG3083. Genosko, Gary: "Félix Guattari and popular pedagogy." In 3034. [Guattari]

GG3084. Geyskens, Tomas: "Gilles Deleuze over Francis Bacon," *Tijdschrift voor Filosofie*, 70ste Jaargang, Nr. 2 (2008), 297-316.

GG3085. Geyskens, Tomas: "Painting as hysteria: Deleuze on Bacon," *Deleuze Studies*, vol. 2, no. 2 (2008), 140-154.

GG3086. Gough, Noel: "Becoming-cyborg." In 3034.

GG3087. Gregoriou, Zelia: "Commencing the rhizome: towards a minor philosophy of education." In 3034.

GG3088. Halsey, Mark: "Molar ecology: what can the (full) body of an eco-tourist do?" In 3015.

GG3089. Herzog, Amy: "Suspended gestures: schizoanalysis, affect and the face in cinema." In 3012.

GG3090. Hickey-Moody, Anna: "Intellectual disability, sensation, and thinking through affect." In 3015.

GG3091. Hickey-Moody, Anna; Peta Malins: "Gilles Deleuze and four movements in social thought." In 3015.

GG3092. Hill, Rebecca: "Phallocentrism in Bergson: life and matter," *Deleuze Studies*, vol. 2 [supplement] (2008), 123-136. [Bergson]

GG3093. Holland, Eugene W.: "Schizoanalysis, nomadology, fascism." In 3011.

GG3094. Honan, Eileen; Marg Sellers: "(E)merging methodologies: putting rhizomes to work." In 3034.

GG3095. Howie, Gillian: "Becoming-woman: a flight into abstraction," *Deleuze Studies*, vol. 2 [supplement] (2008), 83-106.

GG3096. Hristeva, Galina: "George Groddecks Naturbildlichkeit: eine Erwiderung auf Deleuze und Guattari," *Scientia Poetica*, Band 12 (2008), 181-217. [Guattari]

GG3097. Hughes, Joe: "Schizoanalysis and the phenomenology of cinema." In 3012.

GG3098. Kelly, Michael R.: "Husserl, Deleuzean Bergsonism and the sense of the past in general," *Husserl Studies*, vol. 24, no. 1 (2008), 15-30. [Bergson]

GG3099. Kerslake, Christian: "Grounding Deleuze," *Radical Philosophy*, no. 148 (March/April 2008), 30-36.

GG3100. Kouba, Petr: "Two ways to the outside," *Deleuze Studies*, vol. 2, no. 1 (2008), 74-96.

GG3101. Krause, Ralf; Marc Rolli: "Micropolitical associations." In 3011.

GG3102. Lambert, Gregg: "Deleuze and the political ontology of 'the friend'." In 3011.

GG3103. Lambert, Gregg: "Schizoanalysis and the cinema of the brain." In 3012.

GG3104. Lane, David: "The *worldly* and the *otherworldly*: on the 'Utopianism' of Deleuze's thought," *Philament*, vol. 12 (June 2008), [n.p.].

GG3105. Lawlor, Leonard: "Following the rats: becoming-animal in Deleuze and Guattari," *Substance*, vol. 37, no. 3 [no. 117] (2008), 169-187. [Guattari]

GG3106. Lefebvre, Alexandre: "Three Spinozist themes in a Deleuzian jurisprudence. Deleuze and the critique of law." In 3027.

GG3107. Linck, Matthew S.: "Deleuze's difference," *International Journal of Philosophical Studies*, vol. 16, no. 4 (Oct. 2008), 509-532.

GG3108. Lorraine, Tamsin: "Feminist lines of flight from the majoritarian subject," *Deleuze Studies*, vol. 2 [supplement] (2008), 60-82.

GG3109. MacCormack, Patricia: "An ethics of spectatorship." In 3012.

GG3110. Macé, Arnaud: "L'image moins le monde: Gilles Deleuze hanté par André Bazin." In 3021, 43-52. [Bazin]

GG3111. Madelrieux, Stéphane: "Le platonisme aplati de Gilles Deleuze," *Philosophie*, no. 97 (printemps 2008), 42-58.

GG3112. Malins, Peta: "City folds: injecting drug use and urban space." In 3015.

GG3113. Mangue, Philippe: "People and fabulation." In 3011.

GG3114. Manning, Erin: "Sensing beyond security." In 3015.

GG3115. Marshall, Bill: "Cinemas of minor Frenchness." In 3012.

GG3116. Martin-Jones, David: "Schizoanalysis, spectacle and the spaghetti western." In 3012.

GG3117. Martin-Jones, David: "Towards another '-image': Deleuze, narrative time and popular Indian cinema," *Deleuze Studies*, vol. 2, no. 1 (2008), 25-48.

GG3118. May, Todd: "Deleuze and the tale of two intifadas." In 3015.

GG3119. May, Todd; Inna Semetsky: "Deleuze, ethical education, and the unconscious." In 3034.

GG3120. Mussawir, Edward: "Intersex: between law and nature." In 3015.

GG3121. Nail, Thomas: "Expression, immanence and constructivism: 'Spinozism' and Gilles Deleuze," *Deleuze Studies*, vol. 2, no. 2 (2008), 201-219.

GG3122. Narboni, Jean: " Du côté des noms." In 3021, 21-30.

GG3123. Nesme, Axel: "Notes toward a Deleuzian reading of *Transport*," *Wallace Stevens Journal*, vol. 32, no. 2 (Fall 2008), 206-222.

GG3124. Olkowski, Dorothea: "After Alice: Alice and the dry tail," *Deleuze Studies*, vol. 2 [supplement] (2008), 107-122.

GG3125. Olkowski, Dorothea: "Deleuze and the limits of mathematical time," *Deleuze Studies*, vol. 2, no. 1 (2008), 1-24.

GG3126. Païni, Dominique: "De l'expérimental comme une ritournelle." In 3021, 61-64.

GG3127. Papadopoulos, Dimitris; Vassilis Tsianos: "The autonomy of migration: the animals of undocumented mobility." In 3015.

GG3128. Patton, Paul: "Becoming-democratic." In 3011.

GG3129. Pisters, Patricia: "Delirium cinema or machines of the invisible?" In 3012.

GG3130. Powell, Anna: "Off your face: schizoanalysis, faciality and film." In 3012.

GG3131. Presutti, Fabio: "Giorgio Agamben, Gilles Deleuze and the 'idea of language' in the synthesis of 'being'," *Journal of the British Society for Phenomenology*, vol. 39, no. 2 (May 2008), 130-147.

GG3132. Read, Jason: The age of cynicism: Deleuze and Guattari on the production of subjectivity in capitalism." In 3011. [Guattari]

GG3133. Reynolds, Jack: "Transcendental priority and Deleuzian normativity: a reply to James Williams," *Deleuze Studies*, vol. 2, no. 1 (2008), 101-108.

GG3134. Riley, Mark: "Disorientation, duration and Tarkovsky." In 3012.

GG3135. Roffe, Jonathan: "The revolutionary individual." In 3015.

GG3136. Roudinesco, Elisabeth: "Gilles Deleuze: anti-Œdipal variations." In 976, 133-142.

GG3137. Roy, Kaustuv: "Deleuzian murmurs: education and communication." In 3034.

GG3138. Rushton, Richard: "Passions and actions: Deleuze's cinematographic *cogito*," *Deleuze Studies*, vol. 2, no. 2 (2008), 121-139.

GG3139. Scott, David Michael Ryan Davis: "The naivete of thought: the 'critique' of phenomenology in the philosophy of Gilles Deleuze." Diss., Univ. of Memphis, 2008. ix, 314 p.

GG3140. Semetsky, Inna: "(Pre)Facing Deleuze." In 3034.

GG3141. Semetsky, Inna; Terry Lovat: "Knowledge in action: towards a Deleuze-Habermasian critique in/for education." In 3034.

GG3142. Shaw, Spencer: "Deleuze and cinema." In 982.

GG3143. Smith, Dominic: " 'Deleuze's ethics of reading': Deleuze, Badiou, and Primo Levi," *Angelaki*, vol. 12, no. 3 (Dec. 2007), 35-55. [Badiou]

GG3144. St. Pierre, Elizabeth A.: "Deleuzian concepts for education: the subject undone." In 3034.

GG3145. Stivale, Charles J.: "The folds of friendship." In 3041. [Derrida, Foucault]

GG3146. Stivale, Charles J.: "Foucault's folds." In 3041. [Foucault]

GG3147. Thoburn, Nicholas: "What is a militant?" In 3011.

GG3148. Tompkins, Cynthia: "A Deleuzian approach to Carlos Reygadas' *Japón* and *Batalla en el cielo*," *Hispanic Journal*, vol. 29, no. 1 (Spring 2008, 155-169.

GG3149. Vandenberghe, Frédéric: "Deleuzian capitalism," *Philosophy and Social Criticism*, vol. 34, no. 8 (Oct. 2008), 861-887.

GG3150. Vilaseca, David: "Entre Platón y Deleuze: el cine como lo 'virtual' en la autobiografía de Terenci Moix." In 846, 175-190.

GG3151. Watson, Janell: "Theorising European ethnic politics with Deleuze and Guattari." In 3011. [Guattari]

GG3152. Williams, James: "Why Deleuze doesn't blow the actual on virtual priority. A rejoinder to Jack Reynolds," *Deleuze Studies*, vol. 2, no. 1 (2008), 97-100.

GG3153. Woodward, Ashley: "Deleuze and suicide." In 3015.

GG3154. Young, Eugene Brently: "The determination of sense via Deleuze and Blanchot," *Deleuze Studies*, vol. 2, no. 2 (2008), 155-177. [Blanchot]

DELIGNY, Fernand.

GG3155. ● Deligny, Fernand: *Œuvres*. Edition revue et corrigée. Edition établie et prés. par Sandra Alvarez de Toledo. Paris: L'Arachnéen, 2008. 1845 p.

DELISLE, Michael.

GG3156. Mavrikakis, Catherine: "*Dée* de Michael Delisle." In 41, 123-136.

GG3157. Torchi, Francesca: "L'adolescent périphérique. Montréal dans les nouvelles

'Le Pont' de Michael Delisle et "Piercing' de Larry Tremblay," *Etudes Canadiennes*, no. 64 (2008), 175-186. [L. Tremblay]

GG3158. Tremblay, Nicolas: "Michael Delisle, *Le sort de Fille*," *XYZ: La Revue de la Nouvelle*, no. 93 (printemps 2008), 87-92.

DELTEIL, Joseph.

GG3159. ● Briatte, Robert: *Joseph Delteil: une biographie*. Paris: Ed. de Paris, 2008. 272 p.

DEMASY, Paul.

GG3160. Krause, Frank: "Immaculate misconceptions? From Georg Kaiser's *Oktobertag* to Paul Demasy's *L'homme de nuit*." In 464, 161-180.

DENIS, Philippe.

GG3161. Mascarou, Alain: "Philippe Denis: une parenthèse laissée ouverte." In 382, 187-197.

DÉON, Michel.

GG3162. Authier, François-Jean: "Partis pris sans parti, ou la fantasmatique hussarde du militant chez Michel Déon et Jacques Laurent." In 456, 179-189. [Laurent]

DEPESTRE, René. See also 59.

GG3163. Colletta, Antonella: "Depestre lecteur de Pavese: un périple autour du monde," *Interculturel Francophones*, no. 12 (nov.-déc. 2007), 57-76.

GG3164. Constant, Isabelle: "Le lieu onirique dans *Hadriana dans tous mes rêves* de René Depestre." In 59, 107-124.

GG3165. Fallaize, Elizabeth: "Voodoo and the short story in French: Depestre's 'Un nègre à l'ombre blanche'," *Francophone Postcolonial Studies*, vol. 6, no. 2 (Autumn-Winter 2008), 18-33.

GG3166. Lucien, Renée Clémentine: " 'L'écosystème Caraïbe', selon René Depestre." In 118, 261-272.

GG3167. Thiao, Yopane: "Haïti à travers les écrits de René Depestre." In 118, 273-288.

DERMÉE, Paul.

GG3168. Martin-Schmets, Victor: "Paul Dermée et la Section d'or." In 612, 183-190.

DERRIDA, Jacques. See also 378, 397, 4649, 606, 737, 933, 935, 951, 963, 971, 973, 978, 981, 994, 1005, 1008, 1763, 2016, 2021, 2687, 2694, 2699, 3024, 3041, 3145, 3589, 3986, 4513, 5181, 5218, 7497.

GG3169. ● Appelbaum, David: *Jacques Derrida's ghost: a conjuration*. Albany: SUNY Press, 2008.

GG3170. ● Beardsworth, Richard: *Derrida y lo político*. Buenos Aires: Univ. Nacional de la Plata, 2008. 440 p.

GG3171. ● Bennington, Geoffrey: *Derrida*. Paris: Seuil, 2008. 370 p.

GG3172. ● Bradley, Arthur: *Derrida's Of grammatology*. Bloomington: Indiana Univ. Press, 2008. *Indiana philosophical guides*. 166 p.

GG3173. ● Bruckmann, Florian: *Die Schrift als Zeuge analoger Gottrede: Studien zu Lyotard, Derrida und Augustinus*. Freiburg im Breisgau: Herder, 2008. 495 p.

GG3174. ● Buckinx, Sébastien: *Descartes entre Foucault et Derrida: la folie dans la Première méditation*. Paris: L'Harmattan, 2008. *Ouverture philosophique*. 197 p. [Foucault]

GG3175. ● Chérif, Mustapha: *Islam and the West: a conversation with Jacques Derrida*. Trans. Teresa Lavender Fagan. Chicago: Univ. of Chicago Press, 2008. xxii, 114 p.

GG3176. ● *Conjunciones: Derrida y compañía*. Eds. Cristina de Peretti, Emilio Velasco. Madrid: Dykinson, 2007. 396 p.

GG3177. ● Dekens, Olivier: *Derrida pas à pas*. Paris: Ellipses, 2008. 256 p.

GG3178. ● Derrida, Jacques: *The animal that therefore I am*. Ed. Marie-Louise Mallet; trans. David Wills. New York: Fordham Univ. Press, 2008. *Perspectives in continental philosophy*. xiii, 176 p.

GG3179. ● Derrida, Jacques: *Basic writings*. Ed. Barry Stocker. New York: Routledge, 2008. 443 p.

GG3180. ● Derrida, Jacques: *Positionen: Gespräche mit Henri Ronse, Julia Kristeva,*

Jean-Louis Houdebine, Guy Scarpetta. Hrsg. Peter Engelmann. Wien: Passagen, 2008. 2. überarb. Aufl. 178 p.

GG3181. • Derrida, Jacques: *Psyche: inventions of the other*. Ed. Peggy Kamuf, Elizabeth G. Rottenberg. Stanford: Stanford Univ. Press, 2008. *Meridian: crossing aesthetics*. 333 p.

GG3182. • Derrida, Jacques: *Séminaire: La bête et le souverain*. Edition établie par Michel Lisse, Marie-Louise Mallet et Ginette Michaud. Paris: Galilée, 2008. *La philosophie en effet*.

GG3183. • *Derrida à Alger: un regard sur le monde*. Mustapha Chérif [et al.]. Arles: Actes Sud; Alger: Barzakh, 2008. *Bleu*. 191 p.

GG3184. • *Derrida and legal philosophy*. Ed. Peter Goodrich [et al.]. Basingstoke; New York: Palgrave Macmillan, 2008. xv, 257 p.

GG3185. • *Derrida, Deleuze, psychoanalysis*. Ed. Gabriele Schwab. New York: Columbia Univ. Press, 2008. *Critical Theory Institute books*. [Deleuze]

GG3186. • *Derrida: la déconstruction*. Coordonné par Charles Ramond. Paris: PUF, 2008. *Débats philosophiques*. 167 p.

GG3187. • *Derrida, la tradition de la philosophie*. Textes rassemblés par Marc Crépon et Frédéric Worms. Paris: Galilée, 2008. *La philosophie en effet*. 217 p.

GG3188. • *Derrida pour les temps à venir*. Textes réunis par René Major. Paris: Stock, 2007. *L'autre pensée*. 529 p.

GG3189. • *Derrida und Adorno: zur Aktualität von Dekonstruktion und Frankfurter Schule*. Hrsg. Eva L.-Waniek, Erik M. Vogt. Wien: Turia + Kant, 2008. 254 p.

GG3190. • *Derrida und danach?: literaturtheretische Diskurse der Gegenwart*. Hrsg. Gregor Thuswaldner. Wiesbaden: VS, 2008. 195 p.

GG3191. • *Derrida's legacies: literature and philosophy*. Ed. Simon Glendinning, Robert Eaglestone. London: Routledge, 2008. xxviii, 155 p.

GG3192. • Doncel, Alicia: *Los hijos de la luna: Juan José Saer, Jacques Derrida, Paul de Man*. Buenos Aires: De los Cuatro Vientos, 2008. 235 p.

GG3193. • *Edward Said and Jacques Derrida: reconstellating humanism and the global hybrid*. Ed. Mina Karavanta, Nina Morgan. Newcastle-upon-Tyne: Cambridge Scholars, 2008. viii, 361 p.

GG3194. • Fabbri, Lorenzo: *The domestication of Derrida: Rorty, pragmatism and deconstruction*. Trans. Daniele Manni; Ed. Vuslat Demirkoparan, Ari Lee Laskin. London; New York: Continuum, 2008. 150 p.

GG3195. • García Düttmann, Alexander: *Derrida und ich: das Problem der Dekonstruktion*. Bielefeld: Transcript, 2008. *Edition Moderne Postmoderne*. 193 p.

GG3196. • García Masip, Fernando: *Comunicación y desconstrucción: el concepto de comunicación a partir de la obra de Jacques Derrida*. México: Univ. Iberoamericana, 2008. 336 p.

GG3197. • Garritano, Francesco: *La formazione come questione in Jacques Derrida*. Roma: Anicia, 2008. 348 p.

GG3198. • Genève, Max: *Qui a peur de Derrida?*. Paris: Anabet, 2008. 273 p.

GG3199. • *Ghostly demarcations: a symposium on Jacques Derrida's Specters of Marx*. Ed. Michael Sprinker. London; New York: Verso, 2008. *Radical thinkers*. 278 p.

GG3200. • Hägglund, Martin: *Radical atheism: Derrida and the time of life*. Stanford: Stanford Univ. Press, 2008. *Meridian: crossing aesthetics*. x, 255 p.

GG3201. • Hainz, Martin: *Entgöttertes Leid: zur Lyrik Rose Ausländers unter Berücksichtigung der Poetologien von Theodor W. Adorno, Peter Szondi und Jacques Derrida*. Tübingen: Max Niemeyer, 2008. *Conditio Judaica*. vi, 468 p.

GG3202. • Hollander, Dana: *Exemplarity and chosenness: Rosenzweig and Derrida on the nation of philosophy*. Stanford: Stanford Univ. Press, 2008. *Cultural memory in the present*. xxix, 260 p.

GG3203. • Hurst, Andrea: *Derrida vis-à-vis Lacan: interweaving deconstruction and psychoanalysis*. New York: Fordham Univ. Press, 2008. *Perspectives in continental philosophy*. xii, 469 p. [Lacan]

GG3204. • *Jacques Derrida: adesso l'architettura*. A cura di Francesco Vitale. Milano: Libri Scheiwiller, 2008. 373 p.

GG3205. ● *Jacques Derrida-Saint Augustin, des confessions.* Réunis par John D. Caputo et Michael J. Scanlon. Trad. Pierre-Emmanuel Dauzat. Paris: Stock, 2007. 495 p.

GG3206. ● Kaarto, Tomi: *Jacques Derrida and the question of interpretation.* Frankfurt: Peter Lang, 2008. 651 p.

GG3207. ● Kates, Joshua: *Fielding Derrida: philosophy, literary criticism, history, and the work of deconstruction.* New York: Fordham Univ. Press, 2008. *Perspectives in continental philosophy.* xii, 279 p.

GG3208. ● Kennedy, Clare: *Paradox, aphorism and desire in Novalis and Derrida.* London: Maney, 2008. *MHRA texts and dissertations,* 71. 135 p.

GG3209. ● Kimmerle, Heinz: *Jacques Derrida zur Einführung.* Hamburg: Junius, 2008. 7. Aufl. 219 p.

GG3210. ● Lewis, Michael: *Derrida and Lacan: another writing.* Edinburgh: Edinburgh Univ. Press, 2008. xii, 282 p.

GG3211. ● Lotz, Carsten: *Zwischen Glauben und Vernunft: Letztbegründungsstrategien in der Auseinandersetzung mit Emmanuel Levinas und Jacques Derrida.* Paderborn: Schöningh, 2008. 430 p.

GG3212. ● Manithottil, Paul: *Difference at the margin: Derrida's critique of Heidegger's philosophy of the work of art.* New Delhi: Atlantic, 2008. vi, 226 p.

GG3213. ● McCance, Dawne: *Sleights of hand: Derrida writing.* Vernon, B.C.: Kalamalka Press, 2008. *Mackie lecture and reading series.* xiv, 118 p.

GG3214. ● Meier, Angelika: *Die monströse Kleinheit des Denkens: Derrida, Wittgenstein und die Aporie in Philosophie, Literatur und Lebenspraxis.* Freiburg: Rombach, 2008. 580 p.

GG3215. ● Mjaaland, Marium Timmann: *Autopsia: self, death, and God after Kierkegaard and Derrida.* Trans. Brian McNeil. Berlin; New York: Walter de Gruyter, 2008. *Kierkegaard studies,* 17. xiii, 357 p.

GG3216. ● *Mnema: Derrida zum Andenken.* Hrsg. Hans-Joachim Lenger, Georg Christoph Tholen. Bielefeld: Transcript, 2007. 258 p.

GG3217. ● Naas, Michael: *Derrida from now on.* New York: Fordham Univ. Press, 2008. *Perspectives in continental philosophy.* xix, 266 p.

GG3218. ● *Nach Jacques Derrida und Niklas Luhmann.* Hrsg. Gunther Teubner. Stuttgart: Lucius & Lucius, 2008. 198 p.

GG3219. ● Orchard, Vivienne: *Jacques Derrida and the institution of French philosophy.* Leeds: Maney, 2008.

GG3220. ● *Politische Philosophie und Dekonstruktion: Beiträge zur politischen Theorie im Anschluss an Jacques Derrida.* Andreas Niederberger, Markus Wolf, Hrsg. Bielefeld: Transcript, 2007. *Edition Moderne Postmoderne.* 183 p.

GG3221. ● Regazzoni, Simone: *Nel nome di Chora: da Derrida a Platone e al di là.* Genova: Il melangolo, 2008. *Opuscula.* 152 p.

GG3222. ● Richards, Kevin Malcolm: *Derrida reframed: a guide for the arts student.* London; New York: I. B. Tauris, 2008. 149 p.

GG3223. ● Rösch, Thomas: *Kunst und Dekonstruktion: serielle Ästhetik in den Texten von Jacques Derrida.* Wien: Passagen, 2008. 620 p.

GG3224. ● Rosler, Isaac B.: *Jacques Derrida: justicia y hospitalidad.* Lima: Benvenuto, 2008. 109 p.

GG3225. ● Schubbach, Arno: *Subjekt im Verzug: zur Rekonzeption von Subjektivität mit Jacques Derrida.* Zürich: Chronos, 2008. *Legierungen.* 397 p.

GG3226. ● Simon, Rupert: *Die Begriffe des Politischen bei Carl Schmitt und Jacques Derrida.* Frankfurt: Peter Lang, 2008. *Europäische Hochschulschriften.* 216 p.

GG3227. ● *Su Jacques Derrida: scrittura filosofica e pratica di decostruzione.* A cura di Paolo D'Alessandro e Andrea Potestio. Milano: LED, 2008. 344 p.

GG3228. ● Tarditi, Claudio: *Con e oltre la fenomenologia: le "eresie" fenomenologiche di Jacques Derrida e Jean-Luc Marion.* Genova: Il melangolo, 2008. 203 p. [Marion]

GG3229. ● Valisone, Moreno: *Ambiguità e situazione: a partire da Jacques Derrida e Maurice Merleau-Ponty.* Torino: L'Harmattan Italia, 2008. *Psykhé.* 268 p.

GG3230. ● Varghese, Ricky: *Unbearable heartbeat: reading ethics and politics in Derrida, Levinas, and Kundera.* Saarbrücken: Verlag Dr. Müller, 2008. 79 p. [Levinas]

GG3231. ● Vitale, Francesco: *Spettrografie: Jacques Derrida tra singolarità e scrittura.* Genova: Il melangolo, 2008. *Itinera.* 153 p.

GG3232. ● Waniek, Eva: *Derrida und Adorno: zur Aktualität von Dekonstruktion und Frankfurter Schule.* Wien: Turia + Kant, 2008. 254 p.

GG3233. ● Wortham, Simon Morgan: *Derrida: writing events.* London: Continuum, 2008. *Continuum studies in philosophy.* vi, 145 p. [Beckett]

GG3234. ● Yébenes Escardó, Zenia: *Breve introducción al pensamiento de Derrida.* México: UAM, 2008. 172 p.

GG3235. Ahmad, Aijaz: "Reconciling Derrida: *Specters of Marx* and deconstructive politics." In 3199.

GG3236. Alant, Jaco: "Du temps où Derrida était 'pour' Mandela, ou les limites de la littérature engagée," *French Studies in Southern Africa,* no. 38 (2008), 1-17.

GG3237. Al-Kassim, Dina: "Resistance, terminable, and interminable." In 3185. [Deleuze]

GG3238. Arsic, Branka: "The rhythm of pain: Freud, Deleuze, Derrida." In 3185. [Deleuze]

GG3239. Attridge, Derek: "Derrida's singularity: literature and ethics." In 3191, 12-25.

GG3240. Badiou, Alain: "Derrida, ou l'inscription de l'inexistant." In 3187, 171-181.

GG3241. Baldwin, Thomas: "Presence, truth and authenticity." In 3191, 107-117.

GG3242. Balke, Friedrich: "Derrida and Foucault on sovereignty." In 3184. [Foucault]

GG3243. Barber, Bruce: "A deconstructive case study: reading Peter Greenaway's *Z&OO*," *Dalhousie French Studies,* vol. 82 (Spring 2008), 123-139.

GG3244. Barker, Stephen: "Strata/sedimenta/lamina: in ruin(s)," *Derrida Today,* vol. 1, no. 1 (2008), 42-58.

GG3245. Baross, Zsuzsa: "Lessons to live (1): posthumous fragments, for Jacques Derrida," *Derrida Today,* vol. 1, no. 2 (2008), 247-265.

GG3246. Benjamin, Andrew: "Indefinite play and 'the name of man'," *Derrida Today,* vol. 1, no. 1 (2008), 1-18.

GG3247. Benmeziane, Bencheerki: "Derrida et l'épreuve de la mémoire." In 3183, 151-167.

GG3248. Bennington, Geoffrey: "Handshake," *Derrida Today,* vol. 1, no. 2 (2008), 167-189.

GG3249. Bennington, Geoffrey: "In the event." In 3191, 26-35.

GG3250. Bennington, Geoffrey: "Jacques Derrida en Amérique." In 3183, 169-175.

GG3251. Bernet, Rudolf: "La voie et le phénomène." In 3187, 65-85.

GG3252. Bernstein, Richard J.: "The conversation that never happened: Gadamer/Derrida," *Review of Metaphysics,* vol. 61, no. 3 (March 2008), 577-605.

GG3253. Boos, Stephen: " 'In the blink of an eye': Derrida's deconstruction of Husserlian phenomenology," *Dalhousie French Studies,* vol. 82 (Spring 2008), 5-16.

GG3254. Boussaha, Omar: "La mise à nu des pouvoirs de domination." In 3183, 113-116.

GG3255. Bowlby, Rachel: "Derrida one day." In 3191, 76-79.

GG3256. Brandes, Daniel: "Derrida and Heidegger: a lively border dispute," *Dalhousie French Studies,* vol. 82 (Spring 2008), 17-27.

GG3257. Bredeson, Garrett Zantow: "On Dogen and Derrida," *Philosophy East and West,* vol. 58, no. 1 (Jan. 2008), 60-82.

GG3258. Burke, Sean: "The passion of the animal: Derrida." In 933.

GG3259. Calarco, Matthew: "The passion of the animal: Derrida." In 935, 103-149.

GG3260. Calarco, Matthew: "Thinking through animals: reflections on the ethical and political stakes of the question of the animal in Derrida," *Oxford Literary Review,* vol. 29 (2007), 1-15.

GG3261. Callinicos, Alex: "Jacques Derrida and the New International." In 3191, 80-89.

GG3262. Chérif, Mustapha: "Le vivre-ensemble." In 3183, 15-18.

GG3263. Chin, Ken Pa: "Deconstruction and via negativa: Derrida on God as gift," *Sino-Christian Studies*, no. 5 (June 2008), 89-116.

GG3264. Chow, Rey: "Reading Derrida on being monolingual," *New Literary History*, vol. 39, no. 2 (Spring 2008), 217-231.

GG3265. Cisney, Vernon: "Categories of life: the status of the camp in Derrida and Agamben," *Southern Journal of Philosophy*, vol. 46, no. 2 (2008), 161-179.

GG3266. Cixous, Hélène: "Celle qui ne se ferme pas." In 3183, 45-58.

GG3267. Cooper, David E.: "Metaphor and Derrida's philosophy of language." In 3191, 45-53.

GG3268. Courtine, Jean-François: "L'*ABC* de la déconstruction." In 3187, 11-26.

GG3269. Crépon, Marc: "Déconstruction et traduction." In 3187, 27-44.

GG3270. Crépon, Marc: "Les langues du pardon." In 964, 226-238.

GG3271. Critchley, Simon: "Déconstruction et communication." In 3186, 53-70.

GG3272. Critchley, Simon: "Derrida: the reader." In 3191, 1-11.

GG3273. Critchley, Simon: "The reader: Derrida among the philosophers." In 3184.

GG3274. Crowell, Steven: "Fink's untimely Nietzsche: between Heidegger and Derrida," *International Studies in Philosophy*, vol. 38, no. 3 (2006), 15-31.

GG3275. Dastur, Françoise: "Heidegger, Derrida et la question de la différence." In 3187, 87-107.

GG3276. Derrida, Jacques: "The transcendental 'stupidity' ('bêtise') of man and the becoming-animal according to Deleuze." In 3185. [Deleuze]

GG3277. Deuser, Hermann: " ' . . . and moreover, lo, here is a ram.' Genesis 22 in religious-philosophical metacriticism." In 954.

GG3278. Eaglestone, Robert: "Derrida and the legacies of the Holocaust." In 3191, 66-75.

GG3279. Eagleton, Terry: "Marxism without Marxism." In 3199.

GG3280. Edwards, Elizabeth: "Spectres that cannot not spook: work and fear in Derrida," *Dalhousie French Studies*, vol. 82 (Spring 2008), 107-121.

GG3281. Elson, Christopher: "Jacques Derrida and Michel Deguy: 'Knowing what witnessing as a poet means'," *Dalhousie French Studies*, vol. 82 (Spring 2008), 71-83. [Deguy]

GG3282. England, Frank: "Foes: Plato, Derrida, and Coetzee: rereading J. M. Coetzee's *Foe*," *Journal of Literary Studies*, vol. 24, no. 4 (Dec. 2008), 44-62.

GG3283. Flügel, Oliver: "Jenseits von Prozedur und Substanz. Jacques Derrida und die normative Demokratietheorie." In 3220, 119-141.

GG3284. Fudge, Erica: "The dog, the home and the human, and the ancestry of Derrida's cat," *Oxford Literary Review*, vol. 29 (2007), 37-54.

GG3285. Fuggle, Sophie: "Le Parkour: reading or writing the city?" In 575, 159-170. [Foucault]

GG3286. Gaston, Sean: "A palintropoic genealogy of the diaphanous exactitude of pe(n)ser," *Derrida Today*, vol. 1, no. 2 (2008), 212-228.

GG3287. Gearey, Adam: "Thinking, poetics, law." In 3184.

GG3288. Gehring, Petra: "The jurisprudence of the 'force of law'." In 3184.

GG3289. Glowacka, Dorota: "A date, a place, a name: Jacques Derrida's Holocaust translations," *Dalhousie French Studies*, vol. 82 (Spring 2008), 41-58.

GG3290. Goddard, Jean-Christophe: "Œuvre et destruction: Jacques Derrida et Antonin Artaud." In 3186, 71-98. [Artaud]

GG3291. Goldschmit, Marc: "Cosmopolitique du marrane absolu." In 3183, 141-150.

GG3292. Goodrich, Peter: "Un cygne noir." In 3184.

GG3293. Guyer, Sara: "Buccality." In 3185. [Deleuze]

GG3294. Habib, Rafey: "Deconstruction: Jacques Derrida." In 953.

GG3295. Hadj-Aïssa, Zohra: "Traduction et déconstruction chez Derrida." In 3183, 101-111.

GG3296. Hamacher, Werner: "Lingua amissa: the Messianism of commodity-language and Derrida's *Specters of Marx*." In 3199.

GG3297. Heller, Peggy: "Derrida and the idea of Europe," *Dalhousie French Studies*, vol. 82 (Spring 2008), 93-106.

GG3298.   Hobson, Marian: "Derrida's irony?: or, in order that homeland securitiy do not come too early to the case." In 3191, 90-106.

GG3299.   Hoffmann, Florian: "Deadlines: Derrida and critical legal scholarship." In 3184.

GG3300.   Hunter, Ian: "The desire for deconstruction: Derrida's metaphysics of law," *Communication, Politics and Culture*, vol. 41, no. 1 (2008), 6-29.

GG3301.   Hurst, Andrea: "The impotence of pseudo-antagonism: a Derridean response to Zizek's charge of practical irrelevance," *South African Journal of Philosophy*, vol. 27, no. 1 (2008), 10-26.

GG3301a.   Hurst, Rochelle: "Adaptations as an undecidable: fidelity and binarity from Bluestone to Derrida." In 7988.

GG3302.   Ingram, James D.: "Praktische Idee oder vernünftiger Glaube." In 3220, 99-117.

GG3303.   Irizarry, Christine: "Notes about *On touching-Jean-Luc Nancy* by Jacques Derrida," *Derrida Today*, vol. 1, no. 2 (2008), 190-200.

GG3304.   Jameson, Fredric: "Marx's purloined letter." In 3199.

GG3305.   Jang, Sung Shik: "Philosophical textuality and Khoral theology: concursus in the providence of God of Charles Hodge and event in Khora of Jacques Derrida." Diss., Univ. of Glasgow, 2008. vii, 281 p.

GG3306.   Jarvis, Simon: "By heart," *Dalhousie French Studies*, vol. 82 (Spring 2008), 59-68.

GG3307.   Johnson, Christopher: "Derrida and technology." In 3191, 54-65.

GG3308.   Kambouchner, Denis: "La déconstruction et le concept de la culture." In 3183, 185-191.

GG3309.   Kambouchner, Denis: "Hegel en déconstruction." In 3186, 143-161.

GG3310.   Kambouchner, Denis: "Ironie et déconstruction." In 3187, 45-63.

GG3311.   Kamuf, Peggy: "The effect of America." In 3191, 138-150.

GG3312.   Kennedy, Duncan: "European introduction: Four objections." In 3184.

GG3313.   Klein, Judith N.: "Der feine Sand des Gedächtnisses: Spuren verlorener Sprachen in der jüdisch-maghrebinischen Literatur." In 824, 149-168. [Memmi]

GG3314.   Koch, Andrew M.: "Specters of postmodernism: Derrida, Marx, and leftist politics," *International Studies in Philosophy*, vol. 38, no. 4 (2006), 71-96.

GG3315.   Kotsko, Adam: "The sermon on Mount Moriah: faith and the secret in *The Gift of Death*," *Heythrop Journal*, vol. 49, no. 1 (Jan. 2008), 44-61.

GG3316.   Krapp, Peter: "Between forgiveness and forgetting." In 3184.

GG3317.   Lambert, Gregg: "De/territorializing psychoanalysis." In 3185. [Deleuze]

GG3318.   Leavey, John: "From Socrates to electracy and beyond," *Derrida Today*, vol. 1, no. 1 (2008), 59-75.

GG3319.   Lèbre, Jérôme: "Délacement." In 3183, 117-140.

GG3320.   Legrand, Pierre: " 'Il n'y a pas de hors-texte': intimations of Jacques Derrida as comparatist-at-law." In 3184.

GG3321.   Lewis, Tom: "The politics of 'hauntology' in Derrida's *Specters of Marx*." In 3199.

GG3322.   Lucy, Niall: "Running on," *Derrida Today*, vol. 1, no. 2 (2008), 229-246.

GG3323.   Ma, Shaoling: "Echoing the *Politics of Friendship*," *Angelaki*, vol. 12, no. 3 (Dec. 2007), 141-154.

GG3324.   Macherey, Pierre: "Marx dematerialized, or the spirit of Derrida." In 3199.

GG3325.   Macherey, Pierre: "Le Marx intempestif de Derrida." In 3187, 135-154.

GG3326.   Madrid, Raúl: "Hacia una ética de la responsabilidad. Derrida y el otro 'por venir' en Levinas," *Sapientia*, vol. 63, fasc. 223 (2008), 105-142. [Levinas]

GG3327.   Major, René; Chantal Talagrand-Major: "A Samarkand, peut-être." In 3183, 35-43.

GG3328.   Malabou, Catherine: "Polymorphism never will pervert childhood." In 3185. [Deleuze]

GG3329.   Maley, Willy: "A propos of Marx, attribute to Derrida: a note on a note in *Margins of Philosophy*." In 940, 178-196.

GG3330.   Mallet, Marie-Louise: "Une pensée de l'hospitalité." In 3183, 59-67.

GG3331. Marion, Jean-Luc: "L'impossible et le don." In 3187, 155-170.

GG3332. Marzec, Robert P.: "Said, Derrida and the undecidable human: in the name of inhabitancy." In 3193, 304-323.

GG3333. McQuillan, Martin: "Derrida and policy: is deconstruction really a social science?," *Derrida Today*, vol. 1, no. 1 (2008), 119-130.

GG3334. McQuillan, Martin: "Toucher 1: the problem with self-touching," *Derrida Today*, vol. 1, no. 2 (2008), 201-211.

GG3335. Meighoo, Sean: "Derrida's Chinese prejudice," *Cultural Critique*, vol. 68 (Winter 2008), [n.p.].

GG3336. Menke, Christoph: "Subjektivität und Gelingen." In 3220, 61-76.

GG3337. Milesi, Laurent: "*Saint-Je* Derrida," *Oxford Literary Review*, vol. 29 (2007), 55-75.

GG3338. Miller, J. Hillis: "The medium is the maker: Browning, Freud, Derrida, and the new telepathic ecotechnologies," *Oxford Literary Review*, vol. 30, no. 2 (2008), 161-179.

GG3339. Miller, J. Hillis: "Touching Derrida touching Nancy: the main traits of Derrida's hand," *Derrida Today*, vol. 1, no. 2 (2008), 145-166. [Nancy]

GG3340. Mills, Catherine: "Playing with law: Agamben and Derrida on postjuridical justice," *South Atlantic Quarterly*, vol. 107, no. 1 (Jan. 2008), 15-36.

GG3341. Mizuta Lippit, Akira: "The only other apparatus of film." In 3185. [Deleuze]

GG3342. Moazzam-Doulat, Malek: "Future impossible: Carl Schmitt, Jacques Derrida, and the problem of political messianism," *Philosophy Today*, vol. 52, no. 1 (Spring 2008), 73-81.

GG3343. Mocnik, Rastko: "After the fall: through the fogs of the 18th Brumaire of the Eastern Springs." In 3199.

GG3344. Moghith, Anwar: "Le politique dans les textes." In 3183, 69-78.

GG3345. Montag, Warren: "Spirits armed and unarmed: Derrida's *Specters of Marx*." In 3199.

GG3346. Montredon, Jacques [et al.].: "Catchment, growth point, and spatial metaphor: analysing Derrida's oral discourse on deconstruction." In 771, 171-194.

GG3347. Morgan Wortham, Simon: "Law of friendship: Derrida and Agamben," *New Formations*, no. 62 (Autumn 2007), 89-105.

GG3348. Mosès, Stéphane: "Au cœur d'un chiasme." In 3187, 109-133. [Levinas]

GG3349. Moulfi, Mohamed: "Derrida: le sens du monde." In 3183, 177-183.

GG3350. Muir, James R.: "Derrida and post-modern political philosophy," *European Legacy*, vol. 13, no. 4 (July 2008), 425-443.

GG3351. Murdoch, J. Murray, Jr.: "Deconstruction as *Darstellung*: Derrida's subtle Hegelianism," *Idealistic Studies*, vol. 37, no. 1 (Spring 2007), 29-42.

GG3352. Naas, Michael: "Derrida's America." In 3191, 118-137.

GG3353. Nancy, Jean-Luc: "Les différences parallèles." In 3187, 199-215. [Deleuze]

GG3354. Nancy, Jean-Luc: "L'indépendance de l'Algérie, l'indépendance de Derrida." In 3183, 19-25.

GG3355. Negri, Antonio: "The specter's smile." In 3199.

GG3356. O'Connor, Patrick: "Derrida, revolutionary agape, and community," *Kinesis*, vol. 32, no. 2 (Fall 2005), 23-43.

GG3357. Olivier, Bert: "Trauma and literature: Derrida, 9/11 and Hart's *The Reconstructionist*," *Journal of Literary Studies*, vol. 24, no. 1 (March 2008), 32-57.

GG3358. Orford, Anne: "Critical intimacies: reading international law." In 3184.

GG3359. Oventile, Robert Savino: "Jacques Derrida." In 971.

GG3360. Penny, Laura: " 'Who could have oil and kindness enough for them?' A reading of Derrida's *Spurs* and Nietzsche's women," *Dalhousie French Studies*, vol. 82 (Spring 2008), 29-39.

GG3361. Phillips, John W. P.: "Loving love or ethics as natural philosophy in Jacques Derrida's *Politiques de l'amitié*," *Angelaki*, vol. 12, no. 3 (Dec. 2007), 155-170.

GG3362. Quadflieg, Dirk: "Die Frage des Fremden. Derrida und das Paradox der absoluten Gastfreundschaft." In 3220, 27-37.

GG3363. Ramanathan, Vaidehi: "Applied linguistics redux: a Derridean exploration of Alzheimer lifehistories," *Applied Linguistics*, vol. 29, no. 1 (May 2008), 1-23.

GG3364. Ramond, Charles: "Déconstruction et littérature." In 3186, 99-142.

GG3365. Rapaport, Herman: "Deregionizing ontology: Derrida's khora," *Derrida Today*, vol. 1, no. 1 (2008), 95-118.

GG3366. Rheinberger, Hans-Jörg: "Translating Derrida," *Dalhousie French Studies*, vol. 82 (Spring 2008), 85-91. [Also in *CR: The New Centennial Review*, vol. 8, no. 3 (Winter 2008), 175-188]

GG3367. Ronell, Avital: "Saying goodbye: an amateur video." In 3184.

GG3368. Rosenfeld, Michel: "Derrida's ethical turn." In 3184.

GG3369. Ross, Alison: "Derrida's writing-theatre: from the theatrical allegory to political commitment," *Derrida Today*, vol. 1, no. 1 (2008), 76-94.

GG3370. Roudinesco, Elisabeth: "Jacques Derrida: the moment of death." In 976, 143-154.

GG3371. Royle, Nicholas: "Derrida's event." In 3191, 36-44.

GG3372. Rubenstein, Mary-Jane: "Decision: Jacques Derrida." In 978.

GG3373. Salanskis, Jean-Michel: "La philosophie de Jacques Derrida et la spécificité de la déconstruction au sein des philosophies du *linguistic turn*." In 3186, 13-51.

GG3374. Santiago, Silviano: "La troisième rive." In 3183, 27-34.

GG3375. Schink, Philipp: "Von phänomenologischer Reduktion zur Umarbeitung der Epochë." In 3220, 39-59.

GG3376. Schwab, Gabriele: "Derrida, Deleuze, and the psychoanalysis to come." In 3185. [Deleuze]

GG3377. Sheehan, Natalie: "Acknowledging the intermediary: a look at scapegoats, supplements and the temptation of mimetic contagion in Girard, Derrida, and Agamben." In 610, 63-76. [Girard]

GG3378. Simpson, Zachary: "Friendship, the kiss of death, and God: H. Richard Niebuhr and Jacques Derrida on the other," *Heythrop Journal*, vol. 49, no. 1 (Jan. 2008), 62-78.

GG3379. Staikou, Elina: "Justice's last worl: Derrida's post-scriptum to force of law," *Derrida Today*, vol. 1, no. 2 (2008), 266-290.

GG3380. Staten, Henry: "Derrida, Dennett, and the ethico-political project of naturalism," *Derrida Today*, vol. 1, no. 1 (2008), 19-41.

GG3381. Thurschwell, Adam: "Specters and scholars: Derrida and the tragedy of political thought." In 3184.

GG3382. Timme, Samuel: "Inheriting cosmopolitanism: Thomas Pogge and Jacques Derrida on global injustice," *Kinesis*, vol. 34, no. 2 (Fall 2007), 6-16.

GG3383. Tolba, Mona: "Comment Derrida écrit-il 'la religion'?" In 3183, 79-99.

GG3384. Vaughan, William: "Husserl's 'unthought axiomatic' and Derrida's critique." In 988.

GG3385. Vismann, Cornelia: "The archive and the beginning of law." In 3184.

GG3386. Weber, Elisabeth: "Deconstruction is justice." In 3184.

GG3387. Weller, Shane: "Bad violence." In 989.

GG3388. Wills, David: "Friendship in torsion: Schmitt, Derrida." In 990.

GG3389. Wolf, Markus: "Zum Ideal der Demokratie bei John Rawls, Jürgen Habermas und Jacques Derrida." In 3220, 77-98.

GG3390. Worms, Frédéric: 'Derrida ou la transition de la philosophie." In 3187, 199-215.

GG3391. Zantou Bredeson, Garrett: "On Gogen and Derrida," *Philosophy East and West*, vol. 58, no. 1 (2008), 60-82.

DESAUTELS, Denise. See 6085.

DESBIENS, Patrice. See also 324.

GG3392. Hébert, François: "Dans la lune de Patrice Desbiens: de la tumeur à l'oreiller," *Etudes Canadiennes*, no. 64 (2008), 195-204.

DESBIOLLES, Maryline. See also 3416.

GG3393. Desbiolles, Maryline: *Croisée de voix*. Entretiens menés par Denis Lefèvre. Paris: Cherche midi, 2008. 109 p.

DES FORÊTS, Louis-René. See also 606.

GG3394. ● Des Forêts, Louis-René: *Les mégères de la mer: suivi de Poèmes de Samuel Wood.* Préface de Richard Millet. Paris: Gallimard, 2008. *Poésie.* 81 p.

GG3395. Godeau, Florence: "*Opéra* silencieux: texttes et dessins de Louis-René des Forêts." In 418, 179-195.

GG3396. Roudaut, Jean: "La nuit manuscrite," *Théodore Balmoral,* no. 58 (2008), 9-14.

GG3397. Rousselot, Emmanuelle: "L'art du peu d'un 'vieil enfant': étude sur *Pas à pas jusqu'au dernier* de Louis-René des Forêts." In 382, 283-294.

GG3398. Sérié, Hélène: "La conversion rêvée chez Louis-René Des Forêts," *Manchette,* no. 3 (2004), 81-94.

DESGENT, Jean-Marc.

GG3399. David, Carole: "Dans l'atelier de Jean-Marc Desgent: la vérité de la réalité," *Lettres Québécoises,* no. 130 (été 2008), 7-10.

GG3400. Desgent, Jean-Marc: "C'est par intuition que je sais d'avance: c'est une énigme," *Lettres Québécoises,* no. 130 (été 2008), 6.

GG3401. Watteyne, Nathalie: "Les amants sur le ring de la catastrophe," *Lettres Québécoises,* no. 130 (été 2008), 11-12.

DESNOS, Robert. See also 420, 657, 1009.

GG3402. ● Flamel, Louis: *Robert Desnos oder nächtlich gestirnte Augen.* Trémoigne [Dortmund]: Alicorn, 2008. *Miroir de la licorne.* 36 p.

GG3403. Collani, Tania: "L'énigme du sphinx des glaces: réécriture d'un mythe chez Robert Desnos." In 520, 773-786.

GG3404. Lardoux, Jacques: "Genèse du bestiaire amoureux de Robert Desnos." In 439, 41-50.

DESPORTES, Bernard.

GG3405. ● *Bernard Desportes autrement.* Etudes réunies et prés. par Fabrice Thumerel. Arras: Artois presses université, 2008. 113 p.

DESROCHERS, Alfred.

GG3406. Godbout, Patricia: "L'écrivain dans ses lettres." In 44, 221-233.

DES ROSIERS, Joël.

GG3407. Brophy, Michael: "Bris(é)es caraïbes: le souffle d'ex-île de Joël Des Rosiers," *Dalhousie French Studies,* vol. 83 (Summer 2008), 119-126.

DESTREMAU, Didier. See 637a.

DESVIGNES, Lucette. See also 5362.

GG3408. ● Desvignes, Lucette: *Encore toi, Electre!.* A bilingual edition, edited and trans. by Jerry L. Curtis; with a commendatory foreword by Jacqueline Sessa. Lewiston, NY: Edwin Mellen, 2008. xxxi, 182 p.

GG3409. ● Desvignes, Lucette: *Psychological sketches: a collection of short fiction.* Ed. Jerry L. Curtis; commendatory preface by Michael C. Oswald. Lewiston, NY: Edwin Mellen, 2008. 317 p.

GG3410. Curtis, Jerry L.: "The poetry of Lucette Desvignes," *Cincinnati Romance Review,* vol. 26 (2007), 37-62.

GG3411. Pandelescu, Silvia: "Invitation dans le monde de l'innocence: *Petites histoires naturelles,*" *Studies on Lucette Desvignes and the Twentieth Century,* no. 18 (2008), 91-99.

GG3412. Rinciog, Diana: "Traitement de l'Histoire dans deux nouvelles de Lucette Desvignes," *Studies on Lucette Desvignes and the Twentieth Century,* no. 18 (2008), 83-89.

GG3413. Sessa, Jacqueline: "L'Histoire dans les sagas de Lucette Desvignes," *Studies on Lucette Desvignes and the Twentieth Century,* no. 18 (2008), 41-82.

GG3414. Sessa, Jacqueline: "L'Histoire dans le théâtre de Lucette Desvignes," *Studies on Lucette Desvignes and the Twentieth Century,* no. 18 (2008), 127-140.

DEUX, Fred.

GG3415. Deux, Fred: 'Le tracé de l'attente,' *Matricule des Anges,* no. 84 (2007), 28-31. [Entretien]

DEVI, Ananda.

GG3416. Anderson, Jean: "Can the subjected speak? Giving a voice to the voiceless in *Moi, l'interdite* by Ananda Devi and *Une Femme de rien* by Maryline Desbiolles," *Women in French Studies* (2008), 108-115. [Desbiolles]

GG3417.   Compan, Magali: " 'Cette terre qui me ressemble': re-writing the island, re-writing the self in Ananda Devi's *Pagli*." In 92, 41-57.

GG3418.   Devi, Ananda: "Ecrire hor de sa bulle," *Nouvelles Etudes Francophones*, vol. 23, no. 1 (printemps 2008), 12-19.

GG3419.   Effertz, Julia: " 'Le prédateur, c'est moi': l'écriture de la terre et la violence féminine dans l'œuvre d'Ananda Devi." In 617, 71-82.

GG3420.   Lohka, Eileen: "De la terre à la terre, du berceau à la tombe: l'île d'Ananda Devi," *Nouvelles Etudes Francophones*, vol. 23, no. 1 (printemps 2008), 155-162.

GG3421.   Meur, Marie-Caroline: " 'Rodrigues', photo-souvenir et images d'Ananda Devi. Voyage et dévoilement de soi." In 441, 215-229.

GG3422.   Ramharai, Vicram: "La relation fille-père au sein de la famille hindoue dans les œuvres d'Ananda Devi." In 572, 115-124.

GG3423.   Rochmann, Marie-Christine: "Monstruosité et innocence dans *La Vie de Joséphin le fou*," *Nouvelles Etudes Francophones*, vol. 23, no. 1 (printemps 2008), 163-174.

GG3424.   Soobarah Agnihotri, Jeeveeta: "Folie des sens et folie des langues: le pluri-linguisme, stratégie d'écriture dans *Pagli* d'Ananda Devi," *Nouvelles Etudes Francophones*, vol. 23, no. 1 (printemps 2008), 175-183.

DEVILLE, Patrick.

GG3425.   Ernst, Gilles: "Patrick Deville, romancier et philosophe de l'Histoire." In 472, 185-194.

DEVOS, Raymond.

GG3426.   ● Madini, Mongi: *Devos montreur de mots*. Besançon: Presse univ. de Franche-Comté, 2008. 267 p.

DHAINAUT, Pierre.

GG3427.   ● Dhainaut, Pierre: *Pierre Dhainaut*. Prés. Sabine Dewulf. Montreuil-sur-Brèche: Vanneaux, 2008. *Présence de la poésie*. 240 p.

DHÔTEL, André.

GG3428.   ● Dupouy, Christine: *André Dhôtel: histoire d'un fonctionnaire*. Croissy-Beaubourg: Aden, 2008. *Le cercle des poètes disparus*. 315 p.

GG3429.   ● Jaccottet, Philippe: *Avec André Dhôtel*. Saint-Clément-de-Rivière: Fata Morgana, 2008. 105 p.

GG3430.   Arrouye, Jean: "L'insolie selon André Dhôtel." In 439, 97-111.

GG3431.   Bialestowski, Gérard: "L'ombre d'Autun," *Cahiers André Dhôtel*, no. 4 (2006), 15-20.

GG3432.   Blondeau, Philippe: "Dhôtel citadin," *Cahiers André Dhôtel*, no. 4 (2006), 95-102.

GG3433.   Braulx, Claude-Edmond: "A Charleville," *Cahiers André Dhôtel*, no. 4 (2006), 32-34.

GG3434.   Dangy, Isabelle: "La vallée de la lettre blanche," *Cahiers André Dhôtel*, no. 4 (2006), 44-59.

GG3435.   Dupouy, Christine: "Une histoire de lieux," *Cahiers André Dhôtel*, no. 4 (2006), 6-14.

GG3436.   Frankart, Roland: "Un balcon sur la vallée," *Cahiers André Dhôtel*, no. 4 (2006), 21-31.

GG3437.   Grégoire, Jean-François: "Vers d'autres rives," *Cahiers André Dhôtel*, no. 4 (2006), 132-139.

GG3438.   Grosjean, Jean: "Et aussi en Arcadie," *Cahiers André Dhôtel*, no. 4 (2006), 93-94.

GG3439.   Marcipont, Christian: "Le texte et le lieu, le texte ou le lieu," *Cahiers André Dhôtel*, no. 4 (2006), 140-146.

GG3440.   Meynet-Devillers, Marie-Pierre: "La traversée de la forêt," *Cahiers André Dhôtel*, no. 4 (2006), 103-113.

GG3441.   Motoret, Laurence: "L'homme est un lieu pour l'homme," *Cahiers André Dhôtel*, no. 4 (2006), 60-68.

GG3442. Perry, Edith: "Les romans insulaires d'André Dhôtel," *Cahiers André Dhôtel*, no. 4 (2006), 69-82.

GG3443. Pluen, Patrick: "Quelques notes sur *L'Homme de la scierie*," *Cahiers André Dhôtel*, no. 4 (2006), 35-42.

GG3444. Todereo, Marianna Antonella: "Dhôtel: le chercheur d'un nouvel espace," *Cahiers André Dhôtel*, no. 4 (2006), 116-131.

GG3445. Tritsmans, Bruno: "Portulans et broderies: le voyage en mer dans les récits grecs d'André Dhôtel," *Cahiers André Dhôtel*, no. 4 (2006), 83-92.

DIANGO, Sirafily.

GG3446. Le Potvin, Sébastien: "L'Afrique sans complexes de Sirafily Diango," *Cultures Sud*, no. 170 (sept. 2008), 45-50.

DIARRA, Mandé-Alpha.

GG3447. Nissim, Liana: "La fulgurance d'un étonnant voyageur." In 72, 239-258.

DIB, Mohammed. See also 3514.

GG3448. ● Boulafrad-Abudura, Fatiha: *Topique colonialiste et contre-topique dans la triilogie Algérie de Mohammed Dib*. Lille: ANRT, 2008. *Thèse à la carte*. 406 p.

GG3449. Hilliard, Aouicha: "Le rôle de la *çadaqa* dans *Les terrasses d'Orsol* de Mohammed Dib: pour une éthique de la compassion," *Nouvelles Etudes Francophones*, vol. 22, no. 1 (printemps 2007), 140-154.

GG3450. Yelles, Mourad: "De la danse des mots au sourire du chat: l'humour dibien entre *nûtka* et *nonsense*," *Expressions Maghrébines*, vol. 7, no. 2 (hiver 2008), 73-98.

DICKNER, Nicolas.

GG3451. Boisclair, Isabelle: "Trois poissons dans l'eau. Les (non-)relations familiales dans *Nikolski* de Nicolas Dickner." In 572, 277-285.

DI MANNO, Yves.

GG3452. Malnoë, Céline: "Le blanc dans l'esthétique d'Yves Di Manno." In 393, 89-96.

DIOP, Birago. See also 151.

GG3453. Riesz, János: "Birago Diop, écrivain et vétérinaire (1930-1945)." In 127, 209-222.

DIOP, Boubacar Boris.

GG3454. Sarr, Bacary: "Boubacar Boris Diop et Henry Bauchau: revisiter le mythe pour guérir de l'Histoire," *Études de Lettres*, no. 279 [no. 1] (2008), 71-83. [Bauchau]

GG3455. Semujanga, Josias: "*Murambi*. La métaphore de l'horreur ou le témoignage impossible." In 103, 85-101.

DIOP, Ousmane Socé. See 260.

DIVASSA NYAMA, Jean.

GG3456. Clerc, Jeanne-Marie: "Jean Divassa Nyama ou la réappropriation des cultures endogènes," *Cultures Sud*, no. 170 (sept. 2008), 51-56.

GG3457. Clerc, Jeanne-Marie; Lilyane Nzé: "Jean Divassa Nyama, *Le bruit* de l'héritage." In 56, 107-152.

DJAOUT, Tahar.

GG3458. Vallury, Raji: "Walking the tightrope between memory and history: metaphor in Djaout's *L'invention du desert*," *Novel*, vol. 41, no. 2-3 (Spring-Summer 2008), 320-341.

DJAVANN, Chahdortt. See 183.

DJEBAR, Assia. See also 81, 332, 339, 378, 678, 1148, 3646, 4730.

GG3459. ● *Assia Djebar*. Sous la dir. de Najib Redouane, Yvette Bénayoun-Szmidt. Paris: L'Harmattan, 2008. *Autour des écrivains maghrébins*. 378 p.

GG3460. ● Murray, Jenny: *Remembering the (post)colonial self: memory and identity in the novels of Assia Djebar*. Oxford: Peter Lang, 2008. *Modern French identities*. 258 p.

GG3461. ● Rahman, Najat: *Literary disinheritance: the writing of home in the work of Mahmoud Darwish and Assia Djebar*. Lanham, MD: Lexington, 2008. xxiii, 146 p.

GG3462. ● Richter, Elke: *Ich-Entwürfe im hybriden Raum: das "Algerische Quartett" von Assia Djebar*. Frankfurt: Peter Lang, 2008. *Méditerranée*. 303 p.

GG3463. Aït M'Barek, Mina: "*La Femme sans sépulture* ou le lieu de mémoire féminin en mouvement." In 3459, 293-300.

GG3464. Al-Ghadeer, Moneera: "Conquest's spectacle: Djebar's *L'amour, La fantasia* and Lacoue-Labarthe's *Musica Ficta*," *Symploke*, vol. 16, no. 1-2 (2008), 241-271. [Lacoue-Labarthe]

GG3465. Ali-Benali, Zineb: "Ecrire en palimpseste: *Loin de Médine*, aux sources de la première fracture." In 3459, 195-204.

GG3466. Arenberg, Nancy: "Mobile bodies and kindred sisters in Djebar's *Ombre Sultane*," *French Review*, vol. 82, no. 2 (Dec. 2008), 353-367.

GG3467. Assa-Rosemblum, Sonia: "Pour étaler la pièce principale ou rien: démontages de la fiction dans la trilogie maghrébine d'Assia Djebar." In 3459, 359-374.

GG3468. Benhaïm, André: "Pas à pas: *L'œuvre vagabonde* d'Assia Djebar." In 539, 185-198.

GG3469. Bereksi, Lamia: "Lecture de Delacroix dans *Femmes d'Alger dans leur appartement* de Assia Djebar." In 563, 113-117.

GG3470. Bivona, Rosalia: "Villes algériennes et voix sororales." In 3459, 239-262.

GG3471. Blum-Reid, Sylvie: "Voyage dans le passé/présent de *La Femme sans sépulture* d'Assia Djebar." In 3459, 285-292.

GG3472. Boidard Boisson, Cristina: "*La Disparition de la langue française* d'Assia Djebar: le mirage de l'impossible retour?" In 3459, 301-319.

GG3473. Boidard Boisson, Cristina: "Le silence des femmes dans le recueil de nouvelles *Femmes d'Alger dans leur appartement*," *Estudios de Lengua y Literatura Francesas*, no. 17 (2006-2007), 67-79.

GG3474. Bourget, Carine: "La réédition de *Femmes d'Alger dans leur appartement*," *Esprit Créateur*, vol. 48, no. 4 (Winter 2008), 92-103.

GG3475. Brahimi, Denise: "Ruptures et décalages: *Les Alouettes naïves*." In 3459, 129-142.

GG3476. Brândusa-Steiciuc, Elena: "Assia Djebar: *Les Impatients*, une préfiguration de l'œuvre à venir." In 3459, 103-114.

GG3477. Calle-Gruber, Mireille: "Ecrire de main morte ou l'art de la césure chez Assia Djebar," *Esprit Créateur*, vol. 48, no. 4 (Winter 2008), 5-14.

GG3478. Calle-Gruber, Mireille: "La scrittura migrante di Assia Djebar." In 586, 277-281.

GG3479. Case, Frederick Ivor: "Sémiotique de l'espace: les dimensions d'un appartement." In 3459, 165-172.

GG3480. Chikhi, Beïda: "Une visite dans l'atelier itinérant d'Assia Djebar," *Esprit Créateur*, vol. 48, no. 4 (Winter 2008), 117-128.

GG3481. Clerc, Jeanne-Marie: "Choc des cultures, affrontements éthiques et morale de l'écrivain chez Assia Djebar." In 3459, 323-340.

GG3482. Dahan, Danielle: "*L'Amour, la fantasia* ou la construction d'une mémoire algérienne." In 483, 69-84.

GG3483. Diouf Keïta, Anta: "*Vaste est la prison*: l'histoire au cœur du roman." In 3459, 205-226.

GG3484. Donadey, Anne: "African American and Francophone postcolonial memory: Octavia Butler's *Kindred* and Assia Djebar's *La femme sans sépulture*," *Research in African Literatures*, vol. 39, no. 3 (Fall 2008), 65-81.

GG3485. Donadey, Anne: "Introjection and incorporation in Assia Djebar's *La Femme sans sépulture*," *Esprit Créateur*, vol. 48, no. 4 (Winter 2008), 81-91.

GG3486. Elbaz, Robert: "Du corps et de la parole dans *L'Amour, la fantasia* chez Assia Djebar." In 3459, 173-184.

GG3487. Fallaize, Elizabeth: "Translating Delacroix: Assia Djebar's *Les femmes d'Alger dans leur appartement*," *Australian Journal of French Studies*, vol. 45, no. 2 (May-Aug. 2008), 110-124.

GG3488. Faulkner, Rita A.: "Psychoanalysis and anamnesis in the national allegory of Nawal El Saadawi and Assia Djebar," *Esprit Créateur*, vol. 48, no. 4 (Winter 2008), 69-80.

GG3489. Gafaïti, Hafid: "Assia Djebar, l'écriture et la mort." In 3459, 227-238.

GG3490. García Casado, Margarita: "Des pères et des filles à travers l'œuvre de Assia Djebar." In 572, 39-47.

GG3491. Gontard, Marc: "*Les Nuits de Strasbourg* d'Assia Djebar ou l'érotique des langues." In 3459, 273-284.

GG3492. Gruber, Eberhard: "Migrations de l'amour ou *Les nuits de Strasbourg* à la deuxième lecture." In 586, 209-225.

GG3493. Gubinska, Maria: "Assia Djebar et la question de la francophonie." In 76, 205-212.

GG3494. Hannouche, Dalila: "Les pouvoirs de la lecture: trois textes d'Assia Djebar." In 3459, 341-358.

GG3495. Heller-Goldenberg, Lucette: "Ecriture-orature-littérature." In 3459, 275-284.

GG3496. Jones, Christa: "La voix dans le miroir: résistance et identité dans 'Il n'y a pas d'exil' d'Assia Djebar." In 119, 195-214.

GG3497. Laghouati, Sofiane: "Le français, une tunique de Nessus pour vivre: langue marâtre, et langue du père." In 572, 77-85.

GG3498. Laghouati, Sofiane: "Quand le corps s'écrie/s'écrit-il? Manifestations et enjeux des corps féminins dans l'œuvre d'Assia Djebar." In 440, 79-90.

GG3499. Lionnet, Françoise: "Ces voix au fil de soi(e): le detour du poétique," *Esprit Créateur*, vol. 48, no. 4 (Winter 2008), 104-116.

GG3500. McCormack, Jo: "The work of memory in Assia Djebar's *Les Nuits de Strasbourg*," *Australian Journal of French Studies*, vol. 45, no. 2 (May-Aug. 2008), 125-135.

GG3501. Medeiros, Ana de: "The language of exile: haunting desires in Djebar's *La disparition de la langue française*," *Critical Studies*, vol. 30 (2008), 139-150.

GG3502. Medeiros, Ana de: "Mutilation and liberation: filial relationships in Assia Djebar's *L'Amour, la fantasia*." In 458, 163-174.

GG3503. Miraglia, Anne-Marie: "Je(ux) subversifs dans *Ombre Sultane*." In 3459, 185-194.

GG3504. Mohammedi-Tabti, Bouba: "Assia Djebar. *Les enfants du nouveau monde* ou la clôture du lieu." In 3459, 115-128.

GG3505. Mortimer, Mildred: "*La Soif* d'Assia Djebar: exercice de style ou air de flûte." In 3459, 91-102.

GG3506. Murdoch, H. Adlai: "Woman, postcoloniality, otherness: Djebar's discourses of *histoire* and *Algérianité*," *Esprit Créateur*, vol. 48, no. 4 (Winter 2008), 15-33.

GG3507. Ogunyemi, Chikwenye Okonjo: "Talking sister, silenced subaltern: Assia Djebar's *A sister to Scheherazade*." In 110.

GG3508. Pompejano, Valeria: "Il 'terzo spazio' del romanzo: la Strasburgo di Assia Djebar." In 586, 83-96.

GG3509. Redouane, Najib; Yvette Bénayoun-Szmidt, Yvette: "Parole plurielle d'Assia Djebar sur son œuvre." In 3459, 11-87.

GG3510. Restuccia, Laura: "Migrazioni letterarie della parole della notte." In 586, 261-274.

GG3511. Rocca, Anna: "Assia Djebar. La mémoire, le témoin et l'érotisme." In 103, 75-83.

GG3512. Rocca, Anna: "Assia Djebar's *La femme sans sépulture*: anxiety and testimonial writing," *Women in French Studies*, no. 16 (2008), 100-112.

GG3513. Salhi, Zahia Smail: "Between the languages of silence and the woman's word: gender and language in the work of Assia Djebar," *International Journal of the Sociology of Language*, no. 190 (2008), 79-101.

GG3514. Sanson, Hervé: "Imaginer les identités: l'immigré en question." In 586, 73-82. [Dib]

GG3515. Schuchardt, Beatrice: "Fragmenter et faire flotter: à propos de l'esthétique postcoloniale de transition dans *Femmes d'Alger dans leur appartement* d'Assia Djebar." In 483, 85-99.

GG3516. Siassi, Guilan: "Itineraries of desire and the excesses of home: Assia Djebar's cohabitation with 'la langue adverse'," *Esprit Créateur*, vol. 48, no. 4 (Winter 2008), 56-68.

GG3517. Thiel, Véronika: "La querelle des discours: techniques formelles de la réécriture de l'histoire dans *L'Amour, la fantasia*," *Esprit Créateur*, vol. 48, no. 4 (Winter 2008), 34-46.

GG3518. Walker, Muriel: "Femme d'écriture française: la francographie djebarienne," *Esprit Créateur*, vol. 48, no. 4 (Winter 2008), 47-55.

GG3519. Weber-Fève, Stacey A.: "Assia Djebar as film theorist in 'Touchia: ouverture' and *Ces voix qui m'assiègent*," *French Review*, vol. 81, no. 3 (Feb. 2008), 542-551.

GG3520. Wehrs, Donald R.: "Requiem and rebirth: the language of Islamic ethical revolt in Djebar's *Le Blanc de l'Algérie*." In 142.

GG3521. Wehrs, Donald R.: "The sensible, the maternal, and the ethical grounding of feminist Islamic discourse in Djebar's *L'Amour, la fantasia* and *Loin de Médine*." In 142.

GG3522. Yédes, Ali: "*Poèmes pour l'Algérie heureuse* d'Assia Djebar ou la reconquête du patrimoine algérien." In 3459, 143-164.

DJEMAÏ, Abdelkader.

GG3523. Bendjelid, Michèle Faouzia: "Modalités d'énonciation de l'humour dans *Un été de cendres* d'Abdelkader Djemaï," *Expressions Maghrébines*, vol. 7, no. 2 (hiver 2008), 51-71.

DOHO, Gilbert.

GG3524. Dill Palaï, Clément: "Théâtre et perception politique du Cameroun des années 1990: une lecture de *Au-delà du lac des nénuphars* de Gilbert Doho." In 52, 129-146.

DOLTO, Françoise.

GG3525. ● Chapsal, Madeleine: *Ce que m'a appris Françoise Dolto*. Paris: Librairie générale française, 2008. *Livre de poche*. 186 p.

GG3526. ● Chérer, Sophie; Philippe Dumas: *Ma Dolto*. Paris: Stock, 2008. 304 p.

GG3527. ● Dolto, Françoise: *Mère et fille, une correspondance, 1913-1962*. Lettres choisies et prés. par Muriel Djéribi-Valentin; notes de Muriel Djéribi-Valentin et Colette Percheminier. Paris: Mercure de France, 2008. 155 p.

GG3528. ● Guillerault, Gérard: *Comprendre Dolto*. Sous la dir. de Jacques Sédat. Paris: Armand Colin, 2008. *Lire et comprendre*. 252 p.

GG3529. ● Liaudet, Jean-Claude: *Françoise Dolto expliquée aux enfants*. Paris: Archipel, 2008. Nouv. éd. augm. 229 p.

GG3530. ● Pleux, Didier: *Génération Dolto*. Paris: Jacob, 2008. 250 p.

GG3531. ● Sauverzac, Jean-François de: *Françoise Dolto: itinéraire d'une psychanalyste*. Paris: Flammarion, 2008. Ed. augm. d'une postface. *Champs*. 421 p.

GG3532. ● Sauverzac, Odile B. de: *Françoise Dolto*. Toulouse: Milan, 2008. 63 p.

GG3533. ● Tribolet, Serge: *Freud, Lacan, Dolto enfin expliqués!*. Bordeaux: L'Esprit du temps, 2008. *Le monde psy*. 216 p. [Lacan]

DONGALA, Emmanuel.

GG3534. Boudreault, Laurence: "Réel en crise et crise de la représentation," *Itinéraires et Contacts de Cultures*, no. 39 (2007), 155-162. [Bugul]

DORGELÈS, Roland. See also 1353.

GG3535. Hurcombe, Martin: "Guerre du souvenir et guerre des sexes." In 473, 263-274. [Jean Schlumberger]

DORION, Hélène.

GG3536. Bergeron, Carlos: "Hélène Dorion: une faille pour tomber en soi," *Lettres Québécoises*, no. 129 (printemps 2008), 11-12.

GG3537. Dorion, Hélène: "Les paysages, les chemins," *Lettres Québécoises*, no. 129 (printemps 2008), 6.

GG3538. Paquin, Jacques: "Hélène Dorion: pensée du sensible, ouverture du poème," *Lettres Québécoises*, no. 129 (printemps 2008), 7-10.

DORSINVILLE, Roger.

GG3539. Marty, Anne: "Un aspect fondamental de l'œuvre romanesque de Roger Dorsinville: une quête de la Loi orientée par les réminiscences bibliques," *Interculturel Francophones*, no. 12 (nov.-déc. 2007), 169-189.

DOTREMONT, Christian.

GG3540. ● Dotremont, Christian: *Christian Dotremont: 68 37' latitude nord*. Bruxelles: Devillez, 2008. 270 p.

GG3541. Caron, Stéphanie: "Entre legs et dissidence: l'héritage surréaliste de Christian Dotremont," *Mélusine*, no. 28 (2008), 21-32.

GG3542. Hoks, Nathan: "Christian Dotremont," *Circumference*, vol. 4, no. 1 (Autumn 2008), 114-117.

GG3543. Linarès, Serge: "On a touché au mot: plastique de l'écriture chez Christian Dotremont." In 418, 293-310.

GG3544. Okami, Saé: "Le choc interculturel chez Pierre Alechinsky et Christian Dotremont," *Champs du Signe*, no. 24 (2007), 87-108.

DOUBROVSKY, Serge. See also 389.

GG3545. Boulé, Jean-Pierre: "*L'arroseur arrosé*: Doubrovsky, his psychoanalyst and autof(r)iction," *Essays in French Literature and Culture*, no. 45 (Nov. 2008), 149-170.

GG3546. Poirier, Jacques: "Entre catharsis et pharmakon: sur *Fils* de Serge Doubrovsky," *Etudes Epistémè*, no. 13 (printemps 2008), 142-153.

DRACIUS, Suzanne. See also 70.

GG3547. Helm, Yolande: "Suzanne Dracius ou le marronnage au féminin," *Cultures Sud*, no. 170 (sept. 2008), 57-62.

GG3548. Jahn, Jennifer: "*Femmes, féminitude, féminisme*: an afternoon with Suzanne Dracius," *International Journal of Francophone Studies*, vol. 11, no. 3 (2008), 417-450.

DRIEU LA ROCHELLE, Pierre. See also 591.

GG3549. ● Drieu La Rochelle, Pierre: *Blèche*. Préface de Julien Hervier. Paris: Gallimard, 2008. *L'Imaginaire*. 230 p.

GG3550. ● Drieu La Rochelle, Pierre: *Notes pour un roman sur la sexualité: suivi de, Parc Monceau*. Edition établie et prés. par Julien Hervier. Paris: Gallimard, 2008. 94 p.

DUBOIS, Michel. See 1104.

DU BOS, Charles.

GG3551. Pernot, Denis: "Charles Du Bos: relations mondaines et relations critiques," *Revue d'Histoire Littéraire de la France*, tome 108, no. 4 (oct.-déc. 2008), 863-873.

GG3552. Tessier, Andrew T.: "Charles Du Bos: de la *non-littérature* à la *non-œuvre*," *Dalhousie French Studies*, vol. 84 (Fall 2008), 65-74.

DU BOUCHET, André. See also 1033, 1048.

GG3553. Koziej, Alicja: "André du Bouchet spectateur d'une peinture 'réfractaire'." In 563, 108-112.

DUCHARME, Réjean. See also 94.

GG3554. Gyurcsik, Margareta: "Réjean Ducharme, *L'Avalée des avalés*." In 115, 91-106.

GG3555. Hombourger, Juline: "Le grotesque tragique dans l'œuvre de Réjean Ducharme." In 75, 155-166.

GG3556. Hombourger, Juline: "Réjean Ducharme: l'énigmatique signifié." In 441, 187-196.

GG3557. Larochelle, Marie-Hélène: "Fuites et invectives dans les romans de Réjean Ducharme," *Etudes Françaises*, vol. 44, no. 1 (2008), 25-36.

DUHAMEL, Georges.

GG3558. ● Duhamel, Georges: *Vie et aventures de Salavin*. Avant-propos d'Antoine Duhamel. Paris: Omnibus, 2008. xi, 807 p.

GG3559. ● Duhamel, Georges; Blanche Duhamel: *Correspondance de guerre. Tome II, janvier 1917-mars 1919*. Préface par Antoine Duhamel; édition établie et annotée par Arlette Lafay. Paris: Champion, 2008. *Bibliothèque des correspondances, mémoires et journaux*. 1627 p.

GG3560. Campa, Laurence: "D'*Alcools* à *Civilisation*: contributions à l'histoire des relations entre Guillaume Apollinaire et Georges Duhamel." In 612, 43-54. [Apollinaire]

DUJARDIN, Édouard. See 899, 7021.

DUMÉZIL, Georges.

GG3561. ● Pirart, Eric: *Georges Dumézil face aux démons iraniens*. Paris: L'Harmattan, 2008. *Kubaba*. 190 p.

GG3562. Detienne, Marcel; Janet Lloyd: " 'The fact of structure', with Georges Dumézil." In 426.

DUMONT, Fernand.

GG3563. Longre, Jean-Pierre: "La quête de Fernand Dumont: un nouveau Perceval dans *La Région du cœur*." In 553, 227-235.

GG3564. Massicotte, Julien: "Dumont et ce qu'il en reste: présences et absences de Fernand Dumont dans les débats intellectuels québécois contemporains," *Québec Studies*, vol. 45 (Spring/Summer 2008), 107-131.

DUPIN, Jacques.

GG3565. *04.03: mélanges pour Jacques Dupin*. Réunis par Francis Cohen et Nicolas Pesquès. Paris: P.O.L., 2007. 188 p.

GG3566. Villain, Franck: "Valeurs du peu dans *De nul lieu et du Japon*." In 382, 111-124.

DUPRÉ, Louise.

GG3567. ● Jezequel, Anne-Marie: *Louise Dupré: le Québec au féminin*. Paris: L'Harmattan, 2008. 268 p.

DUPUIS, Sylviane.

GG3568. Dupuis, Sylviane: "Le théâtre comme subversion des mythes." In 520, 833-849.

DURAS, Marguerite. See also 546, 705, 2435, 4054.

GG3569. ● Aronsson, Mattias: *La thématique de l'eau dans l'œuvre de Marguerite Duras*. Göteborg: Göteborgs Univ., 2008. *Ropmanica Gothoburgensia*. 202 p.

GG3570. ● Belliot, Emelie; Gaëtane Belliot: *Vietnam song: un voyage sur les traces de Marguerite Duras*. Biarritz: Atlantica, 2008. 97 p.

GG3571. ● Delmar, Michaël: *L'une est l'autre: Duras-Moreau: une amitié littéraire*. Paris: Scali, 2008. 153 p. [Moreau]

GG3572. ● Duras, Marguerite: *Cahiers de guerre et autres textes*. Edition établie par Sophie Bogaert et Olivier Corpet. Paris: P.O.L., 2008. 428 p.

GG3573. ● Duras, Marguerite: *Le Square*. Edition prés., établie et annotée par Arnaud Rykner. Paris: Gallimard, 2008. *Folio théâtre*. 196 p.

GG3574. ● Duras, Marguerite: *Wartime writings: 1943-1949*. Ed. Sophie Bogaert and Olivier Corpet; trans. Linda Coverdale. New York: New Press, 2008. xix, 296 p.

GG3575. ● Fourton, Maud: *Marguerite Duras, une poétique de "l'en allé"*. Dijon: Editions univ. de Dijon, 2008. *Ecritures*. 147 p.

GG3576. ● *In the dark room: Marguerite Duras and cinema*. Ed. Rosanna Maule with Julie Beaulieu. New York: Peter Lang, 2008.

GG3577. ● Jouvenot, Christian: *La folie de Marguerite Duras: Marguerite Duras et sa mère*. Paris: L'Harmattan, 2008. *Espaces théoriques*. 176 p.

GG3578. ● *Marguerite Duras et la pensée contemporaine: actes du colloque des 10-12 mai 2007, La faculté des lettres, Université de Göteborg, Suède*. Textes réunis et prés. par Eva Ahlstedt et Catherine Bouthors-Paillart. Göteborg: Göteborgs Universitet, 2008. 288 p.

GG3579. ● *Marguerite Duras: trajectoires d'une écriture*. Sous la dir. de Jean Cléder. Latresne: Bord de l'eau, 2006. 106 p.

GG3580. ● *Marguerite Duras: visioni veneziane*. A cura di Chiara Bertola, Edda Melon. Padova: Il Poligrafo, 2008. 204 p.

GG3581. Ahlstedt, E.: "Marguerite Duras féministe malgré elle?" In 3578, 157-169.

GG3582. Aronsson, M.: "L'œuvre de Marguerite Duras comme lieu de rencontre entre l'Occident et l'Orient." In 3578, 217-227.

GG3583. Barbé-Petit, F.: "Marguerite Duras, Emmanuel Levinas ou la question d'autrui." In 3578, 63-71. [Levinas]

GG3584. Baum, Alwin: "The love for the other. Le ravissement de l'autre." In 3576.

GG3585. Beaulieu, Julie: "The poetics of cinematic writing." In 3576.

GG3586. Borgomano, Madeleine: "Karl Marx, c'est fini." In 3578, 15-25.

GG3587. Borgomano, Madeleine: "Literature and cinema: the in-betweenness." In 3576.

GG3588. Bougault, Laurence: "Modalisations discursives dans *Le Ravissement de Lol V. Stein* de Marguerite Duras," *Champs du Signe*, no. 21 (2006), 67-78.

GG3589. Bouthors-Paillart, C.: " 'Une différence interne au cœur des significations'." In 3578, 55-62. [Derrida]

GG3590. Calle-Gruber, Mireille: "La chambre noire des différences sexuelles." In 440, 43-57.

GG3590a. Colville, Georgiana M. M.: "Duras ravaged, ravished . . . ravishing." In 8009, 194-213.

GG3591. Conacher, A.: " 'C'est moi la poursuite du vent': le dénouement de la poursuite mystique de Duras dans *C'est tout.*" In 3578, 89-96.

GG3592. Crippa, Simona: "Marguerite Duras, *Un barrage contre le Pacifique*. Géographie de la fuite." In 119, 107-130.

GG3593. Denes, Dominique: "Un lieu à l'œuvre: 'La chambre noire' de Marguerite Duras," *Voix Plurielles*, vol. 5, no. 1 (mai 2008), [n.p.].

GG3594. Dhavernas, Catherine: "Cinema and the destruction of the text in the work of Marguerite Duras." In 3576.

GG3595. Dhavernas, Catherine: "Le poids de l'intelligence ou la futilité du savoir chez Marguerite Duras." In 3578, 97-102.

GG3596. Drissi, Hamida: "La famille chez Marguerite Duras: variations autour d'un mythe." In 571, 343-352.

GG3597. El Maïzi, Myriem: "Chant et mémoire dans *La Mort du jeune aviateur anglais* de Marguerite Duras," *New Zealand Journal of French Studies*, vol. 29, no. 1 (2008), 17-30.

GG3598. Evang Reinton, R.: "Theodor W. Adorno: un lecteur de Marguerite Duras." In 3578, 113-123.

GG3599. Everett, Wendy: "Image, music, film," *Studies in European Cinema*, vol. 5, no. 1 (2008), 7-16. [Godard]

GG3600. Flitterman-Lewis, Sandy: "History, memory, and identity. Nevers, mon souvenir." In 3576.

GG3601. Fox, Albertine: "Writing the rhythms of desire: *Le Ravissement de Lol V. Stein*, *L'Amour* and *L'Amant*," *French Studies Bulletin*, no. 107 (Summer 2008), 39-48.

GG3602. Franzén, C.: " 'La vieille algèbre des peines d'amour'. Duras et la question du désir féminin." In 3578, 139-146.

GG3603. Goldie, Matthew Boyd: "The rhetoric of grief: *Hiroshima mon amour*," *English Language Notes*, vol. 46, no. 1 (Spring/Summer 2008), 61-74. [Resnais]

GG3604. Gorton, Kristyn: "Desire, Duras, and melancholia: theorizing desire after the 'affective turn'," *Feminist Review*, no. 89 (2008), 16-33.

GG3605. Gottesmann, Catherine: "La voix et l'écriture dans *Emily L.* de Marguerite Duras." In 488, 99-114.

GG3606. Günther, Renate: " 'Une femme qui boit, c'est scandaleux'. Marguerite Duras and female alcoholism in France." In 573, 87-100.

GG3607. Hanania, Cécile: "Marguerite Duras au miroir de Barthes." In 3578, 45-54. [Barthes]

GG3608. Hanania, Cécile: "Once upon a time in Hollywood: cinematic references in Marguerite Duras's texts." In 3576.

GG3609. Hauswald, Paul J.: "Une gloire littéraire chez Nicéa," *Rocambole*, no. 42 (2008), 129-131.

GG3610. Hellot, Marie-Christiane: "Femmes, l'amour, la mort, la mer. *Savannah Bay*," *Jeu: Cahiers de Théâtre*, no. 126 (mars 2008), 51-55.

GG3611. Hoppenot, E.: "Maurice Blanchot lecteur de *La Maladie de la mort.*" In 3578, 35-43. [Blanchot]

GG3612. Jeanneret, Sylvie: "Vers la disparition du paysage dans l'œuvre de Marguerite Duras (texte et film)," *Colloquium Helveticum*, no. 38 (2007), 157-170.

GG3613. Kinsey, Tammy A.: " 'You saw nothing': Duras's cinematic language." In 3576.

GG3614. Laverdière, Gabriel: "Ecriture de l'expérience génocidaire dans *Aurélia Steiner* de Marguerite Duras: survoler l' 'infigurable' par une défiguration filmique," *Etudes Littéraires*, vol. 39, no. 1 (hiver 2008), 127-139.

GG3615. Leppick, K.: "Quand l'absolu se retire: écriture, altérité et vide chez Marguerite Duras." In 3578, 103-112.

GG3616.   Lessard, Bruno: " 'Disparaître, dit-elle?': *The Vanishing of Lol V. Stein* as (dis)embodied haunting and invisible spectacle." In 3576.

GG3617.   Liang, Dong: "Redefining image and sound. Marguerite Duras's aural world." In 3576.

GG3618.   Loignon, Sylvie: "Vestiges de l'amour ou l'amour en ruines dans *L'Amour* de Marguerite Duras." In 902, 135-147.

GG3619.   Marion, Esther: "Picturing Proust's *dame en rosse*: notes for framing Duras's *Le Vice-Consul*," *Dalhousie French Studies*, vol. 83 (Summer 2008), 55-68. [Proust]

GG3620.   Maule, Rosanna: "Marguerite Duras, la grande imagière." In 3576.

GG3621.   Mervant-Roux, Marie-Madeleine: "The fragility of beginnings: the first genetic stratum of *Le Square* by Marguerite Duras," *Theatre Research International*, vol. 33, no. 3 (Oct. 2008), 263-275.

GG3622.   Meurée, C.: "Faites vos jeux: déclarer la mourre ou la leçon de Duras à Lacan." In 3578, 127-138. [Lacan]

GG3623.   Mével, Y.: "M. Duras: nuit(s) de la pensée, esthétique(s) de la nuit." In 3578, 209-215.

GG3624.   Mombo, Charles Edgar: "De la relation père-mère-frères et fille dans *L'Amant* de Marguerite Duras." In 571, 179-185.

GG3625.   Muraishi, A.: "Une lecture du *Marin de Gibraltar* à la lumière de la notion de 'désir mimétique' chez René Girard." In 3578, 81-88. [Girard]

GG3626.   Ogawa, Midori: " 'Une Eve marine que la lumière devait enlaidir'," *Revue des Sciences Humaines*, no. 289 [no. 1] (2008), 159-175.

GG3627.   Oliveiera Santos, M.: "Musiques, bruits: l'amour et l'horreur d'*India Song*." In 3578, 229-238.

GG3628.   Patrice, S.: "Duras et la philosophie." In 3578, 239-247.

GG3629.   Quinney, Anne: "A writer under the influence: Duras and the *expérience intérieure*," *Australian Journal of French Studies*, vol. 45, no. 1 (Jan.-April 2008), 33-42.

GG3630.   Rabaté, Dominique: "Evénement et traumatisme." In 590, 169-178.

GG3631.   Rabosseau, Sandrine: "Marguerite Duras: écrire dans la mémoire de l'Occupation et de la Libération." In 103, 119-128.

GG3632.   Ravel, E.: "Duras et Blanchot." In 3578, 29-34. [Blanchot]

GG3633.   Raynal-Zougari: " 'Le chien noir de l'idée': image, cognition et pensée chez Marguerite Duras." In 3578, 195-206.

GG3634.   Remy, M.: "L'influence d'Elio Vittorini sur le communisme de Marguerite Duras." In 3578, 173-180.

GG3635.   Royer, Michelle: "Another type of gaze: writing, the writing self and the cinema of Marguerite Duras." In 3576.

GG3636.   Royer, Michelle: "Féminisme, écriture féminine et féminin dans la parole publique de Marguerite Duras." In 3578, 149-155.

GG3637.   Ruiz, Maria-Luisa: "The house, the car and the child: worlds of Duras, Duras in the world." In 80, 99-107.

GG3638.   Russell-Watts, Lynsey: "Analysing sound and voice: refiguring approaches to the films of the *Indian Cycle*." In 3576.

GG3639.   Rykner, Arnaud: "L'univers quantique de Marguerite Duras et la critique des dispositifs." In 3578, 181-193.

GG3640.   Santini, S.: " 'Je ne sais pas, dit-elle'. Entre voir et dire." In 3578, 73-80. [Deleuze, Foucault]

GG3641.   Spavin, R.: "Pour une lecture de l'adaptation dans *Le camion* de Marguerite Duras." In 3578, 259-267.

GG3642.   Stolz, Claire: "Duras et l'énigme au miroir." In 436, 253-269.

GG3643.   Stubblefield, Thomas: "Love and the burden of memory in Duras's *Ten-thirty on a summer night* and *Moderato cantabile*." In 3576.

GG3644.   Vogt, C.: "L'image sonore: la trouée de l'espace imaginare." In 3578, 249-257.

GG3645.   Wahl, Philippe: "Le discours clivé de *Lol V. Stein*," *Champs du Signe*, no. 22 (2006), 51-79.

GG3646.   Walker, Muriel: "Taboo love between text and image in the works of Marguerite Duras and Assia Djebar." In 3576. [Djebar]

GG3647.   Winston, J.: "Debord and the cinema of Marguerite Duras." In 3578, 269-276. [Debord]

DURKHEIM, Émile.

GG3648.   ● Cherkaoui, Mohamed: *Durkheim and the puzzle of social complexity.* Trans. Peter Hamilton with Toby Matthews. Oxford: Bardwell Press, 2008. *GEMAS studies in social analysis.* xii, 217 p.

GG3649.   ● Dingley, James: *Nationalism, social theory and Durkheim.* New York: Palgrave Macmillan, 2008. vi, 236 p.

GG3650.   ● Durkheim, Emile: *La prohibition de l'inceste et ses origines.* Préface de Robert Neuburger. Paris: Payot, 2008. 139 p.

GG3651.   ● Durkheim, Emile: *Le suicide: étude de sociologie.* Préface de Robert Neuburger. Paris: Payot et Rivages, 2008. 492 p.

GG3652.   ● *Emile Durkheim.* Ed. Roger Cotterrell. Aldershot: Ashgate, 2008.

GG3653.   ● Koenig, Matthias: *Wie weiter mit Emile Durkheim?.* Hamburg: Hamburger Edition, 2008. 39 p.

GG3654.   ● *Suffering and evil: the Durkheimian legacy: essays in commemoration of the 90th anniversary of Durkheim's death.* Ed. W. S. F. Pickering and Massimo Rosati. New York: Durkheim Press; Berghahn, 2008. vi, 195 p.

GG3655.   ● Vázquez Gutiérrez, Juan Pablo: *Autoridad moral y autonomía: une relectura del pensamiento sociológico de Emile Durkheim.* México: Univ. Iberoamericana, 2008. 583 p.

GG3656.   Behrent, Michael C.: "Le débat Guyau-Durkheim sur la théorie sociologique de la religion," *Archives de Sciences Sociales des Religions,* 53e année, no. 142 (avril-juin 2008), 9-26.

GG3657.   Birnbaum, Pierre: "Emile David Durkheim, the memory of Masada." In 799.

GG3658.   Cuin, Charles-Henry: "Emile Durkheim à Bordeaux (1887-1902): un fécond mais pénible exil." In 818.

GG3659.   Deflem, Mathieu: "Emile Durkheim on law and social solidarity." In 941.

GG3660.   "Emile Durkheim: the division of labor." In 882.

GG3661.   Wexler, Philip: "A secular alchemy of social science: the denial of Jewish messianism in Freud and Durkheim," *Theoria,* no. 116 (Aug. 2008), 1-21.

DURRINGER, Xavier. See 1120.

EBERHARDT, Isabelle.

GG3662.   ● Delacour, Marie-Odile; Jean-René Huleu: *Le voyage soufi d'Isabelle Eberhardt.* Paris: J. Losfeld, 2008. 254 p.

GG3663.   ● Eberhardt, Isabelle: *Amours nomades: nouvelles choisies.* Texte établi par Marie-Odile Delacour et Jean-René Huleu; édition prés. et annotée par Martine Reid. Paris: Gallimard, 2008. *Folio; Femmes de lettres.* 138 p.

GG3664.   ● Maâlej, Mohamed: *Isabelle Eberhardt, miroir d'une âme et d'une société.* Paris: L'Harmattan, 2008. *Espaces littéraires.* 163 p.

GG3665.   ● Riéra, Brigitte: *Journaliers d'Isabelle Eberhardt.* Paris: L'Harmattan, 2008. *Classiques francophones.* 130 p.

GG3666.   Clancy-Smith, Julia: "The passionate nomad reconsidered: a European woman in l'Algérie française." In 832, 193-214.

ECHENOZ, Jean. See also 394, 6344, 708, 2652, 2662.

GG3667.   ● Houppermans, Sjef: *Jean Echenoz: étude de l'œuvre.* Paris: Bordas, 2008. *Ecrivains au présent.* 191 p.

GG3668.   ● Vila-Matas, Enrique: *De l'imposture en littérature = De la impostura en literatura.* Dialogue entre Enrique Vila-Matas et Jean Echenoz; dialogue trad. de l'espagnol par Sophie Gewinner et du français par Guadalupe Nettel. Saint-Nazaire: Meet, 2008. *Les bilingues.* 53 p.

GG3669.   Blanckeman, Bruno: "Figure de l'arpenteur, mémoire de l'architecte: *L'occupation des sols* de Jean Echenoz," *Elseneur,* no. 23 (2008), [n.p.].

GG3670. Bonnemason-Richard, Sébastien: "Les filiations insolites: Jean Echenoz, avant-garde l'air de rien." In 2652, 73-79.

GG3671. Cornille, Jean-Louis: "La mort de l'éditeur." In 413. [Lindon]

GG3672. Fournou, Marie: "Représentations du féminin chez Théophile Gautier et Jean Echenoz, une postérité déroutante." In 2652, 37-51.

GG3673. Fourton, Maud: "L'écrivain et son trouble: l'éditeur. A propos de Jérôme Lindon et de Jean Echenoz." In 2652, 63-71.

GG3674. Horvath, Christina: "Eric Laurrent: héritier, pasticheur ou épigone de l'esthétique échenozienne?" In 2652, 95-104. [Laurrent]

GG3675. Laporte, Nadine: "Jean Echenoz: pour une littérature vagabonde." In 2652, 81-93.

GG3676. Motte, Warren: "Jean Echenoz's afterlife." In 900.

GG3677. Mura-Brunel, Aline: "Balzac/Echenoz: un couple insolite." In 2652, 27-36.

GG3678. Panaïté, Oana: "Fiction au conditionnel. L'essai romanesque de Jean Echenoz," *Etudes Littéraires*, vol. 37, no. 2 (printemps 2006), 171-182.

GG3679. Rabenstein, Helga: "Evanescence de l'événement: *Je m'en vais* de Jean Echenoz." In 590, 285-296.

GG3680. Rubichon, Jackie: "*Au piano* de Jean Echenoz: un roman néo-réaliste." In 2652, 53-62.

GG3681. Schlünder, Susanne: " 'Un réalisme en trompe-l'œil': les figures de perception comme principe narratif chez Jean Echenoz," *Roman 20-50*, no. 45 (2008), 145-157.

EDDÉ, Dominique. See 226.

EFFA, Gaston-Paul.

GG3682. Fewou Ngouloure, Jean-Pierre: "L'esthésie comme praxis énonciative: le cas de *Tout ce bleu* de Gaston-Paul Effa," *Itinéraires et Contacts de Cultures*, no. 39 (2007), 61-74.

EFOUI, Kossi. See also 153a, 1108, 4818.

GG3683. Barbolosi, Laurence: "Le théâtre de Kossi Efoui: polyphonie épique ou épopée lyrique," *Esprit Créateur*, vol. 48, no. 3 (Fall 2008), 33-40.

GG3684. Renombo Ogula, Steeve: "Ecriture de la mémoire et simulacres identitaires dans *La Fabrique des cérémonies* de Kossi Efoui." In 103, 239-250.

ELALAMY, Youssef.

GG3685. Pieprzak, Katarzyna: "Bodies on the beach: Youssef Elalamy and Moroccan landscapes of the clandestine." In 92, 104-122.

EL HOUSSI, Majid.

GG3686. Arcoleo, Rossana: "La ricerca del 'Moi' e del "Lieu' nella scrittura d'erranza di Majid El Houssi." In 586, 283-299.

ÉLIADE, Mircea.

GG3687. ● De Martino, Marcello: *Mirceau Eliade esoterico: Ioan Petru Culianu e i "non detti"*. Roma: Settimo sigillo, 2008. 524 p.

GG3688. ● *Mircea Eliade: simbolo de la cultura universal*. Ed. Cataline Elena Dobre, Rafael Garcia Pavón. México: Corinter, 2008. 161 p.

GG3689. ● *Professor Mircea Eliade: reminiscences*. Ed. Mihaela Gligor and Mac Linscott Ricketts. Kolkata: Codex, 2008. 277 p.

GG3690. "Mirceal Eliade." In 984.

GG3691. Oldmeadow, Harry: "Mircea Eliade and C. G. Jung: 'priests without suprlices'?" In 969.

GG3692. Zaidi, Ali Shehzad: "The divine love of Hafiz and Pushkin in Mircea Eliade's 'The captain's daughter'," *International Journal on Humanistic Ideology*, vol. 1, no. 1 (Spring-Summer 2008), 127-144.

GG3693. Zaidi, Ali Shehzad: "Reenchanting the world," *Balkanistica*, no. 21 (2008), 151-157.

GG3694. Zaidi, Ali Shehzad: "Reenchanting the world: Mircea Eliade's *A great man*," *Science Fiction*, vol. 17, no. 1 [no. 45] (2008), 18-23.

EL MALEH, Edmond Amran.

GG3695. Touaf, Larbi: "Memory, history, and narrative ethics in the writing of Edmond Amran El Maleh." In 125, 150-159.

ELSKAMP, Max. See also 681.

GG3696. Bivort, Olivier: "Max Elskamp et la poétique de la ville." In 616, 169-181.

GG3697. Gorceix, Paul: "Max Elskamp (1862-1931), un disciple de Mallarmé." In 83, 175-184. [Mallarmé]

GG3698. Gorceix, Paul: "Réalités flamandes et symbolisme." In 83, 185-198.

GG3699. Gorceix, Paul: "Le 'voyage immobile': Max Elskamp et la symbolique orientale." In 83, 199-214.

ÉLUARD, Paul. See also 420, 1061.

GG3700. • Eluard, Paul: *Capitale de la douleur*. Dossier et notes réalisés par Emilie Frémond; lecture d'image par Alain Jaubert. Paris: Gallimard, 2008. *Folioplus Classiques*. 227 p.

GG3701. • Eluard, Paul: *Le poète et son ombre: prose 1920-1952*. Textes prés. et annotés par Robert D. Valette. Paris: Seghers, 2008. *Poésie d'abord*. 253 p.

GG3702. • *Notre livre, A toute épreuve: a collaboration between Joan Miró and Paul Eluard: 22 February through 29 June 2008, Leonard L. Milberg Gallery for the Graphic Arts, Rare Books and Special Collections, second floor Princeton University Library*. Princeton: Princeton Univ. Library, 2008. 16 p.

EMAZ, Antoine.

GG3703. • *Supplément Triages: actes du colloque Antoine Emaz tenu les 13 et 14 mars 2008 à l'Université de Pau et de l'Adour*. Textes réunis par Jacques Le Gall. Saint-Benoît-du-Sault: Tarabuste, 2008. 192 p.

GG3704. Lloze, Evelyne: "*Le peu importe* d'Antoine Emaz." In 382, 235-246.

EMMANUEL, Pierre.

GG3705. Despax, Arnaud: "Le tyran, le poète et la parole du mal," *Modernités*, no. 29 (2008), 159-174.

EMOND, Paul.

GG3706. Emond, Paul: "Dans la bibliothèque de Paul Emond," *Carnet et les Instants*, no. 153 (2008), 21-25. [Entretien]

ERNAUX, Annie. See also 546, 659, 2833.

GG3707. • Dugast, Francine: *Annie Ernaux: étude de l'œuvre*. Paris: Bordas, 2008. *Ecrivains au présent*. 191 p.

GG3708. Colas-Blaise, Marion: "Temporalité et usages de la photo." In 496, 85-94.

GG3709. Cottille-Foley, Nora: "L'usage de la photographie chez Annie Ernaux," *French Studies*, vol. 62, no. 4 (Oct. 2008), 442-454.

GG3710. Fort, Pierre-Louis: "La filiation inverse: Annie Ernaux et le 'corps glorieux'," *French Studies*, vol. 62, no. 2 (April 2008), 188-199.

GG3711. Garvey, Brenda: "Rhythms, repetitions and rewritings in *Passion simple* by Annie Ernaux." In 575, 75-85.

GG3712. Leclair, Yves: "*Les Années*, de A. Ernaux," *Nouvelle Revue Française*, no. 587 (oct. 2008), 212-216.

GG3713. Mansfield, Charlie: "Paris framed: twentieth-century French writers crossing the city." In 462, 175-186.

GG3714. Parayre, Catherine: "Récits de deuil: Annie Ernaux et Jean-Noël Pancrazi témoignent," *Dalhousie French Studies*, vol. 82 (Spring 2008), 173-179. [Pancrazi]

GG3715. Rabatel, Alain: "La re-présentation des voix populaires dans le discours auctorial chez Annie Ernaux." In 565, 523-546. [Also in 619, 287-325]

GG3716. Romeral Rosel, Francisca: "Annie Ernaux: le retour de la parole refoulée," *Estudios de Lengua y Literatura Francesas*, no. 17 (2006-2007), 139-156.

GG3717. Roussel-Gillet, Isabelle: "Les paradoxes de la photographie chez Ernaux et Le Clézio." In 508, 277-296. [Le Clézio]

GG3718. Roussel-Gillet, Isabelle: "Les photographies dans la liaison au défunt, chez Annie Ernaux et Jean-Marie Gustave Le Clézio." In 571, 157-166. [Le Clézio]

GG3719. Sardin, Pascale: "Towards an ethics of witness, or the story and history of 'une minuscule détresse' in Annie Ernaux's *L'Evénement* and Nancy Huston's *Instruments des ténèbres*," *French Studies*, vol. 62, no. 3 (July 2008), 301-312.

GG3720. Simon, Anne: "Déplacements du genre autobiographique: les sujets Ernaux." In 539, 69-81.

GG3721. Thiel-Janczuk, Katarzyna: "La diversité (culturelle, linguistique, sociale) chez Annie Ernaux et Pierre Pachet." In 76, 297-303. [Pachet]

ESCHOLIER, Raymond.

GG3722. Van den Avenne, Cécile: "Petit-nègre et bambara." In 407, 77-95. [Tharaud]

ESSOMBA, Jean-Roger.

GG3723. Ugochukwu, Françoise: "Quand un roman en éclaire un autre: l'interculturel chez Jean-Roger Essomba." In 52, 111-128.

ETCHART, Salvat.

GG3724. Favre, Marie-Aurélie: " 'Peau blanche, masques noirs'. Salvat Etchart ou les visages d'un écrivain marron." In 441, 97-107.

ÉTIENNE, Gérard.

GG3725. Klaus, Peter: "*La Romance en do mineur de Maître Clo* de Gérard Etienne." In 41, 137-155.

ÉTOKÉ, Nathalie. See 109.

FALL, Aminata Sow. See also 206, 682.

GG3726. • *Emerging perspectives on Aminata Sow Fall: the real and the imaginary in her novels.* Ed. Ada Uzoamaka Azodo. Trenton, NJ: Africa World, 2007. xii, 319 p.

GG3727. Jegede, Olutoyin: "The gender conflict in African literature: a reading of *The Beggar's Strike* and *The Triumph of the Water Lily*," *Journal of African Literature and Culture*, no. 5 (2008), 323-336.

GG3728. Orjinta, Ikechukwu: "Women in Aminata Sow Fall's novels." In 544.

FALLET, René.

GG3729. • Fallet, René: *Romans acides*. Edition établie par Jean-Paul Liégeois; préface de Didier Daeninckx. Paris: Cherche midi, 2008. *Voix publiques*. 985 p.

FANON, Frantz. See also 78, 81, 679, 955, 1002, 1596, 7060, 8304.

GG3730. • Boxill, Ian: *Structure, agency and the influence of Fanon's search for recognition*. Professorial inaugural lecture delivered on April 11, 2008. Kingston, Jamaica: Arawak Publications, 2008. 30 p.

GG3731. • Wideman, John Edgar: *Fanon*. Boston: Houghton Mifflin, 2008. 229 p.

GG3732. Al-Radwany, Marwa: "Radikaler Anti-Imperialismus: Frantz Fanon und die Verdammten dieser Erde." In 839.

GG3733. Basto, Maria-Benedita: "Le Fanon de Homi Bhabha," *Tumultes*, no. 31 (oct. 2008), 47-66.

GG3734. Cherki, Alice: "Frantz Fanon en Algérie: une vision panafricaine," *Cultures Sud*, no. 169 (avril-juin 2008), 95-100.

GG3735. De Lissovoy, Noah: "Stretched dialectic: starting from Frantz Fanon." In 813.

GG3736. Frindéthié, Martial K.: "Fanon's will to unity." In 78, 77-91.

GG3737. Gordon, Lewis R.: "Décoloniser le savoir à la suite de Frantz Fanon," *Tumultes*, no. 31 (oct. 2008), 103-123.

GG3738. Guimarães, Antonio S. A.: "La réception de Frantz Fanon au Brésil," *Tumultes*, no. 31 (oct. 2008), 81-102.

GG3739. Harbi, Mohammed: "Frantz Fanon et le messianisme paysan," *Tumultes*, no. 31 (oct. 2008), 11-15.

GG3740. Koh, Adeline; Frieda Ekotto: "Frantz Fanon in Malaysia: reconfiguring the ideological landscape." In 92, 123-141.

GG3741. Maldonado Torres, Nelson: "Of masters and slaves, or Frantz Fanon and the ethico-political struggle for non-sexist human fraternity." In 512.

GG3742. Marton, Ruchama: "En relisant Fanon. Le droit à la folie," *Tumultes*, no. 31 (oct. 2008), 67-78.

GG3743. Murard, Numa: "Psychiatrie institutionnelle à Blida," *Tumultes*, no. 31 (oct. 2008), 31-45.

GG3743a. Nash, Mark: "Frantz Fanon as film." In 7995.

GG3743b. Petty, Sheila J.: "Transnational gazes in *Frantz Fanon: Black Skin, White Mask*." In 7998, 176-195.

GG3744. Rocchi, Jean-Paul: "Littérature et métapsychanalyse de la race. Après et avec Fanon," *Tumultes*, no. 31 (oct. 2008), 125-144.

GG3745. Snyder, Matthew: "Walking on white nails is something less than a kiss: Frantz Fanon's sister-bashing in *The Marriage Masque*." In 43, 252-274.

GG3746. Stone-Richards, Michael: "Race, Marxism, and colonial experience: Du Bois and Fanon." In 803, 145-160.

GG3747. Wirth, Jason M.: "Lactification and lynching: Fanon and linguistic narcissism," *International Studies in Philosophy*, vol. 38, no. 4 (2006), 143-154.

GG3748. Yacine, Tassadit: "Discrimination et voilence," *Tumultes*, no. 31 (oct. 2008), 17-27.

GG3749. Zaleznik, Abraham: "Frantz Fanon: purgation through violence." In 884.

FARÈS, Nabile.

GG3750. ● Chevalier, Karine: *La mémoire et l'absent: Nabile Farès et Juan Rulfo, de la trace au palimpseste*. Paris: L'Harmattan, 2008. 272 p.

FARGUE, Léon-Paul.

GG3751. ● Fargue, Léon-Paul: *Merveilles de Paris*. Note par Laurent de Freitas. Saint-Clément-de-Rivière: Fata Morgana, 2008. 57 p.

GG3752. Loubier, Pierre: "Dans l'ivresse de la marche: Léon-Paul Fargue et la ville." In 616, 285-294.

GG3753. Pascarel, Barbara: "Fargue contre les alligators de boudoirs." In 564, 137-140.

FARHOUD, Abla. See also 249.

GG3754. Ennaïli, Leïla: "L'écriture migrante et le tremblement de l'écriture dans *Le fou d'Omar* d'Abla Farhoud." In 120, 214-221.

GG3755. Marcheix, Daniel: "Migration, folie, écriture et formes de vie dans les romans d'Abla Farhoud." In 104, 223-236.

GG3756. Steiciuc, Elena-Brandusa: "Une écrivaine 'migrante': Abla Farhoud." In 115, 192-197.

GG3757. Vaucher Gravili, Anne de: "La littérature migrante en Italie: la traduction de *Le bonheur à la queue glissante* d'Abla Farhoud," *Annali di Ca' Foscari*, vol. 46, no. 1 (2007), 127-142.

FEDERMAN, Raymond.

GG3758. ● Federman, Raymond: *Federman hors limites*. Rencontre avec Marie Delvigne. Paris: Argol, 2008. 255 p.

GG3759. Michel Chantal: "L'idiome d'un French qui 'cause pas en Belles lettres', Raymond Federman." In 407, 185-202.

FELLAG, Mohamed.

GG3760. Bivona, Rosalia: "Apologie du couscous. Petit traité sur les rapports franco-maghrébins selon Fellag," *Expressions Maghrébines*, vol. 7, no. 2 (hiver 2008), 143-158.

FELLOUS, Colette.

GG3761. Kassab-Charfi, Samia: "Architecture et histoire chez Colette Fellous," *Revue de Littérature Comparée*, no. 327 [no. 3] (juillet-sept. 2008), 397-406.

FERAOUN, Mouloud.

GG3762. Legendre, Laure: "Mouloud Feraoun entre l'école et le village," *Algérie Littérature/Action*, no. 121-122 (mai-juin 2008), 55-61.

FERNANDEZ, Dominique.

GG3763. ● Fernandez, Dominique: *Discours de réception de Dominique Fernandez à l'Académie française et réponse de Pierre-Jean Rémy*. Paris: Grasset, 2008. 114 p.

FERRÉ, Léo.

GG3764. ● Chabot-Canet, Céline: *Léo Ferré: une voix et un phrasé emblématiques*. Paris: L'Harmattan, 2008. *Univers musical*. 231 p.

GG3765. ● Frot, Maurice: *Léo Ferré: comme si j'vous disais*. Paris: L'Archipel, 2008. 261 p.

GG3766. ● Perraudeau, Michel: *Léo Ferré: poétique du libertaire*. Saint-Geroges d'Oléron: Editions libertaires, 2008. 92 p.

GG3767. ● Perrin, Jean-Eric: *Léo Ferré poète et rebelle*. Monaco: Alphée Jean-Paul Bertrand, 2008. 250 p.

GG3768. ● Valade, Yann: *Léo Ferré: la révolte et l'amour*. Paris: Belles lettres; Valenciennes: Presses univ. de Valenciennes, 2008. *Cantologie*. 244 p.

FERRON, Jacques.

GG3769. ● Cardinal, Jacques: *Le livre des fondatiosn: incarnation et enquébecquoisement dans Le ciel de Québec de Jacques Ferron.* Montréal: XYZ, 2008. 202 p.

GG3770. ● Ferron, Jacques: *Les roses sauvages: petit roman suivi d'une lettre d'amour soigneusement présentée.* Edition préparée par Pierre Cantin, Marie Ferron et Paul Lewis. Montréal: Bibliothèque québécoise, 2008. 187 p.

GG3771. Bednarski, Betty: "Lire-écrire, soigner: les médecins fictifs de Jacques Ferron." In 555, 47-66.

GG3772. Kylousek, Petr: "Les médiateurs de Jacques Ferron." In 76, 237-244.

GG3773. Olscamp, Marcel: "La dernière réconciliation: Jacques Ferron et le souvenir de ses 'années lumineuses'." In 44, 251-261.

FEYDEAU, Georges. See also 1086.

GG3774. ● Feydeau, Georges: *Pièces courtes, monologues, vaudevilles et comédies.* Prés. Henry Gidel. Paris: Omnibus, 2008. ix, 977 p.

GG3775. Heyraud, Violaine: "Principe de répétition et exaspération comique dans *La Puce à l'oreille* de Georges Feydeau," *Humoresques*, no. 26 (2007), 49-62.

GG3776. Ramos Gay, Ignacio: "La prostituta del vaudeville y el pánico burgués." In 866, 131-140.

GG3777. Rittaud-Hutinet, Chantal: "Didascalies et jeu du comédien: comment actualiser l'implicite?" In 605, 495-510.

FIGNOLÉ, Jean-Claude. See also 3950.

GG3778. Tang Samnig, Alice Delphine: "L'influence des traditions orales haïtienne et africaine dans l'écriture romanesque de Jean-Claude Fignolé." In 118, 369-380.

FINKIELKRAUT, Alain. See also 1004.

GG3779. de Wit, Theo W. A.: "Scum of the earth: Alain Finkielkraut on the political risks of a humanism without transcendence," *Telos*, no. 142 (Spring 2008), 163-183.

FLAMMARION, Camille.

GG3780. Bruce, Donald: "Mondes imaginaires et mondes réels: Max Nordau et Camille Flammarion," *Texte*, no. 43-44 (2008), 167-192.

FLEUTIAUX, Pierrette.

GG3781. Bouloumé, Arlette: "Les relations conjugales, familiales et intergénérationnelles dans les contes de Pierrette Fleutiaux." In 894, 165-175.

FOLLAIN, Jean. See also 4654.

GG3782. Farasse, Gérard: "Buissons, brouillons." In 454, 75-85.

GG3783. Kolomiyets, Oléna: "Au sujet de l'imparfait de l'indicatif à partir de l'étude de poèmes de Jean Follain." In 496, 77-83.

FONDANE, Benjamin.

GG3784. ● *Carl Einstein et Benjamin Fondane: avant-gardes et émigration dans le Paris des années 1920-1930.* Dir. Liliane Meffre. Bruxelles: P. Lang, 2008. 218 p.

GG3785. ● Salazar-Ferrer, Olivier: *Benjamin Fondane et la révolte existentielle.* Bruxelles: Corlevour, 2008. 220 p.

FOUCAULT, Michel. See also 24, 397, 923, 933, 936, 946, 948, 949, 952, 970, 997, 1001, 1388, 2017, 2175, 2417, 2424, 2425, 3041, 3055, 3145, 3146, 3174, 3242, 3285, 3640, 5844, 7060.

GG3786. ● Amato, Pierandrea: *Tecnica e potere: Saggi su Michel Foucault.* Milano: Mimesis, 2008. 173 p.

GG3787. ● Beaulieu, Victor-Lévy: *Se dépendre de soi-même: dans les environs de Michel Foucault.* Paroisse Notre-Dame-des-Neiges (Québec): Trois-Pistoles, 2008. 255 p.

GG3788. ● Bellahcène, Driss: *Michel Foucault, ou, l'ouverture de l'histoire à la vérité.* Paris: L'Harmattan, 2008. *La philosophie en commun.* 203 p.

GG3789. ● Bermini, Lorenzo: *Le pecore e il pastore: critica, politica, etica nel pensiero di Michel Foucault.* Napoli: Liguori, 2008. *Profili.* xii, 304 p.

GG3790. ● Cremonesi, Laura: *Michel Foucault e il mondo antico: spunti per una critica dell'attualità.* Pisa: ETS, 2008. 228 p.

GG3791. ● Dahlmanns, Claus: *Die Geschichte des modernen Subjekts: Michel Foucault und Norbert Elias im Vergleich.* Münster: Waxmann, 2008. 264 p.

GG3792. ● De Cristofaro, Ernesto: *Il senso storico della verità: un percorso attraverso Foucault*. Genova: Il melangolo, 2008. 94 p.

GG3793. ● Djaballah, Marc: *Kant, Foucault, and forms of experience*. New York: Routledge, 2008. *Studies in philosophy*. ix, 348 p.

GG3794. ● *Dopo Foucault: genealogie del postmoderno*. A cura di Eleonora de Conciliis. Milano: Mimesis, 2007. 338 p.

GG3795. ● Downing, Lisa: *The Cambridge introduction to Michel Foucault*. Cambridge: Cambridge Univ. Press, 2008. xii, 138 p.

GG3796. ● Fisch, Michael: *Michel Foucault: Bibliographie der deutschsprachigen Veröffentlichungen in chronologischer Folge*. Bielefeld: Aisthesis, 2008. 191 p.

GG3797. ● Foucault, Michel: *The birth of biopolitics: lectures at the Collège de France, 1978-1979*. Ed. Michel Senellart; trans. Graham Burchell. Basingstoke; New York: Palgrave Macmillan, 2008. xvii, 346 p.

GG3798. ● Foucault, Michel: *Le gouvernement de soi et des autres*. Edition établie sous la dir. de François Ewald et Alessandro Fontana par Frédéric Gros. Paris: Seuil; Gallimard, 2008. *Hautes études*. 2 vols.

GG3799. ● Foucault, Michel: *Psychiatric power: lectures at the Collège de France, 1973-1974*. Ed. Jacques Lagrange; trans. Graham Burchell. New York: Picador, 2008. xxiv, 382 p.

GG3800. ● *Foucault and lifelong learning: governing the subject*. Ed. Andreas Fejes, Katherine Nicoll. London; New York: Routledge, 2008. xix, 218 p.

GG3801. ● *Foucault et les lumières*. Sous la dir. de Fabienne Brugère [et al.]. Pessac: Presses univ. de Bordeaux, 2007. 246 p.

GG3802. ● *Foucault Handbuch*. Hrsg. Clemens Kammler [et al.]. Stuttgart: J. B. Metzler, 2008. viii, 454 p.

GG3803. ● *Foucault in an age of terror: essays on biopolitics and the defence of society*. Ed. Stephen Morton, Stephen Bygrave. Basingstoke; New York: Palgrave Macmillan, 2008. ix, 234 p.

GG3804. ● *Foucault in den Kulturwissenschaften eine Bestandsaufnahme*. Hrsg. Clemens Kammler, Rolf Parr. Heidelberg: Synchron, 2007. 276 p.

GG3805. ● *Foucault, oggi*. A cura di Mario Galzigna. Milano: Feltrinelli, 2008. 308 p.

GG3806. ● *Foucault on politics, security and war*. Ed. Michael Dillon and Andrew W. Neal. Basingstoke; New York: Palgrave Macmillan, 2008. viii, 243 p.

GG3807. ● *Foucaults Machtanalytik und soziale Arbeit: eine kritische Einführung und Bestandsaufnahme*. Roland Anhorn, Hrsg. Wiesbaden: Verlag für Sozialwissenschaft, 2007. 367 p.

GG3808. ● Geisenhanslüke, Achim: *Gegendiskurse: Literatur und Diskursanalyse bei Michel Foucault*. Heidelberg: Synchron, 2008. 187 p.

GG3809. ● Gertenbach, Lars: *Die Kultivierung des Marktes: Foucault und die Gouvernementalität des Neoliberalismus*. Berlin: Parodos, 2008. 2. Aufl. 190 p.

GG3810. ● *Gesellschaftstheorie nach Marx und Foucault*. Hrsg. Christina Deckwirth. Münster: Westfälisches Dampfboot, 2008. *Prokla*, Heft 151.

GG3811. ● *Gouvernementalität und Sicherheit: zeitdiagnostische Beiträge im Anschluss an Foucault*. Hrsg. Patricia Purtschert, Katrin Meyer, Yves Winter. Bielefeld: Transcript, 2008. 255 p.

GG3812. ● *Habermas et Foucault: parcours croisés, confrontations critiques*. Dir. Yves Cusset et Stéphane Haber. Paris: CNRS, 2006. 235 p.

GG3813. ● Haeske, U.: *"Kompetenz" im Diskurs*. Berlin: Pro Business, 2008. 332 p.

GG3814. ● Howe, Adrian: *Sex, violence, and crime: Foucault and the "man" question*. New York: Routledge-Cavendish, 2008. viii, 238 p.

GG3815. ● Iacomini, Miriam: *Le parole e le immagini: saggio su Michel Foucault*. Macerata: Quodlibet, 2008. *Estetica e critica*. 284 p.

GG3816. ● Keller, Reiner: *Michel Foucault*. Konstanz: UVK Verlagsgesellschaft, 2008. *Klassiker der Wissenssoziologie*, Band 7. 154 p.

GG3817. ● Kelly, Mark G. E.: *The political philosophy of Michel Foucault*. New York: Routledge, 2008. *Routledge studies in social and political thought*, 61. 192 p.

GG3818. ● Mazumdar, Pravu: *Der archäologische Zirkel: zur Ontologie der Sprache in Michel Foucaults Geschichte des Wissens.* Bielefeld: Transcript, 2008. *Edition Moderne Postmoderne.* 595 p.

GG3819. ● Merquior, José Guilherme: *Foucault.* New ed. London: Fontana, 2008.

GG3820. ● *Michel Foucault: collectif-essai.* Préface de Mathieu Larnaudie. Paris: Inculte, 2007. 253 p.

GG3821. ● *Michel Foucault: savoirs, domination et sujet.* Sous la dir. de Jean-Claude Bourdin [et al.]. Rennes: Presses univ. de Rennes, 2008. 297 p.

GG3822. ● *Michel Foucaults "Geschichte der Gouvernementalität" in den Sozialwissenschaften: internationale Beiträge.* Hrsg. Susanna Krasmann, Michael Volkmer. Bielefeld: Transcript, 2007. 311 p.

GG3823. ● Naumann, Marek: *Die Präsenz Nietzsches im Denken Foucaults.* Saarbrücken: VDM, 2008. 116 p.

GG3824. ● Nealon, Jeffrey T.: *Foucault beyond Foucault: power and its intensifications since 1984.* Stanford: Stanford Univ. Press, 2008. viii, 136 p.

GG3825. ● Novella, Enric J.: *Der junge Foucault und die Psychopathologie.* Berlin: Logos, 2008. 80 p.

GG3826. ● Oksala, Johanna: *How to read Foucault.* New York: W. W. Norton & Co., 2008. x, 116 p.

GG3827. ● Oliveira, Nythamar Fernandes de: *On the genealogy of modernity: Foucault's social philosophy.* Hauppauge, NY: Nova Science, 2008. [Orig. ed., 2003]

GG3828. ● Ottaviani, Didier; Isabelle Boinot: *L'humanisme de Michel Foucault.* Paris: Ollendorff & Desseins, 2008. 155 p.

GG3829. ● *Pensesr avec Michel Foucault: théorie critique et pratiques politiques.* Sous la dir. de Marie-Christine Granjon. Paris: Karthala, 2005. 352 p.

GG3830. ● *Philosophien: Gespräche mit Michel Foucault.* Hrsg. von Peter Engelmann. Wien: Passagen, 2007. 151 p.

GG3831. ● Razac, Olivier: *Avec Foucault, après Foucault: disséquer la société de contrôle.* Paris: L'Harmattan, 2008. *Esthétiques.* 168 p.

GG3832. ● Revel, Judith: *Dictionnaire Foucault.* Paris: Ellipses, 2008. 173 p.

GG3833. ● Ruffing, Reiner: *Michel Foucault.* Paderborn: Fink, 2008. *UTB.* 125 p.

GG3834. ● Sarasin, Philipp: *Wie weiter mit Michel Foucault?.* Hamburg: Hamburger Edition, 2008. 45 p.

GG3835. ● Scherr, Barry J.: *Love and death in Lawrence and Foucault.* New York: Peter Lang, 2008. *Studies on themes and motifs in literature.* 395 p.

GG3836. ● *Sguardo [Lo] di Foucault.* A cura di Michele Cometa, Salvo Vaccaro. Roma: Meltimi, 2007. 162 p.

GG3837. ● Shoemaker, Mary: *Genealogy, from Nietzsche to Foucault: tracing the history of the present.* Saarbrücken: VDM, 2008. 128 p.

GG3838. ● Sorrentino, Vincenzo: *Il pensiero politico di Foucault.* Roma: Heltemi, 2008. 309 p.

GG3839. ● *Space, knowledge and power: Foucault and geography.* Ed. Jeremy W. Crampton, Stuart Elden. Aldershot; Burlington, VT: Ashgate, 2007. x, 377 p.

GG3840. ● *Sphères [Les] du pénal avec Michel Foucault: histoire et sociologie du droit de punir.* Textes dirigés par Marco Cicchini et Michel Porret. Lausanne: Antipodes, 2007. 303 p.

GG3841. ● *Spiel [Das] der Lüste: Sexualität, Identität und Macht bei Michel Foucault.* Hrsg. Marvin Chlada, Marc Christian Jäger. Aschaffenburg: Alibri, 2008. 153 p.

GG3842. ● Stockhammer, Nicolas: *Das Prinzip Macht: Die Rationalität politischer Macht bei Thukydides, Machiavelli und Michel Foucault.* Baden-Baden: Nomos, 2008. 264 p.

GG3843. ● Suárez Müller, Fernando: *Michel Foucault.* Bamberg: Buchner, 2008. 165 p.

GG3844. ● *Travailler avec Foucault: retours sur le politique.* Sous la dir. de Sylvain Meyet, Marie-Cécile Naves et Thomas Ribemont. Paris: L'Harmattan, 2005. 194 p.

GG3845. ● Veyne, Paul: *Foucault, sa pensée, sa personne.* Paris: Albin Michel, 2008. 214 p.

GG3846. ● Vighi, Fabio; Heiko Feldner: *Zizek: beyond Foucault.* Basingstoke: Palgrave Macmillan, 2008. 252 p.

GG3847. ● Volkers, Achim: *Wissen und Bildung bei Foucault*. Wiesbaden: Verlag für Sozialwissenschaft, 2008. 157 p.

GG3848. ● *Widerstand denken: Michel Foucault und die Grenzen der Macht*. Daniel Hechler, Hrsg. Bielefeld: Transcript, 2008. 279 p.

GG3849. Amarasingam, Amarnath: "Foucault, discipline and the self," *Journal of Religion and Film*, vol. 12, no. 2 (April 2008), [n.p.].

GG3850. Bainbridge, Simon: "Poetry must be defended: post-Waterloo responses to 'Power's ode to itself'." In 3803.

GG3851. Biesta, Gert: "Encountering Foucault in lifelong learning." In 3800.

GG3852. Bigo, Didier: "Security: a field left fallow." In 3806.

GG3853. Binnie, Jon: "Locating economics within sexuality studies," *Sexualities*, vol. 11, no. 1-2 (Feb.-April 2008), 100-103.

GG3854. Bové, Paul A.: "Michel Foucault and the critical care of the self." In 399.

GG3855. Boyce, Paul: "Truths and (mis)representations: Adrienne Rich, Michel Foucault and sexual subjectivities in India," *Sexualities*, vol. 11, no. 1-2 (Feb.-April 2008), 110-119.

GG3856. Brownstein, Michael: "Rawls, Foucault, Michael Moore, and 50 Cent on the terms of democratic discourse," *International Studies in Philosophy*, vol. 39, no. 2 (2007), 1-16.

GG3857. Bührmann, Andrea D.: "Vom Begehrens-Subjekt zum unternehmerischen Selbst." In 3841.

GG3858. Bygrave, Stephen: "Foucault, Auden and two New York Septembers." In 3803.

GG3859. Chandler, James: "Foucault and disciplinary authority." In 765, 47-63.

GG3860. Chlada, Marvin: "Lüste des Körpers oder Begehren ohne Organe?" In 3841.

GG3861. Coleman, Mathew; John A. Agnew: "The problem with *empire*." In 3839, 317-339.

GG3862. Colson, Dan: "The pedagogisation of sex, the sexualisation of pedagogy: Foucault, Shakespeare, and adolescent sexuality," *49th Parallel*, no. 22 (Autumn 2008), 49-59.

GG3863. Crampton, Jeremy W.: "Maps, race and Foucault." In 3839, 223-244.

GG3864. Datta, Ronjon Paul: "Foucault and the battle for politics itself." Diss., Carleton Univ., 2008. xii, 598 p.

GG3865. Deuber-Mankowsky, Astrid: "On the concept of the political in Michel Foucault and Carl Schmitt," *Telos*, no. 142 (Spring 2008), 135-161.

GG3866. Deutscher, Penelope: "The inversion of exceptionality: Foucault, Agamben, the 'reproductive rights'," *South Atlantic Quarterly*, vol. 107, no. 1 (Jan. 2008), 55-70.

GG3867. Díaz Marsá, Marco: "¿Qué quiere decir pensar? Acerca de la noción de *problematización* en Michel Foucault," *Daimon*, núm. 43 (enero-abril 2008), 51-70.

GG3868. Dillon, Michael: "Security, race and war." In 3806.

GG3869. Elden, Stuart: "Strategies for waging peace: Foucault as collaborateur." In 3806.

GG3870. Elden, Stuart: "Strategy, medicine and habitat: Foucault in 1976." In 3839, 67-81.

GG3871. Elden, Stuart; Jeremy W. Crampton: "Space, knowledge and power: Foucault and geography." In 3839, 1-16.

GG3872. Fall, Juliet J.: "Catalysts and converts: sparking interest for Foucault among Francophone geographers." In 3839, 107-128.

GG3873. Farley, Margaret A.: "Michel Foucault: the historical constitution of desire." In 946.

GG3874. Fassin, Didier: "The politics of death: race war, biopower and AIDS in the post-apartheid." In 3806.

GG3875. Fensome, Rebecca: " 'Manual for a raid' and 'Henslowe's diary': Foucault and the multiple meanings of the document." In 3803.

GG3876. Flynn, Thomas: "Foucault among the geographers." In 3839, 59-64.

GG3877. Fortanet, Joaquín: "Leer a Foucault. Una crítica de la experiencia," *Daimon*, núm. 43 (enero-abril 2008), 15-32.

GG3878.　Foucault, Michel: "Some questions from Michel Foucault to *Hérodote*." In 3839, 19-21.

GG3879.　Gauntlett, David: "Michel Foucault: discourses and lifestyles." In 830.

GG3880.　Geldof, Koenraad: "Modernité, excès, littérature: une lecture contrastive de Michel Foucault et de Stephen Greenblatt," *Littérature*, no. 151 (sept. 2008), 90-113.

GG3881.　Hannah, Matthew: "Formations of 'Foucault' in Anglo-American geography." In 3839, 83-105.

GG3882.　Hanson, Clare: "Biopolitics, biological racism and eugenics." In 3803.

GG3883.　Hartley, Lucy: "War and peace, or governmentality as the ruin of democracy." In 3803.

GG3884.　Harvey, David: "The Kantian roots of Foucault's dilemmas." In 3839, 41-47.

GG3885.　Hendricks, Christina: "Foucault's Kantian critique: philosophy and the present," *Philosophy and Social Criticism*, vol. 34, no. 4 (May 2008), 357-382.

GG3886.　Houen, Alex: "Sovereignty, biopolitics and the use of literature: Michel Foucault and Kathy Acker." In 3803.

GG3887.　Howell, Philip: "Foucault, sexuality, geography." In 3839, 291-315.

GG3888.　Huxley, Margo: "Geographies of governmentality." In 3839, 185-204.

GG3889.　Jaffro, Laurent: "L'exercice moral est-il assimilable à une technique? Une critique de Michel Foucault," *Revue d'Auvergne*, no. 585 (2007), 73-96.

GG3890.　Jäger, Marc-Christian: "Michel Foucaults Machtbegriff." In 3841.

GG3891.　Jäger, Marc-Christian: "Ordnungen des Sexuellen: Foucaults Unterscheidung von sadistischer Disziplinarmacht und SM-Subkultur." In 3841.

GG3892.　Kearns, Gerry: "The history of medical geography after Foucault." In 3839, 205-222.

GG3893.　Kulick, Don: "Cool heads and hot hearts," *Sexualities*, vol. 11, no. 1-2 (Feb.-April 2008), 80-86.

GG3894.　Lamb, Bethany L.: "*Light in August* in light of Foucault: reexamining the biracial experience," *Arizona Quarterly*, vol. 64, no. 4 (Winter 2008), 51-68.

GG3895.　Legg, Stephen: "Beyond the European province: Foucault and postcolonialism." In 3839, 265-289.

GG3896.　Lewis, Desiree: "Rethinking nationalism in relation to Foucault's *History of sexuality* and Adrienne Rich's 'Compulsory heterosexuality and lesbian existence'," *Sexualities*, vol. 11, no. 1-2 (Feb.-April 2008), 104-109.

GG3897.　Lotringer, Sylvère: "Remember Foucault," *October*, no. 126 (Fall 2008), 3-22.

GG3898.　Luxon, Nancy: "Eethics and subjectivity: techniques of self-governance in the late lecture of Michel Foucault," *Political Theory*, vol. 36, no. 3 (June 2008), 377-402.

GG3899.　Macey, David: "Some reflections on Foucault's 'Society must be defended' and the idea of 'race'." In 3803.

GG3900.　Marks, John: "Michel Foucault: biopolitics and biology." In 3803.

GG3901.　Marroum, Marianne: "Sands of imprisonment, subjugation, and empowerment: reading Foucault in Kobe Abe's *The Woman in the Dunes*," *Comparatist*, vol. 31 (May 2007), 88-104.

GG3902.　Mazower, Mark: "Foucault, Agamben: theory and the Nazis," *Boundary 2*, vol. 35, no. 1 (Spring 2008), 23-34.

GG3903.　Mbembe, Achille: "Necropolitics." In 3803.

GG3904.　McCall, Corey: "Foucault's alleged irrationalism: the legacy of German Romanticism in the thought of Michel Foucault," *Idealistic Studies*, vol. 37, no. 1 (Spring 2007), 1-13.

GG3905.　"Michel Foucault (1926-1981)." In 952.

GG3906.　Mills, Sara: "Geography, gender and power." In 3839, 49-51.

GG3907.　Morton, Stephen: "Torture, terrorism and colonial sovereignty." In 3803.

GG3908.　Mümken, Jürgen: "Wer bin ich? Was bin ich?: Identität und Geschlecht bein Stirner und Foucault." In 3841.

GG3909.　Murakami Wood, David: "Beyond the panopticon? Foucault and surveillance studies." In 3839, 245-263.

GG3910.   Neal, Andrew W.: "Goodbye war on terror?: Foucault and Butler on discourses of law, war and exceptionalism." In 3806.

GG3911.   Nicoll, Katherine; Andreas Fejes: "Mobilizing Foucault in studies of lifelong learning." In 3800.

GG3912.   Osborne, Thomas: "Foucault and the ethics of subjectivity." In 970.

GG3913.   Palladino, Paolo: "Revisiting Franco's death: life and death and biopolitical governmentality." In 3806.

GG3914.   Philo, Chris: " 'Bellicose history' and 'local discursivities': an archaeological reading of Michel Foucault's *Society must be defended*." In 3839, 341-367.

GG3915.   Radner, Hilary: "Compulsory sexuality and the desiring woman," *Sexualities*, vol. 11, no. 1-2 (Feb.-April 2008), 94-100.

GG3916.   Raffestin, Claude: "Could Foucault have revolutionized geography?" In 3839, 129-137

GG3917.   Reid, Julian: "Life struggles: war, discipline and biopolitics in the thought of Michel Foucault." In 3803. [Also in 3806]

GG3918.   Rojas Osorio, Carlos: "Foucault y la locura de Don Quijote," *CIEHL*, no. 9 (2008), 9-15.

GG3919.   Roudinesco, Elisabeth: "Michel Foucault: readings of *History of Madness*." In 976, 65-96.

GG3920.   Sarasin, Philipp: "Vapors, viruses, resistance(s): the trace of infection in the work of Michel Foucault." In 849.

GG3921.   Schlemm, Annette: "Die Sorge um sich selbst: Subjektivität und Homosexualität nach Foucault." In 3841.

GG3922.   Schmitz, Heniz-Gerd: "Macht und Busse: Zur Kritik der von Nietzsche und Foucault vorgetragenen Beurteilung der Strafpraxis." In 929, 47-63.

GG3923.   Schneider, Beth: "Arguments, citations, traces: Rich and Foucault and the problem of heterosexuality," *Sexualities*, vol. 11, no. 1-2 (Feb.-April 2008), 86-93.

GG3924.   Scott, David: "Michel Foucault and power-knowledge." In 864.

GG3925.   Siisiainen, Lauri: "From the empire of the gaze to noisy bodies: Foucault, audition and medical power," *Theory and Event*, vol. 11, no. 1 (2008), [n.p.].

GG3926.   Thomas, Nicholas: "Pedagogy and the work of Michel Foucault," *JAC*, vol. 28, no. 1-2 (2008), 151-180.

GG3927.   Thrift, Nigel: "Overcome by space: reworking Foucault." In 3839, 53-58.

GG3928.   Valveerde, Mariana: "Law versus history: Foucault's genealogy of modern sovereignty." In 3806.

GG3929.   Volbers, Jörg: "Foucaults Genealogie der Philosophie," *Allgemeine Zeitschrift für Philosophie*, 33. Jahrgang, Heft 3 (2008), 297-300.

FOURCADE, Dominique. See also 6875.

GG3930.   Fourcaut, Laurent: "*Est-ce que j'peux placer un mot?* de Dominique Fourcade: la voix de l'infans chapitré au chapitre," *Cuadernos de Filologia Francesa*, no. 19 (2008), 101-121.

GG3931.   Valabrègue, Frédéric: "Dominique Fourcade. 'La page langue monde'," *Critique*, tome 64, no. 735-736 (août-sept. 2008), 710-718.

FRAIGNEAU, André.

GG3932.   ● *André Fraigneau: 1905-2005*. Sous la dir. de Michel Mourlet. Clichy-la-Garenne: France univers, 2007. *Art de lire*. 223 p.

GG3933.   Broche, François: "Malentendu chronique." In 3932, 41-47.

GG3934.   "Chronologie bio-bibliographique." In 3932, 15-29.

GG3935.   Laffly, Georges: "Une trilogie." In 3932, 51-70.

GG3936.   Malfant, Marc-Gabriel: "Fraigneau et Nizan." In 3932, 47-51. [Nizan]

GG3937.   Montety, Etienne de: "Fraigneau et Louis II." In 3932, 35-41.

GG3938.   Poulet, Robert: "André Fraigneau au caléidoscope." In 3932, 31-33.

GG3939.   Sénart, Philippe: "Le souvenir d'une époque." In 3932, 70-83.

GG3940.   "Témoignages." In 3932, 85-116.

GG3941.   Vandromme, Pol: "Le bonheur aux ordres de la grandeur." In 3932, 33-35.

FRANCE, Anatole. See also 5713, 6482.

GG3942. • Todisco, Gino: *Anatole France: dal secondo impero all'Ile des pingouins.* Trento: UNI service, 2008. 60 p.

GG3943. Barilier, Etienne: "Il le faut, pourtant, Dreyfus est innocent!." In 388, 118-126.

GG3944. Chaitin, Gilbert D.: "Contemporary history, by Anatole France: the memory of the present." In 405.

GG3945. Minerva, Nadia: "Enfreindre la clôture: pour une revisitation de la catégorie du temps un utopie, dystopie et alentours." In 386, 251-263.

FRANKÉTIENNE.

GG3946. • *Typo, topo, poéthique: sur Frankétienne.* Dir. Jean Jonassaint. Paris: L'Harmattan, 2008. 368 p.

GG3947. Chancé, Dominique: "Lire *L'Oiseau schizophone* de Frankétienne en écho au *Finnegans Wake* de Joyce," *Interculturel Francophones*, no. 12 (nov.-déc. 2007), 17-40.

GG3948. Douglas, Rachel: "Haitian revolutions in literature: the case of linguistic and visual inventiveness in Frankétienne," *Small Axe*, no. 27 (Oct. 2008), 58-70.

GG3949. Douglas, Rachel: "Transformation of the framing *mise en abyme* in Frankétienne's writing." In 462, 109-124.

GG3950. Gyssels, Kathleen: "Haïti, le dire du spiralisme: entretiens avec Frankétienne et Jean-Claude Fignolé," *Recherches Haitiano-Antillaises*, no. 6 (déc. 2008), 167-188. [Fignolé]

GG3951. Jonassaint, Jean: "On Frankétienne: the course of an opus," *Sirena*, no. 1 (2008), 112-120.

FRÉCHETTE, Carole.

GG3952. Lavigne, Louis-Dominique: "Un singulier conte de fées. *La petite pièce en haut de l'escalier*," *Jeu: Cahiers de Théâtre*, no. 129 [no. 4] (2008), 19-23.

FRÉDÉRIQUE, Madeleine.

GG3953. Hanotte, Xavier; Madeleine Frédérique: "Entretien autour de *Un goût de biscuit au gingembre*," *Degrés*, 36e année, no. 133 (printemps 2008), f1-f15.

FRÉMINVILLE, Claude de.

GG3954. Basset, Guy: "Claude de Fréminville et ses pairs." In 515, 57-66. [Audisio, Amrouche, Roblès, Roy]

FRÉNAUD, André.

GG3955. Courtel, Yannick: " 'Main à pinceau' et 'main à plume'. Notes sur la peinture et la poésie dans l'œuvre d'André Frénaud." In 563, 100-107.

FRISON-ROCHE, Roger.

GG3956. Grave, Jaël: "Quelques figures paternelles chez Frison-Roche," *Cahiers Robinson*, no. 22 (2007), 69-76.

GABILY, Didier-Georges.

GG3957. Serça, Isabelle: "Une figure de ponctuation au théâtre: les didascalies de *Gibiers du temps*." In 605, 511-524.

GADENNE, Paul.

GG3958. Curatolo, Bruno: "Variations sur la figure de l'inspiratrice dans *Les Hauts-Quartiers* de Paul Gadenne." In 419, 417-424.

GAILLY, Christian.

GG3959. • *Christian Gailly, l'écriture qui sauve.* Sous la dir. d'Elisa Bricco et Christine Jérusalem. Saint-Etienne: Publications de l'Univ. de Saint-Etienne, 2008. 184 p.

GG3960. Motte, Warren: "Christian Gailly's dangerous art." In 900.

GARAT, Anne-Marie. See 6402.

GARCIN, Christian.

GG3961. Garcin, Christian: "Affinité élective." In 861, 443-449.

GARMADI, Salah.

GG3962. Hila, Hager: "Présences vocale subversives dans la nouvelle *Le Cireur* de Salah Garmadi," *Revue de Littérature Comparée*, no. 327 [no. 3] (juillet-sept. 2008), 379-386.

GARNIER, Pierre.

GG3963. • Garnier, Pierre: *Œuvres poétiques. I, 1950-1958.* Préface Lucien Wasselin. Montreuil-sur-Brèche: Editions des Vanneaux, 2008. 810 p.

GG3964. ● *Pierre Garnier*. Prés. Cécile Odartchenko. Montreuil-sur-Brèche: Vanneaux, 2007. 257 p.

GARRÉTA, Anne. See also 703.

GG3965. Stemberger, Martina: "*La Disparition* oder Auf der Suche nach dem verschwundenen Geschlecht. Anne Garréta's *Sphinx*," *Weimarar Beiträge*, 54. Jahrgang, Heft 1 (2008), 117-133.

GARRON, Isabelle.

GG3966. Lefebvre, Henri: "Tout corps d'état. Quelques propos sur l'œuvre d'Isabelle Garron," *Critique*, tome 64, no. 735-736 (août-sept. 2008), 697-702.

GARY, Romain. See also 525, 727, 7430.

GG3967. ● Amsellem, Guy: *Romain Gary: les méetamorphoses de l'identité*. Paris: L'Harmattan, 2008. *Psychanalyse et civilisations*. 283 p.

GG3968. ● Degoulet, Miguel: *Etude sur Emile Ajar-Romain Gary, "La vie devant soi"*. Paris: Ellipses, 2008. *Résonances*. 108 p.

GG3969. ● Gary, Romain: *Frühes Versprechen*. Aus dem Franz. von Giò Waeckerlin Induni. Mit einem Nachwort von Sven Crefeld. München: SchirmerGraf, 2008. 415 p.

GG3970. ● Vajda, Sarah: *Gary & co*. Gollion: Infolio, 2008. 332 p.

GG3971. Allamand, Carole: "L'auteur est dans l'escalier. Une relecture de *La Promesse de l'aube* de Romain Gary," *Lettres Romanes*, tome 61, no. 3-4 (2007), 335-348.

GG3972. Almeida, Claudia: "L'enchanteur Romain Gary." In 384, 95-107.

GG3973. Bellos, David: "The new frontier: the human utopia of Romain Gary." In 541, 152-167.

GG3974. Bertrand, Lucie: 'Histoire et fiction dans *Le Grand Voyage* de Jorge Semprún et *La Danse de Gengis Cohn* de Romain Gary." In 904, 259-270. [Semprun]

GG3975. Binder, Anne-Berenike: "Romain Gary, *La Danse de Gengis Cohn*." In 390, 170-230.

GG3976. Brenot, Philippe: "Stendhal, modèle et père de Romain Gary," *Nouveau Cahiers François Mauriac*, no. 16 (2008), 125-132.

GG3977. Chepiga, Valentina: "Jeu suit Romain Gary." In 384, 41-51.

GG3978. Ehrenfreund, Yaël-Catherine: "Répéter à l'envers ou le désespoir des clowns," *Humoresques*, no. 26 (2007), 135-148.

GG3979. Ibsch, Elrud: " 'Nur dem Menschen is das Lachen eigen': Romain Garys satirisch-karevaleske Antwort auf den Holocaust." In 626, 149-161.

GG3980. Luschenkova, Anna: "La réinvention de l'homme par l'art et le rire: *Les Enchanteurs* de Romain Gary." In 442, 141-149.

GG3981. Luschenkova, Anna: "Le rôle de la mère dans le processus créatif ou l'existence de l'artiste par procuration: *La Promesse de l'aube* de Romain Gary." In 571, 19-28.

GG3982. Roland, Geneviève: "La brûlure européenne d'un caméléon francophile." In 384, 77-94.

GG3983. Roumette, Julien: "Romain Gary et le sourire de Prométhée," *Modernités*, no. 29 (2008), 345-365.

GG3984. Roumette, Julien: "Romain Gary ou l'événement à tout prix." In 605, 231-253.

GG3985. Vareille, Arnaud: "Humour et stratégie littéraire dans *La promesse de l'aube*." In 384, 53-75.

GASCHÉ, Rodolphe.

GG3986. McCance, Dawne: "Crossings: an interview with Rodolphe Gasché," *Mosaic*, vol. 41, no. 4 (Dec. 2008), 1-26. [Derrida]

GASPAR, Lorand. See also 2548, 4243.

GG3987. Ben Abdeladhim, Maha: "Visages et paysages chez Lorand Gaspar: traits poétiques d'une errance," *Nouvelles Etudes Francophones*, vol. 22, no. 1 (printemps 2007), 128-139.

GG3988. Wulf, Judith: "Reformulation et variation continue en poésie contemporaine: l'exemple de Lorand Gaspar." In 499, 225-235.

GASQUET, Joachim.

GG3989. Gianinazzi, Willy: "Régionalisme, dreyfusisme et nationalisme. Lettres d'Emile Durkheim et de Georges Sorel au poète Joachim Gasquet (1899-1911)," *Mil Neuf Cent*, no. 26 (2008), 143-162. [Durkheim, Sorel]

GATTI, Armand.

GG3990. Hutchinson, Wesley: " 'Un point d'interrogation qui se voudrait écriture': Gatti's maze," *Etudes Irlandaises*, vol. 33, no. 2 (automne 2008), 53-64.

GAUVIN, Axel.

GG3991. Aït-Aarab, Mohamed: *"Quartier Trois Lettres* d'Axel Gauvin: un roman *réyoné," Nouvelles Etudes Francophones*, vol. 23, no. 1 (printemps 2008), 127-143.

GG3992. Schon, Nathalie: "Ténèbrtes mascareignes." In 72, 551-559.

GAUVIN, Lise.

GG3993. Guenther, Beatrice: "Land and cityscape in Lise Gauvin's and Jacques Poulin's narratives." In 92, 60-87. [Poulin]

GAUVREAU, Claude. See 46.

GAVARRY, Gérard.

GG3994. Motte, Warren: "Gérard Gavarry's hops." In 900.

GENET, Jean. See also 595, 606, 1105, 6707.

GG3995. ● Bührle-Nowikowa, Julia: *Die Neger von Jean Genet*. Saarbrücken: VDM, 2008. 101 p.

GG3996. ● Roy, Ed: *The golden thug*. Toronto: Playwrights Canada Press, 2008. ii, 105 p.

GG3997. ● Shukri, Muhammad: *Jean Genet in Tangier*. Trans. Paul Bowles; foreward by William Burroughs. London; San Francisco: Telegram, 2008. 58 p.

GG3998. ● *Toutes les images du langage: Jean Genet*. Sous la dir. de Frieda Ekotto, Aurélie Renaud, Agnès Vannouvong. Fasano: Schena; Paris: A. Baudry, 2008. 228 p.

GG3999. ● Uvsløkk, Geir: *L'écriture des perversions: les problèmes du mal et de l'identité masculine dans Notre-Dame-des-Fleurs, Miracle de la Rose et le Journal du voleur de Jean Genet*. Oslo: Fac. Of Humanities, Univ. of Oslo, 2008. *Acta humaniora.* 281 p.

GG4000. Adrien, Philippe: "Entretien." In 3998, 151-161.

GG4001. Alves Meira, Cristèle: "Entretien." In 3998, 163-175.

GG4002. Balcázar Moreno, Melina: "Des traces et des spectres: une lecture de *Pompes funèbres* de Jean Genet," *Etudes Françaises*, vol. 44, no. 1 (2008), 147-161.

GG4003. Balcázar Moreno, Melina: *"Mater dolorosa* ou l'écriture de l'événement dans *Un captif amoureux* de Jean Genet." In 440, 59-68.

GG4004. Bougon, Patrice: "La métaphore de la mer dans *Querelle de Brest* de Genet." In 3998, 15-26.

GG4005. Bourseiller, Antoine: "Mise en scène: Jean Genet." In 3998, 149.

GG4006. Boyle, Claire: "Genet inside and out: autobiography, marginality and emmpowerment." In 400, 98-124.

GG4007. Ceccaty, René de: "Le spectre, le neutre, le vide." In 3998, 27-34.

GG4008. Corvin, Michel: "L'être du non-être ou le contretype du stéréotype." In 3998, 35-44.

GG4009. Dreyer, Sylvain: " 'Un millième de seconde'. Stéréotype et fulgurance dans *Un captif amoureux.*" In 3998, 45-61.

GG4010. Ekotto, Frieda: "Lettre à Jean Genet." In 3998, 63-79.

GG4011. Fau, Michel: "Entretien." In 3998, 191-203.

GG4012. Flahutez, Fabrice: "Jean Genet dessinateur." In 3998, 81-89.

GG4013. Guneratne, Kristy: "Framing and authority in Genet's *Miracle de la rose.*" In 462, 91-108.

GG4014. Haney, William S.: "The reality of illusion in Jean Genet's *The Balcony.*" In 1087.

GG4015. Heyndels, Ralph: "Ecrire le tombeau de Jean Genet." In 3998, 91-101.

GG4016. Khélil, Hédi: "Les phrases dans *Les nègres* et *Les paravents* de Jean Genet." In 556.

GG4017. Mercier Leca, Florence: "La (re)sémantisation comme création poétique." In 3998, 103-121.

GG4018. Rajon, Sébastien: "Entretien." In 3998, 177-189.

GG4019.	Ravier, Thomas A.: "Genet, l'homme aux semelles de temps," *Infini*, no. 105 (hiver 2008), 75-89.

GG4020.	Renaud, Aurélie: "L'autre visabe de Carmen dans l'œuvre de Jean Genet." In 3998, 123-133.

GG4021.	Salinas, Marcelo: "Les références à Ganymède dans le *Journal du voleur* de Jean Genet." In 466, 263-272.

GG4021a. Stöhr, Lóránt: "From white page to white light: Fassbinder and self-reflexion in the art of film." In 8016, 187-202.

GG4022.	Vannouvong, Agnès: "Voiler, dévoiler, cacher: de l'art du travestissement dans l'écriture genétienne." In 3998, 135-148.

GERMAIN, Sylvie.

GG4023.	● Germain, Sylvie: *Magnus*. Trans. and with an afterword by Christine Donougher. Sawtry: Dedalus, 2008. 190 p.

GG4024.	● *Sylvie Germain et son œuvre.* Textes réunis et prés. par Jacqueline Michel et Isabelle Dotan. Bucarest: EST-Samuel Tastet, 2006. 151 p.

GG4025.	● *Sylvie Germain: regards croisés sur Immensités.* Sous la dir. de Mariska Koopman-Thurlings. Paris: L'Harmattan, 2008. 212 p.

GG4026.	● *Univers [L'] de Sylvie Germain: actes du colloque de Cerisy, 22-29 août 2007.* Publiés sous la dir. d'Alain Goulet. Caen: Presses univ. de Caen, 2008. 354 p.

GG4027.	Amar, Ruth: "Le sel comme métaphore de l'écriture dans *Eclats de sel.*" In 4024, 121-128.

GG4028.	Armel, Aliette: "Référents bibliques dans l'œuvre de Sylvie Germain." In 4026, 89-97.

GG4029.	Blanckeman, Bruno: "A côté/aux côtés de: Sylvie Germain, une singularité située." In 4026, 19-27.

GG4030.	Boblet, Marie-Hélène: "L'immensité en notre finitude: histoire et humanité." In 4025, 35-45.

GG4031.	Boblet, Marie-Hélène: "Implication éthique et politique." In 4026, 55-67.

GG4032.	Cahne, Pierre: "La saisie du temps dans l'œuvre de Sylvie Germain." In 4026, 147-151.

GG4033.	Chareyron, Hélène: "Voyages au pays des pères." In 4026, 211-221.

GG4034.	Demanze, Laurent: "Sylvie Germain, biographe de la voix." In 4024, 79-87.

GG4035.	Demanze, Laurent: "Sylvie Germain, les plis du baroque." In 4026, 185-195.

GG4036.	Demanze, Laurent: "Les trois coffrets." In 4025, 47-60.

GG4037.	Dotan, Isabelle: "Du *vide* au *Vide*: une révision de la pensée existentialiste." In 4025, 161-174.

GG4038.	Dotan, Isabelle: "Les échappées tragiques de la douleur." In 4026, 263-272.

GG4039.	Dotan, Isabelle: "Narrer la douleur: *La Pleurante des rues de Prague.*" In 4024, 141-146.

GG4040.	Fortin, Jutta E.: "Entre petitesse et immensité." In 4025, 61-78.

GG4041.	Garfitt, Toby: "Les écholalies de Sylvie Germain." In 4025, 97-106.

GG4042.	Garfitt, Toby: "Sylvie Germain et Emmanuel Levinas." In 4026, 79-88. [Levinas]

GG4043.	Germain, Sylvie: "Initialement vôtre." In 861, 453-455.

GG4044.	Goulet, Alain: "Cryptes et fantômes: à la source des fictions de Sylvie Germain." In 4026, 241-256.

GG4045.	Goulet, Alain: "*Magnus*: conte, roman d'apprentissage, fable." In 4024, 89-100.

GG4046.	Goulet, Alain: "Sylvie Germain et son œuvre." In 4024, 13-16.

GG4047.	Hoogen, Toine van den: "Aux toilettes: théo-logie et le contrepoint de la réalité quotidienne." In 4025, 141-160.

GG4048.	Koopman-Thurlings, Mariska: "Dire l'indicible: Sylvie Germain et la question juive." In 4024, 101-109.

GG4049.	Koopman-Thurlings, Mariska: "Du père, du frère et du Saint-Esprit." In 572, 237-244.

GG4050. Koopman-Thurlings, Mariska: "Pour une poétique de la mémoire." In 4026, 223-234.

GG4051. Koopman-Thurlings, Mariksa: "Temps et mémoire." In 4025, 175-189.

GG4052. Lanot, Bénédicte: "Echos du silence." In 4024, 65-75.

GG4053. Lanot, Bénédicte: "Fable du deuil et morale du renoncement." In 4025, 11-33.

GG4054. Lanot, Bénédicte: "Reconstruire, dit-elle: les représentations du désir et du manque." In 4026, 273-285. [Duras]

GG4055. Le Court, Isabelle de: "Sylvie Germain et la peinture." In 4026, 99-117.

GG4056. Lehalle, Béatrice; Anne Clancier; Mareike Wolf-Fedida: "Table ronde." In 4026, 289-307.

GG4057. Leuwers, Daniel: "Sylvie Germain ou le surcroît de réalité." In 4024, 17-20.

GG4058. Logie-Masquelier, Laetitia: "Cris et pépiements dans l'œuvre de Sylvie Germain." In 4026, 137-146.

GG4059. Logie, Laetitia: "Le corps mélancolique: présence de l'androgyne dans l'œuvre de Sylvie Germain." In 4024, 129-140.

GG4060. Mayaux, Catherine; Jacques Houriez: "La grammaire du merveilleux dans quatre romans de Sylvie Germain." In 4024, 53-64.

GG4061. Michel, Jacqueline: "Sylvie Germain et le récit de la couleur." In 4024, 35-42.

GG4062. Michelet-Jacquod, Valérie: "Les mots dans les romans de Sylvie Germain." In 4026, 121-135.

GG4063. Moris-Stefkovic, Milène: "L'écriture de l'effacement dans les romans de Sylvie Germain." In 4026, 167-182.

GG4064. Moyle, Matthew A.: "Places, faces, and the word 'God' in three novels by Sylvie Germain." Diss., Univ. of Wisconsin-Madison, 2008. vi, 224 p.

GG4065. Mulder, Etty: "Musique divine et musique terrestre." In 4025, 107-119.

GG4066. Narjoux, Cécile: "L'extrêmement petit en appelait à l'infiniment grand: lyrisme et ironie dans *Immensités*." In 4025, 79-96.

GG4067. Narjoux, Cécile: " 'Quelle est cette main?' ou l'énonciation paradoxale dans *Les personnages* de Sylvie Germain." In 4026, 153-166.

GG4068. Peeters, Leopold: "Langage et incarnation dans l'œuvre de Sylvie Germain." In 4024, 21-30.

GG4069. Poulouin, Gérard: "Des voix singulières à Prague." In 4026, 41-53.

GG4070. Roche, Anne: "Le rapport à la bibliothèque." In 4026, 29-40.

GG4071. Roelens, Nathalie: "L'acquiescement de Prokop." In 4025, 121-139.

GG4072. Soucy, Pierre-Yves: "Dans les plis de l'œuvre: sensations et perception du monde." In 4024, 43-52.

GG4073. Thoizet, Evelyne: "Des éclats de miroir au miroir du livre." In 4026, 197-210.

GG4074. Travers de Faultrier, Sandra: " 'Etre aimé à vide'." In 4026, 69-77.

GG4075. Tritsmans, Bruno: "Poétique de la brume et du tissage chez Sylvie Germain." In 4024, 113-120.

GERVAIS, Bertrand.

GG4076. Lindberg, Svante: "*Oslo* by Bertrand Gervais: l'américanité as repatriation." In 787, 134-150.

GHELDERODE, Michel de.

GG4077. ● Ghelderode, Michel de: *Correspondance de Michel de Ghelderode. Tome VIII, 1954-1957.* Edition établie, prés. et annotée par Roland Beyen. Bruxelles: AML, 2008. *Archives du futur.* 719 p.

GG4078. ● Ghelderode, Michel de: *Escurial; Barrabas.* Préface de Pierre Debauche; lecture de Michel Autrand. Bruxelles: Luc Pire, 2008. *Espace nord.* 188 p.

GG4079. Asole, Francesco: "Il teatro di Ghelderode e la malinconia," *Bérénice*, anno 15, n. 40-41 (nov. 2008), 152-167.

GG4080. Grodek, Elisabeth: "Les avatars d'un *topos* satirique: la danse macabre et le triomphe de la mort au théâtre et à l'opéra," *Modernités*, no. 27 (2008), 365-380.

GG4081. Malachy, Thérèse: "L'artiste en saltimbanque dans *Dan Juan ou les amants chimériques* de M. de Ghelderode." In 1093.

GG4082. Malachy, Thérèse: "Michel de Ghelderode: espace scénique, espace verbal." In 1093.

GG4083. Pieroopan, Laurence: "Adémar-Adolphe-Louis Martens, *alias* Michel de Ghelderode: construction imaginaire d'un mythe personnel et effets de reconnaissance dans les champs littéraires belge et français." In 441, 13-37.

GG4084. Pop-Curseu, Stefana: "La didascalie: marque d'une présence théâtrale." In 605, 525-537.

GHÉON, Henri.

GG4085. ● Boschian-Campaner, Catherine: *Henri Ghéon, camarade de Gide*. Paris: Presses de la Renaissance, 2008. 375 p. [Gide]

GHIL, René.

GG4086. ● Ghil, René: *De la poésie-scientifique et autres récits*. Textes choisis, prés., et annotés par Jean-Pierre Bobillot. Grenoble: ELLUG, 2008. *Archives critiques*. 299 p.

GG4087. Farasse, Gérard: "René Ghil par intermittence." In 454, 115-125.

GIDE, André. See also 684, 899, 4085, 6253, 6282, 6707.

GG4088. ● Gide, André: *Les faux-monnayeurs*. Dossier et notes réalisés par Frédéric Maget; lecture d'image par Agnès Verlet. Paris: Gallimard, 2008. *Folioplus classiques*. 359 p.

GG4089. ● Gide, André; Léon Blum: *Correspondance 1890-1951*. Edition établie, prés. et annotée par Pierre Lachasse. Lyon: Presses univ. de Lyon, 2008. 215 p. [Blum]

GG4090. ● Royère, Jean; André Gide: *Lettres (1907-1934): "votre affectueuse insistance"*. Lettres réunies, annotées et prés. par Vincent Gogibu. Eaubonne: Clown lyrique, 2008. 145 p.

GG4091. ● Sagaert, Martine; Peter Schnyder: *André Gide: l'écriture vive*. Pessac: Presses univ. de Bordeaux, 2008. *Horizons génétiques*. 162 p.

GG4092. "A la chambre. Débats sur le régime des concessions en Afrique Equatoriale Française (1927-1929)," *Bulletin des Amis d'André Gide*, 41e année, vol. 36, no. 160 (oct. 2008), 461-469.

GG4093. Acquisto, Joseph: "La musique du désir et de la pureté. Gide face à Chopin et Baudelaire," *Bulletin des Amis d'André Gide*, 41e année, vol. 36, no. 157 (janv. 2008), 19-32.

GG4094. Bénilan, Jean: "André Gide à Léré," *Bulletin des Amis d'André Gide*, 41e année, vol. 36, no. 160 (oct. 2008), 439-459.

GG4095. Brosman, Catharine S.: "*La Guirlande des années*, une relique vichyssoise," *Bulletin des Amis d'André Gide*, 41e année, vol. 36, no. 157 (janv. 2008), 57-72.

GG4096. Canonge, Jean-Marc: "A propos de l'affaire Rumeau. André Gide et Maurice Magre. Histoire d'une relation ambiguë," *Bulletin des Amis d'André Gide*, 41e année, vol. 36, no. 157 (janv. 2008), 49-56.

GG4097. "Changement de destinatires . . . (A propos d'une lettre de Gide). Suivi d'une étude de Benjamin Crémieux," *Bulletin des Amis d'André Gide*, 41e année, vol. 36, no. 159 (juillet 2008), 353-366.

GG4098. Claude, Jean: "Gide et les artistes. *Antoine et Cléopâtre*, 1917-1920," *Bulletin des Amis d'André Gide*, 41e année, vol. 36, no. 158 (avril 2008), 149-208.

GG4099. Di Bernardini, Gian Luigi: "Le paradoxe énonciatif du *Thésée* gidien." In 520, 605-616.

GG4100. "Le dossier de presse de *Voyage au Congo* et du *Retour du Tchad*, X," *Bulletin des Amis d'André Gide*, 41e année, vol. 36, no. 160 (oct. 2008), 471-508.

GG4101. "Le dossier de presse des *Nourritures terrestres*, IV. Edmond Jaloux, Léon Blum," *Bulletin des Amis d'André Gide*, 41e année, vol. 36, no. 160 (oct. 2008), 577-587.

GG4102. "Les dossiers de presse des livres d'André Gide: *Corydon*, X (Marcel Réja); *Retour de l'U.R.S.S.* (Robert de Traz)," *Bulletin des Amis d'André Gide*, 41e année, vol. 36, no. 159 (juillet 2008), 385-402.

GG4103. "Les dossiers de presse des livres d'André Gide: *L'École des femmes*, VI," *Bulletin des Amis d'André Gide*, 41e année, vol. 36, no. 157 (janv. 2008), 99-113.

GG4104. "Les dossiers de presse des livres d'André Gide: *Journal*, XI," *Bulletin des Amis d'André Gide*, 41e année, vol. 36, no. 158 (avril 2008), 293-306.

GG4105.   Epron-Denegri, Madeleine: "André Gide dans la vie de tous les jours," *Bulletin des Amis d'André Gide*, 41e année, vol. 36, no. 158 (avril 2008), 223-253.

GG4106.   Foucart, Claude: "André Gide, Bernard Groethuysen et Otto Grautoff ou la définition du politique chez Gide." In 461, 293-307.

GG4107.   Foucart, Claude: "André Gide dialogue avec la nouvelle génération allemande en 1928." In 461, 171-192.

GG4108.   Foucart, Claude: "André Gide et l'Université allemande après 1933." In 461, 377-391.

GG4109.   Foucart, Claude: "André Gide et Otto Braun." In 461, 87-100.

GG4110.   Foucart, Claude: "De la nature et de l'adolescence: Critique du *Corydon* et d'autres œuvres d'André Gide par Hans Henny Jahnn." In 461, 193-211.

GG4111.   Foucart, Claude: "De l'expressionnisme allemand au contact de l'œuvre gidienne." In 461, 247-268.

GG4112.   Foucart, Claude: "Deux Européens: André Gide et Stefan Zweig." In 461, 125-140.

GG4113.   Foucart, Claude: "L'esprit et la réalité: Curtius, Gide et Goethe en 1932." In 461, 141-155.

GG4114.   Foucart, Claude: "L'hebdomadaire *Die Zeit*, ou La réception de l'œuvre d'André Gide en Allemagne au début de la République de Bonn," *Bulletin des Amis d'André Gide*, 41e année, vol. 36, no. 158 (avril 2008), 209-222.

GG4115.   Foucart, Claude: "Un polémiste de la gauche allemande admirateur enthousiaste de la pensée gidienne: Kurt Hiller, 1885-1972." In 461, 213-226.

GG4116.   Foucart, Claude: "Le procès Krantz ou un fait divers qui aurait pu devenir un roman gidien." In 461, 227-246.

GG4117.   Foucart, Claude: "Le triomphe de la 'reconnaissance' ou le classicisme gidien entre Goethe et Racine." In 461, 159-169.

GG4118.   "Gide à Tunis, 1942. Souvenirs de Jacques Galland et Jean Amrouche," *Bulletin des Amis d'André Gide*, 41e année, vol. 36, no. 157 (janv. 2008), 73-86. [J. Amrouche]

GG4119.   Goulet, Alain: "In memoriam Yvonne Davet," *Bulletin des Amis d'André Gide*, 41e année, vol. 36, no. 158 (avril 2008), 255-273.

GG4120.   Goulet, Alain; Claude Maillard: "Gide et Freud, et après . . . Gide dans l'*Almanach der Psychoanalyse 1930*," *Bulletin des Amis d'André Gide*, 41e année, vol. 36, no. 157 (janv. 2008), 33-48.

GG4121.   Grenaud, Céline: "*Isabelle*, ou l'hystérisation du récit," *Bulletin des Amis d'André Gide*, 41e année, vol. 36, no. 159 (juillet 2008), 319-330.

GG4122.   Heidenriech, Rosmarin: "FPG and André Gide: life, art and rifacimento." In 787, 40-54.

GG4123.   Jennings, William: "Escaping from Gide's dystopia." In 541, 141-151.

GG4124.   Jennings, William: "Greek mythology in Gide's *Les Caves du Vatican*," *Dalhousie French Studies*, vol. 83 (Summer 2008), 89-97.

GG4125.   Lacarelle, Bertrand: "Arthur Cravan (enfin) chez André Gide," *Nouvelle Revue Française*, no. 587 (oct. 2008), 233-246. [Cravan]

GG4126.   Lefter, Diana-Adriana: "Le mythe dans le théâtre d'André Gide." In 520, 519-531.

GG4127.   Lefter, Diana-Adriana: "La relation mère-fils dans les œuvres fictionnelles et auto-fictionnelles d'André Gide." In 571, 57-66.

GG4128.   "Lettres retrouvées," *Bulletin des Amis d'André Gide*, 41e année, vol. 36, no. 159 (juillet 2008), 337-348. [Prés. par Jean Claude]

GG4129.   Milne, Anna-Louise: "Gide's polymorphous perversity, or French modernism's arrested development," *Romanic Review*, vol. 99, no. 1-2 (Jan.-March), 103-118.

GG4130.   Minot, Jean-François: "Albert Démarest-André Gide. A chacun son interdit!," *Bulletin des Amis d'André Gide*, 41e année, vol. 36, no. 159 (juillet 2008), 331-336.

GG4131.   Morel, Geneviève: "Gide: masques et sinthome." In 501, 75-114.

GG4132.   "Pages retrouvées," *Bulletin des Amis d'André Gide*, 41e année, vol. 36, no. 159 (juillet 2008), 349-352.

GG4133. Pollard, Patrick: "Gide and Ibsen: a symbolist crossroads," *Modern Language Review*, vol. 103, part 1 (Jan. 2008), 46-56.

GG4134. Pradeau, Christophe: "Eloge de la jachère: Gide et Martin du Gard," *Epistolaire: Revue de l'AIRE*, no. 34 (2008), 59-69. [Martin du Gard]

GG4135. Rouart, Marie-France: "Gide, *Les Faux-monnayeurs*." In 582, 87-112.

GG4136. Schnyder, Peter: "Réflexions sur le rôle de la culture: l'exemple d'André Gide." In 443, 189-197.

GG4137. Van Tuyl, Jocelyn: " 'Un effroyable consommateur de vies humaines'. Témoignages littéraires sur la préhistoire du sida," *Bulletin des Amis d'André Gide*, 41e année, vol. 36, no. 160 (oct. 2008), 509-541.

GG4138. Vivero García, María Dolores: "Jeux et enjeux de l'énonciation humoristique: l'exemple des *Caves du Vatican* d'André Gide," *Etudes Françaises*, vol. 44, no. 1 (2008), 57-71.

GG4139. Wittmann, Jean-Michel: "Gide sur les pas de Novalis. Des *Disciples à Saïs* au *Voyage d'Urien*," *Bulletin des Amis d'André Gide*, 41e année, vol. 36, no. 157 (janv. 2008), 7-18.

GG4140. Zubiate, Jean-Pierre: "Les jardins des *Nourritures terrestres* ou les paradoxes de l'intime gidien." In 487, 411-421.

GILSON, Étienne.

GG4141. ● Gilson, Etienne: *The Gilson lectures on Thomas Aquinas*. Introd. James P. Reilly. Toronto: Pontifical Institute of Mediaeval Studies, 2008. *Etienne Gilson series*, 10. xxix, 246 p.

GG4142. ● Gilson, Etienne: *Three quests in philosophy*. Ed. Armand Maurer; foreword by James K. Farge. Toronto: Pontifical Institute of Mediaeval Studies, 2008. *Etienne Gilson series*. xi, 145 p.

GG4143. Humbrecht, Thierry-Dominique: "Thomisme et antithomisme chez Étienne Gilson," *Revue Thomiste*, tome 108, no. 2 (avril-juin 2008), 327-366.

GIONO, Jean. See also 470.

GG4144. ● Giono, Jean: *L'homme qui plantait des arbres*. Introduction, dossier et notes réalisés par Christine Lhomeau; lecture d'image par Alain Jaubert. Paris: Gallimard, 2008. *Folioplus classiques*. 292 p.

GG4145. ● Giono, Jean: *J'ai ce que j'ai donné*. Lettres établies, annotées et préfacées par Sylvie Durbet-Giono. Paris: Gallimard, 2008. *Haute enfance*. 223 p.

GG4146. ● Ivier, Marica: *De l'errant à l'artiste: le rayonnement d'Ulysse dans l'œuvre romanesque de Jean Giono*. Uppsala: Uppsala University, 2008. 169 p.

GG4147. ● Mallon, Julie: *Du sésie de désordre: les femmes dans les œuvres de fiction de Jean Giono*. Lille: ANRT, 2008. *Thèse à la carte*. 651 p.

GG4148. ● Oulmehdi, Omar: *Le crime dans l'œuvre de Jean Giono*. Lille: ANRT, 2008. 680 p.

GG4149. Abassi, Ahmed: "Le personnage de Janet dans 'Colline' de Jean Giono," *Cahiers de Tunisie*, tome 59, no. 195 (4e trim. 2005), 57-71.

GG4150. Bourgeois, René: "Je finirai par être prisonnier de la musique." In 612, 287-289.

GG4151. Chielens, Piet: "Jean Giono et la bataille du mont Kemmel." In 473, 45-54.

GG4152. Emery, Meaghan: "Jean Giono: the personal ethics of an author writing under the occupation," *Journal of European Studies*, vol. 38, no. 3 (Sept. 2008), 277-320.

GG4153. François, Cyrille: "Récrire l'*Odyssée* au XXe siècle. Mensonge et creation littéraire dans *Naissance de l'Odyssée* de Jean Giono et *Strändernas svali* d'Eyvind Johnson," *Revue de Littérature Comparée*, no. 326 [no. 2] (avril-juin 2008), 151-174.

GG4154. Gazier, Michèle: "Giono: un univers en partage," *Revue Giono*, no. 2 (2008), 173-179.

GG4155. Gramain, Michel: "La réception de l'œuvre de Jean Giono dans la presse (année 1950)," *Revue Giono*, no. 2 (2008), 129-146.

GG4156. Ibanès, Jacques: "Dictionnaire Giono: Abécébête," *Revue Giono*, no. 2 (2008), 91-125.

GG4157. Labouret, Denis: "*Noé* de Jean Giono. Une poétique du monstrueux." In 527, 87-100.

GG4158.   Mény, Jacques: "André Caspari: repérages avec Jean Giono," *Revue Giono*, no. 2 (2008), 149-170.

GG4159.   Mény, Jacques: "Dans la bibliothèque de Jean Giono au Paraïs," *Revue Giono*, no. 2 (2008), 251-256.

GG4160.   Merchant, Peter: " 'Breathed on by the rural Pan': the atmosphere of Arcadia in Giono's *Regain*." In 569, 228-242.

GG4161.   Milcent-Lawson, Sophie: "Mises en scène syntaxiques et art de la surprise dans la phrase gionienne." In 556.

GG4162.   Morello, André-Alain: "La guerre et la paix: Tolstoï, Alain, Giono," *Revue Giono*, no. 2 (2008), 231-247. [Alain]

GG4163.   Salazar-Ferrer, Olivier: "Le mythe de Pan dans l'œuvre de Jean Giono." In 520, 631-642.

GG4164.   Schaffner, Alain: " 'Il y a des guerriers de l'Arioste dans le soleil': romanesque, réécriture et représentation chez Jean Giono." In 506, 283-293.

GG4165.   Thomas-Montesinos, Katia: "Jean Giono et la guerre de 14-18," *Revue Giono*, no. 2 (2008), 183-208.

GG4166.   Tissut, Alain: "Le miroir de la guerre," *Revue Giono*, no. 2 (2008), 209-230.

GG4167.   Vignes, Sylvie: " 'Faust au village': 'le Diable vert' selon Jean Giono," *Modernités*, no. 29 (2008), 193-205.

GG4168.   Vignes, Sylvie: "Poétique des didascalies dans *Le Voyage en calèche* de Jean Giono." In 605, 307-320.

GIRARD, René. See also 942, 983, 3377, 3625, 5783.

GG4169.   • Depoortere, Frederiek: *Christ in postmodern philosophy: Gianni Vattimo, René Girard and Slavoj Zizek.* London: T & T Clark, 2008. viii, 159 p.

GG4170.   • Girard, René: *Mimesis and theory: essays on literature and criticism, 1953-2005.* Ed. and with an introduction by Robert Doran. Stanford: Stanford Univ. Press, 2008. *Cultural memory in the present.* xxvi, 310 p.

GG4171.   • Lopez, Davide: *Il desiderio, il sacrificio, il capro espiatorio.* Costabissara: A. Colla, 2008. 224 p.

GG4172.   • *Male e redenzione: sofferenza e trascendenza in René Girard.* A cura di Paolo Diego Bubbio e Silvio Morigi. Torino: Camilliane, 2008. 270 p.

GG4173.   • Nordhofen, Jacob: *Durch das Opfer erlöst? Die Bedeutung der Rede vom mOpfer Jesu Christi in der Bibel und bei René Girard.* Wien; Berlin: Lit, 2008. 297 p.

GG4174.   • *René Girard.* Cahier dir. par Mark Rogin Anspach. Paris: L'Herne, 2008. 276 p.

GG4175.   Doran, Robert: "Apocalyptic thinking after 9/11: an interview with René Girard," *Substance*, vol. 37, no. 1 [no. 115] (2008), 20-32.

GG4176.   Nelson, Derek: "Sins of commission, sins of omission: Girard, Ricœur, and Armenian genocide." In 945. [Ricœur]

GG4177.   Parrilla, Desiderio: "Las tres versiones rivales de la filosofía en René Girard," *Anuario Filosófico*, vol. 41, n. 3 (2008), 637-660.

GG4178.   Schults, F. LeRon: "Interdisciplinary opportunities." In 983.

GIRAUD, Brigitte.

GG4179.   Giraud, Brigitte: "L'art du détail," *Matricule des Anges*, no. 84 (2007), 19-23. [Entretien]

GG4180.   Guichard, Thierry: "Déminer le silence," *Matricule des Anges*, no. 84 (2007), 18.

GG4181.   Guichard, Thierry: "Vivre, à tous les temps," *Matricule des Anges*, no. 84 (2007), 14-17.

GIRAUDOUX, Jean. See also 420, 536, 694.

GG4182.   • Giraudoux, Jean: *Doppelmemoiren.* Aus dem Franz., mit einem Vorwort und Anmerkungen von Joachim Kalka. Berlin: Berenberg, 2008. 118 p.

GG4183.   • Giraudoux, Jean: *Electre.* Edition prés., annotée et commentée par Françoise Létoublon [et al.]. Paris: Larousse, 2008. *Petits classiques Larousse.* 286 p.

GG4184.   • Giraudoux, Jean: *Ondine.* Préface, commentaires et notes de Colette Weil. Paris: Grasset, 2008. *Livre de poche.* 156 p.

GG4185. Almeida, Pierre d': "La responsabilité de l'écrivain: Giraudoux, d'une guerre à l'autre," *Cahiers Jean Giraudoux*, no. 36 (2008), 349-362.

GG4186. Bernard, Florence: "Collectivité et individu dans la réécriture de *Judith*," *Cahiers Jean Giraudoux*, no. 36 (2008), 209-223.

GG4187. Bernard, Mathias: "L'idée d'Europe dans les années 1920. Etat des lieux," *Cahiers Jean Giraudoux*, no. 36 (2008), 17-27.

GG4188. Besnard, Annie: "Giraudoux et Bernanos observateurs de la France d'avant-guerre," *Cahiers Jean Giraudoux*, no. 36 (2008), 301-316. [Bernanos]

GG4189. Body, Jacques: "Giraudoux et l'A/alliance française," *Cahiers Jean Giraudoux*, no. 36 (2008), 279-286.

GG4190. Bombard, Françoise: "Interférences et singularité, confluences et voies de traverse, le théâtre de Jean Giraudoux dans l'histoire des arts de l'entre-deux-guerres," *Cahiers Jean Giraudoux*, no. 36 (2008), 111-126.

GG4191. Chaudier, Stéphane: "Rhétorique et diplomatie chez Proust et Giraudoux: la crise d'une sainte alliance," *Cahiers Jean Giraudoux*, no. 36 (2008), 287-300. [Proust]

GG4192. Cofidou, Angélique: "Giraudoux et le 'nouveau romantisme'. La formation d'une sensibilité européenne," *Cahiers Jean Giraudoux*, no. 36 (2008), 81-92.

GG4193. Coyault, Sylviane: "Le mot Europe dans l'œuvre de Jean Giraudoux: le rêve d'un lieu," *Cahiers Jean Giraudoux*, no. 36 (2008), 29-35.

GG4194. Duneau, Alain: "Giraudoux sismographe: Argos européen ou la crise de la conscience européenne dans *Electre*," *Cahiers Jean Giraudoux*, no. 36 (2008), 247-270.

GG4195. Edet-Ghomari, Chantal: "De *Siegfried et le Limousin* à *Siegfried*: la levée des ambiguïtés." In 766, 263-272.

GG4196. Giorgi, Giorgetto: "La funzione di Elena ne *La guerre de Troie n'aura pas lieu* de Giraudoux." In 482, 325-335.

GG4197. Hubert, Marie-Claude: "Le théâtre de Giraudoux, entre tradition et modernité," *Cahiers Jean Giraudoux*, no. 36 (2008), 45-54.

GG4198. Ildem, Arzu Etensel: "Le mythe classique, cheval de Troie de Giraudoux," *Cahiers Jean Giraudoux*, no. 36 (2008), 225-236.

GG4199. Job, André: "Giraudoux et la crise de nos idéaux," *Cahiers Jean Giraudoux*, no. 36 (2008), 363-374.

GG4200. Landerouin, Yves: "Giraudoux et le pirandellisme," *Cahiers Jean Giraudoux*, no. 36 (2008), 55-67.

GG4201. Lépron, Myriam: "Mémoire de la guerre dans les romans de Jean Giraudoux," *Cahiers Jean Giraudoux*, no. 36 (2008), 171-183.

GG4202. Malachy, Thérèse: "Jean Giraudoux, *La Guerre de Troie n'aura pas lieu*: politique ou théâtre?" In 1093.

GG4203. Nier, Catherine: "Quand Jouvet inspire Giraudoux," *Cahiers Jean Giraudoux*, no. 36 (2008), 69-80.

GG4204. Prévot, Anne-Marie: "Jean Giraudoux et le surréalisme dans les années 1920-1930: la femme ou les métamorphose du monde," *Cahiers Jean Giraudoux*, no. 36 (2008), 93-108. [Surrealism]

GG4205. Schaffner, Alain: "Portrait de Jean Giraudoux en écrivain européen de l'entre-deux-guerres par Alexandre Vialatte," *Cahiers Jean Giraudoux*, no. 36 (2008), 149-163. [Vialatte]

GG4206. Smadja, Stéphanie: "Giraudoux dans l'histoire de la prose narrative des années 1920: un 'style de la valise'?," *Cahiers Jean Giraudoux*, no. 36 (2008), 127-147.

GG4207. Sozzi, Lionello: "Giraudoux e Diderot." In 423.

GG4208. Sprenger, Scott: "*Sodome et Gomorrhe* et la politique culturelle du mariage chez Jean Giraudoux," *Cahiers Jean Giraudoux*, no. 36 (2008), 317-331.

GG4209. Stefanaki, Katerina: "Les deux Hélène: une histoire d'avant et d'après la guerre selon Jean Giraudoux et George Seféris," *Cahiers Jean Giraudoux*, no. 36 (2008), 237-246.

GG4210. Tatsopoulos, Hélène: "Aspects de 'l'Europe galange' chez Giraudoux et Morand," *Cahiers Jean Giraudoux*, no. 36 (2008), 185-194. [Morand]

GG4211. Vidal, Fabienne: "Giraudoux et la tauromachie," *Cahiers Jean Giraudoux*, no. 36 (2008), 333-347.

GG4212.   Vray, Jean-Bernard: "Giraudoux et le mythe européen de Robinson Crusoé: le regard éloigné," *Cahiers Jean Giraudoux*, no. 36 (2008), 195-208.

GLEIZE, Jean-Marie. See also 735.

GG4213.   Scepi, Henri: "Le sonnet mis à nu par ses . . . mêmes. Jean-Marie Gleize et la forme impraticable," *Formules*, no. 12 (2008), 201-211.

GG4214.   Thomas, Jean-Jacques: "Jean-Marie Gleize ou la poétique de l'aporie herméneutique." In 436, 215-230.

GG4215.   Thomas, Jean-Jacques: "Jean-Marie Gleize's poetic pics," *Esprit Créateur*, vol. 48, no. 2 (Summer 2008), 32-45.

GLISSANT, Édouard. See also 105, 274, 672, 698.

GG4216.   ● *Autour d'Edouard Glissant: lecture, épreuves, extensions d'une poétique de la relation.* Edition préparée par Samia Kassab-Charfi et Sonia Zlitni-Fitouri. Pessac: Presses univ. de Bordeaux; Carthage: Académie tunisienne des sciences des lettres et des arts Beït al-Hikma, 2008. 365 p.

GG4217.   ● Colin, Katell: *Le roman-monde d'Edouard Glissant: totalisation et tautologie.* Québec: Presses de l'Univ. Laval, 2008. *InterCultures.* 311 p.

GG4218.   ● Desportes, Georges: *La paraphilosophie d'Edouard Glissant.* Paris: L'Harmattan, 2008. 72 p.

GG4219.   ● Glissant, Edouard; Alexandre Leupin: *Les entretiens de Bâton Rouge.* Paris: Gallimard, 2008. 167 p.

GG4220.   Ben Abdeladhim, Maha: "Jabès au miroir de Glissant." In 4216, 135-155.

GG4221.   Ben Baya, Abdennebi: "Relations singulier-plurielles: vers une éthique 'glissantillaise' globale." In 4216, 23-30.

GG4222.   Bojsen, Heidi: "La géographie de l'errance." In 4216, 31-48.

GG4223.   Bongie, Chris: "Spectres of Glissant: dealing in relation." In 49.

GG4224.   Britton, Celia: "Langues et langages dans le Tout-Monde." In 4216, 235-245.

GG4225.   Britton, Celia: "Past, future and the maroon community in Edouard Glissant's *Le quatrième siècle*." In 51, 36-54.

GG4226.   Britton, Celia: "Transnational languages in Glissant's 'tout-monde'." In 629.

GG4227.   Bung, Stephanie: "Penser la créolisation en termes de *gender*? Edouard Glissant face à la différence sexuelle." In 440, 151-166.

GG4228.   Cailler, Bernadette: "De ruptures en échos: Virgile, Broch, Glissant." In 4216, 157-171.

GG4229.   Chevrier, Jacques: "Parole indigente/parole pléthorique dans le roman caraïbe contemporain." In 4216, 59-66.

GG4230.   Colin-Thébaudeau, Katell: "Edouard Glissant: entre béance et recomposition du passé." In 103, 129-139.

GG4231.   Coursil, Jacques: "*Monsieur Toussaint* d'Edouard Glissant: poétique de mise en scène." In 4216, 67-86.

GG4232.   Degras, Priska: "Toni Morrison et Edouard Glissant." In 72, 517-528.

GG4233.   Del Fiol, Maxime: "Edouard Glissant/Salah Stétié: immanence ou transcendance de la Relation?" In 4216, 173-189. [Stétié]

GG4234.   Delpech, Catherine: "Edouard Glissant: au zénith de l'exil, une poétique de la démesure." In 4216, 87-105.

GG4235.   Gallagher, Mary: "Relating (in theory) in a globalized world: between Levinas's ethics and Glissant's poetics." In 629. [Levinas]

GG4236.   Gyssels, Kathleen: "Scarlet ibises and the poetics of relation: Perse, Walcott and Glissant," *Commonwealth Essays and Studies*, vol. 31, no. 1 (Autumn 2008), 103-116.

GG4237.   Helmich, Werner: "Des pensées en archipel. A propos du statut textuel de la *Poétique* d'Edouard Glissant." In 423.

GG4238.   Jerad, Nabiha: "La question de la langue chez glissant." In 4216, 247-270.

GG4239.   Kassab-Charpi, Samia: "*Les Indes* métaphoriques." In 4216, 49-57.

GG4240.   Kitenge-Ngoy, T.: "La mémoire de la trace du temps d'avant chez Edouard Glissant." In 103, 157-171.

GG4241.   Lippert, Jean-Louis: "Encyclique des nuages caraïbes." In 4216, 107-117.

GG4242. Malela, Buata B.: "Une 'oblique continuation': Edouard Glissant et le *nomos* de la relation." In 102, 321-366.

GG4243. Malouche, Sarra: "Pour une poétique de la Relation dans l'œuvre de Lorand Gaspar." In 4216, 203-214. [Gaspar]

GG4244. Marchetti, Marilia: "La déchirure linguistique et les poétiques du chaos-monde: *Les Grands Chaos*." In 4216, 271-285.

GG4245. Moatamri, Inès: "Amina Saïd et Edouard Glissant." In 4216, 215-232.

GG4246. Moudileno, Lydie: "Relire *La lézarde*: victoire et mélancolie de la départe-mentalisation," *International Journal of Francophone Studies*, vol. 11, no. 3 (2008), 387-400.

GG4247. Noudelmann, François: "La trame et le tourbillon." In 4216, 119-123.

GG4248. Novivor, Ayelevi: "Des discordances au rapprochement entre Edouard Glissant et les créolistes." In 4216, 287-297.

GG4249. Oakley, Seanna Sumalee: "Commonplaces: rhetorical figures of difference in Heidegger and Glissant," *Philosophy and Rhetoric*, vol. 41, no. 1 (2008), [n.p.].

GG4250. Poiana, Peter: "The competing Caribbean utopias of Edouard Glissant and Patrick Chamoiseau." In 541, 168-179. [Chamoiseau]

GG4251. Villain, Jean-Claude: "La conscience insulaire d'Edouard Glissant." In 4216, 125-132.

GG4252. Vinas del Palacio, Yolanda: "La parole opaque de Glissant." In 4216, 299-305.

GG4253. Witdorn, Michael: " 'Nous ne connaissons même pas si les morts ont donné la main . . .". Desire without an object in Glissant's *Le quatrième siècle*." In 99, 123-138.

GG4254. Zlitni-Fitouri, Sonia: "De l'île de Glissant au désert de Boudjedra." In 4216, 191-201. [Boudjedra]

GODARD, Anne.

GG4255. Duffy, Jean H.: "Commemoration and narcissism in Anne Godard's *L'In-consolable*," *Romance Quarterly*, vol. 55, no. 1 (Winter 2008), 62-79.

GODBOUT, Jacques.

GG4256. Allard, Jacques: "Hommage de l'Académie à M. Jacques Godbout," *Ecrits*, no. 121 (déc. 2007), 7-12.

GOFFETTE, Guy.

GG4257. Thonnerieux, Stéphanie: "Formes du sonnet chez Guy Goffette," *Formules*, no. 12 (2008), 179-189.

GOLDSCHMIDT, Georges-Arthur.

GG4258. ● Goldschmidt, Georges-Arthur: *Un enfant aux cheveux gris: conversations avec François Dufay*. Paris: CNRS éditions, 2008. 121 p.

GG4259. Mugnolo, Domenico: "Vom mühseligen Umgang mit der Muttersprache und von der 'Vergangenheit, die nicht vergehen will': Ruth Klüger und Georges-Arthur Goldschmidt." In 831, 223-230.

GOLL, Yvan.

GG4260. Papparella, Teresa; André Ughetto: "La quête d'identité et le bilinguisme d'Yvan Goll," *Babel*, no. 18 (2008), 151-157.

GONCOURT, Edmond de. See also 689, 719, 738.

GG4261. ● Goncourt, Edmond de; Jules de Goncourt: *Journal des Goncourt. Tome II: 1858-1860*. Edition critique sous la dir. de Jean-Louis Cabanès; texte établi par Christiane et Jean-Louis Cabanès. Paris: H. Champion, 2008. *Bibliothèque des correspondances, mémoires et journaux*. 835 p.

GG4262. Adamy, Paule: "Le silence dans le romans des Goncourt, le silence dans leur vie," *Estudios de Lengua y Literatura Francesas*, no. 17 (2006-2007), 9-28.

GG4263. Bersani, Jacques: "*Idées et sensations* ou les Goncourt en court," *Cahiers Edmond et Jules de Goncourt*, no. 15 (2008), 53-70.

GG4264. Blix, Göran: "Women, heroism, power: the rule of women in the Goncourt brothers' eighteenth-century biographies," *Excavatio*, vol. 23, no. 1-2 (2008), 91-108.

GG4265. Bourgeois, Bertrand: "*La maison d'un artiste* et *A rebours*: du livre comme objet de collection à la maison-œuvre d'art," *Voix Plurielles*, vol. 5, no. 1 (mai 2008), 1-9. [Huysmans]

GG4266.   Cabanès, Jean-Louis: "Les Goncourt moralistes," *Cahiers Edmond et Jules de Goncourt*, no. 15 (2008), 7-23.

GG4267.   Cabanès, Jean-Louis: "L'hystérie ou le théâtre des passions." In 592, 71-85.

GG4268.   Champeau, Stéphanie: "Les Goncourt moralistes dans *Renée Mauperin*," *Cahiers Edmond et Jules de Goncourt*, no. 15 (2008), 95-121.

GG4269.   D'Ascenzo, Federica: "Modulations de la mélancolie chez Edmond de Goncourt," *Bérénice*, anno 15, n. 40-41 (nov. 2008), 184-199.

GG4270.   De Falco, Domenica: "Une poétique du vêtement féminin: lecture de *Chérie* d'Edmond de Goncourt," *Excavatio*, vol. 23, no. 1-2 (2008), 183-194.

GG4271.   Disegni, Silvia: "L'interdiction de la pièce *La Fille Elisa* (1891)." In 360, 277-300.

GG4272.   Dufief, Anne-Simone: "Devenir femme? L'éducation des filles dans l'œuvre des Goncourt," *Cahiers Edmond et Jules de Goncourt*, no. 15 (2008), 123-151.

GG4273.   Dufief, Pierre-Jean: "Les Goncourt moralistes et politiques," *Cahiers Edmond et Jules de Goncourt*, no. 15 (2008), 143-156.

GG4274.   Dufief, Pierre-Jean: "Le silence inaugural. *En 18 . . .* des Goncourt." In 592, 181-193.

GG4275.   Garapon, Jean: "Les Goncourt lecteurs de Saint-Simon dans leur *Journal*," *Cahiers Edmond et Jules de Goncourt*, no. 15 (2008), 41-51.

GG4276.   Gevrey, Françoise: "La Bruyère moraliste: un modèle pour les Goncourt," *Cahiers Edmond et Jules de Goncourt*, no. 15 (2008), 25-40.

GG4277.   Giraud, Barbara: "A reflection of the medical discourse in the Goncourt brothers' *Renée Mauperin*." In 570, 29-39.

GG4278.   Guégan, Stéphane: "Note sur les Goncourt au Salon de 1852: 'Notre réalisme à nous'," *48/14: Revue du Musée d'Orsay*, no. 26 (2008), 6-15.

GG4279.   Laporte, Dominique: " '*Le Démon du foyer* was playing at the time at the Gymnase': inscribing vaudeville in the Goncourts' *Charles Demailly*." In 540, 199-213.

GG4280.   Masse, François: "Passage du personnage romanesque: pour une lecture de la fin de *Manette Salomon* des frères Goncourt." In 586, 131-143.

GG4281.   O'Mahoney, Claire: "*La maison d'un artiste*: the Goncourts, bibelots and fin de siècle interiority." In 630, 187-202.

GG4282.   Palacio, Jean de: "Le Pierrot des Goncourt," *Cahiers Edmond et Jules de Goncourt*, no. 15 (2008), 179-188.

GG4283.   Reverzy, Eléonore: "L'écriture de la généralité," *Cahiers Edmond et Jules de Goncourt*, no. 15 (2008), 71-83.

GG4284.   Rosazza Ferraris, Patrizia: "Collecting and autobiography." In 630, 203-205.

GG4285.   Takai, Nao: "Le corps nu de Manette Salomon: intertextualité et inter-esthéticité," *Cahiers Edmond et Jules de Goncourt*, no. 15 (2008), 189-201.

GG4286.   Tortonese, Paolo: "Elisa et le libre arbitre," *Cahiers Edmond et Jules de Goncourt*, no. 15 (2008), 85-93.

GORODÉ, Déwé. See 181.

GOSCINNY, René.

GG4287.   Davis Vines, Lois: "Teaching Belgian cultural connections with *Astérix*," *French Review*, vol. 81, no. 6 (May 2008), 1224-1238.

GG4288.   Rouvière, Nicolas: "*Astérix et les pirates* ou l'obsession que le pire rate: la conjuration d'un naufrage de l'histoire." In 602, 151-168.

GG4289.   Wilmet, Marc: "Les polyphonies du *Petit Nicholas*." In 503, 217-224.

GOURMONT, Rémy de. See also 403, 681, 763, 899.

GG4290.   ● *Actualité de Remy de Gourmont*. Cahier dirigé par Vincent Gogibu et Nicolas Malais. Eaubonne: Clown lyrique, 2008. 495 p.

GG4291.   ● Dantzig, Charles: *Remy de Gourmont: cher vieux daim*. Paris: Grasset, 2008. Nouv. éd. rev.

GG4292.   ● Gourmont, Remy: *Le chemin de velours*. Texte établi par Thierry Gillybœuf. Paris: Editions du Sandre, 2008. 213 p.

GG4293. ● Gourmont, Remy: *La culture des idées*. Préface de Charles Dantzig. Paris: R. Laffont, 2008. 1124 p.

GG4294. ● Gourmont, Remy de: *Esthétique de la langue française*. Texte prés., établi et annoté par Gabriella Carpinelli. Fasano: Schena; Paris: A. Baudry, 2008. 360 p.

GG4295. Al-Matary, Sarah: " 'L'ours à écrire' et l'arbousier: Remy de Gourmont dans *La Lectura* de Madrid." In 4290, 387-399.

GG4296. Arru, Francesco: "D'Annunzio et Gourmont." In 592, 11-28.

GG4297. Barney, Natalie Clifford: "Autour de la publication des *Lettres intimes à l'Amazone*." In 4290, 433-490.

GG4298. Baronian, Jean-Baptiste: "Petites revues, grands effets." In 4290, 31-33.

GG4299. Buat, Christian: "Un grand Normand." In 4290, 35-51.

GG4300. D'Andrea, Patrizia: "L'ésotérisme chez Remy de Gourmont." In 4290, 175-187.

GG4301. Devaux, Jonathan: "Contribution à l'étude des rapports entre Remy de Gourmont et la Belgique." In 4290, 333-346.

GG4302. Gamalova, Natalia: "La critique littéraire de Remy de Gourmont en Russie." In 4290, 347-359.

GG4303. Gillybœuf, Thierry: "Remy la Science." In 4290, 53-66.

GG4304. Gogibu, Vincent: "Panorama de la correspondance de Remy de Gourmont." In 4290, 67-70.

GG4305. Grillo, Alessandra: "*Chez les Lapons* et ses sources critiques." In 4290, 245-260.

GG4306. Hamot, Odile: "La clef et la cithare: Gourmont et la réception saint-polinienne." In 4290, 71-87.

GG4307. Kalantzis, Alexia: "L'art des jardins et l'idylle symboliste dans l'œuvre de Remy de Gourmont." In 487, 347-356.

GG4308. Kalantzis, Alexia: "La redéfinition du symbolisme à l'aube du XXe siècle et ses conséquences esthétiques." In 4290, 89-101. [Cendrars]

GG4309. Kurakata, Kensaku: "La réception de Remy de Gourmont au Japon." In 4290, 361-370.

GG4310. La Tour, Laure de: "Joris-Karl Huysmans et Remy de Gourmont 'cliniciens ès lettres'?" In 4290, 189-206. [Huysmans]

GG4311. Lucet, Sophie: "A propos de l'article de G. Jean-Aubry." In 4290, 261-278.

GG4312. Lugan, Mikaël: "Remy de Gourmont, *La Nación* et Julio Piquet." In 4290, 371-385.

GG4313. Malais, Nicolas: "Remy de Gourmont, artisan et conscience des revues symbolistes." In 4290, 103-119.

GG4314. Meunier, Jean-Louis: "*L'Imprimerie gourmontienne*: quel Gourmont?" In 4290, 121-129.

GG4315. Poitry, Guy: "Chair et marbre: le corps et la statue chez Remy de Gourmont." In 4290, 279-293.

GG4316. Poulouin, Gérard: "Remy de Gourmont: de la guerre, de la force et des civilisations." In 4290, 295-319.

GG4317. Pound, Ezra: "Remy de Gourmont." In 854.

GG4318. Powys, John Cowper: "Remy de Gourmont." In 4290, 401-417.

GG4319. Prigent, Gaël: "Gourmont et la religion." In 4290, 207-220.

GG4320. Roucan, Carine: "Remy de Gourmont et Joris-Karl Huysmans: deux mystiques fin-de-siècle." In 4290, 221-228. [Huysmans]

GG4321. Schiano-Bennis, Sandrine: "Une tranche d'occultisme." In 4290, 229-243.

GG4322. Vibert, Bertrand: "Don Juan mis à nu par ses amoureuses." In 4290, 321-329.

GG4323. Yaouanq-Tamby, Emilie: "Poétique de la couleur, dans les contes de Remy de Gourmont et de Manuel Díaz Rodríguez." In 4290, 419-432.

GG4324. Young, Sylvie: "Le roman enchâssé, forme textuelle du fantasme." In 4290, 159-171.

GG4325. Entry deleted.

GOUX, Jean-Paul.

GG4326.   Grenouillet, Corinne: "Une histoire de l'âge industriel: les *Mémoires de l'Enclave* de Jean-Paul Goux." In 459, 341-351.

GRACQ, Julien. See also 668, 6414.

GG4327.   • Herzfeld, Claude: *Julien Gracq: préférences médiévales.* Paris: L'Harmattan, 2008. *Espaces littéraires.* 144 p.

GG4328.   • *Julien Gracq 6: Les tensions de l'écriture: adieu au romanesque: persistance de la fiction.* Textes réunis par Patrick Marot. Caen: Lettres modernes Minard, 2008. *Revue des Lettres Modernes.* 265 p.

GG4329.   • Malestroit, Jean de: *Julien Gracq: quarante ans d'amitié, 1967-2007.* Saint Malo: Galodé, 2008. *Univers littératures.* 272 p.

GG4330.   Benoît, Claude: "*Le Roi pêcheur* de Julien Gracq: l'antithèse au service du mythe." In 553, 237-245.

GG4331.   Bergounioux, Pierre: "Un écrivain français," *Fario,* no. 6 (2008), 11-16.

GG4332.   Berthomieu, Gérard: "La lieutenance de l'aspirant Grange," *Information Grammaticale,* no. 116 (2008), 31-40.

GG4333.   Chauvin, Cédric: "Status et fonctions de la référence épique chez Julien Gracq." In 4328, 93-136.

GG4334.   Damade, Jacques: "Vu de l'auto," *Fario,* no. 6 (2008), 53-63.

GG4335.   Damamme-Gilbert, Béatrice: "Julien Gracq (1910-2007), et la Grande-Bretagne," *French Studies Bulletin,* no. 108 (Autumn 2008), 68-71.

GG4336.   Damamme-Gilbert, Béatrice: "Sinuosité, tensions et accidents de parcours dans les chemins de Lettrines." In 4328, 27-49.

GG4337.   Favriaud, Michel: "Les deux-points, pierre de touche de la construction des phrases et de l'écriture gracquiennes d'*Un balcon en forêt,*" *Information Grammaticale,* no. 116 (2008), 25-30.

GG4338.   Fraisse, Luc: "L'énigme des fins de récits chez Julien Gracq," *Revue d'Histoire Littéraire de la France,* tome 108, no. 4 (oct.-déc. 2008), 889-912.

GG4339.   Gur, Adrien: "Julien Gracq *off limits.*" In 4328, 137-190.

GG4340.   Herzog, Christine; Georges Kliebenstein: "Visit en Gracquie." In 379, 79-95.

GG4341.   Margantin, Laurent: "Julien Gracq et la géographie romantique," *Fario,* no. 6 (2008), 33-52.

GG4342.   Marot, Patrick: " 'Fines transcendam': de la transgression à la frontière dans l'œuvre de Gracq." In 4328, 191-240.

GG4343.   Monballin, Michèle: "Romans et fragments paysagers." In 4328, 11-26.

GG4344.   Nagai, Atsuko: "Julien Gracq et sa contribution aux périodiques." In 4328, 241-264.

GG4345.   Pajon, Guillaume: "Le hérisson romanesque." In 908, 191-204.

GG4346.   Pajon, Guillaume: "L'île bleue des Syrtes: Emblème cryptobotanique d'un paysage fantastique," *Etudes Francophones,* vol. 23, no. 1-2 (printemps-automne 2008), 57-72.

GG4347.   Picard, Timothée: "Du rythme de l'histoire au pouls de la nature: Ernst Jünger et Julien Gracq." In 459, 293-305.

GG4348.   Pinchard, Bruno: "Stèle funéraire pour Julien Gracq," *Études,* 152e année, no. 4083 (mars 2008), 383-387.

GG4349.   Proïa, François: "Julien Gracq: la voix mélancolique de l'Histoire," *Bérénice,* anno 15, n. 40-41 (nov. 2008), 120-128.

GG4350.   Riou, Pascal: "Six variations ardennaises," *Fario,* no. 6 (2008), 21-31.

GG4351.   Stétié, Salah: "Dans un cristal de brume," *Fario,* no. 6 (2008), 17-20.

GG4352.   Tritar-Ben-Ahmed, Saloua: "Cohérence et désignation toponymique dans *Le Rivage des Syrtes* de Julien Gracq." In 410, 381-390.

GG4353.   Tritsmans, Bruno: "Brouillards d'automne chez Julien Gracq et Olivier Rolin." In 383, 389-398. [O. Rolin]

GG4354.   Tritsmans, Bruno: "Cartographies et broderies: parcours croisés Malaurie-Gracq-Mialon." In 4328, 73-92.

GG4355.   Vignes-Mottet, Sylvie: "Des 'géographies imaginaires' à la 'mythologie routière' dans l'écriture de Julien Gracq." In 4328, 51-72.

GRAEVE, Laurent de.

GG4356. Seth, Catriona: "Genre et *gender*: des *Liaisons dangereuses* au *Mauvais genre.*" In 766, 163-177.

GRAINVILLE, Patrick. See also 637a.

GG4357. Riesz, János: "*Les Flamboyants* de Patrick Grainville et *La vie et demie* de Sony Labou Tansi. Textes européens et africains à l'époque de la postmodernité." In 127, 349-361. [Labou]

GRAN, Iegor.

GG4358. Diver, Ruth: "Iegor Gran." In 442, 207-213.

GG4359. Durham, Carolyn A.: "My American uncle, America cries uncle, and other fantastic tales from France: Iegor Gran's *Jeanne d'Arc fait tic-tac,*" *Studies in Twentieth and Twenty-First Century Literature*, vol. 32, no. 1 (Winter 2008), 11-36.

GRANDPRÉ, Pierre de.

GG4360. Livernois, Jonathan: "La double direction de la modernité culturelle québécoise: l'exemple de *La Patience des justes,*" *Québec Studies*, vol. 45 (Spring/Summer 2008), 153-165.

GRANDRIEUX, Philippe.

GG4361. Hainge, Greg: "*L'invention du troisième peuple*: the utopian vision of Philippe Grandrieux's dystopias." In 541, 228-239.

GREEN, Julien. See also 2304, 5765.

GG4362. ● Green, Julien: *Sud*. Prés., notes, chronologie et bibliographie par Pascal Aquien. Paris: Flammarion, 2008. *GF Flammarion*. 273 p.

GG4363. ● *Julien Green, diariste et essayiste*. Ed. Michael O'Dwyer. Oxford: Peter Lang, 2007. 263 p.

GG4364. ● *Julien Green: littérature et spiritualité: actes du colloque*. Etudes réunies par Véeronique Grollier. Paris: L'Harmattan, 2008. *Critiques littéraires*.

GG4365. Auroy-Mohn, Carole: "Le désir métaphysique et ses jeux triangulaires dans *Adrienne Mesurat*." In 4364, 89-106.

GG4366. Bouletreau, François: "Variations pascaliennes sur le *Pamphlet contre les catholiques de France* de Julien Green." In 4364, 121-130.

GG4367. Canerot, Marie-Françoise: "Le roman de Julien Green, un roman du crime?," *Bulletin de la Société Internationale d'Etudes Greeniennes*, no. 24 (2008), 11-19.

GG4368. Catelain, Valérie: "Julien Green et la spiritualité franciscaine." In 4364, 17-28.

GG4369. Daudin, Claire: "Culture et religion. Les livres dans *Moïra* et *Chaque homme dans sa nuit*." In 4364, 167-173.

GG4370. Griffin, John: "Le protestantisme dans la vie de Julien Green." In 4364, 9-16.

GG4371. Grollier, Véronique; Marguerite Jean-Blain: "De la nuit de Job au ciel bleu de l'espérance." In 4364, 61-87. [Ionesco]

GG4372. Grzybowska, Aleksandra: "Le cheminement spirituel dans quelques romans de Julien Green." In 4364, 153-165.

GG4373. Maher, Eamon: "L'approche du spirituel dans l'univers romanesque de Jean Sulivan et de Julien Green." In 4364, 51-59. [Sulivan]

GG4374. O'Dwyer, Michael: "Le leitmotiv du ciel étoilé dans la spiritualité greenienne." In 4364, 43-50.

GG4375. Perry, Edith: "Les avatars du boudhisme dans *Varouna*." In 4364, 107-119.

GG4376. Perry, Edith: "De l'incest au parricide. La relation père-fille dans deux romans de Julien Green." In 572, 87-94.

GG4377. Pourcelot, Jérôme: "Résonances jansénistes dans l'œuvre greenienne." In 4364, 29-42.

GG4378. Vultaggio-Grenglet, Nadège: "Perdition ou salut de l'héroïne? La famille dans deux romans de Julien Green." In 571, 253-263.

GG4379. Vultaggio-Grenglet, Nadège: "Spiritualité et fascination du lecteur pour l'héroïne de *L'Autre*." In 4364, 131-152.

GREIF, Hans-Jürgen.

GG4380. Boyer, Marc; Christiane Lahaie: "*Les Divines* de Hans-Jürgen Greif: du 'body art' à la néantisation." In 69, 61-68.

GREIMAS, Algirdas Julien.

GRENIER, Jean. See also 2150.

GG4381. ● Grenier, Jean: *Une attention aimante: écrits sur l'art, 1944-1971.* Textes choisis et édités par Patrick Corneau. Rennes: Presses univ. de Rennes, 2008. *Critique d'art.* 320 p.

GRENIER, Roger.

GG4382. Grenier, Roger: "L'un sans l'autre." In 861, 419-437.

GRIMAUD, Hélène. See 6024.

GRIPARI, Pierre.

GG4383. Camero Perez, Carmen: "La subversion dans la conformité: une lecture du fantastique griparien," *Estudios de Lengua y Literatura Francesas*, no. 16 (2005), 69-82.

GROBÉTY, Anne-Lise. See 179.

GROSJEAN, Jean.

GG4384. Bourgeault, Jean-François: "Défaillances du verset. Réflexions à partir de Jean Grosjean," *Etudes Littéraires*, vol. 38, no. 2 (automne 2007), 57-67.

GG4385. Cohen-Halimi, Michèle: "Puisqu'on ne sait jamais où va aboutir une phrase," *CCP: Cahier Critique de Poésie*, no. 14 (2007), 273-276.

GG4386. Hetzel, Aurélia: "Métamorphoses du sacré: les réécritures bibliques de Jean Grosjean." In 520, 797-806.

GROULX, Lionel.

GG4387. Kolar, Adriana: *La dimension politique de l'histoire: L. Groulx (Québec) et N. Iorga (Roumanie) entre les deux guerres mondiales.* Frankfurt: P. Lang, 2008. *Canadiana.* 184 p.

GRUMBERG, Jean-Claude.

GG4388. Godeau, Florence: "Du conte à la fantaisie théâtrale: *Le Chat botté*, de Perrault à Jean-Claude Grumberg, en passant par Ludwig Tieck." In 766, 211-223.

GUATTARI, Félix. See also 991, 3002, 3005, 3007, 3022, 3034, 3046, 3076, 3083, 3096, 3105, 3132, 3151, 6577.

GG4389. ● Berardi, Franco: *Félix Guattari: thought, friendship and visionary cartography.* Trans. and ed. Giuseppina Mecchia and Charles J. Stivale. Basingstoke; New York: Palgrave Macmillan, 2008. xvi, 188 p.

GG4390. ● Martínez, Francisco José: *Hacia una era post-mediática: ontología, política y ecología en la obra de Félix Guattari.* Matarò: Intervención Cultural, 2008. 196 p.

GG4391. "Entretien avec Félix Guattari," *Chimères: Revue des Schizoanalyses*, no. 69 (2008), 51-63.

GUEDJ, Colette.

GG4392. ● *Ecrire l'identité, écrire la mémoire: rencontre autour du roman de Colette Guedj, Le Journal de Myriam Bloch.* Textes réunis et prés. par Paul Léon. Nice: Editions du Losange, 2006. *Les Mots la Vie*, no. hors série. 193 p.

GUÉHENNO, Jean. See also 6193.

GG4393. ● Guéhenno, Jean: *La jeunesse morte.* Edition établie par Philippe Niogret; avec le concours de Patrick Bachelier et Jean-Kely Paulhan; préfacée par Jean-Kely Paulhan et Philippe Niogret. Paris: C. Paulhan, 2008. *Pour mémoire.* 286 p.

GUÈNE, Faïza. See also 6091.

GG4394. Geesey, Patricia: "Global pop culture in Faïza Guène's *Kiffe kiffe demain*," *Expressions Maghrébines*, vol. 7, no. 1 (été 2008), 53-66.

GG4395. Thomas, Dominic: "New writing for new times: Faïza Guène, banlieue writing, and the post-Beur generation," *Expressions Maghrébines*, vol. 7, no. 1 (été 2008), 33-51.

GUÉNON, René.

GG4396. Oldmeadow, Harry: "René Guénon, metaphysician." In 969.

GUÉRIN, Raymond.

GG4397. Curatolo, Bruno: "Deux exemples littéraires de la déroute du langage." In 554, 237-248. [Céline]

GG4398. Curatolo, Bruno: "Raymond Guérin et la voix médiane. Un exemple du monologue intérieur à la troisième personne," *Cahiers Valery Larbaud*, no. 43 (2008), 165-183.

GUÈVREMONT, Germaine.

GG4399. Addino, Roberto: "La francophonie canadienne: du texte littéraire à l'écran. *Le Survenant* de Germaine Guèvremont," *Annali, Università degli Studi di Napoli "L'Orientale", Sezione Romanza*, anno 49, n. 2 (2007), 571-583.

GUIBERT, Armand.

GG4400. Loreti, Alessio: "Armand Guibert: des liens fraternels entre Maghreb et Italie." In 515, 83-103.

GUIBERT, Hervé. See also 389, 394, 1386.

GG4401. • Orban, Clara: *Body (in) parts: bodies and identity in Sade and Guibert.* Bethlehem, PA: Lehigh Univ. Press, 2008. 164 p.

GG4402. • Poinat, Frédérique: *L'œuvre siamoise: Hervé Guibert et l'expérience photographique.* Paris: L'Harmattan, 2008. *Champs visuels.* 330 p.

GG4403. • Pujade, Robert: *Hervé Guibert, une leçon de photographie.* Villeurbanne: Univ. Claude Bernard, 2008. 105 p.

GG4404. Arouimi, Michel: "Le double et sa violence: *Le Protocole compassionel* d'Hervé Guibert," *Nottingham French Studies*, vol. 47, no. 1 (Spring 2008), 43-60.

GG4405. Genon, Arnaud: "Confusion des âges et nécessité du témoignage de soi dans les derniers textes d'Hervé Guibert." In 379, 291-302.

GG4406. Grauby, Françoise: "La 'maison de verre': utopies corporelles et arts de guérir dans *Le Protocole compassionnel* d'Hervé Guibert." In 541, 211-227.

GUILLEMOT, Cécile. See 1104.

GUILLEVIC, Eugène.

GG4407. Debreuille, Jean-Yves: "Chanter le silence: la rétention dans la poésie de Guillevic." In 382, 149-160.

GUILLOUX, Louis.

GG4408. • *Georges Palante et Louis Guilloux: l'amitié, la fêlure.* Dossier préparé par Pierre-Yves Kerloc'h et Yves Prié. Bédée: Folle avoine, 2008. *Cahiers Louis Guilloux*, 2. 155 p.

GG4409. Kaplan, Alice: "On violent judgment." In 617, 104-122.

GG4410. Le Dimna, Nicole: "La mélancolie de Cripure, héros du *Sang noir* de Louis Guilloux," *Bérénice*, anno 15, n. 40-41 (nov. 2008), 129-142.

GG4411. Martin, Yann: "La réception du *Sang noir*," *Confrontations*, no. 21 (2008), 5-33.

GG4412. Poirot-Delpech, Bertrand: "Maître et modèle de Louis Guilloux," *Confrontations*, no. 21 (2008), 35-38.

GG4413. Signoret, Pierre; Jean Boissieu; Michèle Taddei: "Les œuvres de Louis Guilloux face à la critique," *Confrontations*, no. 21 (2008), 39-46.

GG4414. Vasic, Alexandra: "Figures du militant dans *Le jeu de patience* de Louis Guilloux." In 456, 203-215.

GUITRY, Sacha. See also 1086.

GG4415. • Guitry, Sacha: *La correspondance de Paul Roulier-Davenel.* Avant-propos de Jean-Laurent Cochet. Paris: Fallois, 2008. 152 p.

GG4416. • Guitry, Sacha: *Faisons un rêve.* Paris: Avant-Scène Théâtre, 2008. *Avant-Scène Théâtre*, no. 1247 (1er sept. 2008). 99 p.

GG4417. • Guitry, Sacha: *Mémoires d'un tricheur.* Préface de Jean-Claude Brialy. Paris: Omnibus, 2008. 1158 p. [Orig. ed., 1991]

GG4418. • Guitry, Sacha: *Théâtre, je t'adore.* Préface de Daniel Toscan du Plantier. Paris: Omnibus, 2008. 1185 p. [Orig. ed., 1996]

GG4419. Louis, Stéphanie E.: "Redécouvrir Sacha Guitry," *Vingtième Siècle*, no. 99 (juillet-sept. 2008), 251-253.

GUITTON, Jean.

GG4420. • Creuchet, Anne: *Monsieur Chrétien: souvenirs de Jean Guitton.* Montrouge: Bayard, 2008. 87 p.

GUYOTAT, Pierre.

GG4421. ● Guyotat, Pierre: *Ashby: suivi de Sur un cheval*. Préface de Bernard Comment. Paris: Gallimard, 2008. *Folio*. 255 p.

GG4422. Kendall, Stuart: "Eden and atrocity: Pierre Guyotat's Algeria," *Comparative Studies of South Asia, Africa and the Middle East*, vol. 28, no. 1 (2008), 11-19.

GYP.

GG4423. Barilier, Etienne: "Je les hais de toute mon âme." In 388, 111-117.

GG4424. Pernot, Denis: "Gyp ou la littérature potinière." In 419, 221-232.

HALÉVY, Daniel.

GG4425. ● Rabaud, Henri: *Correspondance avec Daniel Halévy et Max d'Ollone et écrits de jeunesse (1889-1907)*. Prés. et annotés par par Michel Rabaud. Lyon: Symétrie, 2008. 492 p.

HALIMI, Gisèle.

GG4426. Ayari, Ramla: "La fratrie dans *Le lait de l'oranger* et *Fritna* de Gisèle Halimi." In 572, 257-265.

HAMA, Boubou.

GG4427. Diop, Papa Samba: "Boubou Hama: une figure centrale dans l'histoire modern du Niger," *Cultures Sud*, no. 170 (sept. 2008), 63-68.

HAMELIN, Louis.

GG4428. ● Ouellet, François; François Paré: *Louis Hamelin et ses doubles*. Québec: Nota Bene, 2008. 262 p.

HAMP, Pierre.

GG4429. ● *Pierre Hamp, inspecteur du travail et écrivain humaniste, 1876-1962*. Coord. Dominique Guyot. Paris: L'Harmattan, 2005. 252 p.

HAMPÂTÉ BÂ, Amadou. See also 59, 151, 278.

GG4430. Aggarwal, Kusum: "Anthropology and autobiography in Amadou Hampâté Bâ's writings," *Francophone Postcolonial Studies*, vol. 6, no. 2 (Autumn-Winter 2008), 73-91.

GG4431. Azarian, Viviane: " 'Vous avez dit 'Hampâté Bâ le sage' . . . laissez-moi rire'." In 510, 151-164.

GG4432. Bâ, Mamadou: "Les mémoires d'Amadou Hampâté Bâ: une poétique de la tolérance." In 96, 69-76.

GG4433. Constant, Isabelle: "Amadou Hampâté Bâ: *L'Etrange destin de Wangrin*. In 59, 95-106.

GG4434. Le Quellec Cottier, Christien: "Le romanesque africain sous le signe de la ruse," *Études de Lettres*, no. 279 [no. 1] (2008), 103-117. [Kourouma]

GG4435. Magnier, Julien: "D'Amadou Hampâté Bâ à Léonora Miano: une identité déchirée." In 99, 13-26.

GG4436. N'Da, Pierre: "*L'Etrange destin de Wangrin*, un étrange roman." In 72, 393-410.

HANOTTE, Xavier. See also 673.

GG4437. Hanotte, Xavier: "Entretien autour de *Un goût de buiscuit au gingembre*," *Degrés*, no. 133 (2008), f1-f15.

HARDELLET, André.

GG4438. ● *Présence d'André Hardellet*. Dossier dirigé par Pascal Sigoda et Olivier Houbert. Clermont-Ferrand: Au signe de la Licorne, 2008. 265 p.

GG4439. Carn, Hervé: "La grammaire des émotions." In 4438, 25-28.

GG4440. Chateaureynaud, Georges-Olivier: "*Le seuil du jardin*." In 4438, 29-30.

GG4441. Claudel, Philippe: "Vers *L'Ile au trésor*." In 4438, 203-218.

GG4442. Cloux, Patrick: "Les effets secondaires." In 4438, 11-23.

GG4443. Constant, Alexis: "Marge et périphérie." In 4438, 89-112.

GG4444. Darol, Guy: "Tête en l'air." In 4438, 69-86.

GG4445. Demougin, Françoise: "Enfances de l'écriture." In 4438, 187-196.

GG4446. Demougin, Françoise: "Florilège critique." In 4438, 231-238.

GG4447. Dupré, Guy: "André Hardellet: le rêveur éveillé." In 4438, 225-227.

GG4448. Houbert, Olivier: "Le grand stupéfiant." In 4438, 113-125.

GG4449. Lamart, Michel: "Le fantastique d'André Hardellet: un réalisme poétique." In 4438, 147-185.

GG4450. Nucera, Louis: "L'enchanteur." In 4438, 65-67.

GG4451. Réal, Eléonore: "L'écriture du secret." In 4438, 127-146.

GG4452. Taylor, John: "Traces des jours disparus." In 4438, 197-201.

GG4453. Vernet, Joël: "En marchant entre les pages d'Hardellet." In 4438, 219-224.

GG4454. Vers, André: "Le temps du Vecchio." In 4438, 31-55.

GG4455. Walther, Daniel: "Pour saluer André Hardellet," *Presse Littéraire*, no. 11 (2007), 101-108.

HARPMAN, Jacqueline.

GG4456. Amar, Ruth: "*Le bonheur dans le crime* de Jacqueline Harpman: le système de la dissimulation," *Nouvelles Etudes Francophones*, vol. 22, no. 2 (automne 2007), 93-101.

GG4457. Blanckaert, Gina: " 'Admirable tremblement du temps': le vieillir et le créer dans *Récit de la dernière année* de Jacqueline Harpman." In 379, 211-223.

GG4458. Vanbaelen, Sylvie: "L'*Orlanda* de Jacqueline Harpman: Virginia Woolf rencontre Carl Gustav Jung," *Dalhousie French Studies*, vol. 83 (Summer 2008), 81-88.

HARVEY, Pauline. See 221.

HAZOUMÉ, Flore.

GG4459. Gueyes, Léontine: "Flore Hazoumé, romancière du malaise social," *Cultures Sud*, no. 170 (sept. 2008), 69-74.

HAZOUMÉ, Paul.

GG4460. Riesz, János: "De l'ethnographie à la naissance du roman africain. Le cas de *Doguicimi* de Paul Hazoumé." In 127, 249-268.

HÉBERT, Anne. See also 311, 2226.

GG4461. • *Anne Hébert: chronologie et bibliographie des livres, parties de livres, articles et autres travaux consacrés à son œuvre.* Sous la supervision de Nathalie Watteyne en collaboration avec Anne Ancrenat [et al.]. Montréal: Presses de l'Univ. de Montréal, 2008. 315 p.

GG4462. Ancrenat, Anne: "Le corps déserté dans le récit: *Est-ce que je te dérange?* d'Anne Hébert." In 69, 43-59.

GG4463. "Anne Hébert," *Contemporary Literary Criticism*, vol. 246 (2008), 269-382.

GG4464. Batalha, Maria Cristina: "La culture québécoise entre l'Histoire et le mythe." In 496, 141-148.

GG4465. Batalha, Maria Cristina: "La survivance d'un passé collectif et primordial dans *Les Enfants du sabbat*." In 571, 117-125.

GG4466. Bishop, Neil B.: "Empire du mâle ou sexes-solaires? Le sexo-générique dans les premières œuvres d'Anne Hébert," *Cahiers Anne Hébert*, vol. 8 (2008), 37-51.

GG4467. Boisclair, Isabelle: "La solidarité féminine comme réponse à la domination masculine: étude de deux motifs genrés dans l'œuvre d'Anne Hébert," *Cahiers Anne Hébert*, vol. 8 (2008), 15-36.

GG4468. Bouloumié, Arlette: "Espace du corps et corps du désir dans *Les Fous de Bassan* d'Anne Hébert." In 69, 185-197.

GG4469. Dima, Vlad: "Les personnages dans *Les Fous de Bassan*: la *nature* de leurs identités," *Dalhousie French Studies*, vol. 84 (Fall 2008), 75-87.

GG4470. Dimitriu-Panaitescu, Corina: "La lecture poétique d'un roman d'Anne Hébert." In 115, 129-143.

GG4471. Letendre, Evelyne: "Du refoulement du féminin à la prédation: étude du personnage de Stevens Brown des *Fous de Bassan* d'Anne Hébert," *Cahiers Anne Hébert*, vol. 8 (2008), 53-69.

GG4472. Marcheix, Daniel: "Anne Hébert et les incertitudes du masculin." In 69, 127-137.

GG4473. Mauguière, Bénédicte: "L' 'habit de lumière' ou le corps travesti chez Anne Hébert et Pedro Almodóvar." In 69, 227-235.

GG4474. Morency, Catherine: "Emergence et incarnations dans les premiers poèmes d'Anne Hébert," *Cahiers Anne Hébert*, vol. 8 (2008), 137-154.

GG4475. Paterson, Janet M.: "Corps dévoilés dans *Un habit de lumière* d'Anne Hébert." In 69, 237-245.

GG4476. Rea, Annabelle M.: "From *Le Torrent* to *La Cage*: laughter in Anne Hébert's works," *Women in French Studies* (2008), 154-164.

GG4477. Reid, Gregory J.: "Anne Hébert's *La cage*: a masque of liberation," *Text and Presentation* (2008), 132-144.

GG4478. Saint-Martin, Lori: "Femmes et hommes, victimes ou bourreaux? Violence, sexe et genre dans l'œuvre d'Anne Hébert," *Cahiers Anne Hébert*, vol. 8 (2008), 111-133.

GG4479. Salaün, Elise: "Joseph et Julie, jumeaux androgynes. Indifférenciation de genre dans *Les enfants du sabbat*," *Cahiers Anne Hébert*, vol. 8 (2008), 71-90.

GG4480. Sirois, Antoine: "Le regard en arrière dans les romans d'Anne Hébert," *Cahiers Anne Hébert*, vol. 8 (2008), 155-162.

GG4481. Suhonen, Katri: "Les enfancts chargés de songes ou l'illusion patriarcale dans l'œuvre romanesque d'Anne Hébert," *Cahiers Anne Hébert*, vol. 8 (2008), 91-110.

GG4482. Thomas, Jean-Pierre: "Retisser *L'Odyssée*: actualisation d'un motif littéraire fondateur dans *Kamouraska* d'Anne Hébert." In 520, 807-819.

GG4483. Vaucher, Anne de: "Portraits littéraries à l'écran: Anne Hébert et Marie-Claire Blais." In 97, 69-79. [Blais]

HELLENS, Franz.

GG4484. Bagiag, Aurora Manuela: "Franz Hellens, '*Naître ou mourir* ou la fusion avec l'élément maternel'." In 571, 67-75.

GG4485. Ben Ali Memdouh, Sourour: " 'Plus pressé que jamais': *Cet âge qu'on dit grand* de Franz Hellens." In 379, 17-25.

GG4486. Gorceix, Paul: "Le cosmopolitisme du *Disque vert*." In 83, 275-288.

GG4487. Gorceix, Paul: "*Le Disque vert*. Franz Hellens et les écrivains français." In 83, 261-274.

GG4488. Gorceix, Paul: "Les *Essais de critique intuitive*." In 83, 239-252.

GG4489. Gorceix, Paul: "Mélusine: roman fantastique ou roman d'initiation?" In 83, 217-237.

GG4490. Gorceix, Paul: "Mystique et écriture du fantastique." In 83, 253-259.

GG4491. Mortier, Roland: "*En ville morte, les scories* ou le mythe subverti." In 616, 159-168.

HELLO, Ernest.

GG4492. ● Hello, Ernest: *Du néant à Dieu*. Préface de Fabrice Hadjadj. Paris: Sandre, 2008. Nouv. éd. 245 p.

HÉMON, Louis.

GG4493. ● Hémon, Louis: *Marie Chapdelaine: texte intégral*. Prés. Jean Potvin. Saint-Laurent, Québec: Editions du Renouveau pédagogique, 2008. xviii, 166 p.

GG4494. Chovrelat, Geneviève: "Le cas *Maria Chapdelaine* ou une famille dans tous ses états." In 572, 59-67.

GG4495. Mann, J. Debbie: "*Maria Chapdelaine* in literature and film: between tradition and modernity." In 120, 193-203.

GG4496. Morel, Pierre: "*Maria Chapdelaine*." In 115, 81-90.

GG4497. Pageaux, Daniel-Henri: "Eléments pour une lecture de *Maria Chapdelaine* de Louis Hémon," *Rivista di Studi Canadesi*, n. 21 (2008), 81-94.

HENRY, Michel.

GG4498. Audi, Paul: "Michel Henry: entre généalogie et contemporanéité," *Revue Philosophique de Louvain*, tome 106, no. 1 (févr. 2008), 106-128.

GG4499. Calcagno, Antonio: "Michel Henry's non-intentionality thesis and Husserlian phenomenology," *Journal of the British Society for Phenomenology*, vol. 39, no. 2 (May 2008), 117-129.

GG4500. Madou, Jean-Pol: "Roman et phénoménologie: réflexions sur l'œuvre de Michel Henry." In 612, 401-416.

GG4501. Sterlicchi, Paolo: "L'eternità nel tempo. Fenomenologia e cristianesimo nella filosofia di Michel Henry," *Rivista di Filosofia Neo-Scolastica*, anno. 100, fasc. 2-3 (aprile-sett. 2008), 309-334.

HENRY-VALMORE, Simonne.

GG4502. Mossetto, Anna Paola: "L'archipel au cœur de l'île dans *Le Jardinier et le bibliothécaire* de Simonne Henry-Valmore." In 423.

HERGÉ. See also 688.

GG4503. ● Farr, Michael: *Tintin & Cie.* Bruxelles: Moulinsart, 2008. 131 p.

GG4504. ● Goddin, Philippe: *The art of Hergé, inventor of Tintin.* Trans. Michael Farr. San Francisco: Last Gasp, 2008. 3 vols.

GG4505. ● Marchand, Alain Bernard: *Tintin au pays de la ferveur.* Montréal: Les Herbes rouges, 2008. 129 p.

GG4506. ● McCarthy, Tom: *Tintin and the secret of literature.* Berkeley: Counterpoint, 2008. 211 p.

GG4507. Denis, Benoît: "Hergé-Simenon, thirties." In 79, 110-127. [Simenon]

GG4508. Frey, Hugo: "Trapped in the past: anti-semitism in Hergé's *Flight 714.*" In 837.

HOCQUARD, Emmanuel. See also 1042.

GG4509. Cometti, Jean-Pierre: "Emmanuel Hocquard et le rhinocéros de Wittgenstein," *Critique,* tome 64, no. 735-736 (août-sept. 2008), 669-676.

GG4510. Lang, Abigail: "Emmanuel Hocquard/Michael Palmer: une partie de billard sur l'Atlantique," *Revue Française d'Études Américaines,* no. 115 (1er trim. 2008), 72-88.

HOCQUENGHEM, Guy. See also 654.

GG4511. Brossat, Alain: "Une littérature d'interpellation," *Chimères: Revue des Schizoanalyses,* no. 69 (2008), 47-58.

GG4512. Christoffel, David: "Le désir homosexuel: programme poétique," *Chimères: Revue des Schizoanalyses,* no. 69 (2008), 89-101.

GG4513. Desmons, Patrice: "D'Hocquenghem à Derrida et Butler, et retour," *Chimères: Revue des Schizoanalyses,* no. 69 (2008), 183-199. [Derrida]

GG4514. Haas, Ron: "Le sens de l'humour de Guy Hocquenghem," *Chimères: Revue des Schizoanalyses,* no. 69 (2008), 125-132.

GG4515. Hazéra, Hélène: "Guy Hocquenghem au journal, polémiques et vagabondages," *Chimères: Revue des Schizoanalyses,* no. 69 (2008), 157-161.

GG4516. Huard de la Marre, Geoffroy: "Une politique du désir," *Chimères: Revue des Schizoanalyses,* no. 69 (2008), 9-21.

GG4517. Marshall, Bill: "Minorités et indiscernabilité," *Chimères: Revue des Schizoanalyses,* no. 69 (2008), 103-111.

GG4518. Massipe, Alexandre: "Avoir vingt ans dans les années 2000 et lire ' Lettre ouverte à ceux qui sont passés du col Mao au Rotary'," *Chimères: Revue des Schizoanalyses,* no. 69 (2008), 77-87.

GG4519. Nadaud, Stéphane: "Sodome ou Hocquenghem, fils de Vincennes—jusqu'à la mort," *Chimères: Revue des Schizoanalyses,* no. 69 (2008), 5-31.

GG4520. Naze, Alain: "Des couleurs criardes," *Chimères: Revue des Schizoanalyses,* no. 69 (2008), 59-76.

GG4521. Périn, Nathalie: "Géographie du désir," *Chimères: Revue des Schizoanalyses,* no. 69 (2008), 113-123.

GG4522. Querrien, Anne: "Des moments-événements," *Chimères: Revue des Schizoanalyses,* no. 69 (2008), 135-139.

GG4523. Sarfati, Yves: "Phallus, cunus anus: l'enceinte trinité," *Chimères: Revue des Schizoanalyses,* no. 69 (2008), 33-45.

GG4524. Schérer, René: "Etre ailleurs," *Chimères: Revue des Schizoanalyses,* no. 69 (2008), 161-171.

GG4525. Wadbled, Nathanaël: "Devons-nous être des hommes? Faire et se défaire de l'homosexualité," *Chimères: Revue des Schizoanalyses,* no. 69 (2008), 141-156.

HORIA, Vintila.

GG4526. Craciunescu, Pompiliu: *Vintila Horia: translittérature et réalité.* Veauche: L'homme indivis, 2008. 230 p.

HOUELLEBECQ, Michel. See also 1821, 6485.

GG4527. ● Houellebecq, Michel; Bernard-Henri Lévy: *Ennemis publics.* Paris: Flammarion; Grassset & Fasquelle, 2008. 332 p. [Lévy]

GG4528. ● Singh, Stephanie: *Semantik der Krise, Semantik der Zukunft: die kultursemiotische Funktion der zeitgenössischen Literatur am Beispiel der Biotechnologie.* München: Meidenbauer, 2008. 349 p.

GG4529. ● Viard, Bruno: *Houellebecq au scanner: la faute à Mai 68.* Nice: Ovadia, 2008. *Chemins de pensée.* 122 p.

GG4530. Amar, Ruth: "L'ère 'entre-deux' de Michel Houellebecq," *Lettres Romanes*, tome 61, no. 3-4 (2007), 349-356.

GG4531. Barjonet, Aurélie: "Bienifaits de la nouvelle 'littérature putride'? Le cas des *Particules élémentaires* de Michel Houellebecq et des *Bienveillantes* de Jonathan Littell," *Lendemains*, 33. Jahrgang, Heft 132 (2008), 94-108. [Littell]

GG4532. Bridet, Guillaume: "Michel Houellebecq et les montres molles," *Littérature*, no. 151 (sept. 2008), 6-20.

GG4533. Lafargue, Bernard: "Le temps des avatars virtuels." In 508, 297-310. [Sollers]

GG4534. Pröll, Julia: " 'Plus de médium, plus d'image . . .' Le remplacement du lien familial par le clonage dans l'œuvre de Michel Houellebecq: une possibilité de survie?" In 571, 217-226.

GG4535. Roy, Patrick: "Une étrange lumière: la déchirure lyrique dans l'œuvre de Michel Houellebecq." Diss., Univ. Laval, 2008. viii, 277 p.

GG4536. Stemberger, Martina: "(Des-)Illusionen: Skepsis und Stereotypie in Michel Houellebecqs *Extension du domaine de la lutte*," *Romanistische Forschungen*, 120. Band, Heft 2 (2008), 190-200.

GG4537. van Wesemael, Sabine: "Obscénités en littérature: le cas Houellebecq." In 543, 187-201.

HUGNET, Georges. See 1061.

HUSTON, Nancy. See also 183, 888, 1775, 3719.

GG4538. Averis, Kate: "Le 'vrai' moi: Nancy Huston's concern for authenticity," *Essays in French Literature and Culture*, no. 45 (Nov. 2008), 1-18.

GG4539. Daniélou, Catherine: "Nancy Huston ou le 'théâtre de l'exil'." In 119, 319-341.

GG4540. Holmes, Diana: "Ecrire est un verbe transitif: les voix narratives de Nancy Huston." In 539, 83-91.

GG4541. Martens-Okada, Mihoko: "Le roman familial de Nancy Huston. La relation problématique: la fille abandonnée et la mère coupable." In 571, 107-116.

GG4542. Robson, Kathryn: "From beneath the skin: rape and testimony in Nancy Huston's *Histoire d'Omaya*." In 610, 113-127.

GG4543. Tremblay, Mylène: "Le corps, espace-limite entre la jouissance et la vie, l'extatique et l'esthétique dans *La Virevolte* de Nancy Huston et *Cet imperceptible mouvement* d'Aude." In 69, 85-98. [Aude]

HUYSMANS, Joris-Karl. See also 420, 621, 670, 719, 724, 763, 2089, 2213, 4265, 4310, 4320, 5379.

GG4544. ● Huysmans, Joris-Karl: *Against nature.* Trans. with an introduction and notes by Brendan King. Sawtry: Dedalus, 2008. 315 p.

GG4545. ● Huysmans, Joris-Karl: *Ecrits sur l'art.* Prés., notes, chronologie, bibliographie et index par Jérôme Picon. Paris: Flammarion, 2008. *GF.* 476 p.

GG4546. ● Huysmans, Joris-Karl: *Gegen den Strich.* Aus dem Franz. von Brigitta Restorff. Mit einem Nachwort von Ulla Momm. Düsseldorf: Artemis & Winkler, 2008. 251 p.

GG4547. ● Johnstone, Maren: *Desiring Salome: men's fear of power-thieving women.* Saarbrücken: VDM, 2008. 60 p.

GG4548. ● Prigent, Gaël: *Huysmans et la Bible.* Paris: Champion, 2008. *Romantisme et modernités*, 112. 888 p.

GG4549. ● Sicotte, Geneviève: *Le festin lu: le repas chez Flaubert, Zola et Huysmans.* Montréal: Liber, 2008. 325 p. [Zola]

GG4550. ● Solal, Jérôme: *Huysmans et l'homme de la fin.* Caen: Lettres modernes Minard, 2008. *La thèsothèque.* 391 p.

GG4551. Amadieu, Jean-Baptiste; Philippe Barascud: "Huysmans et l'affaire de l'Index, 1898-1899," *Bulletin de la Société J.-K. Huysmans*, no. 100 (2007), 111-148.

GG4552. Barascud, Philippe: "Célébration du centenaire," *Bulletin de la Société J.-K. Huysmans*, no. 100 (2007), 149-157.

GG4553.   Barascud, Philippe: "Huysmans à Saint-Germain-l'Auxerrois," *Bulletin de la Société J.-K. Huysmans*, no. 101 (2008), 87-92.

GG4554.   Barascud, Philippe; Olivier Bivort: " 'M. de Régnier contre J.-K. Huysmans," *Bulletin de la Société J.-K. Huysmans*, no. 100 (2007), 51-63. [Régnier]

GG4555.   Blanchot, Maurice: "Le secret de J.-K. Huysmans," *Bulletin de la Société J.-K. Huysmans*, no. 100 (2007), 103-107.

GG4556.   Dirda, Michel: "J. K. Huysmans." In 430.

GG4557.   Domínguez González, Francisco: "Dandismo y misoginia de Huysmans," *Cuadernos de Filologia Francesa*, no. 19 (2008), 301-319.

GG4558.   Fox, Paul: "Dickens à la carte: aesthetic victualism and the invogoration of the artist in Huysmans's *Against Nature.*" In 381, 62-75.

GG4559.   Giné, Marta: "Huysmans dans le *Journal* de Ricardo Viñes," *Bulletin de la Société J.-K. Huysmans*, no. 101 (2008), 79-86.

GG4560.   Grigorian, Natasha: "Dreams, nightmares, and lunacy in *En rade*," *Comparative Critical Studies*, vol. 5, no. 2-3 (2008), 221-233.

GG4561.   Grojnowski, Daniel: "J.-K. Huysmans et la nouvelle," *Revue d'Histoire Littéraire de la France*, tome 108, no. 4 (oct.-déc. 2008), 849-861.

GG4562.   Guérin, Stéphanie: "L'intimisme au cœur de la poétique de Huysmans," *Bulletin de la Société J.-K. Huysmans*, no. 101 (2008), 45-54.

GG4563.   Guglielmi, Francesca: "Deux pèlerins: Huysmans à la trappe, Loti à Jérusalem," *Bulletin de la Société J.-K. Huysmans*, no. 101 (2008), 55-78. [Loti]

GG4564.   Huysmans, J.-K.: "Lettres à Henri de Régnier, 1885-1890," *Bulletin de la Société J.-K. Huysmans*, no. 100 (2007), 45-50. [Régnier]

GG4565.   Jourde, Pierre: "Le bon objet," *Bulletin de la Société J.-K. Huysmans*, no. 100 (2007), 3-21.

GG4566.   Landuydt, Jan: "Huysmans lu par Lodewijk van Deyssel," *Bulletin de la Société J.-K. Huysmans*, no. 100 (2007), 87-102.

GG4567.   Medrano Dorantes, Ana Maria: "La dualidad artístico personal de Joris-Karl Huysmans en *Certains*," *Thélème*, no. 23 (2008), 87-100.

GG4568.   Pety, Dominique: "Huysmans et la collection," *Bulletin de la Société J.-K. Huysmans*, no. 101 (2008), 17-44.

GG4569.   Redfern, Walter: "Huysmans: back-to-front, and backpacking." In 568.

GG4570.   Régnier, Henri de: "Textes sur Huysmans, 1886-1934," *Bulletin de la Société J.-K. Huysmans*, no. 100 (2007), 23-44.

GG4571.   Reverzy, Eléonore: "Huysmans lecteur de Michelet." In 459, 103-113.

GG4572.   Reverzy, Eléonore: "Huysmans: métapsychologie," *Ritm*, no. 38 (2007), 337-348.

GG4573.   Smeets, Marc "Osmazômes (Huysmans)," *Nineteenth-Century French Studies*, vol. 37, no. 1-2 (Fall-Winter 2008-2009), 97-107.

GG4574.   Solal, Jérôme: "Le Huysmans de Maurice Blanchot," *Bulletin de la Société J.-K. Huysmans*, no. 100 (2007), 108-110. [Blanchot]

GG4575.   Traire, Sylvie: "Corps et graphie: la conversion selon J. K. Huysmans," *Manchette*, no. 3 (2004), 241-268.

GG4576.   Valazza, Nicolas: "Fleurs pour des Esseintes," *Bulletin de la Société J.-K. Huysmans*, no. 101 (2008), 3-16.

GG4577.   Van Deyssel, Lodewijk: "Trois comptes rendus (1891, 1895, 1898)," *Bulletin de la Société J.-K. Huysmans*, no. 100 (2007), 65-85.

GG4578.   Walbecq, Eric: "Huysmans chez les libraires," *Bulletin de la Société J.-K. Huysmans*, no. 100 (2007), 159-168.

GG4579.   Ziegler, Robert: "The climb into dream and the fall into meaning: Huysmans's *En rade*," *Excavatio*, vol. 23, no. 1-2 (2008), 61-73.

HYVERNAUD, Georges.

GG4580.   Farasse, Gérard: "De l'inconvénient d'être mou." In 454, 137-144.

HYVRARD, Jeanne.

GG4581.   Vassallo, Helen: "Metaphors of dis(-)ease: malady and malaise in Jeanne Hyvrard's *Les Prunes de Cythère* and *Le Cercan*." In 573, 133-144.

GG4582. Wardle, Cathy: "Controlling the female body: medicine, technology and maternity in the work of Jeanne Hyvrard." In 573, 145-161.

IMACHE, Tassadit. See 1817.

IONESCO, Eugène. See also 4371, 4939.

GG4583. ● Haskell, Stephen: *Rhinoceros: Eugène Ionesco.* Updated and revised by Adam Kissel. Cambridge, MA: GradeSaver, 2008. 64 p.

GG4584. ● Ionesco, Eugène: *Jacques ou la soumission; L'avenir est dans les œufs.* Edition prés., établie et annotée par Marie-Claude Hubert. Paris: Gallimard, 2008. *Folio Théâtre.* 160 p.

GG4585. ● Mitroi, Anca; Scott Sprenger; Brant Stewart: *Bibliographie Eugène Ionesco.* Bucuresti: Editura Univ. din Bucuresti, 2008. xxi, 296 p.

GG4586. Bénard, Johanne: "Les accommodements de la raison. *Rhinocéros*," *Jeu: Cahiers de Théâtre,* no. 127 [no. 2] (2008), 42-47.

GG4587. Fromilhague, Catherine: "Les didascalies dans le théâtre de Ionesco: un espace de liberté auctoriale?" In 605, 435-449.

GG4588. Guérin, Jeanyves: "Les jeux du temps et le procès de l'histoire dans *Macbett* d'Eugène Ionesco." In 459, 307-318.

GG4589. Haney, William S., II: "Eugène Ionesco's *Rhinoceros*: defiance vs. conformism," *Interactions: Ege University Journal of British and American Studies,* vol. 17, no. 1 (Spring 2008), 85-101.

GG4590. Jongy, Béatrice: "Le journal de la vieillesse: la voie du salut? Etude de *La Quête intermittente* d'Eugène Ionesco." In 379, 39-53.

GG4591. Negro, Francesca: "La maison vivante: voyage architectural à travers les œuvres d'Eugène Ionesco," *Voix Plurielles,* vol. 5, no. 1 (mai 2008), [n.p.].

GG4592. "*Rhinoceros*, Eugène Ionesco." In 1083.

GG4593. Sangsue, Daniel: "Parodie et satire: l'exemple de *Macbett* d'Eugène Ionesco," *Modernités,* no. 27 (2008), 349-364.

IRIGARAY, Luce. See also 955, 2725, 5837, 5869.

GG4594. ● Bainbridge, Caroline: *A feminine cinematics: Luce Irigaray, women and film.* Basingstoke; New York: Palgrave Macmillan, 2008. ix, 223 p.

GG4595. ● *French feminists: critical evaluations in cultural theory. Vol. III: Luce Irigaray.* Ed. Jennifer Hansen, Ann Cahill. London; New York: Routledge, 2008. xi, 428 p.

GG4596. ● Gray, Frances: *Jung, Irigaray, individuation: philosophy, analytical psychology, and the question of the feminine.* London; New York: Routledge, 2008. xii, 188 p.

GG4597. ● Irigaray, Luce: *Conversations.* With Stephen Pluhécek [et al.]. London; New York: Continuum, 2008. xii, 188 p.

GG4598. ● *Luce Irigaray: teaching.* Ed. Luce Irigaray with Mary Green. London; New York: Continuum, 2008. xi, 285 p.

GG4599. Burke, Carolyn: "Irigaray through the looking glass." In 4595.

GG4600. Butler, Judith: "Bodies that matter." In 4595.

GG4601. Caldwell, Anne: "Transforming sacrifice: Irigaray and the politics of sexual difference." In 4595.

GG4602. Chisholm, Dianne: "Irigaray's hysteria." In 4595.

GG4603. Cornell, Drucilla: "Adoption and its progeny." In 4595.

GG4604. Deutscher, Penelope: "*Between East and West* and the politics of 'cultural ingénuité'." In 4595.

GG4605. Deutscher, Penelope: "Irigaray anxiety." In 4595.

GG4606. Deutscher, Penelope: "Recastings: on Alison Stone's *Luce Irigaray and the Philosophy of Sexual Difference*," *Differences,* vol. 19, no. 3 (Fall 2008), 139-149.

GG4607. Fuss, Diana J.: " 'Essentially speaking': Luce Irigaray's language of essence." In 4595.

GG4608. Gallop, Jane: "*Quand nos lèvres s'écrivent*: Irigaray's body politic." In 4595.

GG4609. Green, Mary: "The maternal order read through Luce Irigaray in the work of Diamela Eltit." In 4598, 93-102.

GG4610. Grosz, Elizabeth: "The hetero and the homo: the sexual ethics of Luce Irigaray." In 4595.

GG4611. Harrington, Laine M.: "On rivers, words and becoming an other: the importance of style in Luce Irigaray's work." In 4598, 181-188.

GG4612. Hill, Rebecca: "Interval, sexual difference: Luce Irigaray and Henri Bergson," *Hypatia*, vol. 23, no. 1 (Winter 2008), [n.p.]. [Bergson]

GG4613. Hope, Trevor: "Sexual indifference and the homosexual male imaginary." In 4595.

GG4614. Jones, Serene: "Divining women: Irigaray and feminist theologies." In 4595.

GG4615. Khader, Serene J.: "When equality justifies women's subjection: Luce Irigaray's critique of equality and the fathers' rights movement," *Hypatia*, vol. 23, no. 4 (Fall 2008), [n.p.].

GG4616. Landes, Donald A.: "Expression and speaking-*with* in the work of Luce Irigaray." In 4598, 169-180.

GG4617. Mader, Mary Beth: "Somatic ontology: comments on Alison Stone's *Luce Irigaray and the Philosophy of Sexual Difference*," *Differences*, vol. 19, no. 3 (Fall 2008), 126-138.

GG4618. Markotic, Lorraine: "The object of desire speaks: Ingeborg Bachmann's 'Undine geht' and Luce Irigaray's 'Woman'," *German Life and Letters*, vol. 61, no. 2 (April 2008), 231-243.

GG4619. Moi, Toril: "Patriarchal reflections: Luce Irigaray's looking-glass." In 4595.

GG4620. Plaza, Monique: " 'Phallomorphic power' and the psychology of 'woman'." In 4595.

GG4621. Poe, Danielle: "Replacing just war theory with an ethics of sexual difference," *Hypatia*, vol. 23, no. 2 (Spring 2008), [n.p.].

GG4622. Poxon, Judith L.: "Corporeality and divinity: Irigaray and the problem of the ideal." In 4595.

GG4623. Schor, Naomi: "This essentialism which is not one: coming to grips with Irigaray." In 4595.

GG4624. Shukla, B. A.: "Luce Irigaray and French feminism." In 1500.

GG4625. Shukla, B. A.: "Luce Irigaray on 'The nation of sexuality'." In 1500.

GG4626. Stephenson, Katherine: "A dialogics and ethics of love: Luce Irigaray's *The way of love*," *Women in French Studies* (2008), 135-143.

GG4627. Stone, Alison: "The sex of nature: a reinterpretation of Irigaray's metaphysics and political thought." In 4595.

GG4628. Stone, Alison: "Unthought nature: reply to Penelope Deutscher and Mary Beth Mader," *Differences*, vol. 19, no. 3 (Fall 2008), 150-157.

GG4629. Weir, Allison: "The subversion of identity: Luce Irigaray and the critique of phallogocentrism." In 4595.

GG4630. Wheeler, Andrea: "Architectural issues in building community through Luce Irigaray's perspective on being-two." In 4598, 61-68.

GG4631. Whitford, Margaret: "Irigaray's body symbolic." In 4595.

GG4632. Whitford, Margaret: "Rereading Irigaray." In 4595.

GG4633. Xu, Ping: "Irigaray's mimicry and the problem of essentialism." In 4595.

GG4634. Zaplana, Esther: "Music and the voice of the other: an engagement with Irigaray's thinking and feminine artistic musical performance." In 4598, 39-49.

ISOU, Isidore.

GG4635. Sabatier, Robert: "Isidore Isou: la problématique du dépassement," *Mélusine*, no. 28 (2008), 47-58.

ISTRATI, Panaït.

GG4636. ● *Deux migrants de l'écriture: Panaït Istrati et Felicia Mihali*. A cura di Gisèle Vanhese. Rende: Univ. della Calabria, 2008. 349 p.

GG4637. ● Vasilescu, Diane: *Panaït Istrati: images d'Orient*. Nice: Vaillant, 2008. 205 p.

GG4638. Schaffner, Alain: "Quelques images du militant et de l'action politique chez Panaït Istrati." In 456, 127-135.

JABÈS, Edmond. See also 633, 6567.

GG4639. Benoît, Eric: "Dans l'aporie du comment dire," *Modernités*, no. 29 (2008), 389-406.

GG4640. Israel-Pelletier, Aimée: "Edmond Jabès, Jacques Hassoun, and melancholy: the second exodus in the shadow of the Holocaust," *Modern Language Notes*, vol. 123, no. 4 (Sept. 2008), 797-818.

GG4641. Marchetti, Adriano: "Edmond Jabès et l'errance de la parole." In 502.

GG4642. Rothenberg, Jerome: "Edmond Jabès's return to the book." In 581.

JACCOTTET, Philippe. See also 657, 1012, 1019.

GG4643. ● Iakoubovitch, Maria: *Ossip Mandelstam, Paul Célan, Philippe Jaccottet: trois poètes-traducteurs, leurs positions historiques et leurs interférences.* Lille: ANRT, 2008. *Thèse à la carte.* 588 p.

GG4644. ● Jaccottet, Philippe: *Jaccottet traducteur d'Ungaretti: correspondance 1946-1970.* Edition établie, annotée et prés. par José-Flore Tappy. Paris: Gallimard, 2008. *Les cahiers de la NRF.* 245 p.

GG4645. ● Monte, Michèle; André Bellatorre: *Le printemps du temps: poétiques croisées de Francis Ponge et Philippe Jaccottet.* Aix-en-Provence: Publications de l'Univ. de Provence, 2008. *Textuelles.* 350 p. [Ponge]

GG4646. ● Née, Patrick: *Philippe Jaccottet: à la lumière d'ici.* Paris: Hermann, 2008. 419 p.

GG4647. Campion, Pierre: " 'Dieu perdu dans l'herbe'. L'expérience du sacré chez Philippe Jaccottet," *Travaux de Littérature*, tome 21 (2008), 489-500.

GG4648. Farasse, Gérard: "Navette." In 454, 161-175.

GG4649. Frölicher, Peter: "La métaphore *in fieri*: acte discursif et expérience esthétique dans quelques textes de Philippe Jaccottet." In 550, 27-38.

GG4650. Lebrat, Isabelle: " 'Rien q'une note ou deux': l'art du peu dans les poèmes 'A Henry Purcell' de Philippe Jaccottet." In 382, 341-351.

GG4651. Palamara, Enza: "Philippe Jaccottet-Giorgio Morandi: 'le croisement de deux clairs regards'." In 382, 453-466.

JACOB, Max. See also 623, 5531.

GG4652. ● Pédron, François: *Max Jacob, le fou de Dieu.* Paris: Belle Gabrielle, 2008. *La légende de Montmartre.* 127 p.

GG4653. Bédu, Jean-Jacques: "Max Jacob, personnage de roman dans l'œuvre de Francis Carco," *Cahiers Max Jacob*, no. 8 (2008), 51-62. [Carco]

GG4654. Germain, Alain: "Jean Follain et Max Jacob en correspondance," *Cahiers Max Jacob*, no. 8 (2008), 93-98. [Follain]

GG4655. Gojard, Jacqueline: "Septime Febur alias Max Jacob dans *La Négresse du Sacré-Cœur* d'André Salmon," *Cahiers Max Jacob*, no. 8 (2008), 41-50. [Salmon]

GG4656. Hirsch, Yaël: "L'ambivalence figure de Max Jacob chez Maurice Sachs," *Cahiers Max Jacob*, no. 8 (2008), 63-76. [Sachs]

GG4657. Mousli, Béatrice: "Maxime Lévy, apôtre ou martyr," *Cahiers Max Jacob*, no. 8 (2008), 11-24. [Soupault]

GG4658. Pelletier, Christian: "Max Jacob sous le signe de l'amitié," *Cahiers Max Jacob*, no. 8 (2008), 109-116.

GG4659. Rodriguez, Antonio: "La vie dans les romans à clés: les figurations de Max Jacob et la cohérence d'un genre," *Cahiers Max Jacob*, no. 8 (2008), 77-90.

GG4660. Sibilio, Elisabetta: "Max Jacob e 'l'art romanesque'," *Confronto Letterario*, anno 23, n. 2 [n. 47] (2007), 159-170.

GG4661. Sustrac, Patricia: "Max Jacob, un personnage romanesque?," *Cahiers Max Jacob*, no. 8 (2008), 3-8.

GG4662. Tudal, Antoine: "J'avais douze ans, Max Jacob," *Cahiers Max Jacob*, no. 8 (2008), 103-107.

GG4663. Vassevière, Maryse: "Le fantôme de Max Jacob dans *Anicet ou le Panorama* de Louis Aragon," *Cahiers Max Jacob*, no. 8 (2008), 25-40. [Aragon]

JACOB, Suzanne.

GG4664. Eibl, Doris G.: "*Fugueuses* de Suzanne Jacob." In 41, 157-178.

GG4665. Eibl, Doris G.: "Maternal filiation and 'métissage' in Suzanne Jacob's novels." In 121.

JAMMES, Francis.

GG4666. • Démolin, Claire: *Francis Jammes: une initiation à la simplicité.* Paris: Editions du Cygne, 2008. 150 p.

GG4667. Barthe, Claude: "Francis Jammes: Lourdes, où le ciel se rend familier," *Travaux de Littérature,* tome 21 (2008), 383-390.

GG4668. Henriot, Emile: "L'ami de Clara d'Ellébeuse," *Bulletin de l'Association Francis Jammes,* no. 47 (2008), 49-56.

GG4669. Jammes, Geneviève: "La maladie et la mort du poète," *Bulletin de l'Association Francis Jammes,* no. 47 (2008), 7-28.

GG4670. Zabalo, abbé Joseph: "Le roman du rossignol," *Bulletin de l'Association Francis Jammes,* no. 47 (2008), 61-76.

JARRY, Alfred. See also 468.

GG4671. • *Alfred Jarry et la culture tchèque.* Ed. Mariana Kunesová. Ostrave: Ostravská univerzita, 2008. 343 p.

GG4672. • *Alfred Jarry lu par les livreurs: livre & CD audio.* Sous la dir. de Pierre Jourde. Apt: Archange Minotaure, 2008. 28 p.

GG4673. • Jarry, Alfred: *Ubu roi.* Notes, prés. et appareil pédagogiques préparés par Annie Rousseau et Marie-Eve St-Denis. Mont-Royal, Québec: Groupe Modulo, 2008.

GG4674. • Pascarel, Barbara: *Barbara Pascarel commente Ubu roi, Ubu cocu, Ubu enchaîné, Ubu sur la butte d'Alfred Jarry.* Paris: Gallimard, 2008. *Foliothèque.* 257 p.

GG4675. • Rachilde: *Alfred Jarry: le surmâle de lettres.* Prés. Edith Silve. Paris: Arléa, 2008. 172 p. [Rachilde]

GG4676. Bailly, Jean-Louis: "Jarry et la 'Pataphysique," *303: Arts, Recherches, Créations,* no. 95 (2007), 30-39.

GG4677. Beaume, Diana: "Le Père Ubu comme exercice d'admiration ou le devoir de liberté," *Etoile-Absinthe,* no. 119-120 (2008), 75-81.

GG4678. Béhar, Henri: "Alfred Jarry, homme de lettres," *303: Arts, Recherches, Créations,* no. 95 (2007), 6-21.

GG4679. Besnier, Patrick: "Alfred Jarry, Alain Jans et les pains d'épice." In 418, 157-166.

GG4680. Chevrier, Alain: "Des vers cachés dans *L'Amour en visites*: prose rythmiée et prose rimée chez Jarry," *Etoile-Absinthe,* no. 119-120 (2008), 63-74.

GG4681. Fresneau, Estelle: "Hommage à Gauguin," *303: Arts, Recherches, Créations,* no. 95 (2007), 52-63.

GG4682. Gonzalez Menendez, Maria: "Le rôle de l'illustration dans l'œuvre de Jarry et son héreitage dans l'art," *303: Arts, Recherches, Créations,* no. 95 (2007), 40-51.

GG4683. Hartigan, Ryan: " 'They watch me as they watch this': Alfred Jarry, symbolism and self-as-performance in fin-de-siècle Paris," *Australasian Drama Studies,* no. 52 (April 2008), 165-179.

GG4684. Krzywkowski, Isabelle: "Catalogue centenairique perpétuel," *Etoile-Absinthe,* no. 119-120 (2008), 7-60.

GG4685. Michaud, Olivier: "Comment Laval célèbre Alfred Jarry," *303: Arts, Recherches, Créations,* no. 95 (2007), 22-29.

GG4686. Richards, Shaun: "Synge and the 'savage God'," *Etudes Irlandaises,* vol. 33, no. 2 (automne 2008), 21-30.

GG4687. Schuh, Julien: "Alfred Jarry lecteur de Marco Polo," *Etoile-Absinthe,* no. 119-120 (2008), 83-99.

GG4688. Schuh, Julien: "Articles non réportoriés sur les premières représentations d'*Ubu roi*," *Etoile-Absinthe,* no. 119-120 (2008), 101-105.

GG4689. Schuh, Julien: "Jarry le jeune Daim." In 4290, 143-158.

GG4690. Stas, André; Marc Ways: "Des collections de Marc Ways le 'patagité du bocal'," *303: Arts, Recherches, Créations,* no. 95 (2007), 86-91.

GG4691. Taylor, Michael R.: "The regenerative legacy of Alfred Jarry's *Ubu roi*." In 856.

JAUFFRET, Régis.

GG4692. Mura-Brunel, Aline: "La défaite du processus de défection dans *Les Jeux de plage* de Régis Jauffret." In 902, 241-256.

JAURÈS, Jean.

GG4693. • Jaurès, Jean: *Studies in socialism.* Introd. J. E. Mortimer, Leon Trotsky, J. Ramsay MacDonald. Nottingham: Spokesman, 2008. *Socialist classics.* xvi, 174 p.

GG4694. • Lemke, Matthias: *Repulikanischer Sozialismus: Positionen von Bernstein, Kautsky, Jaurès und Blum.* Frankfurt: Campus Verlag, 2008. *Campus Forschung*, Band 932. 433 p.

GG4695. • Rioux, Jean-Pierre: *Jean Jaurès.* Paris: Perrin, 2008. *Tempus.* 326 p.

JOLICŒUR, Louis.

GG4696. Chassay, Jean-François: *"Le siège du Maure* de Louis Jolicœur." In 41, 179-197.

JOUHANDEAU, Marcel.

GG4697. Dupont, Jacques: "Jouhandeau: pouvuoirs et puissances du mal," *Modernités*, no. 29 (2008), 261-275.

JOUVE, Pierre Jean. See also 420, 1009, 1017.

GG4698. • Bonhomme, Béatrice: *Pierre Jean Jouve: la quête intérieure.* Croissy-Beaubourg: Aden, 2008. *Le cercle des poètes disparus.* 458 p.

GG4699. • *Pierre Jean Jouve: voyage au bout de la psyché.* Dir. Gilles Haéri. Paris: Flammarion, 2008. *Atelier du Roman*, no. 56. 235 p.

GG4700. • Sable, Lauriane: *Pierre Jean Jouve, une poétique du secret: étude de Paulina 1880.* Paris: L'Harmattan, 2008. *Structures et pouvoirs des imaginaires.* 124 p.

GG4701. Boileau, Rose: "Le blanc dans l'œuvre de Pierre Jean Jouve." In 393, 45-52.

JULIA, Lucie. See 117.

JULIET, Charles. See also 2831.

GG4702. • *Attentivement Charles Juliet: lettres d'ami(e)s.* Réunies par Marie-Thérèse Peyrin. Lyon: J. André, 2008. 217 p.

GG4703. Juliet, Charles: "Entretien," *Croquant*, no. 59-60 (2008), 156-161.

GG4704. Ni Mhainnin, Máire-Aine: "Charles Juliet: écrire pour agandir l'espace intérieur." In 618.

JUMINER, Bertène.

GG4705. Olivencia, Rodrigo: "La représentation de la bâtardise chez Bertène Juminer: genèse d'une double prise de conscience," *Nouvelles Etudes Francophones*, vol. 23, no. 2 (automne 2008), 44-54.

KACIMI EL-HASSANI, Mohammed.

GG4706. Kacimi el-Hassani, Mohammed: "Entretien." In 431, 189-195.

KADEL, Yusuf.

GG4707. Makhélé, Caya: "Yusuf Kadel, au cœur d'une parole révélatrice de soi," *Cultures Sud*, no. 170 (sept. 2008), 75-80.

KANE, Cheikh Hamidou. See also 149, 227.

GG4708. Brambilla, Cristina: "Les 'Gardiens du Temple' ou le roman de la Négritude." In 72, 411-420.

GG4709. Gbanou, Sélom Komlan: "L' 'aventure ambiguë' de l'identitaire: la fortune du personnage de Samba Diallo." In 103, 251-264.

GG4710. Meka Obam, Jean Marcel: *La structure symbolique dans "L'Aventure ambiguë" et "Le monde s'effondre".* Paris: L'Harmattan, 2008. *Littératures et savoirs.* 84 p.

GG4711. Nyemb, Elise Nathalie: *L'Afrique et l'Europe dans l'œuvre de Cheikh Hamidou Kane.* Stuttgart: Ibidem, 2008. 83 p.

GG4712. Wehrs, Donald R.: "Islamic ethics, anticolonialism, and the perils of mdernity and its repudiation: Cheikh Hamidou Kane's *L'Aventure ambiguë*." In 142.

KAPLAN, Leslie.

GG4713. Lasserre, Audrey: "Les prostituées philosophes de Leslie Kaplan ou les pratiques transgressives d'une pensée nomade." In 539, 121-135.

KAPLAN, Nelly.

GG4714. • Kaplan, Nelly; Abel Gance: *Et Pandore en avait deux!: roman; Mon cygne, mon signe (correspondances Abel Gance-Nelly Kaplan).* Monaco: Rocher, 2008. 84, 64 p.

KARCH, Pierre Paul. See 324.

KARONE, Yodi.

GG4715. Ndinda, Joseph: *"A la recherche du cannibale amour* de Yodi Karone: écrivain, création et folie." In 99, 43-58.

KATTAN, Naïm.

GG4716. Matic, Ljiljana: "Naïm Kattan écrivain de passage et passeur de cultures." In 115, 228-238.

KEMEID, Olivier.

GG4717. Bourdages, Etienne: "Les fées sont ivres. *Bacchanale*," *Jeu: Cahiers de Théâtre*, no. 128 [no. 3] (2008), 18-22.

GG4718. Olivier, Aurélie: "Nous sommes tous des exilés. *L'Enéide*," *Jeu: Cahiers de Théâtre*, no. 127 [no. 2] (2008), 31-34.

KESSEL, Joseph.

GG4719. ● *Entretiens avec Joseph Kessel: un témoin inspiré.* Carouge-Genève: Zoé, 2008.

GG4720. ● Eyriès, Alexandre: *L'imaginaire de la guerre dans l'œuvre de Joseph Kessel.* Paris: Manuscrit, 2008. *Essais et documents.* 289 p.

GG4721. ● Kessel, Joseph: *Ami, entends-tu?.* Propos recueillis par Jean-Marie Baron; lettre-préface de Maurice Druon. Paris: Gallimard, 2008. *Folio.* 346 p.

GG4722. Laurent, Thierry: "Joseph Kessel (1898-1979)." In 442, 77-83.

GG4723. Ozwald, Thierry: "*Le Lion* de Joseph Kessel, roman éthologique, roman ethnologique," *Roman 20-50*, no. 45 (2008), 123-133.

GG4724. Tassel, Alain: "Poétique du reportage dans *Témoin parmi les hommes* (1956-1969) de Joseph Kessel," *Revue d'Histoire Littéraire de la France*, tome 108, no. 4 (oct.-déc. 2008), 913-929.

KHADRA, Yasmina. See also 230.

GG4725. Baffet, Roselyne: "Larvatus prodeo: qu'arrive-t-il lorsqu'un écrivain, Yasmina Khadra, retire un masque?" In 441, 75-85.

GG4726. Chemla, Yves: " 'Je suis incapable d'imaginer l'Afrique'. Entretien avec Yasmina Khadra," *Cultures Sud*, no. 169 (avril-juin 2008), 63-67.

GG4727. Chossat, Michèle: "A quoi rêvent les loups?: de l'animal et de l'humain selon Khadra." In 617, 143-151.

GG4728. Garand, Dominique: "Que peut la fiction? Yasmina Khadra, le terrorisme et le conflit israélo-palestinien," *Etudes Françaises*, vol. 44, no. 1 (2008), 37-56.

KHAÏR-EDDINE, Mohammed. See 5560.

KHATIBI, Abdelkébir. See also 332.

GG4729. ● Khkatibi, Abdelkébir: *Œuvres de Abdelkébir Khatibi.* Paris: Editions de la Différence, 2008. 3 vols. Avec des textes de Jacques Derrida, Marc Gontard, Roland Barthes.

GG4730. El Nossery, Névine: "Hybridité textuelle chez Abdelkébir Khatibi et Assia Djebar," *Expressions Maghrébines*, vol. 7, no. 2 (hiver 2008), 187-203. [Djebar]

GG4731. Kamara, Mohamed: "The use of palimpsest in Abdelkébir Khatibi's *La mémoire tatouée.*" In 43, 332-346.

GG4732. Khatibi, Abdelkébir: Interface avec Jacques; Derrida on Khatibi," *CELAAN*, vol. 6, no. 3 (Fall 2008), 119-123.

GG4733. Shereen, Faiza: "Host and guest in Khatibi's language," *CELAAN*, vol. 6, no. 3 (Fall 2008), 96-102.

GG4734. Siassi, Guilan: "Dreaming the body into words: translating affect between cultures in Khatibi's *Amour bilingue*," *Yearbook of Comparative and General Literature*, vol. 53 (2007), 169-175.

KHOURY-GHATA, Vénus.

GG4735. Darwiche Jabbour, Zahida: "Réception et stratégies d'écriture dans *Le Moine, l'ottoman et la femme du grand argentier* de Vénus Khoury-Ghata," *Interculturel Francophonies*, no. 14 (2008), 51-63.

GG4736. Brunel, Pierre: "Une heure avec Vénus Khoury-Ghata: entretien." In 61, 63-73.

GG4737. Khoury-Ghata, Vénus: "Nomadisme littéraire." In 539, 17-18.

KLAT, Yasmine. See 226.

KLÉBANER, Daniel.
GG4738. Dupouy, Christine: "Daniel Klébaner, entre baroque et art du peu." In 382, 23-40.

KLOSSOWSKI, Pierre. See also 2039.
GG4739. ● Abad Cuesta, José Manuel: *Clausuras de Pierre Klossowski.* Madrid: Circulo de Bellas Artes de Madrid, 2008. 128 p.
GG4740. ● Klossowski, Pierre: *Unter dem Diktat des Bildes . . . ein Gespräch mit Rémy Zaugg.* Hrsg. Horst Ebner und Walter Seitter. Wien: Turia + Kant, 2008. 157 p.
GG4741. ● *Pierre Klossowski.* Paris: Inculte, 2006. *Collectif-essai.* 220 p.
GG4742. Amstutz, Patrick: "Le bain chrétien de Diane ou les enjeux d'un paratexte ambigu." In 520, 247-260.
GG4743. Tremblay, Thierry: "Métamorphose, tropologie et anagogie: à propos du *Bain de Diane* de Pierre Klossowski." In 520, 643-653.

KOFMAN, Sarah.
GG4744. ● *Sarah Kofman's corpus.* Ed. Tina Chanter and Pleshette DeArmitt. Albany: SUNY Press, 2008. *SUNY series in gender theory.* vii, 148 p.
GG4745. Clementi, Federica K.: "Re-centering the mother: Shoah autobiography in Ruth Klüger, Edith Bruck, Sarah Kofman." Diss., CUNY, 2008. xii, 250 p.
GG4746. Chanter, Tina: "Playing with fire: Kofman and Freud on being Jewish, feminine, and homosexual." In 4744.
GG4747. DeArmitt, Pleshette: "The lifework of Sarah Kofman." In 4744.
GG4748. DeArmitt, Pleshette: "Sarah Kofman's art of affirmation." In 4744.
GG4749. Deutscher, Penelope: "Becoming: devenir-femme in the work of Sarah Kofman." In 4744.
GG4750. Faulkner, Joanne: " 'Keeping it in the family': Sarah Kofman reading Nietzsche as a Jewish woman," *Hypatia*, vol. 23, no. 1 (Winter 2008), [n.p.].
GG4751. Horowitz, Sara R.: "Sarah Kofman et l'ambiguïté des mères." In 602, 101-120.
GG4752. Large, Duncan: "The question of art: Sarah Kofman's aesthetics." In 4744.
GG4753. Naas, Michael: "Fire walls: Sarah Kofman's pyrotechnics." In 4744.
GG4754. Schrift, Alan D.: "Le mépris des anti-sémites: Kofman's Nietzsche and Nietzsche's Jews." In 4744.
GG4755. Smock, Ann: "Sarah Kofman's wit." In 4744.

KOJÈVE, Alexandre.
GG4756. ● Filoni, Marco: *Il filosofo della domenica: la vita e il pensiero di Alexandre Kojève.* Torino: Bollati Boringhieri, 2008. 259 p.
GG4757. Ritter, Henning: "Alexandre Kojève." In 975.
GG4758. Vegetti, Matteo: "Stato totale, imperialismo, impero. Sul pensiero politico di Alexandre Kojève," *Rivista di Storia della Filosofia*, anno 63, no. 4 (2008), 621-651.

KOKIS, Sergio.
GG4759. Ertler, Klaus-Dieter: "Les écritures migrantes ou néo-québécoises dans le système littéraire contemporain du Québec: Sergio Kokis et 'l'amour du lointain'." In 115, 72-80.
GG4760. Ertler, Klaus-Dieter: "*La gare* de Sergio Kokis." In 41, 199-215.
GG4761. Ireland, Susan; Patrice J. Proulx: "Representations of urban space in Sergio Kokis' *Un sourire blindé* and Mauricio Segura's *Côte-des-Nègres*." In 104, 287-304. [Segura]
GG4762. Maddox, Kelly-Anne: "Espaces mémoriels, espaces identitaires." In 103, 217-227. [Lise Tremblay]
GG4763. Maindron, André: "Dans sa noirceur, le Montréal de Sergio Kokis," *Etudes Canadiennes*, no. 64 (2008), 167-173.

KOLTÈS, Bernard-Marie.
GG4764. ● *Bernard-Marie Koltès.* Lucien Attoun [et al.]. Paris: La Comédie-Française, L'Avant-Scène Théâtre, 2007. 104 p.
GG4765. Job, André: *Koltès: la rhétorique vive.* Paris: Hermann, 2008. *Savoir lettres.* 133 p.
GG4766. Patrice, Stéphane: *Koltès subversif.* Paris: Descartes & Cie, 2008. 218 p.

GG4767.   Salino, Brigitte: *Bernard-Marie Koltès*. Paris: Stock, 2008. 250 p.

GG4768.   Sandt, Nicole: *Dealer und Kunden im Theater: bei Koltès und Brecht*. Berlin: Lavallée, 2008. 2., überarb. Aufl. 145 p.

GG4769.   Job, André: "L' 'autre scène' koltésienne: paratexte, didascalie et décentrement multiple de l'énonciation." In 605, 335-349.

KOUMA, Albakaye Ousmane.

GG4770.   Chevrier, Jacques: "Les chroniques maliennes d'Albakaye Ousmane Kouma," *Cultures Sud*, no. 170 (sept. 2008), 81-86.

KOUROUMA, Ahmadou. See also 64, 206, 268, 278, 1321, 4434.

GG4771.   ● *Donsomana [Un] pour Kourouma*. Dir. Pierre Kadi Sossou, Bernadette Kass-Krécoum. Berlin: Wissenschaftlicher Verlag Berlin, 2007. 193 p.

GG4772.   Colvin, Margaret E.: " 'Cette vaste et multiple Afrique': Le périple néobaroque de Maclédio dans *En attendant le vote des bêtes sauvages*," *Nouvelles Etudes Francophones*, vol. 22, no. 2 (automne 2007), 25-33.

GG4773.   Constant, Isabelle: "*Quand on refuse on dit non*: roman du dire cruel, ou comment écrire la guerre," *Nouvelles Etudes Francophones*, vol. 22, no. 2 (automne 2007), 34-43.

GG4774.   Corcoran, Patrick: "Bâtardise de la politique: pour une critique génétique des *Soleils des indépendances*," *Francophone Postcolonial Studies*, vol. 6, no. 1 (Spring-Summer 2008), 40-61.

GG4775.   Kadi Sossou, Pierre: "En voiture avec Kourouma: pour une prospection du *road novel* africain," *Nouvelles Etudes Francophones*, vol. 22, no. 2 (automne 2007), 58-68.

GG4776.   Kassi-Krécoum, Bernadette: "Bibliographie indicative d'Ahmadou Kourouma," *Nouvelles Etudes Francophones*, vol. 22, no. 2 (automne 2007), 79-92.

GG4777.   Koulibaly, Adama: "*Allah n'est pas obligé*, ou la parole injurieuse," *Nouvelles Etudes Francophones*, vol. 22, no. 2 (automne 2007), 11-24.

GG4778.   Lemoine, Geneviève: "L'écriture comme reconfiguration identitaire: la mémoire polyphonique dans *Monnè, outrages et défis* d'Ahmadou Kourouma." In 103, 61-71.

GG4779.   Lievois, Katrien: "*Monnè, outrages et défis*. Kourouma entre traduction et création," *Nouvelles Etudes Francophones*, vol. 22, no. 2 (automne 2007), 44-57.

GG4780.   Ndiaye, Aloyse-Raymond: "La narration et l'idée d'humanité chez Ahmadou Kourouma et Annick Kajitesi." In 533, 51-59.

GG4781.   Walsh, John: "Coming of age with an AK-47: Ahmadou Kourouma's *Allah n'est pas obligé*," *Research in African Literatures*, vol. 39, no. 1 (Spring 2008), 185-197.

GG4782.   Wehrs, Donald R.: "Political economy, cultural despair, and the crisis of the language of revolt: Kourouma's *Les soleils des indépendances*." In 142.

GG4783.   Yapo, Louis P.: "The dynamics of subversion and resistance in Ahmadou Kourouma's novels." Diss., The Univ. of Albany, 2008. vi, 192 p.

GG4784.   Zakrajsek, Katja: "Le texte postcolonial et sa traduction: l'exemple d'*Allah n'est pas obligé* traduit en slovène," *Itinéraires et Contacts de Cultures*, no. 39 (2007), 181-193.

GG4785.   Zamora, Alejandro: "Ahmadou Kourouma, ou la problématique du devoir de critique," *Nouvelles Etudes Francophones*, vol. 22, no. 2 (automne 2007), 69-78.

KRISTEVA, Julia. See also 775, 999, 2725.

GG4786.   ● Chen, Szu-chin Hestia: *French feminist theory exemplified through the novels of Julia Kristeva*. Foreword by Jeanette Den Toonder. Lewiston, NY: Edwin Mellen, 2008. iv, 317 p.

GG4787.   ● *French feminists: critical evaluations in cultural theory. Vol. IV: Julia Kristeva*. Ed. Jennifer Hansen, Ann Cahill. London; New York: Routledge, 2008. x, 439 p. [Philosophy]

GG4788.   Ahmed, Sara: "The skin of the community: affect and boundary formation." In 4744.

GG4789.   Beardsworth, Sara: "From revolution to revolt culture." In 4744.

GG4790.   Bjelic, Dusan I.: "Julia Kristeva: exile and geopolitics of the Balkans," *Slavic Studies*, vol. 67, no. 2 (Summer 2008), 364-383.

GG4791.   Boer, Roland: "Julia Kristeva, Marx and the singularity of Paul." In 961.

GG4792.   Butler, Judith: "The body politics of Julia Kristeva." In 4744.

GG4793.   Chakravorty Spivak, Gayatri: "French feminism in an international frame."
In 4744.
GG4794.   Childress, Cynthia A.: "Unwinding the double helix." Diss., Univ. of Loui-
siana at Lafayette, 2008. viii, 179 p.
GG4795.   Fraser, Nancy: "The uses and abuses of French discourse theories for femi-
nist politics." In 4744.
GG4796.   Grosz, Elizabeth: "The body of signification." In 4744.
GG4797.   Honig, Bonnie: "Ruth, the model emigrée: mourning and the symbolic poli-
tics of immigration." In 4744.
GG4798.   Jardine, Alice: "Pre-texts for the transatlantic feminist." In 4744.
GG4799.   Jones, Ann Rosalind: "Julia Kristeva on femininity." In 4744.
GG4800.   Kuykendall, Eleanor H.: "Questions for Julia Kristeva's ethics of linguis-
tics." In 4744.
GG4801.   Nye, Andrea: "Woman clothes with the sun: Julia Kristeva and the escape
from/to language." In 4744.
GG4802.   Moi, Toril: "Marginality and subversion: Julia Kristeva." In 4744.
GG4803.   Oliver, Kelly: "Julia Kristeva's feminist revolutions." In 4744.
GG4804.   Rose, Jacqueline: "Julia Kristeva: take two." In 4744.
GG4805.   Rubin Suleiman, Susan: "Writing and motherhood." In 4744.
GG4806.   Snyder, Charles: "La psychanalyse et le problème de la métaphysique: Julia
Kristeva, l'identification primaire," *Infini*, no. 104 (automne 2008), 97-110.
GG4807.   Shukla, B. A.: "Julia Kristeva and feminism." In 1500.
GG4808.   Shukla, B. A.: "Julia Kristeva and feminist theory." In 1500.
GG4809.   Shukla, B. A.: "Julia Kristeva and the female subjectivity." In 1500.
GG4810.   Ziarek, Ewa: "The uncanny style of Kristeva's critique of nationalism." In
4744.
KRISTOF, Agota. See 525.
KSIKES, Driss.
GG4811.   Zekri, Khalid: "Entre éthique et philosophie: l'écriture selon Driss Ksikes,"
Cultures Sud, no. 170 (sept. 2008), 87-92.
KUITCHE FONKOU, G.
GG4812.   Bassi, M.: "Ecriture romanesque et défi de normalisation de la langue
française." In 52, 47-60.
KURTOVITCH, Nicolas.
GG4813.   Powell, Sarah: "Perpetual motion: the search for the self and the other in
the works of Nicolas Kurtovitch," *New Zealand Journal of French Studies*, vol. 29, no. 2
(2008), 20-34.
KWAHULÉ, Koffi. See also 153a, 1108.
GG4814.   Asaah, Augustine H.: "Avant-gardisme, jeu et contre-discours dans *Baby-
face* de Koffi Kwahulé," *Lettres Romanes*, tome 61, no. 3-4 (2007), 357-366.
GG4815.   "Brothers in sound: Koffi Kwahulé and jazz. Interviews with Gilles Mouël-
lic," *Esprit Créateur*, vol. 48, no. 3 (Fall 2008), 97-108.
GG4816.   Le Guen, Fanny: "Les voix de femmes dans l'œuvre de Koffi Kwahulé,"
Esprit Créateur, vol. 48, no. 3 (Fall 2008), 119-128.
GG4817.   Mouëllic, Gilles: "*Cette vieille magie noire* de Koffi Kwahulé: un pacte avec
le jazz," *Esprit Créateur*, vol. 48, no. 3 (Fall 2008), 89-96.
GG4818.   Ngilla, Sylvie: "Frapper les rythmes, frapper les corps: dramaturgie du k.o.
chez Koffi Kwahulé et Kossi Efoui," *Esprit Créateur*, vol. 48, no. 3 (Fall 2008), 66-75.
[Efoui]
GG4819.   Soubrier, Virginie: "Une physique de la voix: réflexions sur le théâtre de
Koffi Kwahulé," *Esprit Créateur*, vol. 48, no. 3 (Fall 2008), 25-32.
KYELEM, Mathias.
GG4820.   Sanou, Salaka: "Mathias Kyelem: littérature et développement," *Cultures
Sud*, no. 170 (sept. 2008), 93-98.
LAABI, Abdellatif.
GG4821.   ● Alessandra, Jacques: *Abdellatif Laâbi: traversée de l'œuvre*. Paris: La
Différence, 2008. 184 p.

GG4822. • Babana-Hampton, Safoi: *Réflexions littéraires sur l'espace public marocain dans l'œuvre d'Abdellatif Laâbi*. Birmingham: Summa, 2008. xviii, 177 p.

LABERGE, Marie. See 249.

LABOU TANSI, Sony. See also 4357.

GG4823. Gbouablé, Edwige: "Langage du corps et voix d'auteur dans le théâtre de Sony Labou Tansi: une écriture de l'alibi," *Esprit Créateur*, vol. 48, no. 3 (Fall 2008), 17-24.

GG4824. Giguère, Caroline: "*La vie et demie* de la mémoire." In 103, 141-155.

GG4825. Ogunfolabi, Kayode Omoniyi: "History, horror, reality: the idea of the marvelous in postcolonial fiction." Diss., Michigan State Univ., 2008. vii, 217 p.

GG4826. Ojo, Philip A.: "L'esthétique de la satire et de la subversion dans *La Parenthèse de sang* de Sony Labou Tansi," *Nouvelles Etudes Francophones*, vol. 23, no. 2 (automne 2008), 208-221.

GG4827. Sperti, Valeria: "Le bouleversement des mots de *Machin la Hernie* à *L'Etat honteux*." In 423.

GG4828. Symington, Micéala: "Comparatisme, francophonie et partage: 'Faire signe à l'autre'." In 96, 29-32.

LABRÈCHE, Marie-Sissi.

GG4829. Ledoux-Beaugrand, Evelyne: "Colmater la brèche. Le corps filial dans *Borderline* de Marie-Sissi Labrèche." In 69, 99-109.

LACAN, Jacques. See also 552, 926, 932, 951, 955, 991, 996, 3203, 3210, 3533, 3622, 5859.

GG4830. • Allegretto, Manuela: *Lacan e l'amore cortese*. Roma: Carocci, 2008. 126 p.

GG4831. • Azari, Ehsan: *Lacan and the destiny of literature*. London: Continuum, 2008. *Continuum literary studies*. ix, 205 p.

GG4832. • Batour, Charbel: *How can Lacan and Vasse inform a Christian understanding of desire?*. Saarbrücken: VDM, 2008. 418 p.

GG4833. • Brivic, Shelly: *Joyce through Lacan and Zizek: explorations*. New York: Palgrave Macmillan, 2008. *New directions in Irish and Irish American literature*. xv, 267 p.

GG4834. • Calais, Vincent: *La théorie du langage dans l'enseignement de Jacques Lacan*. Préface Cyril Veken. Paris: L'Harmattan, 2008. *Sémantiques*. 187 p.

GG4835. • Cléro, Jean-Pierre: *Dictionnaire Lacan*. Paris: Ellipses, 2008. 250 p.

GG4836. • Cochet, Alain; Gilles Herlédan: *Jouissez, c'est capital: essai psychanalytique sur l'économie libinale moderne*. Paris: Sextant, 2008. 109 p.

GG4837. • Danis, Juana: *Einführung in J. Lacan*. München: Ed. Psychosymbolik, 2008. 237 p.

GG4838. • *Discursos [Los] de Lacan: seminario del Colegio de psicoanálisis de Madrid*. Madrid: Colegio de psicoanálisis de Madrid, 2007. 151 p. [Conference publication]

GG4839. • Dor, Joël: *Introdução à leitura de Lacan o inconsciente estsruturado como linguagem*. Trad. Carlos Eduardo Reis. Porto Alegre: Artmed, 2008. 203 p.

GG4840. • Duportail, Guy-Félix: *Les institutions du monde de la vie: 1. Merleau-Ponty et Lacan*. Grenoble: Millon, 2008. *Krisis*. [Merleau-Ponty]

GG4841. • *Ella Sharpe, lue par Lacan: textes choisis et commentaires*. Sous la dir. de Marie-Lise Lauth. Paris: Hermann, 2007. 199 p.

GG4842. • Faladé, Solange: *Le moi et la question du sujet: séminarie 1988-1989*. Transcrit par Emmanuel Koerner et Marie-Lise Lauth. Paris: Economica-Anthropos, 2008. viii, 278 p.

GG4843. • Geblesco, Elisabeth: *Un amour de transfert: journal de mon contrôle avec Lacan, 1974-1981*. Texte établi et prés. par Branko Aleksic. Paris: EPEL, 2008. *Des traces*. 271 p.

GG4844. • Grigg, Russell: *Lacan, language, and philosophy*. New York: SUNY Press, 2008. *Insinuations: Philosophy, Psychoanalysis, Literature*. xiv, 199 p. [Badiou]

GG4845. • Hammermeister, Kai: *Jacques Lacan*. München: Beck, 2008. 127 p.

GG4846. • Holm, Lorens: *Brunelleschi, Lacan, Le Corbusier: the architecture of the self*. London: Routledge, 2008.

GG4847. • *Jacques Lacan*. Catherine Clément [et al.]. Paris: Inculte, 2008. Réed. corrigée et augmentée. *L'Arc-Inculte*. 215 p.

GG4848. • Julien, Philippe: *La psychanalyse et le religieux: Freud, Jung, Lacan.* Paris; Cerf, 2008. 93 p.

GG4849. • Kantzá, Giuliana: *Il nome-del-padre nella psicoanalisi: Freud, Jung, Lacan.* Milano: Ares, 2008. 231 p.

GG4850. • Krutzen, Henry: *Jacques Lacan, séminaire 1952-1980: index référentiel.* 3e édition revue et augm. Paris: Economica-Anthropos, 2008. 983 p.

GG4851. • Lacan, Jacques: *The ethics of psychoanalysis, 1959-1960: the seminar of Jacques Lacan, book VII.* Ed. Jacque-Alain Miller; trans. with notes by Dennis Porter. London; New York: Routledge, 2008. ix, 422 p.

GG4852. • *Lacan in context: psychoanalysis and the politics of memory.* Taiwan: Dept. of Foreign Languages and Literatures, National Taiwan Univ., 2008. 3 vols.

GG4853. • *Lacan: Trieb und Begehren.* Hrsg. Christian Kupke. Berlin: Parodos, 2007. 269 p.

GG4854. • *Lacaniana: los seminarios de Jacques Lacan 1964-1979.* Moustapha Safouan; con la colaboración de Roland Chemama [et al]. Trad. Eva Tabakian. Buenos Aires: Paidós, 2008. 379 p.

GG4855. • Laurent, Eric: *Lost in cognition: psychanalyse et sciences cognitives.* Nantes: Cécile Defaut, 2008. *Psyché.* 136 p.

GG4856. • Levine, Steven Z.: *Lacan reframed: a guide for the arts student.* London; New York: I. B. Tauris, 2008. xvii, 150 p.

GG4857. • *Livre compagnon de l'envers de la psychanalyse: Séminaire 1969-1970 de Jacques Lacan.* Paris: Association lacanienne internationale, 2007. 254 p.

GG4858. • Louka, Jean-Michel: *De la notion au concept de transfert de Freud à Lacan.* Paris: L'Harmattan, 2008. *Psychanalyse et civilisations.* 229 p.

GG4859. • Lussier, Mark: *Blake and Lacan.* New York: Peter Lang, 2008. *Studies in nineteenth-century British literature.*

GG4860. • Melman, Charles: *La linguisterie: séminaire 1991-1993.* Paris: Association lacanienne internationale, 2008. 523 p.

GG4861. • Melman, Charles: *Trois leçons: Lacan et les anciens.* Paris: Association lacanienne internationale, 2008. *Logos.* 76 p.

GG4862. • Michaux, Ginette: *De Sophocle à Proust, de Nerval à Boulgakov: essai de psychanalyse lacanienne.* Prés. Pierre Piret. Ramonville-Saint-Agne: Erès, 2008. *Psychanalyse et écriture.* 239 p.

GG4863. • Moncayo, Raul: *Evolving Lacanian perspectives for clinical psychoanalysis.* London: Karnac, 2008. xvii, 284 p.

GG4864. • Monetti, Stefano: *Jacques Lacan e la filosofia.* Pref. Silvana Borutti. Milano: Mimesis, 2008. *Itinerari filosofici.* 230 p.

GG4865. • Porge, Erik: *Des fondements de la clinique psychanalytique.* Ramonville-Saint-Agne: Erès, 2008. 168 p.

GG4866. • Roseboro, Donyell L.: *Jacques Lacan and education: a critical introduction.* Rotterdam: Sense, 2008. *Transgressions.* ix, 103 p.

GG4867. • Schroeder, Jeanne Lorraine: *The four Lacanian discourses, or, Turning law inside-out.* Abingdon; New York: Birbeck Law Press, 2008. vi, 199 p.

GG4868. • Seifert, Edith: *Seele-Subjekt-Körper: Freud mit Lacan in Zeiten der Neurowissenschaft.* Giessen: Psychosozial-Verlag, 2008. 326 p.

GG4869. • Shepherdson, Charles: *Lacan and the limits of language.* New York: Fordham Univ. Press, 2008. xvii, 222 p.

GG4870. • Thomas, Marie-Claude: *Lacan lector de Melanie Klein.* Trad. Silvia Pasternac. México: Epeele, 2008. *Ecole lacanienne de psychanalyse.* 333 p.

GG4871. • Tribolet, Serge: *Plotin et Lacan: la question du sujet.* Paris: Beauchesne, 2008. 86 p.

GG4872. • Willemart, Philippe: *De l'inconscient en littérature.* Montréal: Liber, 2008. *Voix psychanalytiques.* 144 p.

GG4873. • Zizek, Slavoj: *Enjoy your symptom!: Jacques Lacan in Hollywood and out.* With a new preface by the author. New York: Routledge, 2008. xxiii, 280 p.

GG4874. • Zizek, Slavoj: *Lacan: eine Einführung.* Aus dem Engl. von Karen Genschow und Alexander Roesler. Frankfurt: M. Fischer-Taschenbuch, 2008. 170 p.

GG4875.   Badiou, Alain: "Lacan and Plato." In 387.

GG4876.   Chen, Fu-Jen: "A Lacanian reading of *No-No-boy* and *Obasan*," *Comparatist*, vol. 31 (May 2007), 105-129.

GG4877.   Cheng, Sinkwan: "Comparative philosophies of tragedy: Buddhism, Lacan, and ashes of time," *MLN*, vol. 123, no. 5 (Dec. 2008), 1163-1187.

GG4878.   Grigg, Russell: "Lacan and Badiou: logic of the *pas-tout*." In 4844, 81-93. [Badiou]

GG4879.   Habbi, Rafey: "Psychoanalytic criticism: Freud and Lacan." In 953.

GG4880.   Hoeveler, Diane Long: "Teaching 'The purloined letter' and Lacan's seminar: introducing students to psychoanalysis through Poe." In 789, 109-114.

GG4881.   Johnston, Adrian: "A blast from the future: Freud, Lacan, Marcuse, and snapping the threads of the past," *Umbr(a)* (2008), 67-84.

GG4882.   Johnston, Adrian: "Lacanian theory has legs: structures marching in the streets," *South Atlantic Review*, vol. 72, no. 2 (Spring 2007), 99-105.

GG4883.   Leeb, Claudia: "Toward a theoretical outline of the subject: the centrality of Adorno and Lacan for feminist political theorizing," *Political Theory*, vol. 36, no. 3 (June 2008), 351-376.

GG4884.   Malchow, Timothy B.: "Indispensable, inadequate narratives: on reading Grass's œuvre with Lacan." In 805, 36-48.

GG4885.   Olehla, Richard: "The quest for the holy word: Lacan's name-of-the-father, paranoia and possible madness in *The Crying of Lot 49*," *Litteraria Pragensia*, vol. 18, no. 35 (2008), 58-76.

GG4886.   Oltarzewska, Jagna: "Flights of theory: the Lacanian letter and its translations," *Revue Française d'Études Américaines*, no. 115 (1er trim. 2008), 89-101.

GG4887.   Richard, Robert: "Lacan le môme," *Liberté*, no. 280 (avril 2008), 48-55.

GG4888.   Schneider, Christoph: "The transformation of eros: reflections on desire in Jacques Lacan." In 944.

GG4889.   Sigler, David: "The rhetoric of anti-pedagogical Sadism in Jacques Lacan's *Seminar VII*," *Interdisciplinary Literary Studies*, vol. 9, no. 2 (Spring 2008), 71-86.

GG4890.   Sinnerbrink, Robert: "Everything you always wanted to know about Lynch, but were afraid to ask Lacan," *South Atlantic Review*, vol. 72, no. 4 (Fall 2007), 128-132.

GG4891.   Sörman, Richard: "Molière et Lacan aux Etats-Unis et en France." In 509, 173-181.

GG4892.   Tuhkanen, Mikko: "The wager of death: Richard Wright with Hegel and Lacan," *Postmodern Culture*, vol. 18, no. 2 (Jan. 2008), [n.p.].

GG4893.   Van Haute, Philippe: "Lacan reads Klein: some remarks on the body in psychoanalytic thought," *Philosophy Today*, vol. 52, supplement (2008), 54-62.

GG4894.   Ziser, Michael: "Animal mirrors: Poe, Lacan, von Uexküll, and Audobon in the zoosemiosphere," *Angelaki*, vol. 12, no. 3 (Dec. 2007), 11-33.

GG4895.   Zizek, Slavoj: "Lacan's four discourses: a political reading." In 943, 81-97.
LACHAUD, Denis. See also 1178.

GG4896.   Caron, David: "Masculinité et altertemporalité dans *J'apprends l'allemand* de Denis Lachaud," *Itinéraires* (2008), 177-189.
LACOUE-LABARTHE, Philippe.

GG4897.   ● Lacoue-Labarthe, Philippe: *La vraie semblance*. Edition revue par Leonid Kharlamov. Paris: Galilée, 2008. *La philosophie en effet.* 78 p.

GG4898.   ● Nancy, Jean-Luc: *Nach der Tragödie: in memoriam Philippe Lacoue-Labarthe.* Aus dem Franz. von Jörn Etzold und Helga Finter. Mit einem Vorwart von Helga Finter. Stuttgart: Legueil, 2008. 39 p.
LADRIÈRE, Jean. See also 959.

GG4899.   Malherbe, Jean-François: "In memoriam Jean Ladrière," *Laval Théologique et Philosophique*, vol. 63, no. 3 (oct. 2007), 441-443.

GG4900.   Taminiaux, Jacques: "In memoriam Jean Ladrière," *Revue Philosophique de Louvain*, tome 106, no. 2 (mai 2008), 242-247.

GG4901.   Van Parijs, Philippe: "Jean Ladrière, philosophe de toutes les sciences, penseur de l'espérance," *Revue Philosophique de Louvain*, tome 106, no. 2 (mai 2008), 239-241.
LAFERRIÈRE, Dany. See also 194, 672.

GG4902. ● Vasile, Benjamin: *Dany Laferrière, l'autodidacte et le processus de création*. Paris: L'Harmattan, 2008. *Critiques littéraires*. 285 p. [Includes interview with Laferrière]

GG4903. Braziel, Jana Evans: "Trans-American constructions of black heteromasculinity: Dany Laferrière, le nègre, and the late-capitalist American racial machine-désirante." In 50.

GG4904. Mathis-Moser, Ursula: "*Le cri des oieseaux fous* de Dany Laferrière." In 41, 217-241.

GG4905. Prandota, Maria: "L'imaginaire diasporique dans le roman migrant au Québec. L'entre-deux dans *Pays sans chapeau* de Dany Laferrière." In 76, 273-280.

GG4906. Sadkowski, Piotr: "L'écrivain 'transamérican' se met en scène québécoise." In 115, 156-166.

GG4907. Walcott-Hackshaw, Elizabeth: "Dancing at the border: cultural translations and the writer's return." In 67, 149-162.

LAFORGUE, Jules. See also 670, 1027.

GG4908. Bazile, Sandrine: " 'Un Hamlet de moins!' ou la déroute satirique du poète décadent," *Modernités*, no. 27 (2008), 119-129.

GG4909. Holmes, Anne: " 'De nouveaux rythmes': the free verse of Laforgue's 'Solo de Lune'," *French Studies*, vol. 62, no. 2 (April 2008), 162-172.

GG4910. Laroche, Hugues: "Mort de l'automne?" In 383, 93-108.

GG4911. Lesage, Virginie: "Ecarts ironiques: de Jules Laforgue à Thomas Stearns Eliot," *Textuel*, no. 53 (2008), 73-88.

GG4912. Murat, Michel: "L'oubli de Laforgue," *Romantisme*, no. 140 (2e trim. 2008), 111-124.

GG4913. Patterson, Anita: "Hybridity and the new world: Laforgue, Eliot and the Whitmanian poetics of the frontier." In 549.

GG4914. Ruiz de Chastenet, Jonathan: "Une transposition incongrue: le mythe de Salomé revue par Jules Laforgue." In 439, 67-82.

GG4915. Surace, Elisabeth: "Des notes inédites de Jules Laforgue," *Histoires Littéraires*, no. 36 (oct.-nov.-déc. 2008), 5-17.

GG4916. Surace, Elisabeth: "Ecriture et simulacre: 'Le miracle des roses' de Jules Laforgue," *Littératures*, no. 58-59 (2008), 295-320.

LAGARCE, Jean-Luc.

GG4917. ● *Ebauche d'un portrait: d'après le journal de Jean-Luc Lagarce*. Adaptation de François Berreur. Besançon: Solitaires intempestifs, 2008. 107 p.

GG4918. ● *Jean-Luc Lagarce dans le mouvement dramatique*. Sous la dir. de Jean-Pierre Sarrazac et Catherine Naugrette. Besançon: Les solitaires intempestifvs, 2008. 303 p.

GG4919. ● *Traduire Lagarce: langue, culture, imaginaire*. Avant-propos de Bruno Curatolo. Besançon: Les solitaires intempestifs, 2008. 175 p.

GG4920. Bouchardon, Marianne: " 'Sur les cimes de la grande forêt racinienne'." In 4918, 95-109.

GG4921. Boula de Mareuil, Marie-Isabelle: "Narration, rétrospective et rêve dans *De Saxe*." In 4918, 41-57.

GG4922. Daniels, Barry: "Jean-Luc Lagarce," *Western European Stages*, vol. 20, no. 1 (Winter 2008), 65-70.

GG4923. Diaz, Sylvain: "L'action mises en crise dans *Les Prétendants*." In 4918, 29-39.

GG4924. Duret-Pujol, Marie: "Le mouvement vaudevillesque des *Prétendants*." In 4918, 123-135.

GG4925. Fix, Florence: "Seuils de lecture, portes fermées: essai de comparaison de deux traductions allemandes de *J'étais dans ma maison et j'attendais que la pluie vienne*." In 4919, 69-84.

GG4926. Folco, Alice: "Lagarce/García Lorco: dramaturgies du confinement." In 4918, 159-173.

GG4927. Hemmerle, Marie-Aude; Céline Hersant: "Crébillon/Lagarce: 'précisions'." In 4918, 175-189.

GG4928.　Jolly, Geneviève: "La choralité ou la mise en mouvement de la parole théâtrale." In 4918, 221-235.

GG4929.　Jongy, Béatrice: "Habiter l'image: Lagarce à la lueur de Kafka." In 4919, 123-143.

GG4930.　Kuntz, Hélène: "Aux limites du dramatique." In 4918, 11-28.

GG4931.　Le Pors, Sandrine; Jonathan Chatel: " 'C'est donc un amoureux qui parle et qui dit': des *Fragments* de Roland Barthes aux 'chapitres' de Jean-Luc Lagarce." In 4918, 111-121. [Barthes]

GG4932.　Meschonnic, Henri: "Traduire le théâtre c'est traduire l'oralité." In 4919, 11-24.

GG4933.　Migeot, François: "*Les Règles du savoir-vivre dans la société moderne* ou la comédie du parlêtre." In 4919, 85-102.

GG4934.　Moreira da Silva, Alexandra: "Briser la forme: vers un 'paysage fractal'." In 4918, 59-76.

GG4935.　Motte, Emmanuel; Jean-Pierre Ryngaert: "S'essayer à des rôles: l'identité en question." In 4918, 200-219.

GG4936.　Pignon, Raphaëlle: "La fabrication d'un objet théâtral de l'intertextualité absolue." In 4918, 191-207.

GG4937.　Ruggiero Perrino, Vicenzo: "Jean-Luc Lagarce: l'impotenza della lingua," *Annali, Università degli Studi di Napoli "L'Orientale", Sezione Romanza*, anno 49, n. 2 (2007), 425-459.

GG4938.　Sarrazac, Jean-Pierre: "De la parabole du fils prodigue au drame-de-la-vie." In 4918, 271-296.

GG4939.　Sermon, Julie; Anaïs Bonnier: "A propos, et *La Cantatrice chauve*?" In 4918, 137-158. [Ionesco]

GG4940.　Sugiera, Malgorzata; Mateusz Borowski: " 'Non, ça ne se passe pas là, devent moi': la mimèsis reformulée dans le théâtre-récit lagarcien." In 4918, 77-93.

GG4941.　Talbot, Armelle: "L'épanorthose: de la parole comme expérience du temps." In 4918, 255-269.

GG4942.　Toudoire-Surlapierre, Frédérique: "Lagarce: happy end." In 4919, 145-168.

GG4943.　Vacher, Pascal: "Face à ce qui s'absente, le chœur, de la parole au poème." In 4919, 103-122.

GG4944.　Valero, Julie: "Diarisme et écriture dramatique." In 4918, 247-253.

GG4945.　Zaragoza, Georges: "Jean-Luc Lagarce, une langue faite pour le théâtre." In 4919, 25-44.

GG4946.　Zurbach, Christine: "Enjeux théâtraux de la traduction: la réception portugaise de Lagarce." In 4919, 45-68.

LAGIER, Bernard.

GG4947.　Brault, Marie-Andrée: "Hurler à la lune. *Moi chien créole*," *Jeu: Cahiers de Théâtre*, no. 126 (mars 2008), 16-17.

LAHENS, Yanick. See 281, 293, 7432.

LALONDE, Robert.

GG4948.　Goilan-Sandu, Liliana: "La relation père-fils ou la condition masculine dans *Le Fou du père* de Robert Lalonde." In 572, 193-198.

GG4949.　Jarosz, Krzysztof: "Pour saluer Marguerite Yourcenar. *Un jardin entouré de murailles* de Robert Lalonde." In 76, 213-219. [Yourcenar]

GG4950.　Laforest, Daniel: "Robert Lalonde, *Espèces en voie de disparition*," *XYZ: La Revue de la Nouvelle*, no. 94 (été 2008), 91-93.

GG4951.　Lépine, Stéphane: "Robert Lalonde, entretien," *Lettres Québécoises*, no. 132 (hiver 2008), 6-10.

GG4952.　Lord, Michel: "Robert Lalonde nouvellier," *Lettres Québécoises*, no. 132 (hiver 2008), 11-12.

LAMARCHE, Caroline.

GG4953.　Lamarche, Caroline: "Dans l'intimité d'une bibliothèque d'écrivain: chez Caroline Lamarche," *Carnet et les Instants*, no. 151 (2008), 14-18. [Entretien]

LAMARCHE-VADEL, Bernard.

GG4954. ● Robert-Guédon, Danielle: *La Rongère; Le Désespoir du singe, suivi de Mercedes*. Préface de Jean-Loup Trassard. Paris: Argol, 2008. 215 p.

LAMBRICHS, Louise L.

GG4955. Semeniako, Michel: "Genèse d'un projet: du texte à l'image, à propos d'*Exil*." In 508, 541-545.

LANSON, Gustave.

GG4956. Panaïté, Oana: "Gustave Lanson et Marcel Schwob: anachronies contemporaines," *Dix-Neuf*, no. 10 (avril 2008), 35-46. [Schwob]

LAPEYRE, Patrick.

GG4957. Motte, Warren: "Patrick Lapeyre's waiting game." In 900.

LARBAUD, Valery. See also 1020, 6395.

GG4958. ● Larbaud, Valery: *200 chambres, 200 salles de bains*. Préface d'Alberto Manguel. Paris: Sonneur, 2008. 57 p.

GG4959. Aigouy, Sandrine: "Valery Larbaud préfacier," *Cahiers Valery Larbaud*, no. 43 (2008), 141-149.

GG4960. Bataille, Christophe: "*Gwenny-toute-seule* de V. Larbaud," *Cahiers Valery Larbaud*, no. 43 (2008), 53-63.

GG4961. Berquin, François: "Altera ego," *Cahiers Valery Larbaud*, no. 43 (2008), 89-102.

GG4962. Brémond, Mireille: "Le fil d'Ariane de Bonsignor," *Cahiers Valery Larbaud*, no. 44 (2008), 63-81.

GG4963. Chabrol-Gagné, Nelly: "Enfance et enfants dans les journaux intimes de Valery Larbaud," *Cahiers Valery Larbaud*, no. 44 (2008), 25-49.

GG4964. Charbonnier, Gil: "L'élégie dans le *Journal* d'Alicante de Valery Larbaud," *Cahiers Valery Larbaud*, no. 43 (2008), 65-80.

GG4965. Curatolo, Bruno: "Notes sur la vie littéraire: le *Journal* (1931-1935) de Valery Larbaud," *Cahiers Valery Larbaud*, no. 44 (2008), 83-100.

GG4966. Froloff, Nathalie: "Retrouver la voix perdue de l'enfance," *Cahiers Valery Larbaud*, no. 43 (2008), 215-227.

GG4967. Froloff, Nathalie: "Les travaux et les jours: présence de Samuel Butler dans le *Journal* d'Alicante de Valery Larbaud," *Cahiers Valery Larbaud*, no. 44 (2008), 119-133.

GG4968. Gardes Tamine, Joëlle: "La variété d'une écriture," *Cahiers Valery Larbaud*, no. 44 (2008), 135-146.

GG4969. Lioure, Françoise: "*Le Cœur de l'Angleterre*: 'vrai-faux journal'?," *Cahiers Valery Larbaud*, no. 4443 (2008), 101-118.

GG4970. Moron, Paule: "Les diverses publications du *Journal* de Larbaud et de pages du *Journal*," *Cahiers Valery Larbaud*, no. 44 (2008), 13-23.

GG4971. Moron, Paul: "Le *Journal intégral* de Larbaud," *Cahiers Valery Larbaud*, no. 43 (2008), 33-51.

GG4972. Vanorio, Maria Laura: "Le monologue du traducteur," *Cahiers Valery Larbaud*, no. 43 (2008), 81-88.

GG4973. Viellard, Delphine: "Larbaud et Rome," *Cahiers Valery Larbaud*, no. 44 (2008), 51-61.

GG4974. Visuvalingam, Elizabeth Ch.: "Les monologues intérieurs ou l'épreuve de l'identité et de l'altérité," *Cahiers Valery Larbaud*, no. 43 (2008), 119-138.

LA ROCQUE, Gilbert. See 6029.

LAROUI, Fouad.

GG4975. Calargé, Carla: "Les limites de l'appartenance: composition, intertextualité et langue dans *Les dents du topographe* et *Méfiez-vous des parachutistes* de Fouad Laroui," *Présence Francophone*, no. 70 (2008), 154-168.

GG4976. Lievois, Katrien: "La traduction de l'allusion ironique dans *La fin tragique de Philomène Tralala* de Fouad Laroui," *Expressions Maghrébines*, vol. 7, no. 2 (hiver 2008), 113-128.

LARUE, Monique. See also 290.

GG4977. Lüsebrink, Hans-Jürgen: "*La gloire de Cassiodore* de Monique LaRue." In 41, 243-262.

LA TOUR DU PIN, Patrice de.

GG4978. Le Han, Marie-Josette: " 'Il faut qu'Il croisse et que je diminue': Patrice de La Tour du Pin ou l'écriture de l'effacement," *Travaux de Littérature*, tome 21 (2008), 459-472.

LAUDE, André.

GG4979. ● Laude, André: *Œuvre poétique*. Avant-dire de Abdellatif Laâbi; préface de Yann Orveillon. Paris: La Différence, 2008. 733 p.

LAURENT, Jacques. See also 3162.

GG4980. ● Authier, François-Jean: *Poétique du travestissement: Jacques Laurent romancier*. Paris: Champion, 2008. *Littérature de notre siècle*, 35. 737 p.

LAURRENT, Éric. See 3674.

LAYE, Camara.

GG4981. ● Diallo, Mahamadou: *Translation: culture, power, psyche*. Paris: L'Harmattan, 2008. 111 p.

GG4982. ● Dieng, Babacar: *Reclaiming history: a study of the emerging postcolonial consciousness in mid-century novels of the African diaspora*. Saarbrücken: VDM, 2008. v, 191 p.

GG4983. Hayes, Jarrod: "Idyllic masculinity and national allegory: unbecoming men and anticolonial resistance in Camara Laye's *L'Enfant noir*." In 449, 224-250.

GG4984. Morrison, Toni: "On *The radiance of the king* by Camara Laye." In 847.

GG4985. Wehrs, Donald R.: "Gendering the subject and engendering the self: Mande acculturation, Islamic piety, and the forging of ethical identity in Camara Laye's *L'Enfant noir*." In 142.

LE, Linda. See also 584, 5070.

GG4986. Barnes, Leslie: "Literature and the outsider: an interview with Linda Lê," *World Literature Today*, vol. 82, no. 3 (May-June 2008), 53-56.

GG4987. Lê, Linda: "Franchir les frontières," *Matricule des Anges*, no. 86 (2007), 18-23. [Entretien]

LÉAUTAUD, Paul. See 5994.

LEBEAU, Suzanne.

GG4988. Belzil, Patricia: "Pieds nus dans l'aube. *Souliers de sable*," *Jeu: Cahiers de Théâtre*, no. 128 [no. 3] (2008), 23-24.

LEBLANC, David.

GG4989. Clerson, David: "David Leblanc, *La descente du singe*," *XYZ: La Revue de la Nouvelle*, no. 93 (printemps 2008), 85-87.

LEBLANC, Maurice.

GG4990. ● Morel, Gérard: *Les repères d'Arsène Lupin*. Saint-Cyr-sur-Loire: C. Pirot, 2008. 146 p.

GG4991. ● Ruaud, André-François: *Les nombreuses vies d'Arsène Lupin*. Lyon: Moutons électriques, 2008. 351 p.

GG4992. Chelebourg, Christian: "Arsène en scène: poétique et théâtre chez Maurice Leblanc." In 425, 51-77.

LE BRIS, Michel.

GG4993. Glaux, Raphaëlle: "Michel Le Bris, de vagues et de granit," *Spectacle du Monde*, no. 548 (sept. 2008), 64-67.

LE BRUN, Annie. See 691a.

LE CLÉZIO, Jean-Marie Gustave. See also 673, 3717, 3718.

GG4994. ● *A propos de Nice*. Coordonné par Isabelle Roussel-Gillet et Marina Salles. *Les cahiers J.-M. G. Le Clézio*, no. 1 Paris: Complicités, 2008. 209 p.

GG4995. ● *J. M. G. Le Clézio: ailleurs et origines, parcours poétiques*. Dirigé par Bernardette Rey Mimoso-Ruiz. Toulouse: Editions universitaires du Sud, 2006.

GG4996. ● Mbassi Aterba, Raymond: *Identité et fluidité dans l'œuvre de Jean-Marie Gustave Le Clézio: une poétique de la mondialité*. Paris: L'Harmattan, 2008. 386 p.

GG4997. ● Van Acker, Isa: *Carnets de doute: variantes romanesques du voyage chez J. M. G. Le Clézio*. Amsterdam; New York: Rodopi, 2008. 294 p.

GG4998. Amar, Ruth: "La communication orale dans le roman leclézien." In 4995, 8.

GG4999. Andersson, Kajsa: "Colette selon J.-M. G. Le Clézio." In 4995, 53-63. [Colette]

GG5000.	Anoun, Abdelhaq: "L'empathie ou les esprits télescopés." In 4995, 189-199.

GG5001.	Balint Babos, Adina: "La rencontre fils-père dans *L'Africain* de Jean-Marie Gustave Le Clézio." In 572, 143-151.

GG5002.	Balint Baros, Adina: "Le rituel de la Kataviva dans *Révolutions*," *Cahiers J.-M. G. Le Clézio*, no. 1 (2008), 115-129.

GG5003.	Beckett, Sanddra L.: "Le Clézio et les 'vrais lecteurs'," *Cahiers Robinson*, no. 23 (2008), 23-34.

GG5004.	Bedon, Thierry: "Nice, 1940-1944: décor en trois teintes et carton peint," *Cahiers J.-M. G. Le Clézio*, no. 1 (2008), 61-68.

GG5005.	Bedrane-Tsalpatouros, Sabrinelle: "Les romances lecléziennes, une poétique du renouvellement générique." In 4995, 177-187.

GG5006.	Ben: "Je me souviens de Le Clézio," *Cahiers J.-M. G. Le Clézio*, no. 1 (2008), 43-44.

GG5007.	Benjelloun, Mohammed: "Le regard et le fantasme: l'attrait des objets dans les premiers récits de Le Clézio." In 4995, 75-83.

GG5008.	Benjelloun, Mohammed: "Structure de la phrase et élaboration du sens dans un texte du *Déluge* de J. M. G. Le Clézio." In 556.

GG5009.	Bernabe Gil, Maria Luisa: "La création littéraire de Le Clézio: du récit biblique au mythe de l'éternel retour." In 4995, 259-269.

GG5010.	Borgomano, Madeleine: "Nice et son Haut-Pays," *Cahiers J.-M. G. Le Clézio*, no. 1 (2008), 17-32.

GG5011.	Brière, Emilie: "Sans passé, quel avenir? Les enfants de *Poisson d'or*," *Cahiers Robinson*, no. 23 (2008), 109-120.

GG5012.	Cavallero, Claude: "Echo-système du récit." In 4995, 169-176.

GG5013.	Cavallero, Claude: "*Ville Aurore* ou le jardin d'enfance," *Cahiers J.-M. G. Le Clézio*, no. 1 (2008), 131-147.

GG5014.	Damamme-Gilbert, Béatrice: "Les enjeux de la mémoire dans *Onitsha* et *L'Africain* de J. M. G. Le Clézio," *Australian Journal of French Studies*, vol. 45, no. 1 (Jan.-April 2008), 16-32.

GG5015.	Demeulenaere, Alex: "Science ou aventure? Analyse de deux récits de voyage en Afrique noire." In 453, 226-241.

GG5016.	Devilla, Lorenzo: "Du plus loin que je me souvienne, j'ai entendu la mer: poétique de l'espace et nostalgie des origines chez Le Clézio." In 4995, 31-39.

GG5017.	Devilla, Lorenzo: "Récits d'enfance et autofiction," *Cahiers Robinson*, no. 23 (2008), 171-184.

GG5018.	Dohollau, Tanguy: "Les Plomarc'h," *Cahiers J.-M. G. Le Clézio*, no. 1 (2008), 167-171.

GG5019.	Dutton, Jacqueline: "Le mythe de l'éternel retour dans l'œuvre de Le Clézio." In 4995, 271-284.

GG5020.	Gazier, Michèle: "J.-M. G. Le Clézio: enfant lecteur, enfant écrivain," *Cahiers Robinson*, no. 23 (2008), 17-22.

GG5021.	Girolamo Sinna, Amina de: "Suryavati ou 'la force du soleil'." In 4995, 239-248.

GG5022.	Gortfi, Ouafae: "A la recherche de l'identité perdue. Les femmes marocaines de Le Clézio." In 4995, 119-124.

GG5023.	Henky, Danièle: "J.-M. G. Le Clézio édité en jeunesse," *Cahiers Robinson*, no. 23 (2008), 35-48.

GG5024.	Imbert, Jean-Philippe: "Les meurtres sacrés du Michoacán." In 4995, 201-208.

GG5025.	Issur, Kumari: "Les îles indianocéaniques de Le Clézio." In 4995, 227-235.

GG5026.	Jarlsbo, Jeana: "Le réseau intertextuel dans *La Quarantaine* de J.-M. G. Le Clézio." In 4995, 249-257.

GG5027.	Jeannet, Frédéric-Yves: "Jean-Marie Le Clézio ou le Nobel immérité," *Monde* (19-20 octobre 2008), 18.

GG5028.	Kern-Oudot, Catherine: "Poétique du chant dans l'œuvre de J.-M. G. Le Clézio." In 4995, 147-159.

GG5029.   Latendresse-Drapeau, Myra: "Les Maîtres, le Supermarché et le Premier Empereur." In 4995, 135-143.

GG5030.   Le Clézio, Jean-Marie Gustave: "Entretien," *Cahiers J.-M. G. Le Clézio*, no. 1 (2008), 33-40.

GG5031.   Léger, Thierry: "L'arrière-pays niçois et les collines dans l'espace imaginaire leclézien," *Cahiers J.-M. G. Le Clézio*, no. 1 (2008), 101-114.

GG5032.   Léger, Thierry: "L'Œdipe dans *Onitsha*," *Cahiers Robinson*, no. 23 (2008), 151-159.

GG5033.   Lohka, Eileen: "*Raga: approches du continent invisible*," *Cahiers J.-M. G. Le Clézio*, no. 1 (2008), 179-181.

GG5034.   Mabanckou, Alain: "Le Clézio, Nobel mérité," *Monde* (25 octobre 2008), 21.

GG5035.   Macé, Marie-Anne: "*Les Géants* ou le chariot du monde." In 4995, 67-74.

GG5036.   Martin, Serge: "Les enfants de Le Clézio," *Cahiers Robinson*, no. 23 (2008), 77-88.

5036a.   Maurus, Véronique: "Querelle littéraire," *Monde* (26-27 octobre 2008), 19.

GG5037.   Mbassi Ateba, Raymond: "Le Clézio et le thème de l'Afrique dans *Onitsha* et *Désert*." In 4995, 209-218.

GG5038.   Nouchi, Franck: "Un prof en colère," *Monde* (25 octobre 2008), 6.

GG5039.   Perry, Edith: "Les prisons de l'enfance," *Cahiers Robinson*, no. 23 (2008), 129-139.

GG5040.   Pettiti-Morvan, Magali: "Processus initiatique et rencontre avec l'altérité." In 4995, 125-134.

GG5041.   Plu, Christine: "Petite Croix transfigurée: Georges Lemoine illustrateur de *Peuple du ciel*," *Cahiers Robinson*, no. 23 (2008), 93-106.

GG5042.   Poulet, Elisabeth: "La faille identitaire chez les personnages leczéliens." In 4995, 111-118.

GG5043.   Poulet, Régis: "L'Inde de Le Clézio: héritages et choix." In 4995, 219-226.

GG5044.   Roussel-Gillet, Isabelle: "Des saisons et des lisières, de *Printemps* à La Saison des pluies," *Cahiers Robinson*, no. 23 (2008), 141-148.

GG5045.   Roussel-Gillet, Isabelle: "Deux créations théâtrales de récits de Le Clézio: pour enfants?," *Cahiers Robinson*, no. 23 (2008), 201-205.

GG5046.   Roussel-Gillet, Isabelle: "Dialogue avec Edmond Baudouin," *Cahiers J.-M. G. Le Clézio*, no. 1 (2008), 47-60.

GG5047.   Roussel-Gillet, Isabelle: "*Envisager* l'autre: les res-sources d'un héritier." In 4995, 21-30.

GG5048.   Roussel-Gillet, Isabelle: "Le Clézio, passeur au monde: l'écriture et le passage des seuils," *Nouvelles Etudes Francophones*, vol. 22, no. 2 (automne 2007), 152-164.

GG5049.   Salles, Marina: "Jeux d'enfants," *Cahiers Robinson*, no. 23 (2008), 49-60.

GG5050.   Salles, Marina: "*La Mer intérieure* de J.-M. G. Le Clézio," *Cahiers J.-M. G. Le Clézio*, no. 1 (2008), 149-166.

GG5051.   Salles, Marina; Isabelle Roussel-Gillet: "Ecrire une ville," *Cahiers J.-M. G. Le Clézio*, no. 1 (2008), 7-14.

GG5052.   Silva Camarani, Ana Luiza: "La magie de l'enfance chez Le Clézio," *Cahiers Robinson*, no. 23 (2008), 63-74.

GG5053.   Simonffy, Zsuzsa: "La métamorphose en métamorphose." In 4995, 85-95.

GG5054.   Sjöblom, Margareta Kastberg: "La phrase leclézienne et son rythme." In 556.

GG5055.   Stanesco, Corina: "Le mythe des Argonautes dans *Le Chercheur d'or* de Le Clézio." In 520, 655-668.

GG5056.   Thibault, Bruno: "Souvenirs d'en France: l'écriture du désastre dans *Ourania*," *Cahiers Robinson*, no. 23 (2008), 161-170.

GG5057.   Thibault, Bruno: "La ville de Nice en mots et en images," *Cahiers J.-M. G. Le Clézio*, no. 1 (2008), 82-100.

GG5058.   Thoizet, Evelyne: "Remémorations d'enfance," *Cahiers Robinson*, no. 23 (2008), 185-199.

GG5059.   Van Acker, Isa: "Ecrire l'aventure aujourd'hui." In 4995, 41-52.

GG5060. Van Acker, Isa: "Enfance et déchéance dans *Cœur brûle et autres romances*," *Cahiers Robinson*, no. 23 (2008), 121-127.

GG5061. Van Acker, Isa: "*Ourania*: petite victoire sur fond de débris," *Cahiers J.-M. G. Le Clézio*, no. 1 (2008), 174-178.

GG5062. Westerlund, Fredrik: "La musique qui transporte et transforme: fonction de la musique dans *Révolutions*." In 4995, 161-168.

GG5063. Woollen, Geoff: "Tropic bird of the Mascarenes," *Francophone Postcolonial Studies*, vol. 6, no. 2 (Autumn-Winter 2008), 1-17.

GG5064. Yillah, Dauda: "Envisioning difference in Le Clézio's *Onitsha*," *French Studies*, vol. 62, no. 2 (April 2008), 173-187.

LECOMTE, Marcel.

GG5065. Collani, Tania: "Merveilleux et fantastique chez deux surréalistes francophones," *Etudes Francophones*, vol. 23, no. 1-2 (printemps-automne 2008), 127-140.

LEDUC, Violette. See 1621.

LEFEBVRE, Henri. See also 5794.

GG5066. ● Lefebvre, Henri: *Critique of everyday life. Volume II*. Trans. John Moore; preface by Michel Trebitsch. London: Verso, 2008. xxix, 380 p.

GG5067. ● *Space, difference, everyday life: Henri Lefebvre and radical politics*. Ed. Kanishka Goonewaedena [et al.]. London: Routledge, 2007. xiv, 329 p.

GG5068. Conant, Chloé: " 'Faire avec' et 'faire sans': les hypotextes problématiques de la fiction contemporaine." In 506, 409-418.

LEFÈVRE, Kim.

GG5069. Nguyen, Nathalie Huynh Chau: "Landscapes of war: traumascapes in the works of Kim Lefèvre and Phan Huy Duong." In 92, 88-103.

GG5070. Selao, Ching: "Deuils et migrations identitaires dans les romans de Kim Lefèvre et de Linda Lê." In 119, 275-297. [Lê]

LE GUILLOU, Philippe.

GG5071. Ruivo Coppin, Michelle: "La relation père/fils dans le triptyque de Philippe Le Guillou." In 572, 185-192.

LEIRIS, Michel. See also 420, 639, 737, 962, 11423, 1433.

GG5072. ● Becdelièvre, Laure; Sophie Chassat: *Les énigmes du moi, en trente dissertations corrigées*. Paris: Sedes, 2008. *Impulsion*. 233 p.

GG5073. ● *Enigmes [Les] du moi*. Coordination Sophie Rochefort-Guillouet. Paris: Ellipses, 2008. *Fiches et méthodes*. 252 p.

GG5074. ● *Enigmes [Les] du moi*. Denis Collin [et al.]. Paris: Sedes, 2008. *Prépas scientifiques*. 237 p.

GG5075. ● *Giacometti, Leiris et Iliazd: portraits gravés: catalogue de l'exposition présentée au Musée des Beaux-Arts de Caen, du 17 mai au 31 août 2008*. Sous la dir. de Véronique Wiesinger. Lyon: Fage; Paris: Fondation Alberto et Annette Giacometti, 2008. 87 p.

GG5076. ● Sorel, Mathilde: *Les énigmes du moi, en trente textes commentés*. Paris: Sedes, 2008. *Impulsion*. 174 p.

GG5077. ● Ton-That, Thanh-Vân: *Michel Leiris, L'Age d'homme*. Rosny: Bréal, 2008. *Connaissance d'une œuvre*. 126 p.

GG5078. Albers, Irene: "Mimesis and alterity: Michel Leiris's ethnography and poetics of spirit possession," *French Studies*, vol. 62, no. 3 (July 2008), 271-289.

GG5079. Berissi, Marianne: "Manières de critiquer," *Cahiers Robinson*, no. 24 (2008), 175-184.

GG5080. Bub, Stefan: "Ein einzig rotes Schnürchen: Cet unique ruban rouge: Zur Wirkungsgeschichte eines Bildmotivs aus Goethes *Faust* bein Michel Leiris," *Germanisch-Romanische Monatsschrift*, 58. Jahrgang, Heft 4 (2008), 471-481.

GG5081. Cornille, Jean-Louis: "Le soi disant (Leiris entre Descartes et Roussel)." In 413. [Roussel]

GG5082. Janis, Michael: "Leiris in Africa: the psychoanalysis of exoticism." In 486.

GG5083. Peppiatt, Michael: "A strange fascination: the friendship between Michel Leiris and Francis Bacon." In 852.

GG5084. Russo, Adelaide M.: "Michel Leiris: le peitnre comme modèle." In 583, 107-122.

GG5085. Sasso, Luigi: "Nomi ed errori in Michel Leiris," *Nome nel Testo (II)*, no. 8 (2006), 661-673.

GG5086. Surlapierre, Nicolas: "Des articles de mercerie: le fini à partir de lui-même dans *Le Ruban au cou d'Olympia* de Michel Leiris." In 379, 155-174.

GG5087. Westley, Hannah: "The *autoportrait*: Michel Leiris's *L'Age d'homme*." In 625, 49-80.

LEJEUNE, Paul.

GG5088. Pioffet, Marie-Christine: "Le rire de Paul Lejeune: du rire jaune à l'humour noir," *Nouvelles Etudes Francophones*, vol. 22, no. 2 (automne 2007), 122-134.

LEMAHIEU, Daniel. See 1120.

LEMAIRE, Jean-Pierre.

GG5089. Frank, Evelyne: "Jean-Pierre Lemaire: un art du peu biblique." In 382, 177-186.

LENOIR, Hélène. See also 7018.

GG5090. Motte, Warren: "Hélène Lenoir's still life." In 900.

LENORMAND, Henri-René.

GG5091. • Lenormand, Henri-René: *Le temps est un songe, suivi de Les Ratés*. Paris: Avant-Scène Théâtre, 2008. *Avant-Scène Théâtre*, no. 1235-1236 (1er janv. 2008). 158 p.

LEPAGE, Robert.

GG5092. • Lepage, Robert; Stéphan Bureau: *Stéphan Bureau rencontre Robert Lepage*. Verdun, Québec: Amérik média, 2008. 200 p.

GG5093. Bovet, Jeanne: "Prendre sa place dans le monde: dynamiques interculturelles et stratégies interlinguistiques du théâtre de Robert Lepage," *Études de Lettres*, no. 279 [no. 1] (2008), 17-35.

GG5094. Fouquet, Ludovic: "L'envol du dragon. *Le dragon bleu*," *Jeu: Cahiers de Théâtre*, no. 128 [no. 3] (2008), 25-28. [Marie Michaud]

GG5095. Fricker, Karen: "Robert Lepage." In 860, 233-250.

LEROUX, Gaston.

GG5096. • *Gaston Leroux: de Rouletabille à Chéri-Bibi*. Publié à l'occasion de l'exposition présentée par la Bibliothèque nationale de France du 7 octobre 2008 au 4 janvier 2009. Sous la dir. de Guillaume Fau. Paris: Bibliothèque nationale de France, 2008. 142 p.

GG5097. • Leroux, Gaston: *La machine à assassiner*. Préface de Francis Lacassin. Toulouse: Privat-le Rocher, 2008. 315 p.

GG5098. • Leroux, Gaston: *Le mystère de la chambre jaune*. Edition préfacée, annotée et commentée par Jean-Pierre Naugrette. Paris: Librairie générale française, 2008. *Le livre de poche*. 350 p.

GG5099. • Leroux, Gaston: *Romans mystérieux*. Texte de Pierre Lépine. Paris: Omnibus, 2008. 1115 p.

GG5100. Assouline, Pierre: "La contrebande invisible: Gaston Leroux et le journalisme." In 5096, 12-17.

GG5101. Fau, Guillaume: "Rouletabille à la Bibliothèque: le fonds Gaston Leroux du département des Manuscrits." In 5096, 19-25.

GG5102. Lacassin, Francis: "Lettre à Gaston Leroux sur les ogres, les gnomes et les italiques qui agrémentent son œuvre." In 5096, 58-67.

GG5103. Rivière, François: "Gaston Leroux ou la magie de l'outrance." In 5096, 70-77.

LEVARAY, Jean-Pierre.

GG5104. Geneste, Philippe: "L'œuvre en cours de Jean-Pierre Levaray," *Plein Chant*, no. 83-84 (2008), 169-175.

LEVÉ, Édouard. See 2329.

LÉVEILLÉE, J. R. See 2915.

LEVINAS, Emmanuel. See also 928, 949, 959, 978, 1004, 1382, 1604, 2022, 2023, 2360, 3211, 3230, 3326, 3348, 3583, 4042, 4235, 7054.

GG5105. • *Awakening [The] to the other: a provocative dialogue with Emmanuel Levinas*. Ed. Roger Burggraeve. Leuven; Dudley, MA: Peeters, 2008. xv, 339 p.

GG5106. ● Bensussan, Gérard: *Ethique et expérience: Levinas politique*. Strasbourg: Phocide, 2008. 105 p.

GG5107. ● Clemente, Luigi Francesco: *Un idealismo senza ragione: la fenomenologia e le origini del pensiero di Emmanuel Levinas*. Verona: Ombre corte, 2008. *Culture*. 233 p.

GG5108. ● *Emmanuel Levinas-Maurice Blanchot*. Edition établie sous la dir. d'Eric Hoppenot et Alain Milon. Nanterre: Presses Univ. de Paris 10, 2008. 553 p.

GG5109. ● *Emmanuel Levinas, la question du livre*. Sous la dir. de Miguel Abensour et Anne Kupiec. Saint-Germain-la-Blanche-Herbe: IMEC, 2008. 156 p.

GG5110. ● *Emmanuel Levinas: phénoménologie, éthique, esthétique et herméneutique*. Sous la dir. de Philippe Fontaine et Ari Simhon. Paris: Cercle herméneutique, 2007. 247 p.

GG5111. ● *Emmanuel Levinas: prophetic inspiration and philosophy: atti del convegno internazionale per il centenario della nascità: Roma, 24-27 maggio 2006*. A cura di Irene Kajon [et al.]. Firenze: Giuntina, 2008. 414 p.

GG5112. ● Franck, Didier: *L'un-pour-l'autre: Levinas et la signification*. Paris: PUF, 2008. *Epiméthée*. 284 p.

GG5113. ● Hand, Seán: *Emmanuel Levinas*. New York: Routledge, 2008. *Routledge critical thinkers*. xiv, 138 p.

GG5114. ● Hansel, Georges: *De la Bible au Talmud: suivi de l'itinéraire de pensée d'Emmanuel Levinas*. Paris: Jacob, 2008. 336 p.

GG5115. ● *Heidegger's Jewish followers*. Ed. Samuel Fleischacker. Pittsburgh: Duquesne Univ. Press, 2008. ix, 302 p.

GG5116. ● Horowitz, Asher: *Ethics at a standstill: history and subjectivity in Levinas and the Frankfurt school*. Pittsburgh: Duquesne Univ. Press, 2008. xx, 404 p.

GG5117. ● *Kierkegaard and Levinas: ethics, politics, and religion*. Ed. J. Aaron Simmons and David Wood. Bloomington: Indiana Univ. Press, 2008. *Indiana series in the philosophy of religion*. xiii, 270 p.

GG5118. ● Kleinberg-Levin, David Michael: *Before the voice of reason: echoes of responsibility in Merleau-Ponty's ecology and Levinas's ethics*. Albany: SUNY Press, 2008. *SUNY series in contemporary French thought*. xiv, 289 p. [Merleau-Ponty]

GG5119. ● Levinas, Emmanuel: *Ethik und Unendliches: Gespräche mit Philippe Nemo*. Aus dem Franz. von Dorothea Schmidt; Hrsg. von Peter Engelmann. Wien: Passagen, 2008. 4. überarb. Aufl. 96 p.

GG5120. ● *Levinas*. Sous la dir. de Danielle Cohen-Levinas. Paris: Bayard, 2006. 321 p.

GG5121. ● *Levinas à Jérusalem*. Sous la dir. de Joëlle Hansel. Paris: Klincksieck, 2007. 418 p.

GG5122. ● *Levinas and education: at the intersection of faith and reason*. Ed. Danise Egéa-Kuehne. New York: Routledge, 2008. *Routledge international studies in the philosophy of education*, 18. xii, 301 p.

GG5123. ● *Levinas and the ancients*. Ed. Brian Schroeder and Silvia Benso; with a foreword by Adriaan Peperzak. Bloomington: Indiana Univ. Press, 2008. *Studies in continental thought*. xvi, 254 p.

GG5124. ● *Levinas: Chinese and Western perspectives*. Ed. Nicholas Bunnin, Dachun Yang and Linyu Gu. Malden, MA: Wiley-Blackwell, 2008. Journal supplement series to the *Journal of Chinese Philosophy*. ii, 194 p.

GG5125. ● *Levinas, law, politics*. Ed. Marinos Diamantides. London: GlassHouse, 2006. vi, 220 p.

GG5126. ● Marcus, Paul: *Being for the other: Emmanuel Levinas, ethical living and psychoanalysis*. Milwaukee: Marquette Univ. Press, 2008. *Marquette studies in philosophy*. 278 p.

GG5127. ● Martos, Andrés Alonso: *Emmanuel Levinas: la filosofía como ética*. Valencia: Univ. de València, 2008. 289 p.

GG5128. ● Meir, Ephraim: *Levinas's Jewish thought: between Jerusalem and Athens*. Jerusalem: Hebrew University Magnes Press, 2008. viii, 301 p.

GG5129. ● Nodari, Francesca: *Il male radicale tra Kant e Levinas*. Firenze: Giuntina, 2008. 164 p.

GG5130. ● Nordmann, Sophie: *Philosophe et judaïsme: H. Cohen, F. Rosenzweig, E. Levinas*. Paris: PUF, 2008. *Philosophies*. 154 p.

GG5131. ● Ombrosi, Orietta: *Le crépuscule de la raison: Benjamin, Adorno, Horkeimer, et Levinas face à la catastrophe*. 2e éd., rev. et corr. Préface de Catherine Chalier. Paris: Hermann, 2008. 192 p.

GG5132. ● Perpich, Diane: *The ethics of Emmanuel Levinas*. Stanford: Stanford Univ. Press, 2008. *Cultural memory in the present*. xvi, 230 p.

GG5133. ● Pfeuffer, Silvio: *Die Entgrenzung der Verantwortung: Nietzsche, Dostojewskij, Levinas*. Berlin; New York: Walter De Gruyter, 2008. *Monographien und Texte zur Nietzsche-Forschung*, 56. viii, 287 p.

GG5134. ● Ponzio, Augusto: *Tra Bachtin e Levinas: scrittura dialogo alterità*. Bari: Palomar, 2008. 440 p.

GG5135. ● Putnam, Hilary: *Jewish philosophy as a guide to life: Rosenzweig, Buber, Levinas, Wittgenstein*. Bloomington: Indiana Univ. Press, 2008. *The Helen and Martin Schwartz lectures in Jewish studies*. x, 121 p.

GG5136. ● *Responsabilità di fronte alla storia: la filosofia di Emmanuel Levinas tra alterità e terzietà*. A cura di Massimo Durante. Genova: Il Melangolo, 2008. 251 p.

GG5137. ● *Responsibility, God, and society: theological ethics in dialogue: festschrift, Ruger Burggraeve*. Ed. Johan de Tavernier [et al.]. Leuven; Dudley, MA: Peeters, 2008. *Bibliotheca Ephemeridum theologicarum Lovaniensium*, 217. xlv, 413 p.

GG5138. ● Schaufelberger, Philipp: *Emmanuel Levinas, Philosophie des "ich": gravierende Spuren menschlicher Freiheit*. Wien: Lit, 2008. 257 p.

GG5139. ● Schmidt, Katharina: *Zum Verhältnis von Verantwortung und Kritik in der Pädagogik: Versuch einer Neubefragung in Anschluss an Emmanuel Levinas*. München: Fink, 2008. *Phänomenologische Untersuchungen*. 453 p.

GG5140. ● Shaw, Joshua James: *Emmanuel Levinas on the priority of ethics: putting ethics first*. Amherst, NY: Cambria, 2008. xxxviii, 194 p.

GG5141. ● Vinokur, Val: *The trace of Judaism: Dostoevsky, Babel, Mandelstam, Levinas*. Evanston: Northwestern Univ. Press, 2008. *Studies in Russian literature and theory*. xii, 190 p.

GG5142. ● Westphal, Merold: *Levinas and Kierkegaard in dialogue*. Bloomington: Indiana Univ. Press, 2008. *Indiana series in the philosophy of religion*. xiii, 185 p.

GG5143. Achtenbreg, Deborah: "The eternal and the new: Socrates and Levinas on desire and need." In 5123.

GG5144. Alford, C. Fred: "Levinas and the limits of political theory." In 5125, 107-126.

GG5145. Altizer, Thomas J. J.: "Ethics and predestination in Augustine and Levinas." In 5123.

GG5146. Baccarini, Emilio: "La devozione del dire Dio altrimenti." In 5111, 367-386.

GG5147. Banon, David: "Penseur juif ou Juif qui pense?" In 5111, 223-236.

GG5148. Baracchi, Claudia: "Ethics as first philosophy." In 5123.

GG5149. Barash, Jeffrey Andrew: "Après Davos. L'éthique à l'épreuve du politique chez Ernst Cassirer et Emmanuel Levinas," *Critique*, tome 64, no. 728-729 (janv.-févr. 2008), 145-157.

GG5150. Barber, Michael: "Epistemic and ethic intersubjectivity in Brandom and Levinas," *Levinas Studies*, vol. 3 (2008), [n.p.].

GG5151. Batnitzky, Leora: "Enjoymenet and boredom: what Levinas took from Heidegger." In 5115.

GG5152. Benso, Silvia: "The breathing of the air: presocratic echoes in Levinas." In 5123.

GG5153. Bensussan, Gérard: "Justice et proximité." In 5111, 171-182.

GG5154. Bergo, Bettina: "A site from which to hope?: notes on sensibility and meaning in Levinas and Nietzsche," *Levinas Studies*, vol. 3 (2008), [n.p.].

GG5155.   Bergo, Bettina: "The time and language of messianism: Levinas and Saint Paul." In 5123.

GG5156.   Bernasconi, Robert: "Extra-territoriality: outside the state, outside the subject," *Levinas Studies*, vol. 3 (2008), [n.p.]. [Also in 5124]

GG5157.   Biesta, Gert J. J.: "Pedagogy with empty hands: Levinas, education, and the question of being human." In 5122.

GG5158.   Brezzi, Francesca: "Reinterrogando Levinas." In 5111, 255-272.

GG5159.   Brumlik, Micha: "Vom Obskurantismus zur Heiligkeit: 'Ostjüdisches' Denken bei Buber, Heschel, Levinas," *Osteuropa*, 58. Jahrgang, Heft 8-10 (2008), 97-109.

GG5160.   Bugaite, Elena: "Verità e giustizia, separazione e assoluto in *Totalità e infinito* di Emmanuel Levinas," *Freiburger Zeitschrift für Philosophie und Theologie*, 55. Jahrgang, Heft 2 (2008), 380-400.

GG5161.   Burggraeve, Roger: "Affected by the face of the other." In 5111, 273-308.

GG5162.   Burggraeve, Roger: "Awakened into vigilance: in conversation with a recalcitrant thinker." In 5105.

GG5163.   Burggraeve, Roger: "Une générosité qui donne à penser. Mes rencontres avec Emmanuel Levinas," *Cahiers d'Etudes Lévinassiennes*, no. 7 (2008), 193-224.

GG5164.   Burggraeve, Roger: 'No one can save oneself without others': an ethic of liberation in the footsteps of Emmanuel Levinas." In 5105.

GG5165.   Burke, Sean: "Facing the other animal." In 933.

GG5166.   Burns, Lawrence: "Identifying concrete ethical demands in the face of the abstract other: Emmanuel Levinas' pragmatic ethics," *Philosophy and Social Criticism*, vol. 34, no. 3 (March 2008), 315-335.

GG5167.   Carrero de Salazar, M. Carmen: "Levinas' asymmetry and the question of women's oppression: response to Borgerson's 'feminist ethical ontology'," *Feminist Theory*, vol. 9, no. 1 (2008), 109-115.

GG5168.   Casper, Bernhard: " 'Autrement que' Husserl et 'au-delà de' Heidegger." In 5111, 399-414.

GG5169.   Caygill, Howard: "Levinas's silence." In 5125, 83-92.

GG5170.   Chalier, Catherine; Ami Bouganim: "Emmanuel Levinas school master and pedagogue." In 5122.

GG5171.   Chanter, Tina: "Hands that give and hands that take: the politics of the Other in Levinas." In 5125, 71-80.

GG5172.   Chinnery, Ann; Heesoon Bai: "Justice in the name of the Other." In 5122.

GG5173.   Ciglia, Francesco Paolo: "Fra interlocuzione dialogica e responsabilità etica." In 5111, 317-338.

GG5174.   Cohen, Richard A.: "Heidegger, Kant, Levinas and the end of the world." In 5137.

GG5175.   Cohen, Richard A.: "Signifying a spiritual politics in the age of secularity." In 5111, 183-196.

GG5176.   Cornell, Drucilla: "Who has the right to die?" In 5125, 165-177

GG5177.   Craig, Megan: "Lights in the dark: the radical empiricism of Emmanuel Levinas and William James," *Pli: The Warwick Journal of Philosophy*, vol. 18 (2007), 84-107.

GG5178.   Crépon, Marc: "Le mal absolu et la fraternité," *Cahiers d'Etudes Lévinassiennes*, no. 7 (2008), 11-23.

GG5179.   Critchley, Simon: "Five problems in Levinas's view of politics and a sketch of a solution to them." In 5125, 93-105.

GG5180.   Critchley, Simon: "The split subject." In 5124.

GG5181.   Davenport, John J.: "What Kierkegaardian faith adds to alterity ethics." In 5117. [Derrida]

GG5182.   Desfossés, François: "Une tout autre parole: au croisement des pensées de Heidegger et de Levinas." Diss., Univ. du Québec à Rimouski, 2008. x, 602 p.

GG5183.   Dewitte, Jacques: "Le mystère du Mal et la beauté du monde," *Cahiers d'Etudes Lévinassiennes*, no. 7 (2008), 25-49.

GG5184.   Diamantides, Marinos: "Levinas and critical legal thought." In 5125, 179-215.

GG5185. Diedrich, W. Wolf: "Levinas' Christian readers." In 5105.

GG5186. Dillen, Annemie: "Infinite responsibility and 'good enough parenting': the challenge of Levinas's thought for family ethics." In 5105.

GG5187. Direk, Zeynep: "Levinas and Kierkegaard: ethics and politics." In 5117.

GG5188. Drabinski, John: "On subjectivity and political debt," *Levinas Studies*, vol. 3 (2008), [n.p.].

GG5189. Dreizik, Pablo: "The phenomenology of violence in Levinas." In 5111, 309-316.

GG5190. Dudiak, Jeffery: "The greatest commandment? Religion and/or ethics in Kierkegaard and Levinas." In 5117.

GG5191. Dudiak, Jeffery: "Peace as being taught: the philosophical foundations of a culture of peace." In 5122.

GG5192. Duns, Ryan G.: "Being in the face of nameless mystery: Levinas and the trace of doctrine," *Heythrop Journal*, vol. 49, no. 1 (Jan. 2008), 97-109.

GG5193. Edwards, Laurence L.: " 'Extreme attention to the real': Levinas and religious hermeneutics," *Shofar*, vol. 26, no. 4 (Summer 2008), 36-53.

GG5194. Egéa-Kuehne, Denise: "Levinas's quest for justice." In 5122.

GG5195. Eikels, Kai van: "Dankbar für nichts: Gibt es eine Ethik ohne Erfahrung?" In 380, 9-24.

GG5196. Eisenstadt, Oona: "Anti-Utopianism revisited," *Shofar*, vol. 26, no. 4 (Summer 2008), 120-138.

GG5197. Eppert, Claudia: "Emmanuel Levinas, literary engagement, and literature education." In 5122.

GG5198. Eskenazi, Tamara Cohn: "Re-reading the Bible with Levinas." In 5137.

GG5199. Fabenblat, Michael: "Ethics and *Halakhah* in Levinas," *Shofar*, vol. 26, no. 4 (Summer 2008), 97-119.

GG5200. Fagniez, Guillaume: "Levinas et Heidegger, côte à côte et face à face. Sur la question de l'habitation," *Revue Philosophique de Louvain*, tome 106, no. 4 (nov. 2008), 747-770.

GG5201. Faulconer, James E.: "The past and future community: Abraham and Isaac, Sarah and Rebekah," *Levinas Studies*, vol. 3 (2008), [n.p.].

GG5202. Ferreira, M. Jamie: "Kierkegaard and Levinas on four elements of the biblical love commandment." In 5117.

GG5203. Ferretti, Giovanni: "Dal sacro al santo." In 5111, 47-66.

GG5204. Finkielkraut, Alain; Gilles Hanus: "Il y a quelque chose à dire en faveur de la honte," *Cahiers d'Etudes Lévinassiennes*, no. 7 (2008), 267-299.

GG5205. Folens, Tomas: "The other as oneself: a confrontation between Paul Ricœur and Emmanuel Levinas." In 5105.

GG5206. Franks, Paul: "Ontology and ethics: questioning first philosophy in Levinas, Heidegger, and Fichte." In 5115.

GG5207. Freize, Donna-Lee: "The death of the suffering other: responding to Holocaust survivors through the philosophy of Emmanuel Levinas." In 604.

GG5208. Fuchs, Wolfgang: "Love and lust after Levinas and Lingis," *Philosophy Today*, vol. 52, no. 1 (Spring 2008), 45-51.

GG5209. García-Baró, Miguel: "De l'émotion. La phénoménologie contre l'ontologie." In 5111, 339-350.

GG5210. Garrison, Jim: "Ethical obligation and avoiding self-sacrifice in caring for the Other: reflections on Levinas." In 5122.

GG5211. Goetschel, Roland: "Levinas et Hermann Cohen." In 5111, 67-76.

GG5212. Gonzalez, Francisco J.: "Levinas questioning Plato on eros and maieutics." In 5123.

GG5213. Goodhart, Sandor: " 'A land that devours its inhabitants': Midrashic reading, Emmanuel Levinas, and prophetic exegesis," *Shofar*, vol. 26, no. 4 (Summer 2008), 13-35.

GG5214. Gordon, Peter Eli: "Fidelity as heresy: Levinas, Heidegger, and the crisis of the transcendental ego." In 5115.

GG5215. Goud, Johan F.: " 'What one asks of oneself, one asks of a saint': a dialogue with Emmanuel Levinas, 1980-1981," *Levinas Studies*, vol. 3 (2008), [n.p.].

GG5216. Gregoriou, Zelia: "How hospitable can dwelling be? The folds of spatiality in Levinas." In 5122.

GG5217. Gross, Benjamin: "Religious discourse and the language of ethics." In 835.

GG5218. Hammerschlag, Sarah: "Another, other Abraham: Derrida's figuring of Levinas's Judaism," *Shofar*, vol. 26, no. 4 (Summer 2008), 74-96. [Derrida]

GG5219. Handerek, Joanna: "Relations with others in the face of Levinas' *il-y-a*," *Analecta Husserliana*, vol. 95 (2008), 409-418.

GG5220. Hanley, Catriona: "Aristotle and Levinas on war and peace." In 5123.

GG5221. Hansel, Georges: "Emmanuel Levinas and Christianity." In 5137.

GG5222. Hansel, Joëlle: " 'Proches et lointains': Emmanuel Levinas et Vladimir Jankélévitch." In 5111, 121-134.

GG5223. Hanus, Gilles: "Le mal, entre facticité et théodicée," *Cahiers d'Etudes Lévinassiennes*, no. 7 (2008), 51-64.

GG5224. Harvey, Warren Zev: "Levinas on the vocation of Jewish philosophy." In 5111, 77-82.

GG5225. Hayatshahi, Maryam: "Zur Kategorie der Situation im Denken von Emmanuel Levinas." Diss., Frankfurt (Main) Univ., 2008. 201 p.

GG5226. Heng, Wang: "Levinas's phenomenology of sensibility and time in his early period." In 5124.

GG5227. Izzi, John: "Proximity in distance: Levinas and Plotinus." In 5123.

GG5228. Jie, Shang: "The phenomenology of death." In 5124.

GG5229. Kaarto, Tomi: "The decision of Kafka's 'Explorer': Derrida on the notions 'ethics' and 'politics' in Levinas." In 588, 2-23. [Derrida]

GG5230. Kajon, Irene: "Levinas and Platonic humanism." In 5111, 95-108.

GG5231. Kangas, David; Martin Kavka: "Hearing, patiently: time and salvation in Kierkegaard and Levinas." In 5117.

GG5232. Kodelja, Zdenko: "Autonomy and heteronomy: Kant and Levinas." In 5122.

GG5233. Korhonen, Kuisma: "Towards a post-Levinasian approach to narrativity," *Partial Answers*, vol. 6, no. 2 (June 2008), 459-480.

GG5234. Krewani, Wolfgang Nikolaus: "A propos de la notion de justification." In 5111, 109-120.

GG5235. Krueger, Joel W.: "Levinasian reflections on somaticity and the ethical self," *Inquiry*, vol. 51, no. 6 (Dec. 2008), 603-626.

GG5236. Lamarche, Pierre: "Of a non-saying that says nothing: Levinas and Pyrrhonism." In 5123.

GG5237. Lechner, Elsa: "Subjectivity, displacement and the ethics of ethnographic representation." In 588, 333-348.

GG5238. Lescourret, Marie-Anne: "Un air de visage." In 5111, 35-46.

GG5239. Lescourret, Marie-Ange: "Desire by Levinas." In 5124.

GG5240. Levinas, Emmanuel; France Guwy: "What no one else can do in my place: a conversation with Emmanuel Levinas." In 974.

GG5241. Lévy, Benny: "Philon et le langage de la philosophie. Dieu et la création du mal," *Cahiers d'Etudes Lévinassiennes*, no. 7 (2008), 65-72.

GG5242. Liping, Wang: "Transcendence or immanence?" In 5124. [Bergson]

GG5243. Lissa, Giuseppe: "Dal primato della politica al primato dell'etica." In 5111, 135-170.

GG5244. Llewelyn, John: "Who or what or whot?" In 5117.

GG5245. Lombardi, Ivan: "Defenomenalizzazione e rifenomenolizzazione del mondo. Levinas tra Husserl e Heidegger (1930-1948)," *Studi Filosofici*, tomo 30 (2007), 291-303.

GG5246. Love, Kevin: "Emmanuel Levinas and the question of theophany," *Angelaki*, vol. 12, no. 3 (Dec. 2007), 65-79.

GG5247. Lucchetti Bingemar, Maria Clara: "Otherness as path toward overcoming violence: a comparative study of Emmanuel Levinas and Simone Weil," *Levinas Studies*, vol. 3 (2008), [n.p.]. [Weil]

GG5248.   Manderson, Desmond: "Here I am: illuminating and delimiting responsibility." In 5125, 145-164.

GG5249.   Marder, Michael: "Terror of the ethical: on Levinas' *Il y a*," *Postmodern Culture*, vol. 18, no. 2 (Jan. 2008), [n.p.].

GG5250.   Martin, Betsan: "Dehiscence: a dispersal of Levinas in the South Pacific." In 5122.

GG5251.   Marty, Éric: "Emmanuel Levinas avec Shakespeare, Proust et Rimbaud," *Temps Modernes*, 63e année, no. 649 (avril-juin 2008), 224-243. [Proust, Rimbaud]

GG5252.   Matustik, Martin Beck: " 'More than all the others': meditation on responsibility." In 5117.

GG5253.   McPherson, Ian: "Other than the other: Levinas and the educational questioning of infinity." In 5122.

GG5254.   Meir, Ephraim: "Athens and Jerusalem in Levinas's *Difficult Freedom*." In 5111, 83-94.

GG5255.   Mendes de Menezes, Magali: "Um dizer feminino: a maternidade como expressão da subjetividade no pensamento de Emmanuel Levinas." In 965.

GG5256.   Minister, Stephen: "World of justice, works of love." In 5117.

GG5257.   Monseu, Nicolas: "De la philosophie de l'existence à la phénoménologie existentielle: l'attention à Chestov dans les premiers travaux de Levinas," *Cahiers d'Etudes Lévinassiennes*, no. 7 (2008), 227-245.

GG5258.   Morrison, Glenn: "The (im)possibilities of Levinas for Christian theology." In 5137.

GG5259.   Morrison, Glenn: "Renewing Christian theology with Levinas." In 5105.

GG5260.   Moyaert, Marianne: "In responses to the religious other." In 5105.

GG5261.   Naas, Michael: "Lending assistance always to itself: Levinas' infinite conversation with Platonic dialogue." In 5123.

GG5262.   Navarro, Olivia: "El 'rostro' del otro: una lectura de la ética de la alteridad de Emmanuel Levinas," *Contrastes*, vol. 13 (2008), 177-194.

GG5263.   Neppi, Enzo: "Bibbia e modernità nell'opera di Levinas e di Primo Levi." In 5111, 197-210.

GG5264.   Nordmann, Sophie: "Hermann Cohen, Emmanuel Levinas et la question de la souffrance," *Cahiers d'Etudes Lévinassiennes*, no. 7 (2008), 73-98.

GG5265.   Papastephanou, Marianna: "The priority of ethics over ontology, the issue of forgiveness and education." In 5122.

GG5266.   Peñalver Gómez, Patricio: "Mal radical et responsabilité infinie," *Cahiers d'Etudes Lévinassiennes*, no. 7 (2008), 99-136.

GG5267.   Peperzak, Adriaan T.: "Transfigurations." In 5111, 351-366.

GG5268.   Petrosino, Silvano: "La topologia di Levinas." In 5111, 19-34.

GG5269.   Piering, Julie: "Stoic ethics and totality in light of Levinasian alterity." In 5123.

GG5270.   Ponzio, Julia: "Politics not left to itself: recognition and forgiveness in Levinas's philosophy." In 5125, 35-48.

GG5271.   Prairat, Eirick: "Thinking educational ethics with Levinas and Jonas." In 5122.

GG5272.   Richter, Silvia: "Language and eschatology in the work of Emmanuel Levinas," *Shofar*, vol. 26, no. 4 (Summer 2008), 54-73.

GG5273.   Riemslagh, Marina: "The face-to-face as asymmetrical and reciprocal revelation." In 5105.

GG5274.   Rosenberg, Shalom: "Levinas and infinity." In 5111, 13-18.

GG5275.   Rubenstein, Mary-Jane: "Openness: Emmanuel Levinas." In 978.

GG5276.   Schonfeld, Eli: "Sur le Mal élémental," *Cahiers d'Etudes Lévinassiennes*, no. 7 (2008), 137-153.

GG5277.   Schroeder, Brian: "Politics and transcendence." In 5125, 127-141.

GG5278.   Schroeder, Brian: "A trace of the eternal return? Levinas and Neoplatonism." In 5123.

GG5279.   Simmons, J. Aaron: "Existential appropriations: the influence of Jean Wahl on Levinas's reading of Kierkegaard." In 5117.

GG5280. Slaughter, Marty: "Levinas, mercy, and the Middle Ages." In 5125, 49-69.
GG5281. Smit, Christopher R.: "A collaborative aesthetic: Levinas's idea of responsibility and the photographs of Charles Eisenmann and the late nineteenth-century freak-performer." In 878, 283-311.
GG5282. Smith, Nicholas H.: "Levinas, Habermas and modernity," *Philosophy and Social Criticism*, vol. 34, no. 6 (July 2008), 643-664.
GG5283. Stähler, Tanja: "Getting under the skin: Platonic myths in Levinas." In 5123.
GG5284. Standish, Paul: "Levinas's language and the language of the curriculum." In 5122.
GG5285. Taminiaux, Jacques: "Levinas and Heidegger." In 5124.
GG5286. Tangjia, Wang: "The concepts of death in Heidegger and Levinas." In 5124.
GG5287. Tardivel, Emilie: "Transcendance et liberté: Levinas, Patocka et la question du mal," *Cahiers d'Etudes Lévinassiennes*, no. 7 (2008), 155-175.
GG5288. Todd, Sharon: "Welcoming and difficult learning: reading Levinas with education." In 5122.
GG5289. Topolski, Anya: "On freedom in Athens and jerusalem: Arendt's political challenge to Levinas' ethics of responsibility." In 5105.
GG5290. Van Daele, Emilie: "From humanism to anti-humanism and back again: Levinas' redefinition of subjectivity and responsibility." In 5105.
GG5291. Vanheessen, Jean: "A agapeic ethics without eros?: Emmanuel Levinas on need, happiness and desire." In 5105.
GG5292. Vaughan, William: "Community of those who are going to die: on Levinas." In 988.
GG5293. Veltri, Giuseppe: "Philosophy versus philosophy: a critical analysis of Levinas' interpretation of 'translatability' in his commentary on Bavli Megillah 8b-9b." In 5111, 211-222.
GG5294. Veulemans, Sophie: "On time: Levinas' appropriation of Bergson." In 5105. [Bergson]
GG5295. Vinokur, Val: " 'And I most of all': Levinas in *The Brothers Karamazov*." In 5141.
GG5296. Vinokur, Val: "Levinas and Russian literature." In 5141.
GG5297. Visker, Rudi: "In praise of visibility," *Levinas Studies*, vol. 3 (2008), [n.p.].
GG5298. Vogel, Lawrence: "Emmanuel Levinas and the Judaism of the Good Samaritan," *Levinas Studies*, vol. 3 (2008), [n.p.].
GG5299. Von Wolzogen, Christoph: "Das Wort als Geschichtlichkeit. Heinrich Barth, Emmanuel Levinas und Julius Schaaf. Eine Vergegenwärtigung," *Freiburger Zeitschrift für Philosophie und Theologie*, 55. Jahrband, Heft 1 (2008), 185-204.
GG5300. Weimin, Mo: "Phenomenology of anti-phenomenology? A study of the subject in Levinas." In 5124.
GG5301. Weitzman, Erica: "Necessary interruption: traces of the political in Levinas," *Theory and Event*, vol. 11, no. 2 (2008), [n.p.].
GG5302. Welz, Claudia: "Welche Macht is mächtiger als Ohnmacht?" In 1028, 165-185.
GG5303. Wenzler, Ludwig: "Ausbrechen aus der Totalität der Geschichte." In 5111, 387-398.
GG5304. Weston, Michael: "Kierkegaard, Levinas and 'absolute alterity'." In 5117.
GG5305. Westphal, Merold: "The many faces of Levinas as a reader of Kierkegaard." In 954. [Also in 5117]
GG5306. Wigoda, Shmuel: "The moon and the goat: Levinas on Kenosis." In 5111, 237-254.
GG5307. Wills, David: "Facades of the other: Heidegger, Althusser, Levinas." In 990. [Althusser]
GG5308. Wimmer, Michael: "Thinking the other—the other thinking." In 5122.
GG5309. Wiszniewski, Dorian: "Levinas and architecture." In 5124.
GG5310. Wolfs, Toren: "Levinas, euthanasia and the presence of non-sense." In 5105.
GG5311. Wolin, Richard: "Levinas and Heidegger: the anxiety of influence." In 5115.

GG5312. Wright, John W.: "Levinasian ethics of alterity." In 870, 50-68.

GG5313. Wyschogrod, Edith: "The challenge of justice." In 5117.

GG5314. Xiangchen, Sun: "Emmanuel Levinas and the critique of modern political philosophy." In 5124.

GG5315. Xiaozhen, Du: "The philosophy of saintliness." In 5124.

GG5316. Yampolskaya, Anna: "Levinas en Russie: une philosophie inattendue, dérangeante, incontournable," *Cahiers d'Etudes Lévinassiennes*, no. 7 (2008), 317-339.

GG5317. Yang, Dachun: "Levinas and the three dimensions of surpassing phenomenology." In 5124.

GG5318. Zagury-Orly, Raphael: "Heidegger et Levinas. Questions préalables," *Cahiers d'Etudes Lévinassiennes*, no. 7 (2008), 247-264.

LÉVI-STRAUSS, Claude. See also 962.

GG5319. ● *Abécédaire de Claude Lévi-Strauss*. Sous la dir. de Jean-Philippe Cazier. Mons: Sils Maria, 2008. 198 p.

GG5320. ● *Anthropologie [L'] de Lévi-Strauss et la psychanalyse: d'une structure l'autre*. Sous la dir. de Marcel Drach et Bernard Toboul. Paris: La Découverte, 2008. *Recherches*. 331 p.

GG5321. ● Bertholet, Denis: *Claude Lévi-Strauss*. Paris: O. Jacob, 2008. 465 p.

GG5322. ● Desveaux, Emmanuel: *Au-delà du structuralisme: six méditations sur Claude Lévi-Strauss*. Paris: Complexe, 2008. 158 p.

GG5323. ● Hénaff, Marcel: *Claude Lévi-Strauss, le passeur de sens*. Paris: Perrin, 2008. *Tempus*. 233 p.

GG5324. ● Imbert, Claude: *Lévi-Strauss, le passage du nord-ouest*. Paris: Herne, 2008. *Carnets de l'Herne*. 226 p.

GG5325. ● Joulia, Emilie: *Claude Lévi-Strauss: l'homme derrière l'œuvre*. Paris: Lattès, 2008. 203 p.

GG5326. ● Kauppert, Michael: *Claude Lévi-Strauss*. Konstanz: UVK, 2008. 150 p.

GG5327. ● Lévi-Strauss, Claude: *Œuvres*. Préface par Vincent Debaene; édition établie par Vincent Debaene [et al.]. Paris: Gallimard, 2008. *Bibliothèque de la Pléiade*. lxii, 2063 p.

GG5328. ● Nattiez, Jean-Jacques: *Lévi-Strauss musicien: essai sur la tentation homologique*. Arles: Actes sud, 2008. 241 p.

GG5329. ● Passetti, Dorothea Voegeli: *Lévi-Strauss, antropologia e arte*. São Paulo: Edusp, 2008. 488 p.

GG5330. ● Paz, Octavio: *Claude Lévi-Strauss, o El nuevo festín de Esopo*. Barcelona: Seix Barral, 2008.

GG5331. ● Reinhardt, Thomas: *Claude Lévi-Strauss zur Einführung*. Hamburg: Junius, 2008. 187 p.

GG5332. ● *Siècle [Le] de Lévi-Strauss*. Avant-propos de Jean Daniel. Paris: CNRS, 2008. 190 p.

GG5333. ● Stoczkowski, Wiktor: *Anthropologies rédemptrices: le monde selon Lévi-Strauss*. Paris: Hermann, 2008. *Société et pensées*. 347 p.

GG5334. ● Tremlett, Paul-François: *Lévi-Strauss on religion: the structuring mind*. London; Oakville, CT: Equinox, 2008. *Key thinkers in the study of religion*. ix, 121 p.

GG5335. ● *Wirkungen des wilden Denkens: zur strukturalen Anthropologie von Claude Lévi-Strauss*. Hrsg. Michael Kauppert und Dorett Funcke. Frankfurt: Suhrkamp, 2008. 446 p.

GG5336. Baron, Ulrich: "Zur Aktualität von Claude Lévi-Strauss," *Neue Gesellschaft Frankfurter Hefte*, Nr. 11 (2008), 66-68.

GG5337. Benoist, Jocelyn: "Le 'dernier pas' du structuralisme: Lévi-Strauss et le dépassement du modèle linguistique," *Philosophie*, no. 98 (été 2008), 54-70.

GG5338. Clément, Catherine: "Lévi-Strauss et la France, ou les nouvelles rêveries d'un promeneur solitaire," *Règle du Jeu*, no. 37 (mai 2008), 81-96.

GG5339. Descola, Philippe: "Sur Lévi-Strauss, le structuralisme et l'anthropologie de la nature. Entretien avec Marcel Hénaff," *Philosophie*, no. 98 (été 2008), 8-36.

GG5340. Doja, Albert: "From neolithic naturalness to *Tristes Tropiques*: the emergence of Lévi-Strauss's new humanism," *Theory, Culture and Society*, vol. 25, no. 1 (Jan. 2008), 77-100.

GG5341.   Hauschild, Thomas: "Der alte Meister: Claude Lévi-Strauss zum 100. Geburtstag," *Saeculum*, 59. Jahrgang, 2. Halbband (2008), 169-176.

GG5342.   Jardel, Jean-Pierre: "Deux récits d'une escale à la Martinique." In 453, 192-207.

GG5343.   Maniglier, Patrice: "La condition symbolique," *Philosophie*, no. 98 (été 2008), 37-53.

GG5344.   Massonet, Stéphane: "La salamandre sur l'Olympe," *Nouvelle Revue Française*, no. 586 (juin 2008), 122-134.

GG5345.   Massonet, Stéphane: "Voyage dans l'œil de l'ethnographe," *Nouvelle Revue Française*, no. 586 (juin 2008), 105-121.

GG5346.   Ritter, Henning: "Claude Lévi-Strauss." In 975.

GG5347.   Salmon, Gildas: "Les incongruities de la pensée symbolique," *Philosophie*, no. 98 (été 2008), 71-90.

GG5348.   Smith, Douglas: "A river runs through it: Lévi-Strauss and Renoir in India," *Francophone Postcolonial Studies*, vol. 6, no. 1 (Spring-Summer 2008), 62-79.

GG5349.   Spies, Werner: "Claude Lévi-Strauss." In 596.

GG5350.   Zehentreiter, Ferdinand: "Jenseits des 'Alterns der neuen Musik': Ausdrucksästhetische Korrespondenzen zwischen Theodor W. Adorno, Claude Lévi-Strauss und Brian Ferneyhough." In 801.

LÉVY, Bernard-Henri. See also 4527, 6102.

GG5351.   Romano, Carlin: "A French intellectual star considers what's right about the left," *Chronicle of Higher Education*, vol. 55, no. 2 (Sept. 5, 2008), B6-B7.

LEWINTER, Roger.

GG5352.   Roubaud, Jacques: "Roger Lewinter. Une virgule suivie du mot 'vers'," *Critique*, tome 64, no. 735-736 (août-sept. 2008), 719-723.

LIKING, Werewere.

GG5353.   Forsing Fondjo, Luc: "*Orphée-Dafric*: le mythe d'Orphée revisité par Werewere Liking." In 520, 669-684.

LILAR, Suzanne.

GG5354.   Quaghebeur, Marc: "Maria Van Rysselberghe et Suzanne Lilar: deux façons d'indiquer et de voiler le nom de l'auteur." In 441, 161-177.

LIMBOUR, Georges. See 737.

LINDON, Jérôme. See 3671, 3673.

LINERT, Auguste.

GG5355.   Leroux, Nicolas: "Auguste Linert: dix ans de littérature (1885-1894)," *Œil Bleu*, no. 5 (2008), 40-44.

LITTELL, Jonathan. See also 4531.

GG5356.   ● Daxner, Michael: *Die Wohlgesinnten, ein Roman von Jonathan Littell*. Oldenburg: BIS-Verlag, 2008. 31 p.

GG5357.   ● Littell, Jonathan: *Die Wohlgesinnten: Marginalien*. Mit Beiträgen von Jürg Altwegg [et al.]. Berlin: Berlin Verlag, 2008. 99 p.

GG5358.   Boblet, Marie-Hélène: "Roman historique et vérité romanesque." In 908, 221-240.

GG5359.   Breton, Philippe: "Nazisme: une fascination déplacée. A propos de l'ouvrage de Jonathan Littell, *Les Bienveillantes*," *Raison Présente*, no. 167 (2008), 99-108.

GG5360.   Hausmann, Frank-Rutger: "Jonathan Littells Holocaustroman *Les bienveillantes* im "Reading-Room'," *Romantische Zeitschrift für Literaturgeschichte*, 32. Jahrgang, Heft 3-4 (2008), 447-465.

GG5361.   Lyle, Louise: "Ideology and the individual in Jonathan Littell's *Les Bienveillantes*," *French Studies Bulletin*, no. 109 (Winter 2008), 85-88.

GG5362.   O'Neil, Mary Anne: "Myth and the French historical novel: Littell's *Les Bienveillantes* and Desvignes' *American saga*," *Studies on Lucette Desvignes and the Twentieth Century*, no. 18 (2008), 101-109. [Desvignes]

GG5363.   Scheller, Wolf: "Zu Jonathan Littells Roman *die Wohlgesinnten*," *Neue Gesellschaft Frankfurter Hefte*, Nr. 5 (2008), 65-68.

LODS, Jean. See 1160.

LOPES, Henri. See also 7211.

GG5364. ● Nzete, Paul: *Les langues africaines dans l'œuvre romanesque de Henri Lopes*. Paris: L'Harmattan, 2008. 99 p.

GG5365. Coulibalyk, Adama: "Identité métisse, mémoire et fictions chez Henri Lopes." In 103, 33-43.

GG5366. Dianga, Larissa: "La tribalique métisse." In 521, 89-93.

GG5367. Kavwahirehi, Kasereka: "L'écriture, la mémoire et l'identité: Henri Lopes et le métier à métisser." In 103, 45-59.

LORANGER, Jean-Aubert.

GG5368. Bonenfant, Luc: "Modernité générique et usages formels du verset dans *Les atmosphères* de Jean-Aubert Loranger," *Etudes Littéraires*, vol. 38, no. 2 (automne 2007), 69-81.

LORRAIN, Jean. See also 558, 6535.

GG5369. ● *Jean Lorrain (1885-1906): autour et alentours: actes du premier colloque Jean Lorrain, Yport, 26 novembre 2005.* Intervention d'ouverture, Thierry Rodange. Fécamp: Société des Amis de Jean Lorrain, 2007. 93 p.

GG5370. ● Lorrain, Jean: *Histoires de batraciens.* Etablissement des textes, notes, postface et bibliographie par Pascal Noir. Paris: L'Harmattan, 2008. *Les introuvables.* 140 p.

GG5371. ● Lorrain, Jean: *Lettres à Henry Kistenmaeckers.* Réunies, annotées et prés. par Eric Walbecq. Eaubonne: Clown lyrique, 2008. *Les inédits.* 173 p.

GG5372. Anthonay, Thibaut d': "Lorrain et Maupassant." In 5369, 73-81. [Maupassant]

GG5373. Bourrelier, Paul-Henri: "Lorrain et *La Revue Blanche.*" In 5369, 63-72.

GG5374. Brunel, Pierre: "De des Esseintes à Monsieur de Phocas." In 5369, 19-25. [Huysmans]

GG5375. Grivel, Charles: "Lorrain photographique." In 529, 195-210.

GG5376. Lair, Samuel: "Lorrain et Mirbeau." In 5369, 53-62. [Mirbeau]

GG5377. Lowrie, Joyce O.: "Man mirrors toad, or vice-versa: decadent narcissism in Jean Lorrains' œuvre." In 511.

GG5378. Mathieu, Xavier: "Jean Lorrain: le poseur impénitent." In 5369, 29-41.

GG5379. Néry, Alain: "Lorrain, Huysmans et la décadence." In 5369, 11-81. [Huysmans]

GG5380. Ricard, Jean-Pierre: "Une fin d'année fin de siècle: l'automne chez Jean Lorrain." In 383, 159-174.

GG5381. Rodange, Thierry: "Jean Lorrain et Hugues Rebell: vers une certaine aristie." In 5369, 43-49.

GG5382. Ziegler, Robert: "The mask of the blinded toad: Jean Lorrain 1900," *Dalhousie French Studies*, vol. 84 (Fall 2008), 29-40.

LOTI, Pierre. See also 636, 4563.

GG5383. ● Loti, Pierre: *Aziyadé; suivi de Fantôme d'Orient.* Edition préparée par Claire Labouygues. Clermont-Ferrand: Editions Paleo, 2008. *La collection de sable.* 312 p.

GG5384. ● Loti, Pierre: *La Galilée.* Prés. Jean-Claude Bourlès. Paris: Payot et Rivages, 2008. 206 p.

GG5385. ● Loti, Pierre: *L'Inde, sans les Anglais; précédé de Mahé des Indes.* Edition prés. par Jean-Claude Perrier. Paris: Phébus, 2008. 342 p.

GG5386. ● Loti, Pierre: *Jérusalem.* Prés. de Jean-Claude Bourlès. Paris: Payot et Rivages, 2008. 206 p.

GG5387. ● Loti, Pierre: *Journal. Volume II, 1879-1886.* Edition établie, prés. et annotée par Alain Quella-Villéger et Bruno Vercier. Paris: Indes savantes, 2008. *Rivages des Xantons.* 811 p.

GG5388. ● Nipi-Robin, Jacqueline: *L'autofiction dans les récits du cycle turc de Pierre Loti.* Lille: ANRT, 2008. 717 p.

GG5389. ● Quella-Villéger, Alain: *Chez Pierre Loti: une maison d'écrivain-voyageur.* Poitiers: CRDP de Poitou-Charentes, 2008. 139 p., videodisc. 139 p.

GG5390. ● Toma, Dolores: *Pierre Loti: le voyage, entre la féérie et le néant.* Paris: L'Harmattan, 2008. *Espaces littéraires.* 253 p.

GG5391. • Turberfield, Peter James: *Pierre Loti and the theatricality of desire.* Amsterdam: Rodopi, 2008. *Faux titre*, 309. 264 p.

GG5392. Bann, Stephen: "A nomadic investment in history: Pierre Loti's house at Rochefort-sur-Mer." In 630, 207-219.

GG5393. Berrong, Richard M.: "Painting with words as painters paint: Pierre Loti's concern with perspective," *Studi Francesi*, anno 52, fasc. 2 (maggio-agosto 2008), 396-404.

GG5394. Dureau, Guy: "Les amertumes de l'âme dans *Les Désenchantées* de Pierre Loti." In 417, 137-155.

GG5395. Pénot-Lacassagne, Olivier: "Loti, Claudel et l'amer Japon." In 417, 157-167. [Claudel]

LOUIS-COMBET, Claude. See also 644, 711, 2030, 5892.

GG5396. • *Visions visitations passions: en compagnie de Claude Louis-Combet.* Dir. Stéphanie Boulard. Clichy: Corlevour, 2008. 314 p.

GG5397. Lavauzelle, Stéphane: "Claude Louis-Combet et l'enlisement automnal." In 383, 119-130.

GG5398. Marchal-Ninosque, France: "*Anima* et animal de Claude Louis-combet au service de l'hermaphrodisme." In 419, 425-434.

LOUVET, Jean.

GG5399. Doquire Kerszberg, Annik: "Entretien avec Jean Louvet," *French Review*, vol. 81, no. 6 (May 2008), 1198-1209.

LOUYS, Pierre. See also 706.

GG5400. • Louÿs, Pierre: *Les aventures du roi Pausole.* Prés., notes, variantes, annexes, chronologie et bibliographie par Jean-Paul Goujon. Paris: Flammarion, 2008. *GF*. 381 p.

GG5401. Urzáiz Ramírez de Haro, Isabel: "Pierre Louÿs y las ironías del amor: *Danaë ou le malheur*," *Anales de Filología Francesa*, n. 15 (2006-2007), 287-296.

LUBAC, Henri de.

GG5402. • De Vita, Alberto: *La svolta ecclesiologica di Henri de Lubac.* Roma: Viverein, 2008. 263 p.

GG5403. • Lubac, Henri de: *Augustinisme et théologie moderne.* Sous la dir. de Georges Chantraine, avec la collab. de Patrick Descourtieux; prés. de Michael Figura. Paris: Cerf, 2008. *Œuvres complètes, Henri de Lubac*, 13. xxv, 488 p.

GG5404. • Lubac, Henri de: *La foi chrétienne: essai sur la structure du Symbole des apôtres.* Prtés. De Peter Bexell. Paris: Cerf, 2008. *Œuvres complètes, Henri de Lubac*, 5: *Deuxième section.* l, 610 p.

GG5405. • Lubac, Henri de: *Œuvres complètes. Claudel et Péguy. Henri de Lubac avec Jean Bastaire.* Sous la dir. de Georges Chantraine. Paris: Cerf, 2008. xi, 213 p. [Claudel, Péguy]

GG5406. • Lubac, Henri de: *Œuvres complètes. XXVI, septième section.* Sous la dir. de Jean-Pierre Wagner. Paris: Cerf, 2008. 442 p. [Blondel, Teilhard de Chardin]

GG5407. • Nicoloso, Alfio Domenico: *Libertà verità tra appello, ricerca e obbedienza: una rilettura del pensiero di Henri de Lubac.* Roma: Collegio S. Lorenzo da Brindisi, 2008. 333 p.

GG5408. • Voderholzer, Rudolf: *Meet Henri de Lubac.* Trans. Michael J. Miller. San Francisco: Ignatius, 2008. 222 p.

GG5409. "A master who had never been a disciple: Henri de Lubac." In 790.

GG5410. Mayer, Rupert Johannes: "Zum desiderium naturale visionis Dei nach Johannes Duns Scotus und Thomas de Vio Cajetan: eine Anmerkung zum Denken Henri de Lubacs," *Angelicum*, vol. 85, no. 3 (2008), 737-763.

LUCA, Ghérasim.

GG5411. • *Ghérasim Luca.* Conception éditoriale et suivi, Benoît Decron; assisté de Lydie Joubert et Michelle Massuyeau. *Cahiers de l'Abbaye Sainte Croix*, no. 110. 132 p. [Exhibition catalog]

GG5412. • Luca, Ghérasim: *The passive vampire.* Trans. and introd. Krysztof Fijalkowski. Prague: Twisted Spoon, 2008. 139 p.

GG5413. Fullenbaum, Max: "Dans l'entre-deux de la langue: Gherasim Luca." In 521, 27-32.

LYOTARD, Jean-François. See also 928, 981, 1008, 5857, 6623.

GG5414. ● *Afterwords: essays in memory of Jean-François Lyotard.* Ed. Robert Harvey. Stony Brook, NY: Humanities Institute, 2000. 101 p.

GG5415. ● Gallo, Francesca: *Les Immatériaux: un percorso di Jean-François Lyotard nell'arte contemporanea.* Roma: Aracne, 2008. 200 p.

GG5416. ● *Jean-François Lyotard: critical evaluations in cultural theory.* Ed. Victor E. Taylor, Gregg Lambert. London; New York: Routledge, 2006. 3 vols.

GG5417. ● Sander, Sabine: *Der Topos der Undarstellbarkeit: ästhetische Positionen nach Adorno und Lyotard.* Erlangen: Filos, 2008. 310 p.

GG5418. ● *Transformateurs [Les] Lyotard.* Sous la dir. de Corinne Enaudeau [et al.]. Paris: Sens & Tonka, 2008. 396 p.

GG5419. ● Wunderlich, Antonia: *Der Philosoph im Museum: Die Ausstellung "Les Immatériaux" von Jean-François Lyotard.* Bielefeld: Transcript, 2008. 262 p.

GG5420. Deleuze, Gilles: "Lettre à Jean-François Lyotard," *Europe,* no. 949 (mai 2008), 264. [Deleuze]

GG5421. Harvey, Robert: "Témoinité," *Europe,* no. 949 (mai 2008), 284-295.

GG5422. Kolbuszewska, Zofia: "Pynchon, Kant, Lyotard, and the sublime." In 788, 163-168.

GG5423. Marcus, Amit: "Narrative ethics and incommensurable discourses. Lyotard's *The Differend* and Fowles's *The Collector,*" *Mosaic,* vol. 41, no. 4 (Dec. 2008), 77-94.

GG5424. Ronell, Avital: "Ravages de l'impossible," *Europe,* no. 949 (mai 2008), 274-283.

GG5424a. Rose, Sven-Erik: "Auschwitz as hermeneutic rupture, differend, and image malgré tout." In 8015, 114-137.

GG5425. Sanderson, Matthew: "Catastrophic time: Kant and Lyotard on sublime temporality," *International Studies in Philosophy,* vol. 39, no. 1 (2007), 43-57.

GG5426. Thomassen, Lasse: "The violence of consensus: Jean-François Lyotard." In 986.

GG5427. Tomiche, Anne: "Le philosophe, l'œuvre littéraire et la psychanalyse," *Europe,* no. 949 (mai 2008), 265-273.

GG5428. Vandenabeele, Bart: "Aesthetic solidarity 'after' Kant and Lyotard," *Journal of Aesthetic Education,* vol. 42, no. 4 (Winter 2008), 17-30.

5428a. Wald Lasowski, Aliocha: "Signé Lyotard," *Europe,* no. 949 (mai 2008), 255-260.

MAALOUF, Amin.

GG5429. Ette, Ottmar: "Arab-Caribbean origins: on the transareal dimension in Amin Maalouf's literary work." In 53, 143-165.

GG5430. Ette, Ottmar: " 'Ma patrie est caravane'. Amin Maalouf, die Frage des Exils und das ZusammenLebenswissen der Literaturen ohne festen Wohnsitz," *Romantische Zeitschrift für Literaturgeschichte,* 32. Jahrgang, Heft 3-4 (2008), 413-445.

GG5431. Ette, Ottmar: " 'Vivre dans une autre langue, une autre réalité.' Entretien avec Amin Maalouf, Ile d'Yeu, 15 septembre 2007," *Lendemains,* 33. Jahrgang, Heft 129 (2008), 87-101.

GG5432. Solon, Pascale: "Le Liban d'Amin Maalouf," *Interculturel Francophonies,* no. 14 (2008), 83-101.

MABANCKOU, Alain.

GG5433. Boisseron, Bénédicte: "Potlatch transnational dans *Bleu-blanc-rouge* d'Alain Mabanckou," *Dalhousie French Studies,* vol. 84 (Fall 2008), 113-119.

GG5434. Thomas, Dominic: "New technologies and the popular: Alain Mabanckou's blog," *Research in African Literatures,* vol. 39, no. 4 (Winter 2008), 58-71.

MACÉ, Gérard. See also 422, 754.

GG5435. Demanze, Laurent: "Gérard Macé: une hantise biographique." In 391, 219-229.

MAC ORLAN, Pierre.

GG5436. ● Mac Orlan, Pierre: *Le Rire jaune et autres textes.* Edition établie par Sylvain Goudemare. Paris: Sillages, 2008. 407 p.

5436a.	Blondeau, Philippe: "Pierre Mac Orlan et 'les mélancolies de l'âge mûr'." In 379, 99-111.

MAETERLINCK, Maurice. See also 681, 2761.

GG5437. • Capiteyn, André: *Maeterlinck: un prix Nobel.* Gand: Snoeck, 2008. 112 p.

GG5438. • Laoureux, Denis: *Maurice Maeterlinck et la dramaturgie de l'image.* Brasschaat: Pandora, 2008. 287 p.

GG5439. Bouchardon, Marianne: "La didascalie chez Maeterlinck ou la représentation déchirée." In 605, 265-277.

GG5440. Di Donato, Carla: "Alexandre Salzmann et *Pelléas et Mélisande* au Théâtre des Champs-Elysées," *Revue d'Histoire du Théâtre,* no. 238 [no. 2] (2008), 153-170.

GG5441. Gorceix, Paul: "De la mystique médiévale à la psychologie des profondeurs: *Onirologie.*" In 82, 175-185.

GG5442. Gorceix, Paul: "Une dramaturgie de la mort: *L'Intruse* et *Intérieur.*" In 82, 207-228.

GG5443. Gorceix, Paul: "M. Maeterlinck et W. Kandinsky." In 82, 207-218.

GG5444. Gorceix, Paul: "Maurice Maeterlinck et l'analogie." In 82, 125-143.

GG5445. Gorceix, Paul: "Maurice Maeterlinck et l'ésotérisme." In 82, 275-288.

GG5446. Gorceix, Paul: "Maurice Maeterlinck et la forme fragmentaire." In 82, 145-160.

GG5447. Gorceix, Paul: "Maurice Maeterlinck, l'entomologiste." In 82, 267-274.

GG5448. Gorceix, Paul: "Maurice Maeterlinck, vecteur du concept de 'mystique' chez Hermann Bahr, Hugo von Hofmannsthal et Rainer Maria Rilke." In 82, 289-306.

GG5449. Gorceix, Paul: "*L'Oiseau bleu:* un *Märchen* initiatique." In 82, 243-266.

GG5450. Gorceix, Paul: "*Pelléas et Mélisande* au miroir de la lecture de V. Meyerhold." In 82, 229-241.

GG5451. Gorceix, Paul: "La poétique du mystère: *Serres chaudes, Douze chansons, La Princesse Maleine.*" In 82, 187-205.

GG5452. Johach, Eva: "Schwärmen nach der fernen Geliebten: Naturpoesie und Geschlechtermetaphysik in Maurice Maeterlincks 'Das Leben der Bienen' (1919)," *Zeitschrift für Germanistik,* 18. Jahrgang, Heft 2 (2008), 308-317.

GG5453. Martin-Schmets, Victor: "Le triangle Claudel-Maeterlinck-Mockel," *Bulletin de la Société Paul Claudel,* no. 191 (3e trim. 2008), 8-19.

GG5454. Otten, Michel: "Maurice Maeterlinck: de la mystique à la sagesse." In 510, 115-122.

GG5455. Rykner, Arnaud: "Maeterlinck and the search for music." In 79, 23-29.

MAGANI, Mohammed.

GG5456. Slimani Aït-Saada, Eldjamhouria: "La mémoire contemporaine des *Mille et une nuits*: la *Meddaha*, une autre figure de Schéhérazade." In 431, 179-188.

MAHANY, Habiba.

GG5457. Le Boucher, Dominique: "A quand un Bardamu des banlieues?," *Algérie Littérature/Action,* no. 119-120 (mars-avril 2008), 41-43.

MAILLART, Ella.

GG5458. • Forsdick, Charles: *Oasis interdites d'Ella Maillart.* Carouge-Genève: Zoé, 2008. 112 p.

GG5459. Barthélémy, Tiphaine: "Ella Maillart en Russie: les limites du dépaysement." In 453, 164-175.

MAJDALANI, Charif.

GG5460. Amadessi, Veronica: "Entretien avec Charif Majdalani," *Francofonia,* n. 55 (autunno 2008), 103-109.

MAKINE, Andreï.

GG5461. • *Andreï Makine: le sentiment poétique.* Textes réunis par Margaret Parry [et al.]. Paris: L'Harmattan, 2008. *Critiques littéraires.* 280 p.

GG5462. Andrieux, Nicole: "Andreï Makine et le mythe de la France rêvée." In 5461, 87-93.

GG5463. Bellemare-Page, Stéphanie: "Formes et expressions d'un imaginaire nordique chez Andreï Makine." In 5461, 113-123.

GG5464. Bellemare-Page, Stéphanie: "La littérature au temps de la post-mémoire:

écriture et résilience chez Andreï Makine," *Etudes Littéraires*, vol. 37, no. 2 (automne 2006), 49-55.

GG5465. Caratozzolo, Marco: "Le concept d'épiphanie dans l'œuvre de Bounine et de Makine." In 5461, 163-174.

GG5466. Clément, Murielle Lucie: "Andreï Makine: le mensonge, l'amour et la mort en musique." In 442, 177-194.

GG5467. Clément, Murielle Lucie: "Makine, Bounine, Tchekhov, Tolstoï: rhétorique de la séduction, sémiologie du ciel." In 5461, 195-209.

GG5468. Clément, Murielle Lucie: "La musique d'Andreï Makine." In 384, 109-135.

GG5469. Clément, Murielle Lucie: "Nasi ljudi. De la famille chez Andreï Makine." In 571, 205-216.

GG5470. Duffy, Helena: "L'écrivain ne se meurt pas ou la résurrection comme triomphe sur la mélancolie dans l'œuvre d'Andreï Makine." In 384, 153-167.

GG5471. Duffy, Helena: "*La France que j'oublie d'aimer*: the foreigner's vision of his *pays d'accueil* in the works of Andreï Makine," *Essays in French Literature and Culture*, no. 45 (Nov. 2008), 19-42.

GG5472. Gonfond, Claude: "*Au temps du fleuve Amour* d'Andreï Makine ou le désir d'ailleurs." In 119, 255-274.

GG5473. Grandjean, Monique: "François Mauriac et la Russie ou des 'affinités électives'." In 5461, 15-29. [Mauriac]

GG5474. Harmath, Erzsébet: "La France de Makine," *Verbum*, vol. 10, no. 1 (2008), 189-198.

GG5475. Hecham, Claude: "La symbolique des couleurs chez la femme." In 5461, 139-145.

GG5476. Hogenhuis, Anne: "Ivan Bounine, Andreï Makine et le sentiment poétique de la nature." In 5461, 33-41.

GG5477. Ivassioutine, Taras: "Analyse intertextuelle des œuvres d'Anton Tchekhov et d'Andreï Makine." In 5461, 125-137.

GG5478. Jacquet, Marie-Line: "Poétique du temps et de l'espace dans *La terre et le ciel de Jacques Dorme.*" In 5461, 185-193.

GG5479. Laurent, Thierry: "La poésie de l'amour humain dans l'œuvre d'Andreï Makine." In 5461, 211-219.

GG5480. Mosakowski, Marek: "*Le crime d'Olga Arbélina* d'Andreï Makine." In 571, 11-18.

GG5481. Nazarova, Nina: "Makine et Bounine, otages du passé." In 5461, 95-110.

GG5482. Ollivier, Sophie: "Regards sur la nature russe chez Makine et Bounine." In 5461, 55-70.

GG5483. Parry, Margaret: "La poésie du 'domaine déserte' dans l'œuvre de Bounine et de Makine." In 5461, 175-183.

GG5484. Roederer, Christiane: "La poésie de la chanson russe chez Ivan Bounine et Andreï Makine." In 5461, 147-160.

GG5485. Schneidhauer, Marie Louise: "Tchekhov, Bounine, Makine, chantres de la terre russe." In 5461, 43-54.

GG5486. Van Acker, Isa: "De Proust à Belmondo: figures de l'artiste chez Andreï Makine." In 384, 137-151. [Proust]

GG5487. von Knorring, Katya: "*Le Crime d'Olga Arbélina* d'Andreï Makine: hommage poétique à Ivan Bounine." In 5461, 73-86.

GG5488. Wanner, Adrian: "Russian hybrids: identity in the translingual writings of Andreï Makine, Wladimir Kaminer and Gary Shteyngart," *Slavic Review*, vol. 67, no. 3 (Fall 2008), 662-681.

MAKHALI-PHAL.

GG5489. Radar, Emmanuelle: "L' 'inceste patriphore', ou la relation fille-père dans *La Favorite de dix ans* de Makhali-Phal." In 572, 27-37.

MALAQUAIS, Jean.

GG5490. ● Malaquais, Jean; Norman Mailer: *Correspondance 1949-1986*. Trad. Hélène Ancel; édition établie, annotée et préfacée par Elisabeth Malaquais et Geneviève Nakach. Paris: Le Cherche Midi, 2008. 285 p.

GG5491. Rannoux, Catherine: "L'écriture polémique dans le journal d'écrivain au XXe siècle: le *Journal de guerre* de Jean Malaquais." In 768, 217-229.

MALET, Léo. See also 916.

GG5492. Perolini, Cédric: "Léo Malet revient au bercail," *Rocambole*, no. 45 (2008), 143-153.

MALINCONI, Nicole.

GG5493. Bainbrigge, Susan: "Nicole Malinconi: breaching a Belgian taboo," *French Studies Bulletin*, no. 109 (Winter 2008), 83-85.

GG5494. Gousseau, Josette: "Nicole Malinconi et l'expérience de l'émigration." In 586, 125-135.

GG5495. Malinconi, Nicole: "Ecrire l'insoutenable," *Carnet et les Instants*, no. 151 (2008), 25-27. [Entretien]

MALLARMÉ, Stéphane. See also 598, 633, 1027, 1033, 1805, 3697, 6254, 6802.

GG5496. ● Becdelièvre, Laure: *Nietzsche et Mallarmé: rémunérer le "mal d'être deux"*. Chatou: Editions de la Transparence, 2008. 190 p.

GG5497. ● Bersani, Leo: *La mort parfaite de Stéphane Mallarmé*. Trad. Isabelle Châtelet. Paris: EPEL, 2008. *Les grands classiques de l'érotologie moderne*. 153 p.

GG5498. ● Durand, Pascal: *Mallarmé: du sens des formes au sens des formalités*. Paris: Seuil, 2008. 297 p.

GG5499. ● Kumagai, Kensuke: *La fête selon Mallarmé*. Paris: L'Harmattan, 2008. 508 p.

GG5500. ● Maár, Judit: *Mallarmé: de l'œuvre parfaite au fragment*. Budapest: Eötvös Univ. Press; Paris: Univ. Paris III, Sorbonne Nouvelle, 2008. 326 p.

GG5501. ● Mallarmé, Stéphane: *Penser les arts et la politique*. Textes choisis, prés., et annotés par André Stanguennec. Nantes: C. Defaut, 2008.

GG5502. ● Millan, Gordon: *Les mardis de Stéphane Mallarmé: mythes et réalités*. Saint-Genouph: Nizet, 2008. 134 p.

GG5503. ● Takeda, Noriko: *The modernist human: the configuration of humanness in Stéphane Mallarmé's Hérodiade, T. S. Eliot's Cats, and modernist lyrical poetry*. New York: Peter Lang, 2008. xii, 166 p.

GG5504. ● Zhang, Gen: *Le négatif chez Mallarmé*. Saint-Cloud: Globe Press, 2008. 212 p.

GG5505. Abbott, Helen: "Reading and deciphering: Mallarmé's rhythmic sensation." In 575, 29-41.

GG5506. Accardi, Andrea: "Bufalino e Mallarmé: la ricerca e il dolore," *Esperienze Letterarie*, anno 33, n. 2 (2008), 91-109.

GG5507. Badiou, Alain: "Mallarmé's method: subtraction and isolation." In 387.

GG5508. Blaise, Marie: "Mallarmé, Poe: des anges et des démons," *Manchette*, no. 3 (2004), 269-300.

GG5509. Boschian, Catherine: "L'*Hérodiade* de Mallarmé à travers la figure revisitée de saint Jean-Baptiste," *Etudes Littéraires*, vol. 38, no. 2 (automne 2007), 151-165.

GG5510. Charles Worth, Michael: "Monet re-states and Mallarmé suggests the subject matter." In 406.

GG5511. Clark, Nora: " 'In the Goddess's name': symbolist and modernist revisions of the Aphrodite myth." In 569, 193-209.

GG5512. Compagnon, Antoine: "Soupirs de Mallarmé. Sur l'apposition métaphorique anticipée." In 592, 97-111.

GG5513. Eckel, Winfried: "Ballett der Zeichen: Poesie und Tanz bei Stéphane Mallarmé." In 504, 84-100.

GG5514. Foucart, Claude: "Principes de l'esthétique métaphysique chez Nietzsche et Mallarmé." In 461, 63-76.

GG5515. Franko, Mark: "Mimique." In 524, 241-258.

GG5516. Greaney, Patrick: "Poetic rebellion in Mallarmé." In 476.

GG5517. Illouz, Jean-Nicolas: "Fragments d'un discours sur la mort: éloge funèbre, tombeaux et écriture du deuil dans l'œuvre de Mallarmé." In 1014, 375-390.

GG5518. Jones, Susan: "Knowing the dancer: modernism, choreography, and the question of authority." In 765, 193-222.

GG5519. Kossack, Ariane: "Between poetry and philology: rhythms of the Orphic myth in Mallarmé's aesthetics." In 575, 59-71.

GG5520. Kumagai, Kensuke: "L' 'anti-nature' mallarméenne? Les attaques de Maurice Pujo et d'Adolphe Retté," *Revue d'Histoire Littéraire de la France*, tome 108, no. 2 (avril-juin 2008), 407-419.

GG5521. Landy, Joshua: "Mallarméan magic: retrospective necessity, lucid illusion, and the re-enchantment of the world," *Symbolism*, no. 8 (2008), 251-278.

GG5522. Martin, Catherine: "The gift of the poem: Mallarmé and Robert Duncan's *Ground Work: Before the War*," *Modern Language Review*, vol. 103, part 2 (April 2008), 364-382.

GG5523. Por, Peter: "Un fragment littéro-musical et son calque littéro-pictural: *L'Après-midi d'un faune* de Mallarmé et *La Mort du Titien* de Hofmannsthal." In 766, 285-298.

GG5524. Reynolds, Dee: "Kinesthetic rhythms: participation in performance." In 575, 103-118.

GG5525. Roger, Thierry: "La réception immédiate du *Coup de dés*: chronique d'un relatif silence," *Romantisme*, no. 139 (1er trim. 2008), 133-154.

GG5526. Sanz, Teofilo: "Reprendre la langue de l'autre? Mallarmé et la musique wagnérienne." In 521, 47-52.

GG5527. Shingler, Katherine: "Framing the text: Mallarmé's *Un coup de dés* and the arts of the book." In 462, 53-70.

GG5528. Simon, John: "Mallarmé's wanderings," *New Criterion*, vol. 26, no. 7 (March 2008), 30-35.

GG5529. Steland, Dieter: "Poétique humaniste et poétique symboliste," *Zeitschrift für Französische Sprache und Literatur*, Band 118, Heft 3 (2008), 258-266.

GG5530. Vaillant, Alain: "Le lyrisme du vers syllabique: de Lamartine à Mallarmé," *Romantisme*, no. 140 (2e trim. 2008), 53-66.

GG5531. Warren, Rosanna: "Mallarmé and Max Jacob: a tale of two dice cups." In 1030. [Jacob]

GG5532. Wilker, Jessica: "La scission du signe ou l'irréductible ambiguïté du mot silence," *Estudios de Lengua y Literatura Francesas*, no. 17 (2006-2007), 189-204.

MALOT, Hector.

GG5533. ● *Hector Malot en Seine*. Textes rassemblés par Anne de La Brunière et Agnès Thomas-Maleville. Paris: Magellan, 2007. 143 p.

GG5534. ● *Hector Malot et le métier d'écrivain*. Etudes réunies par Francis Marcoin. Paris: Magellan & Cie, 2008. 206 p.

GG5535. Aiglon, Laurent: "L'épisode cévenol entre réalité sociale et pédagogie romantique." In 5534, 149-156.

GG5536. Aranda, Daniel: "Le praticien du retour des personnages." In 5534, 28-40.

GG5537. Cojez, Anne-Marie: "Le dossier préparatoire de *En famille*." In 5534, 85-99.

GG5538. Delahaye, Christa: "La question du romanesque." In 5534, 17-27.

GG5539. Fauvel, Aude: "La voix de fous. Hector Malot et les 'romans d'asile'," *Romantisme*, no. 141 (2008), 51-64.

GG5540. Garnerin, Fabienne: "*Sans famille* et la vie dans la Creuse vers le milieu du XIXe siècle." In 5534, 128-148.

GG5541. Grumetz, Jean-Paul: "La maison Saint-Frères et la question sociale dans *En famille*." In 5534, 114-127.

GG5542. Guillaume, Isabelle: "Le modèle anglais dans *Sans famille* et *En famille*." In 5534, 64-84.

GG5543. Largesse, Pierre: "Les sources locales de *Baccara*." In 5534, 157-170.

GG5544. Marcoin, Francis: "Hector Malot, libre et bourgeois." In 5534, 7-16.

GG5545. Michel-Jones, Françoise: "Une écriture de l'histoire immédiate, paysage industriel et mondialisation dans *En famille*." In 5534, 100-113.

GG5546. Parinet, Elisabeth: "Gérer son succès littéraire." In 5534, 171-190.

GG5547. Pottier, Jean-Michel: "Hector Malot: écrivain classé/déclassé." In 5534, 191-207.

GG5548. Santoro, Adriana: "Les notes de voyage en Italie." In 5534, 58-63.

GG5549.   Tison, Guillemette: "L'avocat des 'droits de l'enfant'." In 5534, 41-57.
MALRAUX, André. See also 349, 591, 779, 2035.
GG5550.   ● Bahmer, Claudia: *Weltkunst: Formpsychologie und Kulturanthropologie in André Malraux' Kunstschriften.* Berlin: Kulturverlag Kadmos, 2008. 317 p.
GG5551.   ● Blanchard, Maxime: *S'engager: l'intellectuel dans l'œuvre d'André Malraux.* Arras: Artois Presse Univ., 2008. 133 p.
GG5552.   ● Clerc, Christine: *De Gaulle-Malraux: une histoire d'amour.* Paris: Nil, 2008. 389 p.
GG5553.   ● Duval-Stalla, Alexandre: *André Malraux, Charles de Gaulle, une histoire, deux légendes: biographie croisée.* Préface de Daniel Rondeau. Paris: Gallimard, 2008. *L'infini.* 403 p.
GG5554.   ● Hervier, Dominique: *André Malraux et l'architecture.* Paris: Moniteur, 2008. *Architextes.* 295 p.
GG5555.   ● Lacouture, Jean: *Malraux: itinéraire d'un destin flamboyant. Entretiens avec Karin Müller.* Bruxelles: A. Versaille, 2008. 167 p.
GG5556.   ● Saint-Cheron, Michaël de: *André Malraux, comopagnon de route d'Israël.* Paris: Desclée de Brouwer, 2008. 250 p.
GG5557.   ● Saint-Cheron, Michaël de: *Malraux et les juifs: histoire d'une fidélité.* Paris: Desclée de Brouwer, 2008. 176 p.
GG5558.   Allan, Derek: "An intellectual revolution: Malraux's account of the temporal nature of art," *Revue André Malraux Review,* vol. 35 (2008), 149-161.
GG5559.   Baecque, Antoine de: "Malraux en son royaume farfelu." In 349, 99-138.
GG5560.   Benzakour Chami, Anissa: "Malraux: un modèle pour Mohammed Khaïr-Eddine (suite et fin)," *Awal,* no. 37 (2008), 95-102. [Khaïr-Eddine]
GG5561.   Couprie, Alain: "L'oraison funèbre et la politique: Bossuet et Malraux." In 768, 231-237.
GG5562.   Dirdo, Michel: "André Malraux." In 430.
GG5563.   Fabre-Lluce, Alfred: "Malraux en jugement," *Commentaire,* no. 122 (2008), 521-529.
GG5564.   Fumaroli, Marc: "Malraux et la fin du système français des Beaux-Arts," *Commentaire,* vol. 31, no. 124 (hiver 2008-2009), 1045-1064.
GG5565.   Khémiri, Moncef: "André Malraux et les ruines ou la métamorphose à l'œuvre," *Revue André Malraux Review,* vol. 35 (2008), 182-202.
GG5566.   Lantelme, Michel: " 'La vieillesse des maîtres': Malraux et le chant du cygne." In 379, 267-278.
GG5567.   Lantonnet, Évelyne: "Les métamorphoses du regard," *Revue André Malraux Review,* vol. 35 (2008), 162-179.
GG5568.   Larrat, Jean-Claude: "Nature et artifice dans l'œuvre d'André Malraux," *Revue André Malraux Review,* vol. 35 (2008), 28-47.
GG5569.   Liao, Jun-Pei: "La Chine comme théâtre des valeurs spirituelles chez André Malraux," *Revue André Malraux Review,* vol. 35 (2008), 122-136.
GG5570.   Loehr, Joël: "*L'Espoir*: un roman d'apprentissage politique?" In 456, 51-60.
GG5571.   Nitsch, Wolfram: "Der Bürgerkireg als Medien-Ereignis. Kommunikationstechniken in Malraux' Roman *L'Espoir*," *Zeitschrift für Französische Sprache und Literatur,* Band 118, Heft 2 (2008), 125-140.
GG5572.   Pillet, Claude: "Les voyages des *Antimémoires*: sens géographique et significations littéraires," *Revue André Malraux Review,* vol. 35 (2008), 101-121.
GG5573.   Radar, Emmanuelle: "*La Voie royale*: spectacle et hors-champ de l'aventure coloniale," *Revue André Malraux Review,* vol. 35 (2008), 48-67.
GG5574.   Ritter, Henning: "André Malraux." In 975.
GG5575.   Rouart, Marie-France: "Malraux, *La condition humaine*." In 582, 167-192.
GG5576.   Solé Castells, Cristina: "Malraux et la guerre civile espagnole: la mythification de la révolte," *Revue André Malraux Review,* vol. 35 (2008), 137-148.
GG5577.   Suleiman, Susan Rubin: "Commemorating the illustrious dead: Jean Moulin and André Malraux." In 600.
GG5578.   Tame, Peter: " Les deux André et le concept de la durée: André Chamson

et André Malraux dans le même combat pour les valeurs spirituelles," *Revue André Malraux Review*, vol. 35 (2008), 82-100. [Chamson]

GG5579. Tannery, Claude: "Le pommier de *L'Espoir*," *Revue André Malraux Review*, vol. 35 (2008), 14-27.

GG5580. Thompson, Brian: " 'Nul n'est prophète': Malraux et son fameux 'XXIe siècle'," *Revue André Malraux Review*, vol. 35 (2008), 68-8-1.

MALRIEU, Jean. See also 1012.

GG5581. ● *Jean Malrieu, l'inquiétude et la ferveur.* Textes rassemblés par Michèle Monte. La Garde: Univ. du Sud Toulon-Var, Faculté des lettres et sciences humaines, Laboratoire Babel, 2008. 303 p.

GG5582. Auroux, Guy: "L'eau de la passion." In 5581, 185-206.

GG5583. Broussard, Yves: "Jean Malrieu, défenseur de la civilisation du Sud." In 5581, 73-79.

GG5584. Caminade, Pierre: "Son pays préféré." In 5581, 97-98.

GG5585. Dazzan, Eric: "L'amour et l'effroi dans l'œuvre de Jean Malrieu." In 5581, 155-184.

GG5586. Dhainaut, Pierre: " 'Le meilleur moyen d'être fidèle à Breton'." In 5581, 99-116.

GG5587. Labrusse, Hughes: "Préfacement." In 5581, 81-96.

GG5588. Lefort, Régis: "Jean Malrieu: une langue de menuisier." In 5581, 127-141.

GG5589. Martin, Taffy: "Une traduction en anglais de 'Possible imaginaire'." In 5581, 261-284.

GG5590. Monte, Michèle: "Figures de l'énonciation dans 'Vesper' et 'Approches d'un village'." In 5581, 207-228.

GG5591. Saulnier, Tristan: "Jean Malrieu, un sourcier de l'incandescence." In 5581, 245-260.

GG5592. Soulier, Catherine: "L'épitaphe a fresco." In 5581, 229-244.

GG5593. Tixier, Jean-Max: "La voix qui monte des pierres." In 5581, 65-72.

GG5594. Ughetto, André: "Le bestiaire de Jean Malrieu." In 5581, 143-153.

MAMMERI, Mouloud.

GG5595. Chibani, Ali: "*Le Banquet* et *La fin absurde des Aztèques* de Mouloud Mammeri. Lorsqu'une mascarade en dévoile une autre." In 441, 57-74.

GG5596. Himeur, Ouarda: "Les médiateurs culturels: le cas Mouloud Mammeri," *Awal*, no. 37 (2008), 83-93.

MAN, Paul de.

GG5597. ● *Legacies of Paul de Man.* Ed. Marc Redfield. New York: Fordham Univ. Press, 2007. vii, 226 p.

GG5598. Balfour, Ian: "History against historicism, formal matters, and the event of the text: de Man with Benjamin." In 5597, 49-61.

GG5599. Benfey, Christopher: "Stopping by Paul de Man," *Yale Review*, vol. 96, no. 3 (July 2008), 72-85.

GG5600. Chase, Cynthia: "Double-take: reading de Man and Derrida writing on tropes." In 5597, 17-28.

GG5601. Guyer, Sara: " 'At the far end of this ongoing enterprise . . .'." In 5597, 77-92.

GG5602. Mieszkowski, Jan: "Reading, begging, Paul de Man." In 5597, 29-45.

GG5603. Plotnitsky, Arkady: "Thinking singularity with Immanuel Kant and Paul de Man." In 5597, 129-161.

GG5604. Redfield, Marc: "Professing literature: John Guillory's misreading of Paul de Man." In 5597, 93-126.

GG5605. Terada, Rei: "Seeing is reading." In 5597, 162-177.

GG5606. Warminski, Andrzej: "Discontinuous shifts: history reading history." In 5597, 62-73.

MANCHETTE, Jean-Patrick.

GG5607. Gérault, Jean-François: *Jean-Patrick Manchette: parcours d'une œuvre.* 2e éd. Amiens: Encrage, 2008. 134 p. [Orig. ed., 2000]

MANSOUR, Joyce.

GG5608. • Mansour, Joyce: *Essential poems and writings of Joyce Mansour*. Trans., introd. Serge Gavronsky. Boston: Black Widow, 2008. 439 p.

MARAN, René.

GG5609. Malela, Buata B.: "René Maran ou le syndrome de Véneuse." In 102, 27-100.

MARCEL, Gabriel. See also 966.

GG5610. • Marcel, Gabriel: *Thou shall not die*. Selected and arranged by Anne Marcel; trans. Katharine Rose Hanley; introd. Xavier Tilliette, s.j. South Bend, IN: St. Augustine's Press, 2008.

GG5611. • Sweetman, Brendan: *The vision of Gabriel Marcel: epistemology, human person, the transcendant*. Amsterdam: Rodopi, 2008. *Philosophy and religion*. xvi, 187 p.

GG5612. Burchland, Bernard: "Dramatist of a broken world: the soft theism of Gabriel Marcel." In 966.

MARGUERITTE, Victor.

GG5613. Di Meo, Nicolas: "Un pacifisme spécifique: le cas de Victor Margueritte," *Aden*, no. 7 (2008), 97-115.

MARIN, Louis.

GG5614. • *Louis Marin: le pouvoir dans ses représentations*. Paris: INHA, 2008. 96 p.

GG5615. Cantillon, Alain: "Louis Marin, sémiologie et histoire," *Critique*, tome 64, no. 738 (nov. 2008), 889-903.

MARION, Jean-Luc. See also 1341, 3228.

GG5616. • *Amore [L'] tra filosofia e teologia: in dialogo con Jean-Luc Marion*. Nicola Reali, ed. Città del Vaticano: Lateran Univ. Press, 2007. 199 p.

GG5617. • *Counter-experiences: reading Jean-Luc Marion*. Ed. Kevin Hart. Notre Dame, IN: Univ. of Notre Dame Press, 2007. ix, 478 p.

GG5618. • Gschwandtner, Christina: *Reading Jean-Luc Marion: exceeding metaphysics*. Bloomington: Indiana Univ. Press, 2008. xxiii, 320 p.

GG5619. • Marion, Jean-Luc: *The visible and the revealed*. Trans., Christina M. Gschwandtner [et al]. New York: Fordham Univ. Press, 2008. *Perspectives in continental philosophy*. xvii, 181 p.

GG5620. • *Von der Ursprunglichkeit der Gabe: Jean-Luc Marions Phänomenologie in der Diskussion*. Hrsg. Michael Gabel, Hans Joas. München: K. Alber, 2007. 279 p.

GG5621. Caputo, John D.: "The hyperbolization of phenomenology." In 5617, 67-93.

GG5622. Carlson, Thomas A.: "Blindness and the decision to see." In 5617, 153-179.

GG5623. Falque, Emmanuel: "*Larvatus pro Deo*: Jean-Luc Marion's phenomenology and theology." In 5617, 181-199.

GG5624. Gschwandtner, Christina M.: "Love as a declaration of war?: on the absolute character of love in Jean-Luc Marion's phenomenology of eros." In 987.

GG5625. Hankey, Wayne J.: "Misrepresenting neoplatonism in contemporary Christian Dionysian polemic: Eriugena and Nicholas of Cusa versus Vladimir Lossky and Jean-Luc Marion," *American Catholic Philosophical Quarterly*, vol. 82, no. 4 (Fall 2008), 683-703.

GG5626. Horner, Robyn: "The weight of love." In 5617, 235-251.

GG5627. Jones, Tamsin: "Apparent darkness: Jean-Luc Marion's revival of the Greek apophatic tradition." Diss., Harvard Univ., 2008. ix, 277 p.

GG5628. Kessler, Michael: "Responsibility within politics." In 5617, 357-379.

GG5629. Marion, Jean-Luc: "L'impouvoir," *Revue de Métaphysique et de Morale*, no. 4 (oct. 2008), 439-445. [Interview]

GG5630. McKenny, Gerald: "(Re)placing ethics." In 5617, 339-353.

GG5631. Milbank, John: "The gift and the mirror: on the philosophy of love." In 5617, 253-317.

GG5632. O'Regan, Cyril: "Jean-Luc Marion: crossing Hegel." In 5617, 95-150.

GG5633. "Primary bibliography of Jean-Luc Marion." In 5617, 419-441.

GG5634. Romano, Claude: "Love in its concept." In 5617, 319-335.

GG5635. "Secondary bibliography of Jean-Luc Marion." In 5617, 443-469.

GG5636. Tanner, Kathryn: "Theology at the limits of phenomenology." In 5617, 201-231.

GG5637. Tracy, David: "Jean-Luc Marion: phenomenology, hermeneutics, theology." In 5617, 57-65.

GG5638. Wardley, Kenneteh Jason: " 'A desire unto death': the deconstructive thanatology of Jean-Luc Marion," *Heythrop Journal*, vol. 49, no. 1 (Jan. 2008), 79-96.

MARITAIN, Jacques. See also 1909, 2069.

GG5639. ● *Amitiés et collaborations intellectuelles autour de Jacques Maritain*. Sous la dir. de Marie-Bruno Borde et Bernard Hubert. Toulouse: Institut catholique de Toulouse, 2007. 188 p.

GG5640. ● Caria, Roberto: *Lo stato nelle teorie politiche di I. Kant e J. Maritain*. Roma: Pontificia università gregoriana, 2008. 301 p.

GG5641. ● Doria, Piero: *La condanna della "dottrina Maritain"*. Roma: Aracne, 2008. 157 p.

GG5642. ● Farías, Victor: *La muerte del camaleón: la democracia cristiana chilena y su descomposición: Jacques Maritain, Eduardo Frei Montalva y el populismo cristiano*. ?: Maye, 2008. 260 p.

GG5643. ● *Jacques Maritain, philosophie dans la cité: mondialisation et diversités culturelles*. Ed. Vincent Aucante, Roberto Papini. Paris: Parole et silence, 2007. 227 p.

GG5644. ● Journet, Charles; Maritain, Jacques: *Correspondance. Volume VI, 1965-1973*. Edition publiée par la fondation du cardinal Journet. 1075 p.

GG5645. ● *Laicità [La] ne Le Paysan de la Garonne di Jacques Maritain*. A cura di Gennaro Giuseppe Curcio. Soveria Mannelli: Rubbettino, 2008. 111 p.

GG5646. ● Maritain, Jacques; Raïssa Maritain: *Œuvres complètes. Volume 17, Bibliographie et index*. Dir. Jean-Marie Allion. Fribourg: Academic Press, 2008. 600 p. [R. Maritain]

GG5647. ● Maritain, Jacques; Yves Simon: *Correspondance. Tome 1. Les années françaises, 1927-1940*. Edition établie et annotée par Florian Michel; introd. Philippe Chenaux. Tours: CLD, 2008. [Y. Simon]

GG5648. ● Smith, Brooke Williams: *Contemplating overflowing the roads of the world: love and friendship in the lives of Jacques and Raïssa Maritain*. Houston: Univ. of St. Thomas, 2008. 39 p.

GG5649. ● Viotto, Piero: *Grandi amicizie: i Maritain e i loro contemporanei*. Roma: Città nuova, 2008. 479 p. [R. Maritain]

GG5650. ● *Vladimir Soloviev, Jacques Maritain et le personnalisme chrétien*. Sous la dir. de Don Patrick de Laubier. Paris: Parole et silence; Presses univ. de l'IPC, 2008. 169 p.

GG5651. Dougherty, Jude P.: "Maritain in context: a selection from *Man and the State*," *Logos*, vol. 11, no. 2 (Spring 2008), [n.p.].

GG5652. Guéna, Sylvain: "*Le feu nouveau*, la controverse du *Paysan de la Garonne*," *Notes et Documents*, no. 10 (janv.-avril 2008), 50-76.

GG5653. Radin, Giulia: "Ungaretti-Maritain via Severini: una corrispondenza inedita," *Lettere Italiane*, anno 60, num. 3 (2008), 352-382.

MARITAIN, Raïssa. See 5648, 5649.

MARTIN DU GARD, Roger. See also 734, 779, 4134.

GG5654. ● Martin du Gard, Roger: *Le lieutenant-colonel de Maumort*. 2e éd. rev. et corr. Edition établie par André Daspre. Paris: Gallimard, 2008. 1058 p.

GG5655. ● Pandelescu, Silvia: *Techniques narratives et descriptives dans l'œuvre de Roger Martin du Gard*. Bucuresti: Editura Universitatii, 2008. 293 p.

GG5656. Andrieux, Charlotte: "La réception de la littérature russe par la *Nouvelle Revue Française*." In 5461, 223-238.

GG5657. Barilier, Etienne: "Et cette preuve, je l'ai vue!" In 388, 153-164.

GG5658. Baty-Delalande, Hélène: " 'Ce n'est pas une enclave; c'est un noyeau': l'affaire Dreyfus dans *Jean Barois*." In 904, 387-405.

GG5659. Baty-Delalande, Hélène: "La représentation désenchantée du militant chez Martin du Gard." In 456, 137-145.

GG5660. Daspre, André: "Roger Martin du Gard et Tchekhov, un accord parfait." In 5461, 265-277.

GG5661. Delobel, Cécile: "Roger Martin du Gard et Tolstoï." In 5461, 239-263.

GG5662. Lengu, Ilia: "Les relations père-fils dans le roman-fleuve *Les Thibault* de Roger Martin du Gard." In 572, 135-141.

GG5663. Rubino, Gianfranco: "L'espace peternel dans *Les Thibault* de Roger Martin du Gard." In 612, 339-354.

MASPERO, François.

GG5664. Cooke, Dervila; "Maspero et Franz: voyages vers l'autre en photographie et en texte." In 508, 473-485.

MASSIGNON, Louis.

GG5665. Mason, Herbert W.: "Louis Massignon, Catholicism and Islam: a memoir reflection," *Spiritus*, vol. 8, no. 2 (Fall 2008), 202-206.

GG5666. Meesemaecker, Laure: "Louis Massignon: des bergers de *L'Astrée* au '*dur Coran*', itinéraire franciscain," *Travaux de Littérature*, tome 21 (2008), 427-439.

MATVEEV, Michel.

GG5667. Zanotti, Raffaele: "Le son de l'est de Michel Matveev." In 442.

MAUCLAIR, Camille.

GG5668. ● Yeoland, Rosemary Hamilton: *La contribution littéraire de Camille Mauclair au domaine musical parisien*. Lewiston, NY: Edwin Mellen Press, 2008. xxii, 331 p.

GG5669. Giraud, Nadine: "De l'automne à 'l'Aube livide' dans *Le Soleil des morts* de Camille Mauclair." In 383, 107-117.

MAULNIER, Thierry.

GG5670. Antliff, Mark: "Classical violence: Thierry Maulnier, French fascist aesthetics and the 1937 Paris World's Fair," *Modernism/Modernity*, vol. 15, no. 1 (Jan. 2008), 45-62.

MAULPOIX, Jean-Michel.

GG5671. Bancquart, Marie-Claire: "Poésie, réflexion poétique: le cheminement du 'lyrisme critique' de Jean-Michel Maulpoix." In 612, 225-229.

GG5672. Giraux, Jean-Paul: "Dis, M'sieur, c'est quoi la poésie: Jean-Michel Maulpoix en 10 questions," *LittéRéalité*, vol. 20, no. 1 (printemps/été 2008), 21-25.

GG5673. Labidoire, Monique W.: "Jean-Michel Maulpoix: ranimer la lumière, ranimer le paysage," *LittéRéalité*, vol. 20, no. 1 (printemps/été 2008), 9-19.

GG5674. Schneider, Ulrike: "Dichtungskkonzeption im Zeichen des lyrisme: Jean-Michel Maulpoix' Antwort auf die 'Krise der Poesie' im ausgehenden 20. Jahrhundert." In 1028, 429-449.

MAUPASSANT, Guy de. See also 398, 558, 621, 689, 5372.

GG5675. ● Bashkirtseff, Marie: *The last confessions of Marie Bashkirtseff and her correspondence with Guy de Maupassant*. Foreword by Jeannette L. Gilder. Whitefish, MT: Kessinger, 2008. 157 p.

GG5676. ● *Guy de Maupassant*. Sous la dir. de Noëlle Benhamou, Yvan Leclerc, Emmanuel Vincent. Paris: Memini, 2008. 1688 p.

GG5677. ● Helms, Laure: *Laure Helms commente Pierre et Jean de Guy de Maupassant*. Paris: Gallimard, 2008. *Foliothèque*. 245 p.

GG5678. ● Lefebvre-Bertrand, Liliane: *Le statut littéraire de la Normandie chez Flaubert et Maupassant*. Lille: ANRT, 2008. 411 p.

GG5679. ● Maupassant, Guy de: *Afloat*. Trans., introd. Douglas Parme. New York: New York Review Books, 2008. xx, 105 p.

GG5680. ● Maupassant, Guy de: *Bel-Ami*. Chronologie, prés., notes, dossier, bibliographie mise à jour par Adeline Wrona. Paris: Flammarion, 2008. 432 p.

GG5681. ● Maupassant, Guy de: *Chroniques*. Textes choisis, prés. et annotés par Henri Mitterand. Paris: Librairie Générale Française, 2008. *Le livre de poche*. 1758 p.

GG5682. ● Maupassant, Guy de: *The collected stories of Guy de Maupassant*. Introd., notes by Richard Fusco. New York: Barnes & Noble, 2008. xxxi, 346 p.

GG5683. ● Maupassant, Guy de: *Contes de la Bécasse*. Edition prés., annotée et commentée par Evelyne Amon. Paris: Larousse, 2008. *Petits classiques Larousse*. 270 p.

GG5684. ● Maupassant, Guy de: *Notre cœur.* Introduction, commentaires et notes de Francis Marcoin. Paris: Librairie générale française, 2008. *Le livre de poche.* 285 p.

GG5685. ● Maupassant, Guy de: *Nouvelles d'Afrique.* Edition critique de Noëlle Benhamou. Lyon: Palimpseste, 2008. 3e éd. rev. et augm. 144 p.

GG5686. ● Maupassant, Guy de: *On horseback and other stories.* Selection by Edmund Howard; foreword by Anthony Guise. London: Capuchin Classics, 2008. 123 p.

GG5687. ● Maupassant, Guy de: *La parure; Le horla et autres contes.* Prés. Nancy Desjardins, François Guénette. Saint-Laurent, Québec: Editions du renouveau pédagogique, 2008. xvi, 86 p.

GG5688. ● Maupassant, Guy de: *La peur et autres contes fantastiques.* Edition prés., annotée et commentée par Joël Planque. Paris: Larousse, 2008. Nouvelle éd. *Petits classiques Larousse.* 159 p.

GG5689. ● Maupassant, Guy de: *Pierre et Jean.* Edition présentée, annotée et commentée par Christian Michel. Paris: Larousse, 2008. *Petits classiques Larousse.* 235 p.

GG5690. ● Maupassant, Guy de: *Pierre et Jean.* Prés., établissement du texte, notes, variantes, dossier, chronologie, bibliographie par Antonio Fonyi. Paris: GF-Flammarion, 2008. *GF.* 285 p.

GG5691. ● Maupassant, Guy de: *Un réveillon; Contes et nouvelles de Normantie; Contes et nouvelles.* Edition prés., annotée et commentée par Joël Planque. Paris: Larousse, 2008. *Petits classiques Larousse.* 223 p.

GG5692. ● Maupassant, Guy de: *Toine.* Edition présentée, établie et annotée par Louis Forestier. Paris: Gallimard, 2008. *Folio.* 240 p.

GG5693. ● Maupassant, Guy de: *Une vie.* Edition prés., annotée et commentée par Joël Planque. Paris: Larousse, 2008. *Petits classiques Larousse.* 319 p.

GG5694. Baron, Anne-Marie: "Maupassant, conteur ou romancier?" In 7963.

GG5695. Benhamou, Noëlle: "De qui se moque-t-on? La satire dans les 'contes du prétoire' de Maupassant," *Modernités,* no. 27 (2008), 165-181.

GG5696. Benhamou, Noëlle: "Le Moyen Age dans l'œuvre de Maupassant. Histoire, légende, poétique," *Etudes Littéraires,* vol. 37, no. 2 (printemps 2006), 133-149.

GG5697. Benhamou, Noëlle: "Nihilisme et anarchisme vus par Maupassant," *Bulletin Flaubert-Maupassant,* no. 21 (2007), 5370.

GG5698. Bollack, Jean: "Un sonnet, une poétique: Mallarmé." In 516, 581-594.

GG5699. Botterel-Michel, Catherine: "De la musique dans *Fort comme la mort*: art décadent, art de la décadence," *Bulletin Flaubert-Maupassant,* no. 20 (2007), 21-32.

GG5700. Campaignolle-Catel, Hélène: "Modèles picturaux, modèles descriptifs dans *Bel-Ami,*" *Poétique,* no. 153 (févr. 2008), 81-106.

GG5701. Cornille, Jean-Louis: "Minutes apocryphes." In 413.

GG5702. Counter, Andrew J.: "The epistemology of the mantelpiece: subversive ornaments in the novels of Guy de Maupassant," *Modern Language Review,* vol. 103, part 3 (July 2008), 682-696.

GG5703. Delaisement, Gérard: "Maupassant chroniqueur politique," *Bulletin Flaubert-Maupassant,* no. 21 (2007), 31-39.

GG5704. Demont, Bernard: "Maupassant, un conteur-géographe," *Bulletin Flaubert-Maupassant,* no. 21 (2007), 91-109.

GG5705. Disegni, Silvia: "Poèmes autographes sur kakemonos," *Bulletin Flaubert-Maupassant,* no. 21 (2007), 65-98.

GG5706. Dulau, Alexandra Viorica; Marlo Johnston: "Adrien Le Corbeau et une autre 'amie' de Maupassant, Mme de D.," *Histoire Littéraires,* no. 34 (avril-mai-juin 2008), 5-28.

GG5707. Farnlof, Hans: "La poétique du parasite: quelques exemples d'éléments motivants dans les nouvelles de Maupassant," *Bulletin Flaubert-Maupassant,* no. 21 (2007), 131-144.

GG5708. Fawell, John W.: "Maupassant's 'Idyll': the art of the simple tale," *Midwest Quarterly,* vol. 49, no. 3 (Spring 2008), 314-325.

GG5709. Grandadam, Emmanuèle: "Maupassant journaliste littéraire," *Bulletin Flaubert-Maupassant,* no. 21 (2007), 111-130.

GG5710. Hadlock, Philip G.: "Le jardin des fantasmes chez Maupassant." In 487, 303-310.

GG5711. Harst, Joachim: "Zopfgeist: Guy de Maupassant, 'La Chevelure'." In 479, 22-32.

GG5712. Helms, Laure: "*Il se fait tard*: l'automne dans les romans de Maupassant." In 383, 411-422.

GG5713. Helms, Laure: "Le roman de la jalousie: Maupassant, Bourget, France," *Ritm*, no. 38 (2007), 113-128. [Bourget, France]

GG5714. Himber, Elisabeth: "Dansez maintenant! Figures musicales et danses dans l'œuvre de Guy de Maupassant," *Bulletin Flaubert-Maupassant*, no. 20 (2007), 33-44.

GG5715. Johnston, Marlo: "*Madame Thomassin*," *Bulletin Flaubert-Maupassant*, no. 20 (2007), 59-64.

GG5716. Lacoste, Francis: "Maupassant et la République," *Bulletin Flaubert-Maupassant*, no. 21 (2007), 19-29.

GG5717. Lambart, Michel: "Maupassant et la politique coloniale ou Maupassant le pacifique," *Bulletin Flaubert-Maupassant*, no. 21 (2007), 41-51.

GG5718. Lowrie, Joyce O.: "Kaleidoscopic reflections in guise of a conclusion." In 511.

GG5719. Makropoulou, Marie: "L'espace du jardin dans la création romanesque de Guy de Maupassant." In 487, 311-322.

GG5720. Makropoulou, Marie: "Maupassant et 'le tragique de répétition,'" *Humoresques*, no. 26 (2007), 25-37.

GG5721. Marquer, Bertrand: "De Charcot à Poe: l'innovation paradoxale du fantastique chez Maupassant," *Ritm*, no. 38 (2007), 99-112.

GG5722. Nolan, Elizabeth: "*The Awakening* as literary innovation: Chopin, Maupassant and the evolution of genre." In 802, 118-131.

GG5723. Ozaeta, María Rosario: "En torno a la traducción de un relato de Maupassant: *Sur l'eau*," *Anales de Filología Francesa*, n. 15 (2006-2007), 205-220.

GG5724. Petrone, Mario: "La mélancolie dans *Pierre et Jean* de Maupassant," *Bérénice*, anno 15, n. 40-41 (nov. 2008), 143-151.

GG5725. Poyet, Thierry: "L'intellectuel, la République et l'ego. Maupassant dans ses chroniques," *Bulletin Flaubert-Maupassant*, no. 21 (2007), 7-18.

GG5726. Prévost, Maxime: "Maupassant, juste après Charcot," *Texte*, no. 43-44 (2008), 147-165.

GG5727. Rabatel, Alain: "Analyse énonciative et interactionnelle de la confidence." In 565, 255-273.

GG5728. Rabatel, Alain: "Points de vue et narration dans 'La mère sauvage' de Maupassant." In 565, 275-287.

GG5729. Rajoy Feijoo, María Dolores: "Breve/largo, del folletín a dos cuentos de Maupassant," *Anales de Filología Francesa*, n. 15 (2006-2007), 253-264.

GG5730. Tourrette, Eric: "Rêves de Jeanne," *Revue d'Histoire Littéraire de la France*, tome 108, no. 2 (avril-juin 2008), 387-406.

GG5731. Vallury, Rajeshwari S.: "*Pierre et Jean*, or the erring of Œdipus." In 615, 8-41.

GG5732. Vieuxtemps, Jeannine: "Maupassant et la musique," *Bulletin Flaubert-Maupassant*, no. 20 (2007), 45-58.

GG5733. Zouaghi-Keime, Marie-Anne: "L'élitisme de Maupassant," *Bulletin Flaubert-Maupassant*, no. 21 (2007), 71-89.

MAURIAC, Claude. See also 2314, 5473.

GG5734. • Mauriac, Claude: *Quand le temps était mobile: chroniques, 1935-1991*. Edition établie, prés. et annotée par Jean Touzot. Paris: Bartillat, 2008. xxii, 343 p.

GG5735. Boblet, Marie-Hélène: "*L'Agrandissement* ou *Le Balcon (détail)*: le roman-photo à la Mauriac." In 508, 217-231.

GG5736. Boblet, Marie-Hélène: "Claude Mauriac, lecteur de Jung," *Cahiers de Malagar*, no. 15 (automne 2006), 101-113.

GG5737. Boblet, Marie-Hélène: "Portrait de Claude Mauriac en 'alittérateur'." In 902, 161-178.

GG5738. Boblet, Marie-Hélène: "Le roman métaphysique de Claude Mauriac ou la machine à immobiliser le temps," *Revue d'Histoire Littéraire de la France*, tome 108, no. 2 (avril-juin 2008), 433-445.

GG5739. Canérot, Marie-Françoise: "Quand *Le temps immobile* se fait éternité," *Cahiers de Malagar*, no. 15 (automne 2006), 169-184.

GG5740. Hecquet, Anne-Marie: "De Claude à François Mauriac: 'le temps immobile' de la Révolution française," *Cahiers de Malagar*, no. 15 (automne 2006), 147-167. [F. Mauriac]

GG5741. Lacouture, Jean: "Claude Mauriac et de Gaulle," *Cahiers de Malagar*, no. 15 (automne 2006), 123-131.

GG5742. Lejeune, Philippe: "Visites," *Cahiers de Malagar*, no. 15 (automne 2006), 73-85.

GG5743. Leroy, Claude: "Le peintre au miroir de ses modèles," *Cahiers de Malagar*, no. 15 (automne 2006), 87-99.

GG5744. Lis, Jerzy: "La conception du dialogue total dans *Le temps immobile* de Claude Mauriac," *Cahiers de Malagar*, no. 15 (automne 2006), 33-45.

GG5745. Pinelli, Pier Luigi: "Les romans de François dans *Le temps immobile* de Claude," *Cahiers de Malagar*, no. 15 (automne 2006), 133-146. [F. Mauriac]

GG5746. Praicheux, Marie-Chantal: "L'espace, dans *Le temps immobile* de Claude Mauriac," *Cahiers de Malagar*, no. 15 (automne 2006), 63-71.

GG5747. Rached, Nachwa: "*Le temps immobile*, une œuvre ouverte," *Cahiers de Malagar*, no. 15 (automne 2006), 19-31.

GG5748. Rigaud, Jacques: "Claude Mauriac ou la difficulté d'être," *Cahiers de Malagar*, no. 15 (automne 2006), 13-17.

GG5749. Swift, Bernard C.: "*Le temps immobile*: y a-t-il un style du journal intime?," *Cahiers de Malagar*, no. 15 (automne 2006), 57-61.

GG5750. Touzot, Jean: "Claude Mauriac et ses pères spirituels: Maurice Clavel, Xavier Emmanuelli, José Cabanis," *Nouveau Cahiers François Mauriac*, no. 16 (2008), 13-22. [Cabanis, Clavel]

GG5751. Touzot, Jean: "Jean Cocteau dans *Le temps immobile*," *Cahiers de Malagar*, no. 15 (automne 2006), 185-195. [Cocteau]

GG5752. Vas-Deyres, Natacha: "*Le temps immobile* ou l'autobiographie éclatée," *Cahiers de Malagar*, no. 15 (automne 2006), 47-56.

GG5753. Zabojnikova, Hviezdoslava: "Claude Mauriac et Jiri Mucha," *Cahiers de Malagar*, no. 15 (automne 2006), 115-122.

MAURIAC, François. See also 779, 22314, 5473, 5740, 5745.

GG5754. ● Behrens, Hilke: *Identität und Beziehung in ausgewählten Romanen François Mauriacs*. Frankfurt: P. Lang, 2008. *Europäische Hochschulschriften*. 304 p.

GG5755. ● *Culture [La] religieuse de François Mauriac*. Sous la dir. de Jean-François Durand. Paris: L'Harmattan, 2008. *Mauriac et son temps*. 314 p.

GG5756. ● Des Garets, Eric: *Petit dictionnaire Mauriac*. Bordeaux: Le Festin, 2008. *Les cahiers de l'éveilleur*. 244 p.

GG5757. ● *François Mauriac: un journaliste engagé*. Jean Daniel [et al.]. Bordeau: Confluences, 2007. 138 p.

GG5758. ● Mauriac, François: *Le désert de l'amour; de La vengeance de narcisse au Désert de l'amour; les manuscrits et leur genèse*. Prés., transcription et notes par Pier Luigi Pinelli. Fasano: Schena; Paris: Baudry, 2008. 638 p.

GG5759. ● Mauriac, François: *Journal; Mémoires politiques*. Edition établie et prés. par Jean-Luc Barré; édition du *Journal* par Jean Touzot; édition du *Bâillon dénoué* et des *Mémoires politiques* par Laurence Granger. Paris: R. Laffont, 2008. *Bouquins*. xii, 1136 p.

GG5760. ● Mauriac, François: *On n'est jamais sûr de rien avec la télévision: chroniques 1959-1964*. Edition établie, prés. et annotée par Jean Touzot avec la collab. de Marryl Moneghetti. Paris: Bartillat, 2008. 652 p.

GG5761. ● Mauriac, Jean: *François Mauriac à Malagar*. Entretien avec Eric des Garets. Paris: Fayard, 2008. Edition rev. et augm. 109 p.

GG5762. Bourcheix, Jean-Paul: "La *Vie de Jésus* de François Mauriac." In 5755, 7-28.

GG5763.   Bréant, Pierre: "L'éveil politique de François Mauriac dans la France du 'ralliement'." In 5755, 29-45.

GG5764.   Bressolette, Michel: "François Mauriac et Simon-Pierre." In 5755, 47-61.

GG5765.   Canérot, Marie-Françoise: "Faut-il tuer le fils? Méditations sur *Le Sagouin* de François Mauriac et *Epaves* de Julien Green," *Nouveau Cahiers François Mauriac*, no. 16 (2008), 87-98. [Green]

GG5766.   Casseville, Caroline: "Mauriac, les pas du fils dans les traces du père," *Nouveau Cahiers François Mauriac*, no. 16 (2008), 55-68. [C. Mauriac]

GG5767.   Chafik, Hassan: "Une lecture du *Nœud de vipères*." In 5755, 63-85.

GG5768.   Chalaye, Gérard: "Le sillon de François Mauriac." In 5755, 103-132.

GG5769.   Dazet-Brun, Philippe: "MRP et RPF sous le regard croisé de François et Claude Mauriac, 1944-1953," *Nouveau Cahiers François Mauriac*, no. 16 (2008), 23-38. [C. Mauriac]

GG5770.   Dyé, Michel: "Fondements et spécificités de la foi mauriacienne." In 5755, 87-101.

GG5771.   Fukuda, Kosuke: "Le fils, rédempteur du père dans les romans de François Mauriac," *Nouveau Cahiers François Mauriac*, no. 16 (2008), 69-86.

GG5772.   Hecquet, Anne-Marie: "L'éducation marianiste de François Mauriac." In 5755, 133-148.

GG5773.   Imhoff, Guy: "Les romans dits catholiques de François Mauriac." In 5755, 148-170.

GG5774.   Jaques, François: "Jansénisme et culpabilité chez François Mauriac." In 5755, 171-182.

GG5775.   Le Corre, Elisabeth: " 'Explorateurs et témoins d'un monde invisible': Mauriac et les mystiques." In 5755, 183-220.

GG5776.   Mérand, Pierre-Emmanuel: "La tentation du modernisme chez François Mauriac." In 5755, 221-257.

GG5777.   Olsen, Michel: "Jean-Paul Sartre linguiste à l'attaque de François Mauriac," *Nouveau Cahiers François Mauriac*, no. 16 (2008), 185-218.

GG5778.   Praicheux, Marie-Chantal: "L'écrivain journaliste François Mauriac," *Nouveau Cahiers François Mauriac*, no. 16 (2008), 39-54.

GG5779.   Shillony, Helena: "François Mauriac: des salons littéraires à la création romanesque." In 419, 137-142.

GG5780.   Touzot, Jean: "François Mauriac: spectateur de la comédie politique," *Cahiers de Malagar*, no. 16 (automne 2007), 61-70.

GG5781.   Touzot, Jean: "Mauriac et le procès du rire," *Cahiers de Malagar*, no. 17 (automne 2008), 31-38.

GG5782.   Voronina, Elena: "François Mauriac et Vatican II." In 5755, 259-275.

GG5783.   Williams, Timothy J.: "Images sacrificielles: François Mauriac à la lumière de René Girard." In 5755, 277-295. [Girard]

MAURRAS, Charles. See also 489.

GG5784.   ● Chiron, Yves: *Ixixe, le grand amour de Maurras*. Niherne: BCM, 2008.

GG5785.   ● Giocanti, Stéphane: *Charles Maurras: le chaos et l'ordre*. Paris: Flammarion, 2008. Edition corrigée. *Grandes biographies*. 575 p.

GG5786.   ● *Lettres à Charles Maurras: amitiés politiques, lettres autographes: 1898-1952*. Dirigé par Agnès Callu et Patricia Gillet. Villeneuve-d'Ascq: Presses univ. du Septentrion, 2008. *Histoire et civilisations*. 256 p.

GG5787.   Grondeux, Jérôme: "Maurras et la crise du spirituel républicain." In 348.

GG5788.   Rocca, Daniele: "Charles Maurras," *Belfagor*, anno 63, n. 378 [fasc. 6] (30 nov. 2008), 687-704.

GG5789.   Serry, Hervé: "Les revues intellectuelles et l'Action française après 1918: hégémonie de la pensée maurrassienne et ajustements catholiques." In 348.

GG5790.   Surette, Leon: "Eliot and humanism: Charles Maurras, J. M. Robertson, and Bertrand Russell." In 872.

MAUSS, Marcel.

GG5791.   ● Gaume, Josette: *Le don en didactique: approche épistémologique à partir de l'Essai sur le don de Marcel Mauss*. Cortil-Wodon: Modulaires européennes, 2008. 151 p.

GG5792. ● Godelier, Maurice: *L'énigme du don*. Paris: Flammarion, 2008. *Champs*. 315 p.

GG5793. ● Viard, Bruno: *La littérature ou la vie!: Marcel Mauss du côté de Proust*. Nice: Ovadia, 2008. 125 p. [Proust]

GG5794. Moore, Gerald: "Clockwork politics: rhythm and the production of time in Mauss, Benjamin and Lefebvre." In 575, 133-144. [Lefebvre]

GG5795. Pecora, Vincent P.: "Inheritances, gifts, and expectations," *Law and Literature*, vol. 20, no. 2 (Summer 2008), 177-196.

MAVRIKAKIS, Catherine.

GG5796. Dumontet, Danielle: "*Fleurs de crachat* de Catherine Mavrikakis." In 41, 263-282.

MAXIMIN, Daniel. See also 190.

GG5797. Britton, Celia: "Community, nature and solitude in Daniel Maximin's *L"Ile et une nuit*." In 51, 111-130.

GG5798. Chevalier, Karine: "Daniel Maximin: le carnaval de Narcisse." In 441, 207-213.

GG5799. Donadey, Anne: "Beyond departmentalization: feminist Black Atlantic reformulations of *outre-mer* in Daniel Maximin's *L'Isolé soleil*," *International Journal of Francophone Studies*, vol. 11, no. 1-2 (2008), 49-65.

GG5800. Oppici, Patrizia: "La contrainte de l'île: *Tu, c'est l'enfance* de Daniel Maximin." In 423.

MBANCKOU, Alain. See 109.

MEDDEB, Abdelwahab. See 1844.

MEDDI, Adlène.

GG5801. Chehat, Fayçal: "Adlène Meddi, un sillon à creuser," *Cultures Sud*, no. 170 (sept. 2008), 99-104.

MELQUIOT, Fabrice.

GG5802. Wickham, Philip: "La guerre à distance. *Le diable en partage*," *Jeu: Cahiers de Théâtre*, no. 126 (mars 2008), 25-28.

MEMMI, Albert. See also 81, 679.

GG5803. ● Memmi, Albert: *La statue de sel*. Préface d'Albert Camus. Paris: Gallimard, 2008. Ed. revue et corr. *Folio*. 377 p.

GG5804. ● Saba, Nathalie: *Les paradoxes de la judéité dans l'œuvre romanesque d'Albert Memmi*. Paris: EdilivreAParis, 2008. 179 p.

GG5805. Macho Vargas, Azucena; Ana Soler: "La révolte individuelle face à l'emprise du groupe: la lutte contre courant comme *Leitmotiv* de l'œuvre memmienne," *French Studies in Southern Africa*, no. 38 (2008), 95-110.

MÉNIL, René.

GG5806. Gottin, Katia: "A travers le miroir: la départementalisation, paravent de l'impérialisme culturel français chez René Ménil," *International Journal of Francophone Studies*, vol. 11, no. 1-2 (2008), 211-227.

MERLE, Robert.

GG5807. ● Merle, Pierre: *Robert Merle, une vie de passions*. La Tour d'Algues: Editions de l'Aube, 2008. 442 p.

GG5808. Germoni, Karine: "*L'Assemblée des femmes* d'Aristophane à Robert Merle: de la scène athénienne à la scène moderne," *Revue d'Histoire du Théâtre*, no. 238 [no. 2] (2008), 127-152.

MERLEAU-PONTY, Maurice. See also 950, 2013, 3229, 4840, 5118, 7061.

GG5809. ● Alloa, Emmanuel: *La résistance du sensible: Merleau-Ponty, critique de la transparence*. Paris: Kimé, 2008. *Philosophie en cours*. 127 p.

GG5810. ● Carman, Taylor: *Merleau-Ponty*. London; New York: Routledge, 2008. *Routledge philosophers*. xi, 261 p.

GG5811. ● Colì, Maria Lucia: *La natura e l'ontologia in alcuni inediti dell'ultimo Merleau-Ponty*. Milano: Mimesis, 2008. *Filosofie*. 141 p.

GG5812. ● Comerci, Nicola: *La deiscenza dell'altro: intersoggettività e comunità in Merleau-Ponty*. Milano: Mimesis, 2008. 439 p.

GG5813. ● De Leo, Daniela: *La relazione percettiva: Merleau-Ponty e la musica.* Milano: Mimesis, 2008. *Filosofie.* 152 p.

GG5814. ● Dupond, Pascal: *Dictionnaire Merleau-Ponty.* Paris: Ellipses, 2008. 233 p.

GG5815. ● Förster, Yvonne: *"Die Zeit als Subjekt und das Subjekt als Zeit": zum Zeitbegriff Merleau-Pontys.* Saarbrücken: VDM, 2008. 86 p.

GG5816. ● Hackermeier, Margaretha: *Einfühlung und Leiblichkeit als Voraussetzung für intersubjektive Konstitution.* Hamburg: Kovac, 2008. 310 p.

GG5817. ● Hass, Lawrence: *Merleau-Ponty's philosophy.* Bloomington: Indiana Univ. Press, 2008. *Studies in continental thought.* xi, 254 p.

GG5818. ● *Intertwinings: interdisciplinary encounters with Merleau-Ponty.* Ed. Gail Weiss. Albany: SUNY Press, 2008. ix, 292 p.

GG5819. ● Jaoua, Mohamed: *Merleau-Ponty critique du Marxisme.* Tunis: Centre de publication universitaire, 2008. 250 p.

GG5820. ● Marshall, George J.: *A guide to Merleau-Ponty's Phenomenology of perception.* Milwaukee: Marquette Univ. Press, 2008. *Marquette studies in philosophy.* 314 p.

GG5821. ● *Maurice Merleau-Ponty.* Sous la dir. d'Emmanuel de Saint Aubert. Paris: Hermann, 2008. 458 p.

GG5822. ● Merleau-Ponty, Maurice: *The world of perception.* Trans. Oliver Davis; foreword by Stéphanie Ménasé; introd. Thomas Baldwin. London; New York: Routledge, 2008. viii, 95 p.

GG5823. ● *Merleau-Ponty.* Ed. Ten Toadvine. London; New York: Routledge, 2006. 4 vols.

GG5824. ● *Merleau-Ponty.* Textes de Pierre Rodrigo [et al]. Dijon: Alter, 2008. *Alter: Revue de Phénoménologie,* no. 16. 362 p.

GG5825. ● *Merleau-Ponty: de la perception à l'action.* Ed. Ronald Bonan. Aix-en-Provence: Publications de l'Univ. de Provence, 2005. 156 p.

GG5826. ● *Merleau-Ponty: key concepts.* Ed. Rosalyn Diprose and Jack Reynolds. Stocksfield: Acumen, 2008. xiv, 255 p.

GG5827. ● Peillon, Vincent: *La tradition de l'esprit: itinéraire de Maurice Merleau-Ponty.* Paris: B. Grasset, 2008. *Livre de poche.* 317 p.

GG5828. ● Tauber, Justin: *Invitations: Merleau-Ponty, cognitive science and phenomenology.* Saarbrücken: VDM, 2008. viii, 198 p.

GG5829. Ales Bello, Angela: " 'Essere grezzo' e hyletica fenomenologica. L'eretidà filosofica del visibile e l'invisibile," *Chiasmi International,* no. 10 (2008), 139-162.

GG5830. Angelino, Lucia: "L'*a priori* du corps chez Merleau-Ponty," *Revue Internationale de Philosophie,* vol. 62, no. 2 [no. 244] (2008), 167-187.

GG5831. Angelino, Lucia: "Between phenomenology and psychoanalysis: the meaningful body," *Philosophy Today,* vol. 52, supplement (2008), 63-73.

GG5832. Aranda Torres, Cayetano: "Reverberaciones bergsonianas en Merleau-Ponty," *Daimon,* núm. 44 (mayo-agosto 2008), 61-72. [Bergson]

GG5833. Barbaras, Renaud: "Les trois sens de la chair: sur une impasse de l'ontologie de Merleau-Ponty," *Chiasmi International,* no. 10 (2008), 19-33.

GG5834. Bello, Eduardo: "¿Qué filosofía elogia Merleau-Ponty?," *Daimon,* núm. 44 (mayo-agosto 2008), 11-27.

GG5835. Belot, David: "Dialectique, ontologie et histoire dans les notes préparatoires aux cours sur *La philosophie dialectique,* 1956," *Revue Internationale de Philosophie,* vol. 62, no. 2 [no. 244] (2008), 189-206.

GG5836. Bouffioux, Ingrid: "Les propos politiques de Merleau-Ponty: philosophie et politique," *Enseignement Philosophique,* vol. 58, no. 5 (2008), 11-31.

GG5837. Butler, Judith: "Sexual difference as a question of ethics: alterities of the flesh in Irigaray and Merleau-Ponty," *Chiasmi International,* no. 10 (2008), 331-346. [Irigaray]

GG5838. Carbone, Mauro: "Le idee sensibile fra vita e filosofía," *Daimon,* núm. 44 (mayo-agosto 2008), 75-83.

GG5839. Carbone, Mauro: "The mythical time of the ideas: Merleau-Ponty and Deleuze as readers of Proust," *Journal of the British Journal for Phenomenology*, vol. 39, no. 1 (Jan. 2008), 12-26. [Deleuze, Proust]

GG5840. Carbone, Mauro: "Pistorius, l'estetica e il rovesciamento del platonismo. Pensare con Merleau-Ponty (l')oggi," *Chiasmi International*, no. 10 (2008), 35-46.

GG5841. Carron, Guillaume: "Imaginaire, symbolisme et réversibilité: une approche singulière de l'inconscient chez Merleau-Ponty," *Revue Philosophique de la France et de l'Etranger*, no. 4 (oct.-déc. 2008), 443-464.

GG5842. Cormann, Grégory: "Pour une lecture rapprochée de Merleau-Ponty," *Daimon*, núm. 44 (mayo-agosto 2008), 45-59.

GG5843. Dastur, Françoise: "Merleau-Ponty and the question of the other," *Journal of the British Journal for Phenomenology*, vol. 39, no. 1 (Jan. 2008), 27-42.

GG5844. Davis, Duane H.; Tony O'Connor: "Intentionality, indirect ontology and historical ontology: reading Merleau-Ponty and Foucault together," *Journal of the British Journal for Phenomenology*, vol. 39, no. 1 (Jan. 2008), 57-75. [Foucault]

GG5845. Deranty, Jean-Philippe: "Witnessing the inhuman: Agamben or Merleau-Ponty," *South Atlantic Quarterly*, vol. 107, no. 1 (Jan. 2008), 165-186.

GG5846. Dupond, Pascal: "Descartes et le labyrinthe de notre ontologie," *Revue Internationale de Philosophie*, vol. 62, no. 2 [no. 244] (2008), 207-225.

GG5847. Escoubas, Eliane: "Merleau-Ponty et Maldiney: deux figures de la phénoménologie," *Chiasmi International*, no. 10 (2008), 289-304.

GG5848. Escoubas, Eliane: "Merleau-Ponty: the body of the work and the principle of Utopia," *Journal of the British Journal for Phenomenology*, vol. 39, no. 1 (Jan. 2008), 43-56.

GG5849. Flynn, Bernard: "Lefort in the wake of Merleau-Ponty," *Chiasmi International*, no. 10 (2008), 249-258.

GG5850. Garcés, Marina: "Anonimato y subjetividad. Una lectura de Merleau-Ponty," *Daimon*, núm. 44 (mayo-agosto 2008), 133-142.

GG5851. Garelli, Jacques: "Remarques sur mon rapport à l'œuvre de Merleau-Ponty," *Chiasmi International*, no. 10 (2008), 195-204.

GG5852. Goulding, Jay: "Wu Kuang-Ming and Maurice Merleau-Ponty: daoism and phenomenology." In 938.

GG5853. Groe, Matthew: "Merleau-Ponty's pragmatist ethics," *Southern Journal of Philosophy*, vol. 46, no. 4 (2008), 519-536.

GG5854. Hiltmann, Gabrielle: "L'ailleuers de la pensée: Bernhard Waldenfels et la postérité en pays de langue allemande de la philosophie de Merleau-Ponty," *Chiasmi International*, no. 10 (2008), 259-288.

GG5855. Hirose, Koji: "La fonction heuristique de la notion philosophique: sur la traduction de la notion de chair en japonais," *Chiasmi International*, no. 10 (2008), 129-138.

GG5856. Invitto, Giovanni: "Merleau-Ponty par lui-même: un filosofo parla di sé," *Chiasmi International*, no. 10 (2008), 59-84.

GG5857. Johnson, Galen A.: "The beautiful and the sublime in Merleau-Ponty and Lyotard," *Chiasmi International*, no. 10 (2008), 205-224. [Lyotard]

GG5858. Johnson, Galen A.: "The voice of Merleau-Ponty: the philosopher and the poet," *Journal of the British Journal for Phenomenology*, vol. 39, no. 1 (Jan. 2008), 88-102.

GG5859. Kim-Reuter, Jonathan: "Merleau-Ponty, Lacan, and the wandering shadow of the body," *Philosophy Today*, vol. 52, supplement (2008), 74-84. [Lacan]

GG5860. Lau, Kwok-Ying: "La folie de la vision: le peintre comme phénoménologue chez Merleau-Ponty," *Chiasmi International*, no. 10 (2008), 163-182.

GG5861. Lawlor, Leonard: " 'Benign sexual variation': an essay on the late thought of Merleau-Ponty," *Chiasmi International*, no. 10 (2008), 47-58.

GG5862. Leoni, Federico: "L'esperienza della filosofia. Senso e significato della parola filosofica nell'ultimo Merleau-Ponty," *Chiasmi International*, no. 10 (2008), 183-194.

GG5863. Lisciani Petrini, Enrica: "Oltre la persona. Merleau-Ponty e l' 'impersonale'," *Daimon*, núm. 44 (mayo-agosto 2008), 119-132.

GG5864. Lisciani Petrini, Enrica: "Per un 'dérèglement de tous les sens'. Merleau-Ponty: le sinestesie e l'impersonale," *Chiasmi International*, no. 10 (2008), 109-128.

GG5865.   López Sáenz, María Carmen: "Merleau-Ponty: imbricación en el mundo con los otros," *Daimon*, núm. 44 (mayo-agosto 2008), 173-184.

GG5866.   Low, Douglas: "Merleau-Ponty between Sartre and postmodernism," *Journal of Philosophical Research*, vol. 31 (2006), 343-360. [Sartre]

GG5867.   Matos Días, Isabel: "Croisement de regards. La phénoménologie de M. Merleau-Ponty et l'art vidéo de Bill Viola," *Daimon*, núm. 44 (mayo-agosto 2008), 85-92.

GG5868.   Moreno Pestaña, José Luis: "Merleau-Ponty y el sentido de la enfermedad mental," *Daimon*, núm. 44 (mayo-agosto 2008), 143-154.

GG5869.   Murphy, Ann V.: "Rethinking the ethical. An introduction to Judith Butler's 'Sexual difference as a question of ethics'," *Chiasmi International*, no. 10 (2008), 319-330. [Irigaray]

GG5870.   Noble, Stephen A.: "De la conscience et du comportement à la conscience perceptive: critiques et enjeux d'une pensée en devenir. Inédits de et sur Merleau-Ponty, 1940-1945," *Revue Internationale de Philosophie*, vol. 62, no. 2 [no. 244] (2008), 127-147.

GG5871.   Noras, John: "A reconsideration of Husserl's notion of transcendental reflection from a Merleau-Pontian perspective," *New Yearbook for Phenomenology and Phenomenological Research*, vol. 7 (2007), 63-76.

GG5872.   Nuti, Marco: "Merleau-Ponty et la quête cézannienne: pour une ontologie de la vision." In 542, 163-184.

GG5873.   Parades Martín, María del Carmen: "Merleau-Ponty y la fenomenología," *Daimon*, núm. 44 (mayo-agosto 2008), 29-43.

GG5874.   Pinto Pardelha, Irene: "L'horizon de l'expérience perceptive en tant que mémoire sensible," *Daimon*, núm. 44 (mayo-agosto 2008), 93-103.

GG5875.   Robert, Franck: "Écriture et vérité," *Revue Internationale de Philosophie*, vol. 62, no. 2 [no. 244] (2008), 149-166.

GG5876.   Rodríguez García, J. L.: "La visión como fundamento último de la intersubjetividad," *Daimon*, núm. 44 (mayo-agosto 2008), 157-172.

GG5877.   Saint Aubert, Emmanuel de: "Conscience et expression chez Merleau-Ponty," *Chiasmi International*, no. 10 (2008), 85-108.

GG5878.   Saint Aubert, Emmanuel de: " 'L'incarnation change tout'. Merleau-Ponty critique de la 'théologie explicative'," *Archives de Philosophie*, tome 71, cahier 3 (juillet-sept. 2008), 371-405.

GG5879.   Shaw, Spencer: "Merleau-Ponty's embodiment." In 982.

GG5880.   Silverman, Hugh J.: "Excessive responsibility and the sense of the world (Merleau-Ponty and Nancy)," *Chiasmi International*, no. 10 (2008), 305-318. [Nancy]

GG5881.   Slatman, Jenny: "Maurice Merleau-Ponty, 1908-2008. Filosofie als herdenking," *Tijdschrift voor Filosofie*, 70ste Jaargang, Nr. 3 (2008), 453-456.

GG5882.   Stoller, Silvia: "Konstruktionen von Geschlecht. Wiederholung und Wiederaufnahme bei Butler und Merleau-Ponty," *Tijdschrift voor Filosofie*, 70ste Jaargang, Nr. 3 (2008), 563-588.

GG5883.   Su, Chiu-hua: "Back to the world of light: on tactile subject in Melville and Merleau-Ponty," *NTU Studies in Language and Literature*, no. 20 (Dec. 2008), 97-130.

GG5884.   Trilles Calvo, Karina P.: "M. Merleau-Ponty, un pensador en guerra," *Daimon*, núm. 44 (mayo-agosto 2008), 185-198.

GG5885.   Vanzago, Luca: "Process and events of nature. Merleau-Ponty and Deleuze as readers of Whitehead," *Chiasmi International*, no. 10 (2008), 225-248. [Deleuze]

GG5886.   Verano Gamboa, Leonardo: "Sentido encarnado y expresión en Merleau-Ponty," *Daimon*, núm. 44 (mayo-agosto 2008), 105-116.

GG5887.   Vetö, Miklos: "L'eidétique de l'espace chez Merleau-Ponty," *Archives de Philosophie*, tome 71, cahier 3 (juillet-sept. 2008), 407-438.

GG5888.   Waldenfels, Bernhard: "The central role of the body in Merleau-Ponty's phenomenology," *Journal of the British Journal for Phenomenology*, vol. 39, no. 1 (Jan. 2008), 76-87.

GG5889.   Wambacq, Judith: "Het differentiële gehalte van Merleau-Ponty's ontologie," *Tijdschrift voor Filosofie*, 70ste Jaargang, Nr. 3 (2008), 479-508.

GG5890.   Yliraudanjoki, Virpi: "Merleau-Ponty in northern feminist education context," *Analecta Husserliana*, vol. 95 (2008), 291-309.

MERTENS, Pierre.

GG5891. • Desorbay, Bernadette: *L'excédent de la formation romanesque: l'emprise du mot sur le moi à l'exemple de Pierre Mertens.* Bruxelles: PIE-Peter Lang, 2008. *Documents pour l'histoire des francophonies.* 536 p.

GG5892. Sounac, Frédéric: "Le 'moi tardif'. Gottfried Benn et Georg Trakl au miroir de Pierre Mertens et Paul Louis-Combet," *Revue d'Histoire Littéraire de la France,* tome 108, no. 1 (janv.-mars 2008), 183-195. [Louis-Combet]

MESCHONNIC, Henri.

GG5893. Eastman, Andrew: "Entretien avec Henri Meschonnic," *Revue Septet,* no. 1 (2008), [n.p.].

GG5894. Eyriès, Alexandre: "Henri Meschonnic ou la saveur de l'écoute." In 1026, 93-108.

GG5895. Martin, Serge: "Henri Meschonnic et Bernard Vargaftig: le poème relation de vie après l'extermination des Juifs d'Europe." In 602, 137-150. [Vargaftig]

GG5896. Martin, Serge: "La traduction comme poème-relation avec Henri Meschonnic." In 1026, 131-143.

GG5897. Mourey, Laurent: "*Embibler, taamiser:* avec les premiers gestes d'*Au commencement,* notes sur le traduire et le poème Meschonnic." In 1026, 109-130.

MIANO, Leonora.

GG5898. Tchumkam, Hervé: "Logiques profanatoires: *L'intérieur de la nuit* de Leonora Miano." In 52, 215-230.

MICHAUX, Henri. See also 420, 497, 698, 1013, 2031.

GG5899. • Bäckström, Per: *Le grotesque dans l'œuvre d'Henri Michaux: Qui cache son fou, meurt sans voix.* Trad. Max Stadler et Matthias Tauveron. Paris: L'Harmattan, 2008. *Critiques littéraires.* 209 p.

GG5900. • *Conversations avec Henri Michaux.* Sous la dir. de Pierre Vilar, Françoise Nicol et Guénaël Boutouillet. Nantes: Cécile Defaut, 2008. 197 p.

GG5901. • Michaux, Henri: *Exorzismen und andere Texte.* Aus dem Franz. von Dieter Hornig [et al.]. Nachwort von Dieter Hornig. Graz; Wien: Literaturverlag Droschl, 2008. 303 p.

GG5902. • Vrydaghs, David: *Michaux l'insaisissable.* Genève: Droz, 2008. *Histoire des idées et critique littéraire.* 198 p.

GG5903. Alexandre, Didier: "L'événement et le corps, chez Michaux et Supervielle." In 590, 191-206. [Supervielle]

GG5904. Caligaris, Nicole: "Deux tympans pour Henri Michaux." In 5900, 19-44.

GG5905. Caligaris, Nicole: "La logique floue." In 5900, 13-16.

GG5906. Charbagi, Haydée: " 'Peu ici compose. Tout le contraire m'y décompose . . .' Henri Michaux musicien." In 5900, 123-149.

GG5907. Chatelier, Patrick: "Henri Michaux et le jeune écrivain." In 5900, 53-57.

GG5908. Berranger, Marie-Paule: "L'aphorisme en poésie: de l'autorité de la parole au peu d'être." In 382, 59-76.

GG5909. Danou, Gérard: "Henri Michaux: le souffle au cœur." In 555, 193-205.

GG5910. Devigne, Nicolas: "Devant, derrière, autour des frottages d'Henri Michaux." In 5900, 99-121.

GG5911. Fintz, Claude: "De la 'sagesse' dans la troisième section de *Poteaux d'angle*: du spirituel dans le langage chez Henri Michaux." In 510, 123-139.

GG5912. Getz, Jasmine: "Ecrire de tout son corps." In 501, 11-26.

GG5913. Hachette, Pauline: "Agir, dit-il. Les malédictions selon Henri Michaux." In 564, 175-178.

GG5914. Halpern, Anne-Elisabeth: " 'Il se croit Maldoror' et il n'a pas tort," *Revue des Sciences Humaines,* no. 292 [no. 4] (2008), 41-60.

GG5915. Kurtos, Karl: "Ekphraseis de l'aliénation: *Les Ravagés* de Henri Michaux." In 516, 437-456.

GG5916. Noland, Carrie: "Miming signing: Henri Michaux and the writing body." In 524, 133-183.

GG5917. Pessan, Eric: "A la faveur de la nuit." In 5900, 45-52.

GG5918. Roger, Jérôme: " 'Le phrasé même de la vie' ou la vie plastique d'Henri 5951Michaux." In 5900, 75-98.

GG5919. Santi, Sylvain: "Face à *Plume*: penser son moi." In 612, 291-304.

GG5920. Spies, Werner: "Henri Michaux." In 596.

GG5921. "Témoignages." In 5900, 153-189.

GG5922. Trudel, Jean-Sébastien: "Origine et inconsistance du l'être et du sens chez Henri Michaux." In 587, 109-129.

GG5923. Vadé, Yves: "Henri Michaux dans l'esplumoir." In 614, 261-299.

GG5924. Vilar, Pierre: "Michaux, danse, dessin." In 5900, 61-73.

MICHEL, Georges.

GG5925. Olivier, Aurélie: "Bon appétit! *Rhapsodie béton*," *Jeu: Cahiers de Théâtre*, no. 126 (mars 2008), 29-31.

MICHON, Pierre. See also 422, 708, 753, 754.

GG5926. ● Richard, Jean-Pierre: *Chemins de Michon*. Lagrasse: Verdier, 2008. 91 p.

GG5927. Berquin, François: " 'Les yeux dans les yeux'," *Revue des Sciences Humaines*, no. 292 [no. 4] (2008), 135-151.

GG5928. Bertini, Jean-Luc: "Tiré à part," *Carnets de Chaminadour*, no. 3 (2008), 193-196.

GG5929. Blot, Bernard: "*Vies minuscules* ou la réalisation de l'impossible accomplissement," *Siècle 21*, no. 12 (2008), 15-16.

GG5930. Bonnaffe, Jacques: "Après une lecture, *Le Roi du bois*," *Carnets de Chaminadour*, no. 3 (2008), 171-173.

GG5931. Castiglione, Agnès: "Le sentiment géographique dans *La Grande Beune* de Pierre Michon," *Siècle 21*, no. 12 (2008), 22-35.

GG5932. Cochard, Jean-Christophe: "L'expérience théâtrale de *Vies minuscules*, 1993-2008," *Carnets de Chaminadour*, no. 3 (2008), 179-186.

GG5933. Godefroy, Stéphane: "Lire *Vies minuscules*: les jouer?," *Carnets de Chaminadour*, no. 3 (2008), 187-191.

GG5934. Hofstede, Rokus: "La beauté difficile: quelques problèmes de lecture dans *Vies minuscules*," *Carnets de Chaminadour*, no. 3 (2008), 15-29.

GG5935. Istratova, Arina: "Pierre Michon, écrivain russe," *Carnets de Chaminadour*, no. 3 (2008), 197-199.

GG5936. Michon, Pierre; Florence Delaporte; Daniel Mesguich: "Conversation," *Carnets de Chaminadour*, no. 3 (2008), 174-177.

GG5937. Michon, Pierre; Pierre-Marc de Biasi: "A quoi sert la littérature?: dialogue," *Carnets de Chaminadour*, no. 3 (2008), 77-93.

GG5938. "Pierre Michon, l'écriture autobiographique: 1," *Carnets de Chaminadour*, no. 3 (2008), 97-122.

GG5939. "Pierre Michon, l'écriture autobiographique: 2," *Carnets de Chaminadour*, no. 3 (2008), 125-139.

GG5940. "Pierre Michon, l'écriture autobiographique: 3," *Carnets de Chaminadour*, no. 3 (2008), 141-162.

GG5941. Podalydes, Denis: "Après une lecture, 'Le ciel est un très grand homme'," *Carnets de Chaminadour*, no. 3 (2008), 165-169.

GG5942. Préclaire, Florian: "*Vies minuscules* de Pierre Michon, résurrections familiales et avénement littéraire." In 572, 343-349.

GG5943. Tamassia, Paolo: "Pierre Michon: deux poétiques du passé." In 561, 217-229.

GG5944. Tobiassen, Elin Beate: " La Sibylle des Cards. Propos sur le *Scipturire* de *Vies minuscules*," *Littérature*, no. 151 (sept. 2008), 34-51.

GG5945. Viart, Dominique: "Puissances du désir: pour une anthropologie érotique et sociale de Pierre Michon," *Siècle 21*, no. 12 (2008), 36-45. [Also in *Carnets de Chaminadour*, no. 3 (2008), 61-75]

MICONE, Marco. See 216.

MILICEVIC, Ljubica.

GG5946. Novakovic, Jelena: "Un roman sur le temps: *Les douze jours de l'année* de Ljubica Milicevic." In 155, 198-207.

MILLET, Catherine. See also 546.

GG5947. Grauby, Françoise: "De 'ceci n'est pas un corps' à 'ceci est mon corps': le body-art de Catherine Millet," *Nottingham French Studies*, vol. 47, no. 1 (Spring 2008), 61-74.

GG5948. Le Bras-Chopard, Armelle: "*Le Sabbat* de Catherine Millet." In 539, 137-146.

GG5949. Millet, Catherine: "La souffrance exquise de Catherine M.," *Livres Hebdo*, no. 742 (2008), 94-97. [Entretien]

GG5950. Morello, Nathalie: "Subject and space in Catherine Millet's *La Vie sexuelle de Catherine M.*," *Modern Language Review*, vol. 103, part 3 (July 2008), 715-727.

MILLET, Richard. See also 1830.

GG5951. • *Richard Millet: la langue du roman*. Etudes réunies par Christian Morzewski. Arras: Artois Presses Université, 2008. 180 p.

GG5952. Coyault, Sylviane: "Richard Millet: une poétique du dénouement." In 5951, 159-172.

GG5953. Desportes, Bernard: "Un chant crépusculaire." In 5951, 33-41.

GG5954. Houppermans, Sjef: "Un 'né de goupil'." In 5951, 147-157.

GG5955. Jackson, Alan: "En traduisant *La Voix d'alto*." In 5951, 117-126.

GG5956. Lapeyre-Desmaison, Chantal: "L'espace romanesque de Richard Millet, un manifeste antimoderne?" In 5951, 17-31

GG5957. Laurichesse, Jean-Yves: "Richard Millet: entre le mal et l'innocence," *Modernités*, no. 29 (2008), 423-435.

GG5958. Laurichesse, Jean-Yves: "Le sentiment géographique de Richard Millet." In 5951, 65-75.

GG5959. Majdalani, Charif: "Les trois Liban de Richard Millet." In 5951, 77-83.

GG5960. Mattar, Marylin: "Le murmure ou la *taisure*." In 5951, 85-102.

GG5961. Morzewski, Christian: "Richard Millet: langue du roman et roman de la langue." In 5951, 9-15.

GG5962. Pons, Gilbert: "D'un clavier à l'autre, notes sur la musique dans l'œuvre de Richard Millet." In 5951, 127-146.

GG5963. Smadja, Robert: "Faulkner, *Absalon, Absalon!* et Richard Millet, *L'Amour des trois sœurs Piale*." In 506, 397-405.

GG5964. Thoizet, Evelyne: "Le retentissement de la parole conteuse." In 5951, 103-115.

GG5965. Thumerel, Fabrice: "Une *Vie parmi les ombres* ou une écriture de l'entre-deux." In 5951, 43-63.

MILOSZ, Oscar Vladislas.

GG5966. Ivaskevicius, Marius: "*Madagaskaras*; entretien," *Cahiers de l'Association des Amis de Milosz*, no. 47 (2008), 83-87.

GG5967. Kohler, janine: "Milosz et Philéas Lebesgue," *Cahiers de l'Association des Amis de Milosz*, no. 47 (2008), 26-34.

GG5968. Laget, Francis: "5-6-7: bouclier de David, sceau de Salomon," *Cahiers de l'Association des Amis de Milosz*, no. 47 (2008), 69-76.

GG5969. Mauclair, Camille: " 'J'ai connu Milosz'," *Cahiers de l'Association des Amis de Milosz*, no. 47 (2008), 88-89.

GG5970. Naujokaitiene, Elina: "Le poète mystique et hermétique O. V. de L. Milosz: la tradition de la technique allégorique," *Cahiers de l'Association des Amis de Milosz*, no. 47 (2008), 53-60.

GG5971. Roditi, Edouard: "Une note," *Cahiers de l'Association des Amis de Milosz*, no. 47 (2008), 61-65.

GG5972. Vaiciulenaite-Kaselioniene, Nijolé: "Des identités nationales difficiles," *Cahiers de l'Association des Amis de Milosz*, no. 47 (2008), 35-48.

MIRBEAU, Octave. See also 692, 5376.

GG5973. • *Aller simple [Un] pour l'Octavie: Ateliers d'écritures interculturels autour de la 628-E8 d'Octave Mirbeau*. Coordonné par Kinda Mubaideen. Angers: Société Octave Mirbeau, 2007. 61 p.

GG5974. • Herzfeld, Claude: *Octave Mirbeau: aspects de la vie et de l'œuvre*. Paris: L'Harmattan, 2008. *Espaces littéraires*. 345 p.

GG5975. • Herzfeld, Claude: *Octave Mirbeau: Le calvaire: étude du roman*. Paris: L'Harmattan, 2008. *Critiques littéraires*. 119 p.

GG5976. • Lair, Samuel: *Mirbeau, l'iconoclaste*. Paris: L'Harmattan, 2008. *Critiques littéraires*. 331 p.

GG5977. Arnoult, Clémence: "Deux écrivains libertaires: Han Ryner juge Octave Mirbeau," *Cahiers Octave Mirbeau*, no. 15 (2008), 256-267.

GG5978. Barilier, Etienne: "Cette ignominie, je la porte joyeusement." In 388, 92-98.

GG5979. Barraud, Cécile: "Octave Mirbeau, un 'batteur d'âmes' à l'horizon de la *Revue Blanche*," *Cahiers Octave Mirbeau*, no. 15 (2008), 92-101.

GG5980. Beauvalot, Chantal: 'Un critique d'art et un peintre, Octave Mirbeau et Albert Besnard," *Cahiers Octave Mirbeau*, no. 15 (2008), 125-138.

GG5981. Bermudez Medina, Lola: "Un violon cassé: *Sébastien Roch* d'Octave Mirbeau," *Estudios de Lengua y Literatura Francesas*, no. 17 (2006-2007), 49-66.

GG5982. Brillant, Marie: "La mise en scène de *Familière Famille*," *Cahiers Octave Mirbeau*, no. 15 (2008), 282-284.

GG5983. Cipriani, Fernando: "*Sébastien Roch*: du roman d'enfance au roman de formation," *Cahiers Octave Mirbeau*, no. 15 (2008), 34-53.

GG5984. Coutelet, Nathalie: "Le théâtre populaire de la 'Coopération des idées'," *Cahiers Octave Mirbeau*, no. 15 (2008), 139-150.

GG5985. Dyvorne, Eric-Noël: "Tempête autour du *Foyer* à Nantes," *Cahiers Octave Mirbeau*, no. 15 (2008), 234-239.

GG5986. Garban, Dominique: "Octave Mirbeau et Jacques Rouché," *Cahiers Octave Mirbeau*, no. 15 (2008), 240-243.

GG5987. Garreau, Bernard-Marie: "Présence d'Octave Mirbeau dans la correspondance alducienne," *Cahiers Octave Mirbeau*, no. 15 (2008), 244-255.

GG5988. Gural-Migdal, Anna: "Entre naturalisme et frénétisme: la représentation du féminin dans *Le Calvaire*," *Cahiers Octave Mirbeau*, no. 15 (2008), 4-17.

GG5989. Herzfeld, Claude: "Kierkegaard et Mirbeau face à l'angoisse," *Cahiers Octave Mirbeau*, no. 15 (2008), 151-165.

GG5990. Lair, Samuel: "Une illustration littéraire du mythe de l'Eternel Retour: 'Le jardin des supplices', d'Octave Mirbeau (1899)," *Studia Romanica Posnaniensia*, no. 35 (2008), 49-65.

GG5991. Lair, Samuel: "*La 628-E8*, 'le nouveau jouet de Mirbeau'," *Cahiers Octave Mirbeau*, no. 15 (2008), 54-67.

GG5992. Lemarié, Yannick: "*L'Abbé Jules*: la colère et le Verbe," *Cahiers Octave Mirbeau*, no. 15 (2008), 18-33.

GG5993. Masse, François: "L'automobile 'vous met en communication directe' avec le monde: la relation au proche et au lointain dans le voyage automobile d'Octave Mirbeau," *Cahiers Octave Mirbeau*, no. 15 (2008), 68-76.

GG5994. Michel, Pierre: "Aristide Briand, Paul Léautaud et *Le Foyer*," *Cahiers Octave Mirbeau*, no. 15 (2008), 218-233. [Léautaud]

GG5995. Michel, Pierre: "Bibliographie mirbellienne," *Cahiers Octave Mirbeau*, no. 15 (2008), 353-364.

GG5996. Michel, Pierre: "Janer Cristaldo et *Le jardin des supplices*," *Cahiers Octave Mirbeau*, no. 15 (2008), 192-200.

GG5997. Michel, Pierre: "Octave Mirbeau et Bertha von Suttner," *Cahiers Octave Mirbeau*, no. 15 (2008), 180-191.

GG5998. Michel, Pierre; Jean-Claude Delauney: "Les épreuves corrigées de *La 628-E8*," *Cahiers Octave Mirbeau*, no. 15 (2008), 208-217.

GG5999. Muller, Charles: "Le vocabulaire automobile d'Octave Mirbeau," *Cahiers Octave Mirbeau*, no. 15 (2008), 88-91.

GG6000. Poulouin, Gérard: "Octabe Mirbeau et Camille Claudel." In 804, 293-319.

GG6001. Samiou, Antigone: "L' 'Autre' dans *La 628-E8* d'Octave Mirbeau," *Cahiers Octave Mirbeau*, no. 15 (2008), 77-87.

GG6002. Vareille, Arnaud: "Un usage particulier de la caricature chez Mirbeau: le contre-type," *Cahiers Octave Mirbeau*, no. 15 (2008), 102-124.

MIRON, Gaston. See also 6699.

GG6003. ● Gasquy-Resch, Yannick: *Gaston Miron: tel un naufragé*. Croissy-Beaubourg: Aden, 2008. *Le cercle des poètes disparus*. 301 p.

GG6004. ● *Universel [L'] Miron*. Sous la dir. de Jean-Pierre Bertrand et François Hébert. Québec: Nota bene, 2007. 237 p.

GG6005. Hébert, François: "Les restes de Miron." In 69, 19-29.

GG6006. Morel, Pierre: "Gaston Miron, *L'Homme rapaillé*." In 115, 116-128.

GG6007. Sainte-Marie, Mariloue: "La parole épistolaire comme événement: les lettres de Gaston Miron, 1949-1970." In 44, 235-250.

GG6008. Warren, Jean-Philippe; Pierre Nepveu: " 'Moi, pan de mur céleste'. Autour de Gaston Miron," *Liberté*, no. 280 (avril 2008), 56-72.

MISTRAL, Frédéric.

GG6009. ● Mistral, Frédéric: *Mes origines: mémoires et récits*. Préface, notes et dossier de Martine Reid. Arles: Actes sud, 2008. *Babel*. 349 p.

GG6010. ● Mistral, Frédéric: *Mirèio = Mireille*. Prés. et annexes de Claude Mauron. Monfaucon: Librairie contemporaine, 2008. 460 p.

GG6011. ● Soulet, Joseph: *Correspondance: à Frédéric Mistral, 1882-1912*. Puylaurens: Institut d'estudis occitans, 2008. 185 p.

MKPATT, Bidoung.

GG6012. Pangop Kameni, Alain Cyr: "La dramaturgie de la corruption dans *Les Charognards* et *Les Parasites* de Bidoung Mkpatt." In 52, 147-172.

MNOUCHKINE, Ariane. See 1124.

MODIANO, Patrick. See also 585, 721, 743, 761, 7250, 8249.

GG6013. ● Butaud, Nadia; Patrick Modiano; Jacques Chancel: *Patrick Modiano*. Paris: Textuel; Bry-sur-Marne: INA, 2008. 141 p.

GG6014. Arato, Franco: "Patrick Modiano," *Belfagor*, anno 63, n. 377 [fasc. 5] (30 sett. 2008), 549-560.

GG6015. Blanckeman, Bruno: "Patrick Modiano: une mémoire empoisonnée," *Elseneur*, no. 22 (2008), [n.p.].

GG6016. Böhm, Roswitha: "Sur les traces du passé: la littérarisation d'une histoire familiale dans l'œuvre narrative de Patrick Modiano." In 483, 229-239.

GG6017. Dye, Michel: "La blessure d'une relation primordiale chez Patrick Modiano et Michel del Castillo," *Nouveau Cahiers François Mauriac*, no. 16 (2008), 167-184. [del Castillo]

GG6018. Kahn, Robert: "Les lambeaux de la mémoire: *Dora Bruder* de Patrick Modiano et *Austerlitz* de W. G. Sebald." In 414, 401-408.

GG6019. Meyer-Bolzinger, Dominique: "Investigation et remémoration: l'inabouti de l'enquête chez Patrick Modiano." In 436, 231-239.

GG6020. Ngamassu, David: "Quête identitaire et écriture de la mémoire dans le roman de Patrick Modiano." In 103, 103-118.

GG6021. Rose, Sven-Erik: "Remembering *Dora Bruder*: Patrick Modiano's surrealist encounter with the postmemorial archive," *Postmodern Culture*, vol. 18, no. 2 (Jan. 2008), [n.p.].

MOKEDDEM, Malika.

GG6022. El-Badr Tirenifi, Mohamed: "Mythe féminin et réalité autobiographique dans l'œuvre de Malika Mokeddem," *Algérie Littérature/Action*, no. 117-118 (janv.-févr. 2008), 17-23.

GG6023. Green, Mary Jean: "Reworking autobiography: Malika Mokeddem's double life," *French Review*, vol. 81, no. 3 (Feb. 2008), 530-541.

GG6024. Miller, Margot: "Writing home: Malika Mokeddem and Hélène Grimaud, witnesses on the journey in search of home." In 80, 46-54. [Grimaud]

GG6025. Morel, Dominique: "Malika Mokeddem: 'Ces ici et là-bas d'une même intranquillité'," *Algérie Littérature/Action*, no. 125-126 (nov.-déc. 2008), 57-61.

MONÉNEMBO, Tierno. See also 278.

GG6026. Monénembo, Tierno: "Les pores du Haggar," *Cultures Sud*, no. 169 (avriljuin 2008), 107-109.

GG6027. Pageaux, Daniel-Henri: "Ombres noires et guignols blancs (ou l'inverse . . .). Regards sur l'exil intérieur chez Tierno Monenembo." In 72, 283-298.

GG6028. Stockhammer, Robert: "Conditions of identity in writing, or: About a genocide," *Arcadia*, 43. Jahrgang, Heft 1 (2008), 114-123.

MONETTE, Madeleine.

GG6029. Tremblay, Roseline: "*Le Double Suspect* de Madeleine Monette et *Les Masques* de Gilbert La Rocque. Une écriture thérapeutique." In 441, 1979-206. [La Rocque]

MONFERRAND, Hélène.

GG6030. Rouanet-Herlt, Nathalie: "La traduction littéraire: conversion, alchimie ou faux-monnayage?," *Manchette*, no. 3 (2004), 371-389.

MONNIER, Adrienne.

GG6031. Robert, Sophie: "Adrienne Monnier et l'esprit moderne," *Romanic Review*, vol. 99, no. 1-2 (Jan.-March), 143-154.

MONTALBETTI, Christine.

GG6032. Motte, Warren: "Christine Montalbetti's showdown." In 900.

MONTHERLANT, Henry de.

GG6033. Adinolfi, Pierangela: "L'idea di finzione nella letteratura francese degli anni Venti: Montherlant e Cocteau," *Studi Francesi*, anno 52, fasc. 1 (genn.-aprile 2008), 147-156. [Cocteau]

GG6034. Al-Matary, Sarah: "Mithra le tauroctone: un mythe antimoderne?" In 520, 261-272.

GG6035. Brown, Jennifer Stafford: "Sympathy for the Devil: the problem of Montherlant and the Medieval," *Papers on Language and Literature*, vol. 44, no. 2 (2008), 193-223.

GG6036. Duroisin, Pierre: "Aux origines du dernier roman de Henry de Montherlant: Alger dans *Un assassin est mon maître*," *Lettres Romanes*, tome 61, no. 3-4 (2007), 261-303.

MORAND, Paul. See also 699, 4210.

GG6037. Di Meo, Nicolas: "Fascination et contestation: les ambiguïtés du discours satirique chez Paul Morand pendant l'entre-deux-guerres," *Modernités*, no. 27 (2008), 419-429.

MORENCY, Pierre.

GG6038. Lepage, Elise: "De la domestication: la maison-le corps-le livre dans la poésie de Pierre Morency et de Pierre Nepveu," *Voix Plurielles*, vol. 5, no. 1 (mai 2008), [n.p.]. [Nepveu]

MORIN, Edgar. See also 8349.

GG6039. • Annacontini, Giuseppe: *Pedagogia e complessità: attraversando Morin*. Pref. di Isabella Loiodice. Pisa: ETS, 2008. *Scienze dell'educazione*. 198 p.

GG6040. • *Edgar Morin, plans rapprochés*. Dir. Nicole Lapierre. Paris: Seuil, 2008. 187 p.

GG6041. • Fortin, Robin: *Penser avec Edgar Morin: lire La méthode*. Québec: Presses de l'Univ. Laval, 2008. x, 244 p.

GG6042. • Morin, Edgar: *La complexité humaine*. Textes rassemblés et prés. par Heinz Weinmann. Paris: Flammarion, 2008. *Champs*. 380 p.

GG6043. • Morin, Edgar: *Mon chemin*. Entretiens avec Djénane Kareh Tager. Paris: Fayard, 2008. 361 p.

MOUAWAD, Wajdi. See also 1108.

GG6044. Belzil, Patricia: "Jeune homme en colère. *Assoiffés*," *Jeu: Cahiers de Théâtre*, no. 128 [no. 3] (2008), 9-11.

GG6045. Lindberg, Svante: "*Visage retrouvé* de Wajdi Mouawad." In 41, 283-301.

GG6046. Parisse, Lydie: "Œdipe par temps de catastrophe: *Incendies*, de Wajdi Mouawad." In 572, 335-341.

GG6047. Torchi, Francesca: " 'Des ciels, il peut y en avoir plusieurs, je commence à le comprendre': entretien avec Wajdi Mouawad," *Francofonia*, n. 55 (autunno 2008), 111-124.

MOUFFE, Chantal.

GG6048. ● *Diskurs-radikale Demokratie-Hegemonie: zum politischen Denken von Ernesto Laclau und Chantal Mouffe.* Martin Nonhoff, Hrsg. Bielefeld: Transcript, 2007. 247 p.

GG6049. Thomassen, Lasse: " 'Back to the rough ground': Chantal Mouffe." In 986.

MOUNIER, Emmanuel.

GG6050. ● *Agir avec Mounier: une pensée pour l'Europe.* Dri. Jean-François Petit, Rémy Valléjo. Lyon: Chronique sociale, 2006. 139 p.

GG6051. ● Coq, Guy: *Mounier: l'engagement politique.* Paris: Michalon, 2008. *Le bien commun.* 121 p.

GG6052. ● *Emmanuel Mounier: persona e umanesimo relazionale nel centenario della nascita (1905-2005): atti del convegno di Roma, UPS, 12-14 gennaio 2005.* A cura di Mario Toso, Zbigniew Formella, Attilio Danese. Roma: LAS, 2005.

GG6053. ● Illiceto, Michele: *La persona: dalla relazione alla responsabilità.* Troina: Città aperta, 2008. 398 p.

GG6054. ● *Pensée [Une] libérale, critique ou conservatrice?: actuality de Hannah Arendt, d'Emmanuel Mounier et de George Grant pour le Québec aujourd'hui.* Dir. Lucille Beaudry et Marc Chevrier. Québec: Presses de l'Univ. Laval, 2007. 220 p.

GG6055. ● Petit, Jean-François: *Petite vie d'Emmanuel Mounier: la sainteté d'un philosophe.* Paris: Desclée de Brouwer, 2008. 111 p.

GG6056. ● *Trahison [La] de Munich: Emmanuel Mounier et la grande débâcle des intellectuels.* Prés. Michel Winock; édition par Nora Benkorich. Paris: CNRS, 2008. 184 p.

MOUSSIRO-MOUYAMA, Auguste.

GG6057. Renomb'Ogula, S. R.: "L'invention scripturale de l'Afrique dans *Parole de vivant* de A. M.-Mouyama." In 72, 259-281.

MOUTOUSSAMY, Ernest.

GG6058. Fontaine-Xavier, Laurence: "Discours informatif, écriture du réel: la mise en scène des rites pour dire l'identité," *Itinéraires et Contacts de Cultures*, no. 39 (2007), 123-134.

MUDIMBE, Valentin. See 278.

MUNIER, Roger.

GG6059. Colomb, Chantal: "L'art du moins de Roger Munier." In 382, 95-110.

NAFFAH, Fouad Gabriel.

GG6060. Khoriaty, Georges: "La quête poétique dans l'œuvre de Fouad Gabriel Naffah," *Présence Francophone*, no. 71 (2008), 121-138.

NAJEM, Tania Yazigi. See 226.

NANCY, Jean-Luc. See also 397, 978, 3339, 5880, 8168.

GG6061. ● Domanov, Oleg: *Between myth and nihilism: community in Jean-Luc Nancy's philosophy.* Saarbrücken: VDM, 2008. 75 p.

GG6062. ● Heikkilä, Martta: *At the limits of presentation: coming-into-presence and its aesthetic relevance in Jean-Luc Nancy's philosophy.* Frankfurt: Peter Lang, 2008. *Europäische Hochschulschriften.* 309 p.

GG6063. Bax, Chantal: "The fibre, the thread, and the weaving of life: Wittgenstein and Nancy on community," *Telos*, no. 145 (Winter 2008), 103-118.

GG6064. Gabriel, Markus: "Der 'Wink' gottes. Zur Rolle der 'Winke des letzten Gottes' in Heideggers *Beiträgen* und bei Jean-Luc Nancy," *Jahrbuch für Religionsphilosophie*, Band 7 (2008), 145-173.

GG6065. Michaud, Ginette: "Penser la nuit tombée," *Critique*, tome 64, no. 732 (mai 2008), 422-429.

GG6066. Nault, François: " 'Le secret du commun': Jean-Luc Nancy et la déconstruction du christianisme," *Science et Esprit*, vol. 60, fasc. 1 (janv.-avril 2008), 39-53.

GG6067. Romani, Silvia: " 'Il faut remettre l'homme dans un rapport infini avec lui-même," *Rivista di Filosofia Neo-Scolastica*, anno. 99, fasc. 4 (ott.-dic. 2007), 771-794.

GG6068. Rubenstein, Mary-Jane: "Relation: Jean-Luc Nancy." In 978.

NDIAYE, Marie.

GG6069. Abisong, Andrew: "*Moja sestra*: Marie NDiaye and the transmission of horrific kinship." In 610, 95-112.

GG6070. Demeyère, Annie: "Père amant, père absent . . . la figure paternelle entre absence et imposture dans *Papa doit manger* de Marie Ndiaye." In 572, 69-75.

GG6071. Jordan, Shirley: "La quête familiale dans les écrits de Marie NDiaye." In 539, 147-157.

GG6072. Kackuté, Eglê: "La métaphore de la famille chez Marie NDiaye." In 571, 273-281.

NDJÉKÉRY, Noël Nétonon.

GG6073. Taboye, Ahmad: "L'univers de Noël Nétonon Ndjékéry: entre paradis et exorcisme," *Cultures Sud*, no. 170 (sept. 2008), 105-110.

NDONGO, Jacques Fame.

GG6074. Dolisant-Ebossè, Cécile: "En conversation avec Jacques Fame Ndongo," *Dalhousie French Studies*, vol. 84 (Fall 2008), 121-124.

NEDJMA.

GG6075. Rao, Sathya: "Corps, exils et temporalités dans *L'Amande* de Nedjma," *Nouvelles Etudes Francophones*, vol. 23, no. 2 (automne 2008), 222-233.

NELLI, René.

GG6076. ● Bardou, Franc: *René Nelli, un élan poétique occitan de l'héritage traditionnel à la modernité.* Puylaurens: Institut d'Etudes occitanes, 2008. 559 p.

NELLIGAN, Émile. See also 6699.

GG6077. ● Nelligan, Emile: *Poésies.* Préface de Louis Dantin; texte conforme à l'édition originale de 1904, avec une postface, une chronologie et une bibliographie de Réjean Beaudoin. Montréal: Boréal, 2008. 237 p.

NÉMIROVSKY, Irène.

GG6078. ● Epstein, Denise: *Survivre et vivre.* Entretiens avec Clémence Boulouque. Paris: Denoël, 2008. 165 p.

GG6079. ● Kedward, H. R.: *The pursuit of reality: the Némirovsky effect.* Reading: Univ. of Reading, 2008. *The Stenton Lecture.* 12 p.

GG6080. ● Némirovsky, Irène: *Chaleur du sang.* Texte établi et préfaceé par Olivier Philipponnat et Patrick Lienhardt. Paris: Gallimard, 2008. *Folio.* 195 p.

GG6081. ● Némirovsky, Irène: *David Golder; The ball; Snow in autumn; The Courilof affair.* Trans. Sandra Smith; introd. Claire Messud. New York: Everyman's Library, 2008. xxxvii, 363 p.

GG6082. ● *Woman of letters: Irène Némirovsky and Suite Française.* Ed. Olivier Corpet and Garrett White. Published on the occasion of the exhibition at the Museum of Jewish Heritage, Sept. 24, 2008-March 22, 2009. New York: Five Ties Publishing, 2008. 159 p.

GG6083. Friedli-Clapie, Lisa: "*Les chiens et les loups* d'Irène Némirovsky: l'allégorie et l'angoisse de l'assimilation juive dans la France de l'entre-deux-guerres." In 384, 221-232.

GG6084. Kershaw, Angela: "Irène Némirovsky (1903-1942): une Russe française, une Française russe?" In 442, 109-120.

NEPVEU, Pierre. See also 6038.

GG6085. Brouillette, Marc André: "Mouvements et paysages dans la poésie de Pierre Nepveu et Denise Desautels." In 120, 254-263. [Desautels]

NGANANG, Patrice. See also 208.

GG6086. Lefèbvre, Aurélie: "Patrice Nganang et 'la parole des sous-quartiers'," *Itinéraires et Contacts de Cultures*, no. 39 (2007), 35-47.

GG6087. Nzessé, Ladislas: "*Temps de chien* de Patrice Nganang ou la prise en charge des réalités camerounaises." In 52, 61-79.

GG6088. Ottou, Emmanuel: "Des stratégies de résistance littéraire chez Patrice Nganang," *Itinéraires et Contacts de Cultures*, no. 39 (2007), 25-34.

NIMIER, Marie.

GG6089. Dusaillant-Fernandes, Valérie: "Reconstruction de l'image du père: stratégies textuelles dans *La Reine du silence* de Marie Nimier." In 572, 207-216.

GG6090. Nimier, Marie: "A propos des *Inséparables,*" *Nouvelle Revue Française*, no. 587 (oct. 2008), 1-13.

NIMIER, Roger. See 1525, 2070, 7452.

NINI, Soraya.

GG6091. Gale, Beth W.: "Searching for home and self in novels by Soraya Nini and Faïza Guène." In 80, 55-66. [Guène]

NIMROD.

GG6092. Doucey, Bruno: "Silhouette noire sur fond blanc," *Autre SUD*, no. 40 (2008), 33-38.

GG6093. Ekotto, Frieda: "Singulier donc solitaire," *Autre SUD*, no. 40 (2008), 39-42.

GG6094. Nimrod: "Entretien," *Autre SUD*, no. 40 (2008), 28-32.

GG6095. Rice, Alison: "Autoportraits de Nimrod," *Autre SUD*, no. 40 (2008), 43-47.

GG6096. Ughetto, André: "La rivière sans retour," *Autre SUD*, no. 40 (2008), 48-50.

NIZAN, Paul. See also 705, 3936.

GG6097. Arpin, Maurice: "Nizan et les événements de Mai 68 en France," *Aden*, no. 7 (2008), 287-289.

GG6098. Bezace, Didier; Laurent Caillon: "Nizan au Théâtre de la Commune d'Aubervilliers," *Aden*, no. 7 (2008), 311-325.

GG6099. Froloff, Nathalie: "La figure du militant dans *Le Cheval de Troie*, 'une vie sans légendes'." In 456, 39-49.

GG6100. Geldof, Koenraad: "Canonisation, imagologie, non-lecture. A propos de la reception de Paul Nizan, 1905-1940," *Studi Francesi*, anno 52, fasc. 1 (genn.-aprile 2008), 63-79.

GG6101. Leiner, Jacqueline: "La révolution culturelle de mai 68 et les pamphlets des années 1930," *Aden*, no. 7 (2008), 291-296.

GG6102. Mathieu, Anne: "De quelques insulteurs de cadavre. Au sujet des *Chiens de garde* de Paul Nizan, de ses héritiers et de Bernard-Henri Lévy," *Aden*, no. 7 (2008), 299-307. [Lévy]

GG6103. Wittmann, Jean-Michel: "Une désacralisation ambiguë: le lien filial dans l'œuvre romanesque de Paul Nizan." In 572, 227-235.

NOAILLES, Anna de. See also 710, 6404.

GG6104. ● Noailles, Anna de: *Le conseil du printemps*. Textes réunis, annotés et postfacés par Elisabeth Higonnet-Dugua. Paris: Maule, 2008. 141 p.

GG6105. ● Noailles, Anna de: *Le livre de ma vie*. Prés. et notes de François Broche. Paris: Bartillat, 2008. 286 p.

GG6106. Peltre, Christine: "Du *Bain turc* au *Gulistân*: Anna de Noailles et le voyage à Constantinople." In 620, 59-70.

NOËL, Bernard. See also 735, 736, 737.

GG6107. ● *Bernard Noël: le corps du verbe*. Dir. Fabio Scotto. Lyon: ENS, 2008. *Signes*. 348 p.

GG6108. ● *En présence: entretien avec Bernard Noël*. Conduit par Jean-Luc Bayard et filmé par Denis Lazerme. Coaraze: Amourier, 2008. 80 p. CD.

GG6109. Ancet, Jacques: "La coïncidence." In 6107, 85-93.

GG6110. Bennis, Mohammed: "Bernard Noël: écriture et partage." In 6107, 95-101.

GG6111. Bikialo, Stéphane: "Le sonnet comme castration mentale: les *Sonnets de la mort* de Bernard Noël," *Formules*, no. 12 (2008), 155-166.

GG6112. Bishop, Michael: "Désir, rhétorique, non-savoir et fumée: l'art de la présence." In 6107, 185-198.

GG6113. Brophy, Michael: "Bernard Noël et l'ange du négatif." In 6107, 171-181.

GG6114. Carn, Hervé: "Gravir le silence: parole et silence dans les récits de Bernard Noël." In 6107, 143-163.

GG6115. Charnet, Yves: "Un peu d'air dans les yeux." In 6107, 245-267.

GG6116. Collot, Michel: "Le monde n'est pas fini." In 6107, 37-53.

GG6117. Dominguez Rey, Antonio: "La rumeur de l'absence." In 6107, 103-111.

GG6118. Frémon, Jean: "L'outrage." In 6107, 287-330.

GG6119. Malaprade, Anne: "Le corps dans tous les sens, corps en tous sens." In 6107, 55-68.

GG6120. Marchal, Hugues: "Des corps en extension." In 6107, 129-140.

GG6121. Ollier, Claude: "Le nom et son contexte." In 6107, 165-169.

GG6122. Peyre, Yves: "L'intensité poétique et son extension aux diverses formes de l'expression." In 6107, 233-243.

GG6123. Rothwell, Andrew: "Bernard Noël et l'autre corps aéré de la peinture." In 6107, 213-232.

GG6124. Russo, Adelaïde: "Collage incipit atelier." In 6107, 199-212.

GG6125. Scott, Fabio: "De la représentation à l'irreprésentable." In 6107, 269-283.

GG6126. Westley, Hannah: "Textual imagery: visualizing the self in the writing of Bernard Noël and Gisèle Prassinos." In 625, 113-159. [Prassinos]

GG6127. Winspur, Steven: "Convertir le temps en espace." In 6107, 113-127.

NOËL, Francine. See also 221.

GG6128. Nkunzimana, Obed: "L'exil ou l'invention de l'autre et la réinvention de soi." In 104, 305-322.

NOËL, Marie. See also 691a.

GG6129. Galmiche, Xavier: "Un 'miracle': *Le Jugement de Don Juan* (1955) de Marie Noël." In 432, 115-126.

NOTHOMB, Amélie. See also 659.

GG6130. Blumenkamp, Katrin: "Authentizität in literarischem Text und Paratext: Alexa Henning von Lange und Amélie Nothomb." In 505.

GG6131. Chevillot, Frédérique: "Rira bien qui rira pour la primultième fois: *Les Catilinaires* d'Amélie Nothomb," *Women in French Studies* (2008), 165-177.

GG6132. Dewez, Nausicaa: "La Belle, la (vieille) bête et la princesse charmante: sur *Mercure* d'Amélie Nothomb." In 894, 235-246.

GG6133. Illanes Ortega, Inmaculada: "Discurso y silencio en *Les Catillnaires* de Amélie Nothomb," *Estudios de Lengua y Literatura Francesas*, no. 17 (2006-2007), 99-117.

GG6134. Jones, Katie: "Literature as consumption and expulsion: Amélie Nothomb's 'esthétique du vomissement'." In 458, 174-191.

GG6135. Malgorzata Wierzbowska, Ewa: "Les relations familiales dans le roman d'Amélie Nothomb *Antéchrista*." In 571, 235-244.

GG6136. McCall, Ian: " 'Merry Christmas Amélie-san': filmic intertext in Nothomb's *Stupeur et tremblements*," *Nottingham French Studies*, vol. 47, no. 1 (Spring 2008), 75-88.

GG6137. Presada, Diana: "Histoire et actualité dans *Péplum* d'Amélie Nothomb," *Studies on Lucette Desvignes and the Twentieth Century*, no. 18 (2008), 189-199.

GG6138. Revial, Gaëlle: "Amélie Nothomb: *Mon portrait entouré de masques*." In 441, 179-185.

GG6139. Velázquez Ezquerra, José Ignacio: "*La Lucidez* de Amélie Nothomb," *Cuadernos de Filologia Francesa*, no. 19 (2008), 235-265.

NOURISSIER, François.

GG6140. Feutry, Alain: "*Eau-de-feu*, de F. Nourissier," *Nouvelle Revue Française*, no. 587 (oct. 2008), 209-212.

NOVARINA, Valère. See also 548, 1119.

GG6141. Calas, Frédéric: "Paradoxes de la cohérence dans l'œuvre de Valère Novarina." In 410, 409-418.

GG6142. Trudel, Jean-Sébastien: "Empire et verbigération: la portée critique de l'œuvre de Valère Novarina," *Studies in Religion*, vol. 37, no. 3-4 (2008), 509-519.

NYS-MAZURE, Colette.

GG6143. Nys-Mazure, Colette: "Dans la bibliothèque de Colette Nys-Mazure," *Carnet et les Instants*, no. 154 (2008-2009), 24-28. [Entretien]

NYSSEN, Hubert.

GG6144. • Ecrivain [L'] et son double: Hubert Nyssen. Textes réunis par Pascal Durand. Liège: CELIC; Arles: Actes sud, 2006. 180 p.

OBERLÉ, Gérard.

GG6145. Fayet, Agnès: "*Retour à Zornhof* de Gérard Oberlé. Esthétique de la fissure." In 379, 125-133.

OKOUMBA-NKOGHÉ, Maurice.

GG6146. Mbondobari, Sylvère: "Ecriture de l'immédiateté: pouvoir politique et postcolonie dans *Le Chemin de la mémoire* d'Okoumba-Nkoghé," *Neohelicon*, vol. 35, no. 2 (2008), 101-113.

OLLIER, Claude.

GG6147. Houppermans, Sjef: "Les énigmes d'*Enigma*." In 436, 241-251.

GG6148. Houppermans, Sjef: "Parmi les (déc)ombres: Claude Ollier en ruines." In 902, 103-120.

OLLIVIER, Émile.

GG6149. Dahouda, Kanaté: "Emile Ollivier, les tensions de la mémoire et l'expérience de gravité existentielle." In 103, 15-31.

GG6150. Gauvin, Lise: "*La Brûlerie* d'Emile Ollivier." In 41, 303-311.

GG6151. Parisot, Yolaine: "Mémoire occultée, mémoire littéraire: le roman haïtien en puzzle dans *La Brûlerie* d'E. Ollivier et dans *Le Briseur de rosée* d'E. Danticat," *Interculturel Francophones*, no. 12 (nov.-déc. 2007), 209-227.

ORIZET, Jean.

GG6152. Fournier, Bernard; Jean Orizet: "Questionnaire," *LittéRéalité*, vol. 20, no. 1 (printemps/été 2008), 27-37.

OST, François.

GG6153. Ferron, Julie: "L'intelligence moderne s'arrête où commence le tragique: autour de l'*Antigone voilée* de François Ost." In 520, 571-583.

OSTENDE, Jean-Pierre.

GG6154. Guichard, Thierry: "L'antre de l'explorateur," *Matricule des Anges*, no. 87 (2007), 14-17.

GG6155. Guichard, Thierry: "L'imaginaire débridé," *Matricule des Anges*, no. 87 (2007), 18.

GG6156. Ostende, Jean-Pierre: "Dans l'appétit du monde," *Matricule des Anges*, no. 87 (2007), 20-26. [Entretien]

OSTER, Christian.

GG6157. Hermosilla Alvarez, Concepción: "Un regard phénoménologique inconfortable: *Sur la dune*, de Christian Oster," *Cuadernos de Filologia Francesa*, no. 19 (2008), 123-139.

GG6158. Schulman, Peter: "Christian Oster: flight disappearance and the modern bachelor," *Francofonia*, n. 55 (autunno 2008), 33-47.

OSTER, Daniel.

GG6159. Cohen-Halimi, Michèle: "Le fusil biographique de Daniel Oster," *CCP: Cahier Critique de Poésie*, no. 13 (2006), 305-308.

OUELLETTE-MICHALSKA, Madeleine.

GG6160. Sasu, Voichita-Maria: " 'L'écriture prend des risques': Madeleine Ouellette-Michalska." In 115, 239-244.

OULEHRI, Touria. See 347.

OULIPO. See also 745, 759.

GG6161. ● Bisenius-Penin, Carole: *Le roman oulipien*. Préface de Pierre Brunel. Paris: L'Harmattan, 2008. *Littératures comparées*. 287 p.

GG6162. Bloomfield, Camille: "Le sonnet à l'Oulipo: quand une forme fixe n'est plus une contrainte," *Formules*, no. 12 (2008), 51-66.

GG6163. Chaigne, Dominique: "Les sonnets oulipiens: une forme mémoire," *Formules*, no. 12 (2008), 81-94.

GG6164. James, Alison: "The Maltese and the mustard fields: Oulipian translation," *Substance*, vol. 37, no. 1 [no. 115] (2008), 134-147.

GG6165. Morisi, Eve Célia: "The OuLiPoe, or constraint and *(contre-)performance*: 'the philosophy of composition' and the Oulipian manifestos," *Comparative Literature*, vol. 60, no. 2 (Spring 2008), 107-124.

GG6166. Reggiani, Christelle: "Secrets oulipiens." In 436, 317-327.

GG6167. Viers, Carole Anne: "The OULIPO and art as retrieval: copyists and translators in the novels of Raymond Queneau, Italo Calvino, Harry Mathews, and Georges Perec." Diss., UCLA, 2008. xii, 270 p.

OUOLOGUEM, Yambo. See also 268.

GG6168. ● Ouologuem, Yambo: *the Yambo Ouologuem reader*. Ed. Christopher Wise. Trenton, NJ: Africa World Press, 2008. xx, 338 p.

GG6169. Biondo, Alessio: "Yambo Ouologuem, o dei passaggi e delle migrazioni della violenza." In 586, 227-248.

GG6170. Janis, Michael: "African avant-garde: Ouologuem's anti-colonialist anthropology." In 486.

GG6171. Wehrs, Donald R.: "Modernity in revolt against Islam: Ouologuem's *Le Devoir de voilence* and Boudjedra's *La Répudiation.*" In 142. [Boudjedra]

OWONDO, Laurent.

GG6172. Clerc, Jeanne-Marie; Liliane Nzé: "Laurent Owondo, *Au bout du silence.*" In 56, 63-106.

OYONO, Ferdinand.

GG6173. ● Nola, Bienvenu: *Le vieux nègre et la médaille: essai d'analyse argumentaire.* Paris: L'Harmattan, 2008. *Littératures et savoirs.* 256 p.

PACHE, Jean.

GG6174. Fankhauser, Pierre: "Le sexe sous le dictionnaire," *Revue de Belles-Lettres,* no. 1-2 (2008), 67-72.

GG6175. Francillon, Roger: "Jean Pache: poétique et érotique," *Revue de Belles-Lettres,* no. 1-2 (2008), 73-78.

GG6176. Gaillard, Benoît: "Jean Pache chroniqueur," *Revue de Belles-Lettres,* no. 1-2 (2008), 87-92.

GG6177. Lador, Pierre Yves: "A l'ombre du rire," *Revue de Belles-Lettres,* no. 1-2 (2008), 65-66.

GG6178. Lescure, Jean; Jean Pache: "Correspondance," *Revue de Belles-Lettres,* no. 1-2 (2008), 37-48.

GG6179. Tâche, Pierre-Alain: "La preuve par l'image," *Revue de Belles-Lettres,* no. 1-2 (2008), 79-86.

PACHET, Pierre. See 3721.

PAGNOL, Marcel.

GG6180. ● Huster, Francis: *Marcel Pagnol: Le Poquelin de Marseille: notes de mise en scène: César, Fanny, Marius.* Paris: Séguier-Archimbaud, 2008. 115 p.

GG6181. ● Pagnol, Marcel: *Carnets de cinéma.* Textes prés. par Nicolas Pagnol. Paris: Privé; Treille, 2008. 155 p.

GG6182. Klotz, Roger: "Avant *Marius* de Marcel Pagnol: l'Alcazar et la revue marseillaise," *Revue d'Histoire du Théâtre,* no. 240 [no. 4] (2008), 359-366.

PANCRAZI, Jean-Noël. See 3714.

PARADIS, André. See 334.

PARET, Roland.

6182a. Chemla, Yves: "Dans le regard de la Gorgone. Une présentation de l'œuvre de Roland Paret, *Tribunal des grands vents,*" *Interculturel Francophones,* no. 12 (nov.-déc. 2007), 41-55.

PARIAN, Anne.

GG6183. Volniek, Jason: "Anne Parian. Déplacement continu du nom," *Critique,* tome 64, no. 735-736 (août-sept. 2008), 703-709.

PARVULESCO, Jean.

GG6184. Marmin, Michel: "Jean Parvuleesco, de l'empire à l'être," *Spectacle du Monde,* no. 542 (févr. 2008), 60-62.

PASQUALI, Adrien. See 334.

PASQUET, Fabienne.

GG6185. François, Cyrille: "Approches de l'altérité dans les romans de Fabienne Pasquet." In 118, 357-368.

PATEL, Shenaz.

GG6186. Bannerjee, Rohini: "Rompre *Le Silence des Chagos*: entretien avec Shenaz Patel," *Nouvelles Etudes Francophones,* vol. 23, no. 1 (printemps 2008), 198-211.

PATIENT, Serge. See 334.

PAULHAN, Jean. See also 489, 2025, 2458, 2472, 2481, 2491, 7387.

GG6187. ● Paulhan, Jean: *On poetry and politics.* Ed., introd., transl. Jennifer Bajorek, Eric Trudel. Urbana: Univ. of Illinois Press, 2008. xvi, 158 p.

GG6188.   Baillaud, Bernard: "Jean Paulhan et Jacques Rivière: revue des lettres," *Epistolaire: Revue de l'AIRE*, no. 34 (2008), 41-50. [Rivière]

GG6189.   Baillaud, Bernard: "Vers une bibliographie de la correspondance de Jean Paulhan," *Epistolaire: Revue de l'AIRE*, no. 34 (2008), 225-249.

GG6190.   Brisset, Laurence: "La correspondance entre Gaston Gallimard et Jean Paulhan ou les épreuves de *La NRF*," *Epistolaire: Revue de l'AIRE*, no. 34 (2008), 51-58.

GG6191.   Cornick, Martyn: "Défendre la France: la correspondance Jean Paulhan-Armand Petitjean." In 2458, 35-51.

GG6192.   Cornick, Martyn: "Jean Paulhan and the *Nouvelle Revue Française*: modernist editor, modernist review?," *Romanic Review*, vol. 99, no. 1-2 (Jan.-March), 9-26.

GG6193.   Paulhan, Jean-Kély: "Intellectuels désarmés," *Epistolaire: Revue de l'AIRE*, no. 34 (2008), 81-97. [Guéhenno]

PEETERS, Benoît.

GG6194.   Peeters, Benoît: "Dans l'intimité d'une bibliothèque d'écrivain: chez Benoît Peeters," *Carnet et les Instants*, no. 152 (2008), 31-36. [Entretien]

PÉGUY, Charles. See also 491, 1020, 2736, 5405.

GG6195.   ● Péguy, Charles: *L'Argent*. Prés. Antoine Compagnon. Paris: Equateurs, 2008. *Parallèles*. 100 p.

GG6196.   ● Teyssier, Arnaud: *Charles Péguy: une humanité française*. Paris: Perrin, 2008. 328 p.

GG6197.   ● Violette: *Charles Péguy: la réhabilitation d'un écrivain patriote*. Paris: Godefroy de Bouillon, 2008. 130 p.

GG6198.   Abgrall, Marie-Thérèse: "Madeleine Daniélou et Péguy," *Amitié Charles Péguy*, no. 123 (2008), 249-263.

GG6199.   Abgrall, Marie-Thérèse: "Relire Péguy aujourd'hui," *Amitié Charles Péguy*, no. 123 (2008), 283-287.

GG6200.   Barilier, Etienne: "Le mysticisme dreyfusiste fut une culmination." In 388, 127-138.

GG6201.   Bernon, Pauline: "Les jardins de la grâce et de la volonté: une représentation de l'écriture chez Charles Péguy." In 487, 387-400.

GG6202.   Bousquet, François: "Charles Péguy, le croisé antimoderne," *Spectacle du Monde*, no. 551 (déc. 2008), 61-65.

GG6203.   Bouvier Cavoret, Anne: "Le martyre, expression accomplice de la spiritualité chez Péguy," *Travaux de Littérature*, tome 21 (2008), 353-367.

GG6204.   Bruley, Pauline: "Faut-il chasser la rhétorique de la Citér?," *Amitié Charles Péguy*, no. 122 (2008), 186-201.

GG6205.   Bryce Echenique, Alfredo: "El retroceso de lo francés," *Cuadernos Hispanoamericanos*, no. 692 (2008), 9-11. [Sartre]

GG6206.   Cabanel, Patrick: "Charles Péguy et Edmondo de Amicis," *Amitié Charles Péguy*, no. 122 (2008), 131-156.

GG6207.   Comeau, Marie: "Péguy et l'âme populaire," *Amitié Charles Péguy*, no. 123 (2008), 351-357.

GG6208.   Conturie, Christiane: "Quand Charles Péguy donne son nom à des écoles," *Amitié Charles Péguy*, no. 123 (2008), 264-282.

GG6209.   Coutel, Charles: "L'apothéose de l'hospitalité," *Amitié Charles Péguy*, no. 124 (2008), 469-483.

GG6210.   Dadoun, Roger: " 'Elèves, je vous hais!': une psychanalyse, à la Péguy, de la relation pédagogique," *Amitié Charles Péguy*, no. 121 (2008), 60-73.

GG6211.   Daniélou, Madelaine: "Figures de femmes dans l'*Eve* de Péguy," *Amitié Charles Péguy*, no. 123 (2008), 307-318.

GG6212.   Daniélou, Madeleine: "La théologie de Péguy dans *Eve*," *Amitié Charles Péguy*, no. 123 (2008), 319-330.

GG6213.   Daudin, Claire: "Péguy prophète," *Amitié Charles Péguy*, no. 122 (2008), 202-219.

GG6214.   Decrop, Geneviève: "L'utopie de Charles Péguy," *Amitié Charles Péguy*, no. 124 (2008), 399-419.

GG6215. Forestier, Yann: "Charles Péguy et les contradictions de l'école républicaine," *Amitié Charles Péguy*, no. 121 (2008), 38-59.

GG6216. Fraisse, Simon: "Péguy, Lanson et le lansonisme," *Amitié Charles Péguy*, no. 233 (2008), 172-185.

GG6217. Gouttefangeas, Maud: "Représentation(s) du discours politique," *Amitié Charles Péguy*, no. 121 (2008), 83-89.

GG6218. Hubert, Marie-Clotilde: "Aperçu bibliographique, I: juillet 2007-juin 2008," *Amitié Charles Péguy*, no. 123 (2008), 389-394.

GG6219. Jeannet, Anne-Marie: "Au lycée Charles Péguy-République," *Amitié Charles Péguy*, no. 123 (2008), 288-295.

GG6220. Jeannet, Anne-Marie: "Le cœur de Péguy," *Amitié Charles Péguy*, no. 123 (2008), 373-378.

GG6221. Jeannet, Anne-Marie: "Péguy et la Vérité," *Amitié Charles Péguy*, no. 123 (2008), 379-385.

GG6222. Jey, Martine: "Péguy et Lanson," *Amitié Charles Péguy*, no. 122 (2008), 157-171.

GG6223. Klein, Denys: "Mère Geneviève Gallois, illustratrice de Péguy," *Amitié Charles Péguy*, no. 124 (2008), 484-495.

GG6224. Krop, Jérôme: "Péguy et les hussards noirs," *Amitié Charles Péguy*, no. 121 (2008), 24-37.

GG6225. Le Guay, Damien: "Madeleine Daniélou: une révolution pédagogique dans l'esprit de Charles Péguy," *Amitié Charles Péguy*, no. 123 (2008), 239-245.

GG6226. Le Guay, Damien: "La République et la monarchie chez Charles Péguy," *Amitié Charles Péguy*, no. 124 (2008), 446-468.

GG6227. Leroy, Géraldi: "Lettres d'instituteurs aux *Cahiers de la quinzaine*," *Amitié Charles Péguy*, no. 121 (2008), 74-82.

GG6228. Leroy, Géraldi: "Péguy et l'enseignement," *Amitié Charles Péguy*, no. 121 (2008), 6-23.

GG6229. Leroy, Géraldi: "Péguy et Jaurès: questions de fond," *Amitié Charles Péguy*, no. 121 (2008), 106-108.

GG6230. Mongin, Suzanne: "En souvenir de Charles Péguy," *Amitié Charles Péguy*, no. 123 (2008), 333-336.

GG6231. Petré, Hélène: "Le Polyeucte de Péguy," *Amitié Charles Péguy*, no. 123 (2008), 358-372.

GG6232. Ryan, Jerry: "A God who trembles: fear and hope in the poetry of Péguy," *Commonweal*, vol. 135, no. 22 (Dec. 19, 2008), 13-15.

GG6233. Soulié, Rémi: "Péguy de combat: le combat continue," *Amitié Charles Péguy*, no. 121 (2008), 100-104.

GG6234. Teyssier, Arnaud: "Péguy est-il républicain ou monarchiste?," *Amitié Charles Péguy*, no. 124 (2008), 420-445.

GG6235. Vaissermann, Romain: "Le verset et la tentation des alexandrins. L'écriture poétique de Péguy à un moment charnière: 1911," *Etudes Littéraires*, vol. 38, no. 2 (automne 2007), 43-56.

PÉLÉGRI, Jean.

GG6236. Zoppellari, Anna: "Jean Pélégri, écrivain du terroir algérien." In 515, 239-244.

PELLETIER, Jean-Jacques.

GG6237. David, Sylvain: "Apocalypse montréalaise, imaginaire urbain et pouvoir des ténèbres dans l'œuvre de Jean-Jacques Pelletier," *Etudes Canadiennes*, no. 65 (2008), 121-133.

PENNAC, Daniel.

GG6238. ● Lozzi, Nicolas [et al.]: *Les nombreuses vies de Malaussène*. Lyon: Les Moutons électriques, 2008. 191 p.

GG6239. Gamoneda Lanza, Amelia: "Le comique agoraphobe et sa guérison ironique: narration et répétition chez Daniel Pennac," *Humoresques*, no. 26 (2007), 121-132.

PEREC, Georges. See also 519, 552, 585, 721, 743, 759, 760, 6167, 6811.

GG6240. ● Constantin, Danielle: *Masques et mirages: genèse du roman chez Cortá-*

zar, Perec et Villemaire. New York: Peter Lang, 2008. *Currents in comparative Romance languages and literatures*. x, 192 p. [Villemaire]

GG6241. ● Perec, Georges: *L'art et la manière d'aborder son chef de service pour lui demander une augmentation*. Postface de Bernard Magné. Paris: Hachette littératures, 2008. 105 p.

GG6242. ● Perec, Georges: *Jeux intéressants*. Prés. Bernard Magné. Paris: Zulma, 2008. 140 p.

GG6243. ● Perec, Georges: *Nouveaux jeux intéressants*. Prés. Bernard Magné. Paris: Zulma, 2008. 92 p.

GG6244. ● Perec, Georges: *Species of space and other pieces*. Ed. and trans. John Sturrock. London; New York: Penguin, 2008. New edition. *Penguin classics*. xvii, 292 p.

GG6245. ● *"Regarde de tous tes yeux, regarde": l'art contemporain de Georges Perec*. Exposition prés. à Nantes, du 27 juin au 12 octobre 2008. Commissariat scientifique, Jean-Pierre Salgas. Nantes: Joseph K; Musée des beaux-arts de Nantes; Dole: Musée des beaux-arts de Dole, 2008. 126 p.

GG6246. Abdelkéfi, Rabâa: "Mystère et enchâssement des récits dans *53 jours*." In 436, 153-162.

GG6247. Bary, Cécile de: "Le jeu, métaphore du texte énigmatique perecquien." In 436, 305-315.

GG6248. Boyle, Claire: "Perec: autobiography, possession and the dispossessed self." In 400, 66-97.

GG6249. Constantin, Danielle: "Genèse du chapitre XLVI de *La Vie mode d'emploi* de Georges Perec." In 436, 101-114.

GG6250. Constantin, Danielle: "*La Vie mode d'emploi* de Georges Perec: le vestibule du 11, rue Simon-Crubellier." In 411.

GG6251. Cornille, Jean-Louis: "Vestiges et vertiges." In 413.

GG6252. Dangy, Isabelle: "Le mystère du personnage dans *La Vie mode d'emploi*." In 436, 89-99.

GG6253. Escobar, Matthew: "X: identity, reflexivity and potential space in Perec's *W ou le souvenir d'enfance* and Gide's *Les Faux-Monnayeurs*," *Romanic Review*, vol. 98, no. 4 (Nov. 2007), 413-433. [Gide]

GG6254. Goga, Yvonne: "Formes de l'autoréflexivité mallarméenne dans *Un homme qui dort* de Georges Perec." In 436, 127-138. [Mallarmé]

GG6255. Guidée, Raphaëlle: "L'éternel retour de la catastrophe: répétition et destruction dans les œuvres de Georges Perec et W. G. Sebald." In 506, 37-47.

GG6256. Hamaide, Eléonore: "Les enfants cachés, de Georges Perec à Berthe Burkko-Falcman." In 602, 121-135.

GG6257. Hartje, Hans: "Réécrire l'histoire littéraire. Georges Perec et d'autres voyageurs d'hiver." In 506, 431-436.

GG6258. Joly, Jean-Luc: "Pièges de sens. Contrainte et révélation dans l'œuvre de Georges Perec." In 436, 289-304.

GG6259. Magné, Bernard: "Tentative d'argumentaire pour quelques-unes des énigmes qui ont été trouvées dans *La Vie mode d'emploi* au fil des ans." In 436, 71-88.

GG6260. Parayre, Marc: "Formes de l'énigme dans *La Disparition* de Perec." In 436, 139-151.

GG6261. Pare, Daouda: "Ecrire le déchirement: *W ou le souvenir d'enfance* de Georges Perec." In 99, 77-89.

GG6262. Reulecke, Anne-Kathrin: "Fälschung und Intermedialität in Georges Perecs Roman *Un cabinet d'amateur*," *Weimarar Beiträge*, 54. Jahrgang, Heft 1 (2008), 103-116.

GG6263. Suleiman, Susan Rubin: "The edge of memory: experimental writing and the 1.5 generation." In 600.

GG6264. Suleiman, Susan Rubin: "Expérimentation littéraire et traumatisme d'enfance." In 602, 81-99.

GG6265. Thorel-Cailleteau, Sylvie: "Georges Perec: la preuve de la poésie par le désastre," *Roman 20-50*, no. 46 (2008), 135-148.

GG6266. Van Montfrans, Manet: "L'enchâssement des énigmes. *Les Villes invisibles* de Calvino dans *La Vie mode d'emploi* de Perec." In 436, 115-126.

GG6267. Villeneuve, Lisa: "The urban experience of placelessness: perceptual rhythms in Georges Perec's *Un homme qui dort*." In 575, 171-186.

GG6268. Wolf, Nelly: "Georges Perec: la cicatrice ou le visage de l'exil," *Romanistische Zeitschrift für Literaturgeschichte*, 32. Jahrgang, Heft 1-2 (2008), 105-112.

PÉRET, Benjamin.

GG6269. • Spiteri, Richard: *Exégèse de Dernier malheur dernière chance de Benjamin Péret*. Paris: L'Harmattan, 2008. *Poétiques*. 143 p.

PÉROCHON, Ernest.

GG6270. • Pérochon, Ernest: *Œuvres complètes. Tome II*. Préface d'Eric Kocher-Marbœuf. La Crèche: Geste, 2007. 506 p.

PERREAULT, Marilyn.

GG6271. Hellot, Marie-Christiane: "Enfants perdus de la Brusqui. *Roche, papier, couteau*," *Jeu: Cahiers de Théâtre*, no. 127 [no. 2] (2008), 12-15.

PERRET, Jacques.

GG6272. • *Jacques Perret, 1901-1992: documents et témoignages*. Avant-propos Jean-Baptiste Chaumeil. Paris: Godefroy de Bouillon, 2006. 94 p.

PERRIER, Anne.

GG6273. Baude, Jeanne-Marie: "Pauvreté et plénitude dans l'œuvre d'Anne Perrier." In 382, 161-176.

PERROS, Georges.

GG6274. • Perros, Georges; Anne Philipe; Gérard Philipe: *Correspondance: 1946-1978*. Prés. par Jérôme Garcin et annotée par Anne-Marie Philipe et Thierry Boizet. Bordeaux: Finitude, 2008. 167 p.

GG6275. Butor, Michel: "L'école des gisants," *Revue de Belles-Lettres*, no. 3-4 (2008), 23-27.

GG6276. Le Gentil, Michel: "Le squatter de l'avenue Le Gorgeu," *Revue de Belles-Lettres*, no. 3-4 (2008), 31-33.

GG6277. Lüthi, Ariane: "Georges Perros et la paresse," *Revue de Belles-Lettres*, no. 3-4 (2008), 41-51.

GG6278. Nedelec, Jean-Pierre: "Georges Perros en coulisses," *Revue de Belles-Lettres*, no. 3-4 (2008), 35-40.

GG6279. Réda, Jacques: "L'abcisse et l'ordonnée," *Revue de Belles-Lettres*, no. 3-4 (2008), 9-14.

GG6280. Roudaut, Jean: " 'Le jeune homme avec lequel je passai une soirée . . .'," *Revue de Belles-Lettres*, no. 3-4 (2008), 15-22.

PHILIPPE, Charles-Louis.

GG6281. Guisy, Maryan: "Charles-Louis Philippe et l'art de la critique sociale implicite," *Amis de Charles-Louis Philippe*, no. 64 (2008), 31-38.

GG6282. Roe, David: "Ch.-L. Philippe dans la *Correspondance* André Gide," *Amis de Charles-Louis Philippe*, no. 64 (2008), 39-47. [Gide]

GG6283. Roe, David: "Roubert Tournaud, premier universitaire philippien," *Amis de Charles-Louis Philippe*, no. 64 (2008), 48-49.

GG6284. Roe, David: " 'Sur les maladies': Ch.-L. Philippe collaborateur de la (toute) première *NRF*," *Amis de Charles-Louis Philippe*, no. 64 (2008), 17-29.

PIAGET, Jean.

GG6285. • *Cognitive development: neo-Piagetian perspectives*. Sergio Morra [et al.]. New York: Lawrence Erlbaum Associates, 2008. xvi, 430 p.

GG6286. • Fedi, Laurent: *Piaget et la conscience morale*. Paris: PUF, 2008. *Philosophies*. 152 p.

GG6287. • *Jean Piaget and Neuchâtel: the learner and the scholar*. Ed. Anne-Nelly Perret-Clermont, Jean-Marc Barrelet. Hove, England; New York: Psychology Press, 2008. xv, 240 p.

GG6288. • Kohler, Richard: *Jean Piaget*. London; New York: Continuum, 2008. *Library of educational thought*. x, 326 p.

GG6289. • Piaget, Jean: *The language and thought of the child*. Preface by E. Claparède; trans. Marjorie Warden. ?: Goldberg Press, 2008. xxiii, 246 p.

GG6290. ● *Piaget e l'educazione della mente*. A cura di Nando Filograsso, Roberto Travaglini. Milano: F. Angeli, 2007. 220 p.

GG6291. Pfeiffle, Horst: "On the psychogenesis of the a priori: Jean Piaget's critique of Kant," *Philosophy and Social Criticism*, vol. 34, no. 5 (June 2008), 487-498.

PICARD, Michel.

GG6292. Chauveau, Jean-Pierre: "Régionalisme et littérature: les Terres-Froides (Isère) au milieu du XXe siècle d'après le roman de Michel Picard, *A pierre fendre*." In 576, 203-253.

PIEYRE DE MANDIARGUES, André.

GG6293. Lowrie, Joyce O.: "The wheel of fortune as mirror: André Pieyre de Mandiargues's *La Motocyclette*." In 511.

GG6294. Russo, Adelaide M.: "Dialogues et dédicaces 'Pour tout ce que les yeux voient': Bona Tibertelli de Pisis et André Pieyre de Mandiargues." In 583, 197-219.

PINEAU, Gisèle. See also 117, 584.

GG6295. Loichot, Valérie: "Eloge de la barbarie selon Gisèle Pineau," *International Journal of Francophone Studies*, vol. 11, no. 1-2 (2008), 137-149.

GG6296. Novivor, Ayelevi: "L'adoption comme acte rédempteur chez les héroïnes de Gisèle Pineau." In 571, 147-156.

GG6297. Thomas, Bonnie: "Utopia and dystopia in Gisèle Pineau's *L'Exil selon Julia* and *Fleur de Barbarie*." In 541, 180-192.

GG6298. Ueckmann, Natascha: " ' . . . tout part d'une blessure': Gewalt, *Gender* und Geschichte in Gisèle Pineaus Roman *L'Espérance-macadam*. In 440, 167-187.

PINGAUD, Bernard.

GG6299. Pingaud, Bernard: "Ecriture et griffonnage." In 438, 53-74.

PINGET, Robert. See also 7288.

GG6300. Camus, Audrey: "Ecrire avec la cendre: les ruines ménippéennes de Robert Pinget." In 902, 121-133.

GG6301. Perrin, Laurent: "Le récit parmi ses voix chez Robert Pinget." In 619, 491-506.

GG6302. Piégay-Gros, Nathalie: "Pinget et le dessin." In 418, 259-275.

PIROTTE, Jean-Claude.

GG6303. ● Dotan, Isabelle: *Bonheurs de l'errance, rumeurs de la douleur: une lecture de l'œuvre de Jean-Claude Pirotte*. Namur: Editions namuroises, 2008. 129 p.

PLACOLY, Vincent.

GG6304. Britton, Celia: "Singular beings and political disorganization in Vincent Placoly's *L'Eau-de-mort guildive*." In 51, 74-92.

GG6305. Grogan Lynch, Molly: "*Frères volcans* de Vincent Placoly: un document sur l'histoire absente de 1848 à la Martinique," *Etudes Littéraires Africaines*, no. 26 (2008), 27-33.

PLIYA, José.

GG6306. Miller, Judith G.: "Women's voices, women's bodies in José Pliya's theatre," *Esprit Créateur*, vol. 48, no. 3 (Fall 2008), 109-118.

PONGE, Francis. See also 536, 606, 662, 663, 735, 1043, 4645.

GG6307. Doga, Marie: "Cycle des saisons et cycle d'écriture dans l'œuvre de Francis Ponge." In 383, 435-441.

GG6308. Farasse, Gérard: "Circonstances atténuées." In 454, 55-67.

GG6309. Farasse, Gérard: "Ponge et Calet: entre la letter et le cri," *Revue des Sciences Humaines*, no. 292 [no. 4] (2008), 61-72. [Calet]

GG6310. Ponge, Francis; Henry-Louis Mermod: "Correspondance: 1945-1961," *Trajectoires*, no. 4 (2008), 149-310.

POOL, Léa.

GG6311. Pallister, Janis L.: "L'*Angst* de l'adolescente: *Emporte-moi* de Léa Pool," *Nouvelles Etudes Francophones*, vol. 22, no. 1 (printemps 2007), 89-108.

POULET, Georges.

GG6312. Cryle, Peter: "Playful theory: Georges Poulet's phenomenological thematics," *Culture, Theory and Critique*, vol. 19, no. 1 (April 2008), 21-34.

POULET, Robert.

GG6313. ● Delaunois, Jean-Marie: *Robert Poulet*. Grez-sur-Loing: Pardès, 2008.

POULIN, Jacques. See also 311, 3993.

GG6314. Dupuis, Gilles: "L'île aux chats. Incursion dans l'archipel félin de Jacques Poulin." In 423.

GG6315. Fasano, Linda: "Tre personaggi in uno: Jacques Poulin," *Rivista di Studi Canadesi*, n. 20 (2007), 143-171.

GG6316. Samzun, Marie-Béatrice: "Le corps poulinien à l'épreuve du temps ou quand le miroir se brise." In 69, 165-175.

GG6317. Sanaker, John Kristian: "*Les yeux bleus de Mistassini* de Jacques Poulin." In 41, 313-335.

GG6318. Yotova, Rennie: "Jacques Poulin, *Volkswagen blues*." In 115, 144-155.

POURRAT, Henri.

GG6319. ● Pourrat, Henri: *Correspondance Henri Pourrat-Bernard Zimmer. 2, 1943-1959*. Edition établie, prés. et annotée par Claude Dalet. Clermont-Ferrand: Bibliothèque communautaire et interuniversitaire, centre Henri Pourrat, 2008. *Cahiers Henri Pourrat*, 23. 179 p.

GG6320. ● Vialatte, Alexandre; Henri Pourrat: *Correspondances Alexandre Vialatte-Henri Pourrat. De Paris à Héliopolis: mars 1935-juillet 1939*. Sous la dir. de Dany Hadjadj; textes réunis, prés. et annotés par Sylviane Coyault. Clermont-Ferrand: Presses univ. Blaise Pascal, 2008. 253 p.

POZZI, Catherine.

GG6321. ● Diaz-Florian, Mireille: *Catherine Pozzi: la vocation à la nuit*. Préface de Claire Paulhan. Croissy-Beaubourg: Aden, 2008. *Le cercle des poètes disparus*. 347 p.

GG6322. Bacherich, Martine: "C. K./P. V.: Hélas, vous êtes donc l'amour." In 795, 17-38.

GG6323. Bourjea, Serge: "Pozzi/*Valéry*/Rilke: un 'divertissement'," *Revue des Sciences Humaines*, no. 292 [no. 4] (2008), 23-40. [Valéry]

PRASSINOS, Gisèle. See 6126.

PRESCOTT, Marc.

GG6324. Hallion Bres, Sandrine: "*Sex, lies et les Franco-Manitobains* (1993) de Marc Prescott: la minorité franco-manitobaine sous les feux de la rampe." In 1100, 17-30.

PRÉVERT, Jacques.

GG6325. ● *Jacques Prévert, Paris la belle*. Catalogue de l'exposition "Jacques Prévert, Paris la belle" à l'Hôtel de ville de Paris, salle Saint-Jean, 24 octobre 2008-28 février 2009. Dir. Eugénie Bachelot Prévert, N. T. Binh. Paris: Flammarion, 2008. 272 p.

GG6326. ● Lamy, Jean-Claude: *Prévert, les frères amis*. Paris: Albin Michel, 2008. 352 p.

GG6327. ● Prévert, Jacques: *La cinquième saison*. Edition préparée par Arnaud et Danièle Laster; avec le concours de Janine Prévert. Paris: Gallimard, 2008. *NRF; Le point du jou*. 237 p. [Orig. ed. 1984]

GG6328. ● Prévert, Jacques: *Poèmes et chansons de Jacques Prévert: une anthologie*. Proposée par Benoit Marchon. Paris: Bayard jeunesse, 2008. 112 p.

GG6329. ● Prévert, Jacques: *Soleil de nuit*. Edition prép. par Arnaud et Danièle Laster; avec le concours de Janine Prévert. Paris: Gallimard, 2008. *NRF; Le point du jour*. 303 p. [Orig. ed. 1980]

GG6330. Marzouki, Samir: "La poésie au théâtre." In 612, 271-284.

PRÉVOST, Jean.

PRIGENT, Christian.

GG6331. Marchal, Hugues: "Note sur une invective désamorcée: *Grand-mère Quéquette* de Christian Prigent." In 564, 199-204.

PROPHÈTE, Emmelie.

GG6332. Chemla, Yves: "Emmelie Prophète: une blessure en forme d'île," *Cultures Sud*, no. 170 (sept. 2008), 111-116.

PROULX, Monique.

GG6333. Fisher, Dominique D.: "Transculturalité et délocalisation dans *Les aurores montréales* de Monique Proulx." In 120, 308-317.

GG6334. Vignes-Mottet, Sylvie: " 'Corps étrangers' dans *Les aurores montréales* de Monique Proulx." In 69, 261-274.

PROUST, Marcel. See also 398, 420, 468, 558, 657, 692, 711, 1629, 1903, 2824, 2961, 3018, 4191, 4862, 5251, 5486, 5793, 8069.

GG6335. ● Ben Mustapha, Jamila: *La dialectique de l'individuel et du général dans La recherche de Marcel Proust.* Tunis: Centre de Publications Universitaire, 2008. 259 p.

GG6336. ● *Cahier 54: Bibliothèque nationale de France. Nouvelles acquisitions françaises 16694.* Introduction et analyse par Nathalie Mauriac Dyer. Turnhourt, Belgique: Brepols, 2008. 2 vols.

GG6337. ● Carbone, Mauro: *Proust et les idées sensibles.* Paris: Vrin, 2008. *Matière étrangère.* 202 p.

GG6338. ● Deleuze, Gilles: *Proust and signs.* Trans. Richard Howard. London: Continuum, 2008. [Deleuze]

GG6339. ● Finch, Alison: *Proust's additions: the making of A la recherche du temps perdu.* Cambridge: Cambridge Univ. Press, 2008. 2 vols. [Orig. ed., 1977]

GG6340. ● Foschini, Lorenza: *Il cappotto di Proust.* Roma: Portaparole, 2008. *Piccoli saggi.* 104 p.

GG6341. ● Foschini, Lorenza: *Le manteau de Proust.* Trad. Benoît Puttermans. Roma: Portaparole, 2008. *Petits essais.* 104 p.

GG6342. ● Fravalo-Tane, Pascale: *A la recherche du temps perdu en France et en Allemagne (1913-1958): "Dans une sorte de langue étrangère".* Paris: H. Champion, 2008. *Recherches Proustiennes,* 11. 461 p.

GG6343. ● Grimaldi, Nicolas: *Proust, les horreurs de l'amour.* Paris: PUF, 2008. *Perspectives critiques.* 261 p.

GG6344. ● Grossvogel, David I.: *Le journal de Charles Swann.* Paris: Buchet-Chastel, 2008. 328 p.

GG6345. ● Hauptmann-Katsuyama, Yuko: *Proust historien: le temps historique dans la Recherche.* Lille: ANRT, 2008. *Thèse à la carte.* 411 p.

GG6346. ● Ifri, Pascal Alain: *Proust.* Grez-sur-Loing: Pardès, 2008. *Qui suis-je?.* 127 p.

GG6347. ● Karpeles, Eric: *Paintings in Proust: a visual companion to In search of lost time.* London: Thames & Hudson, 2008. 352 p.

GG6348. ● *Korrespondenz der Sinne: wahrnehmungsästhetische und intermediale Aspekte im Werk von Proust.* Hrsg. Uta Felten, Volker Roloff. München: Fink, 2008. 316 p.

GG6349. ● Kosofsky Sedgwick, Eve: *Epistémologie du placard.* Trad. Maxime Cervulle. Paris: Amsterdam, 2008. 257 p.

GG6350. ● Lehrer, Jonah: *Proust was a neuroscientist.* Boston: Houghton Mifflin, 2008. x, 242 p.

GG6351. ● Leonte, Liviu: *La réception de l'œuvre de Marcel Proust en Roumanie.* Lille: ANRT, 2008. *Thèse à la carte.* 273 p.

GG6352. ● *Literarische Gendertheorie: Eros und Gesellschaft bei Proust und Colette.* Hrsg. Ursula Kink-Heer, Ursula Hennigfeld, Fernand Horner. Bielefeld: Transcript, 2006. 285 p.

GG6353. ● *Marcel Proust.* Hélène Gaudy [et al.]. Paris: Inculte, 2007. *Collectif-essai.* 237 p.

GG6354. ● Masecchia, Anna: *Al cinema con Proust.* Venezia: Marsilio, 2008. 190 p.

GG6355. ● Mölk, Renate: *Durch die Blume gesagt: Pflanzen und Blumen in Marcel Prousts A la recherche du temps perdu.* Heidelberg: Winter, 2008. *Studia Romanica.* 497 p.

GG6356. ● Nuti, Marco: *De Combray à Venise: archéologies imaginaires chez Proust.* Roma: Aracne, 2008. 154 p.

GG6357. ● O'Sullivan, Michael: *The incarnation of language: Joyce, Proust and a philosophy of the flesh.* London; New York: Continuum, 2008. *Continuum literary studies.* 184 p.

GG6358. ● Painter, George D.: *Marcel Proust: 1871-1922.* Trad. G. Gattaui, R.-P. Vial. Paris: Tallandier, 2008. *Texto.* 955 p.

GG6359. ● Pinson, Guillaume: *Fiction du monde: de la presse mondaine à Marcel Proust.* Montréal: Presses de l'Univ. de Montréal, 2008. *Socius.* 365 p.

GG6360. • Proust, Marcel: *A la recherche du temps perdu. Le Côté de Guermantes I et II*. Edition établie, prés. et annotée par Bernard Brun. Paris: Librairie générale française, 2008. *Le livre de poche*. 733 p. [Orig. ed., 1992]

GG6361. • Proust, Marcel: *"Cher ami . . .": Marcel Proust im Spiegel siner Korrespondenz*. Hrsg. Jürgen Ritte. Köln: Snoeck, 2008.

GG6362. • Proust, Marcel: *Du côté de chez Swann*. Edition prés. et annotée par Antoine Compagnon. Paris: Gallimard, 2008. xxxv, 527 p.

GG6363. • Proust, Marcel: *La fin de la jalousie, et autres nouvelles*. Edition de Thierry Laget. Paris: Gallimard, 2008. *Folio*. 107 p. [Orig. ed., 1993]

GG6364. • Proust, Marcel: *Petit pan de mur jaune*. Précédé de "Les Ecarts d'une vision" par Jean Pavans. Paris: La Différence, 2008. 59 p.

GG6365. • Proust, Marcel: *Précaution inutile*. Edition prés. par Frédéric Ferney. Bègles: Castor astral, 2008. *Les inattendus*. 173 p.

GG6366. • Proust, Marcel: *La prisonnière*. Edition prés., introduite et annotée par Luc Fraisse. Paris: Librairie générale française, 2008. 570 p.

GG6367. • *Proust et la philosophie aujourd'hui*. Sous la dir. de Mauro Carbone et Eleonora Sparvoli. Pisa: ETS, 2008. 345 p.

GG6368. • *Proust et les moyens de connaissance*. Textes réunis par Annick Bouillaguet. Strasbourg: Presses univ. de Strasbourg, 2008. *Formes et savoirs*. 256 p.

GG6369. • Roudaut, Jean: *Les trois anges: essai sur quelques citations de A la recherche du temps perdu*. Paris: H. Champion, 2008. *Recherches Proustiennes*, 13. 132 p.

GG6370. • Rozzoni, Claudio: *Ricordarsi è creare: l'essenza estetica nella Recherche di Marcel Proust*. Milano: Mimesis, 2008. 174 p.

GG6371. • Schmid, Marion: *Proust dans la décadence*. Paris: Honoré Champion, 2008. *Recherches proustiennes*, 12. 258 p.

GG6372. • Schmidt, Jochen: *Schmidt liest Proust*. Dresden: Voland & Quist, 2008. *Singles*. 608 p.

GG6373. • Stierle, Karlheinz: *Zeit und Werk: Prousts A la recherche du temps perdu und Dantes Commedia*. München: Hanser, 2008. *Akzente*. 270 p.

GG6374. • Tadié, Jean-Yves: *Marcel Proust: Biographie*. Aus dem Franz. von Max Looser. Frankfurt: M. Suhrkamp, 2008. 1265 p.

GG6375. • Townsend, Gabrielle: *Proust's imaginary museum reproductions and reproduction in A la recherche du temps perdu*. Oxford: Peter Lang, 2008. *Cultural interactions*. 232 p.

GG6376. • Tribout-Joseph, Sarah: *Proust and Joyce in dialogue*. London: Legenda, 2008. 184 p.

GG6377. • Van Buuren, Maarten: *Marcel Proust et l'imaginaire*. Amsterdam: Rodopi, 2008. *Chiasma*, 25. 174 p.

GG6378. • Willemart, Philippe: *Tratado das sensações em "A prisioneira" de Marcel Proust*. Pref. Leda Tenório da Motta; trad. Claudia Berliner. ?: Opus Print, 2008. 219 p.

GG6379. Austin, James F.: "Pastiche expelled: a Proustian guide to French pedagogy," *Dalhousie French Studies*, vol. 84 (Fall 2008), 51-63.

GG6380. Azagury, Yaelle: "Dr Jekyll et M. Hyde: Proust et les marges du récit," *Bulletin Marcel Proust*, no. 58 (2008), 81-88.

GG6381. Baldwin, Thomas: "Proust's eyes." In 458, 95-108.

GG6382. Barilier, Etienne: "Mais Jean, lui, écoutait le colonel Picquart." In 388, 82-91.

GG6383. Barilier, Etienne: "Pas le temps de penser à la littérature." In 388, 165-177.

GG6384. Bizub, Edward: "Les intermittences du cœur: entre science et poésie." In 6368, 111-116.

GG6385. Bizub, Edward: "La mémoire proustienne et la psychologie expérimentale," *Ritm*, no. 38 (2007), 348-356.

GG6386. Bizub, Edward: "Proust et Ribot: l'imagination créatrice," *Bulletin Marcel Proust*, no. 58 (2008), 49-56.

GG6387. Boongia Woo, Tomoko: "Lecture de Proust, à travers Freud, par les premiers critiques," *Bulletin Marcel Proust*, no. 58 (2008), 69-79.

GG6388. Bouillaguet, Annick: "Intermittences de la *Recherche*." In 459, 201-210.

GG6389. Boyer-Weinmann, Martine: "Outre-manche et outre-langue: fonctions de la citation (à peu près) anglaise dans *A la recherche du temps perdu*." In 407, 21-33.

GG6390. Boyer-Weinmann, Martine: "Proust 'ultra tombeau': réticence, secret et transgression dans la correspondance." In 391, 195-205.

GG6391. Brun, Bernard: "La *tabula rasa* de Marcel Proust." In 6368, 69-77.

GG6392. Chardin, Philippe: " 'Réminiscences anticipées' et 'ramiers fraternels'." In 506, 115-124.

GG6393. Chaudier, Stéphane: "L'automne proustien." In 383, 377-387.

GG6394. Chaudier, Stéphane: "La cocotte polyglotte chez Bourget, Proust, Larbaud." In 407, 35-51. [Bourget, Larbaud]

GG6395. Chaudier, Stéphane: "Le discrédit de Clio." In 6368, 169-182.

GG6396. Chaudier, Stéphane: "Incohérences de Proust." In 410, 351-360.

GG6397. Cohen, Maxime: "Critique amusée de Marcel Proust." In 409.

GG6398. Compagnon, Antoine: " 'Comme la souffrance va plus loin en psychologie que la psychologie!'," *Ritm*, no. 38 (2007), 357-365.

GG6399. Cornille, Jean-Louis: "Proust à l'heure du pastiche." In 413.

GG6400. Craig, Herbert E.: "Three Proustian subjects reconfigured," *Cincinnati Romance Review*, vol. 26 (2007), 100-107.

GG6401. Dangy, Isabelle: "Proust et le roman spectral: le cas d'Anne-Marie Garat," *Marcel Proust Aujourd'hui*, no. 6 (2008), 255-274. [Garat]

GG6402. Daubigny, Fanny: "Le roman de l'écrivain myope," *Marcel Proust Aujourd'hui*, no. 6 (2008), 127-143.

GG6403. de Agostini, Daniela: "Anna de Noailles, Proust e l' 'antica melopea' wagneriana," *Rivista di Letterature Moderne e Comparate*, vol. 61, fasc. 1 (genn.-marzo 2008), 19-31. [Noailles]

GG6404. Delesalle, Simone: "A force de volonté je m'étais réintégré dans le réel." In 6368, 57-67.

GG6405. Depambour-Tarride, Laurence: "Proust et ses professeurs de droit." In 6368, 151-159.

GG6406. Dezon Jones, Elyane: "Saniette/saintine." In 6368, 229-234.

GG6407. Dubois, Jacques: "Proust et le temps des embusqués." In 473, 205-221.

GG6408. Dubosclard, Geneviève: "De Marcel Proust à Claude Simon: la mémoire de la création," *Marcel Proust Aujourd'hui*, no. 6 (2008), 59-79. [Simon]

GG6409. Duval, Sophie: "Une 'force poétique': les anneaux du style et les alliances de l'humour (suite et fin)," *Bulletin d'Informations Proustiennes*, no. 38 (2008), 109-127.

GG6410. Elkins, Katherine: "Memory and material significance: composing modernist influence," *Modern Language Quarterly*, vol. 69, no. 4 (Dec. 2008), 509-531.

GG6411. Erman, Michel: "Le temps de l'inactuel," *Bulletin d'Informations Proustiennes*, no. 38 (2008), 151-159.

GG6412. Fonvielle, Stéphanie: "Cohérence du discours proustien." In 410, 361-370.

GG6413. Fraisse, Luc: "Changement de paysage: les réécritures de Proust dans les récits de Gracq," *Marcel Proust Aujourd'hui*, no. 6 (2008), 13-36. [Gracq]

GG6414. Fraisse, Luc: "Nerval et le roman dogmatique de Proust: compléments à des découvertes récentes," *Romanistische Zeitschrift für Literaturgeschichte*, 32. Jahrgang, Heft 1-2 (2008), 71-81.

GG6415. Fraisse, Luc: "Proust critique de la peinture italienne." In 563, 70-79.

GG6416. Fraisse, Luc: "Proust et l'esthétique des salons." In 419, 117-135.

GG6417. Fulop, Erika: "Becoming body: sleep and writing in Proust's *A la recherche du temps perdu*." In 458, 109-121.

GG6418. Godeau, Florence: "Muettes rencontres de deux sommités: Marcel Proust, Robert Musil," *Bulletin d'Informations Proustiennes*, no. 38 (2008), 143-150.

GG6419. Goujon, Francine: "Écriture réflexive et genèse d'Albertine dans le Cahier 54," *Bulletin d'Informations Proustiennes*, no. 38 (2008), 73-87.

GG6420. Green, André: "Mémoire et oubli chez Marcel Proust." In 516, 191-202.

GG6421. Grenet, Julie: "Portrait d'Abraham en fleur: étrangeté et exotisme du père dans *A la recherche du temps perdu* de Marcel Proust," *Dalhousie French Studies*, vol. 83 (Summer 2008), 109-117.

GG6422. Guez, Stéphanie: "Proust en faiseur d'ana. L'anecdote et la construction du personnage proustien," *Littérature*, no. 149 (mars 2008), 89-107.

GG6423. Hanhart-Marmor, Yona: "De Proust à Claude Simon: une esthétique de la rature," *Marcel Proust Aujourd'hui*, no. 6 (2008), 37-58.

GG6424. Henrot, Geneviève: "Proust et les savoirs archaïques." In 6368, 127-137.

GG6425. Henry, Anne: "Le kaléidoscope proustien." In 6368, 161-167.

GG6426. Houppermans, Sjef: "Les poses de Marcel Proust dans l'œuvre de Renaud Camus," *Marcel Proust Aujourd'hui*, no. 6 (2008), 211-234. [R. Camus]

GG6427. Hurson, Didier: "Le pouvoir et ses emblèmes: ordre totémique et ordre des castes dans la société selon Marcel Proust." In 457, 139-159.

GG6428. Ippolito, Christophe: " 'Faire Verdurin': formes et extériorité dans *Tropismes* et *Les Fruits d'or*," *Marcel Proust Aujourd'hui*, no. 6 (2008), 81-102. [Sarraute]

GG6429. Jordan, Jack: "Proust et la connaissance du moi." In 6368, 139-148.

GG6430. Joseph, Sarah: "Marcel and Albertine: a Proustian psychoanalysis of listening?" In 610, 161-177.

GG6431. Karpeles, Eric: "Paintings in Proust," *New England Review*, vol. 29, no. 3 (2008), 36-45.

GG6432. Kato, Yasué: "L'unité thématique du Cahier 64: Leconte de Lisle, la sensualité et l'amour," *Bulletin d'Informations Proustiennes*, no. 38 (2008), 29-40.

GG6433. Kaushik, Rajiv: "Phenomenological temporality and Proustian nostalgia," *Analecta Husserliana*, vol. 96 (2008), 225-241.

GG6434. Kear, John: "La chambre mentale: Proust's solitude." In 630, 221-233.

GG6435. Keller, Luzius: "Madeleines et aubépine." In 6368, 39-46.

GG6436. Lambert, Hervé-Pierre: "La mémoire: Proust et les neurosciences," *Texte*, no. 43-44 (2008), 211-226.

GG6437. Lavault, Maya: " 'Voir par la fenêtre éclairée': un motif dans le tapis?," *Bulletin d'Informations Proustiennes*, no. 38 (2008), 129-142.

GG6438. Leriche, Françoise: "Quelle édition pour quel public? Les avatars de l'édition électronique de la correspondance de Proust," *Recherches et Travaux, Université Stendhal, UFR de Lettres*, no. 72 (2008), 59-70.

GG6439. Lerner, L. Scott: "Mourning and subjectivity: from Bersani to Proust, Klein, and Freud," *Diacritics*, vol. 37, no. 1 (Spring 2007), 41-53.

GG6440. Lewis, Pericles: "Proust, Woolf, and modern fiction," *Romanic Review*, vol. 99, no. 1-2 (Jan.-March), 77-86.

GG6441. Maar, Michael: "Spargel mit Fissuren. Marginalien beim Wiederlesen Marcel Prousts," *Merkur*, Nr. 707 (April 2008), 350-354.

GG6442. Matsubara, Yoko: "Les vers raciniens et l'amour illusoire dans *A la recherche du temps perdu*," *Bulletin Marcel Proust*, no. 58 (2008), 89-98.

GG6443. Matz, Aaron: "The years of hating Proust," *Comparative Literature*, vol. 60, no. 4 (Fall 2008), 355-369.

GG6444. Mauriac Dyer, Nathalie: "D'Hypo-Proust en Hyper-Proust? Les 'brouillons' imprimés de l'édition électronique," *Recherches et Travaux, Université Stendhal, UFR de Lettres*, no. 72 (2008), 157-170.

GG6445. Mauriac Dyer, Nathalie: "La reconstitution des cahiers de brouillon du fonds Proust: points de méthode et principes de foliotation complémentaire," *Bulletin d'Informations Proustiennes*, no. 38 (2008), 99-105.

GG6446. Mauriac Dyer, Nathalie: "Les vertèbres de tante Léonie." In 6368, 29-38.

GG6447. Medvedev, Yevgeny: "Problèmes de communication dans la *Recherche* de Marcel Proust," *Dalhousie French Studies*, vol. 85 (Winter 2008), 141-165.

GG6448. Miguet-Ollagnier, Marie: "Journal de Marguerite de Saint-Marceaux, 1894-1926: entre Verdurin et Guermantes," *Bulletin Marcel Proust*, no. 58 (2008), 35-47.

GG6449. Miguet-Ollagnier, Marie: "Madame Straus, correspondante privilégiée de Proust." In 419, 309-318.

GG6450. Miguet-Ollagnier, Marie: "Proust et son expérience du théâtre." In 6368, 219-227.

GG6451. Milly, Jean: "Voir, écrire, lire la *Vue de Delft* de Ver Meer," *Bulletin Marcel Proust*, no. 58 (2008), 13-33.

GG6452. Mimouni, Patrick: "La vocation talmudique de Marcel Proust. Chapitre III," *Règle du Jeu*, no. 37 (mai 2008), 97-131.

GG6453. Mimouni, Patrick: "La vocation talmudique de Marcel Proust. Chapitre II, La substance invisible du temps," *Règle du Jeu*, no. 36 (janv. 2008), 36-55.

GG6454. Moser, Janet: "In search of another way: using Proust to teach first-year composition," *Teaching English in the Two-Year College*, vol. 36, no. 1 (Sept. 2008), 57-68.

GG6455. Muresan, Maria: "Le renversement du paradigme proustien de la mémoire dans *Le grand incendie de Londres* de Jacques Roubaud," *Marcel Proust Aujourd'hui*, no. 6 (2008), 189-209. [Roubaud]

GG6456. Nakano, Chizu: "Le Cahier 54: fil conducteur de la métamorphose d'Albertine," *Bulletin d'Informations Proustiennes*, no. 38 (2008), 89-98.

GG6457. Naturel, Mireille: "Erreurs scientifiques et vérité romanesque." In 6368, 101-109.

GG6458a. Newland, Paul; Gavrik Losey: "An involuntary memory?: Joseph Losey, Harold Pinter, and Marcel Proust's *A la recherche du temps perdu*." In 8008.

GG6458. Nordholt, Annelies Schulte: "Réécritures proutiennes? *L'Interdit* de Gérard Wajcman," *Marcel Proust Aujourd'hui*, no. 6 (2008), 167-187. [Wajcman]

GG6459. Ott, Christine: "Oceani di panna, cremosi naufragi. Per una poetica del latte in Flaubert e Proust," *Strumenti Critici*, anno 23, n. 117 (maggio 2008), 177-197.

GG6460. Palumbo Mosca, Raffaello: "Gadda e Proust o l'ambiguità del matricida," *Levia Gravia*, no. 7 (2005), 113-123.

GG6461. Paradis, Clément; Stéphane Chaudier: "La bourse ou le temps: l'imaginaire financier de Marcel Proust." In 465, 79-91.

GG6462. Pennanech, Florian: "Proust et le roman de Roland Barthes," *Marcel Proust Aujourd'hui*, no. 6 (2008), 235-253. [Barthes]

GG6463. Polack, Jean-Claude: "Proust cinéaste," *Chimères: Revue des Schizoanalyses*, no. 66-67 (2007-2008), 247-256.

GG6464. Quaranta, Jean-Marc: "Du savoir et de son bon usage." In 6368, 17-28.

GG6465. Ridout, Nicholas: "Welcome to the vibratorium," *Senses and Society*, vol. 3, no. 2 (July 2008), 221-231.

GG6466. Rosen, Elisheva: "Dans le voisinage de la presse: satire et roman chez Balzac et chez Proust," *Modernités*, no. 27 (2008), 299-312.

GG6467. Rouart, Marie-France: "Proust, *Du côté de chez Swann*." In 582, 37-60.

GG6468. Serça, Isabelle: "Ecrire le Temps," *Poétique*, no. 153 (févr. 2008), 23-39.

GG6469. Simon, Anne: "Méconnaissance de Proust." In 6368, 117-126. [Foucault]

GG6470. Simon, Anne: " 'Un rendez-vous urgent, capital, avec moi-même'," *Revue des Sciences Humaines*, no. 292 [no. 4] (2008), 123-133.

GG6471. Soubbotnik, Michael A.: "Note sur Schopenhauer et Proust, les moyens de la connaissance et l'acte de création." In 6368, 81-91.

GG6472. Suganuma, Jun: "La naissance des 'intermittences du cœur': lire la section du voyage dans le Cahier 65," *Bulletin d'Informations Proustiennes*, no. 38 (2008), 41-64.

GG6473. Swahn, Sigbrit: "Bestiaire proustien," *Studia Neophilologica*, no. 80 (2008), 236-242.

GG6474. Türk, Johannes: "Interruptions: scenes of empathy from Aristotle to Proust," *Deutsche Vierteljahrschaft für Literaturwissenschaft und Geistesgeschichte*, 82. Jahrgang, Heft 3 (Sept. 2008), 448-476.

GG6475. Urbani, Bernard: "*Du côté de chez Proust* de Curzio Malaparte: une reprise de *A la recherche du temps perdu*?" In 506, 125-137.

GG6476. Ushiba, Akio: "Du repas flaubertien au repas proustien." In 6368, 47-56.

GG6477. Vago, Davide: "Marguerite Yourcenar et Proust," *Marcel Proust Aujourd'hui*, no. 6 (2008), 145-165. [Yourcenar]

GG6478. Van Buuren, Maarten: "Le drame originel dans *A la recherche du temps perdu*." In 571, 187-194.

GG6479. Van der Krogt, Annette: "Nathalie Sarraute et la réécriture de Proust dans *Tropismes*," *Marcel Proust Aujourd'hui*, no. 6 (2008), 103-126. [Sarraute]

GG6480. Vannucci, François: "Proust possédait-il une culture scientifique?" In 6368, 93-100.

GG6481. Vendeuvre, Isabelle de: "Proust et la question du savoir: satire et auto-définition." In 6368, 235-245. [Anatole France]

GG6482. Vendeuvre, Isabelle de: "Proust et l'église. Grandeurs d'établissement et pouvoir du verbe," *Revue d'Histoire Littéraire de la France*, tome 108, no. 2 (avril-juin 2008), 421-431.

GG6483. Vendeuvre, Isabelle de: "Satire et regard clinique dans les œuvres de Proust et de James," *Modernités*, no. 27 (2008), 321-337.

GG6484. Viard, Bruno: "La crise de la filiation chez Proust et chez Houellebecq." In 571, 37-45. [Houellebecq]

GG6485. Wada, Akio: "Proust et Leconte de Lisle," *Gallia*, no. 47 (2007), 69-76.

GG6486. Wada, Eri: "Rachel et Bloch dans le Cahier 44," *Bulletin d'Informations Proustiennes*, no. 38 (2008), 65-71.

GG6487. Wieser, Dagmar: "Fantômes parisiens au bal de têtes: Marcel Proust et le temps des romantiques." In 516, 219-251.

GG6488. Wise, Pyra: "Un nouveau mystère des gravures anglaises: Marcel Proust chez Hopilliart," *Bulletin d'Informations Proustiennes*, no. 38 (2008), 7-25.

GG6489. Wise, Pyra: "Proust tapissier: entre bibeloter et penser une philosophie de l'ameublement." In 6368, 195-203.

GG6490. Yeazell, Ruth Bernard: "Proust's genre painting and the rediscovery of Vermeer." In 631.

GG6491. Yoshikawa, Kazuyoshi: "Proust aux expositions." In 6368, 207-218.

PSICHARI, Ernest.

GG6492. • Psichari, Ernest: *Carnets de route*. Prés. Jean-François Durand avec la collab. de Roger Little. Paris: L'Harmattan, 2008. *Autrement mêmes*. xxix, 229 p.

PUEL, Gaston. See 1012.

PUJADE-RENAUD, Claude.

GG6493. • Vignes, Sylvie: *La plénitude et l'exil: la nouvelle selon Claude Pujade-Renaud*. Touulouse: Presses univ. du Mirail, 2008. 125 p.

GG6494. Vignes-Mottet, Sylvie: "L'événement comme point d'interrogation dans *La Nuit la neige* de Claude Pujade-Renaud." In 590, 271-284.

PULVAR, Audrey.

GG6495. Chaulet Achour, Christiane: " 'La Noiraude même pas d'ici': Nou l'Haïtienne dans *L'Enfant-bois* d'Audrey Pulvar." In 118, 235-248.

PY, Olivier. See 1115.

QUEFFÉLEC, Henri.

GG6496. Gachet, Delphine: "Queffélec: le père, le fils . . . et la mer," *Nouveau Cahiers François Mauriac*, no. 16 (2008), 145-166.

QUEFFÉLEC, Yann. See 6496.

QUENEAU, Raymond. See also 642, 668, 759, 1781, 6167.

GG6497. • Baron, Christine: *La littérature et son autre: utopie littéraire et ironie dans les œuvres de Borges, Calvino et Queneau*. Paris: L'Harmattan, 2008. *Littératures comparées*. 244 p.

GG6498. • Manopoulos, Monique: *Tonneaux à fonds perdus: carnavalesque et tiers-espace chez Rabelais et Queneau*. New York: Peter Lang, 2008. *Currents in comparative Romance languages and literatures*, 157. ix, 145 p.

GG6499. • Queneau, Raymond: *Zazie dans le métro*. Notice de Paul Gayot. Paris: Gallimard, 2008. *Folio*. Ed. aug. de deux fragments. 260 p.

GG6500. • Queneau, Raymond: *Les ziaux*. Trans. with an introd. by Daniela Hurezanu and Stephen Kessler. Boston: Black Widow, 2008. 143 p.

GG6501. Bouygues, Astrid: "Trouille verte et barbouille (infra)rouge: deux queniens chevronnés en proie aux terreurs universitaires," *Amis de Valentin Brû*, no. 50-51 (2008), 57-58.

GG6502. Cherqui, Marie-Claude; Jean-Pierre Pagliano: "René Clément, Louis Malle: une vague nouvelle," *Amis de Valentin Brû*, nouvelle série, no. 45 (2006), 27-36. [Cinema: Clément, Malle]

GG6503. Cherqui, Marie-Claude [et al.]: "Mocky-Queneau: scènes de ménage, retours sur *Un couple*," *Amis de Valentin Brû*, nouvelle série, no. 45 (2006), 51-78. [Mocky]

GG6504. Chevrier, Alain: "La forme du sonnet chez Raymond Queneau," *Formules*, no. 12 (2008), 35-50.

GG6505. Chevrier, Alain: "Une source humoristique possible d'un titre quenellien: l'*Encyclopédie des sciences inexactes*," *Amis de Valentin Brû*, nouvelle série, no. 45 (2006), 37-42.

GG6506. Ferraro, Alessandra: "La dissolution de l'événement dans les écrits de Raymond Queneau." In 590, 221-230.

GG6507. Goto, Kanako: "Les *Exercices de style*: interprétation linéaire et interprétation tabulaire," *Amis de Valentin Brû*, nouvelle série, no. 45 (2006), 27-36.

GG6508. Goto, Kanako: "Les *Exercices de style_*: traduction intralinguale_? Le cas de 'Homophonique'," *Amis de Valentin Brû*, nouvelle série, no. 50-51 (2008), 21-27.

GG6509. Ibrahim Lefevre, Pascal_: "L'effilochement célinien et l'émiettement quenien," *Amis de Valentin Brû*, nouvelle série, no. 45 (2006), 4551. [Céline]

GG6510. Larraburu, Sandrine: "Du nombre au rythme dans *Morale élémentaire I* de Raymond Queneau." In 529, 55-66.

GG6511. Martin, Jean-Pierre: "Queneau en crise," *Amis de Valentin Brû*, nouvelle série (2008), 45-51.

GG6512. Martin, Pierre: " 'Mort à l'élément Terre!' " In 529, 67-82.

GG6513. Moncond'huy, Dominique: "Drôle de stèle, ou: La morale élémentaire comme espace." In 529, 83-114.

GG6514. Montémont, Véronique_: "De l'air_! Exploration frantextuelle du mot 'air' dans le corpus quenien," *Amis de Valentin Brû*, nouvelle série (2008), 29-43.

GG6515. Motte, Warren: "Shapes of things," *Esprit Créateur*, vol. 48, no. 2 (Summer 2008), 5-17.

GG6516. Poucel, Jean-Jacques: "Chi Queneaude: vie brève de la morale élémentaire." In 529, 15-54.

GG6517. Saad, Gabriel: "De Jacques l'Aumône à James Charity: la poétique de l'étranger dans *Loin de Rueil*," *Amis de Valentin Brû*, nouvelle série (2008), 13-20.

GG6518. Tomaszewski, Marek: "Raymond Queneau ou l'exploitation systématique des contraintes." In 385, 220-236.

GG6519. Valarini Oliver, Elide: "Queneau's *Poissons* and Guimarães Rosa's jaguar: two literary contributions on the animal and human conditions," *Mosaic*, vol. 41, no. 4 (Dec. 2008), 129-142.

QUIGNARD, Pascal. See also 394, 639, 753, 754, 7404.

GG6520. ● Kristeva, Julia: *Pascal Quignard: la fascination du fragmentaire*. Paris: L'Harmattan, 2008. *Critiques littéraires*. 345 p.

GG6521. ● Pautrot, Jean-Louis: *Pascal Quignard ou le fonds du monde*. Amsterdam: Rodopi, 2008. *Collection monographique Rodopi en littérature française contemporaine*. 197 p.

GG6522. ● Rabaté, Dominique: *Pascal Quignard: étude de l'œuvre*. Paris: Bordas, 2008. *Ecrivains au présent*. 191 p.

GG6523. Claude, Chrystelle: "Maison-roman et roman-stèle: les figurations livresques chez Peter Ackroyd et Pascal Quignard," *Voix Plurielles*, vol. 5, no. 1 (mai 2008), [n.p.].

GG6524. Farasse, Gérard: "17 juillet." In 454, 15-27.

GG6525. Jérusalem, Christine: " 'J'espère être lu en 1640': de l'histoire et du roman dans l'œuvre de Pascal Quignard." In 904, 285-296.

GG6526. Lapeyre-Desmaison, Chantal: "Les allégories paradoxales de *Dernier royaume*." In 382, 295-309.

6527a. Saint-Onge, Simon: "Le temps contemporain ou le jadis chez Pascal Quignard," *Etudes Françaises*, vol. 44, no. 3 (2008), 159-172.

QUINT, Michel.

GG6527. Graeber, Wilhelm: " 'Les parenthèses n'existent pas dans l'Histoire': les romans métahistoriques de Michel Quint." In 483, 241-251.

GG6528. Rézeau, Pierre: "Les traits régionaux dans l'œuvre romanesque de Michel Quint." In 576, 271-309.

QUINTAL, Patrick.

GG6529. Han, Nathalie de: "Les dragons de la création. *Dragon bleu, dragon jaune*," *Jeu: Cahiers de Théâtre*, no. 129 [no. 4] (2008), 26-28.

RACHILDE. See also 621, 719, 4675.

GG6530. Barstad, Guri Ellen: "Espaces et construction de soi dans *Monsieur Vénus* de Rachilde," *Excavatio*, vol. 23, no. 1-2 (2008), 294-302.

GG6531. Gantz, Katherine: "*Une langue étrangère*: translating sex and race in Rachilde's *La Jongleuse*," *French Review*, vol. 81, no. 5 (April 2008), 944-954.

GG6532. Geat, Marina: "Florence, Sodome, Rome: trois contes de Rachilde." In 616, 147-158.

GG6533. Hyman, Erin Williams: "La grève des ventres: anarchist 'anti-matriotism' and Rachilde's *La Marquise de Sade*." In 415, 128-146.

GG6534. Laporte, Dominique: "Une négociation stratégique du discours littéraire et du discours social: le dévoilement des dessous (in)humains dans l'œuvre Romanesque de Rachilde," *Nineteenth-Century French Studies*, vol. 37, no. 1-2 (Fall-Winter 2008-2009), 108-122.

GG6535. Raoult, Marie-Gersande: "Les représentations viciées de Pygmalion, Narcisse et Hermaphrodite dans les œuvres de Rachilde et de Jean Lorrain." In 520, 433-447. [Lorrain]

GG6536. Sanchez, Nelly: "*Les hors nature*: Rachilde, émule de Remy de Gourmont." In 4290, 131-142.

RACZYMOW, Henri. See also 585, 721, 722.

GG6537. Raczymow, Henri: "Histoire: petit h et grande hache." In 602, 17-24.

RAFENOMANJATO, Charlotte.

GG6538. Ranaivoson, Dominique: " 'Un fragment d'histoire collé sur un tesson de fiction': entretien avec Charlotte Rafenomanjato," *Nouvelles Etudes Francophones*, vol. 23, no. 1 (printemps 2008), 28-34.

RAGON, Michel.

GG6539. Slawy-Sutton, Catherine: "Indochine 1910 et Vendée 1940 dans *Ma sœur aux yeux d'Asie* de Michel Ragon: une mise en scène de l'histoire," *French Cultural Studies*, vol. 19, no. 1 (Feb. 2008), 17-38.

RAHARIMANANA, Jean-Luc.

GG6540. Célérier, Patricia: "Raharimanana: 'Le viol des douceurs'," *Présence Francophone*, no. 70 (2008), 136-153.

RAHMANI, Zahia.

GG6541. Bergé-Joonekindt, Aline: "Trajets d'un souffle nomade: Zahia Rahmani." In 539, 173-183.

RAJIC, Negovan.

GG6542. Matic, Ljiljana: "Negovan Rajic: auteur canadien originaire de Serbie." In 155, 217-227.

RAKOTOSON, Michèle.

GG6543. Gyssels, Kathleen: "Francophonies disparates, non dissonantes: Elles dansent sur la crête des volcans," *Interculturel Francophones*, no. 12 (nov.-déc. 2007), 141-168.

RAMBAUD, Patrick.

GG6544. Scaiola, Anna Maria: "Les jours de brume de Napoléon. Sur la trilogie de Patrick Rambaud." In 561, 141-160.

RAMUZ, Charles-Ferdinand.

GG6545. ● Béguin, Albert: *Patience de Ramuz*. Paris: Isolato, 2008. 63 p.

GG6546. ● Ramuz, C.-F.: *Articles et chroniques*. Dir. Céline Cerny, Virginie Jaton. Genève: Slatkine, 2008. *Œuvres complètes*, 11-12.

GG6547. ● Ramuz, Charles-Ferdinand: *Derborence: 1934*. Trad. Marta Pino Moreno; post., cronología y bibliografía de Déborah Puig-Pey Stiefel. Barcelona: Nortesur, 2008. 202 p.

GG6548. ● Ramuz, C.-F.: *Poésie et théâtre*. Textes établis, annotés et prés. par Doris Jakubec et Alain Rochat. Genève: Slatkine, 2008. *Œuvres complètes*, 10. 672 p.

GG6549. ● Rochette, Stéphane: *Ramuz chez Rey-Millet*. Tours: Amis de Ramuz, 2008. *Etudes critiques*. 195 p.

GG6550.   Chauvy, Laurence; Jacques Muron: "Avis de lecteurs sur *Une main*," *Amis de Ramuz*, no. 27-28 (2007), 43-47.

GG6551.   Guignard, Adrien: "Les assis de Ramuz," *Revue d'Histoire Littéraire de la France*, tome 108, no. 4 (oct.-déc. 2008), 875-888.

GG6552.   Marxsen, Patti M.: "The quest and the question in C. F. Ramuz's *Si le soleil ne revenait pas*," *French Review*, vol. 81, no. 6 (May 2008), 1210-1223.

GG6553.   Morzewski, Christian: "Ramuz au Paraïs," *Amis de Ramuz*, no. 27-28 (2007), 100-105.

GG6554.   Pella, Anne-Laure: "La diversité des langues de traduction de l'œuvre de C. F. Ramuz: approche sociologique," *Amis de Ramuz*, no. 27-28 (2007), 106-163.

GG6555.   Poulouin, Gérard: "Ramuz sur la Toile," *Amis de Ramuz*, no. 27-28 (2007), 28-31.

GG6556.   Rochette, Stéphane: "Georges Besson dans l'objectif," *Amis de Ramuz*, no. 27-28 (2007), 72-99.

GG6557.   Vidal, Anne-Marie: "Proal imitateur de Ramus," *Amis de Ramuz*, no. 27-28 (2007), 164-202.

RANCIÈRE, Jacques. See also 22, 996.

GG6558.   ● May, Todd: *The political thought of Jacques Rancière: creating equality.* Edinburgh: Edinburgh Univ. Press, 2008. 196 p.

GG6559.   Oliver, Anne Marie: "Jacques Rancière, aesthetics against incarnation (interview)," *Critical Inquiry*, vol. 35, no. 1 (Autumn 2008), 172-190.

RANDAU, Robert.

GG6560.   Riesz, János: "Regards critiques sur la société coloniale. A partir de deux romans de Robert Randau et de Robert Delavignette." In 127, 107-131. [Delavignette]

RAULT, Antoine.

GG6561.   Rault, Antoine: *Le diable rouge.* Paris: Avant-Scène Théâtre, 2008. *Avant-Scène Théâtre*, no. 1246 (1er août 2008). 109 p.

RAVALOSON, Johary.

GG6562.   Galibert, Nivoelisoa: "Johary Ravaloson 'entre désir et détermination'," *Cultures Sud*, no. 170 (sept. 2008), 117-122.

RAWICZ, Piotr. See also 519.

GG6563.   Jurgenson, Luba: "Piotr Rawicz: les labyrinthes de la fiction identitaire." In 384, 245-257.

GG6564.   Stevens, Christa: "Histoires de queue: témoignage et alliance dans *Le sang du ciel* de Piotr Rawicz." In 442, 163-176.

RAY, Jean.

GG6565.   Amos, Thomas: "A sulphurous time: *Les contes du whiskey* by Jean Ray, a translation of 'les années folles'." In 79, 78-94.

GG6566.   Durand, Pascal: "Rhétorique de l'explication dans le récit fantastique: une lecture de *La ruelle ténébreuse* de Jean Ray," *Etudes Francophones*, vol. 23, no. 1-2 (printemps-automne 2008), 10-33.

GG6567.   Huftier, Arnaud: "La quête du littéraire à travers l'enquête populaire: Jean Ray et Harry Dickson." In 425, 79-134.

RAZANE, Mohamed.

GG6568.   Puig, Steve: "Interview avec Mohamed Razane," *Expressions Maghrébines*, vol. 7, no. 1 (été 2008), 85-92.

GG6569.   Reeck, Laura K.: "Mohamed Razane: the re-generation of Beur literature," *Expressions Maghrébines*, vol. 7, no. 1 (été 2008), 67-83.

RÉAGE, Pauline.

GG6570.   Hall, Susan Lillian: "Seduction and servitude: the erotics of women's captivity narratives." Diss., Cornell Univ., 2008. vii, 198 p.

REBATET, Lucien.

RÉDA, Jacques.

GG6571.   ● Réda, Jacques: *Beauté suburbaine = Suburban beauty.* Trans. and preface by Peter Schulman. Halifax, NS: Editions VVV Editions, 2008. 59 p.

GG6572.   Di Meo, Philippe: "*Démêlés*, de J. Réda," *Nouvelle Revue Française*, no. 587 (oct. 2008), 193-196.

GG6573. Jocqueviel-Bourjea, Marie: "Former le roman: *Aller au diable*, de Jacques Réda." In 443, 15-31.

GG6574. Jocqueviel-Bourjea, Marie: "Jacques Réda: rencontres au sommet. Le mont Ventoux ou le démon de l'analogie," *Revue des Sciences Humaines*, no. 292 [no. 4] (2008), 153-169.

GG6575. Rougé, Pascale: "Petite suite pour piano à quatre mains: Jacques Réda-Duke Ellington," *Revue des Sciences Humaines*, no. 292 [no. 4] (2008), 173-186.

GG6576. Sheringham, Michael: "Everyday rhythms, everyday writing: Réda with Deleuze and Guattari." In 575, 147-158. [Deleuze, Guattari]

REDONNET, Marie.

GG6577. Motte, Warren: "Marie Redonnet's hospitality." In 900.

RÉGNIER, Henri de. See also 4554, 4564.

GG6578. Lloyd, Rosemary: "Régnier's workshop," *Symbolism*, no. 8 (2008), 233-249.

RENARD, Jean-Claude.

GG6579. Despax, Arnaud: "Avec Jean-Claude Renard. Sur quelques branches d' 'un arbre frais'," *Littératures*, no. 58-59 (2008), 373-384.

RENARD, Jules.

GG6580. • Renard, Jules: *L'Ecornifleur*. Précédé de "Satire intime" par Richard Millet. Paris: Sillage, 2008. 201 p.

GG6581. • Renard, Jules: *The journal of Jules Renard*. Ed. and trans. Louise Bogan and Elizabeth Roget. Portland, OR: Tin House Books, 2008. 304 p.

GG6582. Autrand, Michel: "*Poil de carotte* au théâtre ou la compromission," *Amis de Jules Renard*, no. 9 (2008), 121-128.

GG6583. Barnes, Julian: "Abstract: homage to the writer Jules Renard." In 796.

GG6584. Bolzan, L.: "Su Jules Renard. Frammenti di verità e falsi d'autore," *Rivista di Letterature Moderne e Comparate*, vol. 61, fasc. 2 (aprile-giugno 2008), 159-173.

GG6585. Bugarel, Jean: "Les structures internes de *Poil de carotte*," *Amis de Jules Renard*, no. 9 (2008), 7-120.

REVAZ, Noëlle. See 179.

REVERDY, Pierre. See also 1033, 1048.

GG6586. • Titus-Carmel, Gérard: *Pierres d'attente pour Reverdy*. Saint-Benoît-du-Sault: Tarabuste, 2008. 155 p.

GG6587. Azérad, Hugo: "Parisian literary fields: James Joyce and Pierre Reverdy's theory of the image," *Modern Language Review*, vol. 103, part 3 (July 2008), 666-681.

GG6588. Farasse, Gérard: "12, rue Cortot." In 454, 69-72.

GG6589. Ibo, Lydie: "L'aspectualité et le tempo dans 'Encore l'amour' de Pierre Reverdy," *Semiotica*, vol. 169, no. 1-4 (2008), 93-105.

REYNARD, Jean-Michel.

GG6590. Surya, Michel: "Jean-Michel Reynard," *Critique*, tome 64, no. 735-736 (août-sept. 2008), 646-655.

RICARD, Matthieu. See 688.

RICHARDS-PILLOT, Eunice.

GG6591. Chemla, Yves: "Eunice Richards-Pillot: pour une nécessaire réhabilitation de la Guyane," *Cultures Sud*, no. 170 (sept. 2008), 123-128.

RICHAUD, André de.

GG6592. • Mécif, Yvan: *Visions de Richaud*. Préface de Bernard Noël. Saint-Cyr-sur-Loire: C. Pirot, 2008. 217 p.

RICHEZ, Valérie-Catherine.

GG6593. Halpern, Anne-Elisabeth: "Les marelles magiques de Valérie-Christine Richez." In 418, 373-386.

RICŒUR, Paul. See also 779, 959, 980, 1300, 1517, 4176, 5205, 7488, 7723.

GG6594. • Albertos San José, Jesús E.: *El mal en la filosofía de la voluntad de Paul Ricœur*. Pamplona: Ediciones Univ. de Navarra, 2008. 248 p.

GG6595. • Brugiatelli, Vereno: *Potere e riconoscimento in Paul Ricœur: per un'etica del superamento dei conflitti*. Trento: UNI service, 2008. 171 p.

GG6596. • Busacchi, Vinicio: *Ricœur versus Freud.* Saveria Mannelli: Rubbettino, 2008. 84 p.

GG6597. • Dosse, François: *Paul Ricœur: le sens d'une vie, 1913-2005.* Ed. rev. et augm. Paris: Découverte, 2008. 712 p.

GG6598. • Frey, Daniel: *L'interprétation et la lecture chez Ricœur et Gadamer.* Paris: PUF, 2008. *Etudes d'histoire et de philosophie religieuses.* x, 300 p.

GG6599. • Giorgio, Giovanni: *Spiegare per comprendere: la questione del metodo nell'ermeneutica di Paul Ricœur.* Roma: Casini, 2008. 219 p.

GG6600. • *Homme [L'] capable: autour de Paul Ricœur.* Paris: PUF, 2006. *Rue Descartes.* 192 p.

GG6601. • Jervolino, Domenico: *Per una filosofia della traduzione.* Brescia: Morcelliana, 2008. 264 p.

GG6602. • *La juste mémoire: lectures autour de Paul Ricœur.* Sous la dir. d'Olivier Abel [et al.]. Genève: Labor et Fides, 2006. 213 p.

GG6603. • Lentiampa Shenge, Adrien: *Paul Ricœur: la justice selon l'espérance.* Liminaire de Théoneste Nkeramihigo; préface de Paul Gilbert. Bruxelles: Lessius, 2008. 440 p.

GG6604. • Martinengo, Alberto: *Il pensiero incompiuto: ermeneutica, regione, ricostruzione in Paul Ricœur.* Reggio Emilia: Aliberti, 2008. 285 p.

GG6605. • Mattern, Jens: *Zwischen kultureller Symbolik und allgemeiner Wahrheit: Paul Ricœur interkulturell gelesen.* Nordhausen: Bautz, 2008. 153 p.

GG6606. • *Paul Ricœur and phenomenology.* Ed. Katerina Daniel. Pittsburgh: Simon Silverman Phenomenology Center, Duquesne Univ., 2007.

GG6607. • *Paul Ricœur: bibliographie primaire et secondaire.* Compiled and updated by Frans D. Vansina; in collab. with Pieter Vandecasteele. Leuven; Dudley, MA: Peeters, 2008. xxx, 624 p.

GG6608. • *Paul Ricœur: de l'homme faillible à l'homme capable.* Coord. Gaëlle Fiasse. Paris: PUF, 2008. *Débats philosophiques.* 177 p.

GG6609. • *Paul Ricœur e la psicoanalisi: testi scelti.* A cura di Domenico Jervolino, Giuseppe Martini. Milano: F. Angeli, 2007. 176 p.

GG6610. • Possati, Luca M.: *Ricœur e l'esperienza storica: l'ermeneutica filosofica nella tradizione delle Annales.* Roma: Carocci, 2008. 246 p.

GG6611. • *Reading Ricœur.* Ed. David M. Kaplan. Albany: SUNY Press, 2008. viii, 262 p.

GG6612. • Ricœur, Paul: *An den Grenzen der Hermeneutik: philosophische Reflexionen über die Religion.* Hrsg., übers. und mit einem Nachwort versehen von Veronika Hoffmann. Freiburg; München: Alber, 2008. 141 p.

GG6613. • Ricœur, Paul: *Ecrits et conférences. 1, Autour de la psychanalyse.* Textes rassemblés et préparés par Catherine Goldenstein et Jean-Louis Schlegel. Postface par Vinicio Busacchi. Paris: Seuil, 2008. *La couleur des idées.* 329 p.

GG6614. • Roberge, Jonathan: *Paul Ricœur, la culture et les sciences humaines.* Québec: Presses de l'Univ. Laval, 2008. *Sociologie contemporaine.* x, 319 p.

GG6615. • *Saggezza pratica e riconoscimento: il pensiero etico-politico dell'ultimo Ricœur.* A cura di Mauro Piras. Roma: Meltemi, 2007. 238 p.

GG6616. • Seikkla, Aura: *On the notion of culture and identity: a study of Paul Ricœur's narrative identity.* Saarbrücken: VDM, 2008. iv, 126 p.

GG6617. • Ungheanu, Mihail: *Metapher und Verstehen. Untersuchungen zu Paul Ricœurs Metaphertheorie.* Saarbrücken: VDM, 2008. 178 p.

GG6618. • Vincent, Gilbert: *La religion de Ricœur.* Paris: Atelier, 2008. *La religion des philosophes.* 159 p.

GG6619. • Wenzel, Knut: *Glaube in Vermittlung: theologische Hermeneutik nach Paul Ricœur.* Freiburg: Herder, 2008. 332 p.

GG6620. Abel, Oliver: "Paul Ricœur's hermeneutics: from critique to poetics." In 6611.

GG6621. Barasch, Jeffrey Andrew: "Les enchevêtrements de la mémoire." In 6608, 19-35.

GG6622. Bottone, Angelo: "The ethical task of the translator in the philosophy of Paul Ricœur." In 608, 73-86.

GG6623. Bourgeois, Patrick L.: "Ricœur and Lyotard in postmodern dialogue." In 6611. [Lyotard]

GG6624. Boutin, Maurice: "Virtualité et identité. L'identité narrative selon Paul Ricœur, et ses apories," *Études Théologiques et Religieuses*, tome 83, no. 3 (2008), 367-376.

GG6625. Bugaité, Elena: "Metafora e metafisica nel pensiero di Paul Ricœur," *Rivista di Filosofia Neo-Scolastica*, anno. 100, fasc. 1 (genn.-marzo 2008), 49-72.

GG6626. Dauenhauer, Bernard P.: "What makes us think? Two views." In 6611.

GG6627. Deitch, Judith A.: "Love's hologram: Shakespeare, Ricœur, and the equivocations of erotic identity," *Poetics Today*, vol. 29, no. 3 (Fall 2008), 525-564.

GG6628. Farquhar, Sandy: "Narrative identity: Ricœur and early childhood education." Diss., Univ. of Auckland, 2008. vi, 223 p.

GG6629. Fiasse, Gaëlle: "Asymétrie, gratuité et réciprocité." In 6608, 119-156.

GG6630. Fiasse, Gaëlle: "Paul Ricœur et le pardon comme au-delà de l'action," *Laval Théologique et Philosophique*, vol. 63, no. 2 (juin 2007), 343-376.

GG6631. Ford, David F.: "Paul Ricœur: a biblical philosopher on Jesus." In 956.

GG6632. Gedney, Mark: "A love as strong as death: Ricœur's reading of the Song of Songs." In 987.

GG6633. Grondin, Jean: "De Gadamer à Ricœur." In 6608, 37-62.

GG6634. Hoskins, Gregory: "Augustine and Ricœur on the circle of time and narrative." In 792.

GG6635. Janowski, Christine: "Erinnerung und Vergessen im eschatologischen Horizont der 'schwierigen Vergebung'." In 844.

GG6636. Jervolino, Domenico: "Rethinking Ricœur: the unity of his work and the paradigm of translation." In 6611.

GG6637. Joas, Hans: "God in France: Paul Ricœur as theoretical mediator." In 957.

GG6638. Kaplan, David M.: "Ricœur's critical theory." In 6611.

GG6639. Kearney, Richard: "On the hermeneutics of evil." In 6611.

GG6640. Kearney, Richard: "Vers une herméneutique de la traduction." In 6608, 157-178.

GG6641. Klemm, David E.: "Philosophy and kerygma: Ricœur as reader of the Bible." In 6611.

GG6642. LaCocque, André: "Love proceeds by poeteic amplification." In 6611.

GG6643. Ladmiral, Jean-René: "Hommage à Paul Ricœur," *Revue Septet*, no. 1 (2008), [n.p.].

GG6644. Lamouche, Fabien: "Paul Ricœur et les 'clairières' de la reconnaissance," *Esprit*, no. 346 (juillet 2008), 76-87.

GG6645. Marsh, James L.: "Ricœur's phenomenology of freedom as an answer to Sartre." In 6611. [Sartre]

GG6646. Martínez Lucena, Jorge: "Narratividad y pre-narratividad de la experiencia," *Rivista di Filosofia Neo-Scolastica*, anno. 100, fasc. 1 (genn.-marzo 2008), 73-109.

GG6647. Meessen, Yves: "Penser le verbe 'être' autrement. Lecture d'Exode 3, 14 par Paul Ricœur," *Nouvelle Revue Théologique*, tome 130, no. 4 (oct.-déc. 2008, 759-773.

GG6648. Meza, Sadrac E.: "Theology after ideology: an evangelical theological engagement with ideology as formulated by Paul Ricœur and Juan Luis Segundo." Diss., Trinity InternationalUniv., 2008. vi, 312 p.

GG6649. Michel, Johann: "L'animal herméneutique." In 6608, 63-92.

GG6650. Palazón Mayoral, María Rosa: "Las metáforas refieren un mundo existencial." In 807, 239-253.

GG6651. Piercey, Robert: "How Paul Ricœur changed the world," *American Catholic Philosophical Quarterly*, vol. 82, no. 3 (Summer 2008), 463-479.

GG6652. Rasmussen, David M.: "Justice and interpretation." In 6611.

GG6653. Reagan, Charles: "Binding and loosing: promising and forgiving; amnesty and amnesia." In 6611.

GG6654. Schweiker, William: "Paul Ricœur and the prospects of a new humanism." In 6611.

GG6655. Searle, Alison: "Paul Ricœur on metaphor and 'poetic' language." In 980.

GG6656. Thomasset, Alain: "Au cœur de la tension éthique: narrativité, téléologie, théonomie." In 6608, 93-117.

GG6657. Valdés, Mario J.: "Ricœur, Wittgenstein," *Cincinnati Romance Review*, vol. 26 (2007), 177-190.

GG6658. Vandevelde, Pol: "The challenge of the 'such as it was'." In 6611.

GG6659. Watkin, Christopher: "Paul Ricœur and the possibility of just love." In 987.

GG6660. Westphal, Merold: "Ricœur's hermeneutical phenomenology of religion." In 6611.

GG6661. Williams, Robert R.: "Ricœur on recognition," *European Journal of Philosophy*, vol. 16, no. 3 (Dec. 2008), 467-473.

RIMBAUD, Arthur. See also 467, 598, 643, 5251, 7555, 7572, 7574.

GG6662. ● *Afriques [Les] de Rimbaud.* Textes édités par David Ellison, Ralph Heyndels; avec l'aide de Paulette Hacker. Fasano: Schena; Paris: Presses de l'Univ. de Paris-Sorbonne, 2006. 182 p.

GG6663. ● *Arthur Rimbaud, geographe?: 1854-1891.* Jean Bastié [et al.]. Paris: Société de géographie, 2006. 120 p.

GG6664. ● Brunel, Pierre: *Arthur Rimbaud, 1854-1891.* Paris: PUF, 2008. *Figures et plumes.* 123 p.

GG6665. ● Casado, Miguel: *Rimbaud, el otro.* Madrid: Complutense, 2008. *Académica.* 136 p.

GG6666. ● Claes, Paul: *La clef des Illuminations.* Amsterdam: Rodopi, 2008. *Faux titre,* 323. 359 p.

GG6667. ● Garelli, Jacques: *Fragments d'un corps en archipel; suivi de, Perception et imaginaire: réflexions sur un poème oublié de Rimbaud.* Paris: Corti, 2008. 167 p.

GG6668. ● Hodin, Geneviève: *"Brillé, birilli, bérelle" et autres curiosités rimbaldiennes.* Compiègne: G. Hodin, 2008. 123 p.

GG6669. ● Izambard, Georges: *Rimbaud tel que je l'ai connu.* Préface, Jacques Lardoux. Rennes: Part commune, 2008. 252 p.

GG6670. ● Lefrère, Jean-Jacques: *Les dessins d'Arthur Rimbaud.* Paris: Horay, 2008. 88 p.

GG6671. ● Le Pillouër, Pierre: *Trouver Hortense: journal de lecture à la lettre des Illuminations.* Paris: Virgile, 2008. *Ulysse fin de siècle.* 155 p.

GG6672. ● Marchetti, Adriano: *Rapsodia selvaggia: interpreti francesi di Rimbaud.* Genova: Marietti, 2008. *Collana di saggistica.* xxvii, 315 p.

GG6673. ● Michon, Pierre: *Rimbaud der Sohn.* Aus dem Franz. von Anne Weber. Frankfurt: Suhrkamp, 2008. 115 p.

GG6674. ● Rimbaud, Arthur: *Le bateau ivre.* Übertr. von Paul Celan. Mit Dokumenten und einem Nachwort hrsg. von Joachim Seng. Frankfurt: Leipzig: Insel-Verlag, 2008. 101 p.

GG6675. ● Rimbaud, Arthur: *A season in Hell.* Ed. and trans. Andrew Jary. Maidstone: Crescent Moon, 2008. *European writers.*

GG6676. ● *Rimbaud, el otro.* Ed. Miguel Casado. Madrid: Editorial Complutense, 2008. 134 p.

GG6677. ● Ross, Kristin: *The emergence of social space: Rimbaud and the Paris Commune.* London; New York: Verso, 2008. *Radical thinkers.* xvi, 170 p. [Orig. ed., Univ. of Minnesota Press, 1988]

GG6678. ● Thélot, Jérôme: *La poésie excédée: Rimbaud.* Les Cabannes: Fissile, 2008. *Cendrier du voyage.* 41 p.

GG6679. ● White, Edmund: *Rimbaud: the double life of a rebel.* New York: Atlas & Co., 2008. 192 p.

GG6680. Abaka, Edmund: "The driving forces behind French colonial policy in Africa." In 6662, 23-46.

GG6681. Ahearn, Edward J.: "Spectres de Rimbaud," *Parade Sauvage*, no. spécial (2008), 111-123.

GG6682. Aschione, Marc: "Faurisson-Tintin au Pays des Peaux-Rouges ou l'Action française bouleverse la science. Contribution à l'histoire des lectures de 'Voyelles'," *Parade Sauvage*, no. spécial (2008), 169-196.

GG6683. Badiou, Alain: "Rimbaud's method: interruption." In 387.

GG6684. Bataillé, Christophe: "L'édition originale d'*Une saison en enfer* d'Arthur Rimbaud," *Revue d'Histoire Littéraire de la France*, tome 108, no. 3 (juillet-sept. 2008), 651-665.

GG6685. Bataillé, Christophe: "Le plus haut tour de la Chanson," *Parade Sauvage*, no. spécial (2008), 492-500.

GG6686. Berger, Anne-Emmanuelle: "Sens dessus dessous ou le carnaval de Steve Rimbaud," *Parade Sauvage*, no. spécial (2008), 124-136.

GG6687. Bienvenu, Jacques: " 'Chanson de la plus haute Tour' ou le château romantique," *Parade Sauvage*, no. spécial (2008), 501-513.

GG6688. Bobillet, Jean-Pierre: "Fins de vers (3): les méTamorPHoses de l'Y (pour sTeve murPHY)," *Parade Sauvage*, no. spécial (2008), 288-306.

GG6689. Bordwell, Harold: "Late conversion: was Rimbaud a saint?," *Commonweal*, vol. 135, no. 9 (May 9, 2008), 12.

GG6690. Borel, Pierre: "Et l'autre Rimbaud de Milan à Venise?," *Parade Sauvage*, no. spécial (2008), 642-645.

GG6691. Bourkhis, Ridha: "Syntaxe et littérarité dans *Illuminations*," *Parade Sauvage*, no. spécial (2008), 599-616.

GG6692. Brunel, Pierre: "Aphinar," *Parade Sauvage*, no. spécial (2008), 33-40.

GG6693. Brunel, Pierre: "Intimités rimbaldiennes." In 391, 163-174.

GG6694. Brunel, Pierre: "Rimbaud et l'Orient." In 6662, 11-22.

GG6695. Chambers, Ross: "Rimbaud forain," *Parade Sauvage*, no. spécial (2008), 324-337.

GG6696. Chevrier, Alain: "Sur une source méconnue du 'Dormeur du val' et de 'Chant de guerre parisien'," *Parade Sauvage*, no. spécial (2008), 268-287.

GG6697. Claisse, Bruno: " 'Matinée d'ivresse' sans 'paradis artificiels'," *Parade Sauvage*, no. spécial (2008), 617-627.

GG6698. Collot, Michel: "Autobiographie et fiction," *Rimbaud Vivant*, no. 47 (2008), 7-18.

GG6699. Combe, Dominique: "Rimbaud au Québec, de Nelligan à Miron," *Parade Sauvage*, no. spécial (2008), 98-108. [Miron, Nelligan]

GG6700. Cornille, Jean-Louis: "Béthune! Béthune! (Breton et Rimbaud)." In 413. [Breton]

GG6701. Cornille, Jean-Louis: "Le Rimbaldo-lautréamontisme." In 413.

GG6702. Cornulier, Benoît de: "Style métrique de chant," *Parade Sauvage*, no. spécial (2008), 231-253.

GG6703. Danval, Marc: "Rimbaud et le Grand Hôtel Liégeois à Bruxelles," *Rimbaud Vivant*, no. 47 (2008), 41-44.

GG6704. Dominicy, Marc: " 'Mémoire', *Le Capitaine Fracasse* et 'Le Château du souvenir'," *Parade Sauvage*, no. spécial (2008), 514-524.

GG6705. Dotoli, Giovanni: "Rimbaud photographe africain." In 6662, 149-179.

GG6706. " 'Drunken boat'/Arthur Rimbaud." In 1025.

GG6707. Ekotto, Frieda: "Our ancestors the Gauls: Rimbaud, Gide and Genet in Africa." In 6662, 99-111. [Genet, Gide]

GG6708. Elder, David E.: "Réflexions sur neuf traductions du 'Départ' de Rimbaud," *Revue Septet*, no. 1 (2008), [n.p.].

GG6709. Ellison, David: "Rimbaud au pluriel." In 6662, 113-130.

GG6710. Finidori, Muriel: "La poétique du feu chez Rimbaud," *Rimbaud Vivant*, no. 47 (2008), 53-63.

GG6711. Fongaro, Antoine: "De "Bonne pensée du matin' à 'A quatre heures du matin'," *Parade Sauvage*, no. spécial (2008), 475-491.

GG6712. Frémy, Yann: "Une poétique de la force contrariée," *Parade Sauvage*, no. spécial (2008), 558-570.

GG6713. Ganomeda, Amelia: "Rimbaud: videncia y evidencia." In 467, 47-58.

GG6714. Gleize, Jean-Marie: "El charco negro y frio." In 6676, 67-75.

GG6715. Gouvard, Jean-Michel: "Remarques sur la versification de Rimbaud," *Parade Sauvage*, no. spécial (2008), 254-267.

GG6716. Hacker, Paulette: "*Total Eclipse*: Rimbaud in African as ornamental contrapunto." In 6662, 89-97.

GG6717. Heyndels, Ralph: " 'Voyageur où ça disparu?': les tristes Afriques objectives de Rimbaud." In 6662, 131-147.

GG6718. Hodin, Geneviève: "Rimbaud, lecteur du 'brillant poète de juillet'," *Rimbaud Vivant*, no. 47 (2008), 45-51.

GG6719. Hue, Denis: "Arthur Rimbaud *Les Bons Romans*," *Parade Sauvage*, no. spécial (2008), 374-387.

GG6720. Imura, Manami: "Originalités de 'Sensation', au-delà des modèles et des topoï," *Parade Sauvage*, no. spécial (2008), 309-323.

GG6721. Jesi, Furio: "Lecture du 'Bateau ivre' de Rimbaud," *Po&sie*, no. 124 (2008), 32-45.

GG6722. Karmaoui, Ghazi: "Le soleil, dieu de feu." In 6662, 73-87.

GG6723. Kassab-Charfi, Samia: "Plasticité rhétorique et turbulences de la phrase rimbaldienne dans *Une saison en enfer*." In 556.

GG6724. Kliebenstein, Georges: "Alcide B/bava et la Galaxie Rimbaud," *Parade Sauvage*, no. spécial (2008), 155-168.

GG6725. Kramer, Max D.: "The poetry of inversion: queer metaphor in Arthur Rimbaud, Stefan George, and Federico Garcia Lorca." Diss., Columbia Univ., 2008. viii, 556 p.

GG6726. Lanni, Dominique: "Car c'est en marchant que l'on devient marchand." In 6662, 61-71.

GG6727. Lawler, James: "Le chant dionysiaque: étude de 'Matinées d'ivresse'," *Rimbaud Vivant*, no. 47 (2008), 77-90.

GG6728. Maillard, Chantal: "Eso que dice yo." In 6676, 9-15.

GG6729. Majewski, André: "Un Arthur peut en cacher un autre: Arthur Rimbaud à Vireux," *Rimbaud Vivant*, no. 47 (2008), 113-118.

GG6730. Matucci, Mario: "Une traduction italienne du 'Bateau ivre'," *Parade Sauvage*, no. spécial (2008), 468-471.

GG6731. Mendez Rubio, Antonio: "El otro como nadie." In 6676, 77-85.

GG6732. Metzidakis, Stamos: "Des lyres au délire: Rimbaud dépassant Verlaine," *Rimbaud Vivant*, no. 47 (2008), 65-75. [Verlaine]

GG6733. Minahen, Charles D.: "Je(u d')équivoque et dysphorie du genre dans *Poésies* de Rimbaud," *Parade Sauvage*, no. spécial (2008), 388-403.

GG6734. Moga, Eduardo: "Epica sensible. Un análisis de la influencia de Rimbaud y Perse en la poesía de Antonio Gamoneda," *Insula*, no. 736 (abril 2008), 21-23. [Saint-John Perse]

GG6735. Mora, Vicente Lluis: "Yo es otro. La herencia de Rimbaud." In 6676, 39-45.

GG6736. Moreno Villareal, Jaime: "Arthur Rimbaud: notas sobre una defeción literaria." In 6676, 27-31.

GG6737. Morey, Miguel: "Reterato en negro. Arthur Rimbaud del brazo del Minotauro." In 6676, 113-130.

GG6738. Murat, Michel: "*Une saison en enfer*: la logique des ensembles," *Parade Sauvage*, no. spécial (2008), 543-557.

GG6739. Murphy, Steve: "Fragments d'une géopolitique de Rimbaud: le recueil Demeny," *Parade Sauvage*, no. spécial (2008), 19-31.

GG6740. Nakaji, Yoshikazu: "Sur la 'fatalité de bonheur'," *Parade Sauvage*, no. spécial (2008), 586-595.

GG6741. Palenzuela, Nilo: "Si el cobre de despierta clarín." In 6676, 105-111.

GG6742. Poulin, Isabelle: "L'androgyne d'une langue à l'autre: une politique du sujet. Sur *Les Illuminations* d'Arthur Rimbaud et *Orlando* de Virginia Woolf," *Palimpsestes*, no. 21 (2008), 85-108.

GG6743. Premuda Perosa, Maria Luisa: "En marge de quelques analyses récentes du 'Bateau ivre'," *Parade Sauvage*, no. spécial (2008), 429-444.

GG6744. Ramon, Esther: "Si suceden Grillos Rojos." In 6676, 59-65.

GG6745. Reboul, Yves: "Quatre notes sur 'Dévotion'," *Parade Sauvage*, no. spécial (2008), 628-641.

GG6746. Reboul, Yves: "Rimbaud et le mal," *Modernités*, no. 29 (2008), 131-145.

GG6747. Remillieux, Daniel: "Rimbaud et ses anges: une poétique des apparences," *Parade Sauvage*, no. spécial (2008), 414-426.

GG6748. Richter, Mario: "Editer Rimbaud," *Parade Sauvage*, no. spécial (2008), 197-205.

GG6749. "Rimbaud. Documents complémentaires de *Bérénice* 36-37," *Bérénice*, no. 39 (marzo 2008), 121-129.

GG6750. Rodriguez, Ildefonso: "El africano en París." In 6676, 17-25.

GG6751. Rowe, William: "Breve prefacio a Arthur Rimbaud." In 6676, 87-103.

GG6752. Santolini, Arnaud: " 'Le Bateau ivre', un art poétique révolutionnaire," *Parade Sauvage*, no. spécial (2008), 445-461.

GG6753. Steinmetz, Jean-Luc: "Sur les 'proses évangéliques'," *Parade Sauvage*, no. spécial (2008), 527-542.

GG6754. Taliercio, Patrick: "Rimbaud dans les fossiles," *Parade Sauvage*, no. spécial (2008), 338-344.

GG6755. Tucker, George Hugo: "Poétique et rhétoriques de l'exclamation chez Rimbaud latiniste et dans son œuvre française," *Parade Sauvage*, no. spécial (2008), 209-230.

GG6756. Vaillant, Alain: "Principes d'herméneutique rimbaldienne: gloses en marge de 'Chant de guerre parisien'," *Parade Sauvage*, no. spécial (2008), 137-154.

GG6757. Voellmy, Jean: "Les constructions nominales du 'Bateau ivre' et autres analyses," *Parade Sauvage*, no. spécial (2008), 462-467.

GG6758. Warren, Rosanna: "Rimbaud: insulting beauty." In 1030.

GG6759. Wetzel, Hermann H.: "La 'Lettre du voyant' et ses poèmes," *Parade Sauvage*, no. spécial (2008), 365-373.

GG6760. Whidden, Seth: "Les transgressions de Rimbaud dans l'*Album zutique*," *Parade Sauvage*, no. spécial (2008), 404-413.

GG6761. Whitaker, Marie-Joséphine: "Les 'Délires' de Rimbaud," *Parade Sauvage*, no. spécial (2008), 571-585.

GG6762. Wills, David: "A line drawn in the ocean: Exodus, Freud, Rimbaud." In 990.

GG6763. Zimmermann, Laurent: "Le chemin du papillon," *Poétique*, no. 153 (févr. 2008), 17-22.

GG6764. Zotti, Valeria: "Rimbaud 'sage bâtard' et le Coran." In 6662, 47-59.

RINGUET.

GG6765. Faussié, Daniel: "Le roman de la terre et son évolution: *Trente arpents* ou une ère révolue." In 120, 186-192.

RIO, Michel.

GG6766. Santa, Angels: "Merlin entre Arthur et Morgane d'après Michel Rio." In 553, 283-293.

RISTAT, Jean.

GG6767. "Entretien avec Jean Ristat," *Histoires Littéraires*, no. 33 (janv.-févr.-mars 2008), 65-78.

RIVARD, Yvon.

GG6768. Imbert, Patrick: "*Le siècle de Jeanne* d'Yvon Rivard." In 41, 337-352.

RIVAZ, Alice. See also 179.

GG6769. ● Rivaz, Alice; Jean-Georges Lossier: *Pourquoi serions-nous heureux?: correspondance 1945-1982*. Texte établi et annoté par Françoise Fornerod. Carouge-Genève: Zoé, 2008. 182 p.

RIVIÈRE, Jacques. See also 2895, 6188.

GG6770. Richard-Pauchet, Odile: "La correspondance entre Jacques Rivière et Alain-Fournier," *Epistolaire: Revue de l'AIRE*, no. 34 (2008), 27-40.

GG6771. Rivière, Isabelle; Roger Jézéquel: "Après la mort de Jacques Rivière: une correspondance entre Isabelle Rivière et le pasteur Roger Jézéquel," *Bulletin des Amis de Jacques Rivière et d'Alain-Fournier*, no. 119 (1er sem. 2008), 65-87. [Prés. Michel Leplay]

GG6772. Rivière, Jacques: "Extrait d'une lettre de Jacques Rivière à Jacques Copeau," *Bulletin des Amis de Jacques Rivière et d'Alain-Fournier*, no. 119 (1er sem. 2008), 45-47. [Copeau]

GG6773.   Rivière, Jacques: "Trois lettres inédites de Jacques Rivière à Lucie Gallimard," *Bulletin des Amis de Jacques Rivière et d'Alain-Fournier*, no. 120 (2e sem. 2008), 111-118.

ROBBE-GRILLET, Alain. See also 634, 661, 891, 1419, 8326.

GG6774.   ● Gross, Nathalie: *Autopoiesis: Theorie und Praxis autobiographischen Schreibens bei Alain Robbe-Grillet*. Berlin: Schmidt, 2008. 361 p.

GG6775.   ● Loret, Jean-Philippe: *L'espace romanesque comme expression du sujet de l'écriture dans les romans d'Alain Robbe-Grillet*. Lille: ANRT, 2008. *Thèse à la carte*. 452 p.

GG6776.   ● *Robbe-Grillet cinéaste*. Etudes publiées sous la dir. de René Prédal. Caen: Maison de la recherche en sciences humaines, Univ. de Caen Basse-Normandie, 2005. 181 p.

GG6777.   Broad, Lisa: "Prisoners of possibility: Robbe-Grillet's *La Belle Captive* as 'quantum text'," *Senses of Cinema*, no. 48 (2008), [n.p.].

GG6778.   Dugast-Portes, Francine: "Alain Robbe-Grillet: le nouveau roman et l'Histoire." In 561, 23-41.

GG6779.   Faerber, Johan: "Le dernier mot." In 902, 275-278.

GG6780.   Faerber, Johan: "L'éternel retors." In 902, 268-274.

GG6781.   Fernández Cardo, José María: "Evolución y recepción crítica de la obra de Robbe –Grillet: de la nueva autobiografía a la muerte del autor," *Cuadernos de Filologia Francesa*, no. 19 (2008), 83-100.

GG6782.   Poirier, Jacques: "Dans le labyrinthe de la maison Usher: fissures, fétiches et autres faux-semblants dans l'œuvre d'Alain Robbe-Grillet." In 902, 191-206.

GG6783.   Stoltzfus, Ben: "Robbe-Grillet's and Johns's targets: metafiction, autopoiesis, and chaos theory," *Comparatist*, vol. 29 (May 2005), 5-25.

ROBIN, Armand.

GG6784.   Lilti, Anne-Marie: *Armand Robin: le poète indésirable*. Paris: Aden, 2008. 349 p.

GG6785.   Chevrier, Alain: "Deux poètes qui ont dit merde à Staline." In 564, 101-108. [M. Blanchard]

ROBIN, Régine.

GG6786.   Combe, Dominique: "Ecritures migrantes: Régine Robin." In 539, 19-28.

GG6787.   Mouneimne-Wojtas, Tina: "La parole 'est-européenne' dans *La Québécoite* et dans *L'Immense fatigue des pierres* de Régine Robin." In 76, 265-272.

ROBLÈS, Emmanuel. See also 3954, 7200.

GG6788.   Sayeh, Samira: "Espace et littérature: une lecture de *L'Action* d'Emmanuel Roblès." In 515, 223-236.

GG6789.   Tritsmans, Bruno: "Mythologies méditerranéennes et artisanat chez Emmanuel Roblès." In 515, 183-197.

GG6790.   Tritsmans, Bruno: "Roblès sous le signe d'Icare. Aventures maritimes et mythologies solaires," *Francofonia*, n. 55 (autunno 2008), 65-80.

ROCHE, Denis.

GG6791.   ● Baquey, Stéphane: *Le primitivisme de Denis Roche: lyrique amazonide*. Paris: Editions des archives contemporaines, 2008. 132 p.

GG6792.   Doga, Marie: "Legs surréaliste et création rochienne," *Mélusine*, no. 28 (2008), 235-248.

GG6793.   Thomas, Jean-Jacques: "Photographic memories of French poetry: Denis Roche, Jean-Marie Gleize," *Yale French Studies*, no. 114 (2008), 18-36. [Gleize]

ROCHE, Maurice.

GG6794.   Marez Oyens, Ereic de: "Maurice Roche: les mots de la maladie." In 555, 81-100.

RODENBACH, Georges. See also 724.

GG6795.   ● Rodenbach, Georges: *Œuvres de Georges Rodenbach*. Introd. Camille Mauclair. Paris: Karéline, 2008. 2 vols. [Reproduction en fac-similé de l'édition de 1923]

GG6796. Bertrand, Jean-Pierre: "Les clichés d'une ville: *Bruges-la-Morte*, roman photographique." In 616, 49-57.

GG6797. Gorceix, Paul: "A propos des images collectives de l'Histoire." In 83, 124-137.

GG6798. Gorceix, Paul: "L'autre roman de Rodenbach: *Le Carillonneur.*" In 83, 99-109.

GG6799. Gorceix, Paul: "*Bruges-la-Morte*: un modèle de roman symboliste." In 83, 85-97.

GG6800. Gorceix, Paul: "Du conteur à l'auteur de nouvelles fantastiques." In 83, 111-124.

GG6801. Gorceix, Paul: "Paysages d'âme." In 83, 63-74.

GG6802. Gorceix, Paul: "Le symbolisme et l'esthétique du reflet." In 83, 75-84. [Mallarmé]

GG6803. Lowrie, Joyce O.: "Reversals and disappearance in Georges Rodenbach's *L'Ami des miroirs* and *Bruges-la-morte.*" In 511.

ROGNET, Richard.

GG6804. Labidoire, Monique W.: "Richard Rognet: la poétique de la mémoire," *LittéRéalité*, vol. 20, no. 2 (automne/hiver 2008), 11-20.

ROLIN, Dominique.

GG6805. ● De Haes, Frans: *Les pas de la voyageuse: Dominique Rolin.* Bruxelles: Archives et musée de la littérature, 2008. *Archives du futur.* 270 p.

ROLIN, Jean.

GG6806. Motte, Warren: "Jean Rolin's explosion," *Review of Contemporary Fiction*, vol. 28, no. 3 (Fall 2008), 123-141.

ROLIN, Olivier. See also 761, 4353.

GG6807. ● *Olivier Rolin: littérature, histoire, voyage.* Dir. Luc Rasson, Bruno Tritsmans. Amsterdam: Rodopi, 2008. *CRIN*, 49. 163 p.

GG6808. Amar, Ruth: "Olivier Rolin: les fluctuations d'une écriture transgressive." In 6807, 51-61.

GG6809. Blanckeman, Bruno: "L'écriture périphérique: une étude de *Tigre en papier.*" In 6807, 35-49.

GG6810. Brignoli, Laura: "*Port-Soudan* et la critique de la société." In 6807, 65-74.

GG6811. Dangy, Isabelle: "De la chambre au chapitre: l'hôtel virtuel de *Suite à l'hôtel Crystal*," *Voix Plurielles*, vol. 5, no. 1 (mai 2008), [n.p.]. [Perec]

GG6812. Delcroix, Maurice: "Lectures de *Port-Soudan.*" In 6807, 13-24.

GG6813. Dinter, Karolien van; Eva Ramón: "Valise perdue et retrouvée: lecture de *Suite à l'Hôtel Crystal* d'Olivier Rolin." In 6807, 137-143.

GG6814. Fondo-Valette, Madeleine: "Le militant à l'ère du soupçon d'après *Tigre en papier* d'Olivier Rolin." In 456, 263-270.

GG6815. Hillen, Sabine; Alexander Roose: " 'Comme le signe de l'infini, comme un sablier': entretien avec Olivier Rolin." In 6807, 147-159.

GG6816. Michel, Jacqueline: "Le paysage d'enfance revu par Olivier Rolin." In 6807, 127-135.

GG6817. Pelckmans, Paul: " 'Tout est bien qui finit mal': le souvenir de Gordon dans *Méroé.*" In 6807, 25-34.

GG6818. Rasson, Luc: " 'Se mesurer aux Dieux': *Tigre en papier, Méroé.*" In 6807, 75-82.

GG6819. Roose, Alexander: "Accélération de l'histoire et éclipse du temps: les épaves et les ruines dans les romans d'Olivier Rolin." In 528, 61-71.

GG6820. Rubino, Gianfranco: "La pression du passé: Olivier Rolin." In 561, 103-116.

GG6821. Thibault, Bruno: "Le deuil de la révolution et les ruses de l'histoire dans *Tigre en papier* d'Olivier Rolin et dans *Les trois minutes du diable* de Danièle Sallenave." In 6807, 99-113. [Sallenave]

GG6822. Tritsmans, Bruno: "Tropismes exotiques et petites géographies." In 6807, 117-125.

GG6823. Viart, Dominique: "Des hommes habités d'Histoire." In 6807, 83-97.

ROLLAND, Romain.

GG6824. Barilier, Etienne: "Que mon nom soit flétri." In 388, 139-144.

GG6825. Delaunay, Léonor: "*Liluli* de Romain Rolland." In 1101, 187-191.

ROMAINS, Jules. See also 734.

GG6826. ● Niderst, Alain: *Jules Romains, les illusions perdues*. Paris: Alain Baudry, 2008. *Les voix du livre.* 99 p.

GG6827. Dangy, Isabelle: "Engagement politique et société secrète dans *Les hommes de bonne volonté*." In 456, 27-38.

GG6828. Leblond, Aude: "Le dictateur ou la tentation d'un militant." In 456, 115-126.

ROPS, Félicien.

GG6829. ● Huysmans, Joris-Karl: *Jenseits des Bösen: das erotische Work des Félicien Rops*. Aus dem Franz. übertr. von Peter Priskil. Freiburg: Ahriman-Verlag, 2008. 119 p.

GG6830. ● *Loss of control: Grenzgänge zur Kunst von Félicien Rops bis heute*. Redaktion, Michael Kröger, Friederike Fast. Herford: Marta Herford, 2008. 319 p. [Exhibition catalog]

ROSENTHAL, Olivia.

GG6831. Jolly, Geneviève: "Une partition didascalique plurielle: *Les félins m'aiment bien* d'Olivia rosenthal." In 605, 351-364.

ROSNY, Joseph-Henri aîné.

GG6832. ● Rosny aîné, Joseph-Henri: *Journal: cahiers 1880-1897.* Edition établie et annotée par Jean-Michel Pottier. Tusson: Du Lérot, 2008. 235 p.

GG6833. Bozzetto, Roger: "La préhistoire imaginaire de Rosny aîné," *Otrante*, no. 19-20 (2006), 193-200.

GG6834. Chelebourg, Christian: "Le monde déréglé de J.-H. Rosny aîné ou la griserie de l'inconnu," *Otrante*, no. 19-20 (2006), 65-80.

GG6835. Clermont, Philippe: "Visions d'altérité chez Rosny aîné," *Otrante*, no. 19-20 (2006), 81-95.

GG6836. Compère, Daniel: " 'Moi contre moi': 'L'Assassin surnaturel'," *Otrante*, no. 19-20 (2006), 139-150.

GG6837. Fondaneche, Daniel: "*La Force mystérieuse*: une histoire de communication," *Otrante*, no. 19-20 (2006), 113-138.

GG6838. Gourdet, Anna: "Mélange de genres," *Otrante*, no. 19-20 (2006), 97-111.

GG6839. Guillaud, Lauric: "Les mondes perdus de Rosny aîné," *Otrante*, no. 19-20 (2006), 215-240.

GG6840. Huftier, Arnaud: "Rosny aîné et les formes de l'autre," *Otrante*, no. 19-20 (2006), 7-26.

GG6841. Lysøe, Eric: "Rosny aîné ou le fantastique à pied d'œuvre," *Otrante*, no. 19-20 (2006), 37-64.

GG6842. Picot, Jean-Pierre: "Amour, Lotus, nymphées et nymphéas chez Rosny aîné," *Otrante*, no. 19-20 (2006), 167-191.

GG6843. Quaghebeur, Marc: "Science et nature au cœur de l'analogie dans *La Force mystérieuse* de Rosny aîné." In 616, 255-273.

GG6844. Soncini Fratta, Anna: "Diane ou la séduction narcissique échouée," *Otrante*, no. 19-20 (2006), 151-165.

GG6845. Sudret, Laurence: "Afriques imaginaires chez Jules Verne et Rosny aîné," *Otrante*, no. 19-20 (2006), 201-214. [Verne]

ROSTAND, Edmond de.

GG6846. ● *Edmond Rostand, renaissance d'une œuvre*. Textes rassemblés par Guy Lavorel et Philippe Bulinge. Lyon: CEDIC, 2007.

GG6847. Bourgeois, Jean: "*Cyrano de Bergerac* d'Edmond Rostand: le théâtre dans le théâtre," *Revue d'Histoire Littéraire de la France*, tome 108, no. 3 (juillet-sept. 2008), 607-620.

GG6848. Bulinge, Philippe: "Le manuscrit du *Faust* d'Edmond Rostand." In 6846, 191-215.

GG6849. Contamin, Odile: "Les dessins d'Edmond Rostand." In 6846, 169-190.

GG6850.   Degott, Bertrand: "Mourir (et renaître) pour des idées: le théâtre en vers de Rostand." In 530, 471-490.

GG6851.   Douphis, Pierre-Olivier: "Sur les chemins de la pureté." In 6846, 11-23.

GG6852.   Fabre de Beauchamp, Michel: "Les Pyrénées dans l'œuvre d'Edmond Rostand." In 6846, 219-225.

GG6853.   Fetzer, Glenn W.: "Poésie et patrie chez Edmond Rostand." In 6846, 119-127.

GG6854.   Figuerola, Carmen: "*La Dernière Nuit de Don Juan* ou le chant du cygne." In 6846, 153-165.

GG6855.   Goetz, Olivier: "Edmond Rostand, metteur en scène." In 6846, 43-60.

GG6856.   La Cerda, Alexandra de: "Rostand et les Jeux Floraux." In 6846, 227-233.

GG6857.   Lagarde, Monique; Claude Lachet: "Edmond Rostand dans les manuels scolaires." In 6846, 237-249.

GG6858.   Lavorel, Guy: "Le dédoublement, principe théâtral de *Cyrano de Bergerac*." In 6846, 61-67.

GG6859.   Le Person, Marc: "Réminiscences du Moyen Age dans *La Princesse lointaine*." In 6846, 71-103.

GG6860.   Richer, Laurence: "Tradition et réécriture dans le théâtre d'Edmond Rostand." In 6846, 105-117.

GG6861.   Roger-Vasselin, Denis: "*Cyrano de Bergerac* ou la tragédie de l'ivresse." In 6846, 131-142.

GG6862.   Santa, Angels: "La dimension mythique de l'œuvre d'Edmond Rostand." In 6846, 143-151.

GG6863.   Thomasseau, Jean-Marie: "Dérives romanesques et lyriques des didascalies 'fin de siècle' chez Henry Bataille et Edmond Rostand." In 605, 253-264.

GG6864.   Vogel, Géraldine: "Picturalité et mise en scène chez Edmond Rostand." In 6846, 25-39.

ROUART, Jean-Marie.

GG6865.   ● Rouart, Jean-Marie: *Libertin et chrétien*. Entretiens avec Marc Leboucher. Paris: Librairie générale française, 2008. *Le livre de poche*. 219 p. [Orig. ed., 2004]

ROUAUD, Jean. See also 389, 673.

GG6866.   Bevilacqua, Luca: "Notes de lecture sur *L'Imitation du bonheur* de Jean Rouaud." In 561, 161-176.

GG6867.   Duffy, Jean H.: "Closed up and close(-)up: Jean Rouaud's books of revelation," *Yale French Studies*, no. 114 (2008), 67-79.

GG6868.   Freyermuth, Sylvie: "Ruptures et réintégrations en régime de narration littéraire: l'exemple de l'écriture de Jean Rouaud." In 554, 269-278.

GG6869.   Rouaud, Jean; Denis Deprez; Madeleine Frédéric: "Entretien: *Les champs d'honneur*: du roman à la bande dessinée," *Degrés*, 36e année, no. 133 (printemps 2008), d1-d17.

ROUBAUD, Jacques. See also 404, 1042, 6456.

GG6870.   ● Roubaud, Jacques: *La princesse Hoppy ou le conte du labrador; suivi de Le conte conte le conte et compte, et de L'épluchure du conte-oignon*. Lecture d'Elvira Laskowski-Caujolle. Nancy: Absalon, 2008. *La reverdie*. 169 p.

GG6871.   ● Roubaud, Jacques: *Roubaud*. Rencontre avec Jean-François Puff. Paris: Argol, 2008. *Les singuliers*. 145 p.

GG6872.   Baquey, Stéphane: "Le non-non-vers de *Quelque chose noir*," *Textuel*, no. 55 (2008), 89-102.

GG6873.   Barbarant, Olivier: "La mort photographe," *Textuel*, no. 55 (2008), 49-63.

GG6874.   Conort, Benoit: "Le chiffre du deuil," *Textuel*, no. 55 (2008), 145-167.

GG6875.   Consenstein, Peter: "L'énigme de la signification silencieuse." In 436, 201-212. [Albiach, Fourcade, Royet-Journoud]

GG6876.   Fourcaut, Laurent: "L'épreuve par neuf: Jacques Roubaud." In 612, 259-270.

GG6877.   Larraburu-Bédouret, Sandrine: " 'La forme d'un sonnet change plus vite que le cœur des humains . . .'," *Formules*, no. 12 (2008), 143-154.

GG6878. Lewis, Sophie: "An interview with Jacques Roubaud," *PN Review*, vol. 34, no. 6 (July-Aug. 2008), 24-28.

GG6879. Moncond'huy, Dominique: "Du journal au tombeau ou de 'quelque chose' à 'rien'," *Textuel*, no. 55 (2008), 33-48.

GG6880. Monte, Michèle: "*Quelque chose noir*: de la critique de l'élégie à la réinvention du rythme," *Textuel*, no. 55 (2008), 65-87.

GG6881. Montémont, Véronique: "JR 007 ou le secret chez Jacques Roubaud." In 436, 177-186.

GG6882. Montémont, Véronique: "*Quelque chose noir*: le point de fracture?," *Textuel*, no. 55 (2008), 9-31.

GG6883. Pestourié, Emmanuel: "L'impossible déposition de la parole poétique dans *Quelque chose noir*," *Textuel*, no. 55 (2008), 103-128.

GG6884. Pradeau, Christophe: "Le réseau: traboules, groupes clandestins et bifurcations dans l'œuvre de Roubaud." In 436, 165-175.

GG6885. Puff, Jean-François: "La référence médiévale dans *Quelque chose noir*," *Textuel*, no. 55 (2008), 129-143.

GG6886. Reig, Christophe: "Jacques Roubaud: énigmes du roman/romans à énigmes." In 436, 187-199.

GG6887. Salon, Olivier: "Traces et abandons oulipiens dans *Quelque chose noir*," *Textuel*, no. 55 (2008), 169-180.

ROUD, Gustave.

GG6888. • Roud, Gustave; Georges Borgeaud: *Correspondance 1936-1974*. Edition établie par Anne-Lise Delacrétaz. Lausanne: Association des amis de Gustave Roud, 2008. *Cahiers Gustave Roud*, 12. 136 p.

ROUDINESCO, Élisabeth.

GG6889. Fanelli, Cristiana: "Philosophes dans la tourmente. Sul pensiero di Élisabeth Roudinesco," *Cultura: Rivista di Filosofia, Letteratura e Storia*, anno 46, no. 1 (2008), 149-160.

ROUMAIN, Jacques. See also 194, 1182.

GG6890. • Toussaint, Hérold: *L'utopie révolutionnaire en Haïti autour de Jacques Roumain*. Port-au-Prince: Presses nationales d'Haïti, 2008. 217 p.

GG6891. Britton, Celia: "Restoring lost unity in Jacques Roumain's *Gouverneurs de la rosée*." In 51, 19-35.

GG6892. Martín-Ogunsola, Dellita: "The aesthetics of culture transfer in Langston Hughes's translations of works by Federico García Lorca, Nicolás Guillén, Jacques Roumain," *Foreign Literature Studies*, vol. 30, no. 2 (2008), 21-30.

GG6893. Moulin Civil, Françoise: "La conversation ininterrompue de Jacques Roumain et Nicolás Guillén." In 118, 145-156.

GG6894. Munro, Martin: "Reading rhythm and listening to Caribbean history in fiction by Jacques Roumain and Joseph Zobel," *Journal of Modern Literature*, vol. 31, no. 4 (Summer 2008), 131-144. [Zobel]

GG6895. Patterson, Anita: "From Harlem to Haiti: Langston Hughes, Jacques Roumain and the avant-gardes signifying modernism in Wilson Harris's *Eternity to Season*." In 549.

ROUQUETTE, Max.

GG6896. Casanova, Jean-Yves: "L'absence et la trace," *Europe*, no. 950-951 (juin-juillet 2008), 207-211.

GG6897. Forêt, Jean-Claude: "Paradoxe sur le dramaturge," *Europe*, no. 950-951 (juin-juillet 2008), 224-233.

GG6898. Fraisse, Magali: "La seduction des commencements," *Europe*, no. 950-951 (juin-juillet 2008), 196-206.

GG6899. Gardy, Philippe: "Le voie des songes," *Europe*, no. 950-951 (juin-juillet 2008), 165-170.

GG6900. Gasiglia, Rémy: "La couverture rouge," *Europe*, no. 950-951 (juin-juillet 2008), 234-247.

GG6901. Navarro, Lionel: "Le vieil home et la création," *Europe*, no. 950-951 (juin-juillet 2008), 248-257.

GG6902.   Temple, Frédéric-Jacques: "Max maximus," *Europe*, no. 950-951 (juin-juillet 2008), 171-172.

GG6903.   Torreilles, Claire: "Les roseaux de Midas," *Europe*, no. 950-951 (juin-juillet 2008), 179-195.

GG6904.   Verny, Marie-Jeanne: "Echos entre prose et poésie," *Europe*, no. 950-951 (juin-juillet 2008), 212-223.

ROUSSEL, Raymond. See also 1050, 5081.

GG6905.   ● Colombet, Marie J. A.: *L'humour objectif: Roussel, Duchamp, "sous le capot": l'objectivation du surrealisme.* Paris: Publibook.com, 2008. 547 p. [Surrealism, Breton]

GG6906.   ● *Musicalisation et théâtralisation du texte roussellien.* Textes réunis par Anne-Marie Amiot, Christelle Reggiani, Hermès Salceda. Caen: Lettres modernes, Minard, 2007. *Raymond Roussel*, 3. 292 p.

GG6907.   ● Roussel, Raymond: *L'allée aux lucioles.* Suivie de, "Les corps subtils aux gloires légitimantes" de Jacques Sivan. Dijon: Presses du réel, 2008. *L'espace littéraire.* 183 p.

GG6908.   Abrami, Vittorio: "Raymond Roussel: fra l'estasi e l'angoscia," *Bérénice*, anno 14, n. 38 (dic. 2007), 58-67.

GG6909.   Albani, Paolo: "Raymond Roussel oulipiano per anticipazione," *Bérénice*, anno 14, n. 38 (dic. 2007), 31-43.

GG6910.   Amiot, Anne-Marie: "Roussel et la musique." In 6906, 9-35.

GG6911.   Basset, Anne-Marie: "Roussel lecteur de Valéry." In 6906, 207-232. [Valéry]

GG6912.   Basset, Anne-Marie: "Théâtralisation du corps dans les avant-textes de *Impressions d'Afrique*." In 6906, 141-168.

GG6913.   Bazantay, Pierre: "Quelques notes sur la musique chez Roussel." In 6906, 37-53.

GG6914.   Broi, Gianni: "L'attualità di Raymond Roussel," *Bérénice*, anno 14, n. 38 (dic. 2007), 29-30.

GG6915.   Broi, Gianni: "Presentazione," *Bérénice*, anno 14, n. 38 (dic. 2007), 15-25.

GG6916.   Broi, Gianni: "Il tema del *sauveur* nelle *Nozze* di Raymond Roussel," *Bérénice*, anno 14, n. 38 (dic. 2007), 110-128.

GG6917.   Bullot, Erik: "*Les Enfants de Raymond Roussel*." In 6906, 233-239.

GG6918.   Fadini, Ubaldo: "L'affetto del fuori. Annotazioni a partire dal *Roussel* di Michel Foucault," *Bérénice*, anno 14, n. 38 (dic. 2007), 77-87.

GG6919.   Galluzzi, Francesco: "Raymond Roussel tra le arti visive," *Bérénice*, anno 14, n. 38 (dic. 2007), 68-76.

GG6920.   Gromer, Bernadette: "A la recherche de la voix perdue: phonographes et machines musicales." In 6906, 75-107.

GG6921.   Guerini, Gian Paolo: "Morire, . . . dormire! Forse sognare . . . Per Raymond Roussel," *Bérénice*, anno 14, n. 38 (dic. 2007), 129-140.

GG6922.   Houppermans, Sjef: "Tancrède Boucharessas ou les joies du music-hall." In 6906, 55-73.

GG6923.   Leborgne, Erik: "L'*Hommage à Raymond Roussel* (1971) d'Olivier Greif." In 6906, 109-120.

GG6924.   Lisa, Tommaso: "L'universo è un dettaglio. Note sulla traduzione magrelliana de 'La vue' di Raymond Roussel," *Bérénice*, anno 14, n. 38 (dic. 2007), 44-57.

GG6925.   Magne, Bernard: "Roussel dramaturge, spécialiste des échecs." In 6906, 123-139.

GG6926.   Montier, Jean-Pierre: "Et vint *La Vue*." In 508, 413-430.

GG6927.   Nagata, M.: "L'improbable théâtre de Raymond Roussel," *Histoires Littéraires*, no. 36 (oct.-nov.-déc. 2008), 19-32.

GG6928.   Panella, Giuseppe: "Il sogno della letteratura secondo Raymond Roussel," *Bérénice*, anno 14, n. 38 (dic. 2007), 88-109.

GG6929.   Reggiani, Christelle: "Bibliographie 1999-2005." In 6906, 275-280.

GG6930.   Reggiani, Christelle: "Le théâtre de la mémoire." In 6906, 169-179.

GG6931.   Reig, Christophe: "Mathews/Roussel: 'comment j'ai réécrit certains de ses livres'." In 6906, 181-204.

GG6932.   Salceda, Hermès: "Les calculs des images." In 6906, 241-251.

GG6933.   Salceda, Hermès: "Roussel dans l'univers virtuel." In 6906, 255-273.

GG6934.   "La version théâtrale d'*Impressions d'Afrique* de Raymond Roussel," *Histoires Littéraires*, no. 36 (oct.-nov.-déc. 2008), 33-39.

ROUX, Paul de.

GG6935.   Ortlieb, Gilles: "Pour Paul de Roux," *Théodore Balmoral*, no. 58 (2008), 186-198.

ROY, Gabrielle.

GG6936.   ● Roy, Gabrielle: *Street of riches.* Trans. Henry Binsse; afterword by Miriam Waddington. Toronto: McClelland & Stewart, 2008. *New Canadian library.* 220 p.

GG6937.   ● Roy, Gabrielle: *Windflower.* Trans. Joyce Marshall; afterword by Phyllis Webb. Toronto: McClelland & Stewart, 2008. *New Canadian library.* 159 p.

GG6938.   Hutchinson, Lorna: "Uncovering the grotesque in fiction by Alice Munro and Gabrielle Roy," *Studies in Canadian Literature*, vol. 33, no. 1 (2008), 187210.

GG6939.   Marcotte, Sophie: "Pour la création d'une communauté virtuelle autour de l'œuvre de Gabrielle Roy." In 44, 155-168.

GG6940.   Nodelman, J. N.: "Gabrielle Roy's *La route d'Altamont* and Canadian highway narrative," *Studies in Canadian Literature*, vol. 33, no. 1 (2008), 211-228.

GG6941.   Savic, Maria: "Relation père-fille dans l'œuvre de Gabrielle Roy: dynamique oscillatoire entre rapprochement et éloignement." In 572, 105-113.

ROY, Jules. See also 3954, 7199.

GG6942.   ● *Jules Roy, 100 ans.* Textes réunis par Jean Louis Roy. Paris: L'Harmattan, 2008. 128 p.

GG6943.   Cantier, Jacques: "L'après-guerre de Jules Roy." In 515, 67-82.

GG6944.   Roy, Jean-Louis: "Jules Roy à l'Ecole d'Alger." In 515, 175-182.

GG6945.   Vincent, Daniel-Henri: "Jules Roy et le souvenir de Mox-Pol Fouchet, 105-117.

ROYET-JOURNOUD, Claude. See also 6875.

GG6946.   Hocquard, Emmanuel: "Théorème," *Critique*, no. 735-736 (2008), 587-599.

RUFIN, Jean-Christophe.

GG6947.   Ayed, Kawthar: "L'image de soi et de l'autre dans deux romans d'anticipation dystopique," *Nouvelles Etudes Francophones*, vol. 22, no. 2 (automne 2007), 102-111.

SACHS, Maurice. See 4656.

SACRÉ, James.

GG6948.   Guichard, Thierry: "Le poète affectif," *Matricule des Anges*, no. 75 (2006), 14-17.

GG6949.   Sacré, James: "Ecrire contre, tout contre," *Matricule des Anges*, no. 75 (2006), 18-23. [Entretien]

SADIN, Éric.

GG6950.   Lascaux, Sandrine: "Objets poétiques mobiles." In 819, 185-196.

SADJI, Abdoulaye. See also 260.

GG6951.   Ehora, Clément Effoh: "Intergénération et réécriture du conte traditionnel africain." In 894, 285-297.

SAGAN, Françoise.

GG6952.   ● *Album Sagan.* Avant-propos d'Eric Neuhoff. Paris: L'Herne, 2008. *Carnets.*

GG6953.   ● Lelièvre, Marie-Dominique: *Sagan à toute allure.* Paris: Denoël, 2008. 343 p.

GG6954.   ● Sagan, Françoise: *Bonjour tristesse.* Trans. Irene Ash; introd. Diane Johnson. New York: Harper Perennial Modern Classics, 2008. x, 130 p. [Orig. ed., 2001]

GG6955.   ● Sagan, Françoise: *Bonjour tristesse; A certain smile.* Trans. Irene Ash; introd. Rachel Cusk. London: Penguin, 2008. *Modern classics.* 212 p.

GG6956.   Brun, Frédéric: "Françoise Sagan. Bonjour vitesse," *Spectacle du Monde*, no. 547 (juillet-août 2008), 78-82.

GG6957.   Cusk, Rachel: "*Bonjour tristesse* de Françoise Sagan." In 892, 53-65.

SAINT-DENYS GARNEAU, Hector de. See 46.

SAINT-EXUPÉRY, Antoine de. See also 698.

GG6958. • Des Vallières, Nathalie; Roselyne de Ayala: *Saint-Exupéry: art, writings and musings.* Trans. Anthony Zielonka. New York: Rizzoli, 2008. 215 p.

GG6959. • Pradel, Jacques; Luc Vanrell: *Antoine de Saint-Exupéry: die Wahrheit über sin Verschwinden.* Königswinter: Heel, 2008. 189 p.

GG6960. • Pradel, Jacques; Luc Vanrell: *Saint-Exupéry, l'ultime secret: enquête sur une disparition.* Préface d'Alain Decaux; postface de Xavier Delestre. Monaco: Rocher, 2008. *Un nouveau regard.* 189 p.

GG6961. • Ravoux, Jean-Philippe: *Donner un sens à l'existence, ou, Pourquoi Le petit prince est le plus grand traité de métaphysique du XXe siècle.* Paris: Laffont, 2008. 159 p.

GG6962. • Triebel, Claas: *Der Prinz, der Pilot und Antoine de Saint-Exupéry: das Rätsel um den letzten Flug.* München: Herbig, 2008. 220 p.

GG6963. • Vircondelet, Alain: *La véritable histoire du Petit prince.* Paris: Flammarion, 2008. 219 p.

GG6964. Bourguignon, Annie: "Conquering the Arctic and conquering the sky: views on technical progress and Superman in Saint-Exupéry's *Night Flight* and P. O. Sundman's *The Flight of the Eagle*," *Nordlit,* no. 23 (2008), 39-54.

GG6965. Howley, Richard A.: "Icarus in the modern world: the case of Antoine de Saint-Exupéry." In 481.

SAINT-JOHN PERSE. See also 1019, 4236.

GG6966. • Cluse, Jean-Louis: *Figures et voix du double chez Saint-John Perse.* Lille: ANRT, 2008. 600 p.

GG6967. • Kassab-Charfi, Samia: *Rhétorique de Saint-John Perse.* Tunis: Univ. de Tunis, Faculté des sciences humaines et sociales de Tunis, 2008. 567 p.

GG6968. • Koziej, Alicja: *L'imaginaire de Saint-John Perse.* Lublin: Wydawnictwo Uniw. Marii Curie-Sklodowskiej, 2008. 150 p.

GG6969. • Meltz, Renaud: *Alexis Léger dit Saint-John Perse.* Paris: Flammarion, 2008. *Grandes biographies.* 846 p.

GG6970. • *Saint-John Perse: por los caminos de la tierra.* Selección y notas de Ariel Camejo y Haydée Arango. La Habana: Casa de la Américas, 2008. 231 p.

GG6971. • Servissolle, Nicolas: *Eloges, palimpseste.* Paris: L'Harmattan, 2008. *Critiques littéraires.* 317 p.

GG6972. • Trebesch, Jochen: *Diener zweier Herren: Alexis Saint-John Perse.* Berlin: NORA, 2008. 106 p.

GG6973. Carlet, Yves: "*Vents* et les muses du Nouveau Monde. Saint-John Perse lecteur des transcendentalistes américains," *Souffle de Perse,* no. 13 (2008), 77-90.

GG6974. Carpentier, Alejo: "Saint-John Perse: urbi et orbi." In 6970.

GG6975. Césaire, Aimé: "Cérémonie vaudou pour Saint-John Perse." In 6970.

GG6976. Cleac'h-Chesnot, Corinne; Thaïva Ouaki: "Bibliographie 2006," *Souffle de Perse,* no. 13 (2008), 203-215.

GG6977. Combe, Dominique: "La métaphysique des langues: notes sur Yves Bonnefoy et Saint-John Perse." In 516, 299-308. [Bonnefoy]

GG6978. Condé, Maryse: "Eloge de Saint-John Perse." In 6970.

GG6979. Doumet, Christian: "Modalités de la création poétique chez Saint-John Perse," *Souffle de Perse,* no. 13 (2008), 49-62.

GG6980. Favriaud, Michel: "La relation des unités du discours poétique dans *Vents* de Saint-John Perse," *Champs du Signe,* no. 23 (2007), 59-77.

GG6981. Fels, Laurent: "Saint-John Perse: entre créolité et francité," *Galerie,* no. 4 (2006), 571-582.

GG6982. Fernández Retamar, Roberto: "Allan écrit à liuqui est à Cuba." In 6970.

GG6983. Glissant, Edouard: "Saint-John Perse et les Antillais." In 6970.

GG6984. Gómez Rosa, Alexis: "Message chiffre et lettre." In 6970.

GG6985. Gouvard, Jean-Michel: "Le souffle des *Vents*." In 503, 75-93.

GG6986. Koziej, Alicja: "*Amers* de Saint-John Perse et les forces vitales." In 417, 127-136.

GG6987. Kurts-Woeste, Lia: "Stylistique de la phrase dans *Vents* de Saint-John Perse," *Champs du Signe*, no. 23 (2007), 43-58.

GG6988. Levillain, Henriette: "Saint-John Perse et son temps," *Souffle de Perse*, no. 13 (2008), 91-104.

GG6989. Lezama Lima, José: "Saint-John Perse: historien des pluies." In 6970.

GG6990. Mayaux, Catherine: "La réception critique des poèmes *Vents*, *Chronique, Chant pour un équinoxe*," *Souffle de Perse*, no. 13 (2008), 23-47.

GG6991. Meitinger, Serge: "*Vents* de Saint-John Perse ou la récitation occidentale," *Champs du Signe*, no. 24 (2007), 73-86.

GG6992. Morejón, Nancy: "L'île errante de Saint-John Perse." In 6970.

GG6993. Patterson, Anita: "Transnational topographies in Poe, Eliot and Saint-John Perse." In 549.

GG6994. Radhouane, Nebil: "La phrase dans la poésie de Saint-John Perse: de la structure grammaticale à la figure essentielle." In 556.

GG6995. Sacotte, Mireille: "L'éloge lyrique: la voix de Saint-John Perse." In 1014, 403-423.

GG6996. Sacotte, Mireille: "Une lecture de *Vents*, II, 1: de l'usage des mythes," *Souffle de Perse*, no. 13 (2008), 105-119.

GG6997. Saínz, Enrique: "Saint-John Perse ou de la plénitude." In 6970.

GG6998. Vallin, Marjolaine: "La phrase averbale persienne," *Français Moderne*, no. 2 (2008), 203-211.

GG6999. Zalamena, Jorge: "Offrande." In 6970.

SAINT-POL ROUX.

GG7000. Hamot, Odile: "La théologie hétérodoxe du Verbe chez Saint-Pol Roux," *Travaux de Littérature*, tome 21 (2008), 369-382.

SALACROU, Armand.

GG7001. Hoffert, Yannick: "Boulevard Durand ou le calvaire du militant." In 456, 217-229.

SALLENAVE, Danièle. See also 6821.

GG7002. Long, Imogen: "A journey through art to Amsterdam: referenc5es to painting in Danièle Sallenave's novel *Le voyage d'Amsterdam ou les règles de la conversation*." In 570, 41-53.

SALMON, André. See also 4655.

GG7003. • Salmon, André: *La terreur noire*. Edition établie par Cédric Biagini et Lionel de La Fouchardière, avec l'aide précieuse de Jacqueline Gojard. Paris: Echappée, 2008. 334 p.

GG7004. Gojard, Jacqueline: "André Salmon et le mythe du cosmopolitisme." In 612, 127-138.

SALVAYRE, Lydie.

GG7005. Douzou, Catherine: "L'histoire en écho: *La Compagnie des spectres* de Lydie Salvayre." In 561, 67-84.

GG7006. Motte, Warren: "Lydie Salvayre's literature." In 900.

SARDOU, Victorien.

GG7007. Aquien, Pascal: "Sardoodledom revisited, or a few trivial remarks about Oscar Wilde's *An Ideal Husband* (1895)," *Etudes Irlandaises*, vol. 33, no. 2 (automne 2008), 9-19.

GG7008. Chothia, Jean: " 'Henry and 250 supers': Irving, Robespierre and the staging of the revolutionary crowd." In 836, 117-134.

GG7009. Jardez, Dominique: "Poe en vaudeville: Labiche et Sardou." In 766, 225-235.

GG7010. Urbach, Reinhard: "Schnitzlers Anfänge: was Anatol wollen soll," *Internationales Archiv für Sozialgeschichte der Deutschen Literatur*, 33. Jahrgang, Heft 1 (2008), 113-154.

SARNEY, José.

GG7011. Police, Gérard: "Le mot 'créole' dans *Saraminda* de José Sarney," *Nouvelles Etudes Francophones*, vol. 23, no. 2 (automne 2008), 85-97.

SAROTTE, Georges-Michel.

GG7012.   Lautel-Ribstein, Florence: "Entretien avec Georges-Michel Sarotte," *Revue Septet*, no. 1 (2008), [n.p.].

SARRAUTE, Nathalie. See also 6428, 6479.

GG7013.   Anthony, Sarah: "Le plurilinguisme des ultima verba: un outil intratextuel sarrautien." In 442, 99-108.

GG7014.   Avendaño Anguita, Lina: "*Enfance* de Nathalie Sarraute: la déchirure salutaire," *Women in French Studies*, no. 16 (2008), 39-50.

GG7015.   Ayadi, Sabah: "Poétique de l'incohérence dans *Le Planétarium* de Nathalie Sarraute." In 410, 391-398.

GG7016.   Boyle, Claire: "Sarraute writing the self: the drama of self-possession." In 400, 30-65.

GG7017.   Diver, Ruth: "L'*Enfance* russe de Nathalie Sarraute." In 384, 27-39.

GG7018.   Duffy, Jean H.: "Territoriality disputes, pollution and abjection in Sarraute and Lenoir," *Romanic Review*, vol. 98, no. 4 (Nov. 2007), 387-412. [Hélène Lenoir]

GG7019.   Fau, Guillaume: " 'Loin dans la percée poétique'. Deux lettres de Nathalie Sarraute à René Micha," *Revue de la Bibliothèque Nationale de France*, no. 30 (2008), 81-87.

GG7020.   Jefferson, Ann: "L'argent, l'avarice ou le moyen de se ruiner chez Nathalie Sarraute." In 902, 179-189.

GG7021.   Licari, Carmen: "Poétique de l'instant: du monologue d'Edouard Dujardin au tropisme de Nathalie Sarraute," *Cahiers Valery Larbaud*, no. 43 (2008), 151-161. [Dujardin]

GG7022.   Minogue, Valerie: "La Russie de Nathalie Sarraute." In 384, 11-25.

GG7023.   Schechner, Stéphanie: "Words as subjects: the personification of language in three texts by Nathalie Sarraute," *Nottingham French Studies*, vol. 47, no. 1 (Spring 2008), 14-31.

GG7024.   Spies, Werner: "Nathalie Sarraute." In 596.

SARRAZIN, Albertine. See 595.

SARROUB, Karim.

GG7025.   Yacine Meskine, Mohamed: "L'écriture de l'absurde dans *A l'ombre de soi* de Karim Sarroub," *Algérie Littérature/Action*, no. 125-126 (nov.-déc. 2008), 43-48.

SARTRE, Jean-Paul. See also 24, 81, 484, 536, 552, 668, 679, 705, 755, 779, 948, 950, 966, 967, 1393, 1485, 1532, 1543, 1563, 1607, 1619, 1800, 2407, 5777, 5866, 6205, 6645, 7267, 7290, 8091.

GG7026.   ● Coombes, Sam: *The early Sartre and Marxism.* Oxford: Peter Lang, 2008. *Modern French identities*, 64. 330 p.

GG7027.   ● Contat, Michel: *Pour Sartre.* Paris: PUF, 2008. *Perspectives critiques.* 581 p.

GG7028.   ● Cox, Gary: *The Sartre dictionary.* London: Continuum, 2008. 232 p.

GG7029.   ● Detmer, David: *Sartre explained: from bad faith to authenticity.* Chicago: Open Court, 2008. *Ideas explained.* xi, 233 p.

GG7030.   ● Distler, Anton: *Kein Verstehen ohne fundamentale Ontologie: eine philosophische Analyse des Werks von W. G. Sebald aufgrund der "existentiellen Psychoanalyses" Jean-Paul Sartres.* Würzburg: Königshausen & Neumann, 2008. 128 p.

GG7031.   ● Flajoliet, Alain: *La première philosophie de Sartre.* Paris: H. Champion, 2008. *Travaux de philosophie*, 14. 962 p.

GG7032.   ● Harms, Klaus: *Vor Gott ohne Gott: Freiheit, Verantwortung und Widerstand im Kontext der Religionskritik bei Dietrich: Beitrag zur politischen Ethik.* Berlin; Münster: Lit, 2008. x, 352 p.

GG7033.   ● Hatzimoysis, Anthony: *The philosophy of Sartre.* Chesham: Acumen, 2008. *Continental European philosophy.* 240 p.

GG7034.   ● *Jean-Paul Sartre: ein Philosoph des 21. Jahrhunderts?.* Ulrike Bardt, Hrsg. Darmstadt: Wiss. Buchgest., 2008. 192 p.

GG7035.   ● *Jean-Paul Sartre, la conscience de son temps.* François George [et al.]. Paris: Magazine Littéraire, 2005. 98 p.

GG7036.   ● *Jean-Paul Sartre, violence et éthique.* Dir. Gérard Wormser. Lyon: Sens Public, 2005. 159 p.

GG7037. • Krauss, Bernd: *Jean-Paul Sartre, Huis clos*. Stuttgart: Reclam, 2008. 88 p.

GG7038. • Monnin, Nathalie: *Sartre*. Paris: Belles lettres, 2008. *Figures du savoir*. 285 p.

GG7039. • *Moral [Eine] in Situation*. Hrsg. Peter Knopp, Vincent von Wroblewsky. Frankfurt: Peter Lang, 2008. *Carnets Jean-Paul Sartre*. 321 p.

GG7040. • Morris, Katherine J.: *Sartre*. Malden, MA: Blackwell, 2008. xv, 184 p.

GG7041. • Pépin, Charles: *Les philosophes sur le divan*. Paris: Flammarion, 2008. 349 p.

GG7042. • *Race after Sartre: antiracism, African existentialism, postcolonialism*. Ed. Jonathan Judaken. Albany: SUNY Press, 2008. *SUNY series Philosophy and Race*. x, 240 p.

GG7043. • Russo, Antonino: *Tre laici alla corte del XX secolo: Croce, Sartre, Fromm*. Acireale: Bonanno, 2008. 122 p.

GG7044. • *Sartre*. Sous la dir. de Michel Contat. Paris: Bayard, 2005. 282 p.

GG7045. • *Sartre e la filosofia del suo tempo*. A cura di Nestore Pirillo. Trento: Dipartimento di Filosofia, Storia e Beni Culturali, 2008. xvi, 483 p.

GG7046. • *Sartre, le philosophe, l'intellectuel et la politique*. Sous la dir. de Arno Münster et Jean-William Wallet. Paris: L'Harmattan, 20056. 235 p.

GG7047. • *Sartre und die Medien*. Michael Lommel, Volker Roloff, Hrsg. Bielefeld: Transcript, 2008. 225 p.

GG7048. • *Situating Sartre 2005*. Ed. Tom Bishop, Coralie Girard. New York: New York University, Center for French Civilization and Culture, 2007. 257 p.

GG7049. • Souza, Thana Mara de: *Sartre e a literatura engajada*. São Paulo: Edusp, 2008. 155 p.

GG7050. • Zhang, Chi: *Sartre en Chine, 1939-1976*. Paris: Le Manuscrit, 2008. 280 p.

GG7051. Acarlioglu, Abdullatif: "Les relations familiales dans *Les Séquestrés d'Altona* de Jean-Paul Sartre." In 572, 267-275.

GG7052. Arthur, Paige: "The persistence of colonialism." In 7042.

GG7053. Aumann, Antony: "Sartre's view of Kierkegaard as transhistorical man," *Journal of Philosophical Research*, vol. 31 (2006), 361-372.

GG7054. Bernasconi, Robert: "Sartre and Levinas: philosophers against racism and antisemitism." In 7042. [Levinas]

GG7055. Borges de Meneses, Ramiro Délio: "Vivência do outro segundo Sartre: entre a consciência e a liberdade," *Agora*, vol. 26, no. 2 (2007), 129-144.

GG7056. Bouchard, Simon: "Sartre le maître du soupçon," *Laval Théologique et Philosophique*, vol. 63, no. 3 (oct. 2007), 597-604.

GG7057. Butler, Judith: "Violence, nonviolence: Sartre on Fanon." In 7042. [Fanon]

GG7058. Caeymaex, Florence: "L'existentialisme comme éthique de Heidegger à Sartre," *Temps Modernes*, 63e année, no. 650 (juillet-oct. 2008), 248-269.

GG7059. Calas, Frédéric: "Didascalies expressives et marque d'auteur dans *Huis clos* de Jean-Paul Sartre." In 605, 421-434.

GG7060. Ciccariello-Maher, George: "European intellectuals and colonial difference." In 7042. [Césaire, Fanon, Foucault]

GG7061. Coombes, Sam: "New perspectives on the political dimension of Sartre's first ethics," *Sartre Studies International*, vol. 14, no. 1 (2008), 26-41. [Merleau-Ponty]

GG7062. Darnell, Michelle R.: "Ethics in the age of reason," *Sartre Studies International*, vol. 14, no. 2 (2008), 71-89.

GG7063. Delacampagne, Christian: "Race: from philosophy to history." In 7042.

GG7064. Eshleman, Matthew C.: "Bad faith is necessarily social," *Sartre Studies International*, vol. 14, no. 2 (2008), 40-47.

GG7065. Eshleman, Matthew C.: "The misplaced chapter on bad faith, or reading *Being and Nothingness* in reverse," *Sartre Studies International*, vol. 14, no. 2 (2008), 1-22.

GG7066. Evans Smith, Martha: "Myth and power structures in Sartre's *Les Mouches* and *La Putain respectueuse*," *CLCWeb*, vol. 10, no. 3 (2008), [n.p.].

GG7067. Fautrier, Pascale: "Sartre, du grand écrivain à l' 'intellectuel révolutionnaire médiatique'," *Critique*, tome 64, no. 739 (déc. 2008), 944-958.

GG7068. Figueiredo, Lídia: "O abismo da liberdade: Arendt vs. Kierkegaard e Sartre." In 954.

GG7069. Fuchs, Marko J.: "Grundprobleme endlichen Selbstseins: Hussserl, Heidegger, Sartre, Henrich," *Phänomenologische Forschungen* (2008), 89-111.

GG7070. Gordon, Lewis R.: "Sartre and Black existentialism." In 7042.

GG7071. Guérin, Jeanyves: "Sartre anticommuniste honteux: *Les Mains sales*." In 456, 75-87.

GG7072. Gyllenhammer, Paul: "A despairing duty: the non-reciprocal dimension to Sartre's ethics," *Philosophy Today*, vol. 52, no. 2 (Summer 2008), 165-172.

GG7073. Hamel, Yan: "Ce monsstre sureuropéen, l'Amérique du Nord. Jean-Paul Sartre, les Etats-Unis et la Guerre froide." In 527, 71-85.

GG7074. Hamel, Yan: "Jean-Paul Sartre en colère: autour des 'Animaux malades de la rage'." In 564, 95-100.

GG7075. Hamel, Yan: "Scènes de la vie (anti)américaine. Autour de *La putain respectueuse* de Jean-Paul Sartre," *Etudes Littéraires*, vol. 39, no. 1 (hiver 2008), 99-111.

GG7076. Jakubczuk, Renata: "Relations familiales dans le théâtre de Jean-Paul Sartre." In 571, 303-313.

GG7077. Judaken, Jonathan: "Sartre on racism: from existential phenomenology to globalization and 'the new racism'." In 7042.

GG7078. Kritzman, Lawrence D.: "Hauntological mater and Sartre's family romance." In 449, 179-206.

GG7079. Labidi, Najet: "Mimesis et catharsis dans *Huis clos* de J.-P. Sartre," *Cahiers de Tunisie*, tome 60, no. 196 (1er trim. 2006), 57-69.

GG7080. Leak, Andy: "Creation as non-communication: reflections on the space of creativity in Sartre and Winnicott," *Sartre Studies International*, vol. 14, no. 1 (2008), 1-12.

GG7081. Longuenesse, Béatrice: "Self-consciousness and self-reference: Sartre and Wittgenstein," *European Journal of Philosophy*, vol. 16, no. 1 (April 2008), 1-21.

GG7082. Louette, Jean-François: " 'La chambre' de Sartre, ou la folie de Voltaire," *Poétique*, no. 153 (févr. 2008), 41-61.

GG7083. Lübecker, Nikolaj: "Sartre's silence: limits of recognition in *Why Write?*," *Sartre Studies International*, vol. 14, no. 1 (2008), 42-57.

GG7084. Martin, Jean-Pierre: "L'autodissolution. Benny Lévy et le dernier Sartre," *Critique*, tome 64, no. 739 (déc. 2008), 931-943.

GG7085. Martinot, Steve: "Skin for sale: race and *The respectful prostitute*." In 7042.

GG7086. Melican, Brian; Edward Maxwell: "The ethics of food and environmental challenges." In 828, 207-219.

GG7087. Meyer, Matthew; Gregory J. Schneider: "Being-in-*The Office*: Sartre, the look, and the viewer." In 968.

GG7088. Meyers, Mark: "Liminality and the problem of being-in-the-world: reflections on Sartre and Merleau-Ponty," *Sartre Studies International*, vol. 14, no. 1 (2008), 78-105. [Merleau-Ponty]

GG7089. Monahan, Michael J.: "Sartre's *Critique of dialectical reason* and the inevitability of violence," *Sartre Studies International*, vol. 14, no. 2 (2008), 48-70.

GG7090. More, Mabogo P.: "Sartre and South African apartheid." In 7042.

GG7091. Morelli, Eric James: "Pure reflection and intentional process: the foundation of Sartre's phenomenological ontology," *Sartre Studies International*, vol. 14, no. 1 (2008), 61-77.

GG7092. Murchland, Bernard: "The desire to be God: Sartre and the winding roads of freedom." In 966.

GG7093. Payen, Eric de: "Jean-Paul Sartre, un esprit controversé," *Universitas*, vol. 35, no. 3 (March 2008), 19-35.

GG7094. Pinheiro Machado, Roberto: "Nothingness and the work of art: a comparative approach to existential phenomenology and the ontological foundation of aesthetics," *Philosophy East and West*, vol. 58, no. 3 (April 2008), 244-266.

GG7095. Quinney, Anne: " 'Il faudrait qu'elle soit belle et dure comme de l'acier':

Sartre and the problem of writing," *Dalhousie French Studies*, vol. 83 (Summer 2008), 69-79.

GG7096. Redfern, Walter: "Drôle de philosophie: Sartre." In 568.

GG7097. Rieger, Dietmar: " 'Können wir so erlöst warden?'. Das Problem von Schuld und Reue und die 'deutschen' *Mouches* (1947-1948)," *Romantische Zeitschrift für Literaturgeschichte*, 32. Jahrgang, Heft 3-4 (2008), 343-373.

GG7098. Roudinesco, Elisabeth: "Jean-Paul Sartre: psychoanalysis on the shadowy banks of the Danube." In 976, 33-63.

GG7099. Santoni, Ronald E.: "Is bad faith necessarily social?," *Sartre Studies International*, vol. 14, no. 2 (2008), 23-39.

GG7100. Servoise-Vicherat, Sylvie: "La figure du militant dans *Les Chemins de la liberté*." In 456, 89-99.

GG7101. Silverman, Max: " 'Killing me softly': racial ambivalence in Jean-Paul Sartre's *Réflexions sur la question juive*." In 924.

GG7102. Solomon, Robert C.: "Are we victims of circumstances?: Hegel and Jean-Paul Sartre on corporate responsibility and bad faith." In 811.

GG7103. Stephens, Bradley: "Jean-Paul Sartre, John Steinbeck and the liability of liberty in the post-war period," *Journal of European Studies*, vol. 38, no. 2 (June 2008), 177-192.

GG7104. Suleiman, Susan Rubin: " 'Choosing our past': Jean-Paul Sartre as memoirist of Occupied France." In 600.

GG7105. Tamassia, Paolo: "Hélène dans *Les Troyennes*: entre Euripide et Sartre." In 482, 355-367.

GG7106. Thys, Michel: "Fenomenologie van de fascinatie. Een dialog met Sartre," *Tijdschrift voor Filosofie*, 70ste Jaargang, Nr. 2 (2008), 339-371.

GG7107. Vassilicos, Basil: " 'At what price freedom?': the phenomenological rudiments of Sartre's cost-benefit analysis," *Philosophy Today*, vol. 52, no. 1 (Spring 2008), 36-44.

GG7108. Vaughan, William: "Seriality and Sartre's Marxism." In 988.

GG7109. Wang, Stephen: "Motivation and the establishment of ends in Sartre's act theory," *Sartre Studies International*, vol. 14, no. 1 (2008), 13-25.

SASSINE, Williams. See also 637a.

GG7110. Riesz, Janós: "L'utopie pédagogique dans *Saint Monsieur Baly* de Williams Sassine." In 127, 287-296.

SATIE, Erik.

GG7111. Dayan, Peter: "Erik Satie's poetry," *Modern Language Review*, vol. 103, part 2 (April 2008), 409-423.

SATRAPI, Marjane. See also 8351.

GG7112. Schlegel, Amy Ingrid: "Marjane Satrapi." In 823.

GG7113. Wedeven Segall, Kimberly: "Melancholy ties: intragenerational loss and exile in *Persepolis*," *Comparative Studies of South Asia, Africa and the Middle East*, vol. 28, no. 1 (2008), 38-49.

SAUMONT, Annie.

GG7114. Anderson, Jean: "Fictions of another world: exotic elements in selected stories by Annie Saumont," *New Zealand Journal of French Studies*, vol. 29, no. 1 (2008), 31-44.

GG7115. Beaumier, Jean-Paul: "Annie Saumont, *Gammes*," *XYZ: La Revue de la Nouvelle*, no. 96 (hiver 2008), 81-82.

SAUSSURE, Ferdinand de. See also 926, 1003.

GG7116. ● *Du côté de chez Saussure.* Ed. Michel Arrivé. Limoges: Lambert-Lucas, 2008. 276 p.

GG7117. ● Mejía Quijano, Claudia: *Le cours d'une vie. Tome I: portrait diachronique de Ferdinand de Saussure.* Nantes: Defaut, 2008. *Psyché.* 391 p.

GG7118. ● Suzuki, Takayoshi: *Saussure à la recherche de l'unité réelle.* Lille: ANRT, 2008. *Thèse à la carte.* 329 p.

GG7119. ● Swiggers, Pierre: *Ferdinand de Saussure et Antoine Meillet devant l'objet de la linguistique générale.* Leuven: Katholieke Univ., Departement Linguistiek, 2008. 35 p.

GG7120.   Flournoy, Olivier: "Sigmund Freud et Ferdinand de Saussure. Convergences, divergences de deux contemporains de génie," *Cahiers Ferdinand de Saussure*, no. 60 (2007), 9-29.

GG7121.   Forel, Claire: "Montrer au maître ce qu'il fait," *Cahiers Ferdinand de Saussure*, no. 60 (2007), 125-137.

GG7122.   Gambarara, Daniele: "Ordre graphique et ordre théorique: présentatioin de F. de Saussure, Ms. fr. 3951/10," *Cahiers Ferdinand de Saussure*, no. 60 (2007), 237-280.

GG7123.   Jäger, Ludwig: "Aposème und Parasème: das Spiel der Zeichen: Saussures semiologische Skizzen in den 'Notes'," *Zeitschrift für Semiotik*, Band 30, Heft 1-2 (2008), 49-71.

GG7124.   Koerner, E. F. K.: "Hermann Paul and general linguistic theory," *Language Sciences*, vol. 30, no. 1 (Jan. 2008), 102-132.

GG7125.   Lo Piparo, Franco: "Saussure et les Grecs," *Cahiers Ferdinand de Saussure*, no. 60 (2007), 139-162.

GG7126.   Marchese, Maria Pia: "Tra biografia e teoria: due inediti di Saussure del 1893," *Cahiers Ferdinand de Saussure*, no. 60 (2007), 217-235.

GG7127.   Mejía Quijano, Claudia: "L'adresse et l'écoute, la dualité de la parole. A propos d'un texte politique dans le Ms. fr. 3951/10," *Cahiers Ferdinand de Saussure*, no. 60 (2007), 281-299.

GG7128.   Reznik, Vladislava: "A long rendezvous: Aleksandr Romm's unpublished works on Ferdinand de Saussure," *Slavonic and East European Review*, vol. 86, no. 1 (Jan. 2008), 1-25.

GG7129.   Romagnoli, Chiara: "A new Chinese translation of the *CLG*," *Cahiers Ferdinand de Saussure*, no. 60 (2007), 191-216.

GG7130.   Wasik, Zdzislaw: "Metaphors of form and substance in the academic discourse on language." In 770, 87-98.

SCALÉSI, Mario.

GG7131.   Brunel, Pierre: "Mario Scalési, nouveau poète maudit. Perspectives comparatistes," *Revue de Littérature Comparée*, no. 327 [no. 3] (juillet-sept. 2008), 351-365.

SCHEHADÉ, Georges. See also 1009.

GG7132.   • Hatem, Jad: *Phénoménologie de la création poétique*. Paris: L'Harmattan, 2008. *Philosophie en commun*. 190 p.

GG7133.   Bourkhis, Ridha: "La phrase de Georges Schehadé." In 556.

GG7134.   Calargé, Carla: "*Poésies I* et *II* de Georges Schéhadé_: essai d'une étude scripturale," *French Review*, vol. 81, no. 5 (April 2008), 955-966.

GG7135.   Rustom, Pauline: "Le langage dans le théâtre de Schehadé: une répercussion de l'absurde," *Interculturel Francophonies*, no. 14 (2008), 103-119.

SCHÉHADÉ, Laurice.

GG7136.   Chemla, Yves: "Laurice Schéhadé, 'confidente miraculeuse' de l'âpreté des êtres," *Interculturel Francophonies*, no. 14 (2008), 203-215.

SCHEINERT, David.

GG7137.   Rocton, Nicole: "L'empreinte biblique dans l'œuvre de David Scheinert." In 443, 165-174.

SCHLUMBERGER, Jean. See 3535.

SCHMITT, Eric-Emmanuel. See also 711.

GG7138.   Jullien, Claudia: "Eric-Emmanuel Schmitt, *La Nuit de Valognes*." In 432, 185-194.

GG7139.   Rabsztyn, Andrzej: "Eric-Emmanuel Schmitt ou les voies nouvelles du roman par lettres après 2000," *Cuadernos de Filologia Francesa*, no. 19 (2008), 203-212.

SCHUHL, Jean-Jacques.

GG7140.   Pollin, Karl: "De la mise à nu de quelques poupées mécaniques: l'objet du désir dans les fictions de Jean-Jacques Schuhl," *Revue des Sciences Humaines*, no. 289 [no. 1] (2008), 177-188.

SCHWARZ-BART, André.

GG7141.   Alou, Antoinette Tidjani: "Marine origins and anti-marine tropism in the French Caribbean." In 122, 350-364. [S. Schwarz-Bart]

GG7142. Gyssels, Kathleen: "André Schwarz-Bart: héritage et héritiers dans la diaspora africaine," *Pardès*, no. 44 (2008), 149-173.

GG7143. Kaufmann, Francine: "L'œuvre juive et l'œuvre noire d'André Schwarz-Bart," *Pardès*, no. 44 (2008), 137-148.

SCHWARZ-BART, Simone. See also 70, 242, 2868, 7141.

GG7144. ● Aïta, Mariella: *Simone Schwarz-Bart dans la poétique du réel merveilleux*. Paris: L'Harmattan, 2008. *Critiques littéraires*. 276 p.

GG7145. Britton, Celia: "Living by mistake: individual and community in Simone Schwarz-Bart's *Pluie et vent sur Télumée Miracle*." In 51, 55-73.

GG7146. Constant, Isabelle: "Interview de Simone Schwarz-Bart sur le rêve." In 59, 215-231.

GG7147. Constant, Isabelle: "Le rêve et l'oralité: les chroniques oniriques dans l'œuvre de Simone Schwarz-Bart." In 59, 125-144.

GG7148. Heady, Margaret: "The identity quest of *Ti Jean L'Horizon*: returning to the point of entanglement." In 86, 92-112.

GG7149. Kandji, Alioune Badara: "Enfance et ordre coloniale dans la fiction de Jamaica Kincaid, Jean Rhys et Simone Schwarz-Bart." In 628, 231-243.

GG7150. Paravisini-Gebert, Lizabeth: "Simone Schwarz-Bart's *The bridge of beyond*." In 114.

SCHWOB, Marcel. See also 899, 4956.

GG7151. ● García Jurado, Francisco: *Marcel Schwob: antiguos imaginarios*. Madrid: ELR, 2008. 176 p.

GG7152. ● Schwob, Marcel: *Cœur double; Le livre de Monelle*. Prés., notes, chronologie et bibliographie par Jean-Pierre Bertrand. Paris: Flammarion, 2008. *GF*. 337 p.

GG7153. Dufournet, Jean: "Marcel Schwob et Villon." In 815, 121-161.

GG7154. Fabre, Bruno: "Des vies insolites: les *Vies imaginaires* de Marcel Schwob." In 439, 147-158.

GG7155. Fabre, Bruno: "Un hommage à Marcel Schwob: 'Epitafio' de Juan José Arreola," *Spicilège: Cahiers Marcel Schwob*, no. 1 (2008), 35-39.

GG7156. Fabre, Bruno: "Présences de François Villon dans *Vies imaginaires* de Marcel Schwob," *Spicilège: Cahiers Marcel Schwob*, no. 1 (2008), 11-22.

GG7157. Ghander, Amany: "Diversité générique dans les récits de *Cœur double*," *Spicilège: Cahiers Marcel Schwob*, no. 1 (2008), 45-53.

GG7158. Lassus, Jean-Marie: "Marcel Schwob et l'Amérique latine," *Spicilège: Cahiers Marcel Schwob*, no. 1 (2008), 23-33.

GG7159. Lhermitte, Agnès: " 'L'Art' de Marcel Schwob (1896): une controverse imaginaire," *Otrante*, no. 22 (2007), 117-127.

GG7160. Lhermitte, Agnès: "Lettre de Maurice Schwob à Henry Brokman," *Spicilège: Cahiers Marcel Schwob*, no. 1 (2008), 55-57.

GG7161. Lhermitte, Agnès: "Marcel Schwob à Paris," *Spicilège: Cahiers Marcel Schwob*, no. 1 (2008), 59-68.

SCUTENAIRE, Louis.

GG7162. Hussey, Andrew: "The splendours of hatred: Louis Scutenaire between surrealism and situationism." In 79, 190-198.

SEBBAR, Leïla. See also 183, 339.

GG7163. Howell, Jennifer: "Reconstituting cultural memory through image and text in Leïla Sebbar's *Le Chinois vert d'Afrique*," *French Cultural Studies*, vol. 19, no. 1 (Feb. 2008), 57-70.

GG7164. Leinen, Frank: "Beyond the roots, beyond Orientalism: innovative conceptions of personal and cultural identity in Leïla Sebbar's *Shérazade*." In 534, 119-135.

GG7165. Redfield, James Adam: "Cultural identitiy from *habitus* to *au-delà*: Leïla Sebbar encounters her Algerian father," *Research in African Literatures*, vol. 39, no. 3 (Fall 2008), 51-64.

SEFRIOUI, Ahmed.

GG7166. Riegert, Guy: "Acheminement vers le secret," *Cahiers Henri Bosco*, no. 45-46 (2005-2006), 321-327.

SEGALEN, Victor. See also 497, 699, 1013, 1018, 7737.

GG7167. • Cata, Isabelle: *Le Siddhartha de Victor Segalen: une dés-orientation.* Paris: L'Harmattan, 2008. *Univers théâtral.* 200 p.

GG7168. • Cheng, François: *L'un vers l'autre: en voyage avec Victor Segalen.* Paris: Albin Michel, 2008. 180 p.

GG7169. • Dollé, Marie: *Victor Segalen: le voyageur incertain.* Croissy-Beaubourg: Aden, 2008. *Le cercle des poètes disparus.* 363 p.

GG7170. Dupin, Michèle: "L'œuvre, miroir du lecteur dans *René Leys* de V. Segalen," *Champs du Signe,* no. 22 (2006), 127-138.

GG7171. Zinfert, Maria: "Die kurze Spanne zwischen Aufbruch und Rückkehr: Victor Segalens Reisebuch *Equipée.*" In 613, 195-209.

SEGURA, Mauricio. See 4761.

SEMBÈNE, Ousmane. See also 682, 1322.

GG7172. • *Ousmane Sembène: interviews.* Ed. Annett Busch, Max Annas. Jackson: Univ. Press of Mississippi, 2008. *Conversations with filmmakers.* xxx, 235 p.

GG7173. Adekosan, Akin: "The significance of Ousmane Sembène," *World Literature Today,* vol. 82, no. 1 (Jan.-Feb. 2008), 37-39.

GG7174. Bakari, Imruh: "Ousmane Sembène: 'father of African cinema' (1923-2007)," *Wasafiri,* no. 53 (Spring 2008), 64-65.

GG7175. Case, Frederic Ivor: "L'éthique et l'esthétique chez Ousmane Sembène," *Présence Francophone,* no. 71 (2008), 91-99.

GG7176. Copeland, V. Natasha E.: "Anthills touch the sky: Sembène's topographical aesthetic." In 92, 10-26.

GG7176a. Day, Patrick L.: "Beliefs of a non-believer: spirituality and religion in the films of Ousmane Sembène." In 7976.

GG7177. Day, Patrick L.: "Homeland security: how the community protects the individual from violence in the fiction and films of Ousmane Sembène." In 617, 165-177.

GG7178. Diop, Boubacar Boris: "Ousmane Sembène ou l'art de se jouer du destin," *Présence Francophone,* no. 71 (2008), 8-19.

GG7179. Janis, Michael: "Remembering Sembène: the grandfather of African feminism," *CLA Journal,* vol. 51, no. 3 (March 2008), 248-264.

GG7180. Murphy, David: "Un autre monde est possible: création et résistance dans l'œuvre d'Ousmane Sembène," *Présence Francophone,* no. 71 (2008), 40-55.

GG7181. Niang, Sada: "Du néoréalisme en Afrique: une relecture de *Borom Sarret,*" *Présence Francophone,* no. 71 (2008), 76-90.

GG7182. Owoo, Kwate Nee: "The language of real life: interview with Ousmane Sembène," *Framework,* vol. 49, no. 1 (Spring 2008), 27-29.

GG7183. Petty, Sheila: "Pugnacité et pouvoir: la représentation des femmes dans les films d'Ousmane Sembène," *Présence Francophone,* no. 71 (2008), 20-39.

GG7184. Riesz, Janós: " 'Le dernier voyage du négrier Sirius'. Le roman dans le roman *Le Docker noir.*" In 127, 225-247.

GG7185. Tcheuyap, Alexie: "De la fiction criminelle en Afrique. Relecture des films d'Ousmane Sembène," *Présence Francophone,* no. 71 (2008), 56-75.

GG7186. Thomas, Dominic: "Ousmane Sembène's footprint in context," *International Journal of Francophone Studies,* vol. 11, no. 4 (2008), 657-660.

SEMPRUN, Jorge. See also 420, 525, 3974.

GG7187. • Augstein, Hannah Franziska: *Von Treue und Verrat: Jorge Semprún und sin Jahrhundert.* München: Beck, 2008. 381 p.

GG7188. • Vordermark, Ulrike: *Das Gedächtnis des Todes: die Erfahrung des Konzentrationslagers Buchenwald im Werk Jorge Semprúns.* Köln: Böhlau, 2008. *Europäische Geschichtsdarstellungen,* Band 17. ix, 289 p.

GG7189. Bucarelli, A.: "La lunga genesi di 'Veinte Años y un día' dal racconto di Domingo Dominguín al romanzo di Jorge Semprún," *Rivista di Letterature Moderne e Comparate,* vol. 61, fasc. 2 (aprile-giugno 2008), 185-210.

GG7190. Ette, Ottmar: "Fuga de la vida," *Humboldt,* 50. Jahrgang, Heft 150 (2008), 60-63.

GG7191. Liénard Ortega, María: "Roman familial et donjuanisme chez Jorge Semprún, un écrivain bilingue," *Langues Néo-Latines*, 102e année, no. 2 [no. 345] (juin 2008), 15-30.

GG7192.   Pavis, Marie-Christsine: "Jorge Semprun: le militant du camp." In 456, 253-262.

GG7193.   Rabatel, Alain: "Effacement énonciatif et effets argumentatifs indirects dans l'incipit du *Mort qu'il faut* de Semprún." In 565, 583-594.

GG7194.   Russo, Maria Teresa: "Jorge Semprun: un idioma dall'esilio." In 586, 165-178.

GG7195.   Suleiman, Susan Rubin: "Revision: historical trauma and literary testimony: the Buchenwald memoirs of Jorge Semprun." In 600.

GG7196.   Tanqueiro, Helena; Patricia López López-Gay: "Censorship and the self-translator." In 609, 174-183. [Beauvoir]

GG7197.   Tidd, Ursula: "Exile, language, and trauma in recent autobiographical writing by Jorge Semprun," *Modern Language Review*, vol. 103, part 3 (July 2008), 697-714.

GG7198.   Türschmann, Jörg: "Socialisme délabré et fatalisme littéraire: la 'zone d'Utopie populaire' dans *L'Algarabie* de Jorge Semprun." In 483, 253-269.

SÉNAC, Jean.

GG7199.   Nacer-Khodja, Hamid: "Sénac, Camus, Roy, Audisio . . . jusqu'où la fraternité?" In 515, 257-278. [Audisio, Camus, Roy]

GG7200.   Rivas, Pierre: "Camus, Roblès, Sénac et le triangle identitaire." In 515, 199-209. [Camus, Roblès]

SÉNÉCAL, Patrick.

GG7201.   Brind'Amour, Lucie: "*Sur le seuil*: horreur, psychiatrie et religion." In 120, 238-244.

SENGES, Pierre.

GG7202.   Camus, Audrey: "Anatomie de la fiction: *Veuves au maquillage* de Pierre Senges," *Littérature*, no. 151 (sept. 2008), 21-33.

SENGHOR, Léopold Sédar. See also 227, 260, 318, 7347.

GG7203.   ● Ayala, Luis [et al.]: *Senghor et le socialisme.* Paris: Fondation Jean-Jaurès; L'Harmattan, 2007. 90 p.

GG7204.   ● Dumont, Pierre: *La francophonie autrement, héritage senghorien?.* Préface d'Abdou Diouf. Paris: L'Harmattan, 2008. *Critiques littéraires.* 246 p.

GG7205.   ● Kesteloot, Lilyan: *Comprendre les poèmes de Léopold Sédar Senghor.* Paris: L'Harmattan, 2008. Réédition. 143 p. [Orig. ed., 1986]

GG7206.   ● Lajili, Chaker: *Bourguiba-Senghor: deux géants de l'Afrique.* Paris: L'Harmattan, 2008. *Etudes africaines.* 487 p.

GG7207.   ● *Senghor et sa postérité littéraires: actes du colloque de Cerisy-la-Salle, 27-30 juin 2006.* Textes réunis et prés. par Dominique Ranaivoson. Metz: Univ. Paul Verlaine, Centre de recherches "écritures", 2008. 196 p.

GG7208.   Ananissoh, Théo: "Senghor, hélas." In 7207, 171-182.

GG7209.   Awumey, Edem: "L'Orphée noir et les murs de l'Universel." In 7207, 183-190.

GG7210.   Bachir Diagne, Souleymane: "Bergson in the colony: intuition and duration in the thought of Senghor and Iqbal," *Qui Parle*, vol. 17, no. 1 (Fall-Winter 2008), 125-145. [Bergson]

GG7211.   Bobika, André-Patient: "Henri Lopes et Léopold Sédar Senghor: de la contestation à la célébration." In 7207, 33-40. [Lopes]

GG7212.   Brunel, Pierre: "Grâce(s) noire(s). Au sujet de Baudelaire et Senghor." In 72, 207-220.

GG7213.   Daoud, Mohamed: "Littérature maghrébine et littérature négro-africaine: différence ou indifférence?" In 7207, 135-146.

GG7214.   Delas, Daniel: "Actualité de la négritude ou de la postérité 'américaine' de Senghor." In 7207, 123-134.

GG7215.   Devésa, Jean-Michel: "Senghor aux Antilles." In 7207, 101-121.

GG7216.   Diane, Alioune: "Blancs, hésitations et non-dits dans la poésie senghorienne." In 393, 79-88.

GG7217. Diane, Alioune: "Panser les blessures du temps: Senghor et les valeurs de la poésie." In 521, 13-18.

GG7218. Diawara, Manthia: "David Hammon's *Sheep Raffle* at Dak'Art 2004: reading black art through Léopold Sédar Senghor's Négritude." In 122, 11-19.

GG7219. Ebodé, Eugène: "Mémoires d'outre-ciel." In 7207, 167-170.

GG7220. Gastaldi, Marc: "Horizons senghoriens à l'orée du XXIe siècle." In 96, 77-82.

GG7221. Kandji, Mamadou: "Visage de femmes noires dans la poésie de Langston Hughes et de L. S. Senghor." In 628, 181-195.

GG7222. Lambert, Fernando: "La figure de la femme dans la poésie de Léopold Sédar Senghor," *Nouvelles Etudes Francophones*, vol. 22, no. 1 (printemps 2007), 75-85.

GG7223. Malela, Buata B.: "Le 'rastignaquisme' aofien: Socé et Senghor lamantins." In 102, 137-168.

GG7224. Malela, Buata B.: "Senghor nomothète." In 102, 225-274.

GG7225. Martin-Granel, Nicolas: "Senghor et les écrivains congolais." In 7207, 11-31.

GG7226. Mongo-Mboussa, Boniface: "Peut-on encore célébrer l'Afrique?" In 7207, 41-48.

GG7227. Ndiaye, Ibrahima: "Femme et violence coloniale dans 'Femme nue, femme noire' et 'The Venus Hottentot'." In 628, 163-180.

GG7228. Nganang, Patrice: "Le complexe de Senghor." In 7207, 149-165.

GG7229. Ranaivoson, Dominique: "L'*Anthologie* et ses descendantes." In 7207, 81-100.

GG7230. Ravaloson, Johary: "Senghor et moi ou radotage d'un naïf en bonne compagnie." In 7207, 191-194.

GG7231. Sabourin, Lise; Paul Sabourin: "Le dialogue poétique et francophone de Léopold Sédar Senghor." In 72, 221-238.

GG7232. Saint-Jores, Julien de: "La *primitivité* de Léopold Sédar Senghor." In 7207, 49-79.

GG7233. Scheinowitz, Celina: "Sans erg ni hamada: présentation de l'*Elégie de minuit* de Senghor." In 521, 19-24.

GG7234. Thioune, Birahim: "Evocations de la couleur blanche et parcours d'écriture dans les *Elégies majeures* de Léopold Sédar Senghor." In 393, 39-43.

GG7235. Valantin, Christian: "Léopold Sédar Senghor, tel qu'en lui-même," *Présence Africaine*, no. 174 (2008), 95-99.

SERGE, Victor. See also 595.

GG7236. • Serge, Victor: *Unforgiving years*. Trans. and with an introd. by Richard Greeman. New York: New York Review Books, 2008. xxvi, 341 p.

GG7237. Sontag, Susan: "Unextinguished: the case for Victor Serge." In 868.

SERHANE, Abdelhak. See also 169.

GG7238. • *Abdekhak Serhane: une écriture de l'engagement*. Dir. Khalid Zekri. Paris: L'Harmattan, 2006. 158 p.

SERRES, Michel.

GG7239. • Serres, Michel: *Aufklärungen: fünf Gespräche mit Bruno Latour*. Aus dem Franz. von Gustav Rossler. Berlin: Merve-Verlag, 2008. 300 p.

GG7240. • Serres, Michel: *Conversations on science, culture, and time*. With Bruno Latour; trans. Roxanne Lapidus. Ann Arbor: Univ. of Michigan Press, 2008. *Studies in literature and science*. 204 p.

GG7241. Lueck, Bryan: "Toward a Serresian reconceptualization of Kantian respect," *Philosophy Today*, vol. 52, no. 1 (Spring 2008), 52-59.

SEYNES, Jean-Baptiste de.

GG7242. Lequette, Samuel: " 'Le peu jeté par jour au feu'." In 382, 247-262.

SHIMAZAKI, Aki.

GG7243. Moisan, Clément: "*Hotaru* d'Aki Shimazaki." In 41, 353-358.

SILHOL, Léa.

GG7244. Montoro Araque, Mercedes: "Réécrire les contes aujourd'hui: Léa Silhol ou le ré-enchantement générationnel." In 894, 259-269.

SIMENON, Georges. See also 470, 4507.

GG7245. • Simenon, Georges: *L'homme à barbe et autres nouvelles.* Lecture d'Alain Bertrand. Bruxelles: Luc Pire, 2008. *Espace nord.* 280 p.

GG7246. • Simenon, Georges: *Les obsessions du voyageur.* Textes choisis et commentés par Benoît Denis. Paris: Quinzaine littéraire-Vuitton, 2008. 313 p.

GG7247. • Simenon, Georges: *Tout Maigret 3.* Notes et iconographie de Michel Carly. Paris: Omnibus, 2008. 972 p.

GG7248. • Simenon, Georges: *Tout Maigret. X.* Avant-propos de Dominique Fernandez, Pierre Assouline, Denis Tillinac; notes et iconographie de Michel Carly. Paris: Omnibus, 2008. xv, 766 p.

GG7249. • Simenon, Georges: *The Widow.* Trans. John Petrie; introd. Paul Theroux. New York: New York Review Books, 2008. 152 p.

GG7250. Alavoine, Bernard: "Georges Simenon et Patrick Modiano," *Cahiers Simenon,* no. 22 (2008), 135-147. [Modiano]

GG7251. Baronian, Jean-Baptiste: "L'auto-fiction chez Simenon," *Cahiers Valery Larbaud,* no. 43 (2008), 103-108.

GG7252. Baronian, Jean-Baptiste: "Georges Simenon et Jean Cocteau," *Cahiers Simenon,* no. 22 (2008), 71-79. [Cocteau]

GG7253. Carly, Michel: "Georges Simenon et Jacques Brel," *Cahiers Simenon,* no. 22 (2008), 35-68. [Brel]

GG7254. "Georges Simenon." In 547.

GG7255. Indiana, Gary: "Simenon l'incroyable." In 485.

GG7256. Lemoine, Michel: "Georges Simenon et Pierre Assouline," *Cahiers Simenon,* no. 22 (2008), 9-33. [Assouline]

GG7257. Mercier, Paul: "Georges Simenon et Sir Arthur Conan Doyle," *Cahiers Simenon,* no. 22 (2008), 81-132.

GG7258. Meyer, Jean-Paul: "Trois aspects du décadrage dans la relation texte-image. L'exemple de *Maigret tend un piège* dessiné par Philippe Wurm," *Degrés,* 36e année, no. 133 (printemps 2008), a1-a18.

GG7259. Ousselin, Edward: "La panique de M. Hire," *Cincinnati Romance Review,* vol. 26 (2007), 63-78.

GG7260. Pochet, Jean-Michel: "Georges Simenon ou 'Georges Simenon'," *Cahiers Simenon,* no. 22 (2008), 185-192.

GG7261. Schepens, Michel: "Georges Simenon et Stanislas-André Steeman," *Cahiers Simenon,* no. 22 (2008), 149-182. [Steeman]

SIMEONE, Bernard.

GG7262. Guermès, Sophie: " 'Une vibration aux abords du rien'. La passion de Bernard Simeone," *Francofonia,* n. 55 (autunno 2008), 49-63.

SIMON, Claude. See also 711, 6409, 6423.

GG7263. • *Géorgiques [Les]: une forme, un monde.* Textes réunis et prés. par Jean-Yves Laurichesse. Caen: Lettres modernes Minard, 2008. *Revue des Lettres Modernes; Claude Simon,* 5. 259 p.

GG7264. • *Triptyques [Les] de Claude Simon; ou, l'art du montage.* Mireille Calle-Gruber, éd. Paris: Presses Sorbonne Nouvelle, 2008. 216 p.

GG7265. • Zemmour, David: *Une syntaxe du sensible: Claude Simon et l'écriture de la perception.* Préface de Georges Molinié. Paris: PUPS, 2008. *Travaux de stylistique et de linguistique françaises.* 377 p.

GG7266. Alexandre, Didier: " 'Le fin dessin . . . sur le fond noir'. Le récit malgré le monde dans *Les Géorgiques.*" In 7263, 49-79.

GG7267. Alexandre, Didier: "Quelques réflexions sur les relations de Claude Simon à Jean-Paul Sartre," *Cahiers Claude Simon,* no. 3 (2007), 87-104. [Sartre]

GG7268. Barthélémy, Lambert: " 'Pastoral hide and seek'. Sur la déconstruction de l'univers pastoral." In 506, 61-69.

GG7269. Bertrand, Michel: "De *Hommage à la Catalogne* aux *Géorgiques.*" In 7263, 97-114.

GG7270. Bertrand, Michel: "Formes et enjeux des inscriptions historiques dans *La Bataille de Pharsale* de Claude Simon." In 904, 229-244.

GG7271. Bertrand, Michel: "Inscriptions de l'Histoire dans *L'Herbe* de Claude Simon," *Cahiers Claude Simon*, no. 4 (2008), 111-126.

GG7272. Bertrand, Michel: "Militant, milicien, militaire: le brouillage des signes orchestré par *Les Géorgiques*." In 456, 241-252.

GG7273. Bertrand, Michel: "Rythmes de la guerre et cycles de la terre dans *Les Géorgiques* de Claude Simon." In 459, 269-279.

GG7274. Blanc, Anne-Lise: "Le désastre des événements dans quelques romans de Claude Simon." In 590, 255-270.

GG7275. Blanc, Anne-Lise: "La perspective des ombres." In 7263, 185-208.

GG7276. Bonhomme, Bérénice: "Pour une narration cinématographique de l'Histoire: *La Route des Flandres* de Claude Simon." In 904, 245-257.

GG7277. Camproux, Charles: "La langue et le style des écrivains," *Cahiers Claude Simon*, no. 4 (2008), 129-136.

GG7278. Cazalas, Inès: "Jeux de surimpression: la figure de l'oncle dans l'univers romanesque de Claude Simon." In 572, 305-314.

GG7279. Duncan, Alistair B.: "*L'Acacia* de Claude Simon: roman de deux guerres." In 473, 277-289.

GG7280. Duncan, Alistair B.: "Le 'Claude Simon' de Charles Camproux," *Cahiers Claude Simon*, no. 4 (2008), 137-139.

GG7281. Ferrato-Combe, Brigitte: "Variations sur le tracé et les formes graphiques dans *Les Géorgiques*." In 7263, 161-181.

GG7282. Genazino, Wilhelm: "L'absence des recettes comme recette," *Cahiers Claude Simon*, no. 3 (2007), 141-144.

GG7283. Hell, Bodo: "Lisant dans un paysage," *Cahiers Claude Simon*, no. 4 (2008), 143-149.

GG7284. Houppermans, Sjef: "Par terre et par mer: voyages parallèles." In 7263, 81-96.

GG7285. Isolery, Jacques: "Faire œuvre avec le contre." In 7263, 19-48.

GG7286. Julien, Anne-Yvonne: "Le dire du 'Rien' dans *L'Herbe*," *Cahiers Claude Simon*, no. 4 (2008), 95-110.

GG7287. Klinkert, Thomas: "Claude Simon et la mémoire traumatisée." In 611.

GG7288. Labat-Yapaudjian, Cécile: "Ecriture, deuil et mélancolie dans les derniers textes de Samuel Beckett, Robert Pinget et Claude Simon," *Cahiers Claude Simon*, no. 3 (2007), 153-154. [Beckett, Pinget]

GG7289. Laurichesse, Jean-Yves: "Une météorologie poétique. Le génie du froid dans *Les Géorgiques*." In 7263, 135-160.

GG7290. Louette, Jean-François: "Claude Simon et Sartre: les premiers romans," *Cahiers Claude Simon*, no. 3 (2007), 63-85. [Sartre]

GG7291. Luzi, Christophe: "L'archive simonienne," *Cahiers Claude Simon*, no. 3 (2007), 151-153.

GG7292. Michel, Christian: " 'Des rigoles de sang blanc': du graffiti au palimpseste, selon l'analogie: les corps conducteurs de Claude Simon," *Elseneur*, no. 23 (2008), [n.p.].

GG7293. Nitsch, Wolfram: "Une poétique de la dépense: Claude Simon et le Collège de sociologie," *Cahiers Claude Simon*, no. 4 (2008), 33-52.

GG7294. Nuti, Marco: "Entre lisible et visible: convergences cézanniennes chez Claude Simon." In 542, 123-135.

GG7295. Péroz, Pierre: "*Ouais* dans *La Route des Flandres*: essai de sémantique lexicale appliquée." In 619, 429-460.

GG7296. Renaud, Aurélie: "L'Espagne de Claude Simon sous la lumière de Georges Bataille," *Cahiers Claude Simon*, no. 4 (2008), 53-74. [Bataille]

GG7297. Rioux-Watine, Marie-Albane: "Claude Simon: la mélancolie ou comment parler de la ruine." In 902, 51-67.

GG7298. Rioux-Watine, Marie-Albane: "Le dialogue simonien," *Cahiers Claude Simon*, no. 3 (2007), 23-41.

GG7299. Roubichou, Gérard: "*L'Herbe* face à la critique," *Cahiers Claude Simon*, no. 4 (2008), 77-93.

GG7300. Sarkonak, Ralph: "Claude Simon et la Shoah." In 7263, 209-226.

GG7301. Schoentjes, Pierre: " 'Et voilà la gueerre! Une foutue saloperie!'. Lire la guerre dans *Les Géorgiques*." In 7263, 115-133.

GG7302. Solte-Gresser, Christiane: "Expérience historique et refus historiographique: la perception de la Seconde Guerre mondiale chez Claude Simon et Madeleine Bourdouxhe." In 483, 197-210. [Bourdouxhe]

GG7303. Viart, Dominique: "Sartre-Simon: de la 'littérature engagée' aux 'fictions critiques'," *Cahiers Claude Simon*, no. 3 (2007), 105-126.

GG7304. Yocaris, Ilias: "La discohérence dans *Triptyque* et *Leçon des choses* de Claude Simon." In 410, 399-408.

GG7305. Yocaris, Ilias: "Vers un nouveau langage romanesque: le collage citationnel dans *La Bataille de Pharsale* de Claude Simon," *Revue Romane*, vol. 43, no. 2 (2008), 303-327.

GG7306. Zemmour, David: "Les 'phrases' de Claude Simon," *Cahiers Claude Simon*, no. 3 (2007), 43-59.

SIMON, Njami.

GG7307. Gehrmann, Susanne: "Differenz und Neurose. Schwarze Männlichkeit im transkulturellen Roman: *African gigolo*." In 440, 205-220.

SIMON, Yves. See 5647.

SINADINO, Agostino John.

GG7308. ● Claudel, Paul-André: *Le poète sans visage: sur les traces du symboliste A. J. Sinadino (1876-1956)*. Paris: PUPS, 2008. 409 p.

SISSOKO, Fily Dabo. See also 151.

GG7309. Azarian, Viviane: "*La savane rouge* comme roman de formation." In 72, 299-325.

SKIF, Hamid. See 1851.

SOLLERS, Philippe. See also 760, 4533.

GG7310. Sollers, Philippe: "La littérature, ou le nerf de la guerre," *Études*, 152e année, no. 4085 (mai 2008), 649-661. [Entretien]

GG7311. Thomas, Yves: "*Les dernières nuits de Paris*: le café dans le salon." In 564, 63-75.

SOUCY, Gaétan.

GG7312. Piccione, Marie-Lyne: "Quand l'iconoclasme s'égare: *L'Immaculée Conception* de Gaétan Soucy." In 69, 159-164.

GG7313. Xanthos, Nicolas: "*Music-Hall!* de Gaétan Soucy." In 41, 359-377.

SOUPAULT, Philippe. See also 4657.

GG7314. Russo, Adelaide M.: "La médiation dans la critique artistique de Philippe Soupault." In 583, 83-105.

SOUVESTRE, Pierre. See 1185, 1186, 1187, 8189.

SOUZA, Carl de.

GG7315. Joubert, Jean-Louis: "Histoires de familles, généalogie et parenté dans le roman mauricien." In 72, 575-587.

STEEMAN, Stanislas-André. See also 7261.

GG7316. Huftier, Arnaud: "Vertiges de la série: M. Wens de S.-A. Steeman ou réécrire la répétition." In 506, 383-395.

STÉFAN, Jude.

GG7317. Andriot-Saillant, Caroline: "*Laures* de Jude Stéfan: l'intertextualité entre origine et transgression." In 506, 295-307.

GG7318. Di Meo, Philippe: "*Pandectes*, de J. Stéfan," *Nouvelle Revue Française*, no. 587 (oct. 2008), 200-202.

STEPHENSON, Élie. See 334.

STÉTIÉ, Salah. See also 1009, 4233.

GG7319. ● Annese, Venanzia: *Poésie et "permanences": lire Salah Stétié*. Fasano: Schena, 2008. *Biblioteca della ricerca*. 136 p.

GG7320. Brunel, Pierre: "Une heure avec Salah Stétié: entretien." In 61, 9-30.

GG7321. Del Fiol, Maxime: "L'Islam culturel de Salah Stétié dans la langue française: l'arabesque et le *Coran*," *Interculturel Francophonies*, no. 14 (2008), 35-49.

STIL, André.

GG7322. Deguy, Jacques: "André Stil ou le mineur en chanteur de jazz," *Nord'*, no. 51 (2008), 19-22.

GG7323. Eychart, Marie-Thérèse: "Destins de femmes dans le pays des mines," *Nord'*, no. 51 (2008), 23-33.

GG7324. Gillet, Claude: "André Stil ou l'art de la nouvelle," *Nord'*, no. 51 (2008), 51-58.

GG7325. Gillet, Claude: "André Stil, une vie à lutter et/ou à écrire: bio-bibliographie," *Nord'*, no. 51 (2008), 5-18.

GG7326. Renard, Paul: "*Dieu est un enfant* ou comment retrouver le langage de l'enfance," *Nord'*, no. 51 (2008), 35-40.

GG7327. Renard, Paul: "Stil vu (et débiné) par Jacques Henric," *Nord'*, no. 51 (2008), 41-49.

SUARÈS, André.

GG7328. Baron, Philippe: "Une correspondence André Suarès-Emile Fabre," *Revue d'Histoire du Théâtre*, no. 239 [no. 3] (2008), 209-252.

GG7329. Bernon-Bruley, Pauline: "Regards croisés sur la Croix. Esthétiques spirituelles de la Passion: Suarès-Rouault," *Travaux de Littérature*, tome 21 (2008), 411-426.

SULIVAN, Jean. See also 4373.

GG7330. ● Maher, Eamon: *Jean Sulivan, 1913-1980: la marginalité dans la vie et l'œuvre*. Paris: L'Harmattan, 2008. *Espaces littéraires*. 223 p.

GG7331. Maher, Eamon: "Spirituality on the margins: the writings of Jean Sulivan," *Nottingham French Studies*, vol. 47, no. 1 (Spring 2008), 32-42.

GG7332. Gormaile, Pádraig: "Entre activisme et mysticisme: les coulisses de la pensée chrétienne chez Jean Sulivan." In 618.

SUPERVIELLE, Jules. See also 420, 5903.

GG7333. ● Dewulf, Sabine: *La fable du monde de Jules Supervielle*. Paris: Bertrand-Lacoste, 2008. *Parcours de lecture*. 127 p.

GG7334. Aranjo, Daniel: "Jules Supervielle entre Oloron et Montevideo," *Babel*, no. 18 (2008), 133-149.

GG7335. Davaille, Florence: "Comment devient-on un 'poète de la NRF'? les hommes de la revue, leurs lettres et Jules Supervielle," *Epistolaire: Revue de l'AIRE*, no. 34 (2008), 71-79.

TADJO, Véronique. See also 186.

GG7336. Anyinefa, Koffi; Micheline Rice-Maximin: "Entretien avec Véronique Tadjo, écrivaine ivoirienne," *French Review*, vol. 82, no. 2 (Dec. 2008), 368-382.

GG7337. Dahouda, Kanate: " 'Rendre hommage à la vie'. Entretien avec Véronique Tadjo, écrivaine ivoirienne," *Nouvelles Etudes Francophones*, vol. 22, no. 2 (automne 2007), 179-186.

GG7338. Griffin, Jenelle: "Responding to the shadows: reimagining subjectivity in Tadjo's *L'Ombre d'Imana*," *Women in French Studies*, no. 16 (2008), 113-126.

TAILLANDIER, François.

GG7339. Taillandier, François: " 'Mon roman sert à explorer'," *Presse Littéraire*, no. 14 (2008), 71-88. [Entretien]

TARDE, Gabriel.

GG7340. Debaise, Didier: "Une métaphysique des possessions. Puissances et sociétés chez Gabriel Tarde," *Revue de Métaphysique et de Morale*, no. 4 (oct. 2008), 447-460.

TARDIEU, Jean. See also 548, 1119.

GG7341. Farasse, Gérard: "Monsieur Monsieur Tardieu." In 454, 145-160.

TARDON, Raphaël. See 733.

TAURIAC, Michel. See 733.

TCHAK, Sami.

GG7342. Husti Laboye, Carmen: "Ecriture et déchirement. L'individu postmoderne dans *Hermina* de Sami Tchak," *Itinéraires et Contacts de Cultures*, no. 39 (2007), 49-59.

TCHIBAMBA, Paul Lomami.

GG7343. Mongo-Mboussa, Boniface: "De l'Oubangui-Chari aux rives du fleuve Congo: Paul Lomami Tchibamba (1914-1985)," *Cultures Sud*, no. 170 (sept. 2008), 129-134.

TCHICAYA U TAMSI. See also 492, 2542.

GG7344. • Amuri Mpala-Lutebele, Maurice: *Testament de Tchicaya U Tam'si*. Paris: L'Harmattan, 2008. *Comptes rendus*. 257 p.

GG7345. Alem, Kangni: " 'Omoneh': mère dévorante et principe de relation. Approche de la relation poétique dans une nouvelle de Tchicaya U'Tamsi." In 72, 457-466.

GG7346. Bekri, Tahar: "Tchicaya U Tam'si comme un arbre à pain," *Cultures Sud*, no. 171 (déc. 2008), 75-78.

GG7347. Bokiba, André-Patient: "Tchicaya U Tam'si et la negritude senghorienne," *Cultures Sud*, no. 171 (déc. 2008), 85-88. [Senghor]

GG7348. Chalaye, Sylvie: "Les trois coups de théâtre de Tchicaya U Tam'si," *Cultures Sud*, no. 171 (déc. 2008), 69-74.

GG7349. Chemain, Roger: "Quand Gérald parle de Tchicaya," *Cultures Sud*, no. 171 (déc. 2008), 79-80.

GG7350. Chevrier, Jacques: "Le fonctionnaire et l'écrivain," *Cultures Sud*, no. 171 (déc. 2008), 39-42.

GG7351. Chiappano, Nino: "Fragments d'un portrait enfoui," *Cultures Sud*, no. 171 (déc. 2008), 33-38.

GG7352. Delas, Daniel: "Du faux, du sale et du ventre. De la poésie de Tchicaya U Tam'si," *Cultures Sud*, no. 171 (déc. 2008), 63-68.

GG7353. Douaire, Anne: " 'On n'a plus de totem/alcool à gogo': l'écriture de la béance chez Tchicaya U Tam'si." In 72, 433-454.

GG7354. Garnier, Xavier: "Le roman familial des 'morts-vivants'," *Cultures Sud*, no. 171 (déc. 2008), 51-56.

GG7355. Lopes, Henri: "Le Congo intérieur de Tchicaya U Tam'si," *Cultures Sud*, no. 171 (déc. 2008), 13-16.

GG7356. Martin-Granel, Nicolas: "Prophète malgré lui," *Cultures Sud*, no. 171 (déc. 2008), 89-96.

GG7357. Monenembo, Tierno: "L'isolé soleil," *Cultures Sud*, no. 171 (déc. 2008), 29-32.

GG7358. Mongo-Mboussa, Boniface: "Tchicaya, le mal-aimé," *Cultures Sud*, no. 171 (déc. 2008), 97-100.

GG7359. Mouralis, Bernard: "Tchicaya et l'écriture de l'histoire," *Cultures Sud*, no. 171 (déc. 2008), 57-62.

GG7360. Naumann, Michel: "Mémoire, poésie et libération dans une nouvelle-poème de Tchicaya U Tam'si." In 103, 229-238.

GG7361. Safou Tchimanga, Raphaël: " 'Gérald, mon frère'. Entretien avec Mambou Aimée Gnali," *Cultures Sud*, no. 171 (déc. 2008), 43-47.

GG7362. Safou Tchimanga, Raphaël: "Le poète et son pays intérieur. Entretien avec Jean-Baptiste Tati Loutard," *Cultures Sud*, no. 171 (déc. 2008), 17-20.

GG7363. Sorel, Jacqueline: "U Tam'si: esquisse pour un portrait de Tchicaya en huit visions," *Cultures Sud*, no. 171 (déc. 2008), 101-106.

GG7364. "Témoignages," *Cultures Sud*, no. 171 (déc. 2008), 107-120.

GG7365. Yengo, Patrice: "Tchicaya U Tam'si et la parenthèse de Kin," *Cultures Sud*, no. 171 (déc. 2008), 21-28.

TEILHARD DE CHARDIN, Pierre. See also 5406.

GG7366. • Aczel, Amir D.: *The Jesuit and the skull: Teilhard de Chardin, evolution, and the seaarch for Peking Man.* New York: Riverhead Books, 2008. 302 p.

GG7367. • Boudignon, Patrice: *Pierre Teilhard de Chardin.* Paris: Cerf, 2008. 431 p.

GG7368. • Dupleix, André; Evelyne Maurice: *Christ présent et universel: la vision christologique de Teilhard de Chardin.* Paris: Mame-Desclée, 2008. 378 p.

GG7369. • Honoré, Bernard: *Lecture de Teilhard de Chardin: l'ouverture de la pensée et de la foi.* Saint-Etienne: Aubin, 2008. *Science et spiritualité.* 223 p.

GG7370. • Honoré, Bernard: *Résonances: avec Heidegger et Teilhard de Chardin.* Saint-Etienne: Aubin, 2008. *Science et spiritualité.* 243 p.

GG7371. • King, Thomas M.: *Believers and their disbelief: St. Thérèse of Lisieux, Mother Teresa, and Teilhard.* Chambersburg, PA: American Teilhard Assn., 2008. *Teilhard Studies*, 57. 26 p.

GG7372. • Teilhard de Chardin, Pierre: *Lettres à Edouard Le Roy (1921-1946): maturation d'une pensée.* Introd. François Euvé. Paris: Facultés jésuites de Paris, 2008. 160 p.

GG7373. • *Terre [La] est mon pays: "Au ciel par l'achèvement de la terre," Pierre Teilhard de Chardin.* Bernard Pierrat [et al.]. Saint-Etienne: Aubin, 2008. 121 p.

GG7374. • Vilas, Franklin E.: *Teilhard and Jung: a cosmic and psychic convergence.* Chambersburg, PA: American Teilhard Assn., 2008. *Teilhard Studies*, 56. 30 p.

GG7375. Glick, Thomas F.: "Miquel Crusafont, Teilhard de Chardin and the reception of the synthetic theory in Spain." In 859, 553-568.

GG7376. Miller, Lucien: "Boundary crossings: fieldwork, the hidden self, and the invisible spirit." In 594, 216-243.

TESSON, Stéphanie.

GG7377. Tesson, Stéphanie: *A nous d'œufs.* Paris: Avant-Scène Théâtre, 2008. *Avant-Scène Théâtre*, no. 1237 (1er févr. 2008). 95 p.

THARAUD, Jean et Jérôme. See 3722.

THÉRIAULT, Marie-José. See 546.

THÉRIAULT, Yves.

GG7378. • Benson, Mark: *La quête érotique d'Yves Thériault.* Berne; New York: Peter Lang, 2008. x, 224 p.

GG7379. • Thériault, Yves: *Agaguk.* Dossier rédigé par Renald Bérubé. Paris: Adonis, 2008. *Romans de toujours*. 64 p.

GG7380. • Thériault, Yves: *Contes pour un homme seul.* Préface de Laurent Mailhot. Longueuil, QC: Le dernier havre, 2008. 173 p.

GG7381. • *Yves Thériault: le pari de l'écriture.* Catalogue for an exhibition held at the Grande Bibliothèque in Montréal from Sept. 23, 2008 to Jan. 18, 2009. Commissariat, Renald Bérubé, assisté de Francis Langevin. Québec: Presses de l'Univ. Laval, 2008. 172 p.

THIBAULT, Louis-Jean.

GG7382. Bissonnette, Thierry: "Louis-Jean Thibault, *Reculez falaise*," *Liberté*, no. 281 (sept. 2008), 88-90.

THIBON, Gustave.

GG7383. Algange, Luc-Olivier d': "Hommage à Gustave Thibon," *Presse Littéraire*, no. 16 (2008), 79-87.

THIÉRY, Sébastien.

GG7384. • Thiéry, Sébastien: *Cochons d'Inde.* Paris: Avant-Scène Théâtre, 2008. *Avant-Scène Théâtre*, no. 1254 (15 déc. 2008). 94 p.

THOMAS, Henri.

GG7385. • Thomas, Henri: *Carnets, 1934-1948.* Edition établie par Nathalie Thomas; préfacée par Jérôme Prieur; annotée par Luc Autret. Paris: C. Paulhan, 2008. *Pour mémoire*. 717 p.

GG7386. • Thomas, Henri: *Das Vorgebirge.* Aus dem Franz. Paul Celan; hrsg., ergänzt, mit einem Nachwort versehen von Barbara Wiedemann. Frankfurt: Suhrkamp, 2008. 127 p.

GG7387. Autret, Luc: "Entre Henri Thomas et Jean Paulhan," *Théodore Balmoral*, no. 58 (2008), 137-153. [Paulhan]

GG7388. Lombez, Christine: " 'Le labeur des énergies orchestrales de l'esprit': poésie et traduction chez Henri Thomas." In 1026, 187-196.

TILLION, Germaine.

GG7389. • Laroux, Ariane: *Déjeuners chez Germaine Tillion.* Lausanne: L'Age d'homme, 2008. 104 p.

GG7390. • Wood, Nancy: *Germaine Tillion, une femme-mémoire: d'une Algérie à l'autre.* Paris: Autrement, 2008. 251 p.

TITUS-CARMEL, Gérard.

GG7391. • Titus-Carmel, Gérard: *Titus-Carmel: allée, contre-allées: peintures, œuvres sur papier et estampes.* Paris: Réunion des musées nationaux, 2008. Texte de Marik Froidefond. 95 p.

TJIBAOU, Jean-Marie. See 181.

TOPOR, Roland.

GG7392. • *Topor traits.* Réunis par Daniel Colagrossi. Paris: Scali, 2007. 366 p.

GG7393. Boucharenc, Myriam: "En Topor dans le texte," *Mélusine*, no. 28 (2008), 161-174.

GG7394. Pouget, Jean-Pierre: "Le *Don Juan* d'Alexandre Dumas père et celui de Roland Topor." In 432, 159-183.

GG7395. Pujante Gonzalez, Domingo: "*L'Ambigu* de Roland Topor: 'Don Juan séduit par lui-même ou Narcisse retrouvé'." In 432, 157-168.

TOULET, Paul-Jean.

GG7396. ● Martinez, Frédéric: *Prends garde à la douceur des choses: Paul-Jean Toulet, une vie en morceaux.* Paris: Tallandier, 2008. 350 p.

TOUPIN, Catherine-Anne.

GG7397. Bertin, Raymond: "Alice au pays des cauchemars. *A présent*," *Jeu: Cahiers de Théâtre*, no. 128 [no. 3] (2008), 12-14.

TOURANGEAU, Pierre.

GG7398. Gyurcsik, Margareta: "*La dot de la Mère Missel* de Pierre Tourangeau." In 41, 379-403.

TOURNIER, Michel. See also 711, 1845.

GG7399. ● Eickelkamp, Regina: *Reise, Grenze, Erinnerung: Spruen des Verschwindens und die "Erfindung der Wirklichkeit" in ausgewählten Texten Michel Tourniers.* Heidelberg: Winter, 2008. *Studia Romanica.* 299 p.

GG7400. ● Tournier, Michel: *Vendredi ou les limbes du Pacifique.* Dossier et notes réalisés par Marianne Jaeglé; lecture d'image par Olivier Tomasini. Paris: Gallimard, 2008. *Folioplus classiques.* 313 p.

GG7401. Austin de Drouillard, Jean-Raoul: "*Les Météores* ou le mythe gémellaire revisité," *Revue Romane*, vol. 43, no. 1 (2008), 124-135.

GG7402. Boca, Mariana: "Mentalité postmoderne dans *Le Roi des aulnes* de Michel Tournier." In 572, 361-365.

GG7403. Cozic, Alain: "*Le Médianoche amoureux* de M. Tournier: une reprise des *Entretiens d'émigrés allemands* de J. W. Goethe?," *Champs du Signe*, no. 21 (2006), 119-135.

GG7404. Foucart, Claude: "Le triomphe de la curiosité: les écrivains actuels à la recherche des réalités allemandes." In 461, 409-433. [Quignard]

GG7405. Keskinen, Mikko: "Voice doubles: auditory identities in Michel Tournier's *Tristan Vox*." In 493.

GG7406. "Michel Tournier," *Contemporary Literary Criticism*, vol. 249 (2008), 54-184.

GG7407. Nobili, Paola: "Educazione e linguaggio in *Vendredi ou la Vie sauvage* di Michel Tournier." In 423.

GG7408. Pardo Jimenez, Pedro: " 'To read or not to read': sous la piste de Michel Tournier," *Estudios de Lengua y Literatura Francesas*, no. 16 (2005), 83-92.

GG7409. Posthumus, Stephanie: " 'Deux truites frémissant flanc à flanc': le structuralisme et l'écologisme chez Michel Tournier," *Dalhousie French Studies*, vol. 85 (Winter 2008), 167-181.

GG7410. Redfern, Walter: "Approximating man: Michel Tournier's play with language." In 568.

GG7411. Tchumkam, Hervé: "De la dialectique du maître et de l'esclave d'Hegel. De Kojève à *Vendredi ou les limbes du Pacifique* de Michel Tournier." In 99, 179-190.

TOUSSAINT, Jean-Philippe.

GG7412. ● Kauss, Anja: *Der diskrete Chamre der Prokrastination: Aufschub als literarisches Motiv und narrative Strategie.* München: Martin Meidenbauer, 2008. 584 p.

GG7413. Bewes, Timothy: " 'Form resists him': the event of *Zidane's Melancholy*," *New Formations*, no. 62 (Autumn 2007), 18-21.

GG7414. Macey, David: "Un coup de boule n'abolira jamais . . . ," *New Formations*, no. 62 (Autumn 2007), 15-17.

GG7415. Ravindranathan, Thangam: "The song of Zidane," *New Formations*, no. 62 (Autumn 2007), 22-26.

GG7416. Schneider, Ulrike: "Fluchtpunkte des Erzählens. Medialität und Narration in Jean-Philippe Toussaints Roman *Fuir*," *Zeitschrift für Französische Sprache und Literatur*, Band 118, Heft 2 (2008), 141-161.

TOUSSAINT, Patrick.

GG7417.   Dufournet, Jean: "*François Villon et les Dames du temps jadis* de Patrick Toussaint (1959) ou comment écrire un roman populaire sur Villon." In 815, 181-199.

TREMBLAY, Larry. See also 3157.

GG7418.   Olivier, Aurélie: "Les matriochkas de Larry Tremblay," *Jeu: Cahiers de Théâtre*, no. 129 [no. 4] (2008), 7-11.

TREMBLAY, Lise. See also 221, 290, 4762.

GG7419.   Chartier, Daniel: "*La danse juive* de Lise Tremblay." In 41, 405-425.

TREMBLAY, Michel.

GG7420.   Burns, Cory Alan: "Le théâtre de Michel Tremblay et l'impasse communicative dans la relation frère/sœur." In 571, 293-301.

GG7421.   Cardy, Michael: "Michel Tremblay's experiments in naturalist theatre," *Modern Language Review*, vol. 103, part 4 (Oct. 2008), 996-1005.

GG7422.   Klokov, Vassili: "Michel Tremblay, *Les Belles-sœurs*." In 115, 107-115.

GG7423.   Piccione, Marie-Lyne: "*Le trou dans le mur* ou la ville répudiée de Michel Tremblay," *Etudes Canadiennes*, no. 64 (2008), 153-158.

GG7424.   Rabillard, Sheila: "Encore/*en corps*: staging mother in Michel Tremblay's *For the pleasure of seeing her again* and the maternal rhetoric of twentieth-century drama," *Essays in Theatre*, vol. 21, no. 1-2 (Nov. 2002-May 2003), 79-98.

GG7425.   Vigeant, Louise: "Mondes parallèles ou convergents? *Le vrai monde?*," *Jeu: Cahiers de Théâtre*, no. 126 (mars 2008), 42-46.

GG7426.   Yotova, Rennie: "Michel Tremblay." In 115, 167-179.

GG7427.   Zawada, Kinga: "L'espace familial de l'enfermement dans le théâtre de Tremblay: l'exemple de Marcel." In 571, 283-292.

TRIOLET, Elsa.

GG7428.   Bellemare-Page, Stéphanie: "Elsa Triolet: au carrefour des lettres françaises et russes." In 442, 69-76.

GG7429.   Montier, Jean-Pierre: "Effets de cadrage et de décernement dans *Ecoutez-voir* d'Elsa Triolet," *Degrés*, 36e année, no. 133 (printemps 2008), g1-g21.

GG7430.   Van Wesemael, Sabine: "La névrose post-traumatique éclairée par Elsa Triolet et Emile Ajar." In 384, 183-204. [Gary]

TROUILLOT, Evelyne.

GG7431.   Fremin, Marie: "*Rosalie l'Infâme* d'Evelyne Trouillot. Comment inscrire l'esclavage dans la fiction?" In 118, 221-234.

GG7432.   Pessini, Alba: "Insularité: enfermement et ouverture." In 423. [Yannick Lahens]

TROUILLOT, Lyonel. See 281.

TROYAT, Henri. See 727.

TUÉNI, Nadia.

GG7433.   Ippolito, Christophe: "Engendering poetic memory: Nadia Tuéni's *Sentimental Archives of a War in Lebanon*," *LittéRéalité*, vol. 20, no. 2 (automne/hiver 2008), 77-89.

TURCOTTE, Élise.

GG7434.   Caland, Fabienne C.: "La part manquante dans la poésie d'Elise Turcotte." In 69, 31-41.

GG7435.   Oberhuber, Andrea: "*La Maison étrangère* d'Elise Turcotte." In 41, 427-451.

TZARA, Tristan. See also 1068.

GG7436.   ● Tzara, Tristan: *The gas heart: the Dada masterpiece of drama*. Introduction, commentary, staging, and a new translation by Eric v. d. Luft. North Syracuse, NY: Gegensatz Press, 2008. 64 p.

GG7437.   Bordes, Henri: "Tout n'est pas Rrose: Duchamp et Tzara, ensemble séparément," *Etant Donné Marcel Duchamp*, no. 8 (2007), 264-275.

GG7438.   Garner, Jr., Stanton B.: "*The Gas Heart*: disfiguration and the Dada body," *Modern Drama*, vol. 50, no. 4 (Winter 2007), 500-516.

GG7439.   "Kunst und Bühne: Tristan Tzara und die Robes poèmes." In 812.
UGUAY, Marie.
GG7440.   Miron, Isabelle: "Faire partie: corps et monde dans *Autoportraits* et *Poèmes inédits* de Marie Uguay." In 69, 151-158.
VACHÉ, Jacques.
GG7441.   • Rosemont, Franklin: *Jacques Vaché and the roots of surrealism; including Vache's war letters and other writings.* Chicago: Charles H. Kerr, 2008.
VAILLAND, Roger. See also 705.
GG7442.   • *Critiques des romans: Vailland et les lecteurs de son temps, 1955-1965.* Textes choisis par Jean Sénégas. Pantin: Le temps des cerises, 2007. 257 p.
GG7443.   • Delorieux, Franck: *Roger Vailland: libertinage et lutte des classes.* Pantin: Le Temps des cerises, 2008. 83 p.
GG7444.   • Leduc, Alain: *Roger Vailland (1907-1065): un homme encombrant.* Paris: L'Harmattan, 2008. *Socio-anthropologie.* 225 p.
GG7445.   Ballet, René: "Roger Vailland parricide ou la nécessité d'être parricide," *Cahiers Roger Vailland*, no. 28 (2008), 295-299.
GG7446.   Bertrand, Michel: "Militantisme, dilettantisme: la contradiction érigée en complémentarité," *Cahiers Roger Vailland*, no. 28 (2008), 277-293.
GG7447.   Boyer-Weinmann, Martine: "Roger Vailland et la guerre d'Algérie," *Cahiers Roger Vailland*, no. 28 (2008), 9-26.
GG7448.   Bridet, Guillaume: "Vailland et Bataille," *Cahiers Roger Vailland*, no. 28 (2008), 85-107. [Bataille]
GG7449.   Chaudier, Stéphane: " 'L'amoralisme oblige': Vailland entre Nietzsche et Marx," *Cahiers Roger Vailland*, no. 28 (2008), 203-227.
GG7450.   Collomb, Michel: "Grand reportage et expérience du drame dans *Boroboudour; Choses vues en Egypte; La Réunion*," *Cahiers Roger Vailland*, no. 28 (2008), 71-83.
GG7451.   Cordenod, Emmanuelle: "Vailland et Aragon au regard des *Lettres françaises*," *Cahiers Roger Vailland*, no. 28 (2008), 109-134. [Aragon]
GG7452.   Dambre, Marc: "Roger Nimier, les Hussards et Roger Vailland," *Cahiers Roger Vailland*, no. 28 (2008), 145-159. [Nimier]
GG7453.   Dédet, André: "Roger Vailland, un écrivain dans le siècle," *Cahiers Roger Vailland*, no. 28 (2008), 195-202.
GG7454.   Koeppel, Philippe: "Roger Vailland: libertin d'esprit, libertin de corps," *Cahiers Roger Vailland*, no. 28 (2008), 249-253.
GG7455.   Leduc, Alain: "Roger Vailland et la peinture," *Cahiers Roger Vailland*, no. 28 (2008), 167-178.
GG7456.   Not, André: "*325 000 francs*, histoire d'un prolétaire ou roman prolétarien?," *Cahiers Roger Vailland*, no. 28 (2008), 43-56.
GG7457.   Nott, David: "Vailland psychanalyste et psychanalysé," *Cahiers Roger Vailland*, no. 28 (2008), 229-247.
GG7458.   Petr, Christian: "Une balance," *Cahiers Roger Vailland*, no. 28 (2008), 135-144.
GG7459.   Pircar, Mélanie: "Temps, rythme, histoire: la dramatisation du récit dans *La Loi*," *Cahiers Roger Vailland*, no. 28 (2008), 179-194.
GG7460.   Sénégas, Jean: "Sur les hommes nus," *Cahiers Roger Vailland*, no. 28 (2008), 255-275.
GG7461.   Steinova, Dagmar: "Vailland et Prague," *Cahiers Roger Vailland*, no. 28 (2008), 37-42.
GG7462.   Virmaux, Alain: "Roger Gilbert-Lecomte, ses apparitions récurrentes dans les écrits de Vailland," *Cahiers Roger Vailland*, no. 28 (2008), 27-36.
GG7463.   Zamagni, Elena: "Don Cesare dans *La Loi* et Don Fabrizio dans *Le guépard*: figures de l'exil volontaire de l'histoire," *Cahiers Roger Vailland*, no. 28 (2008), 57-69.
VALÉRY, Paul. See also 420, 536, 779, 6324.
GG7464.   • *Di là dalla storia: Paul Valéry: tempo, mondo, opera, individuo.* A cura di Felice Ciro Papparo. Macerata: Quodlibet, 2007. 220 p.
GG7465.   • Durante, Erica: *Poétique et écriture: Dante au miroir de Valéry et de Borges.* Paris: Champion, 2008. *Bibliothèque de littérature générale et comparée*, 76. 549 p.

GG7466. • Gautreau, Jean-Loup: *Le cimetière marin*. Sète: Editions singulières, 2008. 140 p.

GG7467. • Jarrety, Michel: *Paul Valéry*. Paris: Fayard, 2008. 1366 p.

GG7468. • Kimura, Masahiko: *Le mythe du savoir: naissance et évolution de la pensée scientifique chez Paul Valéry (1880-1920)*. Frankfurt: Peter Lang, 2008. *Rostocker romanistische Arbeiten*, Band 13. 359 p.

GG7469. • Le Lannou, Jean-Michel: *La forme souveraine: Soulages, Valéry et la puissance de l'abstraction*. Paris: Hermann, 2008. *Hermann philosophie*. 141 p.

GG7470. • Masson, Jean-Yves: *Trois poètes face à la crise de la tradition au tournant du siècle (1890-1929): Hugo von Hofmannsthal, Paul Valéry, Rainer Maria Rilke*. Lille: ANRT, 2008. *Thèse à la carte*. vi, 770 p.

GG7471. • *Paul Valéry: "regards" sur l'histoire*. Etudes réunies par Robert Pickering avec la collaboration éditoriale de Micheline Hontebeyrie. Clermont-Ferrand: Presses univ. Blaise Pascal, 2008. 366 p.

GG7472. • Perrot, Marie-Claude: *Allegro con spirito*. Paris: Godefroy de Bouillon, 2008. 346 p.

GG7473. • Valéry, Paul: *Corona & coronilla: poèmes à Jean Voilier*. Postface par Bernard de Fallois. Paris: Fallois, 2008. 218 p.

GG7474. • *Valéry et Léonard: le drame d'une rencontre*. Ed. Christina Vogel. Frankfurt: P. Lang, 2007. 324 p.

GG7475. Allain-Castrillo, Monique: "Le présent du passé: entre Pétain et de Gaulle, lecteurs simultanés de Paul Valéry." In 7471, 139-163.

GG7476. Aubry, Laurence: "Enigme et temporalité dans 'Enfance aux cygnes' de Paul Valéry." In 436, 59-67.

GG7477. Bastet, Ned: "Valéry et la discordance des temps." In 7471, 223-232.

GG7478. Bluher, Karl Alfred: "Valéry et Nietzsche critiques de l'Histoire." In 7471, 109-123.

GG7479. Bourjéa, Serge: "Paul de Man 'lecteur' des dessins de Valéry." In 418, 105-117. [de Man]

GG7480. Broche, Laurent: "Les *Annales* et Paul Valéry: une rencontre manquée?" In 7471, 281-293.

GG7481. Celeyrette-Pietri, Nicole: "La genèse de l'idée européenne chez Paul Valéry." In 7471, 163-176.

GG7482. Chalier, Agnès: "Lire Paul Valéry en Chine." In 7471, 295-300.

GG7483. Dabezies, André: "Valéry: *Mon Faust* entre l'esprit et le cœur." In 379, 187-207.

GG7484. Ernst, Gilles: "Paul Valéry et la mort face à l'Histoire." In 7471, 245-265.

GG7485. Fallois, Bernard de: "Paul Valéry et l'histoire de *Corona*," *Commentaire*, vol. 31, no. 124 (hiver 2008-2009), 1027-1038.

GG7486. Fathy, Rania: "Poésie et Histoire." In 7471, 335-348. [Aragon]

GG7487. Foucart, Claude: "La mise en scène de l'Histoire ou l'événement après coup." In 7471, 125-135.

GG7488. Gifford, Paul: "Les 'lieux de mémoire' de Paul Valéry." In 7471, 301-313. [Ricœur]

GG7489. Goldfarb, Lisa: "Poetics of variation: Wallace Stevens' and Paul Valéry's poems of the sea," *Wallace Stevens Journal*, vol. 32, no. 2 (Fall 2008), 256-274.

GG7490. Guerlac, Suzanne: "Valéry: modernist myths and (anti) modernist states of mind," *Romanic Review*, vol. 99, no. 1-2 (Jan.-March), 69-76.

GG7491. Hainaut, Jean: "Pour un discours historique: un programme valéryen, une stylisation thomienne, deux analogies pascaliennes?" In 7471, 43-62

GG7492. Houpert, Jean-Marc: "Une île environnée d'elle-même, l'écriture." In 386, 355-368.

GG7493. Hufnagel, Henning: " 'Avec tous les mauvais sentiments utiles': Paul Valéry als Leser Neitzsches," *Germanisch-Romanische Monatsschrift*, 58. Jahrgang, Heft 3 (2008), 299-318.

GG7494. Imai, Tsutomu: "Au-delà de l'eurocentrisme: Valéry est-il possible dans le contexte postcolonial?" In 7471, 211-220.

GG7495. Laurenti, Huguette: "Valéry et l'enseignement." In 7471, 63-74.

GG7496. Mairesses, Anne: "Faute de poétique, une théorie de l'Etat." In 7471, 201-210.

GG7497. Mattiussi, Laurent: "Le moi intempestif: Valéry après Derrida." In 7471, 233-243. [Derrida]

GG7498. Neiva, Saulo: "La poésie épique contemporaine et la pensée sur l'Histoire de Paul Valéry: le cas brésilien." In 7471, 349-357.

GG7499. Phitoussi, Edwige: "D'une liaison assumée: entrelacement des arts et de l'écriture chez Paul Valéry." In 563, 8-19.

GG7500. Pietra, Régine: "Valéry et l'Ecole des *Annales*." In 7471, 269-279.

GG7501. Ryan, Paul: "Paul Valéry: visual perception and an aesthetics of landscape space," *Australian Journal of French Studies*, vol. 45, no. 1 (Jan.-April 2008), 43-58.

GG7502. Schmidt-Radefeldt, Jürgen: "Nation, Etat, Peuple: trois notions-clés chez Valéry." In 7471, 187-200.

GG7503. Sierro, Maurice: "L'homme de l'esprit et la culture." In 7471, 33-42.

GG7504. Tsukamoto, Masanori: "La modernité et la simulation chez Valéry." In 7471, 327-334.

GG7505. Tsukamoto, Masanori: "*Les Paradis artificiels* et *Monsieur Teste*: la théâtralisation de la conscience," *Licorne*, no. 83 (2008), 193-203.

GG7506. Tsunekawa, Kunio: "Utopie politique valéryenne." In 7471, 177-186.

GG7507. Vogel, Christina: "L'Histoire: 'sous le signe SI'." In 7471, 317-325.

GG7508. Zaccarello, Benedetta: "Le 'Moi' et le 'Nous': limites et enjeux de l'épistémologie de l'histoire chez Paul Valéry." In 7471, 75-94.

VALLÈS, Jules. See also 738, 2489.

GG7509. ● Vallès, Jules: *Jacques Vingtras. 2, Le bachelier*. Préface de Michel Tournier; notices et notes de Jean-Louis Lalanne. Paris: Gallimard, 2008. *Folio*. 492 p.

GG7510. Costa Colajanni, Giuliana: "Ecrire le réel: le fait divers et la chronique populaire selon Vallès," *Autour de Vallès*, no. 38 (2008), 47-56.

GG7511. Disegni, Silvia: "Censure et autocensure dans les avant-textes réalistes." In 619, 241-259.

GG7512. Disegni, Silvia: "Idéologie et réalisme chez Vallès," *Autour de Vallès*, no. 38 (2008), 91-106.

GG7513. Dubois, Jacques: "Franc-parler et réalité du factice," *Autour de Vallès*, no. 38 (2008), 107-117.

GG7514. Durand, Pascal: "Vallès au sujet de Baudelaire," *Autour de Vallès*, no. 38 (2008), 119-132.

GG7515. Feutry, Alain: "Redécouvrir Jules Vallès," *Nouvelle Revue Française*, no. 584 (janv. 2008), 190-198.

GG7516. Jourdan, Maxime: "Jules Vallès, patron de presse," *Autour de Vallès*, no. 38 (2008), 133-177.

GG7517. Melmoux-Montaubin, Marie-Françoise: "De l'actualité à l'actualisme: poétique de la chronique vallésienne," *Autour de Vallès*, no. 38 (2008), 31-46.

GG7518. Redfern, Walter: "Blague hard! Vallès." In 568.

GG7519. Saminadayar-Perrin, Corinne: "Irréguliers, saltimbanques et réfractaires: Vallès et la mythologie bohémienne." In 532, 315-343.

GG7520. Saminadayar-Perrin, Corinne: " 'Trois heures en ballon': politique du voyage fantaisiste," *Autour de Vallès*, no. 38 (2008), 73-90.

GG7521. Thérenty, Marie-Eve: "Dante reporter. La création d'un paradigme journalistique," *Autour de Vallès*, no. 38 (2008), 57-72.

VAN DER MEERSCH, Maxence.

GG7522. ● *Maxence Van der Meersch: écrivain engagé*. Contributions de Paul Renard [et al.]. Vimy: Roman 20-50, 2008. 286 p.

VANDROMME, Pol.

GG7523. Ghysen, Francine: "Pol-le-vif, Vandromme-le-fidèle," *Carnet et les Instants*, no. 150 (2008), 2-7.

VAN LERBERGHE, Charles.

GG7524. Gorceix, Paul: "*La Chanson d'Eve* de Charles Van Lerberghe ou l'objectivation obsessionnelle du moi." In 83, 153-159.

GG7525. Gorceix, Paul: "Charles Van Lerberghe et les *Contes hors du temps*." In 83, 161-174.

GG7526. Gorceix, Paul: "Charles Van Lerberghe ou le modèle de l'esthétique symboliste." In 83, 139-152.

VANMAI, Jean.

GG7527. Do, Tess: "Exile: rupture and continuity in Jean Vanmai's *Chân Dang* and *Fils de Chân Dang*," *Critical Studies*, vol. 30 (2008), 151-172.

VARGAFTIG, Bernard. See 735, 5895.

VARGAS, Fred.

GG7528. Gaspari, Séverine: "Fred Vargas: une archéozoologue en terrain littéraire." In 539, 41-50.

GG7529. Vargas, Fred: " 'Les polars, comme les contes, servent à déjouer l'angoisse de la mort'," *Télérama*, no. 3030 (2008), 14-18. [Entretien]

VAUTRIN, Jean. See 761.

VEINSTEIN, Alain.

GG7530. Laroque, Françoise de: "Alain Veinstein ou le chien des mots," *Critique*, tome 64, no. 735-736 (août-sept. 2008), 638-645.

VELTER, André.

GG7531. ● Nauleau, Sophie: *Un verbe à cheval: la poésie équestre d'André Velter dans le sillage de Bartabas*. Mont-de-Marsan: Atelier des brisants, 2008. *Chambre d'échos*. 107 p.

VERCORS (pseud. of Jean Bruller).

GG7532. ● Bartillat, Christian de: *Vercors: l'homme du siècle à travers son œuvre, 1902-1991*. Etrépilly: Presses du village, 2008. 174 p.

GG7533. ● *Vercors, résistance et résonances*. Sous la dir. de Philippe Hanus et Gilles Vergon. Paris: L'Harmattan, 2008. 239 p.

GG7534. Foucart, Claude: "Vercors face à l'Allemagne." In 461, 393-406.

GG7535. Hamel, Yan: "Renouveau du théâtre humaniste. *Le Silence de la mer*," *Jeu: Cahiers de Théâtre*, no. 127 [no. 2] (2008), 35-38.

VERHAEREN, Émile.

GG7536. ● Verhaeren, Emile: *De Baudelaire à Mallarmé; suivi de, Parnassiens et symbolistes*. Avant-propos de Jean-Baptiste Baronian. Lausanne: L'Age d'homme, 2008. *La petite Belgique*. 116 p. [Poetry]

GG7537. ● Verhaeren, Emile: *Poésie complète. 5, Les Flamandes, Les Moines*. Edition critique établie par Michel Otten; prés. par Véronique Jago-Antoine. Bruxelles: Archives et musée de la littérature, 2008. 382 p.

GG7538. ● Verhaeren, Emile: *Poésie complète. 6, Les bords de la route. Les vignes de ma muraille*. Edition critique établie par Michel Otten; prés. par Christian Angelet. Bruxelles: Archives et musée de la littérature, 2008. 263 p.

GG7539. Ducrey, Guy: "Survivre à Offenbach: *Hélène de Sparte*, tragédie d'Emile Verhaeren." In 482, 279-293.

GG7540. Galand, David: "La mort envisagée: l'insolite dans les *Poèmes* (nouvelle série) d'Emile Verhaeren." In 439, 83-95.

GG7541. Gorceix, Paul: "Emile Verhaeren critique littéraire." In 83, 27-41.

GG7542. Gorceix, Paul: "Emile Verhaeren entre le récit et le poème en prose." In 83, 15-26.

GG7543. Gorceix, Paul: "L'imaginaire décadent chez Emile Verhaeren." In 83, 7-14.

GG7544. Gullentops, David: "Anarchisme et avant-garde chez Emile Verhaeren." In 612, 139-152.

GG7545. Gullentops, David: "Structure, lecture et génétique des *Villes tentaculaires* de Verhaeren." In 503, 61-74.

VERLAINE, Paul. See also 741, 6732.

GG7546. ● Baronian, Jean-Baptiste: *Verlaine*. Paris: Gallimard, 2008. *Folio biographies*. 221 p.

GG7547. ● Goffette, Guy: *L'autre Verlaine: récits*. Paris: Gallimard, 2008. 97 p.

GG7548. ● *Premiers [Les] recueils de Verlaine: Poèmes saturniens, Fêtes galantes, Romances sans paroles.* André Guyaux, dir. Paris: PUPS, 2008. *Colloque de la Sorbonne.* 212 p.

GG7549. ● Verlaine, Paul: *Œuvres complètes. Tome VII, 1886-1887, les mémoires d'un veuf.* Edition prép. par Marc Le Roux. Clermont-Ferrand: Paleo, 2008. *La collection de sable.* 218 p.

GG7550. ● Verlaine, Paul: *Poëmes saturniens.* Edition critique de Steve Murphy. Paris: Champion, 2008. *Textes de littérature moderne et contemporaine.* 676 p.

GG7551. ● Verlaine, Paul: *Poèmes saturniens.* Edition prés., annotée et commentée par Alexandre Gefen. Nouvelle prés. Paris: Larousse, 2008. *Petits classiques Larousse.* 172 p.

GG7552. Ballière, C.-A.: "Une visite à Paul Verlaine," *Œil Bleu*, no. 6 (2008), 57-61.

GG7553. Bernadet, Arnaud: " 'Des propos fades': grammaire et poétique de la conversation dans 'Les Indolents'," *Information Grammaticale*, no. 116 (2008), 46-50.

GG7554. Bernadet, Arnaud: "Une machine à fabriquer le peuple: *Bruxelles, Chevaux de bois*." In 7548, 81-97.

GG7555. Bernadet, Arnaud: "Verlaine à la manière de Rimbaud," *Parade Sauvage*, no. spécial (2008), 67-89. [Rimbaud]

GG7556. Billy, Dominiquë"La rime dans les premiers recueils de Verlaine." In 7548, 137-166.

GG7557. Bivort, Olivier: "Le 'goût Watteau' des *Fêtes galantes*." In 7548, 41-53.

GG7558. Buffard-Moret, Brigitte: " 'De vieilles formes forger un métal vierge et neuf'." In 7548, 69-80.

GG7559. Cavallin, Jean-Christophe: "Dialogisme métrique dans les *Poèmes saturniens*." In 7548, 9-23.

GG7560. Cornulier, Benoît de: "Aspects de la versification dans les *Fêtes galantes*." In 7548, 55-68.

GG7561. Dubiau-Feuillerac, Mylène: "Discours poétique et discours musical: interférences, lectures interprétatives," *Champs du Signe*, no. 24 (2007), 11-70.

GG7562. Dufour, Philippe: "Naïveté de Paul Verlaine," *Information Littéraire*, 60e année, no. 1 (janv.-mars 2008), 51-58.

GG7563. Dupas, Solenn: "Poétique et politique de l'allégorie en vers: à propos du 'Monstre' de Verlaine," *Romantisme*, no. 140 (2e trim. 2008), 85-98.

GG7564. Dupas, Solenn: "Poéetiques de l'intime dans 'Amour'," *Studi Francesi*, anno 52, fasc. 1 (genn.-aprile 2008), 122-135.

GG7565. Gallet, Olivier: "La rime entre actualisation et virtualisation." In 7548, 123-135.

GG7566. Gardes-Tamine, Joëlle: "La répétition dans *Poèmes saturniens, Fêtes galantes* et *Romances sans paroles*." In 7548, 167-178.

GG7567. Murphy, Steve: "Au-delà de la rivière réelle: notes en marge de *Streets II* de Verlaine." In 503, 27-39.

GG7568. Murphy, Steve: "Métrique et pragmatique du 'Sonnet boiteux' de Verlaine," *Studi Francesi*, anno 52, fasc. 1 (genn.-aprile 2008), 41-62.

GG7569. Reboul, Yves: "L'enjeu de *Beams*." In 7548, 99-121.

GG7570. Richard, Elisabeth; Claire Doquet-Lacoste: "La galanterie des fêtes: décrochements énonciatifs et syntagmatiques dans les *Fêtes galantes*," *Information Grammaticale*, no. 116 (2008), 41-45.

GG7571. Rocher, Philippe: " 'Beams': figuration et configuration du mouvement." In 503, 41-60.

GG7572. Rocher, Philippe: "Rimbaud en sourdine: les *Romances sans paroles* et la présence d'Ophélie," *Parade Sauvage*, no. spécial (2008), 23-52. [Rimbaud]

GG7573. Steinmetz, Jean-Luc: "Verlaine au cœur." In 7548, 193-206.

GG7574. Tremblay, Charles-Etienne: "La poire de Rimbaud: la lettre du 24 août 1875," *Parade Sauvage*, no. spécial (2008), 53-66. [Rimbaud]

GG7575. Troulay, Marcel: "Le *Caen-Caen* de juin 1895," *Œil Bleu*, no. 6 (2008), 53-56.

GG7576. Viegnes, Michel: "Ironie et dérision dans *Poèmes saturniens, Fêtes galantes* et *Romances sans paroles.*" In 7548, 179-191.

GG7577. Wanlin, Nicolas: "Les références artistiques dans *Poèmes saturniens* et *Fêtes galantes.*" In 7548, 25-39.

VERNE, Jules. See also 581, 700, 6845.

GG7578. ● Dupuy, Lionel: *Drôle de Jules Verne!: humour, ironie et dérision dans l'œuvre de Jules Verne.* Dole: La Clef d'argent, 2008. 39 p.

GG7579. ● Gauthier, Guy: *Edouard Riou dessinateur: entre le Tour du monde et Jules Verne, 1860-1900.* Paris: L'Harmattan, 2008. *Champs visuels.* 185 p.

GG7580. ● *Jules Verne, le partage du savoir.* Ed. Michel Fabre et Philippe Mustière. Nantes: Coiffard, 2008. 406 p.

GG7581. ● Paumier, Jean-Yves: *Jules Verne: voyageur extraordinaire.* Grenoble: Glénat, 2008. *La bibliothèque des explorateurs.*

GG7582. ● Thadewald, Wolfgang: *"Ich war Jules Verne": Deutsche Jules Verne Persiflagen aus den Jahren 1872-1914.* Dortmund: Synergen, 2008. 200 p.

GG7583. ● Verne, Jules: *Around the world in 80 days.* Introd. James Hynes. New York: Barnes & Noble Books, 2008. xvi, 205 p.

GG7584. ● Verne, Jules: *The golden volcano.* Trans., ed. by Edward Baxter; preface to the French edition by Olivier Dumas. Lincoln: Univ. of Nebraska Press, 2008. *Bison frontiers of imagination.* xvi, 340 p.

GG7585. ● Verne, Jules: *L'invasion de la mer.* Préface de Francis Lassasin. Monaco: Motifs, 2008. 282 p.

GG7586. ● Verne, Jules: *Journey to the center of the earth.* Supplementary materials written by Heather Wilkinson. New York: Pocket Books, 2008. *Enriched classic.* xxi, 330 p.

GG7587. ● Verne, Jules: *Journey to the centre of the earth.* Trans. Robert Baldick, introd. Diana Wynne Jones. London; New York: Puffin, 2008. vi, 337 p.

GG7588. Alonso, Ana: "Jules Verne et le fantastique technologique. Une lecture de *Maître Zacharius ou l'horloger qui avait perdu son âme,*" *Etudes Francophones,* vol. 23, no. 1-2 (printemps-automne 2008), 180-190.

GG7589. Bailbé, Joseph-Marc: "Voix et images musicales dans *Le Château des Carpathes,*" *Revue Jules Verne,* no. 24 (2007), 103-111.

GG7590. Bouloumié, Arlette: "Le mythe de l'Atlantide." In 423. [H. Bosco]

GG7591. Brin, David: *"Journey to the centre of the earth,* by Jules Verne." In 401.

GG7592. Cathe, Philippe: "La culture musicale de Jules Verne à travers son œuvre," *Revue Jules Verne,* no. 24 (2007), 41-57.

GG7593. Chiles, James R.: "Jules Verne in a suitcase." In 806.

GG7594. Dehs, Volker: "Jules Verne entre Léo Delibes, Halévy et Victor Massé," *Revue Jules Verne,* no. 24 (2007), 97-102.

GG7595. Dehs, Volker: " 'Maby Dick' et Cie, fautes et erreurs dans l'œuvre vernienne," *Revue Jules Verne,* no. 26 (2007), 145-161.

GG7596. Dirda, Michael: "Jules Verne." In 430.

GG7597. Dupuy, Lionel: "Inter et intrasémioticité dans l'œuvre de Jules Verne," *Applied Semiotics,* no. 20 (2008), 29-42.

GG7598. Dupuy, Lionel: "Ubiquité temporelle et imaginaire géographique. *Voyage au centre de la Terre* et dans le temps," *Revue Jules Verne,* no. 26 (2007), 119-143.

GG7599. Fitzgerald, Michael: "Oscar Wilde and Jules Verne." In 827.

GG7600. Gondolo della Riva, Piero: "Le problème des variantes entre les différentes éditions des œuvres de Jules Verne en vue de la publication du corpus vernien," *Revue Jules Verne,* no. 26 (2007), 63-74.

GG7601. Lepagnez, Claude: "Jules Verne connaissait-il la musique?," *Revue Jules Verne,* no. 24 (2007), 113-121.

GG7602. Lepagnez, Claude: "Le verne est-il toujours vernal?: de Jean Chesneaux à Roland Barthes," *Revue Jules Verne,* no. 26 (2007), 195-200. [Barthes]

GG7603. Marcetteau-Paul, Agnès: "Les manuscrits conservés à Nantes," *Revue Jules Verne,* no. 24 (2007), 45-61.

GG7604. Marcetteau-Paul, Agnès: "Sur les traces de Jules Verne," *Revue Jules Verne,* no. 26 (2007), 210-215.

GG7605. Mollier, Jean-Yves: "Le contexte éditorial du XIX siècle," *Revue Jules Verne*, no. 26 (2007), 19-43.

GG7606. Paumier, Jean-Yves: "Jules Verne en chantant," *Revue Jules Verne*, no. 24 (2007), 136-143.

GG7607. Pédauge, Mireille: "La musique dans l'œuvre de Jules Verne," *Revue Jules Verne*, no. 24 (2007), 23-38.

GG7608. Pourvoyeur, Robert: "*Monsieur de Chimpanzé*, c'est aussi du Jules Verne!," *Revue Jules Verne*, no. 24 (2007), 85-94.

GG7609. Sadaune, Samuel: "*Monsieur Ré-dièse et Mademoiselle Mi-bémol*: petite ouverture de grande portée sur la symphonie vernienne," *Revue Jules Verne*, no. 24 (2007), 7-20.

GG7610. Sadaune, Samuel: "*Les Voyages extraordinaires*: un autre regard sur l'origine et le devenir du monde," *Revue Jules Verne*, no. 26 (2007), 105-117.

GG7611. Santa, Angels: "Lieux mythiques de l'amour chez *Mathias Sandorf* de Jules Verne." In 502.

GG7612. Sauzereau, Olivier [et al.]: "Table ronde: éditer Jules Verne aujourd'hui," *Revue Jules Verne*, no. 26 (2007), 77-103.

GG7613. Seillan, Jean-Marie: "Petite histoire d'un révolution épistémologique: la captation de l'héritage d'Alexandre Dumas par Jules Verne." In 360, 199-218.

GG7614. Tarrieu, Alexandre: " La musique du corps," *Revue Jules Verne*, no. 24 (2007), 123-134.

GG7615. Valetoux, Philippe: "Le livre que Jules Verne n'a pas écrit: 'Les Voyages ordinaires du *Saint-Michel*'," *Revue Jules Verne*, no. 26 (2007), 163-171.

GG7616. Weber, Anne-Gaëlle: "La place de Jules Verne dans la littérature de vulgarisation scientifique," *Cahiers Robinson*, no. 24 (2008), 101-117.

VERNET, Joël.

GG7617. Pierrot, Jean: "Joël Vernet et la poétique de l'infime." In 382, 211-234.

VIALATTE, Alexandre. See also 4205, 6320.

GG7618. ● Vialatte, Alexandre: *1968: chroniques*. Introd. Philippe Meyer. Paris: Julliard, 2008. 335 p.

VIAN, Boris.

GG7619. ● Bertolt, Nicole; François Roulmann: *Boris Vian: le swing et le verbe*. Préface de Marc Lapprand. Paris: Textuel, 2008. 218 p.

GG7620. ● Dufaud, Marc: *Monsieur Boris Vian, je vous fais une lettre . . . : la chanson du Déserteur*. Paris: Scali, 2008. 206 p.

GG7621. ● Mitura, Magdalena: *L'écriture vianesque: traduction de la prose*. Bern: Lang, 2008. *Europäische Hochschulschriften*. xi, 249 p.

GG7622. ● Vian, Boris: *Je voudrais pas crever: poèmes illustrés en hommage à Martin Matje*. Préface d'André Marois. Montréal: Les Allusifs, 2008. 71 p.

VICTOR, Gary.

GG7623. Mininni, Maria Isabella: "Le réalisme merveilleux de Gary Victor," *Interculturel Francophones*, no. 12 (nov.-déc. 2007), 191-207.

GG7624. Pageaux, Daniel-Henri: "*A l'angle des rues parallèles* de Gary Victor. Entre témoignage et invention romanesque." In 118, 381-388.

VIEL, Tanguy.

GG7625. Houppermans, Sjef: "Tanguy Viel: from word to image," *Yale French Studies*, no. 114 (2008), 37-50.

VIGÉE, Claude.

GG7626. ● Vigée, Claude: *Mélancolie solaire: nouveaux essais, cahiers, entretiens inédits, poèmes (2006-2008)*. Avant-propos et édition d'Anne Mounic. Paris: Orizons, 2008. *Profils d'un classique*. 314 p.

GG7627. ● Vigée, Claude: *Mon heure sur la terre: poésies complètes, 1936-2008*. Préface de Michèle Finck; introd. Anne Mounic. Paris: Galaade, 2008. 925 p.

VIGNEAULT, Gilles.

GG7628. Soucy, Diane: "Gilles Vigneault, chansonnier médiéval, troubadour moderne: les traces du passé dans une œuvre contemporaine." In 120, 358-367.

VIGNEAULT, Guillaume.

GG7629.　Dupuis, Gilles: "*Carnets de naufrage* de Guillaume Vigneault." In 41, 453-474.

VILAIN, Philippe.

GG7630.　Faerber, Johan: "Une vie sans histoire. Ou l'impact autobiographique dans l'œuvre de Philippe Vilain," *Revue de Littérature Comparée*, no. 325 [no. 1] (janv.-mars 2008), 131-140.

GG7631.　Wesemael, Sabine van: "Philippe Vilain se penche sur le miroir de son enfance." In 571, 47-56.

VILAR, Jean. See 1124.

VILDRAC, Charles.

GG7632.　Monnet, Georges: "Les écrits de Charles Vildrac: essai de 'bibliographie sentimentale'," *Cahiers de l'Abbaye de Créteil*, no. 26 (2007), 103-156.

GG7633.　Stahl, August: " 'Französisch gedacht': R. M. Rilke und Charles Vildrac," *Etudes Germaniques*, no. 249 (2008), 49-88.

VILGRAIN, Bénédicte.

GG7634.　Lang, Abigail: "L'interprétation des raves. Lecture de Bénédicte Vilgrain," *Critique*, tome 64, no. 735-736 (août-sept. 2008), 656-668.

VILLEMAIRE, Yolande. See also 6240.

GG7635.　Constantin, Danielle: "*La vie en prose* de Yolande Villemaire: traces, signes et son du soi." In 411.

GG7636.　Lanzolla, Osvaldo: "Yolande Villemaire e il luogo della memoria," *Rivista di Studi Canadesi*, n. 20 (2007), 181-188.

VILLENEUVE, Angélique.

GG7637.　Morello, Nathalie: "Fils perdu, mère . . . délivrée? Etude d'une étrange inquiétude dans *Ne plus y penser* d'Angélique Villeneuve," *Dalhousie French Studies*, vol. 84 (Fall 2008), 89-99.

VILLIERS, Gérard de.

GG7638.　Marmin, Michel: "Gérard de Villiers, le romancier du grand jeu," *Spectacle du Monde*, no. 547 (juillet-août 2008), 74-76.

VILLIERS DE L'ISLE-ADAM. See also 763.

GG7639.　Dufief, Anne-Simone: " 'Et c'était un *crescendo* de silences': Villiers de l'Isle-Adam." In 592, 167-179.

GG7640.　Farasse, Gérard: "Trait pour trait." In 454, 127-134.

GG7641.　Grojnowski, Daniel: "Satire de quoi: Villiers et le conte *cruel*," *Modernités*, no. 27 (2008), 153-154.

GG7642.　Leasure, T. Ross: "Yesterday's Eve and her electric avatar: Villiers's debt to Milton's *Paradise Lost*," *LATCH*, no. 1 (2008), 129-145.

GG7643.　Néry, Alain: "De l'insolite à l'innommable: les *Histoires insolites* de Villiers de l'Isle-Adam." In 439, 137-145.

GG7644.　Orbaugh, Sharalyn: "Emotional infectivity: cyborg affect and the limits of the human." In 845, 150-172.

GG7645.　Rashkin, Esther: "Symbolism and the occulted Jew in Villiers de l'Isle-Adam's *Axël*." In 566.

VILMORIN, Louise de.

GG7646.　● Vilmorin, Louise de; Duff Cooper; Diana Cooper: *Correspondance à trois (1944-1953)*. Edition établie, annotée et commentée par Olivier Muth. Paris: Le Promeneur, 2008. 679 p.

GG7647.　● Wagener, Françoise: *Je suis née inconsolable: Louise de Vilmorin*. Paris: A. Michel, 2008. 549 p.

VINAVER, Michel.

GG7648.　● *Michel Vinaver, côté texte-côté scène*. Catherine Naugrette [et al.]. Paris: Presses Sorbonne nouvelle, 2008. 149 p.

GG7649.　● Vinaver, Michel: *L'ordinaire: pièce en sept morceaux; suivi d'un entretien avec Evelyne Ertel "Michel Vinaver metteur en scène*. Arles: Actes Sud, 2008. *Babel.* 252 p. [Orig. ed., 2002]

GG7650.　Brun, Catherine: "En être ou pas: figures du militant dans l'œuvre théâtrale de Michel Vinaver." In 456, 231-239.

GG7651. Chaperon, Danielle: "Voix plurielles et voix populaires au théâtre." In 519, 143-166.

GG7652. Engélibert, Jean-Paul: "Scènes de l'utopie. *King* de Michel Vinaver." In 386, 283-293.

GG7653. Gracía Martinez, Manuel: "Vinaver's *Par-dessus bord* at the Théâtre de la Colline," *Western European Stages*, vol. 20, no. 3 (Fall 2008), 71-76.

GG7654. Naugrette, Catherine: "Le théâtre de Michel Vinaver ou la prose du monde," *Cuadernos de Filologia Francesa*, no. 19 (2008), 185-201.

VIOLLIER, Yves.

GG7655. Wissner, Inka: "La variation diatopique du français dans l'œuvre littéraire d'Yves Viollier." In 794, 151-158.

VISDEI, Anca.

GG7656. Courtes, Noémie: "Texte à jouer et à transgresser: les didascalies dans l'œuvre d'Anca Visdei." In 605, 393-405.

VITEZ, Antoine. See also 1105.

GG7657. Banu, Georges: "Antoine Vitez: 'Quand tout ça aura été fini, ouvrons une Académie à Bièvres," *Alternatives Théâtrales*, no. 98 (2008), 46-48.

GG7658. Malachy, Thérèse: "Les Molière de Vitez ou la parole non-dite." In 1093.

GG7659. Nantet, Renée; Antoine Vitez: "Correspondance 19975-1990, précédée d'un avant-propos de Jeanne Vitez," *Bulletin de la Société Paul Claudel*, no. 189 (1er trim. 2008), 2-27. [Claudel]

VIVIEN, Renée.

GG7660. • Marçal, Maria-Mercè: *La passió segons Renée Vivien*. Barcelona: Labutxaca, 2008. 397 p.

GG7661. • Vivien, Renée: *Les Kitharèdes*. Avant-propos de Marie-Jo Bonnet. Cassaniouze: Erosonyx, 2008. 175 p.

VIVIER, Robert.

GG7662. • Mignon, Nicolas: *Les Grandes Guerres de Robert Vivier*. Paris: L'Harmattan, 2008. 312 p.

GG7663. Béghin, Laurent: "Robert Vivier et l'Italie," *Lettres Romanes*, tome 61, no. 3-4 (2007), 305-333.

VOILIER, Jean.

GG7664. • Bertin, Célia: *Portrait d'une femme romanesque, Jean Voilier*. Paris: Fallois, 2008. 315 p.

VOISARD, Alexandre.

GG7665. • Buchs, Arnaud: *Le Déjeu d'Alexandre Voisard*. Carouge-Genève: Zoé, 2008. 112 p.

VOLODINE, Antoine.

GG7666. • *Défense et illustration du post-exotisme en vingt leçons: avec Antoine Volodine*. Sous la dir. de Frédérik Detue et Pierre Ouellet. Montréal: VLB, 2008. 399 p.

GG7667. Detue, Frédérik: "Des langues chez Volodine: un drame de la survie," *Littérature*, no. 151 (sept. 2008), 75-89.

GG7668. Ducas, Sylvie: "Ecrire l'insolite pour Antoine Volodine ou l'art du bobard dans *Bardo or not Bardo*." In 439, 159-171.

GG7669. Lamarre, Mélanie: " 'Ici Breughel, il fait très noir: répondez': figures de la communication dans l'œuvre d'Antoine Volodine," *Roman 20-50*, no. 46 (2008), 149-161.

GG7670. Volodine, Antoine: "Volodine disparaît," *Livres Hebdo*, no. 730 (2008), 64-67. [Entretien]

WABERI, Abdourahman A. See also 64.

GG7671. • Waberi, Abdourahman A.: *In den Vereinigten Staaten von Afrika*. Aus dem Franz. mit einem Nachwort von Katja Meintel. Hamburg: Nautilus, 2008. 158 p.

GG7672. Bouba, Aïssatou; Natascha Ueckmann: " 'Ce qui nous rabaisse, c'est la violence du discours sur l'Afrique'. Entretien avec Abdourahman A. Waberi," *Lendemains*, 33. Jahrgang, Heft 132 (2008), 143-155.

GG7673. Narbutovic, Katharina: "Abdourahman A. Waberi," *Sprache im Technischen Zeitalter*, 46. Jahrgang, Heft 185 (März 2008), 91-92.

GG7674. Waberi, Abdourahman A.: "Des récits au canon: la place de l'écrivain afri-cain." In 72, 67-73.

WAJCMAN, Gérard. See 722, 6459.

WAJSBROT, Cécile.

GG7675. Bary, Nicole: "Cécile Wajsbrot, *Mémorial*," *Presse Littéraire*, no. 14 (2008), 64-66.

GG7676. Galea, Claudine: "Des voix et des chemins," *Presse Littéraire*, no. 14 (2008), 66-69.

GG7677. Rozier, Gilles: "Ecriture du sensible," *Presse Littéraire*, no. 14 (2008), 69-70.

GG7678. Schubert, Katja: "Les temps qui tremblent ou un passé possible de ce présent? A propos de l'œuvre de Cécile Wajsbrot." In 602, 231-242.

GG7679. Wajsbrot, Cécile: "Après coup." In 602, 25-29.

GG7680. Wajsbrot, Cécile: " 'Un écrivain ne peut pas ignorer l'époque où il se trouve'," *Presse Littéraire*, no. 14 (2008), 48-64. [Entretien]

WARNER-VIEYRA, Myriam.

GG7681. Ndiaye, Mame Selbée Diouf: "Reconnecting with the ancestors' land: female predicament and the quest for national identity in Myriam Warner-Vieyra's *Juletane*." In 43, 323-331.

WEIL, Éric.

GG7682. ● Sanou, Jean-Baptiste: *Violence et sagesse dans la philosophie d'Eric Weil*. Roma: Editrice Pontoficia Univ. Gregoriana, 2008. 387 p.

WEIL, Simone.

GG7683. ● Adler, Laure: *L'insoumise: récit*. Arles: Actes Sud, 2008. 271 p.

GG7684. ● Avery, Desmond: *Beyond power: Simone Weil and the notion of authority*. Lanham, MD: Lexington Books, 2008. x, 199 p.

GG7685. ● Farina, Paolo: *L'amour divin au fond du malheur: follia di Dio e salvezza dell'uomo in Simone Weil*. Roma: Pontificia Univ. Laternense, 2008. 247 p.

GG7686. ● Minervini, Mauro: *Da una giovinezza lontana: anni Trenta: Simone Weil e la tempesta*. Pref. Ivo Lizzola. Troina: Città aperta, 2008. *Saggi*. 151 p.

GG7687. ● Molard, Julien: *Les valeurs chez Simone Weil*. Paris: Parole et silence, 2008. *Cahiers de l'école cathédrale*. 157 p.

GG7688. ● Plant, Stephen: *Simone Weil: a brief introduction*. Maryknoll, NY: Orbis, 2008. Rev. and expanded ed. xvii, 108 p.

GG7689. ● *Simone Weil: acción y contemplación*. Maria Clara Lucchetti Bingemer, Giulia Paola Di Nicola, editoras. Bilbao: Desclée de Brouwer, 2007. 227 p.

GG7690. ● *Simone Weil, action et contemplation*. Coord. Emmanuel Gabellieri, Maria Clara Lucchetti Bingemer. Paris: L'Harmattan, 2008. 181 p.

GG7691. ● *Simone Weil, le travail comme témoignage*. Sous la dir. de Nadia Taïbi. Lyon: Univ. Jean Moulin, 2008. 114 p.

GG7692. ● *Simone Weil und die religiöse Frage*. Wolfgang W. Müller, Hrsg. Zürich: TVZ, 2007. 203 p.

GG7693. ● Steffens, Martin: *Prier 15 jours avec Simone Weil*. Bruyères-le-Châtel: Nouvelle cité, 2008. 126 p.

GG7694. ● Weil, Simone: *Œuvres complètes. Tome 4, Ecrits de Marseille, vol. 1 (1940-1942)*. Sous la dir. d'André A. Devaux. Paris: Gallimard, 2008. 608 p.

GG7695. ● Weil, Sylvie: *Chez les Weil: André et Simone*. Paris: Buchet-Chastel, 2008. 269 p.

GG7696. ● Wiggins, David: *Solidarity and the root of the ethical*. Lawrence: Dept. of Philosophy, Univ. of Kansas, 2008. *The Lindley Lecture*. 28 p.

GG7697. Avery, Desmond: "Le collectif comme source de lumière et d'aveuglement dans les cahiers de Simone Weil," *Cahiers Simone Weil*, vol. 31, no. 4 (2008), 363-372.

GG7698. Bosi, Alfredo; Ligia Fonseca Ferreira: "Simone Weil: l'intelligence libératrice et ses formes," *Cahiers Simone Weil*, vol. 31, no. 3 (2008), 273-300.

GG7699. Broc-Lapeyre, Monique: "Les cris de l'âme," *Cahiers Simone Weil*, vol. 31, no. 4 (2008), 389-400.

GG7700. Cabaud, Jacques: "Simone Weil: an ethics for esthetics," *Cahiers Simone Weil*, vol. 31, no. 1 (2008), 45-80.

GG7701. Canciani, Domenico: "Marseille la saison des amitiés: le père Perrin et Simone Weil, amis dans la vérité de Dieu," *Cahiers Simone Weil*, vol. 31, no. 1 (2008), 11-26.

GG7702. Concetta Sala, Maria: "Fils conducteurs (1933-1943): le sentiment d'impossibilité et la notion d'impossible," *Cahiers Simone Weil*, vol. 31, no. 2 (2008), 153-173.

GG7703. David, Pascal: " 'Philosophie, chose exclusivement en acte et pratique': l'écriture philosophique des cahiers comme exercice de l'absence," *Cahiers Simone Weil*, vol. 31, no. 2 (2008), 119-151.

GG7704. Drevet, Patrick: "Simone Weil est-elle antisémite?," *Cahiers Simone Weil*, vol. 31, no. 2 (2008), 207-210.

GG7705. Droz, Claude: "L'attention ou la force transformée dans les cahiers," *Cahiers Simone Weil*, vol. 31, no. 4 (2008), 401-416.

GG7706. Estelrich Barcelo, Bartomeu: " 'Le Christ lui-même est descendu et m'a prise'. An approximation of the irruption of Christ in Simone Weil's life as interpreted through the Christian tradition," *Cahiers Simone Weil*, vol. 31, no. 3 (2008), 301-337.

GG7707. Grafe, Adrian: "Simone Weil among the poets." In 816, 161-171.

GG7708. Howe, Christine: "Towards a poetics of hope: Simone Weil, Fanny Howe and Alice Walker." Diss., Univ. of Wollongong, 2008.

GG7709. Lucchetti Bingemer, Maria Clara: "Simone Weil et Joë Bousquet: une amitié sous la signe de la croix," *Cahiers Simone Weil*, vol. 31, no. 1 (2008), 27-44. [Bousquet]

GG7710. Maes, Gabriël: "Dieu qui crie, Dieu qui se tait: vibration déchirante et suprême harmonie: une lecture des cahiers de Simone Weil," *Cahiers Simone Weil*, vol. 31, no. 2 (2008), 187-206.

GG7711. Mallan, Claude: "Au-delà des oppositions: Simone Weil et l'amitié pythagoricienne," *Cahiers Simone Weil*, vol. 31, no. 1 (2008), 1-10.

GG7712. Marchetti, Adriano: "Poétique des cahiers: écriture brève et discontinue," *Cahiers Simone Weil*, vol. 31, no. 2 (2008), 175-185.

GG7713. Mouze, Létitia: "Amère beauté, amère vérité, amère philosophie: notes sur la lecture weilienne de l'*Iliade*." In 417, 211-234.

GG7714. Przybylska, Nelly: "Une expérience ascétique du temps." In 496, 311-319.

GG7715. Russo, Maria Teresa: "La guerra civil española desde el pensamiento femenino: Simone Weil y María Zambrano," *Agora*, vol. 27, no. 1 (2008), 71-89.

GG7716. Rybakova, M.: "Imagination versus attention: Simone Weil translating the *Iliad*," *Arion*, vol. 15, no. 2 (Fall 2007), 29-36.

GG7717. Schweitzer, Erika: "Nelly Sachs découvre Simone Weil," *Cahiers Simone Weil*, vol. 31, no. 3 (2008), 253-263.

GG7718. Schweitzer, Erika: "Nelly Sachs und Simone Weil: ein theologischer Diskurs." In 840.

GG7719. "Simone Weil." In 984.

GG7720. Steffens, Martin: "Le rôle de la volonté dans l'itinéraire spirituel des cahiers," *Cahiers Simone Weil*, vol. 31, no. 4 (2008), 373-387.

GG7721. Tommasi, Wanda; Francis Chiappone: "Christianisme et platonisme dans l'œuvre de Simone Weil," *Cahiers Simone Weil*, vol. 31, no. 3 (2008), 265-272.

GG7722. Vaughan, William: "Indiscretion with regard to the unsayable: Weil to the postmodern." In 998.

GG7723. Villela-Petit, Maria: "Simone Weil présente à la pensée de Paul Ricœur sur l'amitié," *Cahiers Simone Weil*, vol. 31, no. 3 (2008), 235-252. [Ricœur]

GG7724. Vogel, Christina: "De la métaphore comme acte de l'esprit." In 550, 39-48.

GG7725. Vogel, Jeffrey Allan: "The haste of sin, the slowness of salvation: waiting in the theological anthropology of Irenaeus, Gregory of Nyssa and Simone Weil." Diss., Univ. of Virginia, 2008.

WELLENS, Serge.

GG7726. • *Serge Wellens*. Prés. François Huglo. Montreuil-sur-Brèche: Vanneaux, 2008. *Présence de la poésie*. 143 p.

WERTH, Léon.

GG7727. Haddad, Galit: "Comme si lui-même n'appartenait pas à la guerre: Léon Werth, du discours libertaire dans la fiction." In 473, 223-235.

WEYERGANS, François.

GG7728. Fréché, Bibiane: "La double filiation des Weyergans." In 572, 199-206.

WHITE, Kenneth. See also 1019.

GG7729. ● *Horizons de Kenneth White: littérature, pensée, géopoétique.* Paris: Isolato, 2008. 191 p.

GG7730. Bineau, Anne: "La figure de l'oiseau dans l'œuvre de Kenneth White." In 7729, 39-68.

GG7731. Chauche, Catherine: "Géopoétique et temporalité." In 7729, 129-138.

GG7732. Demangeat, Michel: "Au-delà . . . Du sentiment océanique chez Kenneth White." In 7729, 23-38.

GG7733. Duclos, Michèle: "Kenneth White, un 'Ecossais extravagant'." In 7729, 15-22.

GG7734. Gillet, Alexandre: "La montagne dans l'œuvre de Kenneth White." In 7729, 77-95.

GG7735. Lévy, Bertrand: "Poétique de la neige." In 7729, 97-105.

GG7736. Loubes, Jean-Paul: "La géopoétique dans l'espace." In 7729, 139-148.

GG7737. Navarri, Roger: "Physique et poétique du voyage de Victor Segalen à Kenneth White." In 7729, 69-76. [Segalen]

GG7738. Robaye, Hugues: "Reconstitution présumée du dialogue de Kenneth White avec Rainer-Maria Rilke." In 7729, 107-127.

GG7739. Wacrenier, Christian: "Epure topographique ou les voies d'une topologie paradoxale." In 7729, 149-170.

WIESEL, Elie. See also 519.

GG7740. ● Downing, Frederick L.: *Elie Wiesel: a religious biography.* Macon, GA: Mercer Univ. Press, 2008. xiv, 282 p.

GG7741. ● Völker, Andreas: *Elie Wiesel: Zeichen setzen-selbst zum Zeichen werden.* Berlin; Münster: Lit, 2008. 109 p.

GG7742. ● Wiesel, Elie; Michaël de Saint-Cheron. *Entretiens avec Elie Wiesel, 1984-2000; suivi de, Wiesel, ce méconnu.* Paris: Parole et silence, 2008. 149 p.

GG7743. Suleiman, Susan Rubin: "Do facts matter in Holocaust memoirs? Wilkomirski/Wiesel." In 600.

WILLEMS, Paul.

GG7744. Rossion, Laurent: "L'écriture, le fascinant masque du réel chez Paul Willems." In 441, 149-160.

WITTIG, Monique.

GG7745. MacPherson, Pauline: "Constructions of violence: destabilising the fe/male in Wittig and Winterson." In 871, 97-109.

XUEREB, Jean-Claude.

GG7746. Le Boucher, Dominique: "Témoins du soleil," *Algérie Littérature/Action,* no. 125-126 (nov.-déc. 2008), 31-37.

YACINE, Kateb. See also 306a, 643.

GG7747. ● Douiri, Farida: *La sémiologie de la mort dans le roman maghrébin d'expression française: dans Nedjma et Le polygone étoilé de Kateb Yacine.* Lille: ANRT, 2008. *Thèse à la carte.* 284 p.

GG7748. Escafre-Dublet, Angéline: "L'aventure de *Mohamed prends ta valise* de Kateb yacine." In 1100, 87-100.

GG7749. Piriou, Marine: "Retour sur *Le Polygone étoilé,* matrice des *personae* katébiennes." In 441, 39-55.

YAOU, Régina.

GG7750. Sanusi, Ramonu: " 'Contre vents et marées, je mène ma barque'. Entretien avec Régina Yaou, écrivaine ivoirienne," *Nouvelles Etudes Francophones,* vol. 22, no. 2 (automne 2007), 187-197.

YAYA, Dahirou.

GG7751. Dili Palaï, Clément: "Du dysfonctionnement de l'espace urbain dans *Le Diamant maudit* de Dahirou Yaya." In 99, 165-177.

YOURCENAR, Marguerite. See also 420, 470, 779, 4949, 6478.

GG7752. ● Barbier, Catherine: *Etude sur Marguerite Yourcenar, Les nouvelles orientales*. Paris: Ellipses marketing, 2008. 2e éd. 142 p.

GG7753. ● Blanchet-Douspis, Mireille: *L'influence de l'histoire contemporaine dans l'œuvre de Marguerite Yourcenar*. Amsterdam: Rodopi, 2008. *Faux titre*, 310. 513 p.

GG7754. ● Cravio, Graciela: *Marguerite Yourcenar: vocera de antiguos dioses*. Buenos Aires: Capital Intelectual, 2008. 133 p.

GG7755. ● *Elogio al Nero: Marguerite Yourcenar, l'opera al nero, la sua alchimia attraverso le arti*. Catalogo a cura di Claudio Crescentini, Laura Monachesi. Roma: Camera di Commercio industria artigianato e agricoltura, 2005. 190 p.

GG7756. ● *Marguerite Yourcenar et l'univers poétique: actes du colloque international de Tokyo (9-12 septembre 2004)*. Textes réunis par Osamu Hayashi, Naoko Hiramatsu et Rémy Poignault. Clermont-Ferrand: Publications de la Société internationale d'études yourcenariennes, 2008. 396 p.

GG7757. ● *Marguerite Yourcenar sulle tracce des accidents passagers*. A cura di Eleonora Pinzuti. Roma: Bulzoni, 2007. 292 p.

GG7758. ● Viala, Fabienne: *Marguerite Yourcenar, Alejo Carpentier: écritures de l'histoire*. Bruxelles: Peter Lang, 2008. *Yourcenar*, 1. 183 p.

GG7759. Acocella, Joan Ross: "Becoming the emperor: Marguerite Yourcenar." In 786.

GG7760. Alesch, Jeanine S.: "Marguerite Yourcenar, traductrice d'Hortense Flexner." In 7756, 267-276.

GG7761. Andersson, Kajsa: "Marguerite Yourcenar et l'héritage de l'univers poétique paternel." In 7756, 89-108.

GG7762. Baron, Dumitra: " 'Voici que le silence . . .': pour une poétique de l'absence dans *Les Charités d'Alcippe* et *Feux* de Marguerite Yourcenar." In 7756, 75-87.

GG7763. Bonali Fiquet, Françoise: "Choix bibliographique 2008," *Bulletin, Société Internationale d'Etudes Yourcenariennes*, no. 29 (déc. 2008), 111-120.

GG7764. Bonali Fiquet, Françoise: "La dame dans l'île. Construction d'un mythe." In 423.

GG7765. Bouchard, Jacqueline: "Une jeune gothique nommée Électre. *Électre ou la Chute des masques*," *Jeu: Cahiers de Théâtre*, no. 126 (mars 2008), 56-58.

GG7766. Bourgois, Lylian Y.: "Féminin/masculin: ordres et désordres du corps dans l'œuvre de Marguerite Yourcenar." Diss., Univ. of Massachusetts, Amherst, 2008. xii, 450 p.

GG7767. Brémond, Mireille: "Pindare et Yourcenar." In 7756, 145-159.

GG7768. Capusan, Horia: "Deux âmes dans la poitrine du personnage yourcenarien." In 7756, 327-332.

GG7769. Capusan, Horia: "Marguerite Yourcenar et le théâtre poétique." In 7756, 305-316.

GG7770. Caron, Pascal: "Le poème et la danse chez Marguerite Yourcenar." In 7756, 109-122.

GG7771. Castellani, Jean-Pierre: "Réception, traduction et influence des sonnets de Marguerite Yourcenar en Argentine." In 7756, 235-248.

GG7772. Castellani, Jean-Pierre: "Les tribulations d'un livre argentin en Europe," *Bulletin, Société Internationale d'Etudes Yourcenariennes*, no. 29 (déc. 2008), 19-20.

GG7773. Cavazzutti, Maria: "Le mythe d'Ulysse, une métaphore de l'univers poétique de Marguerite Yourcenar." In 7756, 123-134.

GG7774. Cavazzutti, Maria: "Le rapport à l'autre dans l'écriture de Marguerite Yourcenar." In 423.

GG7775. Chehab, May: "Le coup de dés de Marguerite Yourcenar." In 7756, 369-382.

GG7776. Cliche, Elène: "Marguerite Yourcenar et la poésie d'Hortense Flexner." In 7756, 251-266.

GG7777. Counihan, Francesca: "Marguerite Yourcenar, Hortense Flexner: croisements poétiques." In 7756, 291-302.

GG7778. Delcroix, Maurice: "L'île Yourcenar." In 423.

GG7779. Delcroix, Maurice: "La poéticité de la nuit des temps." In 7756, 383-394.

GG7780. Deprez, Bérengère: *"Je ne me trouve plus qu'en me cherchant ailleurs,"* Bulletin, Société Internationale d'Etudes Yourcenariennes, no. 29 (déc. 2008), 35-45.

GG7781. Deprez, Bérengère: " 'Un peu plus près de la vie'. Construction d'un personnage historique de fiction: Zénon dans L'Œuvre au noir de Marguerite Yourcenar." In 904, 57-69.

GG7782. "Dossier Lettres belges," Bulletin, Société Internationale d'Etudes Yourcenariennes, no. 29 (déc. 2008), 127-183.

GG7783. "Dossier: Quatrième version du libretto tiré de Mémoires d'Hadrien par Wells Hively," Bulletin, Société Internationale d'Etudes Yourcenariennes, no. 29 (déc. 2008), 185-235.

GG7784. Fava, Francesca: "Una perfetta alchimia tra critica e creazione letteraria: Le Cerveau noir de Piranèse di Marguerite Yourcenar." In 563, 47-53.

GG7785. Fayet, Agnès: "Dans le sillage de la Contre-Réforme. Poétique visuelle dans Anna, soror . . . de Marguerite Yourcenar." In 7756, 349-360.

GG7786. Fayet, Agnès: "Marguerite Yourcenar et 'les voies secrètes du mysticisme'," Bulletin, Société Internationale d'Etudes Yourcenariennes, no. 29 (déc. 2008), 25-34.

GG7787. Fréris, Georges: "La poéticité mythique dans Feux de Marguerite Yourcenar." In 7756, 49-59.

GG7788. Giorgi, Giorgetto: "L'îlot de marbre de la villa impériale de Tibur dans Mémoires d'Hadrien de Marguerite Yourcenar." In 423.

GG7789. Halley, Achmy: "Marguerite Yourcenar, poète au-delà du poème." In 7756, 135-142.

GG7790. Hayashi, Osamu: "Marguerite Yourcenar et la poésie du haïku." In 7756, 215-224.

GG7791. Hiramatsu, Naoko: " 'Carrefour des songes': la poétique du nô dans l'œuvre théâtrale de Marguerite Yourcenar." In 7756, 317-325.

GG7792. Iwasaki, Tsutomu: "Marguerite Yourcenar au/et le Japon." In 7756, 11-23.

GG7793. Kudawara, Yasuko: "Marguerite Yourcenar et la poéticité du nô." In 7756, 225-234.

GG7794. Lee, Hye-Ok: "La spiritualité poétique dans l'œuvre de Marguerite Yourcenar." In 7756, 333-348.

GG7795. Maindron, André: "L'art du sonnet dans Les Charités d'Alcippe." In 7756, 37-48.

GG7796. Malachy, Thérèse: "Le mythe en devenir: l'Electre de Marguerite Yourcenar." In 1093.

GG7797. "Marguerite Yourcenar," Twentieth-Century Literary Criticism, vol. 193 (2008), 247-369.

GG7798. Mazza, Valentina: "Analyse de la traduction du chant XXVI de l'Enfer de Dante Alighieri, vv 94-142." In 7756, 185-201.

GG7799. Melzi d'Eril, Francesca: "La présence de la poésie italienne de la Renaissance dans l'œuvre de Marguerite Yourcenar." In 7756, 173-184.

GG7800. Molina Romero, Maria Carmen: "Marguerite Yourcenar: entre le silence linguistique et le silence des femmes," Estudios de Lengua y Literatura Francesas, no. 17 (2006-2007), 119-138.

GG7801. Orphanidou-Freris, Maria: "Moderniser la tradition: Marguerite Yourcenar traductrice des poètes grecs de l'Antiquité." In 7756, 161-172.

GG7802. Ouelbani, M. K.: "Naples et la Campanie dans l'écriture de Marguerite Yourcenar," Annali, Università degli Studi di Napoli "L'Orientale", Sezione Romanza, anno 49, n. 2 (2007), 585-613.

GG7803. Ouelbani, Mehdi Karim: "La représentation de Naples et de sa région dans l'écriture yourcenarienne," Bulletin, Société Internationale d'Etudes Yourcenariennes, no. 29 (déc. 2008), 83-110.

GG7804. Poignault, Rémy: "L'île et le pouvoir impérial chez Fronton et Marguerite Yourcenar: résurgence d'une image." In 423.

GG7805. Primozich-Parslow, Loredana: "Les juvenilia yourcenariens entre reniement et remaniement." In 7756, 27-36.

GG7806.   Reggiani, Francesca: " 'Au voisinage du roc et de la vague'. Marguerite Yourcenar traductrice d'Hortense Flexner." In 7756, 277-289.

GG7807.   Romagnolo, Monica: "Marguerite Yourcenar et le poème en prose." In 7756, 61-74.

GG7808.   Smith, Evans Lansing: "The goddess and the underworld in modernism: Marguerite Yourcenar's *Feux*." In 569, 162-176.

GG7809.   Snyman, Elisabeth: "Mémoire et identité dans *Quoi? L'Eternité* de Marguerite Yourcenar," *French Studies in Southern Africa*, no. 38 (2008), 136-158.

GG7810.   Straner, Zsófia: "Formes musicales dans le texte littéraire: analyse des *Nouvelles orientales* de Marguerite Yourcenar," *Verbum*, vol. 10, no. 2 (2008), 413-435.

GG7811.   Terneuil, Alexandre: "L'art du portrait chez Marguerite Yourcenar," *Bulletin, Société Internationale d'Etudes Yourcenariennes*, no. 29 (déc. 2008), 47-64.

GG7812.   Viala, Fabienne: "De l'enquête généalogique à l'enquête historique: *La Vie scélérate* de Maryse Condé et *Le Labyrinthe du monde* de Marguerite Yourcenar." In 571, 265-272.

GG7813.   Viala, Fabienne: "Le 'roman à histoire' de Marguerite Yourcenar." In 904, 71-87.

GG7814.   Vinas del Palacio, Yolanda: "Marguerite Yourcenar ou l'alchimie du verbe." In 7756, 361-368.

GG7815.   Wagner, Michel: "Dialogues entre critique, auteur et traducteur," *Bulletin, Société Internationale d'Etudes Yourcenariennes*, no. 29 (déc. 2008), 21-24.

GG7816.   Wagner, Walter: "Marguerite Yourcenar et Henry David Thoreau," *Bulletin, Société Internationale d'Etudes Yourcenariennes*, no. 29 (déc. 2008), 65-82.

GG7817.   Wagner, Walter: "Sur les traces de Rilke dans *Alexis*." In 7756, 203-213.

ZAMENGA, Batukezanga.

GG7818.   Yoka, Lye M.: "Batukezanga Zamenga: le contour populaire," *Cultures Sud*, no. 170 (sept. 2008), 135-141.

ZELLER, Florian.

GG7819.   ● Zeller, Florian: *Elle t'attend*. Paris: Avant-Scène Théâtre, 2008. *Avant-Scène Théâtre*, no. 1248 (15 sept. 2008). 85 p.

Z'GRAGGEN, Yvette.

GG7820.   Biron Cohen, Cynthia: "Interrogation existentielle d'Yvette Z'Graggen, une écrivaine engagée," *Études de Lettres*, no. 279 [no. 1] (2008), 149-162.

ZOBEL, Joseph. See also 6894.

GG7821.   ● Le Moigne, José: *Joseph Zobel: le cœur en Martinique et les pieds en Cévennes*. Matoury: Ibis rouge, 2008. 172 p.

GG7822.   Hardwick, Louise: "Dancing the unspeakable: rhythms of communication in 'Laghia de la mort' by Joseph Zobel." In 575, 119-131.

GG7823.   Thibault, André: "Français des Antilles et français d'Amérique: les diatopismes de Joseph Zobel, auteur martiniquais," *Revue de Linguistique Romane*, tome 72, no. 285-286 (juin-juillet 2008), 117-156.

ZOLA, Émile. See also 398, 621, 689, 702, 719, 738, 888, 1157, 2945, 2947, 4549.

GG7824.   ● Arnoux-Farnoux, Lucile; Isabelle Gadoin; Chris Rauséo; Catherine Lanone: *Destinées féminines, naturalisme européen: Nana, Tess, Effi Briest*. Neuilly: Atlande, 2008. 250 p.

GG7825.   ● Della Bianca, Luca: *Introduzione alla grandezza di Emile Zola*. Pesaro: Metauro, 2008. *Studi*. 175 p.

GG7826.   ● *Destinées féminines dans le contexte du naturalisme européen*. Ouvrage dirigé par Juliette Vion-Dury. Paris: Armand Colin, 2008. 238 p.

GG7827.   ● *Destinées féminines dans le roman naturaliste européen: Zola, Fontane, Hardy*. Ouvrage coordonné par Sylvie Thorel-Cailleteau. Paris: PUF, 2008. *CNED-PUF, Littérature comparée*. 171 p.

GG7828.   ● Drouin, Michel: *Zola au Panthéon: la quatrième affaire Dreyfus*. Paris: Perrin, 2008. 165 p.

GG7829.   ● Emile-Zola, Brigitte: *Mes étés à Brienne*. Préface d'Alain Pagès. Agneaux: Frisson esthétique, 2008. *Sources*. 189 p.

GG7830. • *Emile Zola: mémoire et sensations*. Véronique Cnockaert, dir. Montréal: XYZ, 2008. 277 p.

GG7831. • Küster, Sabine: *Medizin im Roman: Untersuchungen zu "Les Rougon Macquart" von Emile Zola*. Göttingen: Cuvillier, 2008. 308 p.

GG7832. • Mahjoub-Garbouj, Ghazia: *Réalisme et polémique dans "Pot-Bouille" d'Emile Zola*. Tunis: Centre de publication universitaire, 2008. 119 p.

GG7833. • Mbarga, Christian: *Emile Zola: les femmes de pouvoir dans Les Rougon-Macquart*. Paris: L'Harmattan, 2008. *Approches littéraires*. 229 p.

GG7834. • Mitterand, Henri: *Le Paris de Zola*. Paris: Hazan, 2008. 239 p.

GG7835. • Naccarato, Annafrancesca: *Poétique de la métonymie: les traductions italiennes de "La curée" d'Emile Zola au XIXe siècle*. Roma: Aracne, 2008. 239 p.

GG7836. • Olsson, Eva M.: *L'organisation du lexique dans Thérèse Raquin d'Emile Zola*. Stockholm: Institutionen för franska, italienska och klassiska språk, Stockholms universitet, 2008. 76 p.

7836a. • Pagès, Alain: *Emile Zola: de J'accuse au Panthéon*. Saint-Paul: L. Souny, 2008. 414 p.

GG7837. • Panella, Giuseppe: *Emile Zola: scrittore sperimentale: per la ricostruzione di una poetica della modernità*. Chieti: Solfanelli, 2008. *Micromegas*. 117 p.

GG7838. • Roy-Reverzy, Eléonore: *Eléonore Roy-Reverzy commente Nana d'Emile Zola*. Paris: Gallimard, 2008. *Foliothèque*. 232 p.

GG7839. • Sherard, Robert Harborough: *Emile Zola: a biographical and critical study*. Whitefish, MT: Kessinger, 2008. *Kessinger publishing's rare reprints*. 287 p. [Orig. ed., 1893]

GG7840. • Spieker, Annika: *Der doppelte Blick: Photographie und Malerei in Emile Zolas Rougon-Macquart*. Heidelberg: Winter, 2008. *Studia Romanica*. 255 p.

GG7841. • Zola, Emile: *L'Assommoir*. Chronologie, prés., notes, dossier, bibliographie, lexique par Chantal Pierre-Gnassounou. Paris: Flammarion, 2008. Ed. mise à jour. *GF*. 576 p.

GG7842. • Zola, Emile: *L'Assommoir*. Dossier et notes réalisés par Xavier Bourdenet; lecture d'image par Agnès Varlet. Paris: Gallimard, 2008. *Folioplus classiques*. 544 p.

GG7843. • Zola, Emile: *L'Assommoir*. Edition établie et annotée par Henri Mitterand. Paris: Gallimard, 2008. *Folio classique*.

GG7844. • Zola, Emile: *La conquête de Plassans*. Préface, dossier et notes par Colette Becker. Paris: Librairie générale française, 2008. *Le livre de poche*. 508 p.

GG7845. • Zola, Emile: *Contes et nouvelles*. Choix de textes, prés., notes, vie de Zola, chron. des contes et nouvelles, et bibliographie par François-Marie Mourard. Paris: Flammarion, 2008. *GF*. 2 vols.

GG7846. • Zola, Emile: *De l'Affaire aux Quatre Evangiles (1897-1901)*. Prés., notices, chron., et biblio. par Alain Pagès. Paris: Nouveau monde, 2008. *Œuvres complètes*, tome 18. 671 p.

GG7847. • Zola, Emile: *The fête at Coqueville*. Trans. L. G. Meyer; with an essay by Edmund Gosse about the short stories of Zola. New York: Mondial, 2008. xxxii, 59 p.

GG7848. • Zola, Emile: *La fortune des Rougon (1871)*. Notes et dossier, Anne Cassou-Noguès. Paris: Hatier, 2008. *Classiques & cie*. 447 p.

GG7849. • Zola, Emile: *La fortune des Rougon*. Préface de Maurice Agulhon; édition établie et annotée par Henri Mitterand. Paris: Gallimard, 2008. *Folio classique*. 460 p. [Orig. ed., 1981]

GG7850. • Zola, Emile: *Germinal*. Trans. Peter Collier; introd. Robert Lethbridge. Oxford; New York: Oxford Univ. Press, 2008. *Oxford's world classics*. 538 p. [Orig. ed., 1993]

GG7851. • Zola, Emile: *Germinal*. Chron., prés., notes, dossier, biblio., lexique par Adeline Wrona. Paris: Flammarion, 2008. Ed. mise à jour. *GF*. 622 p.

GG7852. • Zola, Emile: *L'inondation et autres nouvelles*. Etude des œuvres par Chantal Saint-Jarre. Montréal: Beauchemin Chenelière éducation, 2008. *Parcours d'une œuvre*. 286 p.

GG7853. • Zola, Emile: *La joie de vivre*. Préf. Jean Borie; édition établie et annotée par Henri Mitterand. Paris: Gallimard, 2008. *Folio classique*. 442 p.

GG7854. ● Zola, Emile: *The ladies' paradise*. Trans. introd. , notes by Brian Nelson. Oxford; New York: Oxford Univ. Press, 2008. *Oxford world's classics*. xxxi, 438 p. [Orig. ed., 1995]

GG7855. ● Zola, Emile: *The masterpiece*. Trans. Thomas Walton; trans. revised and introduced by Roger Pearson. Oxford; New York: Oxford Univ. Press, 2008. *Oxford world's classics*. xxix, 366 p.

GG7856. ● Zola, Emile: *Nana*. Ed. prés., établie et annotée par Henri Mitterand. Paris: Gallimard, 2008. *Folio classique*. 500 p.

GG7857. ● Zola, Emile: *Paris fin de siècle (1897)*. Prés., notices, chronologie et bibliographie par Jacques Noiray. Paris: Nouveau monde, 2008. *Œuvres complètes*, tome 17. 507 p.

GG7858. ● Zola, Emile: *Thérèse Raquin*. Trans., introd., notes by Andrew Rothwell. Oxford; New York: Oxford Univ. Press, 2008. *Oxford world's classics*. xl, 211 p. [Orig. ed., 1992]

GG7859. ● Zola, Emile: *Thérèse Raquin*. Introd., annexes, chron. et biblio. par Henri Mitterand. Paris: Flammarion, 2008. Ed. mise à jour. *GF*. 302 p.

GG7860. ● Zola, Emile: *Thérèse Raquin*. Prés., notes et dossier par Thierry Corbeau. Paris: Flammarion, 2008. *Etonnants classiques*. 287 p.

GG7861. ● Zola, Emile: *Trois nouvelles: Le grand Michu, Jacques Damour, Angeline*. Dossier et notes réalisés par Marianne Chomienne, Stéphane Chomienne; lecture d'image par sophie Barthélémy. Paris: Gallimard, 2008. *Folioplus classiques*. 162 p.

GG7862. ● Zola, Emile: *Le ventre de Paris*. Commentaire et notes de Philippe Hamon et Marie-France Azéma; introd. Robert Abirached. Paris: Librairie générale française, 2008. *Le livre de poche*. 382 p.

GG7863. ● *Zola, réceptions comiques: le naturalisme parodié par ses contemporains*. Ed. Daniel Compère, Catherine Dousteyssier-Khoze. Paris: Eurédit, 2008. 274 p.

GG7864. Acher, Lionel: "La boucle transgénérique de *Phèdre* chez Zola." In 766, 249-261.

GG7865. Armstrong, Marie-Sophie: " 'Le chapitre de Jenlain', ou la mise en abyme fantasmatique de *Germinal*," *Nineteenth-Century French Studies*, vol. 37, no. 1-2 (Fall-Winter 2008-2009), 81-96.

GG7866. Armstrong, Marie-Sophie: "*Son Excellence Eugène Rougon* et la problématique de l'analité," *Excavatio*, no. 1-2 (2008), 280-293.

GG7867. Aynié, Marie: "Lettres de soutien à Émile Zola dans l'Affaire Dreyfus," *Cahiers Naturalistes*, 54e année, no. 82 (2008), 7-19.

GG7868. Baguley, David: "Histoire et fiction: *Les Rougon-Macquart* de Zola." In 908, 69-82.

GG7869. Baguley, David: "Zola à l'école anglaise? Raison et sensibilité dans *Une page d'amour*." In 7830, 167-175.

GG7870. Bahler, Ursula: "Sur les traces naturalistes de *La Vérité en marche*," *Cahiers Naturalistes*, 54e année, no. 82 (2008), 83-108.

GG7871. Barilier, Etienne: "Que mes œuvres périssent, si Dreyfus n'est pas innocent!" In 388, 68-81.

GG7872a. Baron, Anne-Marie: "Zola. Le roman du peuple." In 7963.

GG7872. Becker, Colette: "La fabrique des *Rougon-Macquart*," *Cahiers Octave Mirbeau*, no. 15 (2008), 167-179.

GG7873. Becker, Colette: " 'Moi, je soutiens que j'ai ma psychologie' (Zola)," *Ritm*, no. 38 (2007), 325-336.

GG7874. Becker, Colette: "La nuit mystérieuse de la chair." In 7830, 131-141.

GG7875. Becker, Colette: "Présentation de l'édition des dossiers préparatoires des *Rougon-Macquart*," *Excavatio*, vol. 23, no. 1-2 (2008), 13-24.

GG7876. Bell, David F.: "La communication instantanée: *Au bonheur des dames*." In 7830, 241-251.

GG7877. Bell, Dorian: "Cavemen among us: genealogies of atavism from Zola's *La Bête humaine* to Chabrol's *Le Boucher*," *French Studies*, vol. 62, no. 1 (Jan. 2008), 53-64. [Chabrol]

GG7878. Benjamin, Andrew: "Experimentation as a defence of literature: Zola's *Le roman expérimental,*" *Australian Journal of French Studies,* vol. 45, no. 1 (Jan.-April 2008), 59-72.

GG7879. Berquin, François: " 'Ne vois-tu pas que nous somme nus?'," *Revue des Sciences Humaines,* no. 289 [no. 1] (2008), 89-104.

GG7880. Bishop, Danielle: "*Au bonheur des dames*: a novel of construction, constructors, and the constructed," *Excavatio,* vol. 23, no. 1-2 (2008), 243-254.

GG7881. Bouarada, Mohamed: "Le concept d'isotopie au service de la cohésion et de la cohérence des textes." In 410, 341-350.

GG7882. Brinton Tildesley, Matthew: "Emile the innocent: a portrait of Zola in a British *fin de siècle* magazine," *Bulletin of the Emile Zola Society,* no. 37-38 (2008), 3-10.

GG7883. Brogowski, Leszek: "*Zola fuit hic* le documentaire: dispositif photographie, dispositif littéraire." In 508, 127-152.

GG7884. Cabanès, Jean-Louis: "A fleur de peau, au fond du corps." In 7830, 143-155.

GG7885. Cardona, Rodolfo: "Note on Zola and Galdós: 1883-1887," *Revista Canadiense de Estudios Hispánicas,* vol. 31, no. 3 (primavera 2008), 475-488.

GG7886. Castagnès, Gilles: "De Musset à Zola: les 'caprices' d'*Une page d'amour,*" *Revue d'Histoire Littéraire de la France,* tome 108, no. 2 (avril-juin 2008), 347-365.

GG7887. Chaitin, Gilbert D.: "Le cauchemar de la *Vérité,* ou le rêve du revenant," *Cahiers Naturalistes,* 54e année, no. 82 (2008), 187-197.

GG7888. Chaitin, Gilbert D.: "*Truth,* by Emile Zola: Zola's daymare and the truth of vérité." In 405.

GG7889. Chalaye, Gérard: "Les jardins de l'Empire. Sand-Zola." In 487, 323-334.

GG7890. Chen, I-Ju Ruby: "Zola's *Nana* and Toulouse-Lautrec's *Elles*: women like many others," *Excavatio,* vol. 23, no. 1-2 (2008), 266-279.

GG7891. Clamor, Annette: "Le rêve, élément narratif dans *Le Docteur Pascal,*" *Cahiers Naturalistes,* 54e année, no. 82 (2008), 139-164.

GG7892. Cnockaert, Véronique: "Mémoire de peau." In 7830, 157-166.

GG7893. Counter, Andrew: "The legacy of the beast: patrilinearity and rupture in Zola's *La Bête humaine* and Freud's *Totem and Taboo,*" *French Studies,* vol. 62, no. 1 (Jan. 2008), 26-38.

GG7894. Cummins, Anthony: "The transmission of Emile Zola in English literary culture, 1877-1895." Diss., Univ. of Oxford, 2008. v, 218 p.

GG7895. Diaz, José-Luis: " 'En nourrice chez les illusions': la correspondance de Zola comme préface à la vie d'écrivain," *Elseneur,* no. 22 (2008), [n.p.].

GG7896. Dirda, Michel: "Emile Zola." In 430.

GG7897. Disegni, Silvia: "Emile Zola all'Indice," *Esperienze Letterarie,* anno 33, n. 4 (ott.-dic. 2008), 47-78.

GG7898. Dotoli, Giovanni: "Zola: écrivain du XXIe siècle," *Presse Littéraire,* no. 16 (2008), 6-30.

GG7899. Dousteyssier-Khoze, Catherine: "*L'Assommoir*: from novel to drama to theatrical parody." In 540, 214-234.

GG7900. Duchêne, Hervé: "Salamon Reinach, Carlos Blacker et l'Affaire," *Cahiers Naturalistes,* 54e année, no. 82 (2008), 49-77.

GG7901. Dufief, Anne-Simone: "Emile Zola critique dramatique," *Annali, Università degli Studi di Napoli "L'Orientale", Sezione Romanza,* anno 49, n. 2 (2007), 461-474.

GG7902. DuPont, Denise: "Decadent naturalism: Eduardo López Bago's response to Emile Zola," *Excavatio,* vol. 23, no. 1-2 (2008), 47-60.

GG7903. Elkabas, Charles: "Mémoire biblique et mémoire poétique: *Le Docteur Pascal* de A à Z." In 7830, 63-75.

GG7904. Emery, Elizabeth: " 'Aux mères heureuses': Zola's compassion for working mothers," *Excavatio,* vol. 23, no. 1-2 (2008), 169-182.

GG7905. Emery, Elizabeth: "Naturalism on stage: the performance and reception of Zola's *Messidor.*" In 540, 126-154.

GG7906. Färnlöf, Hans: "Zola et la motivation," *Cahiers Naturalistes,* 54e année, no. 82 (2008), 199-216.

GG7907. Febles, Eduardo A.: "The anarchic commune as world's fair in Emile Zola's

Travail," *Nineteenth-Century French Studies*, vol. 36, no. 3-4 (Spring-Summer 2008), 286-304.

GG7908. Fougère, Marie-Ange: "La mémoire du lecteur de Zola." In 7830, 253-263.

GG7909. Foulon, Jean-François: "Lire Zola au XXIe siècle?," *Presse Littéraire*, no. 16 (2008), 33-48.

GG7910. Gebet, Gwendoline: "Trois lettres de Zola dans le fonds Labori," *Revue de la Bibliothèque Nationale de France*, no. 29 (2008), 63-72.

GG7911. Gebet, Gwendoline: "Urbain Gohier, polémiste de la panthéonisation," *Cahiers Naturalistes*, 54e année, no. 82 (2008), 79-82.

GG7912. Goux, Jean-Joseph: "Emile Zola: de l'argent de l'écriture à l'écriture de *L'Argent*." In 465, 145-160.

GG7913. Guillemont, Édith: "Un dreyfusard inconnu, Félix Froissart," *Cahiers Naturalistes*, 54e année, no. 82 (2008), 21-48.

GG7914. Harrow, Susan: "Stressing the body, straining narrative: figures at work in the *Rougon-Macquart*," *Dalhousie French Studies*, vol. 84 (Fall 2008), 41-50.

GG7915. Harrow, Susan: "Velocity, vacancy and consciousness: female character as culture critic in *La Bête humaine* and *Au bonheur des dames*," *Excavatio*, vol. 23, no. 1-2 (2008), 214-226.

GG7916. Hennessy, Susie: "Consumption and desire in *Au Bonheur des dames*," *French Review*, vol. 81, no. 4 (March 2008), 696-706.

GG7917. Hinton, Marie-Laure: "Emile Zola photographe." Diss., UCLA, 2008. xi, 179 p.

GG7918. Howell, Keith: "Zola in America," *Bulletin of the Emile Zola Society*, no. 37-38 (2008), 34-40.

GG7919. Larroux, Guy: "La chamber et le bouge," *Poétique*, no. 153 (févr. 2008), 3-15.

GG7920. Laurin, Marie-Eve: "Le personnage-mémoire dans l'univers des *Rougon-Macquart*." In 7830, 77-85.

GG7921. Laville, Béatrice: "La pensée de la chair." In 7830, 177-186.

GG7922. Leduc-Adine, Jean-Pierre: "Topographies zoliennes, ou du référent au dessin et du dessin à l'écriture." In 418, 222-240.

GG7923. Lemarié, Yannick: "Les sons, le réel insolite et le doute dans l'œuvre de Zola." In 439, 125-136.

GG7924. Lintz, Bernadette C.: "Les murs de la mémoire: Hugo dans *La Débâcle*." In 7830, 31-45.

GG7925. Lumbroso, Olivier: "Zola, ou la sensation retrouvée." In 7830, 189-204.

GG7926. Lyotard, Dolorès: "Pudeurs," *Revue des Sciences Humaines*, no. 289 [no. 1] (2008), 105-137.

GG7927. Marzel, Shoshana-Rose: "Female shoppers in *The Ladies' Paradise*," *Bulletin of the Emile Zola Society*, no. 37-38 (2008), 11-19.

GG7928. Ménard, Sophie: "Paradoxes du monstre en régime zolien." In 527, 57-69.

GG7929. Ménard, Sophie: "Les parcours mémoriels et sensitifs de Serge Mouret." In 7830, 87-97.

GG7930. Mitterand, Henri: "*Les Rougon-Macquart*: la violence fondatrice." In 7830, 19-29.

GG7931. Mouanda, Sharon: "*Mise en abyme* and narrative function in Zola's *La Curée*," *Modern Language Review*, vol. 103, part 1 (Jan. 2008), 35-45.

GG7932. Mullier, Sébastien: "Commentaire composée, *Nana*." In 7827, 130-139.

GG7933. Ng, Lisa: "La femme in absentia dans *Les Rougon-Macquart* de Zola," *Excavatio*, vol. 23, no. 1-2 (2008), 227-242.

GG7934. Noiray, Jacques: "Zola, mémoire et vérité de la chair." In 7830, 119-129.

GG7935. Nøjgaard, Morten: "Splendor corporis-splendor veritatis? Le corps féminin comme démonstration ou subversion de la vérité," *Excavatio*, vol. 23, no. 1-2 (2008), 74-90.

GG7936. Nuti, Marco: "Zola et Cézanne: les inquiétudes de la création." In 542.

GG7937. Pagès, Alain: "Les mots témoins." In 7830, 205-218.

GG7938. Pierre-Gnassounou, Chantal: "Fragments d'enfance." In 7830, 99-115.

GG7939. Piton-Foucault, Emilie: "Merveille et monstruosité de l'image photographique dans les *Rougon-Macquart* d'Emile Zola." In 508, 201-215.

GG7940. Piton-Foucault, Emilie: "Un rempart contre le chaos du réel? Jardin et intériorité psychique dans les *Rougon-Macquart* d'Emile Zola." In 487, 335-346.

GG7941. Reverzy, Eléonore: "*Nana*: la fabrique d'un personnage," *Excavatio*, vol. 23, no. 1-2 (2008), 255-265.

GG7942. Ross, James: "Messidor: Republican patriotism and the French revolutionary tradition in Third Republic opera." In 829, 112-130.

GG7943. Rouhier, Amélie: "*Son Excellence Eugène Rougon* ou la rupture selon Zola," *Presse Littéraire*, no. 16 92008), 31-32.

GG7944. Sandras-Fraysse, Agnès; Maria Virgílio Cambraia Lopes: "Zola vu par Rafael Bordalo Pinheiro," *Cahiers Naturalistes*, 54e année, no. 82 (2008), 289-300.

GG7945. Sandu, Corina: "Zola, entre le souvenir vestimentaire et le discours sur le vêtement." In 7830, 229-240.

GG7946. Scarpa, Marie: "De Quasimodo à Marjolin le sot: la mémoire culturelle du roman zolien." In 7830, 47-62.

GG7947. Scharf, Fabian: "Un modèle utopique de *Travail*," *Cahiers Naturalistes*, 54e année, no. 82 (2008), 165-185.

GG7948. Shivanandan, Mary: "Emile Zola: improbable defender of life." In 841.

GG7949. Stone, Barbara M.: "Family law in Zola: the example of the *tutelle*," *New Zealand Journal of French Studies*, vol. 29, no. 1 (2008), 5-16.

GG7950. Szczur, Przemyslaw: "Le sexe du héros: identité sexuelle, mise en intrigue et focalisation dans *La Curée* d'Emile Zola," *Excavatio*, vol. 23, no. 1-2 (2008), 25-38.

GG7951. Thompson, Hannah: "Métaphore et mémoire dans les *Rougon-Macquart*." In 7830, 219-228.

GG7952. Tworek, Agnieszka: "Death masks in *Thérèse Raquin*," *Excavatio*, vol. 23, no. 1-2 (2008), 195-202.

GG7953. Van Tooren, Marjolein: "Neither angel nor she-devil: realism and women's self-determination in Zola's short stories," *Excavatio*, vol. 23, no. 1-2 (2008), 109-122.

GG7954. Vernier-Larochette, Béatrice: "*L'Œuvre*, chimère de la création artistique et précarité humaine," *Cahiers Naturalistes*, 54e année, no. 82 (2008), 127-137.

GG7955. Vinken, Barbara: "Tränen zum Leben, Tränen zum Tode." In 875.

GG7956. Viti, Robert: "Where'd you get those eyes? The role of heredity in Zola's *Le Rêve*," *Excavatio*, vol. 23, no. 1-2 (2008), 39-46.

GG7957. Woollen, Geoff: "Ask Zola TM," *Bulletin of the Emile Zola Society*, no. 37-38 (2008), 41-43.

GG7958. Woollen, Geoff: "Emile Zola, 'fat controller'?," *Bulletin of the Emile Zola Society*, no. 37-38 (2008), 20-33.

GG7959. Worth, Jeremy: "Les corps de bibliothèque montraient les mêmes rangées de volumes," *Voix Plurielles*, vol. 5, no. 1 (mai 2008), 1-9.

GG7960. Worth, Jeremy: "In striated space: Zola's female figures and their symbolic environments," *Excavatio*, vol. 23, no. 1-2 (2008), 203-213.

ZOUARI, Faouzia.

GG7961. Ben Mustapha, Jamila: "L'image de l'intellectuelle maghrébine dans *La Retournée* de Faouzia Zouari," *Cahiers de Tunisie*, tome 59, no. 195 (4e trim. 2005), 73-87.

PART THREE

CINEMA

SECTION I

Cinema in General

See also 756.

GG7962. ● *Auteurs and authorship: a film reader.* Ed. Barry Keith Grant. Oxford: Blackwell, 2008. xv, 322 p. [Barthes, Bazin, Truffaut]

GG7963. ● Baron, Anne-Marie: *Romans français du XIXe siècle à l'écran: problèmes de l'adaptation.* Clermont-Ferrand: Presses univ. Blaise Pascal, 2008. *Cahiers romantiques,* 14. 165 p. [Maupassant, Zola]

GG7964. ● Bloom, Peter J.: *French colonial documentary: mythologies of humanitarianism.* Minneapolis: Univ. of Minnesota Press, 2008. xiii, 265 p.

GG7965. ● *Burning darkenss: a half-century of Spanish cinema.* Ed. Joan Ramon Resina, Andrés Lema-Hincapié. Albany: SUNY Press, 2008. *Latin American and Iberian Thought and Culture.* viii, 310 p. [Buñuel]

GG7966. ● Cardullo, Bert: *Five French filmmakers.* Newcastle: Cambridge Scholars, 2008. xxiv, 168 p. [Bresson, Renoir, Rohmer, Tati, Truffaut]

GG7967. ● Cardullo, Bert: *Soundings on cinema: speaking to film and film artists.* Albany: SUNY Press, 2008. *The SUNY series, Horizons of cinema.* xi, 289 p. [Bresson, Renoir]

GG7968. ● *Chinese connections: critical perspectives on film, identity and diaspora.* Ed. Tan See-Kam, Peter X. Feng, Gina Marchetti. Philadelphia: Temple Univ. Press, 2008. viii, 311 p.

GG7969. ● Chion, Michel: *Le complexe de Cyrano: la langue parlée dans les films français.* Paris: Cahiers du cinéma, 2008. 190 p.

GG7970. ● *Cinémas africains d'aujourd'hui: guide des cinématographies d'Afrique.* Paris: Karthala, 2007. 142 p.

GG7971. ● *Cinematic thinking: philosophical approaches to the new cinema.* Ed. James Phillips. Stanford: Stanford Univ. Press, 2008. ix, 192 p. [Denis]

GG7972. ● *Cities in transition: the moving image and the modern metropolis.* Ed. Andrew Webber, Emma Wilson. London: Wallflower, 2008. ix, 240 p. [Marker, Rivette, Rohmer]

GG7973. ● Coombs, Neil: *Studying surrealist and fantasy cinema.* Leighton Buzzard: Auteur, 2008. Rev. student ed. 160 p. [Surrealism, Buñuel, Cocteau, Jeunet]

GG7974. ● *East Asian cinemas: exploring transnational connections on film.* Ed. Leon Hunt, Wing-Fai Leung. London: Tauris, 2008. 261 p. [Besson]

GG7975. ● *Exile cinema: filmmakers at work beyond Hollywood.* Ed. Michael Atkinson. Albany: SUNY Press, 2008. *Horizons of cinema.* ix, 217 p. [Akerman, Djebar, Marker]

GG7976. ● *Faith and spirituality in masters of world cinema.* Ed. Kenneth R. Morefield. Newcastle: Cambridge Scholars, 2008. xx, 182 p. [Bresson, Dardenne, Rohmer, Sembène]

GG7977. ● *Five directors: auteurism from Assayas to Ozon.* Ed. Kate Ince. Manchester: Manchester Univ. Press, 2008. *French film directors.* viii, 157 p. [Assayas, Audiard, Dardenne, Haneke, Ozon]

GG7978. ● *France cinéma 2008: incontri di Firenze: retrospettiva Carné-Prévert.* A cura di Aldo Tassone. Firenze: Aida, 2008. 144 p. [Prévert, Cinema: Carné]

GG7979. ● *France-Hollywood: échanges cinématographiques et identités nationales.* Dir. Martin Barnier, Raphäelle Moine. Paris: L'Harmattan, 2002. *Champs visuels.* 230 p.

GG7980. ● Gaudreault, André: *Cinéma et attraction: pour une nouvelle histoire du cinématographe, suivi de Les vues cinématographiques, 1907, de Georges Mélès, édité par Jacques Malthête.* Paris: CNRS, 2008. 252 p. [Méliès]

GG7981. ● Grandena, Florian: *Showing the world to the world: political fictions in French cinema of the 1990s and early 2000s.* Newcastle: Cambridge Scholars, 2008. 171 p.

GG7982. ● Grégoire, Gilbert: *Notre cher cinéma. Tome 1, Du parlant à la télédiffusion, 1930-1975.* Paris: L'Harmattan, 2008. 274 p.

GG7983. ● Grégoire, Gilbert: *Notre cher cinéma. Tome 2, A la conquête du modèle français, 1975-2006.* Paris: L'Harmattan, 2008. 556 p.

GG7984. ● Grimblat, Pierre: *Recherche jeune homme aimant le cinéma.* Paris: Grasset, 2008. 380 p.

GG7985. ● Haydock, Nickolas: *Movie medievalism: the imaginary Middle Ages.* Jefferson, NC: McFarland, 2008. ix, 234 p. [Besson]

GG7986. ● Hewitt, Leah Dianne: *Remembering the Occupation in French film: national identity in postwar Europe.* Basingstoke: Palgrave Macmillan, 2008. *Studies in European culture and history.* [Chabrol, Truffaut]

GG7987. ● *Hollywood: les connexions françaises.* Sous la dir. de Christian Viviani. Paris: Nouveau monde, 2007. 402 p.

GG7988. ● *In/fidelity: essays on film adaptation.* Ed. David L. Kranz, Nancy C. Mellerski. Newcastle: Cambridge Scholars, 2008. viii, 251 p. [Akerman, Derrida, Proust]

GG7989. ● *Kompositionen für den Film.* Hrsg. Peter Schweinhardt. Wiesbaden: Breitkopf & Härtel, 2008. *Eisler-Studien,* 3. 280 p. [Resnais]

GG7990. ● *Legend [The] returns and dies harder another day: essays on film.* Ed. Jennifer Forrest. Jefferson, NC: McFarland, 2008. 314 p. [Feuillade, J. Laurent]

GG7991. ● Lichtner, Giacomo: *Film and the Shoah in France and Italy.* Foreword by Richard Bosworth. London; Portland, OR: Vallentine Mitchell, 2008. xii, 244 p. [Gatti, Lanzmann, Malle, Mihaileanu, Ophuls, Pontecorvo, Resnais]

GG7992. ● *Lowering the boom: critical studies in film sound.* Ed. Jay Beck, Tony Grajeda. Urbana: Unniv. Of Illinois Press, 2008. x, 342 p. [Bresson, Buñuel]

GG7993. ● Maule, Rosanna: *Beyond auteurism: new directions in authorial film practices in France, Italy and Spain since the 1980s.* Bristol; Chicago: Intellect, 2008. 294 p. [Assayas, Besson, Denis, Pialat]

GG7994. ● Montagne, Albert: *Histoire juridique des interdits cinématographiques en France, 1909-2001.* Paris: L'Harmattan, 2007. 258 p.

GG7995. ● Nash, Mark: *Screen theory culture.* Basingstoke; New York: Palgrave Macmillan, 2008. *Language, discourse, society.* x, 228 p. [Fanon]

GG7996. ● *North African cinema in a global context: through the lens of diaspora.* Ed. Andrea Flores Khalil. London: Routledge, 2008. xi, 107 p. [Allouache, Moknèche]

GG7997. ● Nowell-Smith, Geoffrey: *Making waves: new cinemas of the 1960s.* New York: Continuum, 2008. x, 230 p. [Godard]

GG7998. ● Petty, Sheila J.: *Contact zones: memory, origin, and discourses in Black diasporic cinema.* Detroit: Wayne State Univ. Press, 2008. 295 p. [Fanon, Hondo, Palcy, Peck]

GG7999. ● *Philosophy [The] of science fiction film.* Ed. Steven M. Sanders. Lexington: Univ. Press of Kentucky, 2008. viii, 232 p. [Godard]

GG8000. ● Prédal, René: *Le cinéma français des années 1990: une génération de transition.* Paris: Armand Colin, 2008. 2e édition. 187 p.

GG8001. ● *Queer cinema in Europe.* Ed. Robin Griffiths. Bristol; Chicago: Intellect Books, 2008. 227 p. [Cyril Collard, Defurne, Ducastel, Martineau, Ozon]

GG8002. ● *Repicturing the Second World War: representations on film and television.* Ed. Michael Paris. Basingstoke: Palgrave Macmillan, 2008. 235 p. [Tavernier]

GG8003. ● Sauteron, François: *Une si jolie usine: Kodak-Pathé Vincennes.* Paris: L'Harmattan, 2008. *Graveurs de mémoire.* 181 p.

GG8004. ● Sellier, Geneviève: *Masculine singular: French new wave cinema.* Trans. Kristin Ross. Durham, NC: Duke Univ. Press, 2008. vi, 269 p. [Bardot, Moreau]

GG8005. ● Serceau, Daniel: *Symptômes du jeune cinéma français.* Paris: Cerf; Condé-sur-Noireau: Corlet, 2008. 289 p.

GG8006. ● Shaw, Spencer: *Film consciousness: from phenomenology to Deleuze.* Jefferson, NC: McFarland, 2008. x, 217 p. [Bergson, Merleau-Ponty, Cinema: Bazin]

GG8007. • Short, Robert: *The age of gold: Dali, Buñuel, Artaud; surrealist cinema.* Los Angeles: Solar Books, 2008. New edition. 197 p. [Surrealism, Artaud, Buñuel]

GG8008. • *Sights unseen: unfinished British films.* Ed. Dan North. Newcastle: Cambridge Scholars, 2008. vi, 213 p. [Proust]

GG8009. • *Situating the feminist gaze and spectatorship in postwar cinema.* Ed. Marcelline Block; preface, Jean-Michel Rabaté. Newcastle upon Tyne: Cambridge Scholars, 2008. lxii, 319 p. [Akerman, Duras, Varda]

GG8010. • *South [The] and film.* Ed. Warren G. French. Jackson: Univ. Press of Mississippi, 2008. vi, 258 p. [Renoir]

GG8011. • Spielmann, Yvonne: *Video: the reflexive medium.* Trans., with a slightly expanded introd. for the English edition by Anja Welle and Stan Jones. Cambridge, MA: MIT Press, 2008. *Leonardo.* viii, 371 p. [Akerman]

GG8012. • Stanzick, Nicolas: *Dans les griffes de la Hammer: la France livrée au cinéma d'épouvante.* Paris: Scali, 2008. 456 p.

GG8013. • Vasse, David: *Le nouvel âge du cinéma d'auteur français.* Paris: Klincksieck, 2008. *50 questions.* 241 p.

GG8014. • Vignaud, Roger: *Henri Verneuil: les plus grands succès du cinéma.* Gémenos: Autres temps, 2008. 314 p.

GG8015. • *Visualizing the Holocaust.* Ed. David Bathrick, Brad Prager, Michael D. Richardson. Rochester, NY: Camden House, 2008. *Screen Cultures.* ix, 336 p. [Cayrol, Lanzmann, Lyotard, Resnais]

GG8016. • *Words and images on the screen: language, literature, moving pictures.* Ed. Agnes Pethö. Newcastle upon Tyne: Cambridge Scholars, 2008. vii, 393 p. [Chéreau, Genet, Godard]

GG8017. Armes, Roy: "Women pioneers of Arab cinema," *Screen,* vol. 48, no. 4 (Winter 2007), 517-520.

GG8018. Badt, Karin: "Cannes 2008: the well-made film," *Film Criticism,* vol. 33, no. 1 (Fall 2008), 64-69.

GG8019. Baecque, Antoine de: "La forme cinématographique de l'histoire dans *Caché* et *La Question humaine,*" *Annales: Histoire, Sciences Sociales,* 63e année, no. 6 (nov.-déc. 2008), 1275-1301. [Haneke, Nicolas Klotz]

GG8020. Bakari, Imruh: "Colonialism and modern lives in African cinema," *Screen,* vol. 48, no. 4 (Winter 2007), 501-506.

GG8021. Baron, Anne-Marie: "Balzac à l'écran." In 7963.

GG8022. Boughedir, Ferid: "Cinémas du Maghreb/cinémas d'Afrique noire: opposés ou complémentaires," *Cultures Sud,* no. 169 (avril-juin 2008), 127-134.

GG8023. Caillé, Patricia: "Actualités cinématographiques "Actualités littéraires de la francophonie," *Nouvelles Etudes Francophones,* vol. 22, no. 1 (printemps 2007), 255-258.

GG8024. Cairns, Lucille: "Sapphism in twentieth to twenty-first century French film: segue or schism?," *Australian Journal of French Studies,* vol. 45, no. 3 (Sept.-Dec. 2008), 264-276.

GG8025. "Le cinéma français en état d'alerte," *Cahiers du Cinéma,* no. 633 (avril 2008), 20-45.

GG8026. Darke, Chris: "Unbelievable but real: the legacy of '68," *Sight and Sound,* vol. 18, no. 5 (May 2008), 28-32.

GG8027. "Dossier: Le cinéma français dans tous ses états," *24 Images,* no. 139 (oct.-nov. 2008), 10-27.

GG8028. Driskell, Jonathan: "The female 'metaphysical' body in poetic realist film," *Studies in French Cinema,* vol. 8, no. 1 (2008), 57-73. [Carné, Jean Grémillon]

GG8029. Durham, Carolyn A.: "Finding France on film: *Chocolat, Amélie* and *Le Divorce,*" *French Cultural Studies,* vol. 19, no. 2 (June 2008), 173-197. [Jeunet]

GG8030. During, Lisabeth; Lisa Trahair: "Film theory," *Year's Work in Critical and Cultural Theory,* vol. 16 (2008), 166-195. [Bazin]

GG8031. Dwyer, Kevin: "Moroccan cinema and the promotion of culture." In 7996.

GG8032. Edwards, Brian T.: "Marok in Morocco: reading Moroccan films in the age of circulation." In 7996.

GG8033. Elstob, Kevin: "Imagined community: the role of popular and critically acclaimed Québécois films in sustaining the nation." In 120, 388-398.

GG8034. Franco, Judith: " 'The more you look, the less you really know': the redemption of white masculinity in contemporary American and French cinema," *Cinema Journal*, vol. 47, no. 3 (2008), 29-47. [L. Cantet, Nicole Garcia]

GG8035. François-Denève, Corinne: "Retour de flamme: Grande Guerre et cinéma français dans le nouveau siècle." In 414, 183-191.

GG8036. Gauthier, Christophe: "L'introuvable critique. Légitimation de l'art et hybridation des discours aux sources de la critique cinématographique," *Mil Neuf Cent*, no. 26 (2008), 51-72.

GG8037. Hainge, Greg: "Three non-places of supermodernity in the history of French cinema: 1967, 1985, 2000," *Australian Journal of French Studies*, vol. 45, no. 3 (Sept.-Dec. 2008), 197-211. [Besson, Roch Stephanik, Tati]

GG8038. Hardwick, Joe: "(Rétro)projections: French cinema in the twenty-first century," *Australian Journal of French Studies*, vol. 45, no. 3 (Sept.-Dec. 2008), 185-196.

GG8039. Hayward, Susan: "Reviewing quality cinema: French costume drama of the 1950s," *Studies in French Cinema*, vol. 8, no. 3 (2008), 229-244.

GG8040. Hilliker, Lee: "Le Québec et la mythologie du cinéma direct." In 120, 380-387.

GG8041. Ince, Kate: "From minor to 'major' cinema? Women's and feminist cinema in the 2000s," *Australian Journal of French Studies*, vol. 45, no. 3 (Sept.-Dec. 2008), 277-288.

GG8042. Lack, Roland-François: "First encounters: French literature and the cinematograph," *Film History*, vol. 20, no. 2 (2008), 133-143.

GG8043. Lecointe, François: "Japon mon amaour: regards croisés France/Japon sur la mémoire filmique de la défaite japonaise de 1945." In 414, 194-202. [Marker, Resnais]

GG8044. Le Pallec-Marand, Claudine: "Du sexuel. Esthétique de l'intimité dans le cinéma contemporain occidental," *Interfaces: Image Texte Langage*, no. 28 (2008), 53-63. [Breillat, Chéreau]

GG8045. Logette, Lucien: "Cannes 2008," *Jeune Cinéma*, no. 317-318 (été 2008), 55-57.

GG8046. Loiselle, André: "Horreur et dépaysement. L'altérité géographique et médiatique comme source de terreur dans trois adaptations cinématographiques de romans d'épouvante québécois." In 97, 81-92.

GG8047. Lowy, Vincent; Jacques Walter: "Primo Levi et le cinéma." In 855.

GG8048. Magnan-Park, Aaron Han Joon: "The HK venture: the Francophone cinelogocentric nexus." In 7968.

GG8049. Maule, Rosanna: "Auteurism and women's cinema in France, Italy, and Spain." In 7993.

GG8050. Mazdon, Lucy; Catherine Wheatley: "Intimate connections," *Sight and Sound*, vol. 18, no. 5 (May 2008), 38-40.

GG8051. McCann, Ben: "Pierced borders, punctured bodies: the contemporary French horror film," *Australian Journal of French Studies*, vol. 45, no. 3 (Sept.-Dec. 2008), 225-237.

GG8052. Murray Levine, Alison J.: "Mapping Beur cinema in the new millennium," *Journal of Film and Video*, vol. 60, no. 3-4 (Fall-Winter 2008), 42-59.

GG8053. Nganang, Alain P.: "Of cameras, trains and roads: French colonial conquest and cinematographic practice." In 43, 291-307.

GG8054. Nowell-Smith, Geoffrey: "France: from nouvelle vague to May 68." In 7997, 1138-151.

GG8055. Penz, François: "From topographical coherence to creative geography." In 7972, 123-140. [Rivette, Rohmer]

GG8056. Prédal, René: "Crise du cinéma et rapport Ferran," *Jeune Cinéma*, no. 319-320 (automne 2008), 6-12.

GG8057. Reeser, Todd W.: "Representing gay male domesticity in French film of the late 1990s." In 8001.

GG8058. Rollet, Brigitte: " 'Paris nous appartient': flânerie in Paris and film," *Film Quarterly*, vol. 61, no. 3 (Spring 2008), 46-51.

GG8059. Romney, Jonathan: "French exceptions," *Sight and Sound*, vol. 18, no. 5 (May 2008), 42-44.

GG8060. Rouxel-Cubberly, Noëlle: "Family resemblances: (en)gendering Claire Denis, Nicole Garcia and Agnès Jaoui's film titles." In 8009, 67-87. [Denis, Garcia, Jaoui]

GG8061. Valcke, Jennifer: "Rhythmical images and visual music: montage in French avant-garde cinema." In 575, 201-215.

SECTION II

Individual Directors, Cinema Authors, Cinema Theorists, and Actors

AKERMAN, Chantal.

GG8062. ● *Chantal Akerman: moving through time and space.* Ed. Terrie Sultan. Houston: Blaffer Gallery, the Art Museum of the Univ. of Houston, 2008. 71 p.

GG8063. ● *Ellipsis: Chantal Akerman, Lili Dujourie, Francesca Woodman.* Curator, Lynne Cooke. Catalogue of an exhibition held at Lunds Konsthall, 9 Feb.-13 Apr. 2008. Lund: Lunds Konsthall, 2008. 129 p.

GG8064. Allen, Sharon Lubkemann: "Chantal Akerman's cinematic transgressions." In 8009, 255-288.

GG8065. Haidu, Rachel: "The city as cipher for the national in the work of Chantal Akerman and Marcel Broodhaers." In 537.

GG8066. Klawans, Stuart: "The not-too-long discourses of Chantal Akerman." In 7975, 189-195.

GG8067. Lebow, Alisa: "Memory once removed: indirect memory and transitive autobiography in Chantal Akerman's *D'Est.*" In 500.

GG8068. Mamula, Tijana: "Matricide, indexicality and abstraction in Chantal Akerman's *News from home* and *Là-bas*," *Studies in French Cinema*, vol. 8, no. 3 (2008), 265-275.

GG8069. Olney, Ian: "A la recherche d'une femme perdue: Proust through the lens of Chantal Akerman's *La captive.*" In 7988. [Proust]

GG8070. Spielmann, Yvonne: "Video installations: Eija-Liisa Ahtila, Chantal Akerman, Gillian Wearing." In 8011.

ALLOUACHE, Merzak.

GG8071. Khalil, Andrea: "The myth of masculinity in the films of Merzak Allouache." In 7996.

ANNAUD, Jean-Jacques.

GG8072. Brownlie, Siobhan: "Using Riffaterre to rehabilitate *The Lover*," *Film/Literature Quarterly*, vol. 36, no. 1 (2008), 52-60.

ARCAND, Denys.

GG8073. ● Loiselle, André: *Denys Arcand's Le déclin de l'empire américain and Les invasions barbares.* Toronto: Univ. of Toronto Press, 2008. *Canadian cinema.* 190 p.

GG8074. Plamondon, Jean-François: "Parcours du littéraire dans *Les invasions barbares* de Denys Arcand." In 97, 121-133.

ASSAYAS, Olivier.

GG8075. Maule, Rosanna: "The difficult legacy of the nouvelle vague: Olivier Assayas and French film authors at the end of auteurism." In 7993.

GG8076. Sutton, Paul: "Olivier Assayas and the cinema of catastrophe." In 7977.

GG8077. Vincendeau, Ginette: "Family ties," *Sight and Sound*, vol. 18, no. 8 (Aug. 2008), 16-20. [Desplechin]

AUBERT, Robin.

GG8078. Beaulieu, Etienne: "La momie, la maman et l'image: *Saints-Martyrs-des-Damnés* de Robin Aubert." In 120, 407-412.

AUDIARD, Jacques.

GG8079. Dobson, Julia: "Jacques Audiard: contesting filiations." In7977.

BARDOT, Brigitte.
GG8080. • Baroni, Maurizio; Marco d'Ubaldo: *BB: Brigitte Bardot: a collection of rare photos, original posters and music from the complete filmography of the divine.* Milan: Mediane Libri, 2008. 129 p.
GG8081. • Crocq, Philippe; Jean Mareska: *Brigitte Bardot, Serge Gainsbourg, ou la véritable histoire de Bonnie & Clyde.* Monaco: Alphée, 2008. 245 p.
GG8082. • Dureau, Christian: *Brigitte Bardot: et le cinéma créa sa star.* Paris: Carpentier, 2008. 126 p.
GG8083. Sellier, Geneviève: "Brigitte Bardot and the new wave: an ambivalent relationship." In 8004.
BATCHEFF, Pierre.
GG8084. Powrie, Phil; Eric Rebillard: "Josephine Baker and Pierre Batcheff in *La Sirène des tropiques*," *Studies in French Cinema*, vol. 8, no. 3 (2008), 245-264.
GG8085. Powrie, Phil; Eric Rebillard: "Pierre Batcheff, the surrealist star," *Studies in French Cinema*, vol. 8, no. 2 (2008), 159-177.
BAZIN, André. See also 3110, 8030, 8349.
GG8086. Andrew, Dudley: "The ontology of a fetish," *Film Quarterly*, vol. 61, no. 4 (Summer 2008), 62-66.
GG8087. "Bazin en Asie," *Cahiers du Cinéma*, no. 640 (déc. 2008), 75-85.
GG8088. Hanisch, Michael: "Was ist Film? 'Vater' einer ganzen Cineasten-Generation: André Bazin," *Film Dienst*, 61. Jahrgang, Heft 8 (10 April 2008), 14-16.
GG8089. Jeong, Seung-Hoon; Dudley Andrew: "Grizzly ghost: Herzog, Bazin and the cinematic animal," *Screen*, vol. 49, no. 1 (Spring 2008), 1-12.
GG8090. Shaw, Spencer: "Bazin's ontology." In 982.
GG8091. Smith, Greg M.: "Reflecting the image: Sartrean emotions in the writings of André Bazin," *Film and Philosophy*, vol. 10 (2006), 117-133. [Sartre]
BENLYAZID, Farida.
GG8092. Bourget, Carine: "Traditions orales et littéraires dans l'œuvre cinématographique de Farida Benlyazid," *French Review*, vol. 81, no. 4 (March 2008), 752-763.
BENOÎT-LÉVY, Jean.
GG8093. Chevallier, Jacques: "Sur Jean Benoît-Lévy," *Jeune Cinéma*, no. 314 (nov. 2007), 30-33.
BESSON, Luc. See also 8037.
GG8094. Cousins, Jennie: "Flesh and fabric: the five elements of Jean-Paul Gaultier's costume design in Luc Besson's *Le Cinquième Elément*," *Studies in French Cinema*, vol. 8, no. 1 (2008), 75-88.
GG8095. Haydock, Nickolas: "Shooting the messenger: Luc Besson at war with Joan of Arc." In 7985.
GG8096. Hunt, Leon: "Asiaphilia, Asianisation and the gatekeeper auteur." In 7974, 220-236.
GG8097. Maule, Rosanna: "Made in Europa: Luc Besson and the question of cultural exception in post-auteur France." In 7993.
BOON, Dany.
GG8098. Mougin, Olivier: "*Les Ch'tis*: quelques raisons d'un succès," *Esprit*, no. 344 (mai 2008), 6-11.
BOUCHAREB, Rachid. See also 8184.
GG8099. Coly, Ayo: "Memory, history, forgetting," *Transition*, no. 98 (2008), 150-155.
BOURDON, Luc.
GG8100. Daudelin, Robert: "Entretien Luc Bourdon," *24 Images*, no. 139 (oct.-nov. 2008), 54-59.
BRAULT, Michel.
GG8101. Desbiens, Marie-Frédérique: "Entre le didactique et le romantique. Les représentations des rébellions des patriotes dans *Quand je serai parti . . . vous vivrez encore* de Michel Brault et *15 février 1839* de Pierre Falardeau." In 97, 53-67. [Falardeau]
GG8102. Koc, Aysesgul: "I'm just a simple filmmaker. An interview with Michel Brault," *Cineaction*, no. 73-74 (2008), 28-31.

BREILLAT, Catherine. See also 8044.

GG8103. ● Breillat, Catherine: *Pornocracy*. Trans. Paul Buck and Catherine Petit; intro. Chris Kraus; afterword by Peter Sotos. Cambridge, MA: London: Semiotext(e), 2008. 135 p.

GG8104. Romney, Jonathan: "Abominable glory," *Sight and Sound*, vol. 18, no. 5 (May 2008), 34-37.

GG8105. Taubin, Amy: "*The last mistress*," *Film Comment*, vol. 44, no. 3 (May-June 2008), 26-29.

BRESSON, Robert. See also 2800, 2810.

GG8106. ● Frodon, Jean-Michel: *Robert Bresson*. Paris: Cahiers du cinéma, 2008. 95 p.

GG8107. Belton, John: "The phenomenology of film sound: Robert Bresson's *A man escaped*." In 7992, 23-35.

GG8108. Cardullo, Bert: "Dostoyevskyan surge, Bressonian spirit: *Une femme douce* and the cinematic world of Robert Bresson." In 7967. [Also in 7966]

GG8109. Cardullo, Bert: "Transcendental style, poetic precision: an interview with Robert Bresson." In 7966, 51-76.

GG8110. Cunneen, Joseph: "Sacred in Bresson: *Au hasard Balthazar*." In 7976.

GG8111. Indiana, Gary: "Robert Bresson: hidden in plain sight." In 485.

BUÑUEL, Luis. See also 8007.

GG8112. ● Abajos de Pablos, Juan Eugenio Julio de: *Luis Buñuel: el cineasta de Calanda*. Valladolid: Castilla, 2008. 127 p.

GG8113. ● Bergala, Alain: *Luis Buñuel*. Paris: Cahiers du cinéma, 2008. 95 p.

GG8114. ● González Requena, Jesús: *Amor loco en el jardín: la diosa que habita el cine de Luis Buñuel*. Madrid: Abada, 2008. 259 p.

GG8115. ● Gutiérrez-Albilla, Julián Daniel: *Queering Buñuel: sexual dissidence and psychoanalysis in his Mexican and Spanish cinema*. London; New York: Tauris Academic Studies, 2008. x, 245 p.

GG8116. ● *Luis Buñuel: Essays, Daten, Dokumente*. Hrsg. Gabriele Jatho. Berlin: Bertz und Fischer, 2008. 184 p.

GG8117. ● *Ola Pepín!: Dalí, Lorca y Buñuel en la Residencia de Estudiantes*. Madrid_: Publicaciones de la Residencia de Estudiantes_; Barcelona_: Funcadió Caixa Catalunya, 2007. 300 p.

GG8118. ● Repetto, Tonino: *Luis Buñuel: la logica irridente dell'inconscio*. Roma: Fondazione Ente dello spettacolo, 2008. 180 p.

GG8119. ● Rucar de Buñuel, Jeanne: *Memoirs of a woman without a piano: my life with Luis Buñuel*. Trans. Marisol Martin del Campo. ?: Five Ties, 2008.

GG8120. Begin, Paul: "Entomology as anthropology in the films of Luis Buñuel," *Screen*, vol. 48, no. 4 (Winter 2007), 425-442.

GG8121. Begin, Paul: "When victim meets voyeur: an aesthetic of confrontation in Hispanic social issue cinema," *Hispanic Research Journal*, vol. 9, no. 3 (June 2008), 261-275.

GG8122. Carrière, Jean-Claude: "San José Purúa. Souvenirs de Luis Buñuel," *Positif*, no. 574 (déc. 2008), 52-54.

GG8123. Catania, Saviour: "Wagnerizing *Wuthering Heights*: Buñuel's *Tristan* storm in *Abismos de Pasión*," *Film/Literature Quarterly*, vol. 36, no. 4 (2008), 272-280.

GG8124. Conley, Tom: "*Viridiana Coca Cola*." In 7965, 43-60.

GG8125. Coombs, Neil: "Surreal auteurs: Luis Buñuel and *The phantom of liberty*." In 7973.

GG8126. Decker, Christof: " 'Irony is a cheap shot': Robert Altman, Luis Buñuel, and the maneuvers of comic deconstruction," *Amerikastudien*, vol. 52, no. 1 O2007), 63-79.

GG8127. Jones, Julie: " 'Above all . . . don't perform!': playing to the camera of Luis Buñuel," *Cineaste*, vol. 33, no. 3 (Summer 2008), 22-27.

GG8128. Kaurismäki, Aki: "Der schönste Film der Welt: Luis Buñuels *Das goldene Zeitalter* (*L'Age d'or*)," *Film Dienst*, 61. Jahrgang, Heft 3 (31 Jan. 2008), 20-21.

GG8129. Mauer, Barry: "Asynchronous documentary: Buñuel's *Land without bread*." In 7992, 141-151.

GG8130. Pflaum, Hans Günther: "Träume von Freiheit und Liebe," *epd Film*, 25. Band, Heft 2 (2008), 22-27.

GG8131. Richards, Rashna Wadia: "Unsynched: the contrapuntal sounds of Luis Buñuel's *L'Age d'or*," *Film Criticism*, vol. 33, no. 2 (Winter 2008), 23-43.

GG8132. Stiglegger, Marcus: "Einschnitte und Tabubrüche: Luis Buñuels Nachwirkungen in der Filmgeschichte," *Film Dienst*, 61. Jahrgang, Heft 3 (31 Jan. 2008), 17-19.

CABRERA, Dominique.

GG8133. Dobson, Julia: "Timely resistance in the documentary work of Dominique Cabrera," *French Studies*, vol. 62, no. 3 (July 2008), 290-300.

CANTET, Laurent. See also 8034.

GG8134. Archer, Neil: "The road as the (non-)place of masculinity: *L'emploi du temps*," *Studies in French Cinema*, vol. 8, no. 2 (2008), 137-148.

GG8135. De Bruyn, Olivier: "*Entre les murs*. République, année zéro," *Positif*, no. 571 (sept. 2008), 25-27.

GG8136. De Raedt, Thérèse: "*Vers le sud*: de la violence, du pouvoir, du sexe et de l'argent." In 617, 123-141.

GG8137. "Entretien avec Laurent Cantet," *Cahiers du Cinéma*, no. 637 (sept. 2008), 7181.

GG8138. "Entretien avec Laurent Cantet," *Positif*, no. 571 (sept. 2008), 28-31.

GG8139. Renzi, Eugenio: "*Entre les murs* de Laurent Cantet," *Cahiers du Cinéma*, no. 637 (sept. 2008), 19-21.

GG8140. Sullivan, Karen: "Laurent Cantet's *Ressources humaines_*: content and class in business French," *French Review*, vol. 81, no. 5 (April 2008), 896-911.

GG8141. Vincendeau, Ginette: "*The Class*: interview," *Sight and Sound*, vol. 18, no. 11 (Nov. 2008), 30-31.

CARLE, Gilles.

GG8142. Harcourt, Peter: "The reality of dreams. A presentation of *L'ange et la femme* (1977)," *Cineaction*, no. 73-74 (2008), 15-19.

CARNÉ, Marcel. See also 8028.

GG8143. Chardère, Bernard: "Carné, avec ou sans Prévert. I, Avec," *Jeune Cinéma*, no. 317-318 (été 2008), 10-27. [Prévert]

GG8144. Chardère, Bernard: "Carné sans Prévert," *Jeune Cinéma*, no. 319-320 (automne 2008), 17-25. [Prévert]

CHABROL, Claude.

GG8145. Hewitt, Leah D.: "Ambiguous national icons in Chabrol's *Story of Women*." In 7986, 125-154.

CHÉREAU, Patrice. See also 8044.

GG8146. Sava, Laura: "Adapting (t0) the letter: Patrice Chéreau's *Gabrielle*." In 8016, 104-118.

CHOMET, Sylvain.

GG8147. McCann, Ben: " 'If it's not Disney, what is it?' Traditional animation techniques in *Les Triplettes de Belleville*," *French Studies Bulletin*, no. 108 (Autumn 2008), 59-62.

CLÉMENT, René. See 6503.

COLLARD, Cyril.

GG8148. Wharton, Steve: "Bars to understanding? Depictions of the 'gay bar' in film." In 8001.

COUZINET, Émile.

GG8149. ● Chevalier, Jean-Claude: *Ces temps de guerre et d'étoiles: 1940-1944: le cinéma sous Vichy: essai sur "Andorra ou les hommes d'airain" d'Emile Couzinet*. Paris: Mare & Martin, 2008. 699 p.

DARDENNE, Luc et Jean-Pierre.

GG8150. ● *Jean-Pierre et Luc Dardenne*. Sous la dir. de Jacqueline Aubenas. Bruxelles: Commissariat général aux relations internationales de la Communauté française de Belgique, 2008. 338 p.

GG8151. Andrew, Geoff: "Emotional rescue," *Sight and Sound*, vol. 18, no. 12 (Dec. 2008), 34-35.

GG8152. Cummings, Doug: "The brothers Dardenne: responding to the face of the other." In 7976.

GG8153. "Entretien avec Jean-Pierre et Luc Dardenne," *Positif*, no. 571 (sept. 2008), 9-14.

GG8154. Morgan, Janice: "The social realism of body language in *Rosetta*," *French Review*, vol. 81, no. 6 (May 2008), 1187-1197.

GG8155. O'Shaughnessy, Martin: "Ethics in the ruin of politics: the Dardenne brothers." In 7977.

DEFURNE, Bavo.

GG8156. Williams, Michael: "The body picturesque: the films of Bavo Defurne." In 8001.

DELVAUX, André.

GG8157. Giukin, Lenuta: "Cinematic transgressions: André Delvaux and the surrealist dilemma," *French Review*, vol. 81, no. 6 (May 2008), 1174-1186.

DEMY, Jacques.

GG8158. ● Clark, James: *Rather have the blues: the novels of Paul Auster, the films of Jacques Demy*. Toronto: Springtime, 2008. xi, 77 p.

GG8159. Becker, Svea; Bruce Williams: "What ever happened to *West Side Story*? Gene kelly, jazz dance, and not so real men in Jacques Demy's *The Young Girls of Rochefort*," *New Review of Film and Television Studies*, vol. 6, no. 3 (Dec. 2008), 303-321.

GG8160. Dupré, Vincent: "Jacques Demy: l'ennui, le néant," *Jeune Cinéma*, no. 321 (déc. 2008), 4-11.

GG8161. Garson, Charlotte: "Jacques Demy en ses œuvres complètes," *Etudes*, 152e année, no. 4096 (déc. 2008), 653-662.

GG8162. Hill, Rodney: "The new wave meets the tradition of quality: Jacques Demy's *The Umbrellas of Cherbourg*," *Cinema Journal*, vol. 48, no. 1 (2008), 27-50.

GG8163. Kermabon, Jacques: "Tout Demy en blancs et en couleurs," *24 Images*, no. 140 (déc. 2008-janv. 2009), 44-47.

DENIS, Claire. See also 8060.

GG8164. ● *Cinéma [Le] de Claire Denis: ou, L'énigme des sens*. Sous la dir. de Rémi Fontanel. Lyon: Aléas, 2008. 284 p.

GG8165. Beugnet, Martine: "Re-enchanting the world: Pascale Ferran's *Lady Chatterley* (2007) and Claire Denis' *Vendredi soir* (2004)," *Australian Journal of French Studies*, vol. 45, no. 3 (Sept.-Dec. 2008), 212-224. [Ferran]

GG8166. Maule, Rosanna: "Female authors and gendered identity in film: Claire Denis's post-subjective representation." In 7993.

GG8167. McMahon, Laura: "The contagious body of the film: Claire Denis's *Trouble Every Day*." In 610, 79-92.

GG8168. McMahon, Laura: "The withdrawal of touch: Denis, Nancy and *L'Intrus*," *Studies in French Cinema*, vol. 8, no. 1 (2008), 29-39. [Nancy]

GG8169. Nancy, Jean-Luc: "Claire Denis: icon of ferocity." In 7971.

GG8170. Newton, Elizabeth: "The phenomenology of desire: Claire Denis's *Vendredi soir*," *Studies in French Cinema*, vol. 8, no. 1 (2008), 17-28.

GG8171. Scholz, Sebastian; Hanna Surma: "Exceeding the limits of representation: screen and/as skin in Claire Denis's *Trouble every day*," *Studies in French Cinema*, vol. 8, no. 1 (2008), 5-16.

DEPARDON, Raymond. See 8314.

DESPLECHIN, Arnaud. See also 8077.

GG8172. ● Desplechin, Arnaud: *Un conte de Noël*. Paris: Avant-Scène Cinéma, 2008. *Avant-Scène Cinéma*, no. 572. 128 p.

GG8173. De Bruyn, Olivier: "*Un conte de Noël*. Le lien défait," *Positif*, no. 568 (juin 2008), 7-9.

GG8174. Domenach, Elise: "*Un conte de Noël*. La nouvelle Arcadie d'Arnaud Desplechin," *Esprit*, no. 347 (août-sept. 2008), 191-207.

GG8175. "Entretien avec Arnaud Desplechin," *Positif*, no. 568 (juin 2008), 10-14.

GG8176. Euvrard, Janine: "Entretien Arnaud Desplechin," *24 Images*, no. 139 (oct.-nov. 2008), 28-29.

GG8177.   Prédal, René: "La greffe et le rejet," *Jeune Cinéma*, no. 317-318 (été 2008), 6-9.

DOILLON, Jacques.
GG8178.   ● Doillon, Jacques: *Les doigts dans la tête*. Edition établie par Chloé Mary. Paris: L'école des loisirs, 2008. 204 p.
GG8179.   ● Doillon, Jacques: *Le jeune Werther*. Edition établie par Chloé Mary. Paris: L'école des loisirs, 2008. 206 p.
GG8180.   ● Doillon, Jacques: *Le petit criminel*. Edition établie par Chloé Mary. Paris: L'école des loisirs, 2008. 203 p.
GG8181.   ● Doillon, Jacques: *Le premier venu*. Edition établie par Chloé Mary. Paris: L'école des loisirs, 2008. 206 p.
GG8182.   "Entretien avec Jacques Doillon," *Cahiers du Cinéma*, no. 633 (avril 2008), 8-16.

DUCASTEL, Olivier.
GG8183.   Pullen, Christopher: "The films of Ducastel and Martineau: gay identity, the family, and the autobiographical self." In 8001. [Jacques Martineau]

DUMONT, Bruno.
GG8184.   Wilson, Emma: "*Days of Glory, Flanders*," *Film Quarterly*, vol. 61, no. 1 (Fall 2007), 16-22. [Rachid Bouchareb]

DUPEYRON, François.
GG8185.   "Entretien avec François Dupeyron," *Positif*, no. 574 (déc. 2008), 25-28.
GG8186.   O'Neill, Eithne: "*Aide-toi, le ciel t'aidera*. Mais où est passé ton mari?," *Positif*, no. 574 (déc. 2008), 23-24.

DUVIVIER, Julien.
GG8187.   Viviani, Christian: "Julien Duvivier entre Paris et Hollywood: le cheminement des images," *Revue Française d'Études Américaines*, no. 115 (1er trim. 2008), 121-135.

FALARDEAU, Pierre. See 8101.
FERRAN, Pascale. See 8165.
FEUILLADE, Louis.
GG8188.   ● Lascault, Gilbert: *Les Vampires de Louis Feuillade: sœurs et frères de l'effroi*. Crisnée: Yellow now, 2008. *Côté films*. 104 p.
GG8189.   Gunning, Tom: "The intertextuality of early cinema: a prologue to *Fantômas*, film and novel." In 7990, 39-56. [Marcel Allain, Pierre Souvestre]

FONTAINE, Anne.
GG8190.   Ritterbusch, Rachel: "Anne Fontaine and contemporary women's cinema in France," *Rocky Mountain Review*, vol. 62, no. 2 (2008), 68-81.

GABIN, Jean.
GG8191.   "Dossier Jean Gabin: des romans au mythe," *Positif*, no. 573 (nov. 2008), 88-111.

GANCE, Abel.
GG8192.   Hourigan, Peter: "On Abel Gance's *J'accuse* and *La Roue*," *Senses of Cinema*, no. 49 (2008-2009), [n.p.].

GARCIA, Nicole. See also 8034, 8060.
GG8193.   Munich, Adrienne: "Architecture and abjection in Nicole Garcia's *Place Vendôme*," *Women: A Cultural Review*, vol. 19, no. 3 (Winter 2008), 297-311.

GARREL, Louis.
GG8194.   "Entretien avec Louis Garrel," *Cahiers du Cinéma*, no. 636 (juillet-août 2008), 12-23.

GIGUÈRE, Serge.
GG8195.   Jean, Marcel: "Entretien avec Serge Giguère," *24 Images*, no. 135 (déc. 2007-janv. 2008), 47-49.

GODARD, Jean-Luc. See also 1063, 3599.
GG8196.   ● Brody, Richard: *Everything is cinema: the working life of Jean-Luc Godard*. New York: Metropolitan, 2008. xv, 701 p.
GG8197.   ● Coureau, Didier: *Jean-Luc Godard 1990-1995: "Nouvelle vague",*

"Hélas pour moi", *"JLG/JLG"*: *complexité esthétique, esthétique de la complexité.* Lille: ANRT, 2008. *Thèse à la carte.* 494 p.

GG8198. ● Drabinski, John E.: *Godard between identity and difference.* New York: Continuum, 2008. xiii, 159 p.

GG8199. ● Péquignot, Bruno: *Recherches sociologiques sur les images.* Paris: L'Harmattan, 2008. *Logiques sociales.* 253 p.

GG8200. ● Robinson, Jeremy Mark: *Jean-Luc Godard: the passion of cinema/la passion de cinéma.* ?: Crescent Moon, 2008.

GG8201. Baetens, Jan: "La novellisation emboîtée: Adrienne Rich et la reprise poétique de *Pierrot le fou,*" *Rivista di Letterature Moderne e Comparate,* vol. 59, fasc. 4 (ott.-dic. 2006), 475-488.

GG8202. Bourseiller, Antoine: "1963-1968. Paris: the Godard years," *Senses of Cinema,* no. 48 (2008), [n.p.].

GG8203. Cohen, Alain J. J.: "Nude vs. naked in films of Kubrick, Godard and Greenaway," *Interdisciplinary Journal for Germanic Linguistics and Semiotic Analysis,* vol. 13, no. 1 (Spring 2008), 1-25.

GG8204. Drabinski, John: "Separation, difference, and time in Godard's *Ici et ailleurs,*" *Substance,* vol. 37, no. 1 [no. 115] (2008), 148-158.

GG8205. Duncan, Sydney: "Portrait of the artist as a pun man: humor and its structures in the films of Jean-Luc Godard," *New Review of Film and Television Studies,* vol. 6, no. 3 (Dec. 2008), 269-284.

GG8206. Gergely, Gabor: "Jean-Luc Godard's film essays of the 1960s: the vitures and limitations of realism theories," *Studies in French Cinema,* vol. 8, no. 2 (2008), 111-121.

GG8207. Harcourt, Peter: "Analogical thinking: organizational strategies within the works of Jean-Luc Godard," *CineAction,* no. 75 (2008), 20-23.

GG8208. Kyburz, Bonnie Lenore: " 'Totally, tenderly, tragically': Godard's contempt and the composition *Qu'il y aurait,*" *Composition Studies,* vol. 36, no. 1 (Spring 2008), 39-55.

GG8209. Lack, Roland-François: "*Vivre sa vie*: an introduction and A to Z," *Senses of Cinema,* no. 48 (2008), [n.p.].

GG8210. Nowell-Smith, Geoffrey: "Young Godard." In 7997, 189-196.

GG8211. Pavsek, Christopher: "What has come to pass for cinema in late Godard," *Discourse,* vol. 28, no. 1 (Winter 2006), 166-175.

GG8212. Pethö, Agnes: "The screen is a blank page: Jean-Luc Godard's word and image plays." In 8016, 159-186.

GG8213. Ramsey, Ramsey Eric; Dianie Gruber: "Do you have a light?: the failures and special effects of Godard's *Alphaville,*" *Film and Philosophy,* vol. 12 (2008), 105-118.

GG8214. Shaw, Debra Benita: "Systems, architecture and the digital body: from *Alphaville* to *The Matrix,*" *Parallax,* vol. 14, no. 3 [no. 48] (July-Sept. 2008), 74-87.

GG8215. Utterson, Andrew: "Tarzan vs. IBM: humans and computers in Jean-Luc Godard's *Alphaville,*" *Film Criticism,* vol. 33, no. 1 (Fall 2008), 45-63.

GG8216. Warner, Charles R.: "Shocking *Histoire(s)*: Godard, surrealism, and historical montage," *Quarterly Review of Film and Video,* vol. 25, no. 1 (2008), 1-15.

GG8217. Williams, James S.: "Histoire(s) du cinéma," *Film Quarterly,* vol. 61, no. 3 (Spring 2008), 10-16.

GG8218. Woolfolk, Alan: "Disenchantment and rebellion in *Alphaville.*" In 7999, 191-205.

GRÉMILLON, Jean. See 8028.

GUÉDIGUIAN, Robert.

GG8219. ● Daniel, Isabelle; Robert Guédiguian: *Conversation avec Robert Guédiguian.* Paris: Carnets de l'info, 2008. 188 p.

GG8220. Anderson, Philip: "Stories of violence, violence of history: the political logic of Guédiguian's cinema from *Dernier Eté* (1980) to *La Ville est tranquille* (2001)," *Australian Journal of French Studies,* vol. 45, no. 3 (Sept.-Dec. 2008), 238-249.

HANEKE, Michael. See also 8019.

GG8221. ● Fogliato, Fabrizio: *La visione negata: il cinema di Michael Haneke.* Alessandria: Falsopiano, 2008. 239 p.

GG8222. • Haneke, Michael: *Michael Haneke: Gespräche mit Thomas Assheuer*. Berlin: Alexander, 2008. 177 p.

GG8223. Austin, Guy: "Drawing trauma: visual testimony in *Caché* and *J'ai 8 ans*," *Screen*, vol. 48, no. 4 (Winter 2007), 529-536.

GG8224. Beugnet, Martine: "Blind spot," *Screen*, vol. 48, no. 2 (Summer 2007), 227-231.

GG8225. Cousins, Mark: "After the end: word of mouth and *Caché*," *Screen*, vol. 48, no. 2 (Summer 2007), 223-226.

GG8226. Cowan, Michael: "Between the street and the apartment: disturbing the space of fortress Europe in Michael Haneke," *Studies in European Cinema*, vol. 5, no. 2 (2008), 117-129.

GG8227. Ezra, Elizabeth; Jane Sillars: "*Hidden* in plain sight: bringing terror home," *Screen*, vol. 48, no. 2 (Summer 2007), 215-221.

GG8228. Gilroy, Paul: "Shooting crabs in a barrel," *Screen*, vol. 48, no. 2 (Summer 2007), 233-235.

GG8229. Khanna, Ranjana: "From Rue Morgue to Rue des Iris," *Screen*, vol. 48, no. 2 (Summer 2007), 237-244.

GG8230. Saxton, Libby: "Close encounters with distant suffering: Michael Haneke's disarming visions." In 7977.

GG8231. Silverman, Max: "The empire looks back," *Screen*, vol. 48, no. 2 (Summer 2007), 245-249.

HAROUN, Mahamat-Saleh.

GG8232. Bray, Maryse; Hélène Gill: "*Abouna* de Mahamat-Saleh Haroun: classicisme ou nouvelle vague dans le cinéma africain francophone?," *Nouvelles Etudes Francophones*, vol. 23, no. 2 (automne 2008), 178-194.

HONDO, Med.

GG8233. Petty, Sheila J.: "Disjunction from self: the politics of arrival in *Soleil O*." In 7998, 104-126.

JAOUI, Agnès. See also 8060.

GG8234. Nettelbeck, Colin: "Regardez-moi: theatre, performance, and directorship in the films of Agnès Jaoui," *Australian Journal of French Studies*, vol. 45, no. 1 (Jan.-April 2008), 3-15.

JEUNET, Jean-Pierre. See also 8029.

GG8235. • Ezra, Elizabeth: *Jean-Pierre Jeunet*. Urbana: Univ. of Illinois Press, 2008. *Contemporary film directors*. xii, 159 p.

GG8236. Coombs, Neil: "Jeunet and Caro and *The city of lost children*." In 7973.

GG8237. Durham, Caroline A.: "*Auteurism* and adaptation in Jean-Pierre Jeunet's *Un long dimanche de fiançailles*," *French Review*, vol. 81, no. 5 (April 2008), 912-929.

GG8238. Morrissey, Jim: "Paris and voyages of self-discovery in *Cléo de 5 à 7* and *Le fabuleux destin d'Amélie Poulain*," *Studies in French Cinema*, vol. 8, no. 2 (2008), 99-110. [Varda]

KECHICHE, Abdellatif.

GG8239. Blatt, Ari J.: "The play's the thing: Marivaux and the *banlieue* in Abdellatif Kechiche's *L'Esquive*," *French Review*, vol. 81, no. 3 (Feb. 2008), 516-529.

GG8240. Köhler, Margret: "Film steht jedem offen: Gespräch mit dem Regisseur Abdellatif Kechiche zu *Couscous mit Fisch*," *Film Dienst*, 61. Jahrgang, Heft 18 (28 August 2008), 15-16.

KIESLOWSKI, Krzysztof.

GG8241. Coates, Paul: "On the dialectics of filmic colors (in general) and red (in particular)," *Film Criticism*, vol. 32, no. 3 (Spring 2008), 2-23.

GG8242. Redner, Gregg: "Fragments of a life: becoming-music/woman in Krzysztof Kieslowski's *Trois couleurs: Bleu*," *Studies in French Cinema*, vol. 8, no. 3 (2008), 277-287.

KLAPISCH, Cédric.

GG8243. • Klapisch, Cédric: *Paris*. Paris: Avant-Scène Cinéma, 2008. *Avant-Scène Cinéma*, no. 569. 128 p.

KLOTZ, Nicolas. See 8019.

LANZMANN, Claude.

GG8244. ● Houdebine, Anne-Marie: *L'écriture de Shoah: une lecture analytique du film et du livre de Claude Lanzmann*. Limoges: Lambert-Lucas, 2008. 89 p.

GG8245. D'Arcy, Michael: "Claude Lanzmann's *Shoah* and the intentionality of the image." In 8015, 138-161.

GG8246. Lichtner, Giacomo: "From recognition to representation: Claude Lanzmann's *Shoah*." In 7991.

LAURENT, Jacques.

GG8247. Sivan, Pierre: "Caroline and Angélique: seductress of the French screen." In 7990, 197-209.

LELOUCH, Claude.

GG8248. ● Lelouch, Claude: *Ces années-là*. Conversations avec Claude Baignères et Sylvie Perez. Paris: Fayard, 2008. 425 p.

MALLE, Louis. See also 6503.

GG8249. ● Malle, Louis; Patrick Modiano: *Lacombe Lucien: scénario*. Dossier réalisé par Olivier Rocheteau; lecture d'image par Olivier Tomasini. Paris: Gallimard, 2008. *Folioplus classiques*. 208 p. [Modiano]

GG8250. ● Nacache, Jacqueline: *Lacombe Lucien de Louis Malle*. Neuilly: Atlande, 2008. *Clefs concours*. 191 p.

GG8251. Lichtner, Giacomo: "Blurred boundaries, 1970-1974: *Il giardino dei Finzi-Contini, Il portiere di notte* and *Lacombe, Lucien*." In 7991.

MAMBETY, Djibril Diop.

GG8252. Oscherwitz, Dayna: "Of cowboys and elephants: Africa, globalization, and the nouveau western in Djibril Diop Mambety's *Hyenas*," *Research in African Literatures*, vol. 39, no. 1 (Spring 2008), 223-238.

MARAIS, Jean.

GG8253. ● Dellatana, Jacqueline: *Jean Marais: le gentleman du Midi*. Gémenos: Autres temps, 2008. 97 p.

MARKER, Chris. See also 8043.

GG8254. ● *Chris Marker: a farewell to movies; Abschied vom Kino*. Ed. Andres Janser. Exhibition catalogue. Zurich: Museum für Gestaltung, 2008. 64 p.

GG8255. ● *Chris Marker et l'imprimerie du regard*. Sous la dir. d'André Habib et Viva Paci. Paris: L'Harmattan, 2008. 305 p.

GG8256. ● Cooper, Sara: *Chris Marker*. Manchester: Manchester Univ. Press, 2008. *French film directors*. x, 204 p.

GG8257. ● Douin, Emmanuel: *Chris Marker*. Paris: Ramsey, 2008. 280 p.

GG8258. ● Lambert, Arnaud: *Also known as Chris Marker*. Cherbourg: Point du jour, 2008. *Champ photographique*. 292 p.

GG8259. ● Marker, Chris: *Chris Marker: Owls at noon prelude: the hollow men*. Exhibition catalogue. Essays, Adrian martin and Raymond Bellour. Brisbane: Institute of Modern Art, 2008. 105 p.

GG8260. Chamarette, Jenny: "A short film about time: dynamism and stillness in Chris Marker's *La Jetée*." In 575, 217-231.

GG8261. Clover, Joshua: "Chris Marker: the return to work at the wonder factory." In 7975, 169-174.

GG8262. Cooper, Sarah: "Time and the city." In 7972, 113-122.

GG8263. Habib, André: "Impressions et figurations du visage dans quelques films de Chris Marker," *Intermédialités*, no. 8 (2006), [n.p.].

GG8264. Kramer, Sven: "Laura und Kinjo: zur Ökonomie des Authentischen in Chris Markers Essayfilm *Level Five*." In 380, 185-202.

GG8265. Martin, Adrian: "Chris Marker: notes in the margin of his time," *Cineaste*, vol. 33, no. 4 (Fall 2008), 6-10.

MARTINEAU, Jacques. See 8183.

MASSON, Laetitia.

GG8266. Devereux Herbeck, Mariah: "Narrative assault in Laetitia Masson's *A vendre*." In 617, 153-164.

MÉLIÈS, Georges.

GG8267. ● *Œuvre [L'] de Georges Mélès*. Coord. éd. Sandrine Bailly. Paris: La Cinémathèque française, 2008. 359 p. [Exhibition catalogue]

GG8268. Masson, Alain: "Georges Méliès, réalisateur," *Positif*, no. 568 (juin 2008), 80-83.

MELVILLE, Jean-Pierre.

GG8269. ● *Jean-Pierre Melville*. A cura di Mauro Gervasini, Emanuela Martini. Torino: Torino Film Festival; Milano: Il castoro, 2008. 208 p.

GG8270. Scott, Jason Mark: " 'When men, even unknowingly, . . . '," *Senses of Cinema*, no. 47 (2008), [n.p.].

MIÉVILLE, Anne-Marie. See 1063.

MIHAILEANU, Radu.

GG8271. Lichtner, Giacomo: "*La vita è bella* and *Train de vie*: 'preventing the eyes from seeing' versus 'cleaning the eyes that have seen to much'." In 7991.

MOCKY, Jean-Pierre. See 6504.

MOKNÈCHE, Nadir.

GG8272. Abderrezak, Hakim: "The modern harem in Moknèche's *Le Harem de Mme Osmane* and *Viva L'Aldgérie*." In 7996.

MOREAU, Jeanne. See also 3571.

GG8273. ● Gorkow, Alexander: *Draussen scheint die Sonne: Interviews mit Jeanne Moreau*. Mit einem Nachwort von Joachim Kaiser. Köln: Kiepenheuer & Witsch, 2008. 359 p.

GG8274. "Hommage à Jeanne Moreau," *Cahiers du Cinéma*, no. 630 (janv. 2008), 71-81.

GG8275. Sellier, Geneviève: "Jeanne Moreau: star of the new wave and icon of modernity." In 8004.

MORIN, Robert.

GG8276. Côté-Fortin, Israël: "Robert Morin, vidéaste du spectacle," *Canadian Journal of Film Studies*, vol. 17, no. 2 (Fall 2008), 48-58.

NGANGURA, Mweze.

GG8277. Konkobo, Christophe: "Espaces contemporains, histoire coloniale: *Pièces d'identité* de Mweze Ngangura," *Nouvelles Etudes Francophones*, vol. 23, no. 2 (automne 2008), 195-207.

OCELOT, Michel.

GG8278. Neupert, Richard: "*Kirikou* and the animated figure/body," *Studies in French Cinema*, vol. 8, no. 1 (2008), 41-56.

OPHULS, Marcel.

GG8279. ● Lowy, Vincent: *Marcel Ophuls*. Entretiens avec Sophie Brunet, Marc Ferro et Marcel Ophuls. Lormont: Bord de l'eau, 2008. 280 p.

GG8280. Bowles, Brett: " 'Ça fait d'excellents montages': documentary technique in *Le Chagrin et la Pitié*," *French Historical Studies*, vol. 31, no. 1 (Jan. 2008), 117-158.

GG8281. Lichtner, Giacomo: "Unveiling the mirror: *Le chagrin et la pitié*." In 7991.

GG8282. Suleiman, Susan Rubin: "History, memory, and moral judgment after the Holocaust: Marcel Ophuls's *Hotel Terminus*." In 600.

OPHULS, Max.

GG8283. Berthomé, Jean-Pierre: "*Lola Montès*: Ophuls et Lola: deux libertés scandaleuses," *Positif*, no. 574 (déc. 2008), 76-78.

GG8284. Berthomé, Jean-Pierre: "La restauration de *Lola Montès*," *Positif*, no. 574 (déc. 2008), 72-75.

OZON, François.

GG8285. ● Asibong, Andrew: *François Ozon*. Manchester; New York: Manchester Univ. Press, 2008. *French film directors*. viii, 157 p.

GG8286. Carruthers, Lee: "Doing time: timeliness and temporal rhetorics in contemporary cinema." Diss., Univ. of Chicago, 2008. vii, 212 p.

GG8287. Cavitch, Max: "Sex after death: François Ozon's libidinal invasions," *Screen*, vol. 48, no. 3 (Autumn 2007), 313-326.

GG8288. Chilcoat, Michelle: "Queering the family in François Ozon's *Sitcom*." In 8001.

GG8289. Handyside, Fiona: "Alternative inheritances: re-thinking what adaptation might mean in François Ozon's *Le temps qui reste*," *Film/Literature Quarterly*, vol. 36, no. 4 (2008), 281-289.

GG8290. Ince, Kate: "François Ozon's cinema of desire." In 7977.

PALCY, Euzhan.

GG8291. Petty, Sheila J.: "Collision of cultures: occulted Caribbean histories in *Sugar Cane Alley*." In 7998, 52-79.

PECK, Raoul.

GG8292. Braziel, Jana Evans: "From Fort Dimanche to Brooklyn: transnational regimes of violence, Duvalierism, and failed heteromasculinity in Raoul Peck's *Haitian corner*." In 50.

GG8293. Petty, Sheila J.: "Locality, memory, and zombification in *The Man by the Shore*." In 7998, 196-223.

PHILIBERT, Nicolas.

GG8294. Andrew, Geoff: "Norman conquests," *Sight and Sound*, vol. 18, no. 2 (Feb. 2008), 26-28.

PHILIPE, Gérard.

GG8295. Barrot, Olivier: *L'ami posthume: Gérard Philipe, 1922-1959*. Paris: Grasset, 2008. 207 p.

PIALAT, Maurice.

GG8296. ● *Dictionnaire [Le] Pialat*. Dir. Antoine de Baecque; avec la collab. d'Angie David. Paris: Léo Scheer, 2008. 314 p.

GG8297. Maule, Rosanna: "The middle generation: Maurice Pialat, Gianni Amelio, and Victor Erice." In 7993.

POIRÉ, Jean-Marie.

GG8298. McMorran, Will: "*Les Visiteurs* and the Quixotic text," *French Cultural Studies*, vol. 19, no. 2 (June 2008), 159-172.

POIRIER, Anne-Claire.

GG8299. Norris, Anna: "L'œuvre filmique d'Anne Claire Poirier ou l'engagement au féminin." In 120, 399-406.

PONTECORVO, Gillo.

GG8300. Behan, Tom: "Gillo Pontecorvo: partisan film-maker," *Film International*, vol. 6, no. 1 (2008), 23-30.

GG8301. Clô, Clarissa: "Revolutionaries of the world unite." In 43, 202-223.

GG8302. Dingeman, Jim: " 'You cannot continually inflict': an interview with Saadi Yacef," *Framework*, vol. 49, no. 2 (Fall 2008), 48-64.

GG8303. Lichtner, Giacomo: "The struggle, not the man: *Kapò* and *L'Enclos*." In 7991.

GG8304. Srivastava, Neelam: "Decolonizing the self: Gandhian non-violence and Fanonian violence as comparative 'ethics of resistance' in *Kanthapura* and *The Battle of Algiers*." In 428, 86-103. [Fanon]

RENOIR, Jean.

GG8305. ● Garson, Charlotte: *Jean Renoir*. Paris: Cahiers du cinéma, 2008. 95 p.

GG8306. ● *Jean Renoir: a conversation with his films 1894-1979*. Christopher Faulkner, Paul Duncan, eds. Köln; London: Taschen, 2007. 192 p.

GG8307. ● Renoir, Jean: *Ma vie et mes films*. Paris: Flammarion, 2008. *Champs*. 265 p. [Orig. ed., 2005]

GG8308. Bear, Jordan: "From magician to metal brain: the embodiment of illusion in early European film theory," *Studies in European Cinema*, vol. 5, no. 1 (2008), 17-29.

GG8309. Cardullo, Bert: " 'Everyone has his reasons': the words and films of Jean Renoir." In 7966, 1-14. [Also in 7967]

GG8310. Cardullo, Bert: "Ruler of the game: a conversation with Jean Renoir." In 7966, 15-36.

GG8311. Faulkner, Christopher: "An archive of the (political) unconscious: Jean Renoir at the FBI." In 526.

GG8312. Faulkner, Christopher: "The phenomenon of the *film raconté* and the novelizations of *La Règle du jeu*," *South Central Review*, vol. 25, no. 2 (Summer 2008), 22-44.

GG8313. Golsan, Katherine: "A Hollywood fairytale: Renoir's *Diary of a chamber-maid*," *South Central Review*, vol. 25, no. 2 (Summer 2008), 45-62.

GG8314. Prédal, René: "De Jean Renoir à Raymond Depardon," *Jeune Cinéma*, no. 315-316 (printemps 2008), 33-39. [Depardon]

GG8315. Sellers, Antony: "Arthur Shields and the politics of Jean Renoir's *The River*," *Senses of Cinema*, no. 49 (2008-2009), [n.p.].

GG8316. Wegner, Hart: "A chronicle of soil, seasons and weather: Jean Renoir's *The Southerner*." In 8010.

RESNAIS, Alain. See also 752, 3603, 8043.

GG8317. ● *Alain Resnais: l'avventura dei linguaggi*. A cura di Roberto Zemignan. Milano: Il castoro, 2008. 299 p.

GG8318. ● Benayoun, Robert: *Alain Resnais, arpenteur de l'imaginaire*. Paris: Ramsey, 2008. Nouvelle éd. 311 p.

GG8319. ● Leutrat, Jean-Louis: *Hiroshima mon amour*. 2e éd. Paris: A. Colin, 2008. 127 p. [Duras]

GG8320. ● Raymond, Hélène: *Poétique du témoignage: autour du film Nuit et brouillard d'Alain Resnais*. Paris: L'Harmattan, 2008. *L'art en bref.* 144 p.

GG8321. Banaji, Ferzina: "Alain Resnais's *Nuit et brouillard* (1955): memory, time and distance." In 610, 129-139.

GG8322. Binder, Anne-Berenike: "Alain Resnais, *Nuit et brouillard*." In 390, 231-277.

GG8323. Kligerman, Eric: "Celan's cinematic: anxiety of the gaze in *Night and Fog* and 'Engführung'." In 8015, 185-210.

GG8324. Le Juez, Brigitte: "War survivors' fractured identities in *Hiroshima mon amour*." In 622, 61-71.

GG8325. Lichtner, Giacomo: "A resistant make-up: the making and reception of *Nuit et brouillard*." In 7991.

GG8326. Reader, Keith: "Another Deleuzian Renais: *L'Année dernière à Marienbad* (1961) as conflict between sadism and masochism," *Studies in French Cinema*, vol. 8, no. 2 (2008), 149-158. [Deleuze, Robbe-Grillet]

GG8327. Wlodarski, Amy Lynn: "Excavating Eisler: relocating the memorial voice in *Nuit et brouillard*." In 7989.

RIVETTE, Jacques. See 8055.

ROHMER, Eric (pseud. of Maurice Schérer). See also 8055.

GG8328. ● *Eric Rohmer 3*. Avant-propos, Yannick Mouren. Caen: Lettres Modernes Minard, 2008. *Etudes cinématographiques.* 168 p.

GG8329. ● *Eric Rohmer: évidence et ambiguïté du cinéma*. Sous la dir. de Jean Cléder. Bordeaux: Bord de l'eau, 2007. 134 p.

GG8330. ● *Rohmer et les autres*. Sous la dir. de Noël Herpe. Rennes: Presses univ. de Rennes, 2007. 307 p.

GG8331. ● Tester, Keith: *Eric Rohmer: film as theology*. Basingstoke: Palgrave Macmillan, 2008. vi, 175 p.

GG8332. Andrew, Geoff: "Late liberty," *Sight and Sound*, vol. 18, no. 10 (Oct. 2008), 30-33.

GG8333. Cardullo, Bert: " 'I am a complete auteur': an interview with Eric Rohmer." In 7966, 139-150.

GG8334. Cardullo, Bert: "Seasons change, or the tales of Eric Rohmer." In 7966, 127-138.

GG8335. Caruana, John: "Cinematic epiphanies: Eric Rohmer and the transcendence of the ordinary." In 7976.

GG8336. Coureau, Didier: "*La Cambrure*. Eloge de la beauté." In 8328, 145-153.

GG8337. Liandrat-Guigues, Suzanne: "*Triple agent*: une fable arithmétique." In 8328, 101-110.

GG8338. Magny, Joël: "Filmographie d'Eric Rohmer (1986-2007); Théâtre et télévision (1987-1989)." In 8328, 155-162.

GG8339. Magny, Joël: "*Triple agent*: amour de l'image, image de l'amour." In 8328, 111-121.

GG8340. Mouren, Yannick: "La série chez Eric Rohmer, principe et illustration." In 8328, 5-61.

GG8341. Nuttens, Jean-Dominique: "*L'Anglaise et le Duc*: le peintre, l'architecte et le cinéaste." In 8328, 83-99.

GG8342. Prédal, René: "*Quatre aventures de Reinette et Mirabelle* et *Les Rendez-vous de Paris*: le langage et la peinture." In 8328, 63-82.

GG8343. Samocki, Jean-Marie: "*Triple agent*: l'autre champ: la fiction avec l'archive?" In 8328, 123-143.

ROUCH, Jean.

GG8344. ● *Building bridges: the cinema of Jean Rouch*. Ed. Joram ten Brink; preface by Michael Renov. London; New York: Wallflower, 2007. xv, 324 p.

GG8345. ● *Jean Rouch: a celebration of life and film*. Ed. William Rothman. Fasano: Schena, 2007. 164 p.

GG8346. ● Piechota, Antje: *Jean Rouch: Innovationen im Spannungsfeld von Ethnologie und Kino*. Saarbrücken: VDM, 2008. 109 p.

GG8347. ● Rouch, Jean: *Alors le noir et le blanc seront amis: carnets de mission, 1946-1951*. Edition établie par Marie-Isabelle Merle des Isles; avec l'aide de Bernard Surugue. Paris: Mille et une nuits, 2008. 310 p.

GG8348. ● Scheinfeigel, Maxime: *Jean Rouch*. Préface de Michel Marie. Paris: CNRS, 2008. 240 p.

GG8349. Di Iorio, Sam: "Total cinema: *Chronique d'un été* and the end of Bazinian film theory," *Screen*, vol. 48, no. 1 (Spring 2007), 25-43. [Bazin, Edgar Morin]

GG8350. Sjöberg, Johannes: "Ethnofiction: drama as creative research practice in ethnographic film," *Journal of Media Practice*, vol. 9, no. 3 (2008), 229-242.

SATRAPI, Marjane.

GG8351. Jaafar, Ali: "Children of the Revolution," *Sight and Sound*, vol. 18, no. 5 (May 2008), 46-47.

SAUVAGE, André.

GG8352. ● Marinone, Isabelle: *André Sauvage, un cinéaste oublié: de La traversée du Grépon à La croisière jaune*. Paris: L'Harmattan, 2008. *Champs visuels*. 254 p.

SCHROEDER, Barbet.

GG8353. Macnab, Geoffrey: "The smiler with a knife," *Sight and Sound*, vol. 18, no. 6 (June 2008), 16-18.

SISSAKO, Abderrahmane.

GG8354. Balseiro, Isabel: "Exile and longing in Abderrahmane Sissako's *La Vie sur terre*," *Screen*, vol. 48, no. 4 (Winter 2007), 443-461.

GG8355. Grugeau, Gérard: "Entretien avec Abderrahmane Sissako," *24 Images*, no. 132 (juin-juillet 2007), 40-45.

STEPHANIK, Roch. See 8037.

TANA, Paul.

GG8356. Jean, Marcel: "Entretien avec Paul Tana," *24 Images*, no. 138 (sept. 2008), 29-30.

TATI, Jacques. See also 8037.

GG8357. Cardullo, Bert: " 'Comedy belongs to everyone': an interview with Jacques Tati." In 7966, 85-100.

GG8358. Cardullo, Bert: "The sound of silence, the space of time: *Monsieur Hulot* and the cinema of Jacques Tati." In 7966, 77-89.

GG8359. McCann, Ben: " 'Du verre, rien que du verre': negotiating Utopia in *Playtime*." In 541, 195-210.

GG8360. Afoumado, Diane: "*Safe conduct*: a tribute to the French film industry during the second world war." In 8002, 70-82.

TÉCHINÉ, André. See also 3058.

GG8361. ● Costeix, Eric: *André Téchiné, le paysage transfiguré*. Paris: L'Harmattan, 2008. *Champs visuels*. 266 p.

GG8362. Pratt, Murray: "Forgetting to remember now and then: AIDS, memory and homosexuality in André Téchiné's *Les Témoins* (2007)," *Australian Journal of French Studies*, vol. 45, no. 3 (Sept.-Dec. 2008), 250-263.

TRUFFAUT, François.
GG8363. ● *François Truffaut: interviews.* Ed. Ronald Bergan. Jackson: Univ. Press of Mississippi, 2008. *Conversations with filmmakers.* 150 p.
GG8364. ● Marchesini, Mauro: *Le grand noir: mancamenti e corpi addolorati nel cinema di François Truffaut.* Recco: Le mani, 2008. *Extralights.* 101 p.
GG8365. Cardullo, Bert: "Alter ego, autobiography, and auteurism: François Truffaut's last interview." In 7966, 109-126.
GG8366. Cardullo, Bert: "Style and meaning in *Shoot the piano player.*" In 7966, 101-108.
GG8367. Hewitt, Leah D.: "Occupational performances in Truffaut's *The Last Metro.*" In 7986, 101-124.
GG8368. Nayar, Sheila J.: "Ecriture aesthetics: mapping the literate episteme of visual narrative," *PMLA*, vol. 123, no. 1 (Jan. 2008), 140-155.
VARDA, Agnès. See also 8238.
GG8369. Darke, Chris: "First person singular," *Film Comment*, vol. 44, no. 1 (Jan.-Feb. 2008), 22-23.
GG8370. DeRoo, Rebecca J.: "Unhappily ever after: visual irony and feminist strategy in Agnès Varda's *Le bonheur,*" *Studies in French Cinema*, vol. 8, no. 3 (2008), 189-209.
GG8371. "Entretien avec Agnès Varda," *Positif*, no. 574 (déc. 2008), 17-21.
GG8372. Flitterman-Lewis, Sandy: "Varda: the gleaner and the just." In 8009, 214-225.
GG8373. Fox Kuhlken, Pam: "Clarissa and Cléo (en)durée: suicidal time in Virginia Woolf's *Mrs. Dalloway* and Agnès Varda's *Cléo de 5 à 7,*" *Comparative Literature Studies*, vol. 45, no. 3 (2008), [n.p.].
GG8374. Kausch, Franck: "*Les plages d'Agnès.* La mer, éternellement recommencée," *Positif*, no. 574 (déc. 2008), 15-16.
GG8375. McKim, Kristi: "Time, scale and cinephilia in the cinematic elegy: Agnès Varda's *Jacquot de Nantes,*" *Studies in French Cinema*, vol. 8, no. 3 (2008), 211-227.
GG8376. Reichart, Wilfried: "Über mich selbst: *Die Strände der Agnès Varda,*" *Film Dienst*, 61. Jahrgang, Heft 13 (19 Juni 2008), 46-47.
VOLCKMAN, Christian.
GG8377. Hdajioannou, Markos: "How does the digital matter? Envisioning corporeality through Christian Volckman's *Renaissance,*" *Studies in French Cinema*, vol. 8, no. 2 (2008), 123-136.